MENTAL HEALTH AND PEOPLE OF COLOR

Mental Health and People of Color

Curriculum Development and Change

Edited by

Jay C. Chunn II

Patricia J. Dunston

Fariyal Ross-Sheriff

HOWARD UNIVERSITY PRESS, Washington, D.C., 1983

Copyright © 1983 by the Howard University School of Social Work and Howard University Press

All rights reserved. No part of this book may be reproduced or utilized in any form without permission in writing from the publisher. Inquiries should be addressed to Howard University Press, 2900 Van Ness Street, N.W., Washington, D.C. 20008.

Printed in the United States of America

Library of Congress Cataloging in Publication Data
Main entry under title:

Mental health and people of color.

  Bibliography: p.
  Includes index.
  1. Minorities—Mental health—United States—Study
and teaching 2. Mental health education—United States.
I. Chunn, Jay C., 1938– . II. Dunston, Patricia J.,
1947– . III. Ross-Sheriff, Fariyal, 1940– .
[DNLM: 1. Curriculum. 2. Mental health. 3. Minority
groups—Psychology. WA 305 M5482]
RC451.5.A2M46 1983   362.2'089   83–295
ISBN 0–88258–097–3

Contents

Part Three
PSYCHIATRY

Part Four
PSYCHIATRIC NURSING

Preface

In our years of training and providing consultation in the core mental health disciplines, it has become increasingly clear that social work, psychology, psychiatry and psychiatric nursing curricula have not prepared practitioners for effective practice among people of color. Since the Civil Rights movement of the sixties there has been concern in the Black community about the mental health of people of color. Parallel concerns among Hispanics, Asian and Pacific Americans, and American Indians have also emerged.

The impetus for this book grew out of several experiences and sources. Accumulating survey data within the core mental health disciplines reveal that, in most instances, university faculties do not include content on people of color in the teaching curriculum. When such content is included the topic is treated in a tangential manner. Simultaneously, accumulating evidence from the field clearly illustrates that mental health professionals lack adequate training for practice among people of color. The President's Commission on Mental Health highlighted this lack of professional training and vividly documented the problems people of color receiving mental health care experience as a result. This emerging reality gave impetus to the concept that practitioners need special training to treat persons of color.

In the 1977–78 academic year, Dr. Jay Chunn, dean of the School of Social Work at Howard University, initiated a dialogue with National Institute of Mental Health (NIMH) officials from the divisions of Manpower and Training and Special Mental Health Programs on setting up a center to train social work educators to develop content relevant to people of color. As the dialogue progressed over the course of a year, it became evident that psychiatry, psychology and psychiatric nursing were in equal need of a focused training approach.

Early in 1979 NIMH, under the joint auspices of Drs. William Denham (Division of Manpower and Training) and Juan Ramos, (Special Mental Health Programs) brought together a group of leading scholars and mental health practitioners to further explore the need for special curriculum training. This consultation group concurred that there was a need for special training. This need was reinforced by the core mental health disciplines' branch chiefs at NIMH. It was agreed that the state of the art of integrating curriculum content on people of color should be thoroughly assessed. Further, deficits in the state of the art needed to be identified, and theoretical and content issues needed to be outlined. It was also agreed that research needs should be identified, guidelines for including minority content explicated and that strategies for implementing content on people of color in professional education–training programs should be posed.

At NIMH's invitation Dr. Chunn submitted a proposal incorporating these objectives. A four–by–four project design was adopted so that input from the four mental health core disciplines and from each of the four racial–ethnic groups of color would be guaranteed. In September 1979 the Howard University School of Social Work was awarded a special project grant to carry out the work. Dr. Jay Chunn was named project director and Dr. Patricia J. Dunston was appointed to the Howard University faculty as the project coordinator. With the continued able assistance of Dr. Fariyal Ross-Sheriff of the Howard University School of Social Work faculty, plans to bring together the sixty-four leading scholars and practitioners selected to guide and carry out this vital effort proceeded rapidly. The conference–workshops convened in November 1979 and March 1980 in Chicago. This volume is the result of these efforts.

The book is divided into four parts: Psychology, Social Work, Psychiatry and Psychiatric Nursing. Each of the four parts contains a chapter from each of the four ethnic groups, resulting in sixteen chapters. The sixteen group leaders are identified in the list of contributors along with the other group members. The book is organized in this manner in order to present the state of the art and other components from a respective disciplinary perspective. However, readers can also gain a clear appreciation of developments across each racial–ethnic group by reading across disciplines by race and ethnicity.

The utilization of the vast amount of material provided in this volume hopefully will not proceed along rigid disciplinary lines. Each core mental health profession can learn from the others and, indeed, incorporate within its own curriculum development and training programs the experiences of the other disciplines. The four–by–four project design allowed an exchange of knowledge among scholars from the same racial–ethnic group *across* the core mental health disciplines. The design also allowed a cross-fertilization of ideas among the different racial–ethnic groups *within* disciplines. Hopefully, this truly interdisciplinary effort will assist each core mental health discipline and racial–ethnic group to look beyond its own body of knowledge and to force linkages with theoretical development efforts within the other core disciplines.

Finally, the charge to the authors and the intent of the editors was not to develop "the" curriculum for any racial–ethnic group within any of the professions. That important work ultimately must rest with faculties, deans and training directors and be supported by accrediting bodies and standard-developing and standard-setting organizations and mechanisms. In addition, each mental health discipline and each racial–ethnic group is in a different phase in the development of curriculum content on people of color. Hence, issues of theoretical orientation, for example, may be resolved for one group but quite unresolved for another. This developmental unevenness is sometimes

reflected in the chapters contained herein and should be viewed as
instructive for future analyses of the state of the art and knowledge
for the particular mental health discipline and racial–ethnic group
being studied.

Jay C. Chunn, II
Patricia J. Dunston
Fariyal Ross-Sheriff

Acknowledgments

We are grateful and deeply indebted to all the authors who contributed to this work. Without their unselfish and steadfast efforts this volume would not have been possible. All of the chapters contained herein were developed specifically for this work and we acknowledge the authors' dedication and devotion to the task. They are, indeed, true scholars.

The development of a book of this type requires tremendous effort on the part of many people. For their steadfast support and encouragement throughout the life of this project, we extend special thanks to Dr. William H. Denham, director of the Division of Manpower and Training, and Dr. Juan Ramos, director of Special Mental Health Programs at the National Institute of Mental Health, through which this project and this book were funded. Dr. Denham assumed lead responsibility for NIMH and we acknowledge his innovative assistance to our collective work. Their colleagues were also extremely helpful, including George White, Donald Fisher and other NIMH staff personnel. The core mental health discipline branch chiefs have all been encouraging and helpful to this publication effort.

There are many technical tasks to be performed in producing a book of this nature. We owe special thanks to Marcella W. Daniels and to Ponnamma S. David of the dean's staff at the Howard University School of Social Work for their assistance in producing this book and for all the many services they have performed throughout this project. We also acknowledge the contributions of our faculty colleagues who have stimulated our thinking and who have made contributions over the years to the art of curriculum content development for people of color. The assistance of our consultants Ianthe C. McMichael, in recruiting project participants and Dr. Marcia E. Lash, in working with the nursing groups, is gratefully acknowledged. We also are grateful to the School of Social Work support staff for typing the manuscript.

The able assistance and help extended through the Howard University Press and its director, Charles Harris, are gratefully acknowledged. His enthusiasm for this publication has been on-going and most beneficial. The technical editing services provided through Renee Mayfield, managing editor at the Howard University Press, have been most helpful in producing this book. Mayfield's sensitivity and skill have made a substantial contribution to the quality of the chapters contained herein.

Finally, we thank and acknowledge with deep appreciation the help, support, and ongoing encouragement of our family members. Without their patience and understanding support, this book would not have been possible. To our readers, we acknowledge responsibility for any technical errors that remain.

Overview

The Black psychology group develops the theme that within psychology there exist fossilized distortions and racist stereotypes of Blacks that make inferior, dehumanize and ignore their historical reality. They examine present curriculum approaches as designs that render Black people "powerless" and serve as barriers to change in the human condition. The authors present a framework for developing Black content in psychology that places the person or family at the center of four interactive subsystems. Each subsystem forms its own essence, new information for curriculum development. They advocate the development of new psychological theory that is based on concrete historical reality and dialectical methodology, and that is reflective and transformative.

The Asian and Pacific American psychology group discusses the total disregard of Asian and Pacific American people and the lack of training materials for this population group in psychology curricula nationally. They contend that this group is a minority within a minority about which persists the widely held false assumption that mental health problems are virtually nonexistent. The authors discuss the difficulty of adopting a psychological frame of reference from an Asian and Pacific American perspective and the development of training center foci for internships and for preparing curriculum content and materials.

The American Indian psychology group asserts that the present knowledge concerning the multitude of psychological difficulties and problems faced by American Indians is alarmingly small and mostly distorted by a lack of understanding of American Indian cultures. They maintain that the rigid anthropological view of American Indians permeates the distortions expressed in the limited literature in sociology, psychology, social work and psychiatry. The authors warn of the grave need to identify, obtain and describe general and specific psychological characteristics, attributes and life styles of American Indians. They attribute the neglect of American Indian psychology to (1) a long standing anthropology-Indian affiliation; (2) the almost complete absence of good psychologically oriented, theoretically based data on American Indian groups; (3) the scant number of American Indian psychologists to serve as representative and facilitative role models; and (4) the almost complete absence of curriculum materials on Indians. The chapter poses a schema for integrating American Indian content into existing psychology curricula.

The Hispanic psychology group posits that it is culturally inappropriate and scientifically myopic to explain the behavior of Hispanics using

Part 1:
Psychology

Chapter 1

Chapter 2

Chapter 3

Chapter 4

systems of categorization developed to describe the majority population. They argue that such systems only perpetuate an ethnocentric
psychological framework of human behavior and that the development
of an integrated curriculum with Hispanic content is necessary. The
authors examine cultural pluralism and the related concepts of acculturation, biculturalism and ethnic identity as the focus of curriculum,
and language, national origin, race, sociodemographics, sociopolitical
history and migration patterns as the focus of content. Further, they
discuss the concept of *la familia*, incorporating family structure and
family function.

**Part 2:
Social Work**

Chapter 5

The Black social work group examines the use of the systems approach
as a method for integrating curriculum content on Blacks in social
work education and for dealing with the simultaneous appraisal of
social systems in transacting with Black individuals and families.
They contend that this approach also provides utility for the five
sequence areas adopted by schools of social work: Human Behavior
and the Social Environment, Social Work Practice, Social Welfare
Policy, Research and Field Work. The authors assert that there is a
need to study Blacks who have coped effectively in certain areas and
to build norms for behavior based on that coping rather than on
comparisons with white norms.

Chapter 6

The Asian and Pacific American social work group addresses issues
relevant to providing and utilizing social work services in the Asian
and Pacific American community. Attention is given to the reality of
Asian and Pacific American communities as distinctively heterogeneous with diverse migration experiences that require differential
social work services. The authors advocate a systems theory perspective
in social work practice and teaching that facilitates a better understanding of how the various Asian and Pacific American social systems—families, organizations and communities—are formed and the
various processes by which they are maintained and/or changed. They
strongly urge scholars and practitioners to look to Asian and Pacific
American communities for definitions of the Asian and Pacific American experience. The authors posit that the consequences of racism
for Asian and Pacific Americans, their ethnic and cultural diversity,
the goal of empowerment and systems theory must serve as the
organizing framework in Asian and Pacific American curriculum
content.

Chapter 7

The American Indian social work group points to the insensitivity
and lack of respect displayed by professional social workers in planning,

developing and delivering social services to American Indian communities and tribes. According to the authors, most of the literature tends toward the myth that Indian cultures, families and communities are biologically and/or culturally "deficient," "ill" or "problematic." They also contend that treatment and service delivery have been influenced by psychological theories and notions that have done more harm than good. The authors recommend that a "liberation" approach rather than a "domestication" approach be used by schools of social work. They also advocate the use of the dual perspective model as an organizing framework and maintain that appropriate research and curriculum developmental activity acceptable to American Indian communities and tribes is necessary.

The Hispanic social work group clearly points out that characteristics of each Hispanic population—Mexican, Puerto Rican and Cuban—vary because of national origin and sociocultural and demographic factors. They examine the psychic structure of such persons of color in the context of diverse roots and vernaculars and intergenerational differences. The authors contend that this diversity makes it difficult to propose a specific theoretical construct or framework. They discuss various options as frameworks for developing Hispanic mental health curriculum and the need to remove the Anglo assumptions and stereotypes deeply embedded in contemporary mental health models. The authors urge those concerned with the reconstruction of curriculum to use paradigms particular to the Hispanic cultures they are intended to serve. They advocate flexibility in thinking, which will aid in replacing Anglo-bound components with Hispanic norms and produce alternative ways of looking at behavior.

Chapter 8

The Black psychiatry group asserts that Freudian theory based on clinical observation and treatment of patients from middle-class white European, Jewish backgrounds holds the fallacious assumption that such theory and psychological requisites are relevant to all groups of people, regardless of ethnic or cultural differences. They question the ability of Freudian theory to draw relevant treatment approaches to the needs of Black patients because of a lack of cross-cultural validation. Further, the authors point to the tendency of psychiatrists to blame the patient when the Freudian treatment approach fails rather than question the validity of the treatment approach, the therapist's competence in using the treatment approach, and the therapist's own acceptance of Black patients. They maintain that psychiatry must address the personality development, socioeconomic conditions and cultural idiosyncracies of individuals belonging to ethnic groups that

Part 3:
Psychiatry

Chapter 9

are different from those of the traditional ideal patient. To increase the quality of instruction psychiatric residents receive, the authors propose that Black curriculum content be part of the learning experience. They argue that this process would generate valid and reliable scientific knowledge of Black people and increase the resident's ability to evaluate and comprehend experiences of Black patients. The authors recommend directions that curriculum should take, including didactic courses on culture and cultural psychology, relevant field learning and experiential group training.

Chapter 10

The Asian and Pacific American psychiatry group points out that psychiatric residency programs have not provided the training or leadership that would enable their graduates to work with underserved Asian and Pacific American patients. They recommend that there be a significant correlation between clinical practice and didactic curriculum and that therapists treating Asian and Pacific American patients and their families recognize cross-cultural and cross-ethnic issues. The authors further advance that trainees often learn best when appropriate role models are involved, and urge that suitable Asian and Pacific American faculty be integrally involved in the teaching of minority content. They propose a four–year curriculum that focuses on cross-cultural seminars, historic knowledge of Asian and Pacific American cultural groups, attitudinal learning and skill enhancement, and advocate the establishment of regional interdisciplinary training centers that focus on training and service to Asian and Pacific American populations.

Chapter 11

The American Indian psychiatry group begins with a discussion of the tremendous deficit that exists in medical school curriculums on Indians, even in areas where there are large Indian populations (in one southwestern state in which 100,000 Indians live, there are only seven hours of instruction on the mental health realities and needs of Indians). They maintain that residents who are interested in and concerned with issues related to Indian content are forced to read on their own and to provide their own clinical supervision. The authors point out the increasing awareness among minority practitioners, educators and others of the need for training to encompass a multitude of conceptual models, diseases, treatments and patient types. They focus on five issues for developing an approach to teaching minority cultural content: material specificity, content foci, personnel issues, transfer to practice and research needs. The authors contend that training that relies on multiple case examples with no conceptual framework creates chaotic training programs, which leave the practitioner with only episodic knowledge and skill for dealing with cultural matters. They recommend a generalist approach that uses multiple precepts based on patients culturally different from the resident and examples from a broad range of cultures as opposed to a specific approach based on one or two cultures. The authors also develop research recommendations that recognize the difference between general and specific approaches to using learning materials and improving patient care.

The Hispanic psychiatry group presents an overview of recent developments in minority content concerns within the context of current psychiatric training standards. They contend that few residency training programs have any focused minority content at all and only a small number address Hispanic content. The authors present an overview of the current state of mental health services that are available to Hispanics and outline theoretical issues that have direct practical implications on how clinical delivery problems arise. They propose a general systems framework, bio-psychosocial model for conceptualizing the relationship among the curriculum, the treatment setting and the characteristics of the therapist and patient. The authors develop a training curriculum model which focuses on understanding the unique experiences that Hispanics have endured in this country at various times in history. They recommend integrating the training mission of the residency training program into the overall service role of the program so that terminal learning objectives incorporate expected competencies. The authors maintain that this approach will enable the stated standards to be integrated into a clinic's quality assurance program.

Chapter 12

The Black psychiatric nursing group points out the dearth of African American nurses and other nurses of color in the United States and suggests the need to have all nurses learn to provide quality nursing care, including care to ethnic people of color. They discuss the slow but constant push in nursing education to incorporate curriculum content on ethnicity in the light of the limited number of class sessions devoted to discussions of ethnicity and the lack of integrated content on ethnicity throughout the entire program. The authors contend that there is a lack of nursing knowledge about the care of African Americans and advocate the use of the systems approach combined with a holistic orientation of nursing in studying issues related to the development of mental health curricula sensitive to African Americans. They discuss three research issues of consequence to African American nurses—institutional racism and its impact, African American coping style, and model psychological responses of African Americans given effective therapeutic interventions—and delineate several content principles—

Part 4:
Psychiatric
Nursing

Chapter 13

among them, self concept, family themes, institutional racism and similar concerns.

Chapter 14

The Asian and Pacific American psychiatric nursing group examines the difficulties in acknowledging cultural plurality and operationalizing its mandates in nursing curriculum. They note that the information presented under the rubric "culture" frequently lends itself to furthering stereotypes instead of truly fostering cultural sensitivity. The authors propose a general framework for working with Asian and Pacific American people that uses a sensitive humanistic approach, which requires the nurse to be knowledgeable about the people served. They advocate the development of client-centered psychiatric nursing practices based upon sound theoretical premises, understanding the clients and their close interpersonal contacts and community dynamics. The authors urge psychiatric nurses to consider the impact of culture, history, politics and socioeconomic influences when identifying factors that shape Asian and Pacific Americans throughout the life cycle. They propose a framework for viewing the Asian and Pacific American client that focuses on the individual, family and community as major independent variables which influence each other and discuss interpersonal theory as a strong component of this framework. The authors examine the problems that stem from the lack of Asian and Pacific American nurses and the need for bilingual, bicultural Asian and Pacific American nurses and also present a policy recommendation for increasing the number of Asian and Pacific American nurses.

Chapter 15

The American Indian psychiatric nursing group contends that the mental health needs of American Indians are as great or greater than those of other cultures and that colleges of nursing are not educating members of the American Indian community who might meet those needs. They also posit that non-Indian mental health personnel are not prepared to offer services to American Indian clients because they hold values which are not compatible with values held by American Indians. The authors document the severe shortage of American Indian psychiatric nurses as well as the lack of cultural content in both undergraduate and graduate nursing education. They use the ecosystem framework as a basis for curriculum development and present two, three-dimensional matrices—the first, an ecosystem for psychosocial nursing and, the second, on nursing education, which embodies the elements of professional nursing both of which can be used to lay the foundations for American Indian content in psychiatric nursing. The authors contend that American Indian cultural content can be meaningfully integrated as a component of curriculum only when there are credit hours attached and where there is a requirement for graduation. They advocate greater involvement of the American Indian community in developing mental health curricula in the nursing profession.

The Hispanic psychiatric nursing group recommends that in designing   *Chapter 16*
curriculum content in psychiatric nursing related to Hispanics, Hispanic content should be integrated into the nursing related content.
They contend that culturally consistent assessment, evaluation and
treatment skills as well as theoretical content must be included in
nursing curricula in order to meet the psychiatric and mental health
needs of Hispanics.

MENTAL HEALTH AND PEOPLE OF COLOR

PART ONE

Psychology

LEWIS M. KING   SARAH MOODY
ODESSA THOMPSON   MAISHA BENNETT

CHAPTER 1

Black Psychology Reconsidered

Notes Toward Curriculum Development

> I, the man of color, want only this: That the tool never possess the man. That the enslavement of man by man ceases forever. That is, of one by another. That it be possible for me to discover and to love man, wherever he may be.
>
> Franz Fanon
> *Black Skin, White Masks* (1956)

> If history is going to be scientific, if the record of human action is going to be set down with that accuracy and faithfulness of detail which will allow its use as a measuring rod and guidepost for the future of nations, there must be set, some standards of ethics in Research and *interpretation.*
>
> William Edward Burghardt DuBois
> *Black Reconstruction* (1915)

Both DuBois and Fanon dedicated their lives not only to social criticism but also to social action in the interest of social transformation. Fanon's hope for mankind is reflected neither in the psychology of Western society nor in the attempts of traditional psychology to mirror the reality of individuals in that society. DuBois clearly warned us that we should not see this lack of reflection as accidental, but rather as the deliberate action of one interest group determined to shape particular images of man and maintain social control of the goods, resources and services of the society, indeed, as the attempt to exclude Blacks from world history. Fanon and DuBois go on to suggest that psychology and history are not value free but are imbedded in the culture and self-interest of the group. Further, a study by Sherwood and Nataupsky, which appeared in the *Journal of Personality and Social Psychology* in 1969, concluded that it is possible to accurately predict the conclusion of Black child–white child intelligence research simply by examining the biographical characteristics of the investi-

3

gator. The political and social significance of this possibility is all too clear. When, therefore, we examine psychology, we must never forget that we are dealing with fundamentally political questions We must examine critical conceptions and assumptions with the intent of understanding what and whose position is being represented as reality. Replacing a curriculum in psychology with another is a political act that must be based on the scientific analysis of the concrete historical reality of the people that the psychology must represent and serve.

This chapter, then, makes no claim to an apolitical posture. It outlines the issues central to developing curricula that allow Black people to more critically focus on their way in the world, their relationships to nature and their position in this society; curricula that allow for a more critical analysis of their condition; curricula that will allow psychologists to engage Black people in a more humane and just way.

Curriculum development must first address the attempt of existing curricula to render Black people "outcasts of evolution." The various curricula do not allow Black people, in any fundamental way, to *represent* themselves as *being in the world*, as a part of the world and in *unity* with it. Black ways of learning, perceiving, developing and motivating are not reflected or examined on the basis of their relative class position or on their cultural reality. What we now have are fossilized distortions and racist stereotypes that serve only to make inferior and dehumanize Blacks and ignore their historical reality. The work of Jensen (1960) and Moynihan (1965) are classic examples of the continuing effort among whites to represent Black people, in these cases children and families, as inferior or pathological. Blacks must have an opportunity to represent themselves at a *national* level.

Second, curriculum development must address existing curricula that are designed to render Black people "powerless." The various curricula not only disallow adequate representations and reflections at the core, but they also preclude the possibility for Black reconstruction of reality and the possibility of placing alternative constructions upon it. At issue here are curricula that are static and fixed and that do not allow the learner to interact with the data in a way that allows movement in both the learner and the curricula. The study of Black personality is a classic example. Despite the psychological motivations that generated the Civil Rights movement, those of Black power advocates in particular, the literature on Black motivation or on locus of control (as defined by laboratory experiments) has not changed. This literature remains fixed, static and stigmatizing. The literature on locus of control primarily represents Blacks as being passive and motivated only by external events and deficient in internal drive to control their destiny.

Third, curriculum development must attend to curricula that do not allow Black people to bring about change in their human condition.

Various curricula now reflect how Black persons *ought to conform* to the needs of society as it is presently ordered. They do not reflect the social conditions nor the disharmonies within society that must be a point of departure for real change. As a result, children and youth, for example, are prescreened and placed into school arrangements designed for their miseducation. School curricula are brilliantly designed for the production of incompetence and social irresponsibility.

These three elements form the core of the problem. They reflect the orientations of educators, researchers and therapists who too often make judgments about and define programs for Black persons and communities with insufficient data on the nature of these persons and communities, their beliefs, values or their abilities and resources. We have almost developed an incapacity to shift from our Anglo American perceptions, to change our attitudes and to foster real change.

The problem, then, is more than the lack of courses or staff. The problem is the lack of curricula that allow Black persons to represent, reconstruct and transform their reality. Introducing a Black perspective into psychology curricula will foster more than the development, analysis and understanding of Black realities. It will not only humanize the learning context and the subject matter of psychology by infusing them with larger social concerns and the role of the individual in human growth and development. It will also encourage the study of other groups and cultures.

In order to develop new knowledge, skills and attitudes that foster a just and humane society for all humans, the curricula we suggest must be introduced into institutions of higher learning. We see the addition at this time of Black content serving to develop deeper levels of analysis, understanding and a more humanistic view of Black reality. This development should foster more open scientific debate as well as the discovery of new knowledge.

The introduction of Black curriculum content is not a magical solution; it is only the initiation of critical scientific examination of the life and struggles of a large group of people who have been systematically excluded from the society and whose ways of *being in the world* have not been seriously considered.

At issue here is Black curriculum content in psychology, in relation to psychiatry, social work and psychiatric nursing. This project is funded by the National Institute of Mental Health (NIMH), and although there is no explicit statement that suggests the focus should be mental health, this is an implicit concern. This presents a problem for curriculum development in psychology since psychology covers, among others, industrial, mathematical, legal and social issues. When

Concepts and Terms

we address Black curriculum content in psychology, we are dealing with the sum total of issues in the psychology of human development specific to a Black reality at the level of higher education.

We are dealing with a Black reality, *Black* meaning people who can trace the origins of their ancestors to Africa, who now reside in the USA geopolitical space and who by virtue of their heritage have been discriminated against by both law and social policy. *African* or *Black* is used in this chapter to connote meaning rather than to denote a racial group. In saying *African*, we imply that we are human like all other men, yet in our individual genetic constitution and personal history we are unique persons different from every other (Nobles, 1976). Between our humanity and our uniqueness lies a large part of us that is created by the culture and historically transmitted to us through our society. *Blacks* as a race is an illusion if one means by it a homogeneous group with common anatomical and psychological characteristics. *Africans*, as we speak of us, defines a people whose detribalization has been much slower and more recent than that of Europeans. We think of *African* here to describe folk people more inclined, as a function of their special and temporal relation to the world, to be "intuitive by participation" or as Sartre (1956) observed, "having a certain affective attitude to the world." *Europeans*, then, would imply people more inclined, possibly as a function of their longer detribilization and, as a result, greater susceptibility to the concept of the world as a machine, to be "analytic by utilization" or, as Fanon (1956) observed, "having a certain mechanistic separation from the world, with diminished capacity for spontaneous and creative enjoyment."

The term *curriculum* is used to mean the content and courses of training that constitute the sphere of learning in schools of higher education. This implies not only the actual courses, but also the philosophy, assumptions, theories, goals, methods and expected outcomes underlying the courses. The curriculum also must represent a comprehensive plan of action for accomplishing some end and for the growth and development of people. *Higher education* refers to the education above high school, including any professional or specialized training or continuing education programs in both private and public institutions.

Three concepts, participation, alteration of the Black condition and transformation, will be used throughout this chapter to imply the growth, development and movement of people from one quality of life to an improved quality of life as defined by a larger social good.

The effort to develop Black content in psychology has a long history. However, we are concerned with efforts by Blacks to define their reality, rather than with the invasion of the Black community by numerous nonresidents eagerly seeking to get another publication out. The two most critical strategies were initiated in 1968 with the formation of the Black and the African psychology movement largely in the Bay area of San Francisco. The first represented a political move to gain recognition for Black professionals in psychology (American Black Psychology Association) and the second represented a struggle to deal with the philosophy and assumptions guiding the study of Black people. While the former was task specific—to get more Black faculty into the major universities, to get more Black labeled courses into institutions of higher education—the latter, more comprehensive, sought a reevaluation and reeducation of Black psychologists and potential Black psychologists in the values and premises they held about Black people and Black reality.

The first movement addressed racism—particularly the continued abuse and misuse of psychological testing to misidentify, misclassify and exclude Black children from educational resources and the issue of the existence of Black language. This movement was strengthened by the community psychology movement, in which Black professionals sought a concrete basis for developing the psychology of Black people. The impetus of this movement was the struggle for integration.

The second movement concerned itself with the continued exclusion of Africa from history. A group of scholars set out to correct this deliberate historical distortion and demonstrated that a recognition of the African roots of American Blacks produced a uniquely different understanding of the ways Black people are in the world, how they represent reality and how they seek to bring about change. This movement got its impetus from the political struggle for Black nationalism and, indeed, separatism.

During the early phases of both movements, the first major text (Jones, 1972) on Black psychology was published. Indeed the authors were in the vanguard in the Black and the African movements. Since 1972, much has been done to further shape and consolidate both positions. Recently, a third movement has begun to emerge largely out of the efforts of new socialist thinkers working with Marxian concepts. The emphasis is on the understanding of class and its historical underpinnings. The impetus for this has come out of the success of Third World struggles for emancipation in Africa and the Caribbean.

We now have in our midst at least three distinct movements in the discipline of Black psychology, each bringing its own Black perspective to the further development of a Black psychology. Debate is frequently

Movements in Black Psychology

waged within Black psychology as to the relative merits of the three distinct movements. Anglo American psychology has largely ignored or has not been aware of this critical debate within Black psychology, which is followed keenly by large groups of young Black people. Thus, the emergence of these movements and the issues germane to them have not played a part in shaping the direction, sensitivity or knowledge base of Anglo American psychology.

Yet another development within Black psychology since the early 1960s has been the serious efforts to increase the numbers of Black professionals. It is common knowledge that there are few social scientists from Black groups because few are admitted to institutions of higher education. Moore (1977) cites Mommser's (1974) estimates of only 3,000 to 3,500 Black Ph.D's. At the time of Mommser's report, only 1.7 percent of all arts and sciences graduate students were Black. Of this percentage, he projected an addition of only 200 new Black Ph.D.'s in the near future.

Epps and Howze (1973) found that there were only 166 Blacks with Ph.D.'s in psychology; Padilla and Ruiz (1973) found that 7.3 percent (348) of the total population of students in doctoral level and clinical psychology training programs were minority and that only 3.3 percent (4) of clinical faculty were Black.

It is reasonable to assume that there is a similar disproportionate representation of Black psychologists in treatment settings. This is a serious problem which leads to misdiagnosis and inadequate treatment, which could be corrected by professionals who are more clinically sensitive to the Black population. Typically, this issue has not been a primary concern of universities and training programs.

Perhaps, quite apart from some degree of unwillingness, there has been some misunderstanding of what must be done to alter the situation, specifically in the university and professional school settings. The next section presents a framework for some specification of issues.

A Model for Developing Black Curriculum Content

Curriculum development becomes more difficult when one considers a curriculum for training in psychology, the discipline which must include itself in its own subject matter (X[Clark], 1973). At one end of the spectrum of psychological theory is the traditional emphasis on the fixed, the immutable and the individual, which constitutes a narrow technological fragment of a science (Guthrie, 1970). It is tied to a philosophical conception of itself that is historical, oppressive and nontransformative, and it clings to a security blanket of mechanistic materialism. At the other end of the spectrum of psychological theory is the growth of a Marxist ideology whose exclusive emphasis on the objective, material social condition limits it as a theory capable of addressing the psychological and the subjective.

Traditional psychology, with its empirical overload or, as Myers (1979) calls it, its pebble picking, defies our scientific understanding because it creates an abstract concept of the abstract individual. Since the bulk of graduate training is under the control of the army of empiricists, this conformist psychology is perpetuated. We must note, however, that the empiricists serve a necessary political function of a class "who make the perfecting of the illusion of that class about itself their chief source of livelihood" (Marx and Engles, 1968).

Marxist ideology, with its reduction of individual concepts to a desiccated notion of history and society (Lukacs, 1971) without penetrating society, in effect amounts to a photograph of an abstract concept of an abstract social order. Marxism attempts to remove us from the moral burden of our basic feelings. Some see it as the new light because they assume that its methods eliminate subjectivity, that some automatic progress in history will be our "salvation." It maintains its appeal because it removes its advocates from the very uncomfortable task of confronting racism as a major social and individual pathology and attempts to install the economic order as the sole monarch on the throne of oppression.

The liberal and conservative utilization of the existing paradigms have produced a false consciousness: the liberal, an abstract conception of man; the conservative, an abstract concept of society. Both lead to impersonal psychologies and depersonalized realities. Because liberal and conservative curriculum builders have so distorted and buried history beneath a mask of scientism and psychologism, the psychology curriculum in reality has become particular to people of color—violent and destructive, the ultimate representation of physically and psychologically damaged people who have a limited sense of history. What we now have as psychology is a displaced white shadow image of Black people. We are forced to ask, "What of the possibility of a radical or even revolutionary perspective for psychology?"

In the next section we suggest an initial framework to break free of the colonial domination, which,

> because it is a systematic negation of the other person and a furious determination to deny the other person all attributes of humanity, . . . forces the people it dominates to ask themselves the question constantly, "In reality, who am I?" (Fanon, 1968).

An Initial Framework for Black Curricula

In developing a perspective or framework for Black curriculum content in psychology the point of departure should be an understanding of the previously defined movements and developments in the light of the present historical reality. One major document recently published (Jones, 1980) sets forth a framework for a Black psychology. This framework is really an effort to bring together the first two movements in "an eclectic approach, presenting a diversity of perspectives and interpretations of the literature on Black Americans." However, Jones seems to stop short of developing the third movement. It is a critical point of departure in this task of developing Black content in curriculum, but a framework must not be limited. Rather, curricula in psychology must be expanded to reflect the political perspective of the dialectical materialists and, indeed, any legitimate effort by Black psychologists to forge a new reality for Black people.

The themes or parameters of this second edition of Jones's *Black Psychology* reflect the following concerns:

- the development and purpose of a Black psychology—the perspectives and directions it should pursue in its movement;
- the formation of Black personality and language—concerned with self-representation of Black individuals in USA society;
- the categorization of people through psychometric concepts or psychological assessments and their role in the misclassification of Black people;
- the intellectual development of Black children and youth— the education of Blacks, the role of schools and other educational institution arrangements;
- the guidance of Black youth—the relations of the helping professions to Black persons seeking help;
- the role of racism in USA life and its persistent manifestation in our daily life;
- the roles of the psychologist and the impact of his or her psychology in the Black community.

A number of critical issues are necessarily left out of Jones's book because of space limitations. Further, the task of developing a Black psychology is too great to be accomplished in one book. These issues, which dramatically affect the Black community and have serious implications for any Black psychology, include—

- the biological formation of the Black person and family— pregnancy, child birth, early infancy, melanin, public health institutions and parenting;
- life span development of Black persons and families—adolescence and youth, the middle years of adulthood, aging and dying;
- the Black family—its development, structure and roles in USA society;
- the migration of Black families within cities and the disruption of family and social networks;
- cross-cultural perspectives on the Black family—Black families as recent migrants from the Caribbean and Africa and Caribbean and African family groupings;

- the political development of Black people and families—the psychology of Black social movements, social groups and leaders;
- the psychological impact of the Black church, religion and spiritual forces in USA life.

These issues do not exhaust the critical areas whose introduction into psychology curricula is urgent. King (1978) suggests a framework for generating issues. In this framework the person or family is in constant interaction with four irreducible social subsystems—the physical or ecological world, the traditional or historical world, the social world, and the social world and the economic world. Each subsystem has its own multiple parameters of interactions with the person or family. Each interaction generates multiple concerns that, together, forge the development of the psychology of the person or family. For example, in the physical or ecological world, the parameters include biology, nutrition, living environment and air. Each parameter allows for an interaction, so that in the biological interaction, for example, one could study the psychophysiology of the Black person and family through the role of melanin, or one could study the psychology of nutritional habits in times of poverty.

This framework is our point of departure for developing Black content in psychology. Figure 1 represents the parameters of the frame of reference. The diagram places the person or family at the center of four interactive subsystems that together constitute the person–system interaction. Each interaction produces its own essence, which is information for curriculum development.

The individual and family are at the center of a dynamic complex of interactions that are continuous and that consist of two or more entities at any given time. Our framework is only a model of specific interactions that can be managed within the limitations of planned education curricula.

The interactions $A \times A'$, $B \times B'$, $C \times C'$ and $D \times D'$ represent the basic interactions. $A \times A'$ is the interaction between the physical environment and the Black person as a biological entity, i.e., between the food, the clothing and the shelter that is in the life space and the biological reality of that person. We can generate a knowledge base that examines this interaction and, in particular, how it produces A', which is the psychophynology of the Black person. Studies may include Ecological Psychology from a Black Perspective; Psychonutrition; the Psychophysiology of the Black Person. Similarly, studies can be generated from interactions $B \times B'$, $C \times C'$ and $D \times D'$.

At a second level, we can generate curricula that examine interactions $(A \times A')$ $(B \times B')$, $(A \times A')$ $(C \times C')$ and so forth. For example we can look at sociocultural, socioeconomic or biosocial influences, which generate a whole new set of courses and questions about a Black reality.

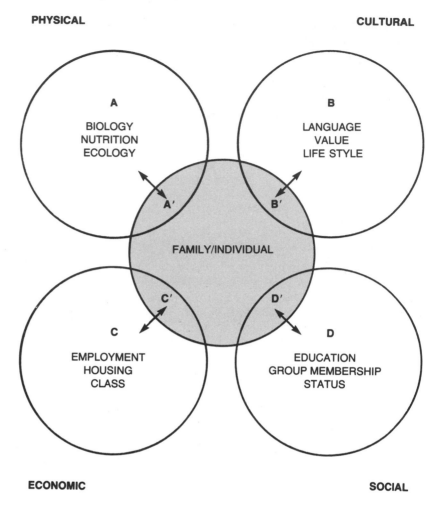

PHYSICAL

CULTURAL

ECONOMIC

SOCIAL

FIGURE 1

Framework for a Black Psychology

At a third level, we can look at the macrophenomenon—starting with the person—and study such specifically defined issues as the effect of culture on cognition, psychopathology and mental health, and development of the personality.

At some levels reflective of the model presented in Figure 1, work has already begun at some universities to develop curricula to include—

- the meaning and significance of culture and social class response patterns on therapist effectiveness and generalization and maintenance of client changes;
- the knowledge, attitudes and skills necessary in working with Black delinquents;

    • the viability of various therapeutic techniques;
    • the qualitative and quantitative learning experiences in mental health service delivery for a specified Black group.

Such attempts connote a fuller appreciation of the needs of the population to be served.

This general model allows us to begin to specify the missing knowledge base needed to train persons who are capable of serving the interests of the Black community.

We must set out to build a new psychology based upon theory that recognizes what we view as the essence of human action: the distillation of history. Four principles are central to this theory:

A New Psychology

1. history—The new psychology must be based in general on the concrete historical reality of humans, and in particular, the circumstances of the group it represents. It must be a history of cognitive maps or world models that groups of humans construct beginning in infancy.

2. dialectics—It must be dialectical in its methodology, requiring only that the analyst of society and the group question everything he or she sees and hears and examine phenomena fully and from every angle. It urges critical examination in the light of ongoing social activity.

3. reflexibility—The new psychology must be reflexive, that is, it must include itself in its own subject matter. Among other things, it must include the creative and the effective, the meaning of people's lives and the spontaneous and dynamic response to experience.

4. transformation—It must be transformative, i.e., it must not only allow for change, it must also have the ability to update or renew itself. It must allow action, movement, change and development.

The ultimate goal of our strategy of development is the radical restructuring of psychology curricula based on these four guiding principles. We must use this strategy to generate a new knowledge base founded on a more comprehensive way of knowing. Radical restructuring raises fundamental methodological questions about how to approach the task. If we accept the arguments presented so far, then a curriculum replacement is indeed needed. The alternative argument, that psychology is fundamentally sound requiring only an update in keeping with the times, requires that we simply intensify our present efforts. We suggest three methodological approaches to radical restructuring.

1. Developing parallel psychologies based on the culture, history and experience of minority groups so as to develop an antithesis to

the traditional psychologies. During the last decade many Black researchers began this process. We need to examine the data bases upon which their research rests and to include these data bases in curriculum for critical examination and analysis. The tools of analysis and the method for evaluating this data must use the framework suggested, which, of course, must also become part of the curriculum.

2. Initiating scientific and scholarly exchange between the proponents of alternative theses in order to discover the fundamental similarities and the particular differences between the data. The purpose of this exercise is to force the debate between the proponents of the various positions, thereby developing new knowledge and shaping the direction of the new psychology.

3. Creating a new paradigm for understanding human behavior. This new paradigm cannot be predefined nor will it necessarily follow that outlined by Khun (1966) for the natural sciences. Kuhn's paradigm suggests a system in which old formulations are completely replaced by new formulations. The conscious action of researchers in psychology ought to lead to an understanding that better explains and transforms the human condition. It is absolutely essential that Black and minority researchers be in the vanguard of developing theory, of defining the questions, of establishing the methods for the generation of new data and of suggesting new solutions to the problems of society.

We have lived for too long with the delusions of "a Black problem." It is a social problem, the decadence of the social ideologies and theories that result in continued war, disease, human exploitation, destruction of our resources, malnutrition, violence and the widening of the gap between the rich and the poor. What the ruling group now postulates as solutions are only delusions. Our very life and liberty depend on adequate research that addresses our interests. We must fight against the internal resistance and the continued exclusion.

Research Requirements

The researcher in this USA society is dominated by the ethic of capitalism. The society of research is maintained by a singular conception of man and human nature. The assumption is that "nature is a machine and nothing but a machine," that the world operates according to strict sets of logical natural laws different from universal order. Truth has become identified with scientific truth. The researcher distorts reality rather than illuminating it when he or she believes in an objective reality independent of the observer and when the method of observation and measurement depends on ritualistic scientism and elaborate statistics based on essentially unreliable data.

Researchers should seek to arrive at an organic conception of the

Black world, which is possible only if we start from the fundamental psychology and physiology of Black people and not from limited European perceptions and psyches. We must inititate research into the historical reality and the concrete human experience. In the ensemble of social relations, the essence of man is eccentric to the individual. We must study the concrete individual as well as the social relations. Rather than conceptualizing the individual and society as two externally related independent structures, we need to see *one* element as determined by the *other*, of which it is also a part (Dixon, 1972).

Critical to the concrete study of human personality is an honest investigation whose primary focus is social relations. Such an investigation requires more than an analysis of the so-called disadvantaged or oppressed. It also requires the study of the systems of domination themselves.

We are talking about the development of a psychology that seeks social transformation; a psychology that views personality development as a "process of progressive development of internal systems toward independent/interdependent regulation of action, manifested by active and increasingly conscious engagement with the natural and social conditions of life" (Moore, 1977). These conditions are material, social ideas (ideology and morality) and expected norms (political, social, occupational) which move the society.

Only through active transaction with one's social condition can the individual acquire behaviors or influence the social condition as well as his formative personality. Development of both personality and society may then be regarded as a dialectical interaction between the internal and the external, the former producing personality change, the latter producing social transformation (Freire, 1970).

But even in creating this psychology, we have to be aware that such a psychology must be conscious of our differing ways in the world. King (1976), writing about the Caribbean, states that our people are governed primarily by laws of intuitive participation. Under these laws, phenomena have the attributes of being themselves and yet partake of other phenomena as well—simultaneously. This think-feeling is in contrast to the dominant form of scientific thinking, which is governed by the "logical law of the contradiction" under which a phenomenon cannot be both itself and not itself at the same time—analytic by utilization. Cohen (1969) speaks of two polar rule sets. Blacks have a relational rule set and whites an analytical one and these, combined with two conflicting resolution styles (flexible and conflict-concrete), produce differing ways of being in the world.

Hilliard (1974) suggests that the inability of "science" to flourish among Blacks can be attributed to extrinsic factors. Science brings an alien ethos to bear on the ethos of intuitive participation. We find that the Haitian population in Florida does not recognize the boundaries between real and unreal experience or between intrapsychic and external phenomena; the real world is visible and invisible; cause is human or magic (Mathewson, 1975).

Riegel (1973), using Bruner's (1964) formulation of enactive, iconic and symbolic modes of representation, places Blacks in the domain of the enactive—a mode of representing past events through appropriate motor responses. He places whites in the iconic domain—the selective organization of percepts and images.

Margaret Mead (1954) states, "Blacks have developed an extrasomatic memory which never allows them to blur and forget their uncomfortable lessons from the past or to forget the pain. They have had to have a continual warning system in an environment, both African and American, which daily threatened their survival." These authors are suggesting the need for specific study of Black reality. In 1971 a NIMH study group did in fact make some significant recommendations on this subject at Meharry Medical College, although the concern was specific to mental health. Another NIMH study group, which met in 1974, followed this up with a further study on policy. A third study group met under the direction of Fanon Center and conceptualized the research requirements; their report (King, 1978), which we now use, outlined eleven concerns:

1. as a top priority, the need for concentrated effort on the relationship between stress (objective and subjective) and the mental health status of the child and family;

2. the study of exceptional competence and health under the objective conditions of stress—the strengths of individuals and family;

3. the persistence of inequality (race, class, sex, age) and its role in human and family dysfunction;

4. the need for Black researchers to continue to pursue vigorously the formulation of alternative theoretical formulations and analytical frameworks for the mental health of Black and poor people, as a means to more fruitful research and development on behalf of these people;

5. the continued thrust toward multidisciplinary, multilevel and interactional research paradigms with more critical specification of the biological, psychological, social and cultural variables that promote individual and family competence and healthy living communities;

6. the continued exploration of the subcultural (ethnic and race) and class variations in values defining social competence and mental health;

7. the promotion of research to prevent individual, family and community mental illness;

8. the examination of the implications for mental health of the profound changes that are taking place in the structure of the family as a consequence of social forces, particularly the apparent new role of women and the continued high unemployment of Black males;

9. the continued analysis of children's special needs, given the new roles of family and social institutions;

10. the urgent need for a group of Black scholars to study one of the most difficult of mental health problems, schizophrenia, emphasizing the biobehavioral coordinates;

11. a systematic and longitudinal study to define the environments and situations that promote ill health and problem behaviors.

These concerns do not exhaust the research directions or requirements, but clearly suggest that the key issues still remain ones of group–self-representation in the world; group–self-community reconstruction of reality from its own vantage point; and, finally, social, group and self-change through this conscious action in the world. Although efforts have already begun, continued research is necessary to address these concerns (e.g., Hill, 1971).

Strategies for Institutional Change

The entrenched and traditional positions of institutions of higher education and state certification–licensing agencies make it difficult at times to gain inroads into their narrow territory, marked by limited expectations and unfounded value premises. Their positions very often preclude the development of new ideas and, integrally a part of this, new or improved faculty and students.

The key strategy used to relax the rigidities must be economic. We must make it costly for institutions of higher learning to ignore the Black reality. They must lose grant funds from state as well as federal institutions for their failure to address Black curriculum content; and on the other hand, there must be funds made available for honest efforts to correct the problems outlined earlier. We must hasten to add, however, that while advocating economic penalties is the key strategy, it must not be separated from an appeal to moral conscience and political will.

A related strategy must be legislative—the appeal for change in existing laws or the enactment of specific laws to correct or update curricula with regard to certification–licensing. This effort would require the careful documentation of the problems, the education of our professional organizations and, perhaps, the creation of new examination–certification–licensing bodies. The task requires an organized and orchestrated approach based on carefully researched data, multiply-focused scholarly documents and consistent and persistent follow-up with the critical bodies, including the community, in order to establish the changes.

Yet another strategy involves using existing faculty and students to bring about a wider education and sensitization of the college community. They are in a position to institute and/or demand courses and content that meet new needs in the community. They can call up precedents in sister institutions or use any other existing body of legitimate information as ammunition in their cause.

Finally, appeals to the moral conscience of the educational community must be made continuously. We must never give up hope that humans have the will to humanize the world.

Even as we begin these strategies to radically restructure psychology, we must immediately address the concrete human condition. It is a fallacy to assume that the examination of these conditions must await the development of a new psychology. This is linear thinking. In fact, it is only in relation to changing human conditions that a new psychology can emerge. Some focus on these realities and the development of priorities for critical social examination are necessary. We do not begin with developing a subdiscipline, but with the social reality and the human conditions. Among the issues we must begin to examine are—

- the criticial data and knowledge needed to deal with the existing and future relations between the person and the social reality of certification bodies, schools, students and funding sources;
- the levels of impact generated by analysis of this data upon services, treatment, research and training;
- the time lines associated with each level of data analysis.

The critical body of data to be studied include the strengths and limits of existing data; the methods for generating new data; the methods for utilization; and the methods for evaluating data and strategies.

Guiding Principles

There are general principles that should guide the development and integration of Black psychology curricula. First, curricula must be based on the study of real Black people in real life situations and not on the attitudes fostered by an "ivory tower" approach or on comparisons with other groups used implicitly as standards. Data must be developed out of scientifically valid research and study.

Curricula must be culturally relative and sensitive, developed within the dynamic context of the living society. Such curricula will facilitate successful negotiation with this living context and avoid the transubstantive error of misinterpreting the cultural meanings of the language, the lifestyle and the values of the group.

The needs of the community and families, ascertained from well-formulated and carefully collected research, must be used to generate curricula. As such, curricula will need to be examined regularly and updated by scholars and citizens of the community to be served.

Institutions of higher learning, through their deans, faculty and students, as well as state certification–licensing bodies, must be part of the curriculum development process. Full discussion and debate should be generated among these groups in the interest of education, sensitization to the issues and exchange of ideas.

As a necessary element in the development of curricula and to ensure full discussion and debate, institutions of higher learning must hire more Black faculty, recruit more Black students and participate more in improving the quality of life of the Black community. It is only through these efforts that legitimate and valid curriculum content, organizationally tied to the needs of community, can be generated.

Psychology has a responsibility to benefit humankind (Nobles, 1978). Given this responsibility, there are serious limitations in psychology today. These limitations are not altered by fiat. Certain public policy issues must be addressed in order to foster the development of research and the expansion of theory and curriculum in the interest of a relevant and useful Black psychology.

A certain amount of this work is already under way, both inside and outside the universities. At present, Black research and development centers are being developed throughout the United States, a strategy which must be strengthened. More support must be given to groups of scholars who have long range plans for developing and implementing legitimate research based on the needs of the community. Specifically, the support of Howard University and Fanon Center should be encouraged. In addition, more effort and support should be given to developing the knowledge base of existing Black sub-institutes, that is, those entities within larger, white institutions. They should be given more resources, staff and the means to recruit more students. It is through these institutions that the necessary building of theory, reconstruction and reconsideration of data will be best facilitated.

Another strategy must involve the Black professional organizations and Black caucuses within the major professional organizations. These groups, particularly the Black psychology organizations, must be informed on the issues, be part of the process and be full participants in any action or deliberation. A related strategy should be to involve sociopolitical groups such as the NAACP, the Urban League and Black women's organizations.

The licensing of psychologists in individual states must be coordinated so that strategies can be designed to influence examination

Policy Recommendations

content, selection of board members, determination of procedures, expectations of professionals and descriptions of professional ethics.

Finally, the media should be approached so as to educate the public, not only via talk shows, radio and newspaper advertisements, but also through community seminars, lectures to high schools, church meetings and so forth. Such communication should be regular and coordinated throughout the country.

Conclusion

This chapter outlines some of the issues critical to the formation, development and implementation of a Black psychology. Our society has a tendency not only to create social problems, but also to measure itself by the number of new social agencies it can create to deal with social problems. To the extent that we accept this proclivity, we perpetuate a relationship of servitude to society.

We must undertake the critical task of humanizing the society by both creating and updating the Black curriculum content in our institutions, which are responsible for developing or transmitting new knowledge of individuals, groups and communities. This is an ideal moment in history, the first time humans have been able to label what is happening to them while it is happening. We have the capacity to research and develop a curriculum based on our collective Black reality. Prior to this moment, curricula were developed primarily by others and then applied to Blacks and other minority people. We can seize this moment to build the kind of social institutions that will not only serve but also transform and humanize our world society.

References

Bruner, J. *Studies in cognitive development.* New York: Oxford University Press, 1964.

Cohen, R. Conceptual style, culture conflict, and nonverbal test of intelligence. *American Anthropologist,* 1969, *71* (5), 825–56.

Dixon, V. J. *Beyond Black and white: An alternative America.* New York: Little Brown and Company, 1972.

DuBois, W. E. B. *Black reconstruction.* New York: Holt, Rinehart and Winston, 1915.

Epps, F. G., & Howze, G. E. *Survey of Black social scientists.* New York: Russell Sage, 1971.

Fanon, F. *Black skin, white masks.* New York: Grove Press, 1956.

Fanon, F. *The wretched of the earth.* New York: Grove Press, 1968.

Freire, P. *Pedagogy of the oppressed.* New York: Herder and Herder, 1970.

Guthrie, R. V. *Even the rat was white.* New York: Harper and Row, 1970.

Hill, R. *Strength of Black families.* New York: National Urban League, 1971.

Hilliard, A. J. The intellectual strengths of Black children and adolescents: A challenge to pseudoscience. *Journal of Non-white Concerns in Personnel and Guidance,* 1974, *2* (4), 178–90.

Jensen, A. R. How much can we boost I.Q., and scholastic achievement? *Harvard Educational Review,* 1960, *39*, 1–123.

Jones, R. L. *Black psychology.* New York: Harper and Row, 1972.

Jones, R. L. *Black psychology* (2nd ed.). New York: Harper and Row, 1980.

Khun, T. *The structure of scientific revolutions.* New York: Harper and Row, 1966.

King, L. M. (Ed.). Mental health and development: Source book II. Los Angeles: Fanon Center, 1978. (Unpublished Report)

King, L. M., & Dixon, V. J. (Eds.). *African philosophy: Assumptions and paradigms in research on Black persons.* Los Angeles: Fanon Center Publications, 1976.

King, L. M. Social and cultural influences in psychopathology. *Annual Review of Psychology,* 1978, *29*, 405–33.

Lukacs, G. *History and class consciousness.* London: Merhn Press, 1971.

Mathewson, M. A. Is crazy Anglo crazy Haitian? *Psychiatric Annals,* 1975, *5* (8), 79–83.

Marx, K., & Engles, F. *Selected works.* New York: International Publishers, 1968.

Mead, M. The swaddling hypothesis: Its reception. *American Anthropologist,* 1954, *56*, 395–409.

Moynihan, D. P. *The Negro family: The case for national action.* U. S. Department of Labor, Office of Policy Planning and Research. Washington, D. C.: U. S. Government Printing Office, 1965.

Mommser, K. G. Black Ph.D.'s in the academic marketplace: Supply, demand, and price. *Journal of Higher Education,* 1974, *45*, 253–67.

Moore, T. Social change and community psychology. In I. Iscoe, B. Bloom, & C. D. Spielberger (Eds.), *Community psychology in transition.* Washington, D. C.: Hemisphere Press, 1977.

Myers, H. F., Psychosocial stress and essential hypertension: A review. Los Angeles: Fanon Center, 1979. (Monograph)

Nobles, W. *A formulative and empirical study of Black families.* Washington, D. C.: Department of Health, Education and Welfare, Office of Child Development, 96-C-255, 1976.

Nobles, W. Africanity in Black families. In L. M. King, & V. J. Dixon (Eds.), *African philosophy: Assumptions and paradigms in research on Black persons.* Los Angeles: Fanon Center Publications, 1976.

Padilla, A. M., & Ruiz, R. A. *Latino mental health: A review of the literature.* Washington, D. C.: U.S. Government Printing Office, 1973. (DHEW Publications No. (HSM) 73-9143)

Riegel, K. F. Dialectic operations: The final period of cognitive development. *Human Development*, 1973, *16* (5), 346–70.

Sartre, J. P. *Being and nothingness.* New York: Philosophical Library, 1956.

Sherwood, J., & Nataupsky, M. Predicting the conclusions of Negro–white intelligence research from the biographical characteristics of the investigator. *Journal of Personality and Social Psychology*, 1968, *8*, 53–58.

X(Clark), C. The role of the white researcher in Black society: A futuristic look. *Journal of Social Issues*, 1973, *29* (1), 109–21.

HERBERT Z. WONG   LUKE I. C. KIM
DONALD T. LIM   JAMES K. MORISHIMA

CHAPTER 2

The Training of Psychologists for Asian and Pacific American Communities

Problems, Perspectives and Practices

The unmet mental health and human services needs of Asian and Pacific Americans are well documented in the literature (*President's Commission on Mental Health*, 1978; Tsai, Teng and Sue, 1979; Murase, 1977) and have become well known to mental health service providers in their day-to-day work. The formation of the Pacific Asian Coalition (PAC) in 1972 and the establishment of the Asian American Psychological Association, also in 1972, heightened awareness of ethnic identity-related psychological issues, mental health and overall quality of life. The National Asian American Psychology Conference, held in 1976, highlighted the need to examine the relationship of psychology to mental health and human services and to explore ways to improve the training of psychologists (Dong, Wong, Callao, Nishimara and Chin, 1976; Sue and Chin, 1976). The conference participants concluded that students need graduate-level training to work with Asian and Pacific American communities and recommended the establishment of one or more training centers in areas with fairly large Asian and Pacific American populations. As its primary tasks, such a center would coordinate field placements, provide bilingual and bicultural training, enhance research skills and offer interdisciplinary approaches in areas such as law, social work, psychiatry, and folk healing methods as well as in clinical, community and social psychology.[1]

The importance of expanding the number of qualified personnel to meet the service needs of Asian and Pacific American communities is echoed in a number of reports, among them the Task Panel Reports of the President's Commission on Mental Health (1978); the proceedings of the 1978 Dulles conference, sponsored by the American Psychological Association, titled "Expanding the Role of Culturally Diverse People in the Profession of Psychology"; and the proceedings

Statement of the Problem

23

of the 1978 Denver conference, titled "National Conference on Minority Group Alcohol, Drug Abuse and Mental Health Issues," sponsored by the Alcohol, Drug Abuse and Mental Health Administration (ADAMHA).

At best, the data on the number of Asian and Pacific Americans in the mental health disciplines generally or in psychology specifically are unreliable; data on the number serving Asian and Pacific American communities are nonexistent. Such information as may exist for psychology results from indirect analysis. The results of surveys by the Asian American Psychological Association and by Padilla, Wagner and Boxley, as well as the findings of Bonneau and Cuca and of Willis are summarized in Sue and Chin (1976). Differences in methodology, conceptual framework, and research design and the changing complexion of what groups are to be included under the rubric "Asian and Pacific American" seem to demonstrate that it is impossible to draw any firm conclusion about the number of Asian and Pacific American psychologists in the United States. For example, since 1978 Asiatic Indians have been brought under this rubric.[2] Further complicating the development of a clearer picture are year-to-year fluctuations in the population, inclusion or exclusion of Asian foreign students, sampling techniques and differences in data base—psychology or subareas of psychology (e.g., clinical).

The crucial question of how many Asian and Pacific American psychologists are serving Asian and Pacific Americans is unanswered. General efforts on the part of agencies serving substantial populations of Asian and Pacific Americans to recruit qualified service providers— whether on the East coast, West coast, in the Northwest or on the Pacific Islands, including the Trust Territories—have resulted in drawing upon the same and very limited pool of psychologists already working in Asian and Pacific American communities and in the unavailability of Asian and Pacific American psychologists or non-APA psychologists to serve this population.[3] While there are Asian and Pacific Americans and other interested students in Ph.D. programs in clinical and/or community psychology who will be available to serve in Asian and Pacific American communities within the next three to five years, the ethnic specific resources to train them for such work are limited.

Despite evidence to the contrary, many Americans still believe that Asian and Pacific Americans experience few mental health problems and have sufficient resources and manpower to meet such needs. The unmet mental health needs and gaps in services are substantial and can be expected to multiply with the known steady increases in Asian and Pacific American populations in the United States (Wong, 1977). Current studies indicate that this minority population is changing, at high risk and growing—predictions forecast close to four million in 1980 (Wong, 1979; Liu, 1979; Kim, 1978; Morishima, Sue, Teng, Zane and Cram, 1979).

Owan (1975) has projected at least a doubling of the Asian and Pacific American population between 1970 and 1980. Ninety-eight percent of all Indochinese, 90 percent of all Korean, 70 percent of all Pilipino, and 60 percent of all Chinese residents in the United States are immigrants. As such they must contend with the multiple problems of language barriers, culture shock, unemployment and underemployment. They must also contend with role and status reversal, intergenerational family conflicts, lack of community support systems and the kinds of emotional distress and concerns of any other American. The most high-risk and vulnerable Asian immigrants are Indochinese refugees.

On the whole, the Asian and Pacific American population continues to be visible and distinct because of commonalities in cultural, life experience and racial backgrounds. However, differing immigration patterns; varying acculturation, adaptation, and assimilation; and community growth and development patterns—all have produced heterogeneous within-group differences. Without a systematic and planned procedure for manpower development and training in the coming decade, the availability pool of psychologists trained to meet mental health needs of Asian and Pacific Americans will be exhausted. Without such psychologists, the unmet mental health needs and gaps in services will be exponentiated.

Mental Health Service and Training Needs

As noted by Morishima et al. (1979), there are some general trends in Asian and Pacific American mental health research. First, there appears to have been a substantial increase in research during the past six or seven years. However, the literature on groups other than Chinese and Japanese Americans is still sparse, although there is evidence of an increase in the literature on Korean and Pilipino Americans. Second, many Asian and Pacific American psychologists dwell on the same themes, particularly in analyzing and criticizing popular beliefs concerning the socioeconomic success and the lack of mental health problems. Third, to reiterate, literature on Asian and Pacific Americans comes from a variety of sources, and material is often published in obscure journals or periodicals. Fourth, the literature is becoming less rhetorical, i.e., more data-based and more substantive. Given the diversity among the groups and the status of the knowledge about each, caution is certainly advised in discussing Asian and Pacific Americans as a single entity. Notwithstanding, a review of the mental health literature reveals dramatic evidences of mental health training and personnel needs.

It is clear from the mounting evidence, documentation and research that emotional problems, mental health distress and mental disorders have bypassed no minority population, and certainly not Asian and

Pacific Americans (President's Commission on Mental Health 1978; Morishima et al., 1979; Tsai, Teng and Sue, 1979; Sue, 1977; Hoang, 1976; Yee, 1975; Morales, 1974; Watanabe, 1973; Berk and Hirata, 1973; Cordova, 1973; Kuramoto, 1971). Unfortunately, not only have researchers and practitioners had to document and state the existing problems and needs for mental health services and the conditions that place Asian and Pacific American subgroups within each of the ethnic groups at risk, they also have had to disprove and counter popular stereotypes and the widespread belief that Asian and Pacific Americans do not suffer the discrimination and disadvantages associated with other minority groups. The research shows that Asian and Pacific Americans, particularly recent immigrants, the young and the elderly, are extremely vulnerable to severe stress, mental and emotional disorder and a variety of life crises (Liu et al., 1978; Aylesworth, Ossorio and Osaki, 1978; Brown et al. 1973; Sue and Frank, 1973; Sue, 1971; Fong and Peskin, 1969).

Research studies also show that Asian and Pacific Americans tend to underutilize more traditional mental health services, drop out after initial contact or terminate treatment prematurely and endure stress to the point of acute breakdown and crisis. Two misinterpretations of underutilization have emerged: patients do not need such services; problems do not warrant continued treatment.

Given the long history of previously untreated and undetected mental health problems within any Asian and Pacific American community, a more likely cause of underutilization is unresponsive services and resources. To the extent that patients are dissatisfied, find the services unresponsive or find little help in treatment, they may discontinue treatment and also discourage others from seeking help.[4] Moreover, the documented evidence shows that the need for mental health services may be greater in the future. Impinging inequities multiply for immigrant Asian and Pacific Americans who are making the tremendous adjustments to the move to the United States, and experiencing the stress of personal, familial and social change compounded by cultural and language barriers.

There is evidence, though limited, that services specifically designed by and targeted for Asian and Pacific Americans help to resolve the mental health problems and concerns of this population (*Task Panel Report,* 1978; Kim, 1978; Wong, 1977; Sue and McKinney, 1975; True, 1975; Hatanaka, Watanabe and Ono, 1975). However, the mere presence or addition of more Asian and Pacific American personnel into the overall mental health system alone does not appear to significantly improve utilization of services. Rather more Asian and Pacific American clients use those mental health centers that both specialize in services to Asian and Pacific Americans and have a higher proportion of Asian and Pacific American mental health professionals. A number of researchers have suggested that the discrepancy between the high incidence of mental disorders and the low utilization of mental health services can be reduced or eliminated through a combination of community outreach, community participation in decision making, bilingual and culturally sensitive therapists, and other similar measures (Kim, 1978; True, 1975; Sue and Wagner, 1973).

A manpower strategy and program are needed to train mental health personnel, specifically in psychology and other core disciplines, for services to Asian and Pacific American communities. Two orienting perspectives frame the selection of our strategy.

Concepts, Terms, and Perspectives

First, the term, *Asian and Pacific American* is almost a travesty. This summarizing label is used only because we are the minority of the minorities. In 1972, the totality of all Asian and Pacific Americans in this country was estimated to be two million, or approximately one percent of the population. Political necessity requires the use of the term. As noted by Morishima (1978), the term *Asian and Pacific Americans* encompasses

> at least the following: (1) the descendents of immigrants from China, Japan, Korea, the Philipines, Southeast Asia (Thailand, Vietnam), East Asia (Tibet, Ryukyu Islands) and Oceania (Samoa, Guam); (2) immigrants from those areas in Asia; and (3) children of "mixed" marriages where one of the parents was Asian American. . . . Given the diversity of languages, norms, mores and immigrant/American born (status), it is evident that to label these peoples [Asian and Pacific Americans] implies a homogeneity which is lacking. Aggregation into one category is similar to aggregating the Irish, the Poles, the Swedes and the Italians into one group—European—ignoring the vast language and cultural differences. (p. 8)

Morishima's definition, then, excludes individuals from Asia and/or the Pacific Islands who reside in the United States with an intention of returning to their homelands—business persons, visitors and diplomatic personnel—as well as those who are in the United States on student visas. What we have are between-group differences (e.g., Chinese, Japanese, Korean, Pilipino and so forth) and within-group differences. Some of the dimensions by which they are different include—

- area of residence in the United States;
- generational status in the United States (first, second, third, fourth generations or more);
- degree of acculturation;
- native language facilities;
- degree of identification with the "home" country and/or region of one's own or one's parents' origin;

- education (number of years overseas in Asia, in the United States and elsewhere);
- age;
- family composition and degree of family intactness or dispersion with accompanying motivation for the particular family constellation;
- sociopolitical identification;
- degree to which groups are embedded in the local formal (e.g., family associations, churches) and informal community network;
- religious beliefs and value orientation;
- economic status and financial standing;
- comfort and competence with the English language;
- children from families in which one of the parents is Asian or Pacific American and the other is not.

The implication of such within-group diversity is that any constellation of a set of these differences describes a particular subgroup within the Asian and Pacific American population, with specific needs and specific demands for services and resources. In order to define services and develop training strategies and curriculum, we will need to be able to specify such differences using valid information.

Second, we need to pay equal attention to the common group experiences that underline the unique individual experiences. These have been labeled as unmeltable issues and unmeltable metaphors in Asian and Pacific American mental health (a wordplay on the melting pot theory—as defined by preemptive assimilation, of yellow man worshipping white man's metaphors, of yellow man importing Western psychology to understand Asian people). Common group experiences are unmeltable in the sense that they are phenomenological choice points for most Asian and Pacific Americans, which they must face and deal with or else suffer the erosion of selfhood—selfhood being the source of the sense of vibrant well-being and mental health.

The point is not that the basic emotions of Asian and Pacific Americans are different from the basic emotions of other groups, but that the existential dilemmas, the life experiences, the perception of what is important and the intensity of the reaction may be different. Differences may exist from person to person, even among persons who have faced the same situation. Given the common life experiences, "are there indigenous Asian mental health models and methods"? We contend definitely yes!

Whereas, in the United States, the repository of notions of mental health were embedded in the religious metaphors and philosophic systems of the Judeo–Christian, European–Americans (as well as of those who became Americans by virtue of immigration), in Asian history, the Zen school of Buddhism became a very accessible and successful therapeutic system.[5] Zen masters functioned as therapists. For example, Chinese philosophers and Zen masters provided unmeltable metaphors that are the basic elements of successful therapeutic systems. From the viewpoint of Western psychotherapy, the notion of emotional conflict or emotional blockage is a key in all insight-oriented psychotherapies. However, conceptualized in non-Western psychotherapy systems, the quintessence of the notion involves a binding of the psychic processes in such a way that growth is thwarted, that functioning is impaired and that the mind becomes diseased. As put by one psychoanalyst, the neurotic is not only emotionally sick, he also has cognitive difficulties. That is simply a "fancy" way of saying that the person can't see straight because of emotional problems.

Some indigenous Chinese therapists had something to say on the subject. From Mencius: "Make whole your heart, actualize your nature, and serve the cosmic purpose." In other words, integrate the fragmented parts of your mind, realize your selfhood and be a fully functioning person. From the earliest Taoist philosophers: "Use your mind as a mirror, it reflects but does not register." That is, the mirror reflects things truly as they are, without distortion by images previously reflected (an analogue of one of Marie Jahoda's concepts of mental health which goes under the ponderous label of "perceptual veridicality"); From the Sixth Patriarch, a Zen master: "Come, go, of themselves, no stoppage, no blockage." Or, don't perish the thought, let your thoughts and associations flow spontaneously, without repression or suppression. In another passage, "seek tranquility . . . dwell on tranquility . . . bound by tranquility . . . seek quietude . . . dwell on quietude . . . bound by quietude . . ." The passage continues with all the self-restrictions that result from denying spontaneity. The implications of these notions of unmeltable issues and unmeltable metaphors are that indigenous mental health practices exist and need to be integrated into any training curriculum and training program. They do not necessarily have to be accepted on face value, but rather should be pitted on even ground with existing therapeutic metaphors for their utility in the mental health services for Asian and Pacific American communities. The question is: "What kind of training strategy will allow for the maximization and integration of our knowledge base (now and to be developed) and the Asian and Pacific American life experiences?"

Models for Regional Mental Health Training Centers

To bring together the clinical and cultural experiences necessary to developing the training, research and knowledge bases that are critical to psychologists who serve Asian and Pacific American communities, we recommend the establishment of a regional multidisciplinary, multiethnic training center. A multidisciplinary approach would provide a sufficient "core mass" for training and knowledge development. As noted by the President's Commission on Mental Health (1978), traditional training programs in the mental health disciplines of psychology, psychiatry, social work and psychiatric nursing have not significantly increased the number of Asian and Pacific American graduates nor adequately equipped them to serve the mental health needs of Asian and Pacific American populations. The vast majority of the traditional training programs have lacked the necessary expertise, interest, qualified training staff and knowledge base. They have tended to provide little opportunity for contact with Asian and Pacific American clients and communities. This situation indirectly discourages service to Asian and Pacific American populations and denies students the necessary training during critical junctures in their professional careers.

Not only is there a lack of sufficient training resources, but most Asian and Pacific American communities usually constitute much less than a majority of the catchment area populations. A larger geographic or demographic area, such as a county or metropolitan area encompassing many catchment areas, is often needed before the number of Asian and Pacific Americans becomes significant.

It is therefore far more efficient and logical, from an organizational standpoint, to pool minority staff and expertise to establish a regional Asian and Pacific American, multidisciplinary mental health training center and service program than to attempt to duplicate efforts within several community mental health centers that have limited resources or within one particular discipline that has insufficient training resources. Ideally, such a center would provide multidisciplinary training for the various mental health disciplines as noted by the President's Commission on Mental Health (1978).

The typical community mental health service center employs few bicultural and bilingual staff, which tends to discourage Asian and Pacific Americans from seeking services. Regional training-service centers are desirable because they would maximize the number of faculty, trainees and Asian and Pacific American clients within a geographical area, resulting in a more efficient and a higher caliber training program. Several training centers—the San Francisco Bay Area Asian Community Mental Health Training Center, the Korean Community Service Center in San Francisco, the Asian American Mental Health Training Center in Los Angeles, and the Bay Area Indochinese Mental Health Project—have demonstrated that increases in the bicultural and bilingual staff correlate significantly with increases in Asian and Pacific American client loads. Where there is adequate minority staffing, for example, at a regional training-service center, there is a greater utilization of mental health services by Asian and Pacific Americans. Conversely, the Asian and Pacific American community must utilize health services in order to provide training and research opportunities for Asian and Pacific American mental health professionals.

To maximize training and research opportunities and fiscal resources, regional training-service centers should be located in geographical areas with a large Asian and Pacific American population. One of the major objectives of these centers should be the training of Asian and Pacific American mental health faculty capable of providing training and mental health services for Asian and Pacific Americans in areas throughout the country. Also, these centers could bring together students from around the country for continuing education seminars.

To maintain the highest educational and training standards, the regional training-service centers should be affiliated with universities or other training institutions. Such programs should produce individuals academically qualified within their disciplines but not necessarily restricted to their areas of special interest nor to serving only Asian and Pacific Americans. In order to maintain the integrity of the goals and objectives of the Asian and Pacific American populations they serve, the centers should have significant representation from the Asian and Pacific American communities on the governing board of directors or advisors.

Wong (1980) has identified system factors for the utilization of mental health services by Asian and Pacific American clients and for the training and manpower development of Asian and Pacific American professionals and paraprofessionals. They are key principles in planning, developing, implementing and evaluating any Asian and Pacific American mental health training center.

Conceptual and Theoretical Principles Relevant to Mental Health Training Centers

- *community-based perspective*—Highly utilized and seemingly effective services tend to be community-based with strong linkages, credibility and good reputations within the particular Asian and Pacific American community and its networks. Service providers tend to be known to or to be members of the ethnic community. Although services may be affiliated with a major institution, more than likely they tend to be free-standing and physically located in or near the particular Asian and Pacific American community. Oftentimes, medical and institutional affiliations and orientations are deemphasized because they are culturally less acceptable.
- *critical mass*—Both a sufficient number of ethnic staff and clients served appear to be necessary for a "successful" program. Differences seem to be found for kinds of staff (e.g., professional field, ethnicity) and kinds of programs (e.g., inpatient, partial day, outpatient, preventive). Programs that merely add one or

two "minority specialists" do not appear to have as much impact. As such, the training center will require a core training staff, located in an area where a sufficient number of trainers, supervisors and Asian and Pacific American clients are available to ensure appropriate training.

• *internship training model*—The training center model is not designed to replace or substitute for more formal academic training. Rather, it is designed to augment and to complement existing academic training programs with specific internship training experiences for the development of special skills in working with Asian and Pacific American populations and communities.

• *multidisciplinary support*—Because of limited manpower skilled in ethnic-minority mental health services, manpower from the core mental health professional staff are oftentimes, by necessity, multidisciplinary. Programs that tend to show shared support and decision making across the disciplines in services, planning and other programmatic functions appear to be more effective. The training center will provide the staffing patterns as well as the trainee disciplines that mirror the ongoing multidisciplinary service agencies.

• *human resource orientation*—There exists a mutual teaching and learning environment where individuals and groups may explore with (and therefore learn from) their peers and subordinates areas of clinical inexperience and weakness and share their skills and strengths. No clinician knows all of the varied, diverse and complex aspects and problem manifestations of Asian and Pacific American populations. Thus, an open learning and growing environment contributes to the development of such programs where staff are viewed as "resources" for the organization.

• *systemic approach*—Services are planned, organized, implemented and evaluated not as the sum of the various program parts and/or individuals that make up those programs but as a coordinated and continuous service delivery system. This reduces the tendency to just add ethnic personnel in a piecemeal fashion to increase the capacity of the agency, as the selection of staff personnel and program elements is geared toward contributing to the total mission of the agency. Likewise, in examining the client system, assessment, treatment and interventions must be viewed from a wider systemic perspective rather than from the status of each client. For Asian and Pacific American populations, the importance of family and community networks needs to be emphasized. A training program must not only provide training from a systemic perspective but must also be organized in such a way that systemic considerations are taken into account.

• *longitudinal and developmental perspective*—Both the training and service program (or agency) and some or many of the personnel have been and continue to be service providers in the particular community. Programs and individuals have positive "track records." The motivations, attitudes, skills and performance of program personnel are relatively known and accepted, and their commitment to the program or service is moderate to high. There is review and evaluation of the present and the past and a goal-directed perspective for future services. Mental health needs are met in a developmental, systematic and goal-directed manner, with resources allocated according to set priorities.

• *outreach orientation*—The training center approach does not limit service provider–client contact to agency facilities or to the training program. Rather, services are provided—within cost constraints and clinical appropriateness—in the home, community or in more familiar settings such as churches, schools and community centers. Staff members are not "penalized" for such work (e.g., by making such services of lower status as in the practice of letting only paraprofessionals do "outreach" while other clinicians are doing "therapy").

• *indirect benefits viewpoint*—Direct clinical services appear to be enhanced when programs and agencies are organized around complementary preventive and indirect services (e.g., consultation, mental health education and information, community organization and program technical assistance). Clients and the community at large, as well as training staff, would benefit from a comprehensive program that includes both direct and indirect services.

• *nonlanguage–translation perspective and monolingual clients*—The organizing viewpoint is that good and skillful translation is not synonymous with the delivery of quality service by a service provider who is fluent (with appropriate bicultural life experiences) in the client's language-of-preference. Language translation may have to be a procedure of necessity—but not one of programmatic choice. As such, the role of language translation and bilingual services needs to be explored in the training center.

The National Asian American Psychology Training Center

The National Asian American Psychology Training Center, recently funded by the National Institute of Mental Health, is the first organized program in the United States for the training of psychologists equipped to provide community-based multiethnic and mental health service to Asian and Pacific Americans. Only recently have the training and skills of Asian and Pacific American service providers been targeted and applied with commitment to their respective communities.

The training program of the National Asian American Psychology Training Center is composed of both supervised clinical-community field work and didactic seminars. The director of training, advised by a board, coordinates three program components: (1) clinical training, (2) educational coordination and (3) research and evolution. The core training is accomplished at field training sites. The field training sites involve at least three separate agencies that offer a broad range of mental health services to the Asian and Pacific American communities in the Bay area. The three agencies are the Richmond Maxi-Center (San Francisco), the Asian Community Mental Health Services (Oakland) and the Northeast Mental Health Center (San Francisco). The different field sites facilitate a broad range of clinical experiences. For example, trainees are able to see Asian and non-Asian clients. Some of the sites are located in urban and others in suburban areas. Some agencies deal mainly with preventive and indirect services (consultation, education, information, community organization) while others offer primarily direct services. The variety of sites offers trainees the opportunity to see clients of all ages and varying degrees of emotional disturbance (crisis to chronic). Furthermore, trainees who have special interests may request an assignment to the Asian and Pacific American-oriented inpatient unit at San Francisco General Hospital, the Counseling Center for Asian Wives (mixed marriages) in Sacramento, Vacaville State Prison or Napa State Hospital.

All trainees attend seminars at the Richmond Maxi-Center, as well as seminars that have been made available in collaboration with other nearby training programs. Seminars address the standard issues in psychological theory and psychotherapy, but also emphasize their relevance and applicability to Asian and Pacific American clients, as well as address psychological issues unique to this population. Issues of prevention, outreach and working with mental health systems are also covered. There are also opportunities for trainees to do research and to explore program administration and planning. Clinical supervision is provided by Asian and Pacific American psychologists; however, all of the four primary sites have a multidisciplinary staff; consultation and extra supervision by Asian and non-Asian mental health staff from other disciplines are also available. The establishment of the field sites and hospitals promotes collaboration.

The training program is conducted in community-based facilities that have had proven effectiveness in providing services to Asian and Pacific American communities. As a service delivery system that is part of the community mental health system of California, these agencies have been able to overcome many of the barriers that have prevented Asian and Pacific Americans from seeking services and to staff the agencies with personnel and resources appropriate to the needs of the unserved and underserved Asian and Pacific American populations. Although the mental health problems and concerns of Asian and Pacific Americans are often interwoven with other problems—cultural, social, vocational and medical—training in these community-accepted mental health programs allows the trained professionals to work in the context of the client-defined problems, with relevant and appropriate mental health service resources in an acceptable service delivery system.

Training also includes exposure to and some experience with the full range of community mental health services of each county in which the agency is located. These services are delivered through three direct treatment modes: (1) twenty-four-hour care, which may include residential care, twenty-four-hour sub-acute care, twenty-four-hour acute hospital care and twenty-four-hour acute nonhospital care; (2) partial day care, which may include hospital day treatment, nonhospital day treatment, sheltered workshop and social activity centers; and (3) outpatient care, which may include individual therapy, group therapy, family therapy, assessment, medication, crisis intervention and collateral services. Also, there are four modes of indirect community services: (1) mental health consultations; (2) mental health information and education; (3) community organization; and (4) community client care. Alcoholism and drug abuse programs are part of the mental health service system of the counties. Such work experience in the community mental health system allows trainees to assess and to transfer similarities and differences in treatment modalities for Asian and Pacific Americans and for clients of both other ethnic and nonminority backgrounds.

Candidates for the training program are predoctoral students already enrolled in a university clinical and/or community psychology doctoral program; the training program combined with placement will serve as a full-time, one-year internship. Two to four students will be trained the first year, and up to the maximum of six students in subsequent years of the program. Some provisions have been made for postdoctoral training as well as special summer outreach programs for masters and undergraduate students. The special programs will be aimed at emerging Asian and Pacific American communities that may not at the present time have candidates ready for predoctoral training.

The primary goals and objectives of the training program are as follows:

- To increase mental health service resources for Asian and Pacific American communities, with special focus on underserved and unserved groups such as children, the elderly and emerging groups—
  - by recruiting and enrolling as trainees qualified bicultural and bilingual Asian and Pacific Americans with backgrounds

in clinical and/or community psychology and who have interests in developing mental health service skills appropriate to Asian and Pacific American communities;

• by providing trainees with supervised multidisciplinary, multiethnic, community-based experiences during their training;

• by carrying out special outreach efforts (such as summer programs and community education) in order to attract members of emerging Asian and Pacific American groups to the field of psychology and mental health services. These efforts will be targeted at persons with minimum training in psychology as well as individuals who have extensive background in nonclinical psychology.

• To increase the relevance and utility of psychological theories and research to Asian and Pacific American communities by examining and/or testing the applicability and relevance of—

• existing psychological theories and models vis-à-vis the Asian and Pacific American populations;

• existing research methodologies for research with Asian and Pacific American communities;

• existing psychological intervention techniques as they relate to the the mental health problems of Asian and Pacific American individuals;

• current psychological assessment methods for Asian and Pacific American groups.

• To increase the awareness of institutions of higher learning, professional training centers, service delivery systems, professional psychologists and mental health service providers of the issues and needs of Asian and Pacific American communities and individuals—

• by collaborating with these institutions, agencies and individuals in meaningful activities, such as joint seminars, colloquia or case discussions;

• by helping and encouraging these institutions to implement courses that are of greater relevance to Asian and Pacific American cultures, psychology and people;

• by encouraging changes in their recruitment methods and admissions policies vis-à-vis Asian and Pacific American applicants, students and trainees;

• by establishing and maintaining systemic linkages with public and private mental health agencies, at least in the geographic area where the training center is located;

• by disseminating to these institutions and agencies and to the community at large information about new research methodologies, intervention techniques and knowledge about Asian and Pacific American communities.

- To promote support and interaction among Asian and Pacific American psychologists as well as other professionals—
  - by developing a social and informational network that will strengthen the ties between Asian and Pacific American psychologists and researchers across cultures and geographic locations;
  - by structuring activities that promote interchange of experiences and knowledge (e.g., newsletters, collaborative research, collaborative community or social action, multi-discipline conferences and workshops and collaborative policy planning).

The Need for Further Research

To date, psychological theories and knowledge have provided an inadequate understanding of Asian and Pacific American communities because researchers have not accounted for the diversity and differentiation among these groups and their problems and concerns. As noted by Morishima et al. (1979) and others, only within the recent past has the research on Asian and Pacific American populations been more data-based; extended to populations beyond one or two groups within the Asian and Pacific American rubric (i.e., beyond only Chinese and Japanese); and focused on Asian and Pacific American research samples beyond those that are more readily available (e.g., Asian and Pacific American college students).

We conclude that much research on Asian and Pacific American populations needs to be done before we can develop curricula that reflect the complexity and depth of the psychological and mental health perspectives of Asian and Pacific American populations. Although some of this information does exist, it needs to be further researched and explored to cover the diversity of life experiences that constitute the Asian and Pacific American psychological domain. Asian and Pacific American and non-Asian and Pacific American psychologists who study these phenomena agree and disagree with particular areas of knowledge. We can truly say that such commonalities and differences among Asian and Pacific American psychologists pervade the entire knowledge enterprise: theory, conceptualization, research design, methodologies, interpretation and evaluation. We foresee, however, that within the next decade research about Asian and Pacific American psychological perspectives will progress significantly, and only from such knowledge can an adequate and representative Asian and Pacific American psychological curricula be developed.

Notes

1. In keeping with the convention used by the Special Population Sub-Panel on the Mental Health of Asian and Pacific Americans, The President's Commission on Mental Health (1978), the term *Asian and Pacific Americans* refers to Cambodians, Chinese, East Indians, Guamanians, Hawaiians, Japanese, Koreans, Laotians, Pakistanis, Pilipinos, Samoans, Thais, Vietnamese and other Asian and Pacific Island Peoples in the United States.

2. The confusion revolving around the inclusion and/or exclusion of Asians within the Asian and Pacific American count is well demonstrated by the Carnegie Council on Policy Studies in Higher Education (1975). The council reported that in 1973, 61 percent of all doctorates awarded to minorities were awarded to individuals of Asian lineage and that 87 percent of these individuals were noncitizens. In actuality, the percent of total doctorates awarded to Asian and Pacific Americans (i.e., American citizens of Asian and Pacific Islander lineage) was not 61 percent, but 22 percent or 1.1 percent of the total doctorates awarded (p. 35).

3. Personal communications by H. Z. Wong with directors and senior staff personnel of mental health programs in New York, Boston, Sacramento, Chicago, San Francisco, Palo Alto, Oakland, Berkeley, Los Angeles, Seattle, Tacoma, Honolulu, Guam and other areas with substantial Asian and Pacific American populations.

4. For example, Atkinson, Moruyama, and Matsui (1978) found Asian and Pacific American students preferred directive counseling approaches and viewed Asian and Pacific American counselors as more credible and approachable.

5. Morishima (1976) pointed out that religious beliefs exhibit substantial differences between Japanese Americans and white Americans. He noted that it is extremely difficult for a white American to simultaneously be Buddhist, Christian, and Shinto, but because of cultural differences, there is no dissonance for a Japanese or Japanese American to claim simultaneous allegiance to the three religions. Given Morishima's report, it is evident that much more research needs to be conducted on a vast array of cultural differences and their implications for the training of psychologists who serve Asian and Pacific American clients.

References

Atkinson, D. R., Moruyama, M., & Matsui, S. Effects of counselor race and counseling approaches on Asian Americans' perception of counselor credibility and utility. *Journal of Counseling Psychology*, 1978, *25*, 63–76.

Aylesworth, L. S., Ossorio, P. G., & Osaki, L. T. *Stress and mental health among Vietnamese in the United States*. Research report, Chicago: Asian American Mental Health Resource Center, 1978.

Berk, B., & Hirata, L. Mental illness among the Chinese: Myth or reality? *Journal of Social Issues*, 1973, *29*, 149–166.

Brown, T. R., Stein, K., Huang, K., & Harris, D. Mental illness and the role of mental health facilities in Chinatown. In S. Sue and N. Wagner (Eds.), *Asian Americans: Psychological perspectives*. Palo Alto, California: Science and Behavior Books, 1973.

Carnegie Council on Policy Studies in Higher Education. *Making affirmative action work in higher education*. San Francisco: Jossey-Bass, 1975.

Cordova, F. The Filipino-American, there's always an identity crisis. In S. Sue & N. Wagner (Eds.), *Asian Americans: psychological perspectives*. Ben Lomond, California: Science and Behavior Books, 1973.

Dong, T., Wong, H., Callao, M., Nishihara, A., & Chin, R. Psychology in action: Asian American psychology training conference. *American Psychologist*, 1978, *33*, 691–92.

Fong, S. L. M., & Peskin, H. Sex role strain and personality adjustment of Chinaborn students in America: A pilot study. *Journal of Abnormal Psychology*, 1969, *74*, 563–67.

Hatanaka, H. K., Watanabe, B. Y., & Ono, S. The utilization of mental health services in the Los Angeles area. In N. H. Ishikawa and N. H. Archer (Eds.), *Service delivery in Pan Asian communities*. San Diego: Pacific Asian Coalition, 1975.

Hoang, T. A. *Mental health needs of Indochinese refugees: A survey*. San Francisco: International Institute, 1976.

Kim, B. L. C. *The Asian Americans: Changing patterns, changing needs*. Urbana, IL.: Association of Korean Christian Scholars in North America, 1978.

Kuramoto, F. What do Asians want? An examination of issues in social work education. *Journal of Education for Social Workers*, 1971, *7*, 7–17.

Liu, W. T. *Transition to nowhere: Vietnamese refugees in America*. Nashville: Charter House, 1979.

Liu, W. T., Rahe, R. H., Looney, J. G., Ward, H. W., & Tung, T. M. Psychiatric consultation in a Vietnamese refugee camp. *American Journal of Psychiatry*, 1978, *135*, 185–190.

Morales, R. *Makibaka: The Pilipino American struggle*. Los Angeles: Mountainview Publishers, 1974.

Morishima, J. K. Cultural differences for Asian/Pacific Americans: Implications for ESL. Paper presented to the Clover Park Public Schools, Tacoma, Washington, 1976.

Morishima, J. K. The Asian American experience: 1850–1975. *Journal of the Society of Ethnic and Special Studies*, 1978, *2*, 8–10.

Morishima, J., Sue, S., Teng, L. N., Zane, N., & Cram, J. *Handbook on Asian American/Pacific American mental health research*. Washington, D.C.: National Institute of Mental Health, 1979.

Murase, K. Delivery of social services to Asian Americans. *Encyclopedia of Social Work*. Washington, D.C.: National Association of Social Workers, 1977.

Owan, T. Asian Americans: A case of benighted neglect. Paper presented at the National Conference of Social Welfare, Los Angeles, 1975.

President's Commission on Mental Health. *Task Panel reports: Mental health of Asian/Pacific Americans, volume 3.* Washington, D.C.: U.S. Government Printing Office, 1978.

Sue, D. W. Counseling the culturally different: A conceptual analysis. *The Personnel and Guidance Journal,* 1977, *55,* 422–45.

Sue, D. W., & Frank, A. A typological approach to the psychological study of Chinese and Japanese college males. *Journal of Social Issues,* 1973, *29,* 129–48.

Sue, S. Community mental health services to minority groups: Some optimism, some pessimism. *American Psychologist,* 1977, *32,* 616–28.

Sue, S., & Chin, R. *The national Asian American psychology training conference.* Report of the conference held July 29–August 1, 1976, Long Beach, California.

Sue, S. & McKinney, H. Asian Americans in the community mental health care system. *American Journal of Orthopsychiatry,* 1975, *45,* 111–18.

Sue, S., & Sue D. W. Chinese-American personality and mental health. *Amerasia Journal,* 1971, *1,* 36–48.

Sue, S., & Wagner, N. (Eds.) *Asian-Americans: Psychological perspectives.* Palo Alto: Science and Behavior Books, 1973.

Tsai, M., Teng, L. N., & Sue, S. Mental health status of Chinese in the United States. In A. Klienman & T. Y. Lin (Eds.), *Normal and deviant behavior in Chinese culture.* Hingham, Mass.: Reidel Publishing Co., 1979.

True, R. H. Mental health services in a Chinese American community. In N. H. Ishikawa and N. H. Archer (Eds.), *Service delivery in Pan Asian communities.* San Diego: Pacific Asian Coalition, 1975.

Watanabe, C. Self-expression and the Asian American experience. *Personnel and Guidance Journal,* 1973, *51,* 390–96.

Wong, H. Z. Community mental health services and manpower and training concerns of Asian Americans. Paper presented to the President's Commission on Mental Health, San Francisco, June 21, 1977.

Wong, H. Z. Demographic and socio-economic characteristics of the Chinese population: Implications and concerns of the Chinese communities for the 1980 census. Paper presented to the Subcommittee on the Census, U.S. House of Representatives, San Francisco, 1979.

Wong, H. Z. Systemic factors affecting the delivery of mental health services to Asian and Pacific Americans. Paper prepared for the Western Interstate Commission on Higher Education (WICHE), 1980.

Yee, A. H. Identity crisis for Asian Americans: A personal view. *Association of Asian American Psychologists Newsletter,* 1975, *1,* 6–11.

Bibliography

Bergin, A. E. Some implications of psychotherapy research for therapeutic practice. *Journal of Abnormal Psychology*, 1966, *71*, 235–46.

Carkhuff, R. R., & Pierce, R. Differential effects of therapist race and social class upon patient depth of self-exploration in the initial clinical interview. *Journal of Consulting Psychology*, 1967, *31*, 632–34.

Kitano, H. Japanese-American mental illness. In Plog and Edgarton (Eds.), *Changing perspectives in mental illness*. San Francisco: Holt, Rinehart and Winston, 1969.

National Institute of Mental Health. *Psychiatric services and the changing institutional scene, 1950–1985*. Washington, D.C.: Government Printing Office, 1977.

Padilla, A. M., Ruiz, R. A., & Alvarez, R. Community mental health services for the Spanish-speaking/surname population. *American Psychologist*, 1975, *30*, 892–905.

San Francisco Community Mental Health Services. *Chinese bilingual mental health task force preliminary report*. San Francisco: Department of Public Health, 1977.

Sue, D. W., & Kirk, B. Asian Americans: Use of counseling and psychiatric services on a college campus. *Journal of Counseling Psychology*, 1975, *22*, 84–86.

Sue, S., & Sue, D. W. Asian Americans as a minority group. *American Psychologist*, 1975, *30*, 906–10.

Sue, S., Wagner, N., Ja, D., Margullis, C., & Lew, L. Conception of mental illness among Asian and Caucasian students. *Psychological Reports*, 1976, *38*, 703–8.

Szasz, T. S. The myth of mental illness. *American Psychologist*, 1960, *15*, 113–18.

Szasz, T. S. *Ceremonial chemistry*. New York: Anchor Press/Doubleday, 1974.

Wong, H. Z. A national Asian American psychology training center. *Asian American Psychological Association Newsletter*, 1978, *4*, 15–19.

Urban Associates. *A study of selected socio-economic characteristics of ethnic minorities based on the 1970 census. Volume II: Asian Americans*. Special report prepared for the Office of Special Concerns, Office of the Secretary, Department of Health, Education and Welfare, Washington, D.C.: Government Printing Office, 1974.

Yamamoto, J., James, Q. C., & Palley, N. Cultural problems in psychiatric therapy. *Archives of General Psychiatry*, 1968, *19*, 45–49.

JOSEPH E. TRIMBLE   DUANE H. MACKEY
TERESA D. LA FROMBOISE   GARY A. FRANCE

CHAPTER 3

American Indians, Psychology and Curriculum Development

A Proposed Reform With Reservations

Several years ago, John Bryde, currently at the University of South Dakota, was asked to organize a psychology text for use with American Indians.[1] In his seminal effort Bryde drew upon basic psychological principles, concepts and terms and related them to traditional and contemporary American Indian life in the Dakotas (Bryde, 1969). The effort, however seminal, attracted a great deal of criticism—many Indian scholars, critics and self-styled experts of Indian history emphasized the author's omissions, misinterpretations and overgeneralizations. The criticisms, however accurate they seemed to be, were challenged by many favorable reactions (e.g., to Bryde's attention to culture as an important variable in counseling those from different cultures; and to his transference of knowledge about Indians into practice) from those who used the text.

Four (of probably many) issues involved in integrating American Indian content in psychology into psychology curricula are reflected in the critical comments launched against John Bryde's effort. First, Indian scholars usually perceive themselves as self-styled experts on the subject of American Indians. Some feel little or no reluctance to speak out and criticize on any subject, regardless of the academic discipline emphasized in the work. Second, no matter which tribal group(s) is included in a treatise reflecting some psychological principle, some individual (or group) will denounce, decry, ridicule or sharply criticize the work for one reason or another. A typical criticism is that one cannot generalize findings from one tribe to another. Third, the study of American Indians is generally thought to be the *sole* property of anthropology. Traditionally, the study of culture has not been considered important to psychology. Further, the implication of treating American Indians without regard to knowledge of their culture has never been an issue psychology felt it should address. Combined, Indian-related information published in sociology, psychology, social work and psychiatry does not approach that in one typical cultural anthropology text. The marriage between anthropology and Indians, often justifiably maligned, is a major obstacle to including Indian content in psychological curricula. Fourth, there simply is very little widespread and representative psychological information available on American Indians. Most focuses on deviant patterns of adjustment (e.g., suicide, alcoholism). Little is available that describes cognitive-affective bases of behavior, social and personality processes and biological bases of behavior. These four problems provide sufficient reasons to explore ways and means to facilitate and expedite inclusion of Indian content into psychological curricula. But there are more profound reasons.

Current Data and Curriculum Development

The bicultural and multicultural challenges facing American Indians now and in the future seem to go quite unnoticed by the helping profession as a whole. This state of affairs is likely to create problems for both American Indian clients and the service provider when effectiveness of service delivery is questioned. Currently the knowledge of the multitude of psychological difficulties among Indians is alarmingly slim (Trimble, Jacobs and Ryan, forthcoming; Dinges, Trimble, Manson and Pasquale, 1980). In the place of knowledge are rigid perceptions, beliefs and practices that must be challenged and overcome if we are to accomplish many of the broad goals of the helping profession. The ignorance of basic Indian lifestyle orientations among many who deliver mental health, educational and occupational services all the more emphasizes the need to identify, obtain and describe general and, if possible, specific psychological characteristics, attributes and processes of American Indians and Alaska Natives.

Institutional Barriers

Psychology's almost exclusive neglect of American Indians stems from the long-standing anthropology-Indian affiliation; the almost complete absence of good psychologically-oriented, theoretically based data on American Indian groups; the scant number of American Indian psychologists to serve as representative and facilitative role models;[2] and the almost complete absence of any curricula materials or procedures for diffusing available information on Indians.

Many colleges and universities around the country offer and promote Indian studies programs in response to demands to sensitize faculty and students. Unfortunately, most Indian studies courses are taught in geocultural areas with "known" concentrations of Indians, (e.g.,

New Mexico, South Dakota, Los Angeles and Denver). They are organized and presented by historians, anthropologists, linguists and local "experts" either through a designated department—history, anthropology—or through an ethnic studies program or department. These courses are usually presented in the "ethnographic present," (i.e., as if the lifestyle orientations of Indians 100 years or so ago are still practiced today). Rarely do psychology departments incorporate these courses as part of the required course of study, which presents a major stumbling block for including Indian content in psychology programs: most psychologists simply do not place understanding American Indians within the purview of their discipline.[3]

Psychology, by definition, is committed through training and research to understand and further the human condition. By any stretch of the imagination the goal is certainly unattainable in our lifetimes. If one reviews the bulk of the information written in the field, however, one could quite legitimately ask psychologists what humans concern them—all humans, the average human or just a few representative humans? Every student of psychology knows that some psychologists try to discover principles by studying lower-order species (rats, pigeons, primates, planaria, spiders, dogs and so forth). Significant findings are typically generalized to humans, in many cases with tongue in cheek.

Omissions of Innocence

Students also know that some psychologists spend a great deal of time with humans, especially student populations. A casual or even an intensive, exhaustive review of the psychology literature of the past century, however, shows that psychologists haven't bothered much with American Indians. Although we may never know precisely why American Indians have been omitted or excluded, there are several possible reasons. To begin with, there were few Indians living around institutions of higher education two decades or so ago as compared to increases, though still small, seen today. Therefore, the Indian could not become part of one's subject pool; hence the absence of a critical mass (or representative sample) ruled out most research possibilities. Second, the notion of including ethnic and cultural variables in psychological research is a very recent consideration. A few good field studies were conducted on child-rearing practices among Indians in the 1940s and 1950s; however, anthropologists seemed more interested in the findings than psychologists. Of course, interest in cross-cultural psychology has increased in the past decade, as witnessed by the formation of approximately four journals and three professional organizations. Third, many psychologists probably viewed the cultural relativism phenomena as too potent and concluded that available psychological research tools were inadequate and inappropriate for use with diverse tribal populations. Fourth, for many psychologists, studying American Indians probably meant living and working in Indian communities, an environment usually thought of as rough, isolated and hostile. Fifth, many psychologists really believe that the study of American Indians belongs within the domain of anthropologists. Considering these possibilities we conclude that the omission of Indian content from psychology was born of innocence and was not deliberate or overtly intentional.

Innocence and ignorance, however, are not worthy excuses for the absence of Indian content in contemporary psychology texts. In fact, an abundance of mental health and psychologically slanted literature is indeed available on Indians (Attneave and Kelso, 1977).[4] The literature, however, does not seem to find its way into present-day psychology textbooks. To profile the distribution of Indian content, we selected twenty-five widely read psychology textbooks representing five core areas: (1) physiological; (2) social developmental; (3) learning-motivation; (4) pathology-testing; and (5) general. Of the twenty-five texts, only two referred specifically to American Indians.[5]

This brief survey clearly shows that information on American Indians does not appear very often in psychology texts. When it appeared in the two texts surveyed, some of the information was historically inaccurate and misinterpreted; in one of the two texts, the results cited from a study were slightly misrepresented. Hence, we must conclude that despite the abundance of research literature omissions continue to occur.

The omissions become all the more disturbing when one considers the possibility that students are not receiving an adequate representation of human behavior and the important contribution cultural factors make in shaping and organizing behavior. Moreover, after taking several psychology courses a student conceivably might believe that psychological findings and principles apply unilaterally to Indians. Of course, they do not. There are a number of studies that clearly show differential response patterns, learning styles and metabolic reactions that can be directly attributed to the different cultural and racial characteristics of Indians. Hundreds of examples can be identified to show that Indian people react, respond and do things quite differently from those portrayed in psychology texts. In the future, innocence cannot be accepted as an excuse for such omissions. The efforts we propose can bring about a much needed change in the field and can serve only to advance, rather than retard, the development of psychological theory.

| The Rationale and Its Implications | What advancements and developments can occur if Indian content is increased in psychology? Who will be the beneficiaries? Is it likely that increases in information will *only* add to the unknowns which already overburden the field? These and probably many more questions |

are legitimate. As we continue to examine the needs of Indians and the deficiencies of information and practicum experiences for meeting those needs, the answers to these questions will become more apparent.

As a prelude, it must be said that Indians have been applying certain psychological concepts and providing psychological services for centuries. The traditional "curing" modes of certain Indian men and women, for example, in essence are straightforward applications of psychology, although not necessarily cast in Western theoretical paradigms. It is presumptuous to assume that there are no parallels between the discipline of psychology and the lifestyle and behavioral and cognitive orientations and perspectives of Indians.

Efforts to impose Western psychiatric and psychological concepts on Indian groups have met with some passive resistance. The resistance probably reflects a folk wisdom, a wisdom tempered by the intuitive understanding that folk concepts and practices usually work, which precludes any need to internalize new, somewhat confusing terminologies and concepts. Learning Western psychiatric principles benefits an Indian student's understanding of non-Indian orientations to psychology but may do little to facilitate the same among individuals steeped in tradition. On the other hand, learning new and unfamiliar concepts may put blinders on those Indians who are also trying to adjust and adapt to the bicultural and sometimes multicultural demands placed upon them, distorting the essence of grounded traditional perspectives.

Increased cultural contact and acculturative pressures are bringing new orientations and generating new demands among Indians. The incidence levels of mental health problems among Indians are statistically well-documented, and there are indications that the incidence levels are increasing despite the best efforts of federal programs.

A survey of Indian-oriented community mental health centers in rural, reservation and urban areas would show that most services are delivered by non-Indians, many of whom have little or no grounded training in working with the Indian residents of the catchment area.[6] Unfamiliarity with lifestyle orientations coupled with culturally insensitive treatment and diagnostic procedures render the non-Indian service provider ill-equipped for success. This argument is not new, of course; however, it bears another airing simply because little has been done to bring about reasonably effective changes. Fortunately, local residents are being trained to deliver some services (Haven and Imotichey, 1979; Beiser and Attneave, 1978), and collaborative arrangements between non-Indian professionals and traditional medicine people are being established (Attneave, 1974).

The increasing mental health needs of Indians require immediate attention from many directions. Training opportunities for paraprofessionals and professionals; sensitive development of assessment instruments; effective application of culturally appropriate research findings;

development of appropriately designed educational experiences—these are but a few issues that merit ongoing, intensive consideration.

The discipline of psychology can no longer ignore the American Indian, especially in the areas of study in which students are trained to deliver psychological services. The problem is not just at the graduate level where the intensive training occurs. Undergraduate psychology students are not given the exposure, unless, of course, they take one or two courses in contemporary Americanist-oriented cultural anthropology. On the basis of the evidence presented thus far, we propose a curriculum reform that provides students, non-Indian and Indian, with the opportunity to learn something about psychology and the behavior and cognitive styles of the first Americans.

Curriculum Organization

Curriculum materials can be organized in a number of ways. Instructors typically sequence the subject matter in an historical, chronological manner or align content along some developmental progression. Course outlines for introductory psychology usually are centrifugal—courses begin with an overview of the biological determinants of behavior and lead up to an exploration of the social bases of behavior. Hence the organization of many courses is lineal, progressive and time dimensional.

Instructors prefer to follow a particular theoretical bent in organizing and teaching the many psychology courses. Learning theorists and staunch behaviorists often prefer to emphasize empirically derived subject matter. In contrast, clinical and counseling psychologists often adopt a less rigorous, scientific perspective and concentrate instruction on more "humanistic" matters. Still others prefer to view psychology solely as a social science and tend to organize instructional materials accordingly. Whatever the theoretical bent, the psychologist will likely follow one or a combination of two or more.

While there are many critics of prevailing instructional and organizational styles in psychology and the related social sciences, none is perhaps more outspoken than the anthropologist, Geertz. He claims that behavioral and social scientists should abandon their views of people as "layers." Geertz (1968) eloquently asserts that:

> As one analyzes man one peels off layer after layer. Each layer being complete and irreducible in itself revealing another quite different sort of layer underneath. Strip off motely forms of culture and one finds structural and functional irregularities of social organization. Peel off these in turn and one finds underlying psychological factors . . . pull off psychological factors and what is left but biological foundations. (p. 20)

If Geertz's assertion is accurate, and there is good reason to assume it is, then adding American Indian content to psychology curricula

could be analogous to adding another layer. Adding another layer—
probably a cultural one which would likely come just before social
organization—would not only compound matters but could very
conceivably strain departmental teaching budgets and alienate conservative curriculum committee members. Moreover, the myopic,
acultural orientation of psychology's purists—the experimentalists—
would protest including courses such as "The Psychology of American
Indians," "The American Indian Personality and Dynamics" and
"Developmental Life Span Perspectives Among the Northwest Coast
Salish Indians." While such course titles might have surface appeal,
they could be viewed as new ethnics in a segregated neighborhood.

The addition of American Indian content to psychology cannot and
should not come about by merely adding another layer. Another model
is required, one that expands and at the same time contributes to the
conventional, somewhat omniscient, lineal orientation. Geertz provides some suggestions, as every good critic should, by asking instructors to look at the human through his or her own *career*, that is,
through the development and growth of people as a result of the
simultaneous influences of internal and external processes. Through
the identification of certain fundamental principles, these influences
can be shown to affect people from varied cultural backgrounds in a
variety of ways. Put another way, available content about certain
groups can be diffused (spread throughout) existing course offerings.
Then we can begin to understand how various internal and external
processes bring about differing modes of adaptation during a constant
flurry of change. Following this suggestion, American Indian content
can be integrated without major modification to the curricula of
psychology departments.

To guide the identification, classification and organization of material, we generated a model using three axes—psychological content,
levels of analysis, and human activities—which form a three-dimensional cube (see Figure 1). Each axis represents an essential factor in
organizing Indian materials for use in psychology, or for that matter
in any academic discipline.[7] The following discussion provides a topical
outline for integrating Indian content within psychology.

Integrating American Indian Content: A Model

A major task in psychology is to identify major categories for classifying
the abundant number of topics and core program areas. One has only
to skim through the table of contents of an introductory psychology
text to get a sense of the magnitude of existing information. A variety
of classifications are currently available. The American Psychological
Association (APA), for example, uses four categories: (1) biological; (2)
cognitive-affective; (3) social; and (4) individual. Although convenient
and simple, the APA's schema condenses into these four categories
certain important topic areas. The first axis of our model forms an
alternative schema of classification with eight categories: (1) neural

50   Psychology

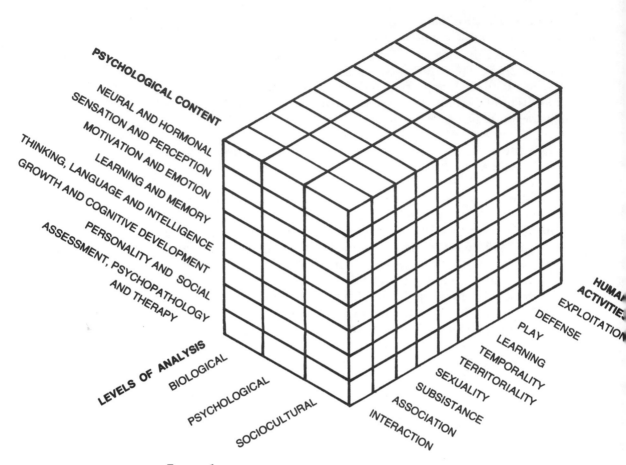

FIGURE 1

Conceptual Framework for the Organization of Cross-Ethnic Psychology Curricular Materials

and hormonal; (2) sensation and perception; (3) motivation and emotion; (4) learning and memory; (5) thinking, language and intelligence; (6) growth and cognitive development; (7) personality and social; (8) assessment, psychopathology and therapy. Although these eight categories certainly are not all-inclusive, it is assumed that the vast majority of psychological information can be tagged to each or to a combination of one or more.

The second axis provides for incorporating and classifying both the existing psychological information on Indians and the mode of analyses used in obtaining the specific information, since not all information is analyzed in the same manner. Some writers, technicians and researchers prefer to study and write about behavior from a biological perspective; others prefer to organize their thoughts in strict psychological or sociocultural terms. Therefore, to further the classification effort, an appeal is made for the use of a "levels of analysis" approach.

The idea of ordering the research perspectives of the physical, natural and social sciences into a "levels" scheme was first suggested by the anthropologist Alfred Kroeber in 1917; his "superorganic" concept suggested the need to order research perspectives according to the manner in which a culture was organized. Variations in the use of the "levels of analysis" concept have been suggested (Bidney, 1947; Hoebel, 1949; White, 1949; and Sherif and Sherif, 1969). The variations include recommendations to use a "systems" scheme (Buckley, 1968), justifying the ordering of the research approaches along hierarchical lines (White, 1949) and separating the "social" level from the "cultural" level (Yinger, 1966). The order of the "levels of analysis" indeed resembles the historical development of the sciences—biological, psychological and sociocultural.

Ordering the "levels of analysis" axis according to the three categories requires more explanation. Any data that pertain to anatomy and physiology and are analyzed or interpreted accordingly fall in the biological level; when information, data and research findings are analyzed and interpreted according to the behavior of the persons in question, they belong to the psychological level; and when humans and their interactions form the basic theme, the information is slotted for the sociocultural axis. The usefulness of levels of analysis becomes apparent when one finds an article dealing with neural and hormonal bases; the article, however, focuses on certain anatomic characteristics of particular Indians. The analysis obviously could not be psychological or sociocultural (even though Indians are the subject matter) and therefore the article would be placed in the biological level.

The two axes presented thus far allow one to categorize existing information by topic and level of analysis. Another dimension is needed to identify the salient human activities prominent among conventional American Indian and Alaska Native groups. The third axis gives attention to the "kinds of things Indian people do." There are numerous categories to choose from but it makes most sense to use the ten categories developed by the anthropologist, Edward Hall. The ten categories include basic activities humans are most likely to engage in: (1) interaction; (2) association; (3) subsistence; (4) sexuality; (5) territoriality; (6) temporality; (7) learning; (8) play; (9) defense; and (10) exploitation (Hall, 1959).

Using the three dimensions of this model the vast amount of mental health reference information available on American Indians can be classified for use by psychologists in preparation for teaching certain courses. The matrix gives order and structure to an otherwise chaotic array of seemingly unrelated information about American Indians. The matrix is not only a guide to organizing the information, it is also a guide to preparing the information for implementation.

Implementing Curriculum Materials

Prior to implementing the curriculum materials a few major tasks should be completed. First, a core group of psychologists and assistants should identify the existing psychologically related literature on American Indians. An extensive annotated bibliography resulted from the work of Attneave and Kelso (1977), and the effort continues under the direction of White Cloud Center (National Center for American Indian and Alaska Native Research and Development) staff in Portland, Oregon. However, the classifications and dimensions listed previously should be given greater emphasis. Second, following the psychology classification schema, references (and abstracts or annotations) should be organized under subtopics for each area of psychology. Following this effort, related resource materials can be identified and included in the core curriculum modules. Films, additional readings and audio visual materials can be listed to supplement the core annotated bibliographies.

Identifying, classifying and organizing materials would require approximately eighteen months. During the early stages of the effort, format, mode of presentation and criteria for abstract content can be developed. Following this, the responsibility for annotating and abstracting information should be assigned to a core group. Finally, an overall editor would provide continuity and control to the total effort. Arising from what on the surface looks like a major undertaking would be eight modules.

The modules should be field-tested to determine the efficacy and ease with which they can be integrated into courses. A small number of academic institutions and/or interested instructors can be identified to test the module concept and content.

Finally, implementation occurs through the distribution of the curriculum materials. Naturally, the institution or organization responsible for developing the materials can double as a distribution and resource outlet; as an alternative the modules can be submitted to a publisher for distribution.

A process for preparing revisions should be included in the total programmatic effort. Mechanisms for monitoring publications and reviewing them should be identified. In addition, a literature retrieval mechanism should be established and maintained. Users of the modules should be informed of the service and advised of the details for upgrading instructional materials. Maintaining an ongoing revision and update process is crucial to achieving the fundamental goals of the program.

An Example of the Integration Process

We investigated the ease with which the proposed curriculum model can be implemented by utilizing a specific aspect of the American Indian family. Family structures and family obligations are major cultural differentials and, therefore, fertile ground for studying the psychology of responsibility delineation, identity development, decision making and problem solving among Indians.

Most Indian tribal groups maintain reliance on extended family role models for the transmission of cultural identity, status and understanding. An Indian, just as a non-Indian, establishes his or her identity while moving among roles during maturation. Roles in Indian cultures place particular emphasis on tribe, clan, family, traditional status and heritage as a means of defining one's individual uniqueness within the cultural system. Roles also define each person's relationship to other tribal members and to the entire tribe. Since roles provide cues for appropriate behavior and clarification of one's status, privileges and responsibilities, psychologists may profit by reviewing traditional perspectives on roles and role modeling in order to understand contemporary Indian behavior and current enactments of traditional roles.

We selected cultural identity confusion within the Indian familial context, a prevalent topic in the psychological literature on Indian adolescents, to test the implementation of our model. However, before one can assess this phenomenon, one must understand the personal and social development of the Indian youth's motivations and behavior within the extended family system. In informal discussions, service providers who work in areas with high Indian populations and have attained respect in the communities they serve frequently emphasize the need for knowledge, respectful attitudes and skills in traditional child-rearing practices; extended family systems; generational roles; enforced separation of parents and children; sex-role identity development; descendency; preferential treatment or special status of favorite children; and numerous other aspects of Indian family life. To work with Indian families without understanding these aspects of Indian culture is not only ineffective but probably unethical.

The levels of analysis selected for this topic were the psychological and sociocultural levels. Each of Hall's human activities were then surveyed in relation to personality and social psychology content to determine which activities were relevant to the understanding of identity development and acceptance of role expectation, both of which influence cultural status and personal worth. The human activities found to be most relevant to the transmission of cultural values, role expectation and sense of identity were association (bonding, status, organization) and learning.

A literature search conducted by the White Cloud Center using the descriptors of social status, traditional social control, role models, extended family, family functioning and traditional child rearing produced citations of 151 published articles relevant to cultural identity confusion. Citations that specifically address the transmission of cultural role expectations within the Indian family are shown in Appendix 1 to this chapter; organizing psychological content in this fashion not only verifies substantial investigatory effort thus far but also highlights the need for more extensive research in psychological content relevant to American Indians.

A survey of the titles of these publications reveals a variety of problematic and difficult aspects of Indian family life. A critical reading of the material presented within the text of each publication may facilitate the development of the psychology student's appreciation for the American Indian's maintenance of strong and enduring beliefs, despite oppression and adversity. When conveyed through curriculum content this information can precipitate respect for a way of life not expressed in Western psychological concepts of modern American family life.

Continuing Initiatives

Some students and psychologists do not take lightly the absence of interest and content on American Indians. Over the past eight to ten years many interested individuals have initiated efforts to foster more concern and awareness for the problem. Both Indians and non-Indians are teaching individual courses or structuring courses to include Indian content. Awareness of their efforts is minimal, largely because there is no outlet for disseminating the information—within the informal network of Indian psychologists most are aware of some program efforts. Nonetheless, this network is small and many efforts are individual and go unnoticed before the larger public.

From time to time, Indian psychologists (and those non-Indians interested and concerned about similar topics) formally convene to discuss mutual concerns. In 1976, a small group met at the White Cloud Center to organize a formal meeting of American Indians to address salient mental health concerns. The following objectives were outlined:

- to identify, define and discuss the common and current issues and problems in the training of American Indians and Alaska Natives in psychology, anthropology, social work, sociology and psychiatry;
- to identify and discuss the most effective and appropriate institutional arrangements for training;
- to determine the directions for training in the social and behavioral sciences and to develop a set of recommendations for their implementation.

In April 1978, the meeting was convened in Seattle, Washington, and was attended by Indian and non-Indian mental health professionals, paraprofessionals and students from a wide variety of disciplines.

A great deal of information was shared at the Seattle meeting. Old social and professional networks were rekindled and new networks were identified and developed.[8] The substance of the set of recommendations drawn up by the participants far exceeds curriculum development issues, the central theme of this chapter, but because they bear directly on the present and future mental health needs of American Indians they are presented in Appendix 2. Curriculum reform, especially in psychology, cannot occur in a vacuum. As course descriptions and content are amended to include Indian material, they can be understood in light of the recommendations presented at the 1978 Seattle meeting (see Appendix 2). The authors have attended several meetings in which the same or similar recommendations have been set forth. However, no action has ever been taken. We strongly advocate that as stated in their entirety, these recommendations be acted upon.

Future Perspectives

Efforts to broaden psychology curricula are frequently met with a great deal of resistance and criticism. A number of the issues and concerns are explored in this chapter. Certainly, the list is by no means exhaustive. We must continue to identify methods to overcome the many forms of resistance.

The future for including American Indian content in psychology can be promising provided psychologists recognize the importance of culture in shaping and directing cognition and behavior; psychologists are willing to legitimize specializations that include work with specific ethnic minorities to the extent that such work is comparable to that typically conducted by researchers; psychologists give attention to the contextual and situational influences associated with ethnopsychological (person) characteristics; psychology departments retrench and critique offerings to reflect contemporary research findings, theoretical issues and social psychological controversies; and that psychologists give attention, time and professional recognition to formulating curricular materials reflecting knowledge and knowledge gaps in the study of American Indians.

The inclusion of materials on Indians cannot be achieved by simply offering courses entitled "Indian Psychology" or "The Psychology of American Indians." Rather, psychologists must attempt to identify and develop procedures for diffusing findings, issues and theories throughout the five substantive areas of psychology—biological bases of behavior, cognitive and affective bases of behavior, social bases of behavior, individual differences and research designs and methodologies. The diffusion process should reflect a social ecological orientation—one that identifies and describes the multitudes of variables and factors that influence and affect contemporary American Indian lifestyle orientations, preferences and characteristics.

Indian content that is integrated into traditional or conventional psychology offerings most likely will be integrated into the applied areas of social, clinical and counseling psychology most often offered at the graduate level. Program planners, educators and practicum supervisors need to anticipate and plan for a number of interrelated problems not the least of which is establishing stable collaborative arrangements with Indian communities. In addition, program planners should identify and develop culturally sensitive competencies, those minimum standards psychologists must meet if they are to work effectively with Indian people.

The positions taken in this chapter represent a basic orientation. It assumes that sensitization and awareness of American Indians cannot be achieved unless students and instructors in psychology begin talking about America's indigenous people in the context of psychology. Obviously, if the effort is successful, further efforts must be initiated to follow up on expressed interests. In addition, we urge students, scholars, planners, politicians and the lay public to keep in mind the necessities for responding positively to the mental health needs of American Indians.

Appendix 1
Selected References on Indian Family and Cultural Identity

Ablon, J. Relocated American Indians in the San Francisco Bay Area: Social interaction and Indian identity. *Human Organization*, 1964, *23*, 296–304.

Ackerman, L. A. Marital instability and juvenile delinquency among the Nez Perces. *American Anthropologist*, 1971, *73*, 595–603.

Berger, A. The education of Canadian Indians: An indepth study of nine families. *Alberta Journal of Educational Research*, 1973, *19*, 334–42.

Berry J. W. Temne and Eskimo perceptual skills. *International Journal of Psychology*, 1966, *1*, 207–29.

Boyer, L. B. Psychological problems of a group of Apaches: Alcoholic hallucinosis and latent homosexuality among typical men. *Psychoanalytic Study of Society*, 1964, *3*, 203–77.

Boyer, R. M. The matrilocal family among the Mescalero: Additional data, part I. *American Anthropologist*, 1964, *66*, 593–602.

Briggs, J. L. The issues of autonomy and aggression in the three-year-old: The Utku Eskimo case. *Seminars in Psychiatry*, 1972, *4*, 317–29.

Bruner, E. M. Primary group experience and the process of acculturation. *American Anthropologist*, 1956, *58*, 605–23.

Collins, J. M. An interpretation of Skagit intragroup conflict during acculturation. *American Anthropologist*, 1952, *54*, 347–55.

Cruikshank, J. Native women in the North: An expanding role. *North/Nord*, 1971, *18*, 1–7.

Demontigny, L. H. Doctor-Indian patient relationships. *Pine Ridge Research Bulletin*, 1969, *8*, 28–39. (Indian Health Service) Washington, D.C.: Government Printing Office.

Devereaux, G. Status, socialization, and interpersonal relations of Mohave children. *Psychiatry*, 1950, *13*, 489–502.

Eggan, D. Instruction and affect in Hopi cultural continuity. *Southwestern Journal of Anthropology*, 1956, *12*, 347–70.

Erikson, E. H. Hunters across the prairie. In E. H. Erikson, *Childhood and society*. New York: W. W. Norton, 1963.

Freeman, D. M. Adolescent crises on the Kiowa-Apache Indian male. In E. Brody (Ed.), *Minority group adolescents in the United States*. Baltimore: Williams and Wilkins, 1968.

Goldfrank, E. S. Socialization, personality, and the structure of Pueblo society (with particular reference to Hopi and Zuni). *American Anthropologist*, 1945, *47*, 516–39.

Hamamsy, L. S. The role of women in a changing Navajo society. *American Anthropologist*, 1957, *59*, 101–11.

Hippler, A. E. The Athabaskans of interior Alaska: A culture and personality perspective. *American Anthropologist*, 1973, *75*, 1529–41.

Hostbjor, S. Social services to the Indian unmarried mother. *Child Welfare*, 1961, 7–9.

Indian Health Service. Oglala Sioux and family organization, a statistical analysis. In *Pine Ridge Research Bulletin*, 1968, *5*, 1–23. Washington, D.C.: Government Printing Office.

Indian Health Service. Family problems and dependency. In *Pine Ridge Research Bulletin*, 1969, 7, 11–17. Washington, D.C.: Government Printing Office.

Jimson, L. B. Parent and child relationships in law and in Navajo custom. In S. Unger (Ed.), *The destruction of American Indian families.* New York: Association on American Indian Affairs, 1977.

Lamphere, L. Ceremonial co-operation and networks: A reanalysis of the Navajo outfit. *Man*, 1970, 5, 39–59.

Levy, J. E. The older American Indian. In E. G. Youmans (Ed.), *Older rural Americans.* Lexington, Ky.: University of Kentucky Press, 1967.

McAllester, D. Water as a disciplinary agent among the Crow and Blackfoot. *American Anthropologist*, 1941, 43, 593–604.

Medicine, B. The changing Dakota family and the stresses therein. In *Pine Ridge Research Bulletin*, 1969, 9, 1–20. (Indian Health Service) Washington, D.C.: Government Printing Office.

Morey, S. M., & Gilliam, O. L. *Respect for life: Report of a conference at Harper's Ferry, West Virginia on the traditional upbringing of American Indian children.* Garden City, N.Y.: Waldorf Press, 1974.

Moyer, D. S. The social context of economic change: A study of Eskimo boat management. *Human Organization*, 1971, 30, 11–24.

Munsell, M. R. Functions of the aged among Salt River Pima. In D. O. Cowgill & L. D. Homnes (Eds.), *Aging and modernization.* New York: Appleton-Century-Crofts, 1972.

Parker, S. Eskimo psychopathology in the context of Eskimo personality and culture. *American Anthropologist*, 1962, 64, 76–96.

Pelletier, W. Childhood in an Indian village. In *For every North American Indian who begins to disappear, I also begin to disappear.* Toronto, Canada: Neewin Publishing Co., 1971.

RedBird, A., & Melendy, P. Indian child welfare in Oregon. In S. Unger (Ed.), *The destruction of American Indian families.* New York: Association on American Indian Affairs, 1977.

RedHorse, J. G., Lewis, R. G., Feit, M., & Decker, J. Family behavior of urban American Indians. *Social Casework*, 1978, 59 (2), 67–72.

Schlegel, A. The adolescent socialization of the Hopi girl. *Ethnology*, 1973, 12, 449–62.

Shore, J. H., & Nicholls, W. M. Indian children and tribal group homes: New interpretation of the Whipper Man. *American Journal of Psychiatry*, 1975, 132, 454–56.

Van Leeuwen, M. S. A cross-cultural examination of psychological differentiation in males and females. *International Journal of Psychology*, 1978, 13, 87–122.

Wallis, R. The overt fears of Dakota Indian children. *Child Development*, 1954, 25, 185–92.

Appendix 2

Recommendations of the 1978 Seattle Meeting

1. Academicians, practitioners and researchers must be sensitive to the broad range of cultural differences existing among American Indians and Alaska Natives. Training methods and research procedures should reflect these differences in the development of curriculum and utilization of techniques.

Awareness

2. Too often educators are completely unaware of the cultural backgrounds and orientations of Indian and Native students. Lack of familiarity with and understanding of cultural ways can contribute to decreases in student motivation and possibly lead to withdrawal from schools and training institutions. Efforts should be taken to increase the cultural awareness and sensitivity of educators, especially at the elementary and secondary school levels. Funds should be made available to develop awareness programs and a mechanism established to implement them.

3. Cultural traditions and customs of American Indians and Alaska Natives are essential factors in the maintenance of social and psychological well-being. Nonetheless, the factors receive limited attention when planners and developers activate environmental protection assessments. Indeed, archeologists and historians are employed to determine the historical importance of certain land areas. The intent is to protect the area from destruction. Rarely, if ever, are the customs and traditions of Indian and Alaska Native people assessed with the same or similar intent in mind. Future environmental protection assessments and statements must address the importance of cultural conflict and contact with an eye to respecting the rights and privileges of a cultural group to maintain their lifestyle in a manner of their own choosing.

4. Efforts should be taken to attract more Indian and Alaska Native students into the mental health fields. Career opportunities earmarked for these students should be identified and highly publicized. Film documentaries can be produced showing the nature and kind of mental health career opportunities available: together with appropriate brochures the film can be distributed to secondary schools and undergraduate institutions for review.

5. Opportunities should be created to permit critical examination of the applicability and appropriateness of contemporary clinical and counseling techniques. Alternative mental health intervention approaches should be investigated, especially those consistent with tribal and village lifestyles. Future training programs should incorporate the results of these examinations into curriculum and practicum offerings.

6. Agencies are encouraged to explore development of mental health training programs in nonacademic, nontraditional settings. Community and village mental health clinics and service delivery units can serve as training centers for paraprofessional counselors, sites for field practicums where students' efforts are supervised by local people, and foster development of curriculum materials sensitive to local cultural orientations.

7. Community and village representatives must be involved in future mental health planning and research ventures. The mainstay of cooperation should be organized around a participatory decision-making framework.

Community Functions

8. Too often American Indian and Alaska Native communities and villages ignore the academic accomplishments of their youth and elders. Communities

should be encouraged to recognize the accomplishments of their students and graduates. Graduates, in like manner, should seek ways to communicate to community and village members ways in which skills can be utilized to effect positive change. So often graduates want to return to their native areas to develop and implement constructive programs; yet many feel they are not needed or wanted. Increased dialogue should occur to foster mutual understanding between both parties.

Research

9. Research measurement on American Indians and Alaska Natives should meet the criteria of reliability and validity. It should also be appropriate to the cultural milieu of the village and community. Validation of old theories based on the Indian and Alaska Native experience is encouraged. Future research development and efforts should be sensitive to community problems. Solutions should be consistent with a community and village lifestyle to the extent that they can be internalized and utilized without violating normative traditions.

10. A code of ethics for conducting mental health related research in Indian communities and Alaska Native villages must be developed and implemented. The code of ethics should be developed by a team of Indian and Alaska Native mental health professionals, paraprofessionals, community and village leaders, and students and be included as an essential consideration of human subjects review committees at the federal and institutional levels.

11. Through collaboration with Indian and Alaska Native mental health professionals and tribal and village representatives and federal agencies, specific mental health research areas should be identified and prioritized. Emphasis should be placed on regional and local community needs. If mental health needs have not been empirically demonstrated, steps should be taken to have them assessed. Accordingly, efforts must be taken by federal agencies to apportion certain funds strictly for meeting the research agenda and priorities.

12. Satellite regional Indian and Alaska Native mental health research and development centers should be established and supported by federal agencies. These centers should work cooperatively and their efforts should form the nucleus for sharing and disseminating information.

13. Federal agencies are encouraged to support research which can lead to an assessment of successful mental health training programs. Emphasis should be placed on the characteristics of faculty, academic climate, curriculum, nature and existence of student support systems and relevance of the educational experience for Indian and Alaska Native students.

14. Massive amounts of research reports, commentary and mental health information exists on American Indians and Alaska Natives. A central clearing house should be established and maintained for processing, collecting and disseminating works. Yearly summaries of research, program developments and training efforts can be prepared and made available for distribution. Development funds should be made available; however, it's possible for the effort to become self-supporting in years to come.

15. For decades numerous theoreticians and practitioners have attempted to define and conceptualize mental health. For the most part, current conceptualizations play down the importance of the Indian and Alaska Native perspective. Efforts, carried out through carefully planned research, should be made to obtain tribal and village conceptualizations of mental health. It could be that the native world view of the concept might provide insights into developing culturally appropriate curriculum and treatment models.

16. Alcoholism is considered to be the main mental health problem among American Indians and Alaska Natives; while NIAAA has devoted some effort

to support training and treatment programs, limited attention has been given to understanding the problem. In other words, the limited empirically based research has taken a backseat to training and treatment efforts. NIAAA should encourage more substantive and appropriate research into the etiology and prevention of alcoholism among Indians and Alaska Natives. While NIAAA has supported a number of programs, little has been done to assess the accomplishments and the impact at the local levels. NIAAA is also encouraged to support an assessment leading to a systematic identification and documentation of Indian and Alaska Native alcoholism and treatment related successes.

17. A large number of Indian and Alaska Native communities are not familiar with useful mental health techniques, services and programs. An intensive educational effort should be developed and implemented.

Federal and State Agencies

18. The prevention of mental health related problems among American Indians and Alaska Natives is a highly neglected area. Federal and state agencies should accelerate efforts to identify appropriate, culturally sensitive prevention strategies. In itself, education is one mechanism; however, there are other approaches that need to be identified, tested, revised and implemented. Continuing technological development on or near reservations and villages is likely to have negative social impacts. Efforts must be stepped up to assess the magnitude of the impact, the consequences to social and psychological well-being and long-term effects on cultural traditions and customs. Negative social and psychological impacts can be prevented with intensive research and development efforts.

19. Prior experience with the federal review of Indian and Alaska Native grant and training applications has demonstrated that retaining a few Indian and Alaska Native members on the review groups is not sufficient. Many applications have been denied approval largely because review-group members fail to see the relevance of cultural orientations and the importance of tribal and village lifestyles. Federal agencies, e.g., NIMH, NIAAA, NIDA, and NIH, should convene separate Indian and Alaska Native groups to review applications particular to their orientation. Groups should consist of professionals, paraprofessionals and appropriate community representatives. There are not enough Indian and Alaska Native professionals to form a separate review group for each agency within ADAMHA. Nonetheless, a separate Indian and Alaska Native review group could be convened at the ADAMHA level to serve the functions outlined above to supplement the typical review procedure.

20. Federal agencies such as NIMH, NIAAA and NIDA, together with representatives of Indian and Alaska Native communities, should explore the feasibility of providing direct funding to tribes and villages. Direct funding procedures can eliminate the competitive nature of grant and training applications where tribes and villages are pitted against one another for limited financial resources. The competitive process often creates unnecessary friction between groups. The mental health needs of tribal and village communities can be served more expeditiously through direct funding mechanisms.

21. Convening American Indian and Alaska Native mental health professionals, paraprofessionals and students to discuss issues, problems and provide recommendations is welcomed. However, many issues and problems surface with little time to devote full attention to them. Annual meetings are encouraged and sorely needed. ADAMHA should set aside support for such events. Both federal agencies and Indian and Alaska Native communities could benefit immensely from sharing information, participation in task-oriented sessions and workshops and generating new and beneficial approaches to solving and preventing future mental health problems.

Academic Institutions

22. Academic institutions should develop and maintain strong Indian and Alaska Native student support systems, especially those with substantial Indian and Alaska Native enrollments. Career opportunities, tutorial opportunities, guidance in the selection of courses and personal counseling should serve as the main components of the system. Counseling and guidance should be initiated early in a student's career with the center taking the initiative in contacting students.

23. Academic institutions should not dismiss lightly the significant folk knowledge and traditional healing practices of American Indians and Alaska Natives. Efforts should be taken to support development of curriculum that incorporated this knowledge into course content. Local spiritual leaders and medicine men should be utilized in the planning and implementation. Non-Indians as well as Indians and Alaska Natives need to be aware of the importance of traditional healing practices in everyday reservation and village life.

24. A large number of Indians and Alaska Natives have received limited mental health training at the paraprofessional level. Efforts should be taken to initiate, develop and maintain continuing education programs for these paraprofessionals. Techniques, advances in mental health knowledge, courses to sharpen counseling and interviewing skills should be part of the curricula. Too often formal paraprofessional education stops with the certificate. Yet the knowledge needs seem to increase with client contact on the job.

General

25. Efforts should be supported to identify, establish and maintain a skills bank of American Indian and Alaska Native mental health professionals and paraprofessionals. The skills bank could be organized to include three substantial areas: research and training, technical assistance and curriculum development. The effort should include the identification of students enrolled in mental health related programs, maintenance of a tracking system and a means for providing guidance and consultation.

Systems Change

26. Colleges and universities should allow students to take courses that are specifically related to the understanding of the American Indian and Alaska Native. Credit for these courses should be given in lieu of a required course of a major field of study.

27. States should require mental health workers to complete successfully one course (three hours) that contributes to the understanding of the cultures of American Indians and Alaska Natives.

28. Federal funding criteria for mental health related grants should include stipulations for developing ethnic minority related curricula, research and programs of study.

Notes

1. The term *Indian* will be used in this chapter to refer to American Indians and Alaska Natives collectively. Use of the single term in this manner is generally acceptable.

2. The American Psychological Association reports that fourteen American Indians are current members or associates. The Society of Indian Psychologists estimates that about eighty Indians have graduate degrees in psychology.

3. The senior author was told that his symposium proposal submitted for consideration as a part of the 1970 regional psychological association meeting was not approved because: "(1) anthropologists, not psychologists, are interested in American Indians; and (2) there are no Indians on reservations in the East so no one would be able to apply your results and suggestions." The program suggested that the same proposal be submitted to a western psychological association where there are greater, known concentrations of Indians.

4. An ongoing research literature retrieval and information program is in operation at the While Cloud Center, the National Center for American Indian and Alaska Native Research and Development. The center, located on the campus of the University of Oregon Health Sciences Center in Portland, periodically publishes bibliographies on certain aspects of Indian mental health.

5. The two were undergraduate social psychology texts. One contained 11 pages out of 579; the other, 9 out of 662.

6. Imagine graduate practicums not providing grounded experiences for students who want to eventually work with the handicapped or the psychotic, for example. Very few, if any, graduate programs provide practicum experiences for those who intend to work in Indian communities.

7. Conceptualizing content, process and things into cubes is certainly not new. Guilford (1959) found it convenient to organize intelligence according to three axes. Cattell (1966) effectively proposes the ordering of multivariate research into three dimensions. Trimble and Medicine (1976), through a three-dimensional ecosystems analysis matrix, argue that future research on American Indians can capture the "ethos" of communities more accurately.

8. A detailed report of the meeting may be obtained from Dr. Robert A. Ryan, White Cloud Center, 840 S.W. Gaines Road, Portland, Oregon 97201.

References

Attneave, C., & Kelso, D. (Eds.). *American Indian annotated bibliography of mental health* (Vol. 1). Seattle: University of Washington, 1977.

Attneave, C. L. Medicine men and psychiatrists in Indian health service. *Psychiatric Annals*, 1974, 4(11), 49–55.

Beiser, M., & Attneave, C. L. Mental health services for American Indians: Neither feast nor famine. *White Cloud Journal*, 1978, 1(2), 3–10.

Bidney, D. On the concept of culture and some cultural fallacies. *American Anthropologist*, 1947, 46, 35–44.

Bryde, J. *Modern Indian psychology*. Vermillion, S. D.: Institute of Indian Studies, University of South Dakota, 1969.

Buckley, W. *Modern systems research for the behavioral scientist: A sourcebook*. Chicago: Aldine, 1968.

Cattell, R. B. (Ed.). *Handbook of multivariate experimental psychology*. Chicago: Rand McNally, 1966.

Dinges, N., Trimble, J., Manson, S., & Pasquale, F. The social ecology of counseling and psychotherapy with American Indians and Alaska Natives. In A. J. Marsella & P. Pedersen (Eds.), *Counseling and psychotherapy: Foundations, evaluation, cultural considerations*. Elmsford, N.Y.: Pergamon, 1980.

Geertz, C. The impact of the concept of culture on the concept of man. In Y. A. Cohen (Ed.), *Man in adaptation: The cultural present*. Chicago: Aldine, 1968.

Guilford, J. P. The three faces of intellect. *American Psychologist*, 1959, 14, 469–79.

Hall, E. T. *The silent language*. New York: Doubleday, 1959.

Haven, G., & Imotichey, P. Mental health services for American Indians: The USET program. *White Cloud Journal*, 1979, 1(3), 3–5.

Hoebel, F. A. *Man in the primitive world*. New York: McGraw-Hill, 1949.

Kroeber, A. L. The superorganic. *American Anthropologist*, 1917, 19, 163–213.

Sherif, M., & Sherif, C. *Social psychology*. New York: Harper and Row, 1969.

Trimble, J., Jacobs, D., & Ryan, R. Psychology in action: American Indian and Alaska Native mental health training. *American Psychologist* (forthcoming).

Trimble, J. E., & Medicine, B. Development of theoretical models and levels of interpretation in mental health. In J. Westermeyer (Ed.), *Anthropology and mental health*. Netherlands: Moltune, 1976.

White, L. A. *The science culture*. New York: Farrar-Strauss, 1949.

Yinger, J. M. *Toward a field theory of behavior*. New York: McGraw-Hill, 1966.

GUILLERMO BERNAL
ANGEL C. MARTINEZ
DAVID SANTISTEBAN

MARTHA E. BERNAL
ESTEBAN L. OLMEDO

CHAPTER **4**

Hispanic Mental Health Curriculum for Psychology

Hispanic is a generic term that refers to all Spanish-speaking or Spanish-surnamed peoples who reside in the United States or Puerto Rico. The three major groups are Mexican Americans or Chicanos, Cuban Americans and Puerto Ricans. There are also substantial numbers of other Hispanics of Central or South American origin.

Definitions

The term *Hispanic* is used in this chapter because it is the official label adopted by the National Hispanic Psychological Association. Traditionally, the label *Hispanic* has been preferred on the East Coast by the Puerto Rican and Cuban communities. On the West Coast, the preferred label has been *Latino,* a Spanish word indicating Latin American origins. *Chicano* is another term predominantly employed on the West Coast and refers to Mexican Americans and to persons of Mexican heritage born in the United States. Two other terms have enjoyed widespread use: *Spanish Speaking-Spanish Surnamed* and *La Raza.* The former is a recognition that a wide number of Hispanics may not be Spanish speaking. The latter is a term associated with political struggles and connotes *el mestizaje* (defined as a crossing of races). *La Raza* refers to all the peoples of the Western Hemisphere who to some degree share a social and a cultural legacy of Spanish colonists, Native Indians and African peoples.

The term *mental health* is broadly defined to include not only issues of diagnosis and treatment of mental disorders but also the social, economic, and cultural factors that can be directly linked to the etiology of mental health problems among Hispanics. Psychology involves the study of behavior and experience and the application of that knowledge to solving human problems; as such, it is both a science and a profession. "Students of psychology study a basic core of knowledge including the biological, mental, emotional, and social bases for human behavior as well as theories which account for individual differences and abnormal behavior. They are also instructed in research design and methodology, statistics, psychological testing, scientific and professional ethics and standards, and a variety of skills applicable to their specialty" (American Psychological Association, 1979, p. 6). As one of the four "core" mental health disciplines, psychology is characterized by its effort to provide a sound scientific basis for the development and delivery of health services.

Statement of the Problem

In an effort to delineate the parameters of the problem of Hispanic mental health curricula for psychology, seven major issues have been identified: (1) nature of U.S. Hispanic population; (2) mental health needs; (3) barriers to service; (4) problems of diagnosis and treatment; (5) personnel needs; (6) accessibility and quality of mental health literature; and (7) the absence of systematic data on integrated curriculum development. These issues indicate the urgent need to develop and implement curricula that properly prepare future psychologists to conduct research, training and to deliver services to the Hispanic population in the United States.

Nature of the U.S. Hispanic Population

A detailed sociodemographic analysis of the U.S. Hispanic population is provided later in this chapter. At this point, it is sufficient to say that the number of Hispanics in the United States is large and rapidly increasing. Projected population estimates for 1985 range from 13.4 to 33.0 million; for the year 2000 the range is between 17.5 and 55.3 million (Macias, 1977). Furthermore, Hispanics constitute a heterogeneous population. Individuals of Mexican, Puerto Rican, Cuban and Central–South American origin have varying sociocultural and demographic characteristics. As a result, their mental health needs also differ. A thorough understanding of the heterogeneous nature of this population is therefore essential.

Mental Health Needs of Hispanics

The mental health needs of Hispanics have been well-documented in the report of the Hispanic panel to the President's Commission on Mental Health (1978):

> They have been found to suffer the full impact of a "culture of poverty" to a much higher extent than the general population. Low income, unemployment, underemployment, undereducation, poor housing, prejudice and discrimination, and cultural/linguistic barriers have been compounded by the low quality and quantity of mental health services available to Hispanics. This situation has perpetuated undue stress on Hispanic Americans and often results

in severe deleterious consequences not only for the Hispanic population, but also for American society at large. (pp. 905–906)

Although the factors described in the preceding excerpt render Hispanics "at risk" in an actuarial sense, Hispanics tend to underutilize the mental health services available. This underutilization has been attributed to structural factors that pertain to availability, accessibility and acceptability of services in terms of their relevance to the socio-cultural characteristics of Hispanics (President's Commission on Mental Health, 1978).

Barriers to Services

In an effort to identify barriers to services, a Delphi survey of Hispanic mental health professionals was conducted recently by the National Coalition of Hispanic Mental Health and Human Services Organizations (COSSMHO, 1980). The following ten "significant barriers" were identified: (1) a shortage of trained bilingual and bicultural clinicians; (2) insufficient training opportunities for Hispanics seeking careers in the mental health fields; (3) the extremely limited emphasis given preventive services in community mental health centers which fail to address cultural factors inhibiting Hispanics from utilizing mental health services; (4) the excessive use of treatment modalities that rarely take into consideration the realities of poverty, housing, food and so forth; (5) a low level of cultural sensitivity among the majority of mental health service providers; (6) discrimination on the part of institutions toward Hispanics seeking mental health services; (7) the organizational rigidity of mental health institutions, which hampers the development of appropriate services for Hispanic populations; (8) the confusion among those responsible for the development of programs, which results from the various opinions regarding what constitutes culturally relevant mental health services; (9) the geographic inaccessibility of many programs to Hispanic populations (including urban and rural); (10) a shortage of research on the effectiveness of the various treatment modalities used with Hispanic consumers of mental health services, on the process of acculturation and related stresses on the individual, on the training of mental health workers who will be working primarily with Hispanic clients, and on factors that deter Hispanics from using mental health facilities.

A significant problem is the misuse of diagnostic procedures that were developed for the Anglo population but that have no demonstrated validity or applicability for Hispanics. A similar misuse is the administration of psychotherapies that are based on models of human functioning that do not reflect Hispanic cultures and values. Thus it is not surprising to find that, under such conditions, Hispanics tend to terminate treatment prematurely (President's Commission on Mental Health, 1978).

Problems of Diagnosis and Treatment

Personnel Needs in Service Delivery and Research

Despite the "affirmative action" efforts of recent years, the shortage of Hispanic mental health personnel continues to be a serious problem (Olmedo and Lopez, 1977). The lack of adequate Hispanic representation among psychology faculty, students and practitioners is pervasive. For example, a recent survey of health service providers in psychology (Gottfredson and Dyer, 1978) indicated that Hispanics constitute only 0.4 percent of service providers at the doctoral level and only 0.5 percent of service providers at the master's level. Similarly, data collected for 1977–1978 on 132 APA-approved doctoral programs in clinical, counseling and school psychology indicated that of a total of 7,264 students, 252 (3.4 percent) were Hispanic. These data also indicated that there were only 28 Hispanic faculty in the 132 programs, resulting in the lowest faculty-student ratio of all ethnic groups (1/9.0). In comparison, there were 4,320 nonminority faculty and 6,189 nonminority students, for a faculty–student ratio of 1/1.4 (Vidato, 1979).

State of the Art in Hispanic Mental Health Literature

Accessibility and Quality of the Literature

As indicated in *Hispanic Mental Health Bibliography II* (Padilla, Olmedo, Lopez and Perez, 1978), the growth rate of literature pertaining to Hispanic mental health has been exponential. However, the extent to which this literature is conveniently available for didactic purposes is a different matter. A great deal of this research is reported, for example, in doctoral dissertations, in government reports and in other sources that are relatively difficult to find, and in a form which is not readily adaptable for didactic purposes. Moreover, the substantial amount of literature available in nonrefereed sources is often of uneven quality, and its adequacy is difficult to discern. Relatively few articles are published in APA journals. For example, examination of the Padilla bibliography indicates that out of 1,723 entries, only 99 (less than 6 percent) have been published in APA journals.

Absence of Systematic Data

At present, there is no information on the extent to which Hispanic mental health literature is being organized and integrated into systematic curricula for the training of Hispanic and other psychologists who will do research on or provide mental health services to Hispanics. It is unknown whether or not "minority content" is being provided in some departments. In the departments in which minority material may be covered, there is no mechanism to examine its level, quality and availability.

For example, according to the 1978–1979 APA survey of graduate departments of psychology, 109 (29.6 percent of the 368 respondents) reported offering courses "specifically directed toward research on minorities." Similarly, of the 319 departments that trained service providers, 110 (34.5 percent) reported offering courses "specifically directed toward service delivery to minorities." Notwithstanding the absence of systematic data, the nature and scope of "minority" curricula would appear to vary widely across departments.

Olmedo recently conducted an informal survey of sixty-four current catalogues from departments with APA-approved programs in clinical psychology. Of these, eleven (17 percent) included one or more courses that could be broadly identified as "minority-related." Course titles and descriptions, however, were quite heterogeneous, ranging from "Cross-cultural Psychology" and "Psychology of Minorities" to "Psychology of Prejudice" and "Psychological Effects of Racism." Bernal has collected data from a nationwide survey of minority curriculum and training in APA-approved clinical training programs (Bernal and Padilla, 1982).

The integration of Hispanic minority content into psychology curricula is a necessary requirement, if we are to develop a science of human behavior that goes beyond the current ethnocentric knowledge base. To understand the variety of human experiences and behaviors, we must understand its social and cultural context.

A Rationale for Minority Content

Frake (1968), cited in Manners and Kaplan stated that culture may be defined as the form by which individuals "organize their experience conceptually so that it may be transmitted as knowledge from person to person" (p.513). Diaz-Guerrero (1977) has suggested that culture is "a system of interrelated sociocultural premises that norm or govern the feelings, the ideas, and hierarchiation of the interpersonal relations, the stipulation of the type of roles to be fulfilled, the rules for the interaction of individuals in such roles, the where's, when's and with whom and how to play them" (p. 81). Important assumptions are inherent in these two definitions. In the former definition the assumption is that experience is organized through communicative behavior—verbal and nonverbal. In the latter definition the assumption is that systems of categorization may vary from culture to culture.

It is both culturally inappropriate and scientifically myopic to explain the behavior of Hispanics using systems that categorize the majority population. Attempts at a Procrustean fit between Anglo models and categories and the behavior of Hispanics will only perpetuate an ethnocentric psychological framework of human behavior. In reference to the development of a cultural relativistic approach with Chicanos, Martinez (1977) has noted that "psychological formulations that adequately explain the behavior of Anglos within an Anglo culture may not necessarily explain the behavior of Chicanos within a Chicano culture. Thus, a situation exists where improperly applied explanations of the behavior of Chicanos may actually do them harm" (p. 11). Martinez's *Chicano Psychology* documents numerous examples of inappropriate explanations that have had deleterious effects on Chicanos. Formulations developed with a majority group have been used to explain the behavior not only of Chicanos but also of Puerto Ricans, Cubans and other Hispanics from Central and South America. The integration of Hispanic content in the general educational curricula would be a step toward a psychological framework that is culturally pluralistic.

Furthermore, the development of integrated curricula with Hispanic content is necessary if we expect to train sensitive professionals, Hispanic or otherwise, who will be involved in the delivery of mental health and health care services. As noted previously, Hispanic Americans underutilize mental health services. When they do seek help, frequently they are offered treatment that does not reflect the needs, expectations and situational constraints of the Hispanic individual and family. In these cases the cultural values, beliefs and norms that are at the base of the Hispanic American's social reality are either considered unimportant or ignored. Therefore, in order to train and sensitize professionals to the needs of this population, basic curriculum content on Hispanic Americans must be designed.

The integration of knowledge about Hispanics within mono- and/or multicultural contexts into overall clinical, research and teaching areas of psychology curriculum would facilitate the development of an empirical knowledge base that is firmly rooted in the social reality of a variety of individuals and groups. Such a knowledge base would constitute an important step toward a genuine "American psychology that would encompass all peoples of the Americas" (Martinez, 1977, p. 13), including North, South and Central Americans.

A Theoretical Framework for Curricula

It must be recognized that what is taught as psychology results from a scientific enterprise conducted, collectively and individually, by psychological researchers primarily within academic settings. Within this setting, it is important to note the emergence of a "sociology of psychological knowledge" which calls for the recognition that psychology, as a scientific enterprise, occurs within a social context. As such, it reflects, at any given time, the world view inherent in the particular sociohistorical setting in which it develops (Buss, 1975; Sampson, 1978). The sociohistorical imprint is perhaps most discernable at the metatheoretical level; that is, the underlying level of implicit assumptions that guide theory as well as empirical research.

It is the level at which, for example, the development of biased concepts such as the "cultural deficit" model are developed for explaining the behavior of Hispanics. As more Hispanics enter the field of psychological research and practice, we witness the broadening of American psychology to reflect a different perspective, one which focuses on the strengths of the Hispanic cultures and which recognizes the diversity inherent in our pluralistic society. Cultural pluralism is the foundation of our theoretical framework, one which allows for the development of psychological knowledge and, consequently, for the development of curriculum content that is relevant and appropriate for Hispanic mental health.

One of the critical characteristics of Hispanic lineage is that Hispanics represent a highly heterogeneous population composed of persons of Spanish, Black and North and South American heritages. In addition, Hispanics have varying social, economic, political, cultural and demographic characteristics. In order to fully understand and study similarities and differences among Hispanics and the similarities and differences between them and other groups, a cross-cultural theoretical framework is required. Such a cross-cultural and pluralistic theoretical framework must encompass psychological, sociological, anthropological and political analyses. Curricula that reflect the cultural heterogeneity of Hispanic heritage and legacies are essential.

Hispanic Issues

Spanish Language as a Common Bond

Language is more than a medium of communication; it embodies how a person thinks, feels and reacts to his or her environment. As part of the Hispanic heritage, the Spanish language serves a unifying function for all Hispanics by providing a link with their cultural roots and a means to perpetuate their values. It has been argued that this historical sense of continuity has a therapeutic benefit. For instance, Szapocznik, Kurtinez and Aranald (forthcoming) have found that the degree to which migrants maintain contact with their own cultural background has important implications for their psychosocial adjustment.

The Bilingual Education Act of 1968 recognized the importance of the Spanish language in helping to remedy the enormous difficulties Hispanic children were having in their school performance. Several studies have shown the beneficial effects of bilingual programs. For example, Offenberg and Lega (1974) found that in the Philadelphia public school system self-esteem was significantly higher for those Spanish-speaking children participating in bilingual programs than for those children participating in English monolingual programs. Since the passage of the bilingual act, some have contended that bilingual education interferes with language acquisition. However, several studies conducted with Mexicans have demonstrated that bilingual children in fact acquire the two languages at a comparable rate to that of monolingual children (Padilla and Liebman, 1975; Padilla and Lindholm, 1976).

Despite the current interest in social policy issues such as bilingual education, other issues have been relatively neglected, such as the role of functioning as a bilingual or the role of using the Spanish language to affirm Hispanic identity and to facilitate bicultural adaptation. For example, while there are substantial numbers of Hispanics in need of psychotherapy, mental health professionals have only recently begun to pay attention to the underutilization by Hispanics of mental health services (Padilla & Ruiz, 1973) and their high dropout rates from psychotherapy. It has been suggested that the English language barrier experienced by Hispanics is one of the underlying factors affecting the underutilization of services and the high dropout rate from psychotherapy.

The experience of bilinguals in psychotherapy has been investigated in several studies. Marcos, Alpert, Urcuyo and Kesselman (1973) summarized the findings of these studies and found that when speaking in English bilinguals display different character traits; recollect different sets of experiences; feel a different sense of identity; and show a diminution of effect. The authors also found that psychiatric ratings of disturbed Hispanic patients reflected more psychopathology when patients were interviewed in English than when they were interviewed in Spanish. They argued that when speaking in English the rater's frame of reference was not applicable to the specific problems of the Hispanic patients. This contention has been stressed in the literature recently and the need for bilingual Hispanic American mental health professionals has been well documented.

In the near future, there will be few Hispanic mental health professionals capable of providing for bilingual-bicultural mental health services to the Hispanic American community. There should be at the very minimum a conversational Spanish language requirement for the Ph. D. in psychology. However, knowledge of the Spanish language is only one aspect of a more important issue: cultural sensitivity. It will be necessary to sensitize and train both professionals and students to understand clearly the specifics of culturally related attitudes, needs and beliefs of Hispanic Americans.

One avenue for developing such cultural sensitivity might be the study of the Latin American literature. Making it available to *all* students enrolled in a graduate program in psychology would increase their familiarity with the history and assets of the Hispanic American people. Specific samples from the literature could be used to illustrate psychological traits within the culture and accepted as well as controversial beliefs, systems and values prevalent in Hispanic American countries. This curriculum content could serve a twofold purpose: (1) to legitimize the Hispanic American student by making him or her feel proud of the heritage; and (2) to help the non-Hispanic American student understand and appreciate the strengths of the Hispanic American culture through its vast literature.

National Origin. Hispanic Americans come from a variety of countries, each having its own traditions, mores, value systems and history. There are twenty-one countries in Latin America. Puerto Rico is a special case, since it is a commonwealth state associated to the United States.

Race. The multicultural background of Hispanics results from a blend of African, European and Indian sociohistorical influence. The colonization of Latin America in the fifteenth and sixteenth centuries, mainly by Spain but also to some extent by England and France, radically changed the Mesoamerican, Andean and Caribbean cultures. The Indians in many countries, particularly in the Caribbean, were almost totally eradicated, and Black slaves were brought from Africa as substitutes to work on plantations. The United States began its interventions in Latin America in the nineteenth century; this added the Anglo American dimensions to the multicultural composition of Hispanics.

Each Hispanic country has its own history of addressing racial and ethnic differences. Knowing the manner in which these differences are handled in the Hispanic individual's country of origin is crucial to understanding how that individual is going to adapt and react to the way Anglos treat people from different racial and ethnic backgrounds.

The various historical, economic, sociopolitical and cultural factors that have played a role in developing and maintaining racism in the Hispanic countries of origin and in the United States should be presented in a course dealing with racial issues. Such a course should also explore the impact of institutional racism and personal prejudice upon the lives and mental health of Hispanic Americans.

Sociodemographics. According to the Bureau of the Census, in March 1978 there were 12 million Hispanic Americans in the United States—7.2 million of Mexican origin; 1.8 million of Puerto Rican origin; 700,000 of Cuban origin; 900,000 of Central or South American origin; and 1.5 million of other Spanish origin. Projected population estimates for 1985 of the Hispanic population range from 13.4 to 33.0 million. It should be noted that the census does not take into account the number of illegal Hispanics in the United States. The Immigration Service estimates that a million illegal aliens a year enter the United States, 90 percent of whom are Hispanics (Jimenez, 1978).

The socioeconomic status of Hispanics of different national origins varies. In general, Cubans and South and Central Americans have relatively higher levels of education and, consequently, higher occupational status. Puerto Ricans, Dominicans and Mexicans have been reported to have relatively lower educational and income levels.

The Hispanic median family income level is about $11,421, whereas the national median is about $16,000. The Hispanic median family

Dimensions of Diversity

income level appears to be weighted down by the lower income levels of Puerto Ricans ($8,000). Mexicans have average family incomes of $12,000, whereas Cubans and other Hispanics have average family income levels of $14,000 and $13,000 respectively. Cubans appear to have higher income levels than the median for all Hispanic Americans (U.S. Bureau of the Census, 1980).

Most Hispanic families live in metropolitan areas. According to the census, 85 percent of all Hispanics reside in urban, highly populated areas, as compared with 65 percent of the total national population. A breakdown of all Hispanic American groups reveals that 81 percent of Mexicans, 95 percent of Puerto Ricans, 97 percent of Cubans and 86 percent of other Hispanic Americans live in metropolitan areas. These differences in socioeconomic status may be best understood by examining the factors underlying the migration phenomenon and the sociopolitical history for each of the different Hispanic American groups.

Sociopolitical History. To understand the diverse experiences and struggles of Chicanos, Mexican Americans, Puerto Ricans, Cubans, Nicaraguans, Salvadorans, Argentinians, Chileans and so on, it is most important to examine Hispanic issues within their sociopolitical context. There are unique social, political and historical factors that differentiate Hispanic groups from each other and, more important, from other migrant ethnic groups. Further, an appreciation of these factors may facilitate a richer understanding of the current status of Hispanics within an Anglo American society. The purpose of this section is not to develop the definitive sociopolitical analysis of Hispanics; rather it is to draw attention to contextual issues so that these may become an integral part of Hispanic mental health curriculum development and implementation for psychology. Because of space limitations, this section will primarily focus on the Mexican American. It is hoped that the brief historical details presented may be used to understand the commonality as well as the diversity of experience among Hispanic groups in the United States.

During the nineteenth century, the rubric "Manifest Destiny" gave the expansionist policy of the United States a reason for being. The zeitgeist of the times was that the United States represented a people chosen by "Providence" (Lopez y Rivas, 1973) to include within the union of states neighboring peoples through annexation, purchase and/or conquest. Subsequent to the U.S. occupation of the Louisiana Territories in 1803, Florida in 1819 and Oregon and its territories (now Washington, Idaho and the western parts of Wyoming and Montana) in 1846, the stage was set for further expansion into Mexico.

The acquisition of additional territories was a necessary basis for further economic development. The western territories would provide land rich for cultivation, virgin forests and mines and inexpensive labor (Lopez y Rivas, 1973; Montiel, 1978). The objectives of territorial expansion were to open new markets and to convert natural and human resources into objects of trade.

When the United States moved to annex Texas in 1845, this precipitated a chain of events that made war with Mexico inevitable. The so-called Mexican-American War ended with the Treaty of Guadalupe Hidalgo in 1848. Mexico received $15 million from the United States and had to give up 45 percent of its land—which included Texas, the territories now known as New Mexico, Arizona and California—and more than 100,000 people.

Given this historical background, it is almost inappropriate to speak of Mexican Americans and Chicanos as migrants. It is difficult to estimate the extent to which the Mexican Americans of today are descendants of Mexicans residing in northern Mexico (Southwest) at the time of its occupation by the United States. Fernandex (1970) has indicated that more than a million Mexican Americans who live in the southwestern United States have roots dating back to 1848. However, about two-thirds of the Mexican American population in the United States are recent migrants or are descendants of persons who migrated to the Southwest after the Mexican Revolution of 1910. Montiel (1978) points out that during the fifty-year period between 1910 and 1960 a number of mass migrations took place, in part because of economic and political changes that resulted from the Mexican Revolution. Subsequently, migration from Mexico to the southwestern United States was stimulated by the demand for cheap labor.

The position of the Mexican American may serve to illustrate the unique and different social reality between many Hispanic Americans and other migrant groups. For example, part of the distinguishing aspect of that reality is that the part of the United States where Mexican Americans are most heavily concentrated previously constituted northern Mexico. The boundaries between Mexico and the United States are viewed as artificial by many Mexican Americans. As Dieppa and Montiel (1978) point out, "The geographic, ecological, and cultural blending of the Southwest with Mexico is perceived as a continuing unity of people whose claim to the Southwest is rooted in the land itself" (p. 3).

Puerto Ricans have been in a position similar to that of the Chicanos in the Southwest. Puerto Ricans share in a legacy characterized by Anglo American expansionism and annexation. At the time of the Spanish-American War of 1898, Puerto Rico was invaded by the United States, as was Cuba, the Philipines and Guam. Unlike Cuba in 1902 and the Philipines in 1949, Puerto Rico was not to achieve its independence. Maldonado-Dennis (1972) in his sociohistorical interpretation of Puerto Rico, points out the misleading nature of comparisons between Puerto Ricans and other white migrant groups that have incorporated themselves in the sociopolitical power structure. While other groups became U.S. citizens by choice, Puerto Ricans "became citizens because they had no other alternatives, given the political status of the island as a colony of the United States" (p. 303).

The legacy of North American expansionism and colonialism is important in the Mexican American social reality, as well as in that of other Hispanic Americans. This legacy must be clearly analyzed in order to modify the conditions that shape social reality for the diverse populations of Hispanics in this country. It is expected that critical evaluations of the sociopolitical history of Hispanics in view of the present conditions and that critical evaluations of the present reality in view of the sociopolitical histories will become part of Hispanic mental health curriculum for psychology.

Migration Patterns. The topic of migration is essential to understanding the patterns of adaptation, acculturation and assimilation of Hispanics in the United States. The history of the migration movement—who migrates, under what conditions and why—is important data (Martinez-Urrutia, 1979). When planning how best to meet the needs of the different Hispanic groups in this country, particularly from a mental health point of view, patterns of migration must be taken into consideration.

Puerto Ricans became U.S. citizens by an act of Congress in 1917 and since then have traveled to the mainland without immigration restrictions. During the 1920s few migrated to the mainland, despite the fact that the per capita income in Puerto Rico was extremely low and unemployment was rampant. The labor shortages during World War II created strong economic pressures in the island people to seek relief elsewhere. Their freedom of travel to the United States and subsidized transportation programs with active recruitment to bring them to the mainland contributed to the mass migration of Puerto Ricans to the United States in the 1940s.

Although Puerto Ricans from all over the island traveled to the United States, 70 percent of them were from rural areas. Thus, this was essentially a rural-to-urban migration. These migrants tended to be young, and there was an almost equal representation from both sexes. Although their level of education and skill was slightly above the island average, the semi-skilled and unskilled predominated. Most had an elementary school education, but the majority could not speak English. Their work experience as farm laborers did not qualify them to find jobs in the urban areas.

In the past decade a significant number of Puerto Ricans have returned to the island after obtaining enough money to fulfill their dream: "To return to my 'tierra' and build my 'casita'." The reason for the return migration has been mainland unemployment. The majority have settled in urban areas, such as in the capital city of San

Juan. Puerto Ricans comprise the Hispanic group that has shown the highest back-and-forth movement between the mainland and the homeland of any migrant Hispanic group in the history of the United States.

Mexican migration may have been punctuated by the Mexican Revolution of 1910, which created political instability and, coupled with the emerging demands for labor, stimulated a migration that reached mass proportions during the 1920s. During the 1930s, with the economic depression, migration subsided. However, after World War II the Mexican Labor Program—known as the "bracero" program—encouraged a large number of Mexicans to enter the United States on work permits for a number of months. The entrance of illegal migrants in search of better jobs was high from the beginning. Even Operation Wetback in 1954, which returned more than a million illegal Mexicans to Mexico, was not effective in deterring the influx of illegal migrants. In 1964 the "bracero" program was terminated and a quota system was implemented. Nevertheless, as previously stated elsewhere, Mexicans have continued to enter the United States both legally and illegally in large numbers.

A large segment of the Mexican American population has migrated from cities near the border. Other segments have representation from almost all of Mexico. Most migrants have been unskilled laborers from the lower socioeconomic stratum. Recent U.S. government efforts to increase migration of professionals in fields where there is a domestic shortage and to prevent the unskilled from entering the country appear to have failed. The educational achievement of migrants has been low, and most have rudimentary or no knowledge of the English language.

There had been a steady migration of Cubans to the U.S. since the nineteenth century (Casal and Hernandez, 1975). However, after the Cuban Revolution of 1959, a large number of Cubans began to leave the island. First to migrate were the very wealthy and those individuals who were directly connected with the defeated dictatorship. After the Bay of Pigs invasion in 1961, a growing number of the middle-class Cubans began to migrate. They included professionals, highly skilled personnel and white collar workers. In 1966 daily "freedom flights" were instituted from Cuba to the United States. This allowed people from the lower-middle class and lower class to leave the island.

The migration patterns of Puerto Ricans, Mexicans and Cubans, as reviewed, point out that there are differences in social class, life experiences and expectations among these groups. Above all, there are differences in the reasons for leaving the old environment and in the amount of stress associated with that life change. These differences have been found to have important implications for the concomitant adjustment of these groups to the new culture and therefore should be taught as basic content in mental health curriculum.

Cultural Pluralism

In the last decade the theory of cultural pluralism has gained significance as a heuristic device to explain sociocultural dynamics in American society. The shift away from the melting pot conception of ethnic minority acculturation into American society is related to various factors. Among these factors is the breakdown of traditional social and cultural norms in American society (Gordon, 1964). The loss of faith in the traditional sociocultural values has given way to the cult of the self and the development of the culture of narcissism. This break with the past, and subsequent emphasis on "doing your own thing," has created social fragmentation, with numerous groups dividing along interest lines. There has been an emergence of social and political action groups as seen in the Black rights movement, Hispanic rights movement, Women's rights movement and Gay rights movement, with each one struggling to get a greater "share of the pie."

Within the cultural pluralism theory the plight of the migrating Hispanic group becomes more complex. As compared with the past, today the right of Hispanics to equal opportunities is upheld along with their right to maintain their language and cultural heritage. However, as the group begins to acculturate into American society, it adopts ethnic identity as its symbol to achieve greater access to power. In this process conflicts ensue between maintaining Hispanic values or adopting American ones. The concepts of acculturation, biculturalism and ethnic identity are clarified in the following discussion.

Acculturation

The term *acculturation* has been used loosely, in part because of the different conceptual orientations of all the disciplines involved in the investigation of its meaning. *Acculturation* was originally defined as comprehending "those phenomena which result when groups of individuals having different cultures come into continuous first-hand contact, with subsequent changes in the original pattern of either or both groups" (Redfield, Linton and Herskovitz, 1936). It should be noted that in order for acculturation to occur there must be a continuous interaction between members of two different cultures and a change in cultural patterns in either or both groups. Keefe (1979) indicates that the more contemporary work on acculturation still utilizes the same definition postulated by Redfield, Linton and Herskovitz.

The concept of acculturation originated in the discipline of anthropology; consequently the focus of the research has been on groups of people over a long period of time. More recently, acculturation has been conceived as also occurring at the individual level (Dohrenwend and Smith, 1962). Graves (1967) has coined the concept "psychological acculturation" to differentiate it from the group phenomenon. However, researchers continue to be ambivalent about what constitutes the proper unit of assessment—the group or the individual—when investigating acculturation.

In a thorough review of the literature on acculturation from a psychometric perspective, Olmedo (1979) emphasizes that the measurement of individual acculturation can meet the conventional criteria of reliability and validity. He also argues that recent developments in quantifying acculturation along multiple dimensions, rather than along arbitrary ethnic group membership or generational typologies, seem more promising. The three major dimensions emerging from factor analytic studies, he indicates, are: (1) language proficiency, preference and/or use; (2) socioeconomic status; and (3) culture specific attitudes and value orientations.

It may be worthwhile at this point to compare the culture-specific value orientations of the Hispanic with those of the Anglo American. There is a discrepancy between the American value of individualism—independence—and the Hispanic's *family-centered* concept of the individual—dependence. This discrepancy creates tension for the Hispanic who is perceived by the larger American society as overly dependent and who is pressured by that larger society to become more independent. Thus, the Hispanic individual is caught in a dilemma: he or she must assume behavior patterns consistent with American values which tend to disrupt close-knit family ties from which the Hispanic individual derives his or her sense of self, or risk becoming a socially marginal person. *La Familia* is a source of strength and identity, as Armas (1972) says: "Our home was like a mighty rock in a stormy sea. It was fun to swim and fight the waves. It was fun to return to the rock. It could even reach out and pluck you from the sea as you were going down."

The American occupational structure and educational and governmental institutions are based on the cultural values of *pragmatism*, *effectiveness* and *efficiency*. As such, the carriers of those cultural values stress systematic, impersonal relationships. In contrast, Hispanics are more attuned to value *personalism*, *idealism* and *informality* in institutional and interpersonal relations.

When the researcher recognizes the Hispanic cultural emphasis upon respect and dignity of the individual, the view that the Hispanic is overly obsequious becomes untenable. Hispanics are taught not to be rude or confronting to avoid offending other human beings. Nevertheless, the Hispanic individual may be perceived as weak and servile because he or she fails to be sufficiently assertive.

Another source of potential conflict for some Hispanic groups is the achievement-oriented Protestant Ethic. In order to adopt the norms of behavior implied in the Protestant Ethic, the Hispanic individual must reverse his or her own religious values, which prescribe a more passive, humanistic code of behavior. Given the organization of

American institutions around the principle that the individual's quest for achievement, particularly in the material realm, has merit and is rewarded on earth as it is in heaven, the Hispanic individual may face the dilemma of adapting to or becoming isolated from the larger society.

For the Hispanic individual who must function within the American social structure, this clash of values creates conflicts and loss of self-esteem. The implications that such cultural conflicts have for the mental health of Hispanic Americans have been noted in the literature. For example, Fitzpatrick (1971) described the Hispanic trying to acculturate: "Frustrated and not fully accepted by the broader social world he wishes to enter, ambivalent in his attitude toward the more restricted social world to which he has ancestral rights, and beset by conflicting social standards, he develops, according to the classic conception, personality traits of insecurity, moodiness, hypersensitivity, excessive self-consciousness, and nervous strain."

Two major acculturation models have been described: one in which changes may occur in one culture, the other in which changes may occur in both cultures. Nevertheless, the predominant model of acculturation has been a unidimensional, unidirectional continuum from one culture (migrant) to another (host). An example of the unidirectional model is the one developed by Szapocznik, et al. (forthcoming). This model postulates that acculturation is a linear function of the amount of time a person has been exposed to the host culture, and that the rate of acculturation is a function of the age and sex of the individual. In applying this model to a research design, they found that intergenerational differences develop when younger members of the family acculturate more rapidly than older ones. It should be noted, however, that this model did not take into consideration the multidimensional aspects of acculturation, nor the phenomenon of biculturalism.

Biculturalism

The unidimensional, unidirectional model of acculturation does not apply in those situations in which individuals migrate to bicultural or multicultural communities. Furthermore, that individuals acquire new sets of norms and characteristics of the new culture does not necessarily imply that they relinquish the old ones associated with the culture of origin (Dohrenwend and Smith, 1962). Padilla (forthcoming) developed a two-dimensional model concerned with cultural awareness and ethnic loyalty. The first dimension of the model refers to an individual's knowledge of specific cultural material of his own origins and culture or his knowledge of the host culture. The second dimension refers to the individual's preference for one cultural orientation over the other. In this model, a "degree of Hispanicity" and a degree of "Anglicity" were considered as orthogonal dimensions.

Szapocznik et al., modified their original model, and therefore their scale, by incorporating items reflecting these two dimensions of biculturalism. More specifically, the first dimension consists of a linear process in which individuals accommodate the host culture. The second dimension is a complex process in which individuals retain or abandon characteristics of the culture of origin. Investigations using this revised model have shown that individuals who migrate to bicultural communities tend to become maladjusted when they remain or become monocultural (Szapocznik and Kurtinez, forthcoming).

Ethnic Identity

The theory of cultural pluralism permits and encourages the maintenance of ethnic identity, while the melting pot ideology pressures the Hispanic individual toward conformity and "Americanization." Consequently, studies on ethnic identity during the melting pot era showed that there was a fairly clear preference for an identity associated with the dominant group (Brand, Ruiz and Padilla, 1974). However, more recent studies reveal that the level of identification with the dominant group tends to be less than the level of identification with the Hispanic group (Levine-Brand and Ruiz, 1978).

By focusing on ethnic identity, it is possible to understand different ethnic groups within their own perspective and reality rather than in comparison to that of other groups. Ethnic identity does not assume a superiority-inferiority dichotomy, since it is embedded in the theory of cultural pluralism. Being proud of one's own ethnic identity is conducive to mental health and, during the acculturation process, affords the Hispanic more freedom to choose. As Tumin and Plotch (1976) have said: "Ethnicity is not to be conceived as a merely primordial fateful, tribal bond; on the contrary, it can be freely chosen, developed as part of a multicultural competence, and rooted in the socially aware individual rather than in the unthinking group." It can be seen in Tumin's description that choosing to maintain ethnic identity creates a "healthy aware" individual and this in turn promotes a healthy society.

In addition to bicultural and ethnic identity, the following content areas associated with acculturation should be addressed. First, a study of the behavior of Hispanic Americans should include values and belief systems, child-rearing practices, sex-role expectations and cognitive styles. A distinction should be made between deviant and normative behavior within the Hispanic culture and between the contrasts of those behaviors to the dominant American culture. Second, the impact of acculturation on the psychological functioning of the Hispanic should be considered. How does an individual cope with the stress associated with the acculturation struggle? Particular areas to look at include alternative healing methods used by Hispanics, such as *Espiritisitas*; the fit of current psychotherapeutic modalities to the needs of Hispanic patients; and the development of new, more effective treatment modalities for the mental health problems of the Hispanic American. Third, the need to develop specific assessment instruments that are sufficiently reliable and valid to test Hispanic Americans in personality and intellectual functioning should be recognized. The unreliability and invalidity of current Anglo-oriented psychological tests vis-à-vis the Hispanic American should be emphasized.

La Familia

In this section we examine some basic processes that concern Hispanic families. These processes need further elaboration, research and development and are noted here to serve as guidelines for areas to be included in Hispanic curriculum.

La familia is perhaps one of the most significant considerations in the delivery of health and mental health services to Hispanics (Duran, 1975). Involvement of the family in the treatment of any one of its members maximizes the success of the treatment. Given the importance of *la familia* to Hispanics, research and clinical efforts should be geared to understanding family processes, as well as to developing and assessing treatment models that are culture-specific and that blend Hispanic values with natural support systems.

The Hispanic family is diversified and heterogeneous. There are wide ranges of important differences related to national origin, race, class, migration and sociopolitical history. Nevertheless, there are important similarities among Puerto Rican, Chicano, Mexican American, Cuban and other Central and South American families. The similarities involve family structure and family function.

Family Structure

The Hispanic family is perhaps most clearly characterized by a bond of loyalty and unity, which includes nuclear and extended family members as well as the network of friends, neighbors and community. The family has its own particular history which is highly valued, and the family moves as a unit in time in accordance with this history. If culture is, as Diaz Guerrero (1977) suggests, a system of sociocultural rules that regulates feelings and behaviors, then the Hispanic family is the principal social unit that transmits cultural knowledge from one generation to the next.

In their examination of Hispanic families, Dieppa and Montiel (1978) noted five characteristics found among Cubans, Mexican Americans, Puerto Ricans and other Hispanics (citing the Illinois State

Advisory Committee to the U.S. Commission on Civil Rights 1974 Report). These general characteristics are the following:

- value orientation to persons vs. abstractions;
- individual independence valued within the context of family and traditional Hispanic values;
- *la familia* as central and hierarchical;
- value orientation to being vs. doing;
- father as primary authority figure.

Taking into account these characteristics along with the findings of Keefe, Padilla and Carlos (1978) with Mexican Americans; of Szapocznik, Scopetta, Arnalde and Kurtinez (1978), in their work with Cuban value structures; and of Marin (1978), and Spiegel (1971) on Puerto Rican family values, we may arrive at the following tentative sketch of the traditional Hispanic family structure.

The Hispanic family is firmly rooted in ties of obligation to the past and future generations. Within this fiber of loyalty bonds, the parent-child relationship emerges as primary. At the very minimum, the children owe *respeto* to the parents. At the other end of the spectrum, the child's existence is owed to the parents and, in the ultimate analysis, this debt of obligation can never be repaid. Traditionally the role of the father has been that of the decision maker and disciplinarian. Father's word is the law and he is not to be questioned. Father is primarily concerned with the economic welfare and well-being of the family. The father may focus more of his attention upon economic issues and less upon expressive and emotional issues. Mother balances father's role through her investment in the welfare of the children and is one of the primary providers of emotional support. Extended family members, such as grandmothers, aunts and uncles, may supplement mother's emotional support. The children become attached to the mother and grow to expect support from her, while the father may appear distant. The older son is traditionally the *primogenito*, who is the principal inheritor and secondary decision maker to the father. The children are expected to live at home until they marry. The relationships between parents and children are embedded in a network of multiple extended relationships that provide economic and emotional support.

All families have a variety of complex functions that must be performed in order to meet the needs of their members. A variety of functions have been identified (e.g., Minuchin, 1974; Howells, 1974) and these are psychological and economic in nature. The psychological functions include psychosocial protection of family members, satisfaction of

Family Function

affectual needs, socialization of children, political and religious up-bringing and sexual satisfaction. The economic functions include material maintenance of family members through economic units, transference of property and survival of members through provision of basic economic needs—food, clothing and shelter.

Hispanic family functioning must be understood not only in terms of structural and intergenerational family processes and specific developmental tasks but also in terms of survival stresses that may have their roots in the current and/or historical context. Given the socio-economic conditions of many Hispanics, the ultimate function of Hispanic families has been economic survival. As indicated in the report of the President's Commission on Mental Health (1978), Hispanics too often "have been found to suffer the full impact of a 'culture of poverty' . . . low income, unemployment, undereducation, poor housing, prejudice, discrimination and cultural-linguistic barriers." The stressors that disrupt Hispanic family functioning constitute an important area of study. The sources of stress that are external to the family and that may condition patterns of dysfunction include discrimination, racism, poverty, forced immigration and language barriers. Intrafamily events—breaks in extended family relations, disorders, substance abuse, and family intergenerational role and acculturation conflicts—may cause disorganization within the family.

Further research is needed to identify sources of stress, to study coping mechanisms and to develop intervention strategies that are effective for dealing with a wide range of stressful situations in Hispanic families. In addition, research is needed to identify the factors and processes of Hispanic families that have coped successfully with stressful situations.

Theory, Research and Practice in Psychology

Psychology has traditionally favored empirical scientific method and an examination of methodological issues in studying human behavior and mental processes. Compared with other disciplines, psychology emphasizes the relationship between theory, research and professional practice. The psychologist, as a "scientist-practitioner," is not unlike the physician who applies in his clinical practice the findings from research laboratories. Ideally, the psychologist is a scientist-practitioner who has integrated clinical, research, theoretical and teaching skills.

Hispanic psychologists trained through the scientist-practitioner model are at the forefront in developing scientific research that focuses on culture, delivering mental health services to Hispanics and teaching courses that are content-integrated with the available literature about Hispanics and other ethnic groups. The link between conceptual models, research and culturally sensitive clinical services is an important one in psychology. Hispanic mental health curricula should reflect the necessity of integrated training in theory, research, clinical practice and community service.

Nevertheless, the scientist-practitioner model must be viewed in its historical context (Bakan, 1956; Gadlin and Ingle, 1975) and from a Hispanic perspective. Twentieth-century psychology was patterned, both in its methods and assumptions, after nineteenth-century physics: methods of study preceded the phenomenon (Gadlin and Ingle, 1975). It is not altogether clear that the traditional model of the scientist-practitioner has benefited psychology (Raush, 1974), or that it has enhanced psychologists' scientific development. We must ask ourselves what does the research produced in the journals offer the individual concerned with application? A rejection of science is not implied here; rather the focus is on questioning the methods and models that have dominated the field of psychology. Can we develop alternatives to traditional research (Bennett et al., 1966) and move toward a model of the psychologist as a "participant-conceptualizer"?

For Hispanic psychologists, it is critical that integrated and rigorous training in research and methodology continue to be provided. However, it is also critical that current conceptions of research be explored and expanded to include conceptual analysis, development of models and a focus on events, processes and experience (e.g., researching phenomena and then searching for the method to fit the phenomena). These explorations can contribute to the development of a pluralistic paradigm of psychology as a science that is integrated in terms of training practitioners and in developing knowledge about theory, practice and research in context.

Guiding Principles

Curricula that are based on empirically derived data must be developed if psychologists are to be adequately educated and trained to work with Hispanics. Clinical impressions, opinions about relations between culture and mental health, and folklore about effective interventions for Hispanics are not substitutes for sound research findings. Padilla and Ruiz (1973) describe the serious deficiencies in the available research, including stereotypic interpretations of data, weak methodological and data analysis techniques, findings that cannot be replicated and the absence of programmatic research. There have been some advances in the field, but a major obstacle to further advancement is the limited number of well-trained Hispanic behavioral scientists. The Hispanic behavioral scientist's education must emphasize equally psychological theory, empirical research methods and findings and professional practice. Such an emphasis removes the expectation that becoming a service provider or administrator precludes becoming a scientist. It also increases the likelihood that the psychologist will develop a critical view of existing literature and practice and engage in scientific activities that permit the generation of empirical answers to questions arising from everyday psychological practice.

The development and implementation of Hispanic content in psychology curricula should take place within departments of psychology in universities in both Puerto Rico and the United States. Emphasis on the integration of such content into the mainstream of the education of psychologists is a vital aspect of this guiding principle. A recent study by Hicks and Ridley (1979) revealed a tendency, over time, for Black studies programs to take over the task of offering Black psychology programs. A trend toward the establishment of satellite units such as junior and community colleges to deal with the educational needs of minorities and the poor (Gamson and Arce, 1978) can be seen in the same light as the teaching of Black psychology by ethnic studies programs. That is, the educational system shifts the burden of responsibility for minority curriculum development and education to satellite units rather than incorporating them into the mainstream of American education. The trend toward ethnic studies programs or other institutions outside the mainstream of higher education in psychology assuming responsibility for Hispanic content is totally unacceptable.

Hispanic mental health curricula may be organized and implemented in departments of psychology in a number of ways. The manner of such organization and implementation should be in accord with the nature of the different institutions. One course or a sequence of courses bearing on Hispanic mental health may be taught separately or integrated into existing courses. While the former approach may legitimate Hispanic curricula as an area of instruction, it may also result in separate or "ghettoized" Hispanic curriculum. The latter approach also has its advantages and disadvantages. It may facilitate integration of Hispanic content into a number of core curriculum areas in psychology, but it also may impede a systematic study of interrelated subjects specific to Hispanic issues. Furthermore, non-Hispanic faculty may resist inclusion of such Hispanic content and lack the knowledge to teach it properly. To facilitate the inclusion of Hispanic curricula, professionals in each educational setting must remain alert to the implications of the manner in which Hispanic curricula are implemented and capitalize on the positive aspects of programs.

Strategies for Change

Strategies for change and implementation in Hispanic mental health education will be discussed at three levels: governmental policy and funding, accrediting and licensing bodies, and educational and training institutions. Whenever possible the proposed strategies will address needed modifications in existing mechanisms which would enhance the implementation process, thus ensuring a pragmatic and reality-conscious approach to the issues.

As discussed in meetings the National Hispanic Committee (NHC) for the Implementation of the Reports and Recommendations of the President's Commission on Mental Health, the process of developing a qualified cadre of Hispanic mental health professionals and a curriculum that meets existing needs is rather complex. It will require short-term strategies that address the present state of affairs, as well as long-term strategies that recognize the mental health needs of this country's rapidly growing Hispanic population. The success of both short-term and long-term strategies requires redirecting existing training resources and targeting new funds.

Governmental Policy and Funding

One of the strategies seeks to ensure that existing funds for training Hispanic psychologists—local, state and especially federal funds—are redirected to educational institutions that focus on minority populations. In allocating funds, agencies should give priority to programs that specialize in minority training, curriculum development and other educational resources. These training programs should emphasize service needs within the Hispanic community and the generation of greater understanding and motivation for service delivery to and research on this population. Training in research activities that have the potential to yield materials for the development of Hispanic mental health curricula should also be supported.

Existing mechanisms within accrediting and licensing bodies and professional associations must also be utilized as vehicles for change. These professional bodies and associations are frequently responsible for establishing training, curriculum and accreditation standards. Government bodies such as ADAMHA should ensure that such standards are sensitive to Hispanics and other minorities by establishing cultural and ethnic appropriateness as criteria for funding. The aim would be to make curriculum content an issue in affirmative action.

Accrediting and Licensing Bodies

The American Psychological Association has recently established an office of Ethnic Minority Affairs with a board composed of professionals from four major ethnic groups (Blacks, Hispanics, Asian and Pacific Americans and American Indians and Alaska Natives). It is proposed that this board be fully utilized in order to affect APA accreditation criteria.

Strategies for change must address those institutions responsible for training and manpower development. There is a need to encourage, foster and direct training programs in psychology that develop more Hispanic professionals (including those specializing in services to

Educational and Training Institutions

special populations, e.g., women, children, youth, the elderly and migrant and rural populations), and curricula relevant to Hispanics. Long-range success in increasing the number of culturally sensitive professionals depends on supporting and enhancing motivation at all educational levels and on integrating minority content into the training of all mental health personnel. Success also requires the retraining of existing personnel to enhance their ability to provide services to Hispanics and other special populations. Curriculum and training needs in psychology have been discussed recently by Bernal (1980). The actions and recommendations proposed by Bernal will be discussed here as they particularly address the major problems that exist at the school and institutional level.

One of the most immediate needs in Hispanic psychology is an increase in the pool of interested and qualified graduate school applicants. This requires training teachers and school counselors to be more sensitive and responsive to Hispanic educational needs and cultural differences. It also requires a concentrated effort to disseminate career information materials to Hispanic students and to involve Hispanic high school and college students in psychological work.

Specifically, ADAMHA should seek to develop programs that identify and support promising Hispanic undergraduates as a means of stimulating their educational development, thereby increasing the number of potential applicants to graduate training. Consistent with this strategy the President's Commission on Mental Health (1978) made two recommendations urging the Department of Health, Education and Welfare—

1. to develop, at the high school level, special projects to interest minority high school students in mental health careers and augment them through a program of summer and part-time internships which provide work opportunities in mental health facilities and programs;

2. to develop, at the college level, a program to provide scholarship support in the social, behavioral and biomedical sciences to outstanding juniors and seniors interested in graduate training in the mental health professions, with stipends also provided for summer jobs in mental health settings.

These two recommendations are critical; they point to the need for programs at the secondary and postsecondary levels to help identify potential Hispanic psychologists, to encourage their interest in this field, to support their involvement in education and to provide the kinds of enrichment opportunities that will help develop them into qualified candidates for graduate training.

We must also address the issue of admissions criteria for graduate training in psychology. It is well known that current criteria not only have low predictive validity but are also discriminatory; therefore, admission criteria that are more accurate and nondiscriminatory must be developed.

Enlarging the pool of undergraduate and graduate psychology students will eventually increase the numbers of Hispanic psychologists interested in academic careers. However, there is a more immediate need for strategies that develop Hispanic faculty as role models for our students. A means of fostering a more appropriate Hispanic faculty-Hispanic student ratio would be the establishment of APA accreditation criteria and National Institute of Mental Health (NIMH) training grant funding criteria that require Hispanic faculty representation in institutions where there are large concentrations of Hispanic students.

In addition to the development of human resources, there also must be changes in curriculum. A strategy proposed by Bernal (1980) is to generate data on the current status of minority content in graduate psychology to determine what curriculum and training experiences exist for minority groups, not just for Hispanics. These data should then constitute persuasive facts to present to groups such as the APA's Education and Training Board and Committee on Accreditation, as well as institutions such as NIMH that fund training programs.

The importance of training and curriculum development issues has also been underscored by the Hispanic Technical Consultant Group in charge of making recommendations to ADAMHA that foster the development of a Hispanic capability throughout ADAMHA and in the field.

The Hispanic Technical Consultant Group proposed two major recommendations in the areas of training and curriculum development. One of the recommendations presents a comprehensive outline: Hispanic Initiative for Training (HIT). The other suggests the need for an organized effort, involving a broad representation of Hispanic organizations and professionals in planning the HIT program. These recommendations are presented here because they outline strategies for implementation that should be encouraged and supported.

1. ADAMHA should convene and conduct a Workshop on Hispanic Training in Mental Health, Drug, and Alcohol Abuse. Workshop objectives should be—

- to reassess training needs;
- to re-evaluate proposed areas of impact of the HIT program;
- to delineate specific strategies and design specific program components and corresponding work plans for implementing the HIT program;
- to ascertain how to interface the HIT Program with each of the ADAMHA Institutes considering the characteristics, philosophy, emphasis and funding strategies of each.

2. There should be established an ADAMHA-wide Hispanic Initiative for Training (HIT) program. Its specific purpose would be to train Hispanics in disciplines relevant to the three ADAMHA Institutes. In

each institute, a Hispanic staff member should be designated to direct the program. The HIT program would focus—

> • on institutional training grants to those institutions with a proven record in training Hispanic students, including funds for faculty to develop and teach courses relevant to Hispanics;
>
> • on student stipend support that is adequate to provide Hispanic students, particularly in the first year of graduate training, with uninterrupted time for study, research, internship opportunities, and with books and training-related material;
>
> • on faculty development grants to assist in the development of Hispanic professionals—in the form of postdoctoral awards, research scientist career awards and other faculty development related programs—who opt for teaching or research careers;
>
> • on curriculum development grants to foster the development of training materials, content modules, training films, a comprehensive handbook on Hispanic mental health, drug and alcohol abuse; curriculum development should be closely tied in with knowledge development;
>
> • on training grants for the development of paraprofessionals, including the development of training programs, curricular materials and stipend support for trainees;
>
> • on regional training center grants that focus on curriculum development, internship training experiences and other relevant training functions.

Clearly, the deliberations and recommendations of this group reflect many of the issues and concerns addressed in this chapter. This fact points to a most important strategy for change: coordination and collaboration with other national groups and organizations working in this area. Liaisons among these various groups should be established as a means of implementing the strategies previously discussed. This is especially the case with such groups as ADAMHA's Hispanic Technical Consultant Group, APA's Office and Board of Ethnic Minority Affairs, the Minority Manpower Development Committee of the National Institute of Drug Abuse (NIDA) and the newly formed National Hispanic Psychological Association.

References

American Psychological Association. *Survey of U.S. graduate departments of psychology.* Washington, D.C.: Author, 1978–79.

American Psychological Association. *Psychology as a health care profession.* Washington, D.C.: Author, 1979.

Armas, J. *La Familia de La Raza.* 1972.

Bakan, D. Clinical psychology and logic. *American Psychologist,* 1956, *11,* 655–81.

Bennett, C. C., Anderson, L. S., Cooper, S., Hassol, L., Klein, D. C., & Rosenblum, A. *Community psychology: A report of the Boston conference in the education of psychologists for community mental health.* Boston: Boston University Press, 1966.

Bernal, M. E. Hispanic issues in curriculum and training in psychology. *Hispanic Journal of Behavioral Sciences,* 1980.

Bernal, M. E., & Padilla, A. M. Status of minority curricula and training in clinical psychology. *American Psychologist,* 1982, *37* (7), 780–87.

Brand, E., Ruiz, R., & Padilla, A. Ethnic identification and preference: A review. *Psychological Bulletin,* 1974, *81* (11), 860–90.

Buss, A. R. The emerging field of the sociology of psychological knowledge. *American Psychologist,* 1975, *30,* 988–1002.

Casal, L., & Hernandez, A. Cubans in the U.S.: A survey of the literature. *Cuban Studies/Estudios Cubanos,* 1975, *5* (2).

Diaz Guerrero, R. A Mexican psychology. *American Psychology,* 1977, *32* (11), 934–44.

Dieppa, I., & Montiel, M. Hispanic families: An exploration. In M. Montiel (Ed.), *Hispanic families: Critical issues for policy and programs in human services.* Washington, D.C.: COSSMHO, 1978.

Dohrenwend, B. P., & Smith, R. J. Toward a theory of acculturation. *Southwestern Journal of Anthropology,* 1962, *18,* 30–39.

Duran R. (Ed.). *Salubridad Chicana: Su preservacion es mantenimiento (The Chicano Plan for Mental Health).* Denver, CO.: Western Interstate Commission of Hispanic Education, 1975.

Fernandex, L. F. *A forgotten American.* New York: Anti-defamation League of B'nai B'rith 1970.

Fitzpatrick, J. P. *Puerto Rican Americans.* New Jersey: Prentice Hall, 1971.

Frake, C. O. The ethnographic study of cognitive systems. In R. A. Manners & D. Kaplan (Eds.), *Theory of anthropology.* Chicago: Aldine Publishing Co., 1968.

Gadlin, H., & Ingle, G. Through the one-way mirror: the limits of experimental self-reflection. *American Psychologist,* 1975, *30,* 1003–1009.

Gamson, Z. S., & Arce, D. H. Implications of the social context for higher education. In M. W. Peterson, R. T. Blackburn, G. S. Gamson, C. H. Arce, R. W. Davenport, & J. Mingle (Eds.), *Black students on white campuses: The impact of increased Black enrollment.* Ann Arbor: Publishing Division of the Survey Research Center, Institute for Social Research, 1978.

Gordon, M. M. *Assimilation in American life.* New York: Oxford University Press, 1964.

Gottfredson, G. D., & Dyer, S. E. Health service providers in psychology. *American Psychologist,* 1978, *33,* 314–38.

Graves, T. D. Psychological acculturation in a tri-ethnic community. *Southwestern Journal of Anthropology,* 1967, *23,* 337–50.

Hicks, H. H., & Ridley, S. E. Black studies in psychology. *American Psychologist,* 1979, *34,* 597–602.

Howells, J. G. *Principles of family psychotherapy.* New York: Brunner/Mazel, Inc., 1975.

Jiminez, R. Sociocultural perspective: How many Hispanics? In *The Hispanic American: Cultural issues in contemporary psychiatry.* Philadelphia: Smith, Kline & French Lab Publications, 1978.

Keefe, S. E. Acculturation and the extended family among urban Mexican Americans. Paper presented at the meeting of the American Association for the Advancement of Science, Houston, 1979.

Keefe, S. E., Padilla, A. M., & Carlos, M. L. Emotional support systems in two cultures: A comparison of Mexican-Americans and Anglo-Americans. Los Angeles: Spanish-speaking Mental Health Research Center, University of California, Los Angeles, Occasional Paper, No. 7, 1978.

Levine-Brand, E. S. & Ruiz, R. An explortaion of multicorrelates of ethnic group choice. *Journal of Cross Cultural Psychology,* 1978, *9,* 179–90.

Lopez y Rivas, G. *The Chicanos.* New York: Monthly Review Press, 1973.

Macias, R. F. U.S. Hispanics in 2000 A. D.—Projecting the number. *Agenda,* 1977, *7,* 16–20.

Maldonado-Dennis, M. *Puerto Rico: A sociohistoric interpretation.* New York: Vintage Books, 1972.

Marcos, L. R., Alpert, M., Urcuyo, L., & Kesselman, M. The effect of interview language on the evaluation of psychopathology in Spanish-American schizophrenic patients. *American Journal of Psychiatry,* 1973, *130,* 549–53.

Marin, P. C. Dependent needy family of San Juan, Puerto Rico. In M. Montiel (Ed.), *Hispanic families: Critical issues for policy and programs in human services.* Washington, D.C.: COSSMHO, 1978.

Martinez, J. L., Jr. (Ed.). *Chicano psychology.* New York: Academic Press, 1977.

Martinez-Urrutia, A. Migration patterns of Cubans, Mexicans, and Puerto Ricans. Unpublished manuscript, 1979.

Minuchin, S. *Families and family therapy.* Cambridge, Mass.: Harvard Press, 1974.

Montiel, M. Chicanos in the United States: An overview of sociohistorical context and emerging perspectives. In M. Montiel (Ed.), *Hispanic families: Critical issues for policy and programs in human service.* Washington, D.C.: COSSMHO, 1978.

National Coalition of Hispanic Mental Health and Human Services Organizations (COSSMHO). *Delphi survey of barriers.* Washington, D.C.: Author, 1980.

Offenberg, R., & Lega, L. L. Title VI Bilingual project: Let us be "amigos." Philadelphia School District of Philadelphia, 1974. (ERIC Ed. No. 109-933).

Olmedo, E. L. Acculturation: A psychometric perspective. *American Psychologist,* 1979, *34* (11), 1061–1070.

Olmedo, E. L., & Lopez, S. (Eds.). *Hispanic mental health professionals.* Monograph No. 5., Spanish Speaking Mental Health Research Center, University of California, Los Angeles, 1977.

Padilla, A. The role of cultural awareness and ethnic loyalty in acculturation. In A. M. Padilla (Ed.), *Acculturation: Theory, models and some new findings.* Boulder, CO.: Westview Press (forthcoming).

Padilla, A. M., & Liebman, E. Language acquisition in the bilingual child. *The Bilingual Review,* 1975, *2,* 34–55.

Padilla, A. M., & Lindholm, K. Acquisition of bilingualism: A descriptive analysis of the linguistic structures of Spanish/English-speaking children. In G. D. Keller, R. Tishner, & S. Viera (Eds.), *Bilingualism in the bicentennial and beyond.* New York: Bilingual Press, 1976.

Padilla, A. M., Olmedo, E. L., Lopez, S., & Perez, R. *Hispanic mental health bibliography*

II. Monograph No. 6, Spanish Speaking Mental Health Research Center, University of California, Los Angeles, 1978.

Padilla, A. M., & Ruiz, R. A. *Latino mental health: A review of literature.* Washington, D.C.: U.S. Government Printing Office, 1973. (DHEW Publications No. (HSM) 73-9143)

President's Commission on Mental Health. *Report of the task panel on special populations (Volume III).* Washington, D.C.: U.S. Government Printing Office, 1978.

Raush, J. L. Research practice and accountability. *American Psychologist,* 1974, *29,* 678–81.

Redfield, R., Linton, R. & Herskovits, M. Memorandum for the study of acculturation. *American Anthropologist,* 1936, *38,* 149–52.

Sampson, E. E. Scientific paradigms and social values: Wanted—A scientific revolution. *Journal of Personality and Social Psychology,* 1978, *36,* 1332–1343.

Spiegel, J. *Transactions: The interplay between individual, family and society.* New York: Science House, Inc., 1971.

Szapocznik, J., & Kurtinez, W. Acculturation, biculturalism and adjustment among Cuban Americans. In A. Padilla (Ed.), *Acculturation: Theory, models and some new findings.* Boulder, CO: Westview Press (forthcoming).

Szapocznik, J., Scopetta, M., Kurtines W., & Aranalde, M. Theory and measurement of acculturation. *Interamerican Journal of Psychology* (forthcoming).

Szapocznik, J., Scopetta, M. A., Arnalde, M., & Kurtines, W. Cuban value structure: Treatment implications. *Journal of Consulting and Clinical Psychology,* 1978, *46* (5), 961–70.

Tumin, M., & Plotch, W. (Eds.). *Pluralism in a democratic society.* New York: Praeger Publishers, 1976.

U.S. Bureau of the Census. Persons of Spanish origin in the United States: 1980. Current Population Reports, Series P-20, No. 328, Washington, D. C.: U.S. Government Printing Office, 1980.

Vidato, D. *A data report on the 1977–78 academic year and trends of APA accredited programs: Student and faculty distributions.* Washington, D.C.: American Psychological Association, 1979.

Bibliography

Horowitz, M. M. (Ed.). *Peoples and cultures of the Caribbean.* New York: The Natural History Press, 1971.

Proshansky, A. M. For what are we training our graduate students? *American Psychologist,* 1972, *27,* 205–12.

Tumin, M. *Caste in a peasant society.* Princeton, N.J.: Princeton University Press, 1952.

PART TWO

Social Work

JAMES A. BUSH   DELORES G. NORTON
CHARLES L. SANDERS   BARBARA B. SOLOMON

CHAPTER 5

An Integrative Approach for the Inclusion of Content on Blacks in Social Work Education

In the mid-1960s, schools of social work struggled to develop an awareness and understanding of the differences between racial and ethnic groups and to integrate minority ethnic content into the curriculum. The struggle has continued for almost twenty years with varying degrees of success. Schools of social work have offered both elective and required courses on minorities and on institutional racism. But these isolated courses, usually taught by minority faculty, often disappeared when their teachers moved on. There has been little or no overall integrative approach to the inclusion of ethnic minority content throughout the entire curriculum.

Meanwhile, increasingly large numbers of minority clients are served by social and mental health agencies. Statistics reveal that Black children probably live in homes where the median income is lower than that in the homes of most white children. In 1979 the white family median income was approximately $20,439 while the Black family median income was approximately $11,609. The increase during 1970–79 was $5,330 for Black families and $10,209 for white families (U.S. Bureau of the Census Current Population Data, 1981). Currently there are more poor Black families than there were a decade ago, but the number of poor white families has decreased. For example, the number of poor white families fell by 2 percent (from 3.6 to 3.5 million between 1969 and 1979) but rose 22 percent for poor Black families (from 1.4 to 1.7 million) (National Urban League, 1981). Also, the proportion of Black families headed by females increased from 34 percent to 37 percent between 1974 and 1977, while the proportion of white families headed by females increased from only 10 to 11 percent (National Urban League, 1981). The problems faced by these Black families continue to challenge social workers, and they imply questions for the social work profession. How are we to expand the curriculum

Statement of
the Problem

97

content on Blacks and how are we to develop effective theories of practice so that students of social work are prepared to serve all their clients?

Integration of minority content on Blacks into the social work curriculum must be based on pragmatic and pedagogical rationales. We need a systematic model to ensure the inclusion of Black content throughout the social work curriculum. Utilizing the fundamental concepts of social work, the model must also consider the following dimensions:

- The model must be compatible with the principles, history and philosophy of social work.
- The model must be applicable across curriculum areas such as intervention and Human Behavior and Social Environment (HBSE).
- The model must encompass practice at several levels, from individual, family and group levels through to communities.
- The model must be capable of program and policy planning at the various levels.

This chapter will address a number of issues. We will explore the forces behind the development of an integrated social work curriculum that includes ethnic and minority content as well as define some major concepts. We will discuss earlier trends in the development of theoretical frameworks for the inclusion of minority content in social work curricula, with particular attention to the history of the development of a Black perspective in social work education. Moreover, we will define commonly used concepts and terms. The use of the systems approach as a method for integrating curriculum content on Blacks in social work education will be examined and guidelines for its use will be suggested. In addition, we will specify what research is needed and propose strategies for institutional change and faculty development in relation to minority ethnic curriculum content.

Mandate for the 1980s: An Integrated Curriculum

The federal government, the National Institute of Mental Health (NIMH) and the Council on Social Work Education (CSWE) have issued mandates for the profession of social work. The mandate of the federal government is twofold. The first part, based on the 1978 task force of the President's Commission on Mental Health, sets the priority of training mental health professionals capable of serving the mental health needs of a pluralistic society, with special attention to the underserved and to minorities. The task force report clearly asserted that the nation's general health and mental health reflected the overall quality of life as well as the effectiveness of the social integration of all subgroups in our population (President's Commission on Mental Health, 1978, p. 11). There was an implicit assumption that the underserved sectors of our society were more vulnerable to mental disorder and a conclusion that minority groups were proportionately more underserved than other groups. The task force report reasoned that there must be a commitment of federal government policies to meet the needs of the underserved sectors of our population in order to have an impact on the mental health of the nation.*

The second part of the federal mandate included the profession of social work as one of the core professions in mental health along with psychiatry, psychology and psychiatric nursing (President's Commission on Mental Health, 1978, p. 452). The task force report recognized that "social work has given more attention to training for cross-cultural values than any of the other professions" (President's Commission on Mental Health, 1978, p. 438) but stressed that increasing the sensitivity of all service providers to the special needs, values and cultures of minorities was imperative for effective work. It bluntly stated that there should be minority content in all mental health training programs.

The National Institute of Mental Health, among whose major purposes are to increase the numbers of trained mental health personnel and to improve the quality of their education, provided the second major mandate for the inclusion of minority content in social work education. Based on the task force report of the President's Commission on Mental Health, the NIMH, has taken a firm stance that at a time of increasingly limited resources, *public* resources must be targeted toward the unserved, the underserved and the inappropriately served client population, of which lower income minorities, residing primarily in ethnically and racially segregated areas, are a large proportion. A recent study revealed that Black neighborhoods, compared with white neighborhoods, consistently have a relative absence of facilities and services (Yancey and Ericksen, 1979). Studies on service utilization rates, which reveal that lower income, urban Blacks and Hispanics are less likely to use what services do exist than are higher income and white groups, raise serious questions about the "middle-class bias" of service programs, as well as about physical and sociocultural barriers to service utilization and access (Cafferty and Chestang, 1976; Perlmutter and Alexander, 1978). If mental health professionals who plan programs, make policy and offer direct treatment do not understand the special needs, values and cultures of minorities, then their programs

---

* The conservative policies of the current Reagan Administration may seriously impede this goal. Mental health training has received a low budget priority.

and treatments will be ineffective and thus continually underutilized even when they exist.

Thus NIMH reasons, quite correctly, that much effort must be devoted to training social workers to meet the special needs of minority populations. NIMH has elected to do this in two ways: it strives to overcome the deficits in knowledge through the stimulation of research and to improve service delivery through the encouragement of more effective educational programs.

The Council on Social Work Education, a representative of the social work profession itself, provides the third mandate for the development and inclusion of content on minorities. The CSWE curriculum policy statement for masters degree programs defines social work as, "a profession that deals with problems and conditions which limit social functioning, through the promotion of social and institutional change and the provision of opportunities which enhance social functioning of individuals, groups, organizations, communities and nations" (Council on Social Work Education, 1972). The goals of social work education become, then, the development of competent professionals who can perform the functions that define their profession. Integral to this education is a provision for students to develop the knowledge, values and skills that prepare them to serve society in the prevention and treatment of problems and in the enhancement of the social well-being of all their clients. In a society such as ours, composed of different racial, ethnic and socioeconomic groups, the total client population can be very diverse. Social workers, at various points in their careers, are called upon to serve members of various socioeconomic, ethnic and racial groups.

Social work education must assume the responsibility to develop the student's understanding of clients and their varying socioeconomic, cultural and racial contexts. We must educate the student to be appreciative of and sensitive to cultural differences. Social workers must understand the dynamics of a community in order to know when and if intervention is needed and what that intervention should be. There needs to be an understanding of how generic social work training can mesh with training for work with specific minority groups.

The CSWE has sought to complement its mandate in regard to inclusion of minority and ethnic content with its accreditation standard 1234 A (CSWE, 1972). Although the language used by CSWE is broad and abstract, it does permit the development of programs with goals fitted to various target populations. There is no mechanism, however, that ensures the development and teaching of such content or that provides flexibility for groups primarily served by a school's curriculum, faculty and students. The question is: What is the theory upon which we can build a framework that permits the appropriate integration of substantive content relative to the client group being served? To help answer this question, let us look at earlier trends in theories that provided for the inclusion of minority content in social work curricula.

A critical issue has been the fragmentation of the knowledge base for social work. There has been heavy dependence on content from other disciplines, particularly psychiatry and clinical psychology. Students in some schools of social work are far more familiar with Erikson, Maslow, Rogers or Eyesenck than with any social work theoretician. In fact, most social work authors tend to develop theories of practice rather than theories of behavior and base their theories of practice on behavioral theories developed by allied applied scientists—psychiatrists and clinical psychologists. That these allied disciplines are more likely than social work to construct their theoretical systems on predominantly white, middle-class client contacts has meant certain theoretical deficits when social workers attempt to apply them in practice.

Prior to the 1960s, ethnic content in social work curricula was addressed primarily by a nod in the direction of "culture" as it was presumed to act as a determinant of behavior. This, however, was the culture of Kluckhohn and Mead with their strong emphasis on cultural variations in value orientations. Values that were not congruent with dominant American values were most often viewed only as the source of dysfunction within American society. In addition to the cultural anthropological theme, there was some inclusion of sociological literature such as Myrdal's *American Dilemma* (1962) or psychological literature like Kardiner and Ovesey's *Mark of Oppression* (1951). These sources, however, were used primarily to identify again the sources of the pathologies that were seen to characterize Blacks in the United States rather than to differentially assess Black clients and differentially plan practice strategies. The result was something Gwendolyn Gilbert has referred to as the "ain't it awful" syndrome (Gilbert and Ryan, 1974).

The late 1960s brought ferment through the Black movement, which placed new pressures on schools of social work to be "more relevant" for minority clients. Grier and Cobb's *Black Rage* (1968) became required reading despite the fact that it was criticized, and rightly so, for its too narrow psychoanalytic interpretation of the Black experience, which the authors overgeneralized from their encounters with their own highly disturbed Black patients. It should be noted, however, that at least they were grappling with the implications of that experience in a way that had not been done before. Furthermore, their modus operandi was no more or no less than that of Freud in his extrapolations from his couch.

Grier and Cobb were followed by authors who rushed into print with books and articles on the Black experience and its significance for mental health practice. Most of the material was informative or descriptive, concentrating on debunking myths (e.g., Billingsley, 1968; Goodman, 1973; Thomas and Sillen, 1972; and Willie, Kramer and

Trends in the Development of Theoretical Frameworks

Brown, 1973). Other literature identified the evil consequences of discrimination on the survival capacities and the life chances of oppressed minorities and called for change (e.g., Chestang, 1972; Cohen, 1969). Still others sought to describe reality through extensive review of the fragmented literature (e.g., Figueira-McDonough, 1979).

This proliferation of literature and the attempts to provide comprehensive and detailed information about all ethnic groups (but particularly about Blacks, who were most consistently applying the pressure) gave rise to one approach to the incorporation of minority content in social work curricula—that which employed behavioral objectives. Crompton (1974) pointed out that the emphasis on "ordering, organizing, [and] classifying content for all minority groups" had not taken into consideration either the specific behavioral objectives or the most effective teaching-learning process that would lead to the achievement of the behavioral objectives. To alleviate the problem of content overload and to establish clear behavioral objectives, Crompton advocated the shifting of focus to the strategies, psychological processes and behavioral capacities used by the student to master the content.

Unlike Crompton, who emphasized behavioral objectives to ensure some accountability for the teaching and learning of minority content, the experiential learning proponents rarely insisted on such rigor. A favorite tool of the experientialists was the encounter group, where role-playing faculty, students and persons from minority communities simulated conflict and crisis situations. This approach was tried in many schools of social work but did not yield clear results. Moreover, its inherent lack of structure and subjectivity tended to be atheoretical if not actually antitheoretical.

Theoretical frameworks have been emerging, however, that more effectively rationalize inclusion of both behavioral and experiential materials in social work curricula. Chestang (1972) suggested that specific aspects of the environment, namely social injustice and societal inconsistency, have consequences for character development. These two dynamic social processes affect the individual's sense of personal powerlessness to influence the environment. Although Chestang's references were particularly directed to the Black community, the implication could easily be drawn that any minority group experiencing social injustice and societal inconsistency has to deal with feelings of powerlessness and evolve two aspects to their character—a depreciated one and a transcendent one. This duality of response stems from the experience of functioning in two environments. The depreciated character results from the incorporation by Blacks of the negative messages from the wider or sustaining environment, while the transcendent character emerges from the incorporation of positive images from the Black family and community, and is supported by that nurturing environment. The specific expression of these abstract processes is shaped by the unique aspects of a particular minority group's experience in the society.

Norton (1978) expanded on this theme, defining dual perspective, as, "The conscious and systematic process of perceiving, understanding and comparing simultaneously the values, attitudes, and behavior of the larger societal system with those of the client's immediate family and community system." The social worker should be able to recognize when these two systems are in conflict and be able to assess the nature and implications of the conflict through cultural knowledge of both systems.

Many of the principles set forth by Chestang and Norton are embodied in Solomon's (1976) framework, which utilizes ethnosystem, power and empowerment as the major integrative concepts. *Ethnosystem* is defined as: "A society which comprises groups which vary in modes of communication, in degree of control over material resources, and in the structure of their internal relationships or social organization. Moreover, these groups must be in a more or less stable pattern of relationships which have characteristics transcending any single group's field of interaction, e.g., the ethnosystem's political, educational or economic subsystems" (p. 45). There is a basic similarity between this concept and the concept of two environments—the immediate or nurturing environment and the wider, sustaining environment.

In addition, Solomon builds upon Chestang's concept of personal impotence to generate a family of concepts in which the pivotal one is power. She argues that if, as Norton (1976) indicated, the larger societal system rejects the minority group's immediate environmental system, then empowerment of the minority group should be the goal. Empowerment is described as the gaining of an ability to manage emotions, knowledge, skills or material resources in a way that makes possible effective performance of valued social roles and receipt of personal gratification. Empowerment as process refers to a set of activities aimed at reducing institutionally derived powerlessness, i.e., powerlessness caused by Chestang's social injustice and societal inconsistency.

There are similar parallels between Norton's (1976) concept of reversible thought (taken from Piaget) and Solomon's (1976) description of the nonracist practitioner. To be capable of reversible thought, according to Norton's concept, one must have the ability and conscious motivation to think about the situation being observed and to look for points of difference, conflict or congruence with the larger society. And Solomon's nonracist practitioner would be one who possesses "the ability to perceive in any behavior—other's or one's own—alternative ways to explain that behavior, particularly those which the self might most strongly reject as false."

These themes are also present in a recent framework developed in Gallegos and Harris (1979) for integrating minority ethnic content into curricula of doctoral programs in social work. They perceive the three major integrative concepts as (1) socialization, which identifies the process whereby "one receives ideas, clues, or direct pressures to adopt attitudes and behaviors"; (2) pluralism, which identifies the multilevel societal structure through which socialization processes flow; and (3) sociocultural dissonance, which is the tension that occurs when levels are in conflict. These emerging frameworks, although applied most often to Blacks, are not minority-specific. They can be utilized in viewing the experience of any oppressed, stigmatized racial or ethnic group in the American social system.

Before we discuss the present approach to an integrative framework, we offer some definitions of terms and an historical overview of the impact of the Civil Rights movement.

Concepts and Terms

A discussion dealing with the broad aspects of the many issues related to the why and how of ethnic minority content in social work education necessitates some common definitions. Among some of the terms which need more clarification are *Black perspective*, *Black culture*, and *ethnic minority*. All of these terms have been used more widely in recent times, given the racial, ethnic and social diversity of our society.

Black Perspective

Black perspective refers to the conscious and systematic process of perceiving and understanding the unique values, attitudes and behavioral patterns of Black Americans, as a subculture embedded within but different from the larger society (Norton, 1978; Sanders, 1971). The premise of this definition is that there is both a majority culture and a minority culture. It simply means that Blacks are viewed within the context of their own sociocultural conditions and in interaction with the dominant culture. The term demands acceptance, sensitivity and understanding of difference. The term *black perspective* is cognitive in that it is theoretical and intellectual. But it is also attitudinal in that it implies, for social work practitioners, the need to be self-aware and nonjudgmental about differences among people. An understanding of the *Black perspective* helps in assessing the problems of Black clients more accurately and in developing solutions and treatment plans. Indeed, the *Black perspective* builds upon the practitioner's use of all social work principles.

Black Culture

An integral relationship exists between the terms *Black perspective* and *Black culture*. The Black perspective derives from the Black culture, and one supports the other. An individual is more cognizant of the Black perspective when he has adequate knowledge of Black culture. The interactions between the two terms, however, are frequently blurred. Although a consensus has yet to emerge, some common themes are identifiable when defining the elements of Black culture. Bishop (1977) observed that "Black people in America comprise a culture markedly distinguishable from other American cultures. Unique to the Black culture are . . . (1) a continuing search for freedom of the group; (2) deeply held religious convictions about deliverance; and (3) a . . . highly expressive lifestyle."

The words of Mayor Richard Hatcher (1976) of Gary, Indiana, reflect not only the diffusion of the terms *Black perspective* and *Black culture* but also the philosophy of *Black culture*.

> When we say Black culture we are not talking about a culture which is racist, or reactionary, which seals off Black society from the rest of the nation, which glorifies separatism, or wants to return to Africa. We are talking about a culture which encourages, develops, subsidizes and pays attention to itself, which takes pride in its color and its past; which rids itself of selfhate, and selfdoubt; which does not mirror and ape a white society, especially the worst of it.

More recently, a more comprehensive view of both the dominant and minority culture has emerged in a synthesis known as the dual perspective (Norton, 1978). Black perspective and Black culture reflect the evolving body of minority- and ethnic-based social work knowledge, skill and practice.

Ethnic Minority

Ethnic minority refers to Blacks, Asians, Hispanics and Native Americans as groups that have been historically oppressed. Color is a dominant factor in the oppression. The term *minority*, for our purposes, refers primarily to a group that because of its physical or cultural characteristics, is singled out from society for differential and unequal treatment. In turn, the group members regard themselves as objects of discrimination. Minority status implies exclusion of certain ethnic groups from full participation in the life of the society (Simpson and Yinger, 1972).

We are in an age of the "new ethnicity." Ethnicity is a phenomenon to be studied in both individuals and in groups and calls for a competent understanding of multicultural consciousness. The concept of ethnic minority lies at the center of this discussion.

Historical Overview

Prior to 1960, there was only minimal consideration in social work education of racial and cultural factors. In the socially conscious 1960s and early 1970s, the period of the tumultuous Civil Rights era, such factors received greater emphasis. The "new ethnicity" in social work, a result of the Civil Rights movement, was coming to the fore.

Past Patterns   The developmental pattern in social work education relative to Blacks appears to have followed the developmental pattern of the larger Civil Rights movement of the 1950s, 1960s and 1970s. Although each movement appears to have influenced the other, it was more often the larger Civil Rights movement that influenced social work education concerning Blacks.

Each movement quickly crystallized around highly visible deficits. Within social work education, as it related to Black curriculum content, these issues were initially the following: (1) lack of awareness and understanding of a dual perspective—one Anglo, one Black (Norton, 1978); (2) the absence of organizing concepts, constructs and theoretical bases for teaching curriculum content about Blacks (Bush, 1972); and (3) the need for teaching strategies in social welfare policy, human behavior and the environment and the need for practice relevant for assisting Blacks. These issues were initially set forth in the Council on Social Work Education's Black Task Force Report of 1973 (Francis, 1973) along with the need for locating responsibility for the integration of curriculum content about Blacks within schools of social work.

The outcomes were significant. For example, by 1971 the number of Black students in graduate schools of social work had increased, the number of Black faculty in a tenured track in graduate schools of social work had greatly increased, and the number of specific courses, as well as the amount of relevant curriculum content about Blacks had grown significantly. In 1960 there were only 326 (13 percent) Black students in graduate schools of social work. By 1968 this number had increased to 700, and one-fourth of all students were nonwhite by 1971. Black faculty increased from 154 to 259 for this same period. Also, by 1971, 59 of the 70 accredited schools of social work had one or more courses on ethnic minority groups (Scott, 1978).

There was resistance in several apparent legitimate guises. These include such statements and questions as "The experience of Blacks is not different from all humans."; "Where is the content and teaching strategies for teaching about Blacks in our curriculum?"; and "If we start to teach content about Blacks we will receive demands to teach separate courses from all the other ethnic groups, and how can we cover all that material in our curriculum?" These statements and questions generated several other relevant questions that merited consideration: "Who should teach the courses and/or be responsible for the content?"; "Should the content be integrated into existing courses or taught separately? And what are the strategies for introducing this content in the various sequences of social policy, human behavior and the environment, and social work practice?" Amid this apprehension, the Council on Social Work Education agreed to use efforts at integrating curriculum content about ethnic minorities as certifying or recertifying criteria for graduate schools of social work.

In the years following 1972, there was a pronounced loss in the sense of urgency that had marked the period of 1966–1972. New issues concerning the rights of groups such as women, the mentally ill, homosexuals, and the handicapped gained prominence. In some ways the change had been predicted. The Civil Rights movement for Blacks had been envisioned as occuring in identifiable phases or stages. These phases were termed *separation, identity, institution-building and control, coalition-building,* and *unity* (Bush, 1977). Within social work education also, there were expected developmental phases in the emerging curriculum content about Blacks. For example, there were initially specific courses about Blacks that tended to highlight the divergence in profit, privilege and power for Black Americans and coping strategies they frequently used in dealing with institutional racism. Later course content tended to emphasize character developments in Blacks (Billingsley, 1972; Chestang, 1972). Also, there were efforts toward institution and community control and empowerment (Glasgow, 1972; Solomon, 1976). Subsequently, comparing experiences among Blacks with a mythological "white norm" was denounced and an effort made to find common goals and strategies for "peoples of color" (Mendes, 1974). The responsibility for continued stimulation for change was more often than not left to evolution or assumed to be self-regulating. Exceptions to this have been the efforts of the Council on Social Work Education (CSWE, 1971) and diverse individual commitments made by various social work professionals and groups.

Professional Social Work Organizations

The Civil Rights movement evolved during a period of pervasive social consciousness, and in the Black community it culminated in what was known as the Black militancy period. This era of dissent not only influenced the traditional, established white organizations but also influenced the newly emerging all-Black groups (Young, 1968).

Within the social work establishment, the thrust for equal rights provoked a reexamination of not only ethnic-based associations but also of several other organizations such as the National Association of Social Workers, the Council on Social Work Education and the National Conference of Social Welfare. The impact of the Civil Rights movement on the National Association of Social Workers, for example, was visible: minority officers were appointed at the policy-making level; by-laws, program priorities and policy statements on issues affecting minorities were written and issued; and a National Committee on Minority Affairs and an affirmative action policy for national and chapter units were created in 1980.

For the purposes of this chapter, we will discuss primary professional organizations, such as the Council on Social Work Education and the National Association of Black Social Workers (NABSW). The CSWE is primarily involved in education, while the NABSW, representing minority interests, is probably more related to practice issues. In addition, we will also look at schools of social work.

Council on Social Work Education. One of the earliest efforts was seen in the CSWE development of the Commission on Minority Groups in 1972. As part of the commission, the Black Task Force was to develop guidelines for inclusion of content on Blacks in social work curriculum. The task force consisted of fifteen nationally based Black members and two students and was chaired by Genevieve T. Hill, dean of the Atlanta University School of Social Work, the oldest Black school of social work in the United States. The group expanded and redefined its mission from simply developing Black curriculum content to designing a format for incorporating it in both Black and non-Black schools of social work (Hill, 1972).

While this was a structural response to the 1960s, CSWE effected an integrative approach in ethnic minority content. As the major accrediting social work education body for graduate and undergraduate schools, CSWE had a wide impact. During the early 1970s, CSWE expanded many ancillary functions, such as recruitment of minority students and faculty; scholarship assistance for minority students; and financial support for faculty publications, newsletters, reports, books, teaching materials, conferences and consultations. This expansion necessitated more involvement with minorities, especially Blacks, as a means of developing ethnic content in educational curriculum. One primary outcome was the review of the criteria by which it set standards, which resulted in a new standard that required every school to make a "special continual effort to enrich its program by providing racial, ethnic, and cultural diversity in its student body, all levels of instructional and research personnel, and by providing corresponding educational support" (Ross-Sheriff, 1979; CSWE, 1971).

A series of meetings, conferences and task forces sponsored by CSWE for almost ten years has consistently provided the impetus for social work educators to explore issues and models for developing minority curriculum content. Following these efforts the concept of the dual perspective was identified as clarifying the issues of both content and methodology (Norton, 1978). The dual perspective as a specific approach will be discussed later.

National Association of Black Social Workers. Seemingly, in both social work practice and education definite stances on the Black perspective have followed organizational lines. Francis's survey of the 1960s to the present revealed "a period of major change in the social work profession as Blacks began to demand proportionate representation in its national organizations, its schools, and the profession itself. Along with the thrust for representation there developed national Black associations to address Black issues and concerns which [they] felt could not be addressed in the established organizations. Though slow, advances have been made in minority representation in those areas of major concern" (Francis, 1978).

Empirical data that assess the impact of NABSW on education (especially as it relates to the inclusion of minority content) are scarce. One might expect this, as the original emphasis of NABSW was on practice issues, such as service delivery and equitable representation in established national practice-oriented organizations. Further, Sanders (1973) noted that perceptions of institutional racism in education and training were not high among surveyed Black social workers. There were few instances when Black social workers remarked on racist practices in education. When noting the NABSW impact on education in the early 1970s Sanders observed:

> The NABSW strategy for a more relevant education and training program has been minimal. . . . While this was not the association's chief area of concern, it did raise hard and fast questions about Black educational opportunities, regarding minority representation, scholarships and awards more so than minority content in curriculum (Sanders, 1973).

Nevertheless, the advocacy provided by NABSW helped to develop a national perspective for minority concerns in social work education, which was implemented by the CSWE.

Schools of Social Work. The 185 schools of social work responded to inclusion of Black content in extremely diversified ways. The two major Black schools of social work, Howard University and Atlanta University, have striven to fulfill their missions. Until recently, however, there have been no specific means of codifying the individual responses of all the schools. Trader observed that most schools had no systematic mechanism for including minority content, and both Trader and Leigh noted that minority content is generally taught outside of the core curriculum (Leigh, 1974; Trader, 1974).

Ross-Sheriff (1979) surveyed schools of social work in an attempt to answer at least some of the following questions:

- How has minority content been taught at undergraduate and graduate schools of social work?
- What were characteristics of schools in terms of composition of faculty and students by minority groupings and by sex?
- How was minority content developed, implemented and monitored?
- What were field placements in relation to minority needs?
- What were programs' needs for minority content?

The results of this study show conclusively that until minority content becomes part of core curricula there will continue to be a great need for supplementary training through summer institutes or for information clearinghouses.

Current Trends

Strategies to increase and integrate Black curriculum content in schools of social work consist of fostering up-to-date information and knowledge on pertinent issues and changes; increasing the knowledge and skills of practicing graduates who were not exposed to Black curriculum content during training; and creating necessary change based on new research, additional knowledge, and new models or frameworks. This last strategy deserves special emphasis. Research is needed to distinguish that knowledge of behaviors that relates Blacks to all other humans in contrast to behaviors that are distinctive to Blacks and based upon unique factors of their experiences (Spiegel, 1975). For example, there is an increasing emphasis on social class among Blacks in America. Also, there is a significant increase in interracial marriages or alliances and in numbers of children resulting from these relationships. At least three approaches to these emerging social issues are being undertaken: the social systems approach, the dual perspective approach and the ethnosystem approach.

The Social Systems Approach. The efforts to integrate Black curriculum content into the curricula of schools of social work reflect change and development at the institutional level. The systems approach seems to be a viable way to conceptualize and develop strategies for change. The systems approach begins with the person-in-environment focus which permeates all social work curricula and can be used to appraise the transactions between social systems and Blacks. When transactions result in problems, the systems approach involves assessment and intervention to effect positive change.

The effect of the environment on the person is the most commonly used mechanism for discussing the Black experience in the United States, especially in terms of racism, discrimination and, in the past, slavery. Thomas and Sillen (1972) suggested that this tends to absolve the practitioner from any responsibility or hope because he or she cannot change something that is a result of a highly institutionalized process that will take years to change. There have been efforts to take a positive rather than a negative view of the effect of an oppressive environment on Blacks. The Civil Rights movement is an example of the effect an oppressive environment had on a people who represented a small number in terms of position and power but who were able to effect a positive change in social services.

In the systems approach, social systems, to be effective and efficient, should be open rather than closed and balanced rather than stressful and adversarial. In social work practice traditional as well as innovative methods should be used for intervention. Traditional methods would include confrontation, debate and regulatory mechanisms such as affirmative actions. Innovative approaches could include empowerment, phased approaches to issues and research and expanded continuing education programs and postgraduate education systems. The intent is to develop a multilevel and multitechnical systems approach to ensure ongoing progress and success.

The Dual Perspective Approach. Norton's (1976) model of the dual perspective is a dynamic and detailed conceptualization of the systems affecting Blacks. It utilizes Chestang's conceptualization that the person's immediate or nurturing system, comprising subsystems of family, neighborhood, peer group, and so forth, interacts with the larger, sustaining system comprising myriad subsystems such as school, place of work, system of justice and so forth. It argues that the social work practitioner must have a dual perspective which forces attention on differences between a minority and a nonminority world.

The Ethnosystem Approach. The ethnosystem approach is the reasoning behind some of the efforts to include minority content in social work education. Solomon's (1976) conceptualization of the ethnosystem assumes that race or ethnicity is the primary organizing principle in U.S. society. She presents society as an ethnosystem comprising smaller groups or collectives of individuals (subsystems) whose ethnicity defines them and their relationship to the whole—either by self-determination or by the determination of other, more powerful subsystems. An ethnosystem is defined as a collective of interdependent ethnic groups sharing unique historical and/or cultural ties and bound together by a single, political system. This is viewed by Valle (1978) as polyculturalism—a variant on the dual perspective theme.

Because no individual represents the entire human race, the ethnosystem approach essentially speaks to the new ethnicity, wherein we learn how to discern and interpret the behavior of others who differ from ourselves. It is, indeed, an ethnic awareness of racial and cultural pluralism and the well-being of mankind (Gambino, 1975).

The common theme shared by all three approaches is that of "social systems," and the social systems approach first discussed has perhaps the greatest potential for incorporating content about the dynamic interactions between Blacks and their environment. The systems approach, however, does not constitute a cohesive theory with tightly connecting propositions and unambiguous concepts. There may still be considerable lack of clarity about the particular nature and consequences of the interaction between different minority groups, such as Blacks and Hispanics. But a systems perspective does provide a framework for studying, for example, how an educational system can support simultaneously the learning needs of children from two ethnic groups. (We avoid the terminology "disadvantaged children," which implies a heterogeneous group defined by poverty rather than ethnicity.) The immediate limitations of a systems approach would recede as further work is done.

*Impact of
Approaches*

Changes can be assessed using frameworks suggested by the three approaches. For example, the behaviors of an ethnosystem can be understood when the framework shown in Figure 1 is used. In this framework, Black families are viewed within the larger context that is formed by the configuration and interacting elements of values, knowledge, and skills—a configuration that is basic to social work. These elements are evident within each family, each community and the larger society. When there is a high degree of congruency between these elements, Black families will experience a sense of winning in life, of control over their destiny and of contributing to the well-being of the various components.

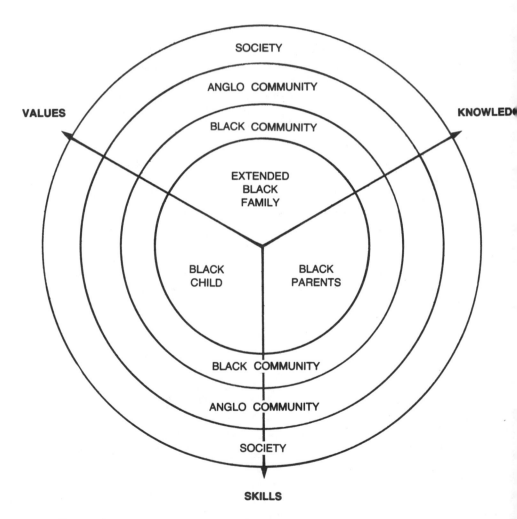

FIGURE 1

A Framework for Understanding the Behaviors of an Ethnosystem

In contrast, when there is discongruency between these elements, Black families will be affected negatively in their efforts to *survive* (physically and psychologically), to *socialize* the members of their family and to pass on the *cultural heritage* to their descendents. Black families will experience rootlessness and a lessened sense of belonging and of contributing to the well-being of society. Where there are ego strengths among and high nourishment from the Black family members and the Black community, discongruency can elicit positive adaptive responses that resist vulnerability to distress, even though the social and psychological price may be high.

In addition, this framework can assist teachers and students in grasping not only the impacts on Black families but also the impact that Black families and Black communities have on the Anglo and larger society, as well as on its individual members.

Frameworks, methods and assessments for integrating curriculum content about Blacks in social work education must be established on multiple levels. Examples of these approaches are the education levels of orientation-induction in social work and social service agencies, in-service training programs, paraprofessional and undergraduate training programs, graduate training and postgraduate and continuing education programs.

The sequences of social work curricula are human behavior and the social environment, social work practice and field work, social welfare policy and services, and research. In each area, a systems perspective generates particular questions related to Black curriculum content. Consideration of these questions leads to the incorporation of Black content into the curricula.

Curriculum Relevance

The major question in this sequence stems from the assumption that race or ethnicity has generated differential social histories, life experiences and social environments for individuals growing up in this society. The question is, to what extent has the differential "Black experience" influenced the growth and development process—regardless of the theoretical models used to define that process? For example, from psychoanalytic or ego psychology theory, the major question can be broken down into more specific ones such as: How is the Oedipal conflict an influencer of the variant structures of Black families? How are ego supports and ego strengths developed under conditions of social stigma and collective discrimination? How are defense mechanisms employed by Black Americans to deal with fears they may have of conforming to racial stereotypes, or with guilt from accepting a negative

Human Behavior and the Social Environment

valuation of the collective? How is the conceptualization of a "pleasure principle" and "reality principle" based on a concept of delayed gratification influenced by the realistic probability of "no gratification"? What is the effect of "growing up Black" on the resolution of each of the psychosocial crises conceptualized by Erikson, e.g. identity formation?

If the faculty member utilizes a behavioral or learning theory approach, there are still specific questions that stem from the major one indicated above. How do value orientations of Blacks influence their perceptions of "reward" and "punishment"? To what extent have interactions between Blacks and the external systems (i.e. systems outside their immediate, nurturing system) reinforced certain behaviors and extinguished others?

If the faculty member uses a humanistic, theoretical framework, again system-related questions emerge. If there is a hierarchy of human needs, how have the external systems supported or failed to support meeting these needs in the immediate, nurturing system of Blacks? How is the development of a sense of responsibility for self, autonomy, free will and so forth influenced by constraints imposed by the environment as in the case of many Blacks? Because feelings of powerlessness are believed to stem from lack of self-esteem and to result in "madness" (May, 1972), what is the impact of the external environment on the self-esteem of Blacks, and, hence, on their mental health?

Although most of the preceding questions have been at the individual growth and developmental level, similar questions can be asked at the level of groups, organizations and communities from the dual perspective. For example, to what extent has the Black experience influenced the development of self-help groups? Do self-help groups in Black communities differ in any way from those outside Black communities? How does race as an intervening variable influence the exercise of power in organizations? Is there differential power in organizations that operate almost exclusively either within or outside the minority group's immediate environment? To what extent do primary group networks developed by Blacks differ from those developed by other groups? The answers to these and similar questions identify the content about Blacks that can be incorporated into the social work human behavior and social environment sequence.

Social Work Practice and Field Work

Social work practice involves understanding how knowledge, value and skill relate to each other as well as their utilization in assessing problems or situations in the provision of professional social work services. From a systems perspective, social work is at the point of transactions between the individual and the environments (both nurturing and sustaining). When those transactions become problematic, it involves assessment and intervention aimed at effecting positive change. This is accomplished within a relationship. The establishment of that relationship, the perceptions incorporated into an assessment of problems and the interventions all require consummate understanding of communication, particularly as it occurs within and across ethnic-system boundaries. How does a practitioner communicate to a Black client that he or she is perceived as a peer? That the practitioner has knowledge and skills and is willing to place them at the client's disposal in seeking solutions to problems? That the practitioner believes in the client's capability to solve his or her own problems? How does a Black client use both verbal and nonverbal language to express feelings of, for example, acceptance, rejection, hostility and friendship. What characteristic of a relationship supports self-disclosure among Blacks? There is little empirical research available that will provide the answers to these questions. Therefore, the exploration of answers can come through experiential exercises that are transracial in nature and that provide an opportunity for faculty and students to obtain more accurate knowledge. Mere speculation or extrapolation from related literature would not be fruitful.

These experiential exercises have been created, utilized and reported in the literature (Norton, 1978; Solomon, 1976). There are some suggestions in the literature for a nontraditional model of social work practice with Blacks based on hypotheses about the answers to these questions. For example, Trader (1974) has suggested a transactional, teaching-learning process between client and practitioner which requires sharing expert knowledge and skills on each side. Solomon has proposed four elements of an "empowerment" model of practice: (1) helping clients perceive themselves as causal agents in achieving solutions to their problems; (2) helping clients to perceive practitioners as having knowledge and skills which clients can use; (3) helping clients to perceive practitioners as peer collaborator or partner in the problem-solving effort; and (4) helping clients to perceive the "power structure" as multipolar, demonstrating varying degrees of commitment to the status quo and therefore open to influence. These models are based on certain notions about the answers to the questions posed previously.

Social Welfare Policy and Services

From the dual perspective, it is important to place the policy-making process in the context of transactions between the immediate and the sustaining systems in our society. It is clear that the major forces for policy development and implementation lie in the sustaining systems—courts, legislatures, schools and so forth. These are the systems that constitute the suprasystem which Solomon describes as having a "life of its own," transcending any group within it and different from the mere sum of behaviors in its component parts. In essence, however, this suprasystem *is* influenced by the differential power of the collective which is part of it. The Anglo subgroup has the greatest power and tends to negatively value the racial minority subgroups, and this is reflected in the policies that emerge from the suprasystem.

As in the other areas of the curriculum, the social welfare policy and services area can incorporate Black content by addressing certain system-related questions. For example, how has the social welfare institution of the suprasystem historically responded to the unmet needs of the Black subsystem? How has the immediate, nurturing system of Blacks responded to the failures of the sustaining system to truly sustain them? What is the impact of recent major social legislation on the Black subsystem? What has been the differential impact of the political process and how does this relate to differential power among the several subsystems of the ethnosystem? What has been the differential impact on Blacks of recent court rulings? How do social policies emerging from the suprasystem reflect differential value orientations among the different ethnic collectives.

There is an excellent summary of content relating to the first two questions in Norton (1978). In contrast to behavior and practice, much of the literature on racism and discrimination in our society has dealt with social welfare services and policies so that the bibliographical supports directly relevant to the social work issues in this area are considerable. At the same time, the area is changing rapidly and therefore requires a constant commitment to scholarship from the dual perspective. For example, in teaching human behavior from an ego-psychology perspective, the basic issues will not change much from year to year. On the other hand, the social welfare policies and services having an impact on Blacks are ever-changing and varying in equitability. The faculty member in this area must be constantly aware of these changes and their implications.

Research

It is only in the past decade that social work has begun to place a priority on research. It is particularly startling to discover that there is no specific discussion nor description of required research in the CSWE curriculum policy statement for the master's degree, written in 1971 (CSWE, 1971). Research is alluded to only in the section on the development of competence in the practice of social work. This section points out a need to provide opportunities designed to help each student "develop a spirit of inquiry and a commitment throughout his professional career to seek, critically appraise, contribute and utilize new knowledge." Though such an indirect allusion to research as late as 1971 is surprising, it is also prophetic in that it is linked to the goal of developing competence in practice for students. Currently there is a major trend in social work education to integrate research and practice.

The Educational System. Many factors have led to a growing concern about the status of research in social work, among them the demand for cost accountability of intervention in a time of scarce resources; growing criticism of existing theory, based on social science literature, which does not provide clear guidelines for practice; and outcome studies which have challenged the effectiveness of social work intervention (Roberts, 1979). These social work concerns to link research with practice coincide with the need for research with regard to social work and minorities.

The first concern, cost accountability, represents a danger in research relating to services to ethnic minority populations. The tendency to emphasize concrete variables such as work units and financial savings to the public as outcome measures overlooks the preliminary efforts that often must be made before these indicators of program "effect" can be rationally applied. Helping clients to achieve higher levels of self-esteem, for example, may not, in the short run, result in a job or improved family relationships but would certainly be necessary if these ultimate benefits are to be attained. The second two factors—clear guidelines for practice and doubt on the effectiveness of intervention—have applicability to intervention in relation to minorities. Social science theory has developed frequently through the study of white, middle-class behavior, and the results of this research has been assumed to be the norm for everyone. Practice models based on such theory can often be ineffective with members of groups of different cultural values and norms. These models need to be tested carefully through research to evaluate what characteristics or variables may prove effective or ineffective with Black clients. Similarly, the frameworks that have emerged to provide a perspective on the experience of minority ethnic groups in our society and to provide a basis for practice with minority clients are still largely untested (Chunn 1974; Norton, 1978; Solomon, 1976; Trader, 1977). Programmatic research is needed to systematically extrapolate hypotheses from these frameworks and to test them in practice. This calls for careful definition of variables and monitoring of practice.

Although the testing of various frameworks of practice is one kind of research needed to improve services to minorities, there is another model for research that should also be pursued. This is the more indicative model that begins in the field, emphasizing practice methods, not testing explanatory frameworks. This model, best explicated by Reid (1980), stresses services to clients, evaluation of one's own practice, and feedback to practice of what is effective. It involves testing by various means of evaluation (such as single subject design) what is effective in practice. In this research, one does not *test* a framework of practice as described earlier, rather one *builds* one. This research approach evolves around the client and his goals and values, not around hypotheses or practice techniques. The result could be new guidelines for practice based on the particular clients served. The information gleaned, a result of practice with minorities, can be fed back to the agencies' service programs and can be extremely valuable in knowledge development on minorities.

The Researchers. Social work and social science researchers, especially Anglo researchers, tend to investigate ethnic minorities, especially Blacks, without an appropriate set of guiding principles and without appropriate frameworks for their methodology. For example, they often compare their findings regarding Blacks with whites, or they assume that all Black families are similar. Many researchers focus on low-income Blacks and compare their findings with middle-class whites. Some researchers display a tendency to use a negative, illness-oriented framework to view the behaviors of Blacks.

Currently, there is dialogue in the literature about whether students have the skills and the clarity of purpose to learn research and practice skills simultaneously (Reid, 1980; Rothman, 1980; Roberts, 1979). The discussion also asks if busy social work practitioners have the time or the skills to do research. Although answers to these questions are beyond the scope of this chapter, we do posit that Black social work faculty will have to assume a major responsibility not only in carrying out this research themselves but in teaching all students, Black and white, how to do such research. They must also take on the responsibility of engaging practitioners in such research efforts. Although this may seem an undue burden when combined with other responsibilities, it is only in this way will there be continued infusion of this vital content into the social work curriculum.

The New Research Required. During the 1970s, several theoretical frameworks were developed to provide perspective on the minority experience and to intervene effectively based on that knowledge. Few of these theoretical frameworks have been tested. There is a need for programmatic research to test hypotheses relating to these theoretical frameworks. Some of these hypotheses may be considered contradictory. For example, if the nurturing environment "protects" the minority child from the full impact of negative valuation from the larger society, should life experiences be primarily within that nurturing environment? Solomon (1976) raises the question, Does this mean that early life experiences should emphasize exposure to positive experiences in order to develop more effective skills at later ages. Powell's (1973) work seems to support Solomon's research. She found that children in a segregated school situation had a higher self-image than children in an integrated situation. Such research needs to be formed into hypotheses and tested.

There is also a need to study what is "effective for Blacks," that is, studying Blacks who have coped effectively and building norms for behavior based on that coping rather than comparing it with white norms. Baumrind (1972), for example, discovered that the authoritarian, rejecting behavior often evidenced in the relationship between Black parents and their small daughters did not have the same quality of meaning (as traditionally interpreted) as such behavior did for whites. The little Black girls' behavior seemed quite different from white norm behavior, and the behavior of the Black parents, which on the surface seemed rejecting, was really very supportive. There needs to be more interpretation of behavior based on culture. Studying the positive aspects of Black life with an understanding of culture and evolving effective intervention techniques will help the social worker in developing better social functioning in other Blacks. We will never move away from the "mark of oppression syndrome" until we move toward the examination of the dynamics of Black life and leave behind structural comparisons with white, middle-class norms.

Strategies for Accomplishing New Research. It is important for minority social workers to have the capability to do research and build theories of practice out of their findings. Minority students at the master's level must be given opportunities to do research of various kinds in their field placement. This research must be integrated with research as taught in the classroom. One must support the other. Minority practitioners must familiarize themselves with research techniques if they are to become critical consumers of research. They must be able to judge the validity of research that others are doing on Blacks.

Strategies for Utilizing and Disseminating Research. The responsibility for utilizing and disseminating minority content in social work education falls primarily on minority faculty and practitioners. They have to be vigilant in including content in all courses where it is necessary. They must also be responsible for sharing bibliographic material not only with minority faculty, but with all faculty, whether they have expressed an interest or not. In the field, social workers must be ready to teach and again to share materials with field instructors. Social work faculty must develop arguments based on the concepts valued by their institutions as to why this information is necessary. They can also join with minority institutions and minority social work organizations to foster collectively the dissemination of such knowledge. They must take the initiative in submitting proposals and in giving workshops and papers at social work conferences and symposia. They must collectively bring pressure on institutions and boards of certification as to the importance of this information.

The authors of this chapter have discussed specific ways of implementing the ideas put forth and present them as, first, guiding principles for ethnic minority curriculum content and, second, as recommendations for the National Institute of Mental Health and the profession of social work.

Guiding Principles

The following seven principles should guide the inclusion of ethnic minority curriculum content about Blacks in schools of social work. Without doubt most of these principles are also applicable to other minorities.

1. Ethnic minorities are the primary source of information about their situation, condition and direction. All efforts directed at identifying, developing, teaching and evaluating ethnic minority content in social work education should involve ethnic minorities appropriately, preferably in a leadership role.

2. Ethnic minority content in social work education should be treated with dignity, respect and responsibility.

3. All educational institutions utilizing ethnic minority content in social work education should have well-defined curriculum and policy statements regarding the content's significance, purpose and thrust.

4. Ethnic minority content should be individualized by relevant groups and linked, when possible, by overarching frameworks in a way that does not lose the viability of the groups.

5. In order to ensure its continuity, viability and priority, the responsibility for ethnic minority content in social work education at each institution should be under an ongoing school committee designated for this purpose.

6. Ethnic minority curriculum content in social work education should be a part of the core curriculum, rather than elective or peripheral in nature.

7. Ethnic minority curriculum content should focus on normative behaviors and wellness, rather than on abnormal and illness reactions.

Recommendations

In addition to the preceding guidelines, the following specific recommendations should facilitate and ensure the integration of ethnic minority content into social work curricula.

1. Accreditation, recertification and membership of a school of social work in their professional organizations should be linked to an affirmative action approach for inclusion of ethnic minority content in the applicant school's core curriculum.

2. Funding bodies, e.g., NIMH, should have as standard review criteria ethnic minority content for programs providing social work education and/or providing social services.

3. Existing standards, i.e., CSWE Accreditation Standards, Sections a, b, and c, should be enforced and each school should be required to add how they will monitor their efforts and success at inclusion of ethnic minority content in the core curriculum.

4. A two-level approach to research relative to integrating ethnic minority content in the curriculum of social work education should exist. The first, or micro-level, approach should be directed at the outcomes relative to the efforts of professional schools. This approach should focus on content taught, methods used, and learning achieved for students. The second, or macro-level, approach should focus on the impact of the students learning and practice on changes in the target group (client-system; group-system; organization/community-system).

5. Regional research centers should be developed and funded by NIMH to identify, develop, test, evaluate and disseminate interdisciplinary research findings relative to ethnic minority content that begins first with a focus on the four major ethnic groups (Blacks, Asians, Hispanics, American Indians) and expands to other ethnic and unserved, underserved and inappropriately served groups. Also, these centers can extend knowledge about the special populations served, what education systems provide and can provide, plus study the existing delivery systems and make recommendations for change.

6. Specific efforts should be made to develop ethnic minority researchers who can provide the unique perspective and talent for research related to ethnic minority curriculum content.

7. The findings of this book should be distributed to each school of social work and each dean should be requested to indicate how the materials will be reviewed and integrated in their curriculum.

8. The findings and recommendations of this book should be distributed to all major universities and schools that operate human services programs or are funded by NIMH branches to provide education in human services.

References

Baumrind, D. An exploratory study of socialization effects on Black children: Some Black-white comparisons. *Child Development*, 1972, *43*, 261–67.

Billingsley, A. *Black females in white America*. Englewood Cliffs, N. J.: Prentice Hall, 1968.

Billingsley, A. *Black families in white America*. Englewood Cliffs, N. J.: Prentice Hall, 1972.

Bishop, C. Culture and the Black administrator. In L. Howard, L. Henderson, & D. Hunt, *Public administration and public policy: A minority perspective*. Pittsburgh, PA.: Public Policy Press, 1977.

Bush, J. A. New colonialism and compensatory justice. An occasional paper, Consortium of the State of Texas Schools of Social Work, April 1972.

Bush, J. S. Suicide and Blacks: A conceptual framework. *Suicide and Life-Threatening Behavior*, 1977, *3* (1), 216–23.

Cafferty, P. S. J., & Chestang, L. (Eds.). *The diverse society: Implications for social policy*. Washington, D.C.: National Association of Social Workers, 1976.

Chestang, L. Character development in a hostile society. Occasional paper, No. 3, School of Social Service Administration, University of Chicago, 1972.

Chunn, J. Integrating minority content in the social work curricula. In *Black perspective on social work education*. New York: Council on Social Work Education, 1974.

Cohen J. Race as a factor in social work practice. In R. R. Miller (Ed.), *Race, research and reason: Social work perspective*. New York: National Association of Social Workers, 1969

Council on Social Work Education. *Manual of accrediting standards*. New York: Author, 1971.

Council on Social Work Education. *Curriculum policy for the master's degree program in graduate schools of social work*. New York: Author, 1972.

Crompton, D.W. Minority content in social work education: Promise or pitfall. *Journal of Education for Social Work*, 1974, *10* (1), 9–18.

Figueira-McDonough, J. Discrimination in social work: Evidence, myth and ignorance. *Social Work*, 1979, *24* (3), 214–24.

Francis, E. *Black task force report: Suggested guidelines for the integration of Black content in social work curriculum*. New York: Council on Social Work Education, 1973.

Francis, E. A. Integration of Black minority content into social welfare policy and services. In D. G. Norton (Ed.), *The dual perspective: Inclusion of ethnic minority content in the social work curriculum*. New York: Council on Social Education, 1978, 48–58.

Gallegos, J. S., & Harris, O. D. Toward a model for the inclusion of ethnic minority content in doctoral social work education. *Journal of Education for Social Work*, 1979, 29–35.

Gambino, R. *A guide to ethnic studies programs in American colleges, universities and schools*. New York: Rockefeller Foundation, 1975.

Gilbert, G. C. Counseling Black adolescent parents. *Social Work*, 1974, *19*, (1), 88–95.

Gilbert, G., & Ryan, R. *Beyond ain't it awful: A working document for leadership into the curriculum of the Ohio State University School of Social Work*. Columbus, OH.: College of Administrative Science, Ohio State University, 1974.

Glasgow, D. Black power through community control. *Social Work*, 1972, *17* (3), 59–64.

Goodman, J. A. (Ed.). *Dynamics of racism in social work practice.* Washington, D.C.: National Association of Social Workers, 1973.

Grier, W. H., & Cobb, P. *Black rage.* New York: Basic Books, 1968.

Hatcher, R. Quoted from a speech delivered at a meeting of the Black Political Science Association, 1976.

Hill, G. T. Report of the CSWE Black Task Force. Report presented at the Commission on Minority Groups, June 1972.

Kardiner, A., & Ovesey, L. *Mark of oppression: Explorations in the personality of the American Negro.* New York: W. W. Norton and Company, Inc., 1951.

Leigh, J. W. Ethnic content in field instruction. In *Black perspective in social work education.* New York: Council on Social Work Education, 1974.

May, R. *Power and innocence: A search for the sources of violence.* New York: Dell Publishing Company, 1972.

Mendes, H. Some religious values held by Blacks, Chicanos, and Japanese-Americans and their implications for casework practice. Monograph No. 4. Boulder, CO: Western Interstate Commission in Higher Education, January 1974.

Myrdal, G. *An American dilemma.* New York: Harper and Row, 1962.

National Urban League. *The state of Black America, 1981.* New York: Author, 1981.

Norton, D. G. Working with minority populations: The dual perspective. In B. Ross and S. K. Khinduka (Eds.), *Social work in practice.* New York: National Association of Social Workers, 1976.

Norton, D. G. *The dual perspective: The inclusion of ethnic minority content in social work curriculums.* New York: Council on Social Work Education, 1978.

Perlmutter, F., & Alexander, L. Exposing the coercive consensus: Racism and sexism in social work. In R. Sarri, & Y. Hasenfeld (Eds.), *The management of human services.* New York: Columbia University Press, 1978.

Powell, G. J. Self-Concept in white and Black children. In C. Willie (Ed.), *Racism and mental health.* Pittsburgh: University of Pittsburgh Press, 1973.

President's Commission on Mental Health. *Task panel reports, Vol. 2,* appendix. Washington, D.C.: U.S. Government Printing Office, 1978.

Reid, W. Integrating research and practice in field work. Unpublished paper, School of Social Service Administration, University of Chicago, 1980.

Roberts, R. W. The relationship between social work research and practice: Toward dissolution or consummation? Unpublished paper, University of Southern California, 1979.

Ross-Sheriff, F. Implementation of minority content in social work education. Paper presented at the Program Meeting, Council on Social Work Education, Boston, Massachusetts, 1979.

Rothman J. *Social research and development in the human services.* Englewood Cliffs, N.J.: Prentice Hall, 1980.

Sanders, C. L. Growth of the association of Black social workers. *Social Casework,* 1970, *51* (5), 277–84.

Sanders, C. L. Reflections on the Black experience. *Black World,* 1971, *20* (10), 75–79.

Sanders, C. L. *Black professionals' perception of institutional racism in health and welfare organizations.* Fairlawn, N.J.: Burdick Publishers, 1973.

Scott, C. Ethnic minorities in social work education. In *The current scene in social work education.* New York: Council on Social Work Education, 1978.

Simpson, G. E., & Yinger, J. M. *Racial and cultural minorities: An analysis of prejudice and discrimination* (4th ed.). New York: Harper and Row, 1972, p. 11.

Solomon, B. B. *Black empowerment: Social work in oppressed communities.* New York: Columbia University Press, 1976.

Spiegel, J. *Transactions: An interplay between the individual, family, and society.* New York: W. W. Norton, 1975.

Thomas, A., & Sillen, S. *Racism and psychiatry.* New York: Brunner/Mazel, 1972.

Trader, H. P. Dilemma for Black faculty teaching Black curriculum content in schools of social work. In *Black perspective on social work education.* New York: Council on Social Work Education, 1974.

Trader H. P. Survival strategies for oppressed minorities. *Social Work,* 1977, *22* (1), 10–13.

U.S. Department of Commerce, Bureau of the Census. *The social and economic status of the Black population in the U.S.: An historical view, 1790–1978.* Washington, D.C.: Author, 1978.

Valle R. The development of a polycultural social policy curriculum from the Latin perspective. In D. G. Norton (Ed.), *The dual perspective: The inclusion of ethnic minority content in social work curriculum.* New York: Council on Social Work Education, 1978.

Willie, C. V., Kramer, B. M., & Brown, B. S. *Racism and mental health.* Pittsburgh: University of Pittsburgh Press, 1973.

Yancey, W., & Ericksen, E. The antecedents of community: The economic and institutional structure of urban neighborhoods. *American Sociological Review,* 1979, *44* (2), 253–62.

Young, A. F. *Dissent: Explorations in the history of America radicalism.* DeKalb, Ill.: Northern Illinois University Press, 1968.

Bibliography

Beckett, J. *Perspectives on social work intervention and treatment with Black clients: A bibliography.* Mimeographed bibliography, School of Social Work, University of Michigan, 1979.

Calnek, M. Racial factors in counter transference: The Black therapist and Black client. *American Journal of Orthopsychiatry*, 1970, *40* (1), 39–45.

Carmichael, S., & Hamilton, C. *Black power: The politics of liberation in America.* New York: Random House, 1967, 4–8.

Council on Social Work Education. *Project papers of project to develop knowledge about the needs of ethnic minority groups of color to be used in strengthening programs which prepare social workers for careers in the aging field.* New York: Author, 1978.

Eysenck, H. J. The effects of psychotherapy. *International Journal of Psychotherapy*, 1965, *1*, 97–179.

Giordana, J. *Ethnicity and mental health.* New York Institute of Human Relations, National Project on Ethnic America of the American Jewish Committee, 1973.

Hill, R. B. *The strengths of Black families.* New York: Emerson Hall, 1972.

Hill, R. B. *Social work research on minorities: Impediments and opportunities.* Mimeographed paper prepared for the Urban League National Conference on the Future of Social Work Research, San Antonio, Texas, 1978.

Powell, G. J., Morales, A., & Yamamoto, J. (Eds.). The psychosocial development of minority group children. New York: Brunner/Mazel, Inc. (forthcoming).

Smith, W. D., Burlew, A. R., Mosely, M. H., & Whitney, W. M. *Minority issues in mental health.* Boston: Addison-Wesley, 1978.

Taylor, R. Black youth and psycho-social development: A conceptual framework. *Journal of Black Studies*, 1976, *6*, 353–72.

Teper, S. Ethnicity, race and human development. In *A report on the state of our knowledge.* American Jewish Committee, Institute on Pluralism and Group Identity, 1977.

Valentine, C. Depict, difference and bicultural models of Afro-American behavior. In *Challenging the myths: The schools, the Black and the poor.* Cambridge, MA.: Harvard Educational Review, Reprint Series No. 5, 1971, *41*, 137–57.

FORD H. KURAMOTO   ROYAL F. MORALES
FAYE U. MUNOZ   KENJI MURASE

CHAPTER 6

Education for Social Work Practice in Asian and Pacific American Communities

This chapter on Asian and Pacific American (AAPA) ethnic curriculum content in social work education addresses the rationale and trends in curriculum development. It further delineates the bases for an ethnic perspective and sets some guiding principles necessary for the development of theories and research issues related to the communities identified. In focusing on the immediate need for institutional changes and faculty development for and from the Asian and Pacific American communities, this study further spells out significant recommendations touching on major public policies affecting the issues identified. It is far from complete, and much work is necessary in curriculum development.

We need to acknowledge our indebtedness to many individuals who have given greater visibility to the need for specialized training and curriculum content for social work practice in Asian and Pacific American communities. The ideological base and thrust for this development must go back to the founders of the "Asian American movement" of the 1960s, who awakened Asian and Pacific Americans to their cultural roots and ethnic identity. The beginnings of the "Asian American movement" took concrete form in the development of Asian American studies programs in various colleges and universities on the West Coast. Many of the graduates of Asian American studies programs then turned to social work as an occupational vehicle for translating into action their commitment to advancing the interests of their particular communities.

The schools of social work, however, were slow to respond to the challenge of meeting the needs of Asian and Pacific American students who sought the training necessary to prepare them to work in their own communities. It was necessary, therefore, to organize and mobilize the Asian and Pacific American communities to put pressure upon the Council on Social Work Education (CSWE), the National Institute of Mental Health (NIMH), and other institutions. Leading this diligent effort was the Asian American Social Workers Association (AASW), based in Los Angeles. The writers acknowledge AASW's leadership for the subsequent developments of curriculum on Asian and Pacific American people.

In the material to follow, we first make a general statement of the problems confronting Asian and Pacific American communities that must be addressed in the curriculum content of social work education for practice in such communities. We then define the term *Asian and Pacific Americans* and provide an overview and historical perspective of trends in the development of Asian and Pacific American content in social work education. This is followed by a statement of guiding principles for Asian and Pacific American curriculum content development. The next section contains suggestions for specific course offerings, including teaching modules. Further theory development needs and the research necessary for such theory development then is discussed, as are some possible strategies for institutional change and faculty development. We conclude with recommendations for major policy implementation.

Statement of the Problem	The state of the art of social work curriculum content specifically designed for Asian, Pacific and Southeast Asian minority people of color is at best an unfinished agenda, unknown to most students, untouched by the majority of the faculty and often misunderstood by many of the social work field instructors and researchers. In professional social work education, inclusion of content about Asian and Pacific Americans is essential for several compelling reasons. First of all, there is a simple matter of equity. In any consideration of ethnic minorities, Blacks, Hispanics and American Indians are generally recognized, while Asian and Pacific Americans are frequently omitted. A case in point is the President's Commission on Mental Health, which did not include Asian and Pacific American representation.

Asian and Pacific Americans constitute a substantial population of close to three million, which is also growing at a rate faster than any other ethnic minority community (Office of Special Concerns, Department of Health Education and Welfare, 1974). The 1970 census reported a 56 percent increase over the 1960 figures for the three major Asian and Pacific American groups—Chinese, Japanese and Pilipino—during a period in which the overall U.S. increase was only 13 percent. The 1980 census is likely to show the Asian and Pacific American population as double the 1970 figure, as Koreans, Pilipinos and

Southeast Asians continue to be the largest among all groups immigrating to this country today. Refugees from Southeast Asia now number close to 450,000, a number that continues to grow at a rate of almost 15,000 a month. The preponderance of immigrants and refugees is significant in that they represent an especially high-risk population that is likely to present a high level of demand for services that require well-trained and culturally sensitive providers.

Second, there are many misconceptions and misleading assumptions made about Asian and Pacific Americans which need to be corrected (Kim, 1973). A common misconception is that Asian and Pacific Americans constitute a single homogeneous group and can be treated all alike. These communities represent a heterogeneity of history, religion, language, culture and appearance. Superimposed upon this diversity of influences are the consequences of differential patterns of immigration and acculturation. For these reasons, each Asian and Pacific American community must be understood as a distinct and separate entity.

Another widespread misconception is that Asian and Pacific Americans, seen as law-abiding, hard working, quiet and clean, are a "model minority" which does not suffer the discrimination and disadvantages associated with other minority groups. The facts are, however, that Asian and Pacific Americans are victims of the same social, economic and political inequities that have victimized Blacks, Hispanics and American Indians. For a substantial number of Asian and Pacific Americans in this country, particularly among the elderly and immigrant populations, ghetto existence and chronic conditions of poverty remain their only way of life. Asian and Pacific Americans are therefore confronted today with very real questions of survival because of such problems as below-subsistence levels of income, high rates of unemployment or underemployment, substandard housing, inferior education, inadequate health and social services, problems of drug abuse and delinquency among their youth, and the insidious and demoralizing effects of prolonged states of alienation and powerlessness (Barth, 1964; McWilliams, 1946; Miller, 1969; U.S. Civil Rights Commission, 1980).

Finally, it must be acknowledged that in order for social work education to be authentic and relevant to the needs of minority communities, the conceptual definitions and program implementation must involve the participation of the minority communities concerned. This means that we must look to Asian and Pacific American communities for their definition of their experience in America from their own perspective and for their perceptions of the strategies necessary for their own liberation and enhancement. It is in this spirit that the materials which follow are derived from the perspective and the definitions of Asian and Pacific Americans with respect to their own problems, needs, resources and aspirations.

Definition of Terms

Although the generic term *Asian Americans* has been commonly used to refer also to Pacific Islander Americans, the more inclusive term *Asian and Pacific Americans* is preferred. The major population groups of Asian and Pacific Americans originate from four geographic areas:

1. East Asia—China, Japan, Korea;
2. South Asia—India, Pakistan, Sri Lanka;
3. Southeast Asia—Cambodia, Laos, Thailand, Vietnam, Philippines, Burma, Malaysia, Indonesia;
4. The Pacific Islands—Guam, Hawaii, Samoa, and Tonga.

Because of different historical, linguistic and sociocultural backgrounds, there is enormous diversity among Asian and Pacific Americans. While asserting their separate ethnic identity, Asian and Pacific Americans share certain common interests and aspirations. They also recognize the political reality that in order to gain public attention and to influence the political process they must unite as an interest group and act collectively. Therefore, acting under the rubric of Asian and Pacific Americans are Americans of Burmese, Cambodian, Chinese, East Indian, Indonesian, Guamanian, Hawaiian, Japanese, Korean, Laotian, Malaysian, Pakistani, Pilipino, Samoan, Sri Lankan, Thai, Tongan and Vietnamese descent.

Trends in Asian and Pacific American Content Development

To date there has been no systematic, orderly or sustained attention directed to the development of curriculum content in social work education with reference specifically to Asian and Pacific Americans. The first major effort to identify problems and issues in social work education for Asian and Pacific Americans was undertaken in 1972 by the Asian American Task Force on Social Work Education, convened by the Council on Social Work Education. The task force's report, published in 1973, marked the beginning of efforts to identify specific curriculum content for the training of social workers for Asian and Pacific American communities (Murase, 1973).

Subsequently, a number of social work training programs designed for Asian and Pacific American students were funded by the National Institute of Mental Health: in Los Angeles in 1972; in San Francisco in 1974; and in Sacramento and New York in 1977. Although the development of curriculum materials was one of the objectives of these training projects, they were not adequately funded for this purpose and their output was limited. The Asian American Mental Health Training Center in Los Angeles was an exception, producing a substantial curriculum document that has been utilized by faculty in several schools of social work (Kushida, Montenegro, Chicahisa and Morales, 1976). Currently, the Los Angeles center and the San Francisco Bay Area Asian American Mental Health Training Center are engaged in developing curriculum materials not only for social work but also for other mental health disciplines.

The Western Interstate Commission for Higher Education (WICHE) has also supported a series of conferences and monographs pertaining to ethnic minority curriculum and faculty development (McCann, 1972). Although not specifically addressed to Asian and Pacific American concerns, the WICHE program involved many Asian and Pacific American social work educators and practitioners.

The Council on Social Work Education, in addition to sponsoring the original Asian American Task Force in Social Work Education, has also supported other efforts of a more specialized nature. Under a grant from the Administration on Aging, the council convened a conference for Asian and Pacific Americans in the field of aging to develop curriculum materials for schools of social work (Nishimura, 1978). This project is expected to produce substantial curriculum materials bearing upon the training of social workers for services to the Asian and Pacific American elderly population. The council has also published a monograph which includes a chapter on "Social Welfare Policy and Services: Asian Americans," by Kenji Murase, with teaching modules on "A Demographic Profile of Asian Americans," "Asians in American History," "Socio-Economic Role and Status of Asian Americans," "Delivery of Social Services to Asian American Communities," and "Culturally Relevant Social Services and Social Work Practice in Asian-American Communities" (Norton, 1978).

Perspective and Guiding Principles

Appropriate guiding principles for Asian and Pacific American content development in social work education may be based upon the following considerations:

- the consequences of racism for Asian and Pacific Americans;
- ethnic and cultural diversity among Asian and Pacific Americans;
- the goal of empowerment for Asian and Pacific Americans;
- systems theory as an organizing framework.

Consequences of Racism

The Asian and Pacific Americans' encounter with racism in the United States is quite different from that of other ethnic minorities, and their responses and adaptations to differing socioeconomic and political circumstances provide the basis for a comparative analysis of institutional racism. For example, the Chinese and Japanese were neither an indigenous people to be conquered and incarcerated, as in the case of American Indians, nor were they forcibly removed from their homeland to build the economic base of a racist society, as in the case of Black Americans. While the arrival of the Chinese and Japanese on these shores was voluntary, the inducements for their passage were designed to exploit them for their labor. As they strove to survive and to better themselves, they were subjected to persecution and oppression unparalleled in American history. Indeed, the racist oppression of the Chinese and Japanese created conditions that formed and perpetuated the Asian ghetto, which may be conceptualized as the urban successor to the plantations of Black Americans and the reservations of American Indians. It may also be argued that by working out its response to the Asian challenge to Anglo-Saxon dominance, America refined and perfected the institutions of modern racism—institutions that had their unorganized beginnings in the treatment of free Blacks in the slave era.

We need to consider further the consequences for Asian and Pacific Americans of their historical and continuing encounters with racism and their exclusion from mainstream America. In terms of the social services, there is a well-documented pattern of low utilization rates for Asian and Pacific Americans (Brown, Stein, Huang and Harris, 1973; Hatanaka, Watanabe and Ono, 1975; San Francisco Community Mental Health Services, 1977; President's Commission on Mental Health, 1978). The low utilization rates, however, do not reflect a low incidence of social services need nor do they reflect the ability of the Asian and Pacific American community to "take care of their own." Rather, the research data point to an underutilization of services despite a high incidence of distress or disorder (Berk and Hirata, 1973; S. Sue, 1977; Sue and Kirk, 1975; Yamamoto, James and Palley, 1968). Indeed, S. Sue's study (1977) of greater Seattle found that the incidence of diagnosed psychosis was much greater among the Asian and Pacific American population than among any other group. These findings, when compared with data documenting low utilization rates, suggest that Asian and Pacific Americans tend to seek services only after having endured considerable stress and after having reached a point of acute crisis.

Not only do Asian and Pacific Americans underutilize social services, but they also tend to unilaterally terminate contacts after an initial visit. S. Sue (1977) reported in a comprehensive study conducted on minority clients that 51 percent of the Asian and Pacific American clients unilaterally terminated contact after the initial visit compared to a 30 percent rate for white clients. One clear implication of the study is that there is a direct and profound consequence of racism in the utilization of social services by Asian and Pacific Americans and that the influence of racism cannot be ignored in the planning and delivery of services to their communities.

According to one stereotype, Asian and Pacific Americans are one homogeneous, monolithic group. This assumption has led to the view, for example, that, because Japanese Americans have a median income higher than that of white Americans or because the proportion of Chinese males attaining higher education is higher than males or females of any other group, all Asian and Pacific Americans must be well off and not in need of social services (Office of Special Concerns, DHEW, 1974). For some white Americans it is easy to overlook or dismiss the fact that there are vast differences among Asian and Pacific American families; consider, for example, the gulf between an affluent, fourth-generation, Japanese American family and the poverty, bewilderment and despair felt by the family of an uneducated fisherman who fled Vietnam in a fishing boat (U.S. Civil Rights Commission, 1980).

Ethnic and Cultural Diversity

An enormous diversity—in ethnicity, cultural heritage, immigration patterns, socioeconomic development, regional distribution—characterizes Asian and Pacific American communities. And differences are not only between groups but also within groups. Distinct ethnic groups, for example, Pilipinos and Koreans, can be further categorized by immigrant status: early or recent arrival. Recent immigrants of one ethnic group may have more in common with other recent immigrants than with earlier immigrants of their own ethnic group. This paradox illustrates the simultaneous commonality and uniqueness among Asian and Pacific American groups.

The immigration patterns of Asian and Pacific Americans have been largely influenced by immigration legislation and by U.S. foreign policy. The largest groups, the Japanese and the Chinese, were the first, in the late nineteenth century, to migrate in large numbers; the Pilipinos and a small number of Koreans followed in the early twentieth century. With the end of World War II and the 1965 repeal of exclusionary immigration legislation, the Chinese and the Pilipinos renewed their high immigration rates. Conversely, Japanese immigration declined markedly. A new development has been a substantial increase in the migration of Koreans, Samoans, Guamanians and, more recently following the end of the Indochinese war, Southeast Asians from Cambodia, Laos and Vietnam (Chikahisa, Cho, Kushida and Morales, 1980; Cordova, 1980; Liu, Lamanna and Murata, 1979).

The early immigrants were generally either students from urban families or uneducated and able-bodied young men from rural backgrounds seeking a better livelihood. In contrast, and because of the preferential category for professionals in immigration regulations, most newer immigrants (excluding those who migrated as dependents of the lower-income early immigrants) are an urban, relatively well educated group (Morales, 1974). Guamanians, Samoans and other Pacific Islanders who are exempt from such regulations are more similar to the earlier immigrants, sharing lower-income and nonurban characteristics and coming to the United States to improve their living standards (Munoz, 1976).

The current upper and lower division in socioeconomic status of Asian and Pacific Americans is in great part due to the above immigration sequence. In general, the newer immigrants from Southeast Asia, Samoa, Korea and the Philippines are lower in socioeconomic status and further from the middle-class American lifestyle experienced by the American-born descendants of earlier Japanese and Chinese immigrants (U.S. Department of Commerce, Bureau of the Census, 1973).

A variation on socioeconomic status and "status role reversal" peculiar to Asian and Pacific Americans applies to those persons who were of high socioeconomic status before immigration but are of lower socioeconomic status in this country (Green and Tong, 1979). An example would be that of a medical doctor from the Philippines who is employed as a hospital orderly in this country, because he is unable to obtain a license to practice medicine. Another example would be a "general" from Southeast Asia, who works in this country as an office manager. For such persons, the self-perception of socioeconomic status is not congruent with their current socioeconomic status in this country but rather with their previous status in their country of origin. A Chinese bank official, for example, who enjoyed high socioeconomic status in Hong Kong and is currently a bank teller would not regard himself as being of lower socioeconomic status; at the same time, he may scorn an earlier immigrant-turned-successful-banker as being of lower socioeconomic status because of that individual's prior rural and impoverished status in China. This situation may apply to the significant roles of the chiefs among the Samoans.

The regional distribution of Asian and Pacific Americans has been influenced by ethnicity, immigration patterns and socioeconomic status. In general, the early immigrants of rural, low socioeconomic status settled on the West Coast. Those of higher socioeconomic status migrated to areas such as Chicago, New York and Boston as these places encouraged the settlement of professionals via foreign student exchange programs. It was also to these areas that large numbers of Japanese Americans were relocated from the concentration camps after World War II. Currently, although official government policy is to disperse widely refugees from Southeast Asia, the refugees themselves are moving in a "secondary migration" to population centers on the West Coast.

In summary, Asian, Pacific and Southeast Asian American populations are undergoing rapid changes due to immigration, acculturation and adaptation. Relatively little in their cultural backgrounds and experiences contributes to homogeneity between the early and recent arrivals. Indeed, each specific Asian and Pacific American ethnic community is becoming more heterogeneous as new immigrants alter the composition, cultural unity and identity of that community. Yet, Asian and Pacific Americans as a whole continue to constitute a distinct population because their varied cultural backgrounds and life experiences are unique and can be differentiated from other minority and larger nonminority populations in the United States. Many have and are contributing to the resources, skills and manpower needed by the country.

Social work education must shed its historic affliction with a misplaced faith in the notion of an American melting pot and its traditional promotion of cultural and ethnic homogeneity in terms dominated by the white middle class. The integrationist bent of the last several decades has had a profound influence on social work education and practice, tending to make social workers seek simplistic solutions to the enormously complex problems that beset members of ethnic minority communities. Simplistic solutions are still reflected in curricula that view what are primarily structural and institutional problems as individual and social malfunctions. We need to develop curricula that view the problems of ethnic minority communities as induced by economic and political forces which transcend individual behavior and local circumstances. Moreover, we need to train social workers who will work with minority communities to empower them to challenge the institutional and structural barriers to their advancement.

Goal of Empowerment

The melting pot mentality fails to perceive not only the enormous diversity among the various ethnic communities but also their growing ethnic self-awareness and political consciousness. This tendency to ignore the reality of pluralistic developments among ethnic minority communities may be attributed not only to expediency and convenience but, more fundamentally, to a deeply ingrained racist thinking within social work education itself (Murase, 1972).

To respond to the needs of Asian and Pacific American communities, social work must critically reexamine traditional methodology. Proceeding from the premise that self-fulfillment and the fulfillment of human potential must be achieved through structural and institutional change, we argue that social work practice must move from the present stress on conformity to established standards of behavior to the amelioration or improvement of social conditions. The teaching of practice must extend beyond the roles of direct service, supervision and consultation, administration, program planning and development, and research. Practitioners must also be knowledgeable about and skilled in strategies required to bring about institutional change—that is the redistribution of power, resources, authority and income and the participation of minority members in decision making

Thus, the practitioner required in Asian and Pacific American communities not only secures services for clients and helps them to function more effectively in their environment but also deals directly with the institutions that attempt to deny Asian and Pacific Americans the rights to self-determination and equal opportunity. Practitioners must strive to increase the accessibility of services for Asian and Pacific Americans, and also be prepared to organize Asian and Pacific Americans into effective advocacy groups. They must assist them in their own community organizing and program development and ultimately enable them to acquire and exercise power on their own behalf. Thus, the practice skills needed for work in Asian and Pacific American communities do not so much facilitate conformity or adjustment to reality as they, more significantly, enable clients and communities to mobilize their own resources to challenge and to change their reality.

Systems Theory as an Organizing Framework

We propose that social systems theory be used as a framework for organizing the Asian and Pacific American content to be developed in social work education. Social systems theory deals with the way in which various social systems, such as families, small groups, organizations, communities and societies, are created and the various processes by which they are maintained and/or changed. Systems theory assumes an interaction and an interdependency between social systems, as well as a high degree of organization within each system. If change occurs in one part of a social system, its effect will be felt in all other parts of the system. If, for example, one member of a family becomes seriously ill, the effects of that illness, both direct and indirect, will be experienced by all family members. Similarly, because of the interdependency of social systems, changes that occur in one system are likely to have effects in other related systems. The seriously ill family member may get help from the informal network of relatives and friends that surrounds the immediate nuclear family (extended family and friendship system) and in addition require financial and other assistance from social service agencies (social welfare system). Finally, enough sick individuals in enough families might create a need great enough to require change in national policy toward family health (society system). Thus, change in one part of a social system may exert a ripple or "domino" effect throughout that system and extend into other systems as well.

Under social systems theory a particular ethnic or cultural system would be viewed as interacting and interdependent with other social systems. Ethnic cultural systems may be conceptualized as consisting of one's cultural heritage, identity and lifestyle, while the individual, family and community comprise other social systems. Conceptually, it is the interfacing of these two systems—the cultural system and the social system—that translates into human and/or organizational behavior. Thus, the social systems concept rejects the premise that behavior can be explained only by either biological or cultural determinism theories. Instead, social systems theory adopts a structural and environmental determinism model to describe the particular ethnic minority group experience.

The role of the social worker operating from a social systems framework is that of an agent for change who intervenes on behalf of a client (the client system) and affects one of the systems: (1) the individual personality system; (2) the face-to-face group system; (3) the organizational system; or (4) the community system. We find highly relevant the concept of the social worker as an agent for change in Asian and Pacific American communities, who intervenes at the individual, family, organizational and community levels.

On the basis of the perspective and the guiding principles developed in the previous section, we now propose specific curriculum content bearing upon Asian and Pacific Americans. This content could either be integrated into existing course materials or offered as distinct modules. Additional materials, with a focus upon courses in the area of social welfare policy and services, have been developed by and are available through Murase (1978). The content to follow is adapted from materials developed by the Asian American Community Mental Health Training Center of Los Angeles (Chikahisa, et al., 1976).

Suggested Curriculum Content

Internal Colonization and Exploitation. The curriculum content should focus on a discussion of the role of "internal colonization" and exploitation by the "white majority" which has utilized institutions as well as political, social and economic means to perpetuate racism and colonization. Contrast and comparison should be made with the various experiences of other ethnic minorities such as Blacks, Chicanos, Puerto Ricans, and American Indians. This approach will aid in the definition and conceptualization of the historical experiences and concerns of Asian and Pacific American people.

General Content Areas

Collective Asian Experience. The collective Asian and Pacific American experience provides an illustration of the difficulties and dilemmas faced by racial minorities, be it within the larger society or within their immediate families and communities. Our thesis is that racial minorities perceive and experience overt and subtle hostilities and racism from the majority group. Besides not tolerating cultural plurality or parity, the majority group also defines cultural differences as deviant or abnormal, by first imposing behavioral expectations and then penalizing those unable to meet such expectations.

Family Experience. Life experiences and interactions within the family may create stress. Examination of resulting contradictions and conflicts should provide the basis for assessment and understanding of the impact of historical events, with the conflicts posed by the dominant group upon the minority Asian and Pacific Americans. The curriculum modules should also focus on the sources of conflicts, the operation of the institutional racism, resultant inequities and injustice, and unequal distribution of resources and services delivery.

Content Objectives

• To look at the institutional responses, programs and alternatives for minority communities and examine systematic attempts to control and suppress power by the social, political and economic institutions that are oppressive to Asian and Pacific American peoples.

• To explore the scope and character of the failure of public policy to respond to "ghetto" and urban concerns affecting Asian and Pacific Americans, and to examine why there is lack of resources in and from the community.

• To demonstrate the evolution of institutional racism, the sociocultural influence of poverty and the role of race or color in American society as they relate to the development of social welfare policies.

• To foster a holistic view of curriculum. The pyramid model in Figure 1 depicts a holistic view of the Asian American Community Mental Health Training Center curriculum. The broken lines represent the interrelation of the nevertheless distinct Asian and Pacific American communities as affected by legislative practices in a culturally pluralistic society. The triangle formed by the broken lines represents the modules of a curriculum syllabus, though not necessarily in numerical sequence. This conceptual model as utilized at the center has been refined and examined in accordance with the student population—graduates, undergraduates and others outside of the social work discipline. The specifics of the modules as enriched by feedback from various consultants and students follow.

Module Specifics

Module 1a. Historical perspectives of the Chinese, Guamanian, Indian, Japanese, Korean, Pakistani, Pilipino, Samoan and South East Asian

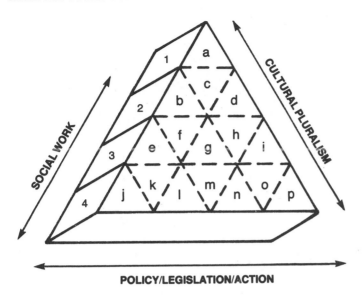

FIGURE 1

A Holistic View of the Asian American Community Mental Health Training Center

communities, including the various periods of immigration; a review and analysis of the underlying social, economic, political and organizational issues; an examination of racism as translated into laws, legislation, ordinances, traditions and attitudes; an examination of experiences at some critical periods of American history as contrasted with the country's cultural pluralism.

Modules 2b, 2c, 2d. An investigation of health, education and welfare needs and concerns of the Asian and Pacific American peoples; a critical look at services, opportunities and resources—what are indigenous, lacking and needed—and the implications for teaching, training, practice and service delivery; also a look at various bicultural and bilingual approaches to prevention and treatment.

Modules 3c, 3f, 3g, 3h, 3i. An examination of the heterogeneity and homogeneity of the Asian and Pacific American bilingual and bicultural values, familial relationships and individual identities; an assessment of generational conflicts, survival and integration with American society; a look at intermarriages, interaction with other ethnic groups and the established and quasi-established linkages developed since the first wave of immigration.

Modules 4j, 4k, 4l, 4m, 4n, 4o, 4p. Views of the specific Asian and Pacific American experiences: Chinese, Guamanian, Japanese, Korean,

Pilipino, Samoan and others; explorations and examinations of specific individual, familial and communal systems.

In developing the syllabus represented by the triangular diagram, the center utilized the growing body of related reference materials and incorporated proven components of the center's current training program, which includes—

• raising the awareness and ethnic identification levels of the students through ethnic-specific seminars and workshops;

• training in the field to identify cultural factors that present barriers to service, such as attitudes toward social services and skills necessary to serve Asian and Pacific Americans.

Because there are only meager, if any, Asian and Pacific American curriculum content materials available in most schools, the proposed curriculum modules rely heavily on the experiences of those practitioners who have adapted, creatively and successfully, traditional modules of service delivery. In addition, seminars, workshops and lectures by such practitioners permit students to compare theoretical classroom material and their own field training with the first-hand experiences of the speakers.

Growing directly out of the center's program and experience, this proposed curriculum can extend its influence far beyond its present parameters, now confined largely to the West Coast. Schools as geographically separated as those at the University of Hawaii, Rutgers, and the State University of New Jersey could enrich their curricular offerings by means of this syllabus. Appropriate bibliographies should be included.

Seminars and workshops should be included in the curriculum. During the few years of operation, many seminars and workshops have been conducted at the training center. The presentations involved consultants and resource people in the fields of community work and service delivery techniques, were informal and, in order to encourage personal interaction, included personal anecdotal experiences and question-and-answer periods. Some workshops used audiovisual materials.

The consultants were composed of professionals, community leaders, "grass roots" community workers and administrators. They covered major ethnic communities of the Los Angeles area: Chinese, Japanese, Korean, Pilipino and Samoan. Content centered on identification of specific needs, problems and concerns of Asians, on service delivery models, and on similarities and differences among the ethnic communities.

Student Participation in Field Work

An important part of any curriculum is practical experience. The training center and the specific field placement agency became the bases from which students operated. Students were required to serve various segments of the community beyond the usual hours. Since there was very little Asian and Pacific American curriculum content in the local schools, the training center and students relied heavily on the experiences of the present practitioners who had modified and adapted traditional models of service delivery. For example, the students had to know not only the usual bicultural and bilingual components of an Asian and Pacific American community but also those factors which made one group in that population significantly different from other Asian and Pacific American groups. Students identified those cultural factors that presented barriers to service (such as attitudes concerning social service or mental illness) and those attitudes and skills necessary to serve an Asian immigrant as opposed to an American-born Asian.

Workshops and seminars were geared to raising the conscious awareness and ethnic identification levels of the students. The interaction with the speakers allowed the students to examine theoretical classroom material and actual experiences related by the participants. One concept the training center emphasized in practice and in its philosophy was "outreach." This concept was essential to the Asian and Pacific American communities, especially in service delivery. For the students, it meant exposure to community-based techniques they were to encounter throughout their participation with the training center and agencies. Some major areas explored included language and cultural barriers, the generational differences between foreign-born and U.S.-born Asians and the attendant systems of social and behavioral values.

Although all of the students had experienced prior involvement in the various Asian and Pacific American communities, it sometimes took many months before the depth of traditional patterns became apparent in treatment relationships. Students stated that being Asian made acceptance easier; despite this fact, however, they needed much more experience before they really understood the nature of effective approaches in working with Asian immigrants and Asian Americans. The students were, on the whole, from middle-class families in which at least one parent was English-speaking. Their childhoods were spent in minority neighborhoods. Their parents were believers in hard work and the necessity of a good education. Parental values were aimed at joining the mainstream of American life.

Several insights into working with Asians were provided by the students. One student found that Japanese clients were often not looking for a direct solution. They wanted to discuss their problems in order to find their independent way to solutions.

This same student also noticed the difficulty some Japanese clients had in verbalizing their feelings. A glance or a gesture often transmitted emotions that could not be properly expressed verbally. The student observed that a listener from the same cultural background as the speaker will either consciously or unconsciously understand the nonverbal signals and will react accordingly. For example, the gesture of a Japanese nodding his head does not always signify agreement, but does imply attentiveness and the assurance that the communication is being heard. The Japanese student automatically understood this gesture. A non-Asian might have misinterpreted or been unaware of the meaning behind this nonverbal communication.

The emphasis on the traditional concepts of pride and dignity, which were often the main values making up the lifestyles of some of the older Asians, greatly affected the students' learning. These values account for the social stigma associated with receiving any kind of government aid, including counseling and other services which have been used for years by the non-Asian communities. This concept was related to the traditional pattern of families taking care of their own and not relying on outside resources. It was part of a family's pride to do well for its own.

One student described the difficulty in locating handicapped Koreans and Japanese, whose families took on the responsibility of care unobtrusively. Interestingly, this student found that the value of family self-reliance held throughout the wider Asian and Pacific American community: people were reluctant to help the agencies locate handicapped persons within their areas. The community also felt a responsibility in helping to maintain the dignity of the family and in wanting to keep the problem within the home. Although family problems and the care of the handicapped had traditionally been kept within the immediate family, the student recognized that there was a tendency toward accepting services from those community agencies that had gained the community's trust through patience, careful outreach and effective service delivery.

Because problems of daily existence and survival are traditionally one's own concern, the poverty and plight of the elderly Issei went unnoticed for years. Once uncovered, social services were made available to them but without much effect. These elderly Issei feared and distrusted outside agencies which suddenly thrust upon them offers of aid. They also felt somewhat disoriented by outsiders being overly concerned with problems which they felt were very private. The student realized that in order to understand the Issei's thoughts and feelings, concerned workers need both time and patience.

Another problem related to this kind of conflict was brought forth by a student who felt that the plight of Chinese women was caused by the underlying social and cultural patterns of the Chinese family. The high suicide rate and drug problems of many Chinese women could be traced to the conflict between the family's traditional expectations and the different values of the dominant society. The student felt that as women's roles became confusing, the women themselves became confused.

Theory development is needed in many areas for the further development of Asian and Pacific American content for social work curriculum. It is difficult to identify and isolate particular problems or issues since they are interrelated. Perhaps one way of conceptualizing the issues is in terms of macro and micro levels of investigation.

Theory Development and Research Needs

At the macro level, theory development is needed to explicate the relationship among such structural or institutional factors as racism, cultural diversity and social change and their consequences for the quality of life of Asian and Pacific Americans. Such theory development, of course, must be derived from conceptualizations that are not corrupted by biases found in Western culture and ideologies. For example, Green and Tong (1979) point out that studies done on acculturation and assimilation of Asians largely fall victim to the same kinds of methodological issues that were demonstrated in the case of Black Americans. Only those Asians who could be viewed as deficient in terms of socialization or internationalization of dominant society values have tended to be regarded as potential candidates for social services. They were simply seen by the researchers as hapless victims of "improper socialization" or as lacking acculturation.

Macro Level

Even studies of Asian delinquent behavior have been based on the premise that dysfunctional behavior merely reflected the failure on the part of the dominant white society to inculcate its values thoroughly enough, or the failure of Asian families to carry out this function (Connor, 1974 and 1975; Fujimoto, 1975). Green and Tong (1979) further note that such studies rarely point out the possible impact that conflicting cultural values or milieus might have on Asian and Pacific American families that are not accustomed to strange new surroundings or customs. For example, recent studies of Asian elderly point out the severe loss in status that most elderly face in this country, in contrast to the revered, esteemed and honorable status accorded the elderly in Asian cultures (Cheng, 1978; Fabros, Kato, and Swanson, 1979; Fujii, 1976). Moreover, with a shift away from the extended family, the role of the elderly has also changed and growing numbers of Asian elderly are living alone and in conditions of extreme poverty and dependency (Pacific Asian Elderly Resource Center Project, 1978). Recent studies have shown a high rate of suicide, psychological dysfunction and depression among the Asian elderly in this country (Cheng, 1978; Chin, 1971; Horikawa and Peralta, 1978; Kalish and Moriwaki, 1973; Lin, 1973). For such phenomena, theory development is needed to provide insights into whether and how such phenomena are related to the absence or loss of cultural and institutional supports.

Theory development is also needed in relation to the role of informal and natural support networks in the help-seeking behavior of Asian and Pacific Americans. What is the potential for such networks to serve as mechanisms for identifying persons requiring services and for facilitating access to and utilization of services? Theory development is needed to comprehend the functions of informal support networks within each Asian and Pacific American community, to suggest ways in which they can be strengthened as resources and to provide the basis for promoting more effective communication between the informal and formal service networks.

Micro Level

At the micro level of interpersonal relationships or human interactions, theory development is needed in relation to the applicability of traditional models of intervention and the development of alternative models for use with Asian and Pacific American clients. We need to know why traditional modes of intervention do not work for some clients and for some problems, and we need to know what will work. What theory, then, accounts for this?

Research under the following two broad categories is needed to develop specific theory for Asian and Pacific American content:

(1) service delivery utilization;
(2) family structure and cultural behavior.

Service Delivery Utilization. Related to theory development on natural support networks is the need for research on service delivery utilization by Asian and Pacific Americans. One of the dilemmas to be resolved by research is whether it is sufficient to make social services delivery systems more culturally relevant to Asian and Pacific American communities or, failing that, to rely upon more indigenous solutions. As have many other ethnic and minority communities, Asian and Pacific American communities have evolved a variety of services for their members based upon internal culturally derived and sanctioned practices. For some, such an alternative reflects cultural self-assertion and a rejection of the racist assumptions of dominant societal organizations and individuals. Others see it as a viable alternative that attempts to integrate folk or indigenous models with conventional methods of service delivery. This method may be augmented by Asian and Pacific American service providers and practitioners who are specifically trained and equipped with the knowledge and skills required for working with a specific Asian and Pacific American population. On the basis of logic and reason, this option would appear to maximize service utilization, but we do not in fact have solid empirical data to support such an assumption.

Indeed, there are vast information gaps that must be remedied by research in order for a clear picture of service utilization to emerge.

Baseline data is needed on the service needs of particular populations, such as Southeast Asian or Indochinese refugees, Pacific Island communities, the developmentally disabled population among Asian and Pacific Americans, Asian wives of U.S. servicemen and rural populations of Asian and Pacific Americans. We know that language is a key factor in service utilization but again we have no body of empirical data on the consequences of English language facility.

Family Structure and Cultural Behavior. Related to theory development on intervention is the need for research on family structure and cultural behavior. Given the enormous demographic and cultural diversity and heterogeneity among Asian and Pacific American groups, social workers must be familiar with differences both within and between each ethnic group. Practitioners should be able to distinguish between different generations of Asian and Pacific Americans, the major historical influences for each generation and the differences in family structure that may be common to each. Similarly, research data are crucial to understanding the nature and consequences of traditional and modern lifestyles, developmental cycles, socialization processes and social values unique to each Asian and Pacific American subgroup. Such knowledge can enable a skillful practitioner to individualize and select the appropriate alternative for each client and to move quickly to develop a helping relationship.

Research, therefore, is needed to provide a basis for conceptualizing differences among Asian and Pacific American populations. We need to be able to conceptualize family lifestyles with regard to generational differences as reflected in such matters as language, socialization, child-rearing practices, religion, cultural values and family roles. One possible conceptualization suggested by Green and Tong (1979) is to identify three models of family lifestyle patterns for Asian and Pacific Americans:

1. Immigrant families, i.e., those Chinese American and Japanese Americans who arrived before the 1924 Exclusion Act, and those Pilipinos, Koreans and others who came shortly thereafter;
2. American-born or the descendants of the first generation of immigrants;
3. New arrivals, i.e., recent immigrants after the 1965 revision of the national origins quota, including recent Indochinese refugees.

Tong suggests that the early immigrant families and the recent arrivals, for the sake of analysis, might be called "traditional" to the extent that the donor cultures dictate normative lifestyles including child-rearing methods, enculturative content, parent-child roles, sibling interaction and the like.

In contrast, the American-born generations of families tend to be acculturated to American norms but many continue a bicultural lifestyle. Utilizing this comparative model, research may show that each pattern represents a different interactive field or environmental context for social service intervention. Thus, in traditional families where extended kinship networks exist, help from significant individuals in the community or religious or family networks may be the preferred mode. American-born families, on the other hand, may be found to be more inclined to use the existing services.

Research is also needed to establish how help-seeking behavior is affected by socioeconomic factors, English-speaking facility and cultural differences related to length of stay in the United States. Our impression is that requests for services tend to vary with the individual's or family's socioeconomic status. Recent arrivals who do not speak English or who may not possess marketable work skills, or both, are often unemployed or underemployed. Their requests tend to be predominantly for concrete services such as information, referrals and advocacy or brokerage types of activities. The same pattern is likely to characterize the older non-English-speaking early immigrants. The American-born offspring or long-term resident families are more likely, because of their greater acculturation and knowledge of the service delivery system, to seek counseling and other forms of services. Research is still needed to establish whether this is one way of conceptualizing help-seeking behavior on the part of the different populations within any single Asian and Pacific American community.

In identifying research needs, we need also to be mindful of the lack of Asian and Pacific American researchers to carry out the research tasks. Therefore, the need to develop and strengthen research capability in Asian and Pacific American communities must be addressed. In practical terms this means the need for funding to support Asian and Pacific Americans in doctoral training in research. Because of diminishing resources for training, we support the concept of regional centers that would integrate Asian and Pacific American training, services and research. Research conducted in such regional training centers could focus upon an analysis and evaluation of the content, processes and outcomes of social work education for practice in Asian and Pacific American communities.

Strategy Recommendations

To secure the curriculum content and professional education called for in this chapter, certain strategies are suggested for institutional change, faculty development and use of regional training centers.

Institutional Change

Accrediting standards need to be strengthened for more aggressive implementation of requirements for minority content. Standards for minority content need greater specificity in substance and structure, identifying basic information, knowledge and skills that are directly related to social work intervention in Asian and Pacific American communities. Funding sources, such as the National Institute of Mental Health (NIMH), should also consider such standards for funding of training projects in professional schools.

Certification and licensure requirements must be identified and established to ensure appropriate levels of skills and competency of staff serving Asian and Pacific American groups. The employment of bilingual and bicultural staff and staff sensitive to the culture of the people they serve should be mandated. These measures will help to provide staff who are sensitive to Asian and Pacific American groups and who provide quality care and services to these groups. Requirements should also be established whereby providers contracting services to Asian and Pacific American communities must be certified as to their sensitivity and competency to deliver services. Continuing education programs should be assessed in terms of content and/or need to meet existing mental health problems and staff requirements for Asian and Pacific American services, programs and communities.

The traditional university setting for professional education must be supplemented by other types of arrangements. Of particular importance would be training programs based in the Asian and Pacific American community itself, with an independent and autonomous governing body made up of community representatives. Prototypes for such a training program would be the Asian American Community Mental Health Training Center in Los Angeles and the San Francisco Bay Area Mental Health Training Center in San Francisco.

Faculty Development

Faculty qualifications and skills for developing and delivering minority content in social work education are often lacking or inadequate. To improve the quality of curriculum content and teaching, faculty need support and opportunities to obtain skills in these areas. There should be faculty workshops, seminars and other opportunities for faculty involved in the teaching of minority content. Faculty development should also be used as a mechanism to ensure compliance of curriculum content with accreditation standards in relation to ethnic minorities. Thus, sharing and agreeing on common content and objectives would facilitate among faculty cross-fertilization of knowledge, skills and methods for social work practice with Asian and Pacific American communities.

Regional Training Centers

As a major strategy, consideration should be given to the development of a regional Asian and Pacific American multidisciplinary mental health training center. Ideally, such centers should also render comprehensive mental health services to Asian and Pacific American populations. The training within such a center would include continuing education, bilingual and bicultural training, seminars, development of teaching materials, research and evaluation. Such training centers, whenever feasible, should be independent of existing institutions. The centers should have a board of directors representative of the Asian and Pacific American communities in the region. However, this should not preclude the establishment of mutually beneficial affiliations with academic institutions.

> The mental health professionals are not to be regarded as guardians of mental health, but as agents of the community—among others—in developing and conserving its human resources in restoring to more effective functioning people whose performance has been impaired. Professional people are valuable allies in the community's quest for the health and well-being of its members, but the responsibility of setting goals and major policies cannot be wisely delegated (Smith and Hobbs, 1966).

The development, planning and implementation of such regional interdisciplinary training centers must actively involve the Asian and Pacific American communities they are to serve. Flexible schedules (e.g., evening and weekend classes and "intensive seminars") should be provided to accommodate those unable to participate on a full-time basis or who need to continue working while attending classes. Such flexibility in planning would integrate the "career-ladder" concept and ensure outcomes that would benefit both participants and the community.

Until recently, few Asian and Pacific American mental health paraprofessionals and professionals have been in service settings and in leadership roles. The scarcity of successful role models with which to identify has tended to discourage Asian and Pacific American trainees from pursuing careers in the mental health field. It is, therefore, urged that qualified Asian and Pacific American paraprofessionals and professionals be identified and considered for appointment to national, state and local committees within their professional organizations in order to increase the number of candidates entering training.

Major Public Policy Recommendations

On the basis of our deliberations and assessments of the current state of curriculum development in social work education for practice in Asian and Pacific American communities, certain public policy recommendations have emerged. These recommendations refer to public policy to be implemented at the federal, state and regional levels.

Federal Public Policy

At the federal level, we recommend the following:

- Title VI of the U.S. Civil Rights Act should be stringently enforced by the appropriate federal authorities. Although NIMH is not an enforcement agency per se, it must take every opportunity to stimulate and support compliance with Title VI, e.g., site visits.

• NIMH must establish a set of minority mental health training "principles." These principles must include the concept that any quality training program will have appropriate minority mental health curriculum content and instruction.

• NIMH should utilize the contract mechanism, when the grant system is not as effective.

• NIMH continuing education funds should be used to upgrade faculty and practitioners regarding minority mental health issues.

• NIMH must make funds available for pilot projects that will be "incentives" for training institutions and facilities to strengthen their minority mental health curricula and instructions.

• An appropriate minority mental health training advisory committee should be established to advise the director of the Division of Manpower and Training.

• NIMH-State Manpower Planning Program must stress the enhancement of minority mental health curriculum and instruction in its funding to state departments of mental health.

• NIMH's Division of Manpower and Training should evaluate its current efforts to enhance minority mental health curricula and instruction.

• The Health Manpower Act, PL 94-484, should be amended to include a requirement for minority mental health training throughout its provisions.

• A national network of minority mental health professionals who provide training should be created to promote information exchange, build strategies for change and collaborate on intergroup problem solving.

At the state and regional levels, we recommend the following:

State and Regional Levels

• National accrediting institutions (e.g., the Western Interstate Commission on Higher Education and the Southern Regional Education Board) must use their influence to stimulate and strengthen minority mental health curricula and instruction.

• State licensing for social workers should require minority mental health knowledge in the licensing examinations. Also there should be a requirement for minority mental health knowledge in renewing licenses for those individuals who already hold state social work licenses. This objective should be reached by requiring continuing education units.

• Each school of social work (undergraduate and graduate) must be evaluated for their minority mental health curricula and instruction by the Council on Social Work Education (CSWE). This data should be updated regularly and should be used for CSWE accreditation, federal and state grant application reviews, monitoring, and endorsements from minority communities.

References

Barth, C. *Bitter strength: A history of the Chinese in the United States, 1850–1870.* Cambridge: Harvard University Press, 1964.

Berk, B., & Hirata, L. C. Mental illness among the Chinese: Myth or reality? *Journal of Social Issues,* 1973, *29* (2), 149–66.

Brown, T. R., Stein, K. M., Huang, K., & Harris, D. E. Mental illness and the role of mental health facilities in Chinatown. In S. Sue & N. Wagner (Eds.), *Asian American psychological perspectives.* Palo Alto, CA.: Science and Behavior Books, 1973.

Cheng, E. *The elder Chinese.* San Diego: Center on Aging, San Diego State University, 1978.

Chikahisa, P., Cho, K., Kushida, A., & Morales, R. *Asian and Pacific American curriculum on social work education.* Los Angeles: Asian American Community Mental Health Training Center, 1976.

Chikahisa, P., Cho, K., Kushida, A., & Morales, R. Southeast Asian American reader. Los Angeles: Asian American Community Mental Health Training Center, 1980. (Unpublished)

Chin, R. New York Chinatown today: Community in crisis." *Amerasia Journal,* 1971, *1* (1), 52–63.

Connor, J. W. Acculturation and changing need patterns in Japanese-American and Caucasian-American college students. *Journal of Social Psychology,* 1974, *93* (2), 293–94.

Connor, J.W. Value changes in third generation Japanese Americans. *Journal of Personality Assessment,* 1975, *39* (6), 597–600.

Cordova, D. L. Immigration issues: Policy, impact and strategies. In U.S. Civil Rights Commission, *Civil rights issues of Asian and Pacific Americans: Myths and realities.* Washington, D.C.: Government Printing Office, 1980.

Fabros, L., Kato, C., & Swanson, L. K. *Proceedings and final report: Pacific Asian elderly resource center development project.* Los Angeles: 1979.

Fujii, S. M. Elderly Asian Americans and use of public services. *Social Casework,* 1976, *57* (3), 202–7.

Fujimoto, T. Social class and crime: The case of the Japanese-Americans. *Issues in Criminology,* 1975, *10* (1), 73–93.

Green, J. W., & Tong, C. (Eds.). *Cultural awareness in the human services: A training manual.* Seattle: University of Washington Center for Social Welfare Research, 1979.

Hatanaka, H., Watanabe, B., & Ono, S. The utilization of mental health services by Asian-Americans in the Los Angeles Area. In W. H. Ishikawa & N. H. Archer (Eds.), *Service delivery in Pan Asian communities.* San Diego: Pacific-Asian Coalition, 1975.

Horikowa, H., & Peralta, V. *Needs and potentialities assessment of Asian-American elderly in Greater Philadelphia.* Chicago: Pacific Asian-American Mental Health Research Center, 1978.

Kalish, R. A., & Moriwaki, S. The worlds of the elderly Asian American. *Journal of Social Issues,* 1973, *29* (2), 187–209.

Kim, B. C. Asian Americans: No model minority. *Social Work,* 1973, *18* (3), 44–53.

Kushida, A. H., Montenegro, M., Chikahisa, P., & Morales, R. F. A training program for Asian and Pacific Islander-Americans. *Social Casework,* 1976, *57* (3), 185–194.

Lin, T. A study of the incidence of mental disorder in Chinese and other cultures. *Psychiatry,* 1973, *16* (4), 313–36.

Liu, W. T., Lamanna, M., & Murata, A. *Transition to nowhere: Vietnamese refugees in America.* Nashville: Charter House Publishers, 1979.

McCann, C. W. (Ed.). *Perspectives on ethnic minority content in social work education.* Boulder, CO.: Western Interstate Commission on Higher Education, 1972.

McWilliams, C. *Brothers under the skin.* Boston: Little, Brown and Co., 1946.

Miller, S. C. *The unwelcomed immigrant: The American image of the Chinese, 1785–1882.* Berkeley, CA.: University of California Press, 1969.

Morales, R. *Makibaka: The Filipino American struggle.* Los Angeles: Mountain View Publishers, 1974.

Munoz, F. U. Pacific Islanders: Perplexed, neglected minority. *Social Casework,* 1976, *57* (30), 179–84.

Murase, K. Ethnic minority content in social work curriculum: Social welfare policy and social research. In C. W. McCann (Ed.), *Perspectives on ethnic minority content in social work education.* Boulder, CO.: Western Interstate Commission on Higher Education, 1972.

Murase, K. (Ed.). *Asian American task force report: Problems and issues in social work education.* New York: Council on Social Work Education, 1973.

Murase, K. Social welfare policy and services: Asian Americans. In D. G. Norton (Ed.), *The dual perspective: Inclusion of minority content in the social work curriculum.* New York: Council on Social Work Education, 1978.

Nishimura, R. T. (Ed.). *Issues and methods for curriculum building in relation to the Asian and Pacific Islands elderly.* New York: Council on Social Work Education, 1978.

Norton, D. (Ed.). *The dual perspective: Inclusion of ethnic content in the social work curriculum.* New York: Council on Social Work Education, 1978.

Office of Special Concerns, Office of the Secretary, Department of Health, Education and Welfare. *A study of selected socioeconomic characteristics of ethnic minorities based on the 1970 census, Volume 2, Asian Americans.* Washington, D.C.: Government Printing Office, 1974.

Pacific Asian Elderly Research Project. *Critical factors in service delivery—Final report.* Los Angeles: Author, 1978.

President's Commission on Mental Health. *Task panel reports, Volume 3.* Washington, D.C.: U.S. Government Printing Office, 1978.

San Francisco Community Mental Health Services, Annual Report. San Francisco: San Francisco Department of Public Health, 1977.

Smith, M. B., & Hobbs, N. The community and the community mental health center. *American Psychologist,* 1966, *21* (6), 449–509.

Sue, D. W., & Kirk, B. A. Asian Americans: Use of counseling and psychiatric services on a college campus. *Journal of Counseling Psychology,* 1975, *22,* 84–86.

Sue, S. Community mental health services to minority groups: Some optimism, some pessimism. *American Psychologist,* 1977, *32,* 616–24.

U.S. Civil Rights Commission. *Civil rights issues of Asian and Pacific Americans: Myths and realities.* Washington, D.C.: U.S. Government Printing Office, 1980.

U.S. Department of Commerce, Bureau of the Census. *Subject reports: Japanese, Chinese and Filipinos in the United States.* Washington, D.C.: Government Printing Office, 1973.

Yamamoto, J., James, Q. C., & Palley, N. Cultural problems in psychiatric therapy. *Archives of General Psychiatry,* 1968, *19,* 45–49.

Bibliography

Abott, K. Chinese-American society. *Amerasia Journal*, 1972, *1* (4), 68–70.

Bok-Lim, C. K. Asian Americans: No model minority. *Social Work*, 1973, *18* (2), 44–53; see also the special issue of *Journal of Social Issues*, 1973, *29* (2), Asian Americans: A success story?

Catapusan, B. T. *The social adjustment of Pilipinos in the United States.* San Francisco: R and E Research Associates, 1972.

Chen, P. The Chinese community in Los Angeles. *Social Casework*, 1970, *51* (10), 591–98.

Chen, P. Samoans in California. *Social Work*, 1973, *18* (2), 41–48.

Chew, A. Treatment implications of cultural attitudes toward dependence/independence. In W. Ishikawa & N. Archer (Eds.), *Service delivery in Pan Asian communities.* San Diego Pacific Asian Coalition, 1975.

Chun-Hoon, L. Jade Snow Wong and the fate of Chinese-American identity. *Amerasia Journal*, 1971, *1* (1), 52–63.

Diamond, M. J., & Bond, J. H. The acceptance of "Barnum" personality interpretations by Japanese, Japanese-Americans, and Caucasian-American college students. *Journal of Cross Cultural Psychology*, 1974, *5* (2), 228–35.

Fong, S. Assimilation and changing social roles of Chinese-Americans. *Journal of Social Issues*, 1973, *29* (2), 115–27.

Ho, D. Y. F. Prevention and treatment of mental illness in the People's Republic of China. *American Journal of Orthopsychiatry*, 1974, *44* (4), 620–36.

Ho, D. Y. F. On the concept of face. *American Journal of Sociology*, 1976, *81* (4), 867–84.

Ho W. Social work with Asian-Americans. *Social Casework*, 1976, *57* (3), 195–201.

Hsa, J., & Tseng, W. Intercultural psychotherapy. *Archives of General Psychiatry*, 1972, *27*, 700–705.

Hsu, F. *The challenge of the American dream: The Chinese in the United States.* Belmont, CA.: Wadsworth Publishing Company, 1971.

Ignacio, L. F. The Pacific/Asian coalitions: Origin, structure, and program. *Social Casework*, 1976, *57* (3), 131–35.

Johnson, C. L. Interdependence, reciprocity and indebtedness: An analysis of Japanese American kinship relations. *Journal of Marriage and the Family*, 1977, *39* (2), 351–63.

Jung, M. Characteristics of contrasting chinatowns. *Social Casework*, 1976, *57* (3), 149–54.

Kalish, R., & Sam, Y. Americans of East Asian ancestry: Aging and the aged. *Gerontologist*, 1971, *2* (1), Pt. 2.

Khinduka, S. K. Social work and the Third World. *Social Service Review*, 1976, *45* (1), 61–73.

Kikumura, A., & Kitano, H. Interracial marriage: A picture of the Japanese Americans. *Journal of Social Issues*, 1973, *29* (2), 67–81.

Kim, B. C. An appraisal of Korean immigrant service needs. *Social Casework*, 1976, *57* (3), 139–48.

Kim, B. C. Casework with Japanese and Korean wives of Americans. *Social Casework*, 1972, *53* (5), 273–79.

Kim, H., & Meijia, C. *The Filipinos in America, 1898–1974: A chronology and fact book.* Dobbs Ferry, N.Y.: Oceana Publications, 1976.

Kim, K. Cross-culture differences between Americans and Koreans in nonverbal behavior. In H. Sohn (Ed.), *The Korean Language: Its structure and social projection.* Honolulu, HI.: The Center for Korean Studies, 1976.

Koran, L. M. Psychiatry in mainland China: History and recent status. *American Journal of Psychiatry,* 1972, *128,* 84–92.

Kuramoto, F. H. What do Asians want? An examination of issues in social work education. *Journal of Education for Social Work,* 1971, 7 (3), 7–18.

Kuramoto, F. U. Lessons learned in the federal funding game. *Social Casework,* 1976, *57* (3), 208–18.

Levine, G. N., & Montero, D. M. Socioeconomic mobility among three generations of Japanese Americans. *Journal of Social Issues,* 1973, *29* (2), 33–48.

Lott, J. T. Migration of a mentality: The Filipino community. *Social Casework,* 1976, *57* (3), 165–72.

Mariano, H. *The Filipino immigrants in the United States.* San Francisco: R and E Research Associates, 1972.

Marsella, A. J., Kinzie, D., & Gordon, P. Ethnic variations in the expression of depression. *Journal of Cross-Cultural Psychology,* 1973, *4* (4), 435–568.

Mass, A. Asians as individuals: The Japanese community. *Social Casework,* 1976, *57* (3), 160–4.

Masuda, M., Hasegawa, R., & Matsumoto, G. The ethnic identity questionnaire: A comparison of three Japanese age groups in Tachikawa, Japan, Honolulu, and Seattle. *Journal of Cross-Cultural Psychology,* 1973, *4* (2), 229–45.

Maykovich, M. K. Political activation of Japanese-American youth. *Journal of Social Issues,* 1973, *29* (2), 167–85.

Melendy, H.B. *Asians in America: Filipinos, Koreans and East Indians.* Boston: Twayne Publishers, 1977.

Meredith, G. M. Interpersonal needs of Japanese-American and Caucasian-American college students in Hawaii. *Journal of Social Psychology,* 1977, *99* (2), 157–61.

Murase, K. Minorities: Asian Americans. In *Encyclopedia of social work.* Washington, D.C.: National Association of Social Workers, 1977.

Norell, I. *Literature of the Filipino-American in the United States: A selective and annotated bibliography.* San Francisco: R and E Research Associates, 1976.

Owan, T. Improving productivity in the public sector through bilingual-bicultural staff. *Social Work Research and Abstracts,* 1978, *14* (1), 10–18.

Shin, L. Koreans in America, 1930–1945. *Amerasia Journal,* 1971, *1* (3), 32–39.

Sidel, R. The role of revolutionary optimism in the treatment of mental illness in the People's Republic of China. *American Journal of Orthopsychiatry,* 1973, *43,* 732–36.

Sue, D. W., & Frank, A. C. A typological approach to the psychological study of Chinese and Japanese American college males. *Journal of Social Issues,* 1973, *29* (2), 129–48.

Sue, S., & Sue, D. Chinese-American personality and mental health. *Amerasia Journal,* 1971, *1,* 36–48.

Sue, W., & McKinney, H. Asian-Americans in the community mental health care system. *American Journal of Orthopsychiatry,* 1975, *45* (1), 111–18.

Tong, B. The ghetto of the mind: Notes on the historical psychology of Chinese-Americans. *Amerasia Journal,* 1971, *1* (3), 1–31.

True, R. Mental health services in a Chinese-American community. In W. Ishikawa & N. Archer (Eds.), *Service delivery in Pan Asian communities.* San Diego: Pacific Asian Coalition, 1975, 15–22.

True, R. Characteristics of contrasting Chinatowns: Oakland, Chinatown. *Social Casework,* 1976, *57* (3), 155–59.

Tseng, W. The development of psychiatric concepts in traditional Chinese medicine. *Archives of General Psychiatry*, 1973, *29* (4), 596–75.

Tseng, W. S., & McDermott, J. F., Jr. Psychotherapy: Historical roots, universal elements, and cultural variations. *American Journal of Psychiatry*, 1975,*32* (4), 378–84.

U.S. Civil Rights Commission. *Asian Americans: Unfulfilled dreams.* Washington, D.C.: Government Printing Office, 1974.

Yanagisaki, S. J. Women-centered kin networks: Urban bilateral kinship. *American Ethnologist*, 1977, *4* (2), 207–26.

Yoshida, R., & Wu, R. E. Intervention techniques and Asian-American identity: The problem of alienation and self-esteem. *International Mental Health Research Newsletter*, 1975, *17* (3), 2–4.

Yun, H. The Korean personality and treatment considerations. *Social Casework*, 1976, *57* (3), 173–8.

EDDIE F. BROWN   RONALD G. LEWIS
JOHN COMPTON   JOHN E. MACKEY

CHAPTER 7

American Indian Content in Social Work Curricula

A Challenge for the 1980s

At all educational levels in the training of a social worker, attempts have been made to incorporate ethnic minority content into the curriculum. It has proven a difficult and complex task, borne principally by faculties of institutions of higher learning which have had to reevaluate their courses in terms of their responsibilities to ethnic minority communities. In the early 1970s the idea of American society as a pluralistic society gained currency, and it became evident that if social work education were to meet the needs of a culturally diverse society, faculties of schools of social work had to critically reappraise their current curricula. Changes would have to be made that would provide for more relevant, realistic interventions in alleviating the extreme social problems faced by millions of people in American society. Providing the traditional manpower for social service agencies was not enough; social work education had to produce professionally equipped service providers able to evaluate and deal with inequality, racism and poverty.

To support this reevaluation, the Council on Social Work Education (CSWE) revised Accreditation Standard 1234A (1973) to read:

> A school must make special, continual efforts to enrich its program by providing racial, ethnic and cultural diversity in its student body and at all levels of instructional and research personnel, and by providing corresponding educational supports. (p. 1)

The overriding purpose of this new standard was to make students aware of the knowledge, attitudes and skills imperative for sensitive and effective social work in a pluralistic society.

Since the accreditation revision, there have been numerous bibliographies, course outlines, and schemata developed for the identifi-

157

cation and inclusion of ethnic minority content in the social work curriculum. These efforts, however, have focused principally on Hispanic, Black and Asian and Pacific Americans. Until recently, little attention has been given to the issue of social work curriculum that is culturally relevant to American Indians and Alaskan Natives, their families and communities.

A frequent complaint of American Indian and Alaskan Native peoples has been the ignorance, insensitivity and lack of respect displayed by professional social workers in the planning, development and delivery of social services to their communities and tribes. Although in general the field of social work has been in the forefront of safeguarding the integrity of family life, these efforts have not included the American Indian family. Historically, social services and child welfare programs, ostensibly designed to benefit the American Indian, have severely attacked and nearly destroyed American Indian family life. Contemporary practices regarding health, education and welfare services for the American Indian have often only aggravated this situation.

Many social service professionals have attempted to discount American Indian cultures, inferring that these cultures are in a state of "entropy" or are dying. Most education literature tends to point toward Indian cultures, families and communities as biologically and/or culturally "deficient," "ill," or at least "problematic." Such stereotypes must be exposed and attacked.

It must be understood that social delivery and treatment have been influenced by negative pathological-oriented theories which have done more harm than good. Faculties of schools of social work must ensure that their institutions emphasize the need for serious consideration, understanding and provision of a humanistic approach which liberates rather than "domesticates" the American Indian and Alaskan Native family and community.

This proposed perspective of American Indian and Alaskan Native families and communities represents a nondeficit approach that concentrates on the strengths of the Indian family and community. It views American Indian and Alaskan Native cultures, communities and families as healthy, dynamic, coping systems in a state of synergy rather than entropy and capable of providing active lives for their members. To incorporate this perspective, a comprehensive strategy is needed to ensure that schools of social work are making adequate attempts to include the identification, development and presentation of American Indian content in their schools.

Despite the revision of Accreditation Standard 1234A, schools of social work have been hard-pressed to find a comprehensive, systematic strategy by which they could include ethnic minority content in the social work curricula. Because of the considerable variation in the degree of commitment and in the philosophies of schools, only limited approaches have evolved for the inclusion of ethnic minority content in the social work curriculum (Chunn, 1974). There have been attempts to educate and recruit ethnic minority faculty members, refine bibliographies, further develop course outlines and sponsor faculty development activities, but these have been principally varied, piecemeal approaches over short periods of time with limited resources and little coordinated support.

A 1975 study addressing the inclusion of ethnic minority content in social work curriculum concluded that both existing social work literature and the faculty of accredited graduate social work programs had failed to provide a comprehensive and systematic strategy by which ethnic minority content could be included in a step-by-step process.

> The faculty of the graduate schools, while expressing the desire to integrate ethnic minority content throughout the total curriculum have lacked a systematic strategy or mechanism through which this can be accomplished. The authors of the literature, while stressing the integration of ethnic minority content, have also failed to explore a systematic strategy. It appears therefore that the faculty of graduate schools, with very few exceptions, have been blocked in their attempt to systematically include ethnic minority content because they lack a strategy which would expedite the actual implementation. (E. F. Brown, 1975, p. 98)

In developing a comprehensive strategy for inclusion of American Indian and Alaskan Native content, there are four major areas to consider (see Figure 1). Although the areas are shown as separate and distinct, they are, in reality, interrelated and interdependent. This chapter will specifically address each of the major components and describe the necessary tasks to be performed.

Development of Appropriate Administration and Policies

The overall purpose for the inclusion of ethnic minority content should be to prepare students—

- to recognize that racism is institutional and maintained in society at the expense of ethnic minorities;
- to recognize that social work practice can and must reduce prejudice;
- to develop commitment to confront and examine personal attitudes that are detrimental to the practice of social work;
- to become aware of cultural and ethnic traits of minority people that affect their ways of negotiating with social systems;
- to enhance the cultural factors among minorities that enrich the larger society;

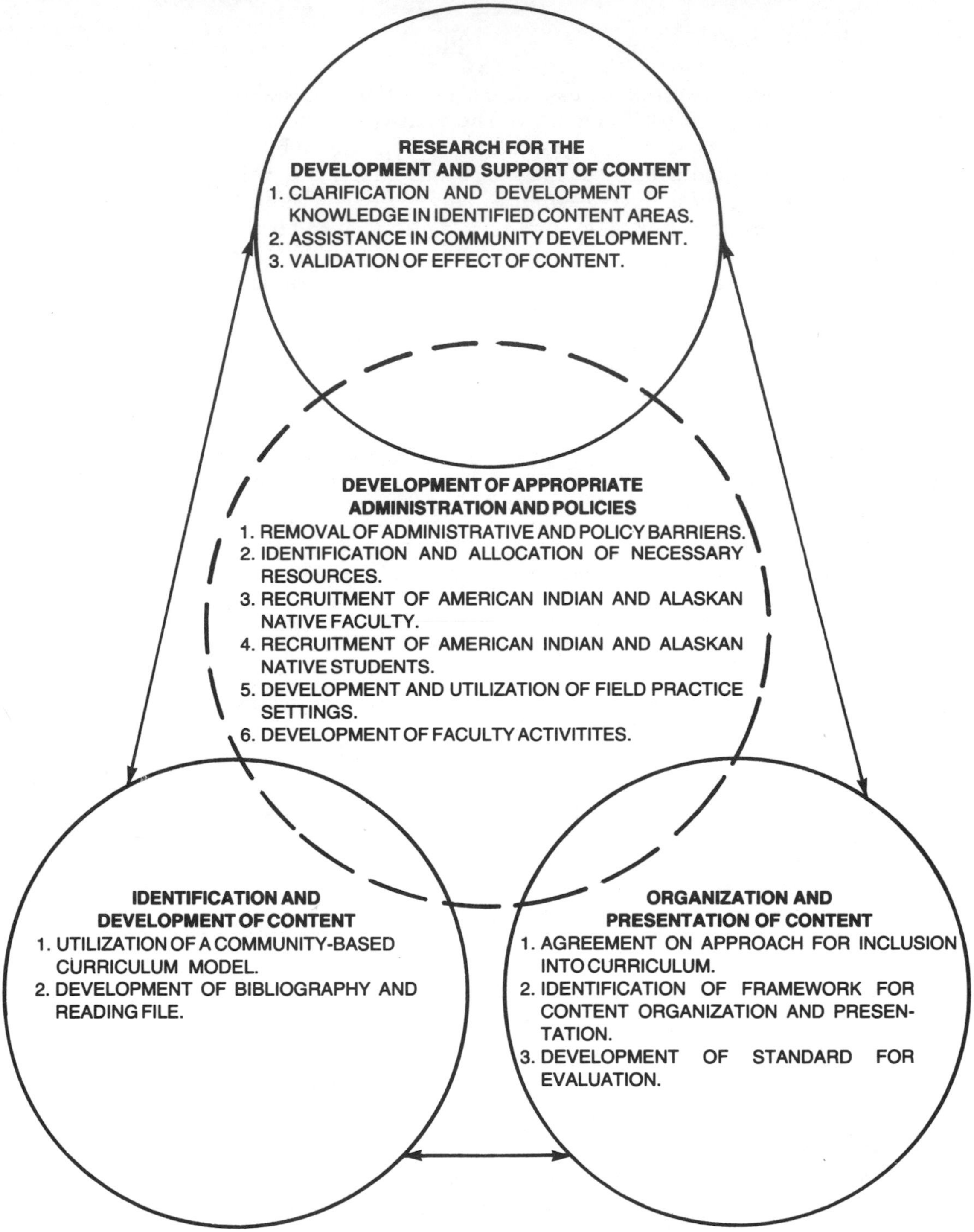

FIGURE 1

A Comprehensive Strategy for Inclusion of American Indian and Alaskan Native Content in Social Work Curriculum

> • to become aware of the interdependence of all people in a culturally pluralistic society.

To achieve these goals, school administrators must be prepared to remove policies and structures that bar successful integration of ethnic minority content into the social work curriculum.

School administrators should be conscious of the following recommended guidelines for effective planned change within their institutions.

> • Two to five years should be allowed for completing the initial planned change. Recognizing that the inclusion of ethnic minority content into the curriculum is an ongoing and continual process, the initial reorganization of the curriculum cannot be accomplished within a single semester or academic year.
> • A variety of programs should be planned which include joint planning with curriculum committee, faculty development, outside consultation and research activities.
> • The support, cooperation and coordination between administration curriculum committees and individual faculty members must be obtained.
> • A "phasing program" must be developed for the inclusion of content across a realistic timeframe (Bennis, Benne and Chin, 1969, p. 19).

These guidelines provide some of the support and policy necessary to allow for an administrative organization along the following lines:

> • Recruit faculty who have demonstrated competence in transethnic social work practice;
> • Recruit students who are committed to transethnic social work practice;
> • Develop and use field practice settings that encourage and serve American Indian and Alaskan Native populations;
> • Devise a standard process for including American Indian and Alaskan Native content in the core curriculum and elective courses;
> • Develop faculty activities around knowledge and curriculum building of American Indian and Alaskan Native content in social work curriculum (Brown and Gilbert, 1977).

There is evidence that the schools of social work that have progressed furthest in planning for and including ethnic minority content in the curriculum are those whose faculties have formally organized special committees to address the task of including American Indian content; devised rationales with goals and objectives; and developed an evaluation plan (E. F. Brown, 1975, p. 98).

Identification and Development of Content

During the past decade, specialized efforts funded by the National Institute of Mental Health have been made to recruit American Indian students and faculty, to develop and utilize field practice settings and to provide development activities for greater faculty awareness. To a degree, these programs have been successful, but they are limited to a few graduate schools of social work and have received limited administrative and faculty support.* A 1976 national survey of American Indian students working toward master of social work (MSW) degrees revealed that more than 50 percent felt their curriculum was not relevant to the needs of their communities and tribes. Of the graduates "most stated that the curriculum paid only token attention to Indians, consisted largely of misinformation about Indians and was over-simplified or too general to be useful. Even schools with formal programs for Indians were judged to be weak in this area" (Compton, 1976, p. 30).

The identification and further development of relevant American Indian content has not been in any depth. Compton identified two major decisions as basic to successful inclusion of minority content. "First, a decision must be made on what content should be included. Second, a decision must be made on how it should be packaged" (Compton, 1976, p. 30).

Identifying the content to be included is not easy: it must be relevant to the current life situations of American Indian and Alaskan Native peoples, and those life situations are undergoing rapid and extensive change in terms of both the individual and the collective. Anthropologist George Kneller (1965) states, "As the rate of cultural change accelerates, educators find it increasingly difficult to adapt the curriculum to the so-called demands of society, since they do not know exactly what their demands are or how long they will last" (p. 136). Logic suggests, thus, that for maximum curricular relevance curriculum developers must draw upon a broad base of community resources.

Like Kneller, Gollattscheck (1976) stresses the importance of the curriculum developer in identifying and utilizing pertinent community input. Gollattscheck notes, for example, that leaders of educational institutions must recognize that the college and community are interdependent. "It seems obvious," says Gollattscheck, "that the college as an agency does not exist in isolation from the community and its many organizations and agencies" (p. 45). He depicts the important advantages of drawing upon community resources:

*Seven graduate schools of social work are presently receiving funds from the National Institute of Mental Health for the recruitment and education of American Indians: Arizona State University, Barry College, Portland University, San Francisco State University, University of Oklahoma, University of Utah, and University of Wisconsin-Milwaukee.

The colleges' and the communities' images of each other will change as the college begins to work with community groups on a partnership basis. The college will gain a better perspective of one or more publics within its community as it loses its "ivory tower" insularity. The college will gain valuable credibility in the eyes of the community as it demonstrates, rather than talks about, its interest in working with groups, agencies, and organizations for community improvement.

In short, the college attempting to become effectively involved with the community in improvement and renewal activities should recognize the great potential of community organizations and agencies (p. 49).

American Indian communities, like their mainstream society counterparts, are undergoing rapid changes. Although the present modification of American Indian community life is obvious in many aspects—agriculture, schooling, business—new approaches to the delivery of social services is an important issue to American Indian and Alaskan Native people and therefore to social work curriculum developers too. The delivery of social services to American Indian and Alaskan Native communities and families cannot be addressed as an isolated concern. Some examples of cultural aspects intricately intertwined with social services delivery are tribal culture, reservation and urban economics, the unique federal trust relationship, the effects and potential of self-determination, tribal sovereignty, family networks and bonds, nutrition, mobility and educational structures.

In addition to emphasizing knowledge of such aspects of American Indian and Alaskan Native life, social work curriculum developers must also stress the accompanying attitudes and skills. Combining cognitive (knowledge), affective (attitudes) and behaviorial (skills) elements produces a three-dimensional schema that is essential for social workers, particularly those who work with Indian populations, to grasp (see Figure 2).

Given the tridimensional curricular framework, the major concern of social work curriculum developers is to identify the specific knowledge, attitudes and skills that must be instilled in social work students and practitioners concerned with social services for American Indians. For relevant input on curriculum content, we should listen to those who are closest to tribal lifestyle, norms and mores and to those who possess the most experience and expertise in social services delivery to American Indians, namely, American Indian social work professionals. McDanfield (1974) affirms, "There seems little question that curriculum design must begin with individuals who are most concerned with that curriculum" (p. 104). It is no longer possible to rely solely on university specialists. Curriculum developers in schools of social work attempting to infuse American Indian or other ethnic content must encourage and use pertinent community resource persons. As the group of educational writers and researchers assembled by the Center for Adaptive Learning stated:

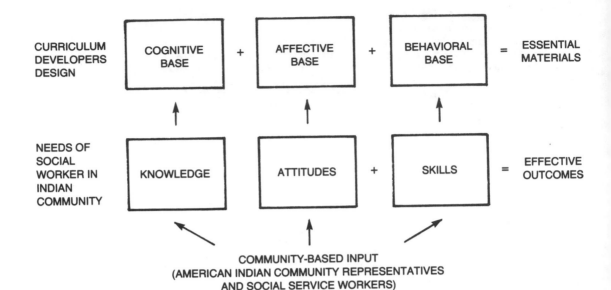

FIGURE 2

A Three-Dimensional Curriculum Model

> We assumed that there is an environment outside the school that is
> related to the curriculum. The core curriculum does not exist in a
> vacuum. If we have a concern for social reality, we must link the
> instructional program implicit in the culture. What has already
> been done by the media of the culture and other socialization
> methods? What is it that the instructional media should do? What
> is it that the media of the culture can do? How can we bring the
> two together? (McDanfield, 1974, p. 109)

"Bringing the two together," that is, the community or cultural
resource persons and academic specialists, is imperative when building
a sound and relevant curriculum dedicated to improving the state of
social services in Indian communities.* Foerster and Soldier (1975)
recommended that Indian people be involved "at every stage" of
curriculum development. "Indians," they assert, "are weary of being
'explained' by non-Indians. They want to tell their own story" (p. 192).
In a final statement they conclude:

> In order to assure authenticity and validity, then, most curriculum
> projects call for direct involvement of Native Americans during
> every phase. Attention is given to such elements as tribal history
> and governments, language, religion, customs, and values (p. 192).

Because of the number and diversity of tribes within the United States,
it is difficult to develop specific American Indian and Alaskan Native
curriculum relevant to all tribal groups. However, given that American

*For more information as to specific processes, refer to Shaughnessy and Brown
(1979) and Brown and Gilbert (1977).

Indians and Alaskan Natives deal with specific federal institutions and policies developed specifically to govern health, education, welfare and economics on reservations, we indeed have points of commonality from which to develop curriculum.

Identifying and developing curriculum materials of genuine relevancy to American Indian and Alaskan Native communities is a difficult and complex challenge that schools of social work must respond to. Schools located in culturally diverse settings must be prepared to offer curriculum that prepares graduates to deliver creative, innovative, sensitive and relevant services.

Organization and Presentation of Content

It is not hard to find a bibliography that says "here is Indian content, here are all the books written, here are all the articles." It is one thing to identify the content. It is another thing to package that content and then teach it from a point that supports Indian perspective (Buffalohead, 1976).

To ensure that the organization and presentation of American Indian content reflects a nondeficit perspective, an overall curriculum approach must be identified, a framework for organization and presentation agreed upon and a standard developed to evaluate goals and objectives.

Curriculum Approaches

Schools of social work throughout the United States have used four major approaches for the inclusion of ethnic minority content in the social work curriculum.

1. Ethnic minority content organized as a separate curriculum entailing: (a) the development of courses on ethnic minority content to be taught as a separate curriculum developed to educate social workers to practice specifically with minorities or minority groups, or (b) a school which specializes in training social workers for one particular ethnic group or groups and has developed its core curriculum to reflect such group or groups.
2. Ethnic minority content taught in specialized courses which would involve the addition of courses specializing in minority content to the total curriculum and not in changing the content of the core curriculum.
3. Ethnic minority content integrated into the sequence areas of the core curriculum, which means that ethnic minority content is not found exclusively in any one part of the curriculum but is woven into the course outlines of all sequences. There is no development of specialized courses pertaining to ethnic minority groups or group.
4. A combination of ethnic minority content integrated into the core curriculum and the addition of specialized courses. This provides ethnic minority content integrated into the core curriculum as well as supplementary ethnic minority content in specialized courses (E. F. Brown, 1975, p. 43).

The majority of graduate schools follow the fourth approach, a combined specialized and integrated approach, in their efforts to include minority content (see Figure 3).

Given the mission statement and rationale of each school, it is recommended that a particular approach be identified and content organized to meet the needs of that approach. For instance, in response to the combined specialized and integrated approach, beginning awareness of American Indian and Alaskan Native families could be integrated into the core curriculum on social work with families, while more indepth content on specific techniques and skills could be presented in a specialized course on social work practice with American Indian and Alaskan Native families.

Frameworks for Organization and Presentation

In organizing and presenting American Indian content, a framework or model helps immensely. At this early stage of inclusion of minority content there is a need to develop and test several frameworks. For example, the dual perspective model, developed by Norton (1978) for use in social work, has great potential for applying American Indian and Alaskan Native content as a generic group or singly as tribal communities. This model employs as major components the values, attitudes and behavior of the larger societal system along with those of the client's family and community. Thus, for the American Indian

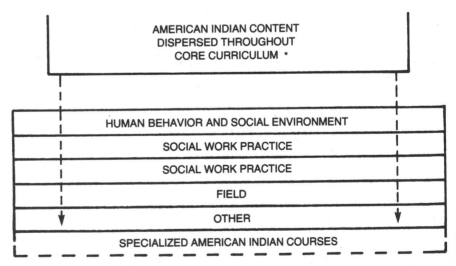

*IF MATERIAL IS SHOWN OUTSIDE "CORE CURRICULUM," STUDENTS DO NOT VIEW MATERIAL AS RELEVANT

FIGURE 3

American Indian Curriculum Integration Model

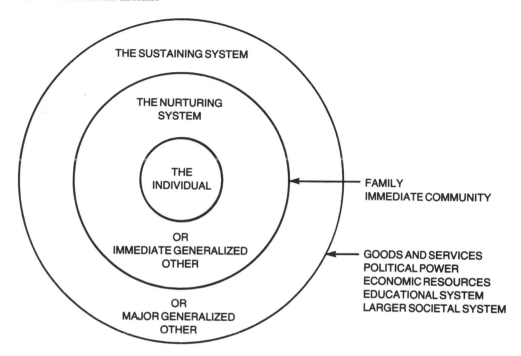

FIGURE 4

The Dual System of All Individuals

or Alaskan Native, the extended family and the tribe are the "nurturing system" and the larger system (the United States) is the "sustaining system" since the bulk of certain resources stem from this system (see Figure 4).

Brown in Brown and Shaughnessy (1978) provides an example of how the dual perspective can be applied to explain the incongruence between the nurturing and sustaining systems.

> Native Americans, as other ethnic minority populations, have experienced much incongruence between the two systems. The nurturing culture has validated the individual and family and generally produces feelings of positive self-worth and being valued. The sustaining system has given messages and structural rigidity which devalued Indian people and their ways. The difference between these two systems has led to institutional racism. To cope with the situation, it becomes necessary for Indians to develop two ways of relating and coping: one set of behaviors for the nurturing system and another set for use in the sustaining system. In the nurturing system, one can have status, respect and clearly-defined roles and contributions. In the sustaining system, the same person or family may be roleless and be judged as worthless, resistant, inadequate or problematic. Self-esteem is high in one system; it is challenged and eroded in the other.

An illustration of that process can be seen in the expectation for self-reliance at an early age for children that is supported and esteemed by the Indian culture, but that same expectation is seen as negligence and exploitation by the Anglo (sustaining) culture. In practice, the young Indian child (6–8 years of age) is expected to contribute to the family by working (herding sheep) or caring for the siblings, even for long periods of time. Both of these tasks are focused on contributing to the family and group and require the child to be at home. Anglo culture would expect the same child to be cared for by an adult, or a much older child; the main "work" of Anglo children is defined as play and formal education. These activities are child or individual-centered, with family support expected for them. Formal education takes place away from the home as does a good deal of the play activity. The conflicts generated from these two expectations based on cultural differences between the nurturing system and the sustaining system are obvious. But the conflict does not end there. Traditional Indian ways support learning by observation and thoughtful contemplation until one arrives at his/her own conclusions; only then is the child expected to speak or share. The formal educational process often expects students to share opinions, to question, to seek ongoing assistance and guidance, and utilize group inputs in arriving at conclusions. The Native American child is expected to utilize the respective coping behaviors if he/she is to be relevant and effective in the two systems (p. 115).

We singled out the dual perspective model not because it is necessarily the best model but because it is an example. There are many other models that can be employed.

Standard for Evaluation

Graduate schools of social work have not developed an instrument to measure the effect of ethnic minority content in the curriculum on graduates (E. F. Brown, 1975). Of the schools that have an evaluation method, the most often used criteria were student evaluations or a combination of faculty and student evaluations (Ross-Sheriff, 1979).

Little in the social work literature deals with the evaluation of ethnic minority content. Recent articles by E. G. Brown (1975) and by Leigh (1972) did not address the issue directly but referred to Mager (1962) and Tyler (1950) concerning development of clearly defined behavioral objectives in relation to the inclusion of ethnic minority content.

Brown stated that, although minority content was included in the curriculum, its use was limited because of the lack of clearly defined objectives. To correct this, he proposed two major steps: (1) the identification of specific, student behavioral objectives in relation to social work practice and minority issues; and (2) the selection of learning experiences to help students to acquire these behavioral objectives. Leigh suggested that this process would help to clarify what was taught in the classroom and would provide a means of evaluating the curriculum by focusing on whether the students were meeting the stated behavioral objectives.

We recommended that minimum standards be developed that specifically address course objectives and selective readings. Course descriptions, objectives, units of study and methods of evaluation (papers, exams and so forth) must include content that provides an understanding and knowledge of American Indians and Alaskan Natives and sensitivity to transethnic social work practice. A percentage of all selective reading and accompanying bibliographies of course syllabi should address American Indian and Alaskan Native transethnic social work practice. As additional standards are developed, they should increasingly focus on assessing student competencies.

Research for Development and Support of Content

As a major component of a comprehensive strategy for the inclusion of American Indian and Alaskan Native content in the social work curriculum, research is necessary in three areas.

First, descriptive research is needed to clarify or further develop identified Indian and Alaskan Native content areas. There are many identified content areas relevant to Indian lifestyles and the field of social work where little background material exists. An example is the present natural support system currently utilized by American Indian families on reservations and in cities. Although anthropological information and extensive descriptive studies are available on traditional American Indian extended family networks, knowledge on contemporary families and on means of assessing this natural support system, both in the reservation and urban setting, is lacking. Research is needed to further identify the values, knowledge and skills related to the study of American Indian and Alaskan Native communities, families and individuals (see Figure 5).

Second, research is needed that assists local Indian and Alaskan Native communities to develop and implement social services delivery systems. As Montiel (1975) states:

> The purpose of research in ethnic communities of color should be to assist people to live their own lives. Minorities need to understand themselves, not in comparison to anyone else, but within their own perspective. This means that the research enterprise for ethnic minorities must be a liberating process since this ethnic perspective has been continuously denied in this society. No other purpose can or should be justified for research in ethnic communities of color (p. 13).

Both the profession and schools of social work need to engage in research and developmental activities that are capable of resolving or alleviating long-standing problems within American Indian and Alas-

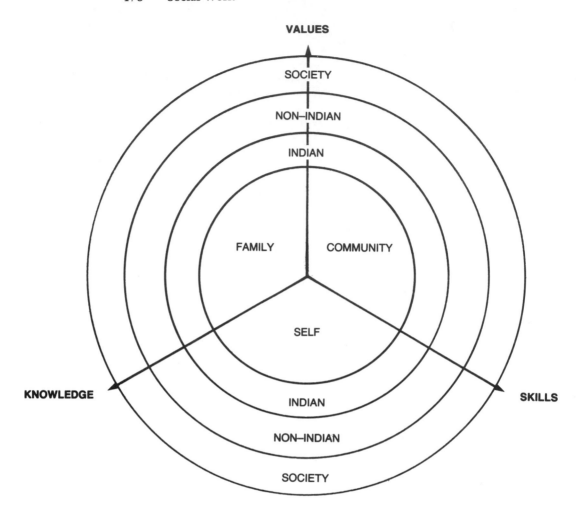

FIGURE 5

Research for Values, Knowledge, and Skills Base

kan Native communities. Such activities should be acceptable to American Indian and Alaskan Native communities and maintain integrity between research and development. Research is inadvertently conducted or research statistics manipulated to prove certain stereotypes about American Indians, such as their alcoholic predisposition and suicidal tendencies. These results are further misused for inappropriate practice or program planning. American Indian professionals have questioned the integrity of such research and development efforts. Without integrity, there exists a credibility gap between the researcher and the practitioner; an incongruity between the theory and the real problem will continue to exist.

Third, research is needed to determine methods of evaluating the effect on students of American Indian and Alaskan Native content in the social work curriculum. The development of an attitude-measuring scale to evaluate awareness before and after the students' encounter with American Indian and Alaskan Native content is presently needed. An instrument of this type could have potential merit in validating methods being used to include American Indian and Alaskan Native content. In addition, the quality, presentation and utilization of content need further research to validate and support the various frameworks being developed. Figure 6 identifies the areas in which research is needed to further validate content.

Concluding Suggestions

There is no one model that can guide educators in the development of American Indian and Alaskan Native content in social work programs. We have attempted, however, to offer a comprehensive strategy by which schools of social work—including those with formal programs for American Indians and Alaskan Natives—could improve their curricula to reflect the current socioeconomic and cultural realities of reservation and off-reservation American Indian and Alaskan Native communities. Essential in this strategy is the need for greater American Indian and Alaskan Native input and participation in the development of social work curricula and educational programs. Following are recommendations that support this direction.

American Indian tribes and Alaskan Native groups must be given a role of responsibility in the development of social work curricula

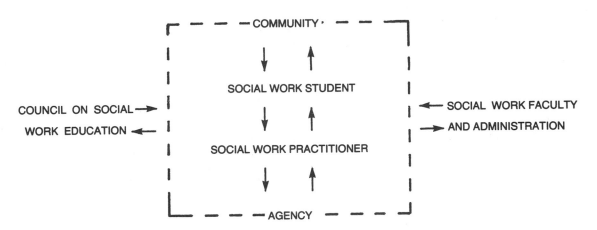

FIGURE 6

Research Areas for Validation of Content

and programs for their communities. Specific programs should have personnel, including directors, who are of American Indian or Alaskan Native descent and who are recognized as such by their communities. To minimize the organizational forces hindering success, program directors should be part of the school's central administration and directly accountable to the dean. The value structure of academia may make it desirable for directors of American Indian programs to have doctorates; from an American Indian standpoint, a doctorate is not necessary to ensure effective functioning of the programs. There are very few American Indians or Alaskan Natives with doctorates in social work at the present time.

A greater number of American Indian and Alaskan Native faculty in schools of social work should enhance the success of social work programs. American Indian and Alaskan Native social workers should seek faculty positions in schools of social work, especially in schools located relatively close to such populations, and should seek, in turn, to influence the students. It is essential to recognize that systemic barriers to the recruitment, retention and promotion of minority faculty continue to exist, despite their identification as early as 1972 by a subcommittee of the Commission on Minority Groups of the Council of Social Work Education. Faculty recruitment efforts should be vigorously pursued and training programs developed. Some social work organizations, such as CSWE, and schools of social work periodically offer faculty development sessions, but these are infrequent and do not always meet the needs of American Indian and Alaskan Native faculty. Black and Hispanic social work groups have proven that such training programs can be successful. The increasing number of qualified Black and Hispanic faculty members at schools of social work is one sign of their success.

Field placement possibilities with American Indian and Alaskan Native populations, both in traditional and nontraditional settings, need to be further identified and developed. Because governmental agencies, especially on the federal level, can offer practicum placements, these should be continually developed, both qualitatively and quantitatively. Indian-controlled organizations, such as urban American Indian centers and tribally run human service agencies, are another major resource. Finally, there are a few off-reservation private social welfare agencies, such as Lutheran or Jewish family services, that work with American Indian communities and that could be used for practicum placement purposes. These agencies have been responsible for American Indian child welfare services, such as adoption, and therefore could develop into special American Indian child welfare practicum placements.

Because the federal government provides the money which supports stipends and scholarships and the development of recruitment and educational programs for American Indian and Alaskan Native social work students, it is imperative that we examine government policies that are promoted by those in positions of influence. There are two policy alternatives that can be pursued. The present policy encourages schools of social work to seek funds from the National Institute of Mental Health and other federal sources for the establishment of a demonstration-type recruitment and educational program for American Indians in the field of social work. The second policy alternative, which is actually a refinement of present policy, would emphasize greater American Indian input into and control over the funds devoted to social work education. It would require that the present number of schools with formal programs for American Indians and Alaskan Natives be maintained and that more be financed if possible. In order to receive federal funds, colleges and universities with these programs would have to devise concrete plans for the gradual replacement of federal money over a set number of years, which would then institutionalize the programs.

Specific to the tasks of identification, development and inclusion of American Indian and Alaskan Native content in the curriculum, the following are recommended:

• Schools of social work within major American Indian regions should adopt a strategy which allows for regional tribal and cultural differences and which provides for the systematic identification and inclusion of American Indian content into the social work curriculum through joint university and community effort. Evidence suggests that schools of social work which have made greatest progress in including ethnic minority content in the curriculum are those that have organized special committees to address the task (E. F. Brown, 1975). In adopting a strategy, a school's administration should allow for a "phasing in" of American Indian and Alaskan Native content, with sufficient time allotted to complete the task (three to five years, depending on past efforts).

• To ensure an American Indian perspective in the identification and inclusion of content areas, an advisory curriculum committee, composed of community practitioners in various specializations and at various levels, can be organized. Although existing American Indian or Alaskan Native faculty may have a general idea of needed content, it may or may not represent those knowledge areas viewed as necessary by tribal groups and communities within certain geographical regions.

• Administrators of schools of social work should make available a variety of resources in planning, consulting, training and researching to ensure the development and inclusion of module courses, selective readings, and greater activities according to content areas identified by the curriculum task force.

• A bibliography of selected American Indian and Alaskan Native references specifically relating to social service topics should be compiled across the major curriculum sequences of the schools of social work. This could be utilized by faculty in strengthening required readings and for further module and course development.

• The curriculum task force should have an ongoing plan to evaluate the attempts of the schools of social work to incorporate into existing curricula the major content areas identified by the task force. This process would not only ensure continuity and consistency but also quality of the content being incorporated into the social work curriculum.

• Research efforts of graduate students, of federal- and state-funded programs and of faculties should be coordinated to address the gaps in current data for curriculum development and to respond to the special concerns of American Indian and Alaskan Native communities.

References

Bennis, W., Benne, K., & Chin. R. *The planning of change* (2nd ed.). New York: Holt, Rinehart, & Winston, Inc., 1969.

Brown, E. F. The inclusion of ethnic minority content in the curricula of graduate schools of social work. Doctoral dissertation, Graduate School of Social Work, University of Utah, Salt Lake City, 1975.

Brown, E. F., & Gilbert, B. *Social work practice with American Indians: A schema for the identification and inclusion of American Indian content in the social work curriculum.* Tempe, AZ.: Arizona State University, School of Social Work, 1977.

Brown, E. F., & Shaughnessy, T. F. (Eds.). *Education for social work practice with American Indian families: Introductory text.* Tempe, AZ.: Arizona State University, School of Social Work, 1978.

Brown, E. G. *Minority content and learning in the first year method classes.* New York: Council on Social Work Education, 1975.

Buffalohead, R. *Higher education of Indian students: 200 years of Indian education.* Tempe, AZ.: Center for Indian Education, Arizona State University, 1976.

Chunn, J. Integrating minority content into the social work curriculum: A model based on Black perspective and principles. In *Black perspectives on social work education.* New York: Council on Social Work Education, 1974.

Compton, J. *Social work education for American Indians.* Denver, CO.: Center for Social Research and Development, University of Denver, 1976.

Council on Social Work Education. *Guidelines for implementation of accreditation 1234A.* New York: Author, 1973.

Foerster, L., & Soldier, D. What's new and good in Indian education. *Educational Leadership*, 1975, 192.

Gollattscheck. J. F. *College leadership for community renewal.* San Francisco: Jossey-Bass, Inc., 1976.

Kneller, G. *Educational anthropology.* New York: John Wiley & Sons, 1965.

Leigh, J. Ethnic content in field instruction. In C. W. McCann (Ed.), *Perspectives on ethnic minority content in social work education.* Boulder, CO.: Western Interstate Commission on Higher Education, 1972.

Mager, R. *Preparing instructional objectives.* Palo Alto, CA.: Fearon Publishers, 1962.

McDanfield, M. Tomorrow's curriculum today. In A. Toffler (Ed.), *Learning for tomorrow.* New York: Vintage Books, 1974.

Montiel, M. Research perspectives in ethnic communities of color. Paper presented at the Graduate School of Social Work, University of Houston, 1976. (Typescript)

Norton, D. G. Implementation of minority content in social work education. A paper presented from a Black perspective at the Annual Program Meeting, Council on Social Work Education, 1978.

Ross-Sheriff, F. Implementation of minority content in social work education. Paper presented at the Annual Program Meeting of the Council on Social Work Education, Boston, Massachusetts, 1979. (Typescript)

Shaughnessy, T. F., & Brown, E. F. Developing Indian content in social work education: A community-based curriculum model. In *Multicultural education and the American Indian.* Los Angeles: University of California, American Indian Studies Center, 1979.

Tyler, R. *Principles of curriculum development.* Chicago: University of Chicago Press, 1950.

Bibliography

Brown, E. F. Self-determination for Indian communities: A dilemma for social work education and practice. In F. J. Pierce (Ed.), *Mental health services and social work education with Native Americans.* Norman, OK.: University of Oklahoma, School of Social Work, 1977.

Brown, E. F. *A conceptual framework for the study and analysis of Indian communities.* Tempe, AZ.: Arizona State University, School of Social Work, 1978. (a)

Brown, E. F. American Indians in modern society: Implications for social policy and services. In D. G. Norton (Ed.), *The dual perspective: Inclusion of ethnic minority content in the social work curriculum.* New York: Council on Social Work Education, 1978. (b)

Brown, E. F., & Shaugnessy, T. F. (Eds.). *Education for social work practice with American Indian families: Instructor's manual.* Tempe, AZ.: Arizona State University, School of Social Work, 1979.

Bryde, J. F. *Indian students and guidance.* Boston: Houghton Mifflin, 1971. (a)

Bryde, J F. *Modern Indian psychology.* Vermillion, SD.: University of South Dakota, 1971. (b)

Dieppa, I. Ethnic minority content in the social work curriculum: A position statement. In *Perspectives on ethnic minority content in social work education.* Boulder, CO.: Western Interstate Commission for Higher Education, June 1972.

Farris, C. E. The American Indian: Social work education's neglected minority. *Journal of Education for Social Work,* 1975, 2, (1), 37–43.

Lewis, R. G., & Man, K. H. Social work with Native Americans. *Social Work,* 1975, 20(5), 379–82.

Longres, J. The impact of racism on social work education. *Journal of Education for Social Work,* 1972, 8 (1), 50–59.

Mackey, J. E. *American Indian task force report.* New York: Council on Social Work Education, 1973.

Pierce, F. J. (Ed.). *Mental health services and social work education with Native Americans.* Norman, OK.: University of Oklahoma, School of Social Work, 1977.

Roberts, R. W. Systemic carriers to recruitment, retention, and promotion of ethnic minority faculty in schools of social work. *Social Work Education Reporter,* 1972.

Robertson, M. E. Inclusion of content on ethnic and racial minorities in the social work curriculum. In *Ethnic minorities in social work education.* New York: Council on Social Work Education, 1970.

Scott, C. A. Ethnic minority content in social work education. In *The current scene in social work education.* New York: Council on Social Education, 1971.

Wanberg, L. D. Historical perspective of the Indian dilemma: The character of Native American culture in modern conflict. DSW dissertation, University of Denver, 1973.

Wright, A. R., & Hammons, M. A. *Guidelines for Peace Corps crosscultural training.* Estes Park, CO.: Center for Research and Education, 1970.

L. YVONNE BACARISSE   RAMON M. SALCIDO

CHAPTER **8**

Integration of Hispanic Content in Social Work Curricula

Leaders in social work education still look forward to the full integration of Hispanic content in mental health curricula. All too often such
content is merely an adjunct to the main body of curricula. Although
course descriptions, syllabi and bibliographies abound with references
to Hispanic content, little of the information is systematized in
instruction, and the resulting sporadic treatment ill equips students
of social work to serve their Hispanic clientele. Inadequate integration
of Hispanic content has serious drawbacks in training social workers
to pay attention to the particular problems and mental health service
needs posed by an increasing Hispanic population and clientele.[1]

The Hispanic population trends during the 1970s bring challenges
to the profession to include Hispanic content and practice throughout
the curricula if social work education programs are to graduate students
capable of meeting the multiple needs of heterogeneous populations
of different Hispanic origins and cultures. In 1970 9.6 million people
of Spanish origin lived in the United States. By 1974 there had been
an increase to 11.2 million and by 1979 to slightly more than 12
million (U.S. Bureau of the Census, 1980). According to the 1979
estimate, 7.3 million of the Hispanic population were of Mexican
origin, 1.7 million of Puerto Rican, 794,000 of Cuban and 840,000 of
Central and South American, while 1.3 million reported they were of
"other" Spanish origin. Added to these are an estimated 6 million
undocumented aliens, predominantly from Mexico (Salcido, 1979d).

These population trends, of course, promise more Hispanic people
to come. Although projections vary widely, it is estimated that by the
year 2000 the number of Hispanic Americans may increase to 55
million (Macias, 1977). More conservative estimates predict that
Hispanics will become the largest ethnic minority in the United States.
The population data also show that the Hispanic population is clustered
in low-income occupational ranks, which makes them a high-risk

population. The impact is already felt in the inordinately increasing numbers of the Hispanic population turning to social and mental health centers, which are all too often staffed by social workers unable to provide culturally relevant services to Hispanic clients. The personnel believe that their professional education is deficient in treatment of Hispanics. Moreover, many social workers abandon this target population in favor of middle-class, mainly white clientele whom their theories of behavior and practice "fit." Just when the need for social workers trained to serve Hispanics is increasing, inadequate education and negative attitudes are turning practitioners away from meeting the mental health needs of Hispanics.

Social work educational programs are necessarily implicated in the flight of social workers from the challenges presented by the Hispanic population. Despite the increasing numbers of Hispanic students and the inclusion of Hispanic descriptive literature, Hispanic content has been "left out in the cold" through good intentions but failing strategies. For example, it is difficult to mandate specific curriculum content in a profession which can choose among myriad roles and tasks for which educational programs have utilized a wide variety of theoretical frameworks. Thus, the pronouncements of the Council on Social Work Education with regard to inclusion of Hispanic content are broad and abstract; concrete and uniform guidelines need to be developed to permeate social work curricula. To date, despite efforts to include Hispanic content, the content has not been incorporated into theories of human behavior and theories of practice and social policy. Hispanic content remains outside the main bodies of thought and practice modalities to the extent that it is relegated to a second-class position in curriculum development. However, attempts to bring Hispanic content into the mainstream of social work curricula show the beginnings of a good faith effort. The problem is how to change those efforts of social work educators into a commitment to include Hispanic content as an integral part of the curriculum.

This chapter provides a partial review of the literature of Hispanic content, a discussion of the theoretical models needed in imparting Hispanic content, recommendations for further research and suggested strategies for developing an integrative framework for culturally relevant Hispanic content for social work practice in mental health.

Review of the Literature

A partial review of the articles in professional social work journals reveals the trends in the literature that is available to students and the profession. Unfortunately, the available material deals only with Chicano and Puerto Rican clients. Seemingly, there has been little attention to other groups.

Much that has been written about the characteristics of Chicanos and Puerto Ricans is of a descriptive nature, with much discussion of racism and of the value differences between Chicano groups and the majority culture. Yet the discussion of value differences includes limited information on the various kinds of knowledge needed for effective cross-cultural social work practice in mental health. In general, the descriptive literature stops short of explaining how to use such knowledge in course development and in practice.

To determine how much of the descriptive literature could be applied to course work and professional practice, we reviewed articles from the *Journal of Education for Social Work, Social Work* and *Social Casework* between January 1964 and October 1979. Twenty-one articles were reviewed on Chicano content and twelve on Puerto Rican content (see Appendix 1). Table 1 shows the total number of articles published in three-year spans from 1964 to 1979. The selection of articles was based on titles and abstracts specifically pointing to Chicano and Puerto Rican content. Using this criterion for the mini-study carries the built-in limitation of excluding other social work articles that may be used in courses and practice. Books and other journals were not covered. By no means does this review of the literature reflect all that social work has to say on Chicano and Puerto Rican content, but it does allow some inferences and statements to be drawn about the state of art during those fifteen years.

Table 1 compares the dates of publication of Puerto Rican and Chicano articles appearing in social work journals. Publication of Puerto Rican articles did not catch up to the publication of Chicano articles until the mid-1970s. The articles on Puerto Ricans published between 1972 and 1975 were concerned with racism, social justice, the Puerto Rican community and social work practice. No articles were written about ex-offenders, gangs or the elderly. Nor were there any articles on divorce, child abuse, sexuality or health needs. The last four articles, published between 1976 and 1979, focused on the Puerto Rican culture, awareness and spiritualism. During the late 1970s no articles were written about research findings that related to the needs of the Puerto Rican or social work practice knowledge needed to work with the population.

The publication dates of Chicano articles in social work journals tell a slightly different story. Of the twenty-one Chicano articles

TABLE 1

Number of Articles on Chicanos and Puerto Ricans, by Year

Articles	1964– 1967	1968– 1971	1972– 1975	1976– 1979	Total
Chicano	—	9	8	4	21
Puerto Rican	—	—	8	4	12

reviewed, 81 percent were published between 1971 and 1975, compared to 66 percent of articles published about Puerto Ricans during the early years of the 1970s. The remaining 29 percent of Chicano articles were spread over eight of the fifteen years studied, with a heavier concentration of articles during the last years of the 1960s and a slackening in number during the last half of the 1970s. No articles were published about Chicanos during the middle years of the 1960s. Considering the Civil Rights movement of the 1960s, it appears that the social work profession was slow to recognize the need for Hispanic content and was reactive in complying with the need. Worse, the overdue recognition was rapidly diminishing as the 1970s came to a close.

But the mid-1970s offered more hope for achievement both within and outside the profession. The articles appearing between 1972 and 1975 were concerned, for the most part, with social justice for Chicanos and the same number of articles showed the same concern for Puerto Ricans. The articles about Chicanos specifically treated Chicanos who were bilingual and bicultural almost to the exclusion of other topics of interest to the profession. Only one article focused on the elderly Mexican American. No articles were written specifically about ex-offenders or gangs. Nor were any articles published about problems such as divorce, child abuse, or health needs among Chicanos—just as none were written about Puerto Ricans. A look at this pattern suggests that some subgroups and subjects of customary social work concern may have been overlooked because of the values and interests of the authors.

Similar conspicuous absences appeared in articles about social work practice. Only three articles gave general suggestions on how to work with Spanish-speaking Chicanos, but they offered no practice principles.[2] Only one article presented a training model in which Chicano content can be applied to mental health training and schools of social work.[3] The lack of articles that describe how to apply Chicano or Puerto Rican content in the practice setting is one of the overall shortcomings of the available literature.

While the literature is somewhat limited in usable practice content, it is abundantly rich in those areas the authors deemed to be more significant kinds of knowledge. Table 2 shows the kinds of knowledge the authors developed in their social work articles, with cultural differences and experiences of racism appearing more frequently than other topics in both Puerto Rican and Chicano literature. Family structure is also a major theme, but it appears slightly less frequently in Puerto Rican than in Chicano literature. Of course, it is only fair to note that cultural differences, racism and family structure are cited in the majority of articles to substantiate the themes of the authors rather than as part of a discussion of kinds of knowledge the social worker needs or its application to mental health practice. Only one

TABLE 2

Major Themes in Articles on Chicanos and Puerto Ricans

Themes	Chicano	Puerto Rican
Cultural differences	6	4
Experience of racism	6	3
Family structure	3	1
Language	1	—
Community structure	1	2
Politics	—	2
Social system theory	1	—
Warmth, empathy, genuineness	1	—

Chicano article undertook the application of knowledge in reporting a study of clients' perceptions of helping relationships formed with social workers of an ethnic background different from their own.[4] The study reported that Anglo clients and Chicano clients were positive in characterizing initial helping relationships with social workers of different cultural backgrounds, but all the Chicano clients who spoke Spanish were excluded from the sample. So were documented and undocumented immigrants. Nor were the clients asked if they preferred social workers of the same ethnic background. No doubt all these factors would have influenced the results of the study had they been included.

Table 2 also shows that politics and interest in the Puerto Rican community have been greater concerns in Puerto Rican than in Chicano literature. One explanation for this anomaly may be the values of the authors favoring these areas.

The abiding concerns of the authors with the effects of racism and cultural differences in both Puerto Rican and Chicano literature provide social workers with background that can help them to become more sensitive to Hispanic populations. It should be noted that there were no articles on Chicano or Puerto Rican content that had any relationship with practice knowledge needed by social workers for working with Hispanic clients. When we view the state of Hispanic content in social work education and in the profession, we find gaps. It will be especially important to gather information about other Hispanic groups, which will undoubtedly increase significantly in American society during the 1980s. Second, Hispanic literature should be developed and the content derived from research that specifically addresses the practice concerns of our profession. Unfortunately, the existing descriptive literature is not being utilized properly in our classrooms, in our field practice or in the delivery of mental health services. By broadening the literature and data base into all areas of social work practice we will spread the content throughout the discipline instead of creating Hispanic matrices that are outside the theories of behavior, practice and policy.

Frameworks

There have been attempts to find a framework to integrate Hispanic content in social work curriculum. Some promising trends as well as problems have emerged as a result of these efforts. Two requirements become apparent if these efforts are to be successful. First, there must be a minority presence in social work education programs. Faculty, students and field placements are necessary to sustain a commitment to the development of an integral Hispanic curriculum. Second, minority content must be placed within the framework of theories of human behavior, theories of practice, research and social policy content. An examination of some prevalent frameworks will give us an idea of where minority content can fit into existing theories of behavior and practice. We will also examine ethnic-specific systems and the use of Hispanic content in seeking a truly viable integrative framework.

Solomon's framework provides one option for integrating Hispanic content into the curriculum. Solomon utilizes ethnosystem and empowerment as the major integrative concepts. She writes:

> Combining the two concepts, we create "ethnosystem," which must by definition then comprise groups which vary in modes of communication, in degree of control over material resources, and in the structure of their internal relationships or social organization. Moreover, these groups must be in a more or less stable pattern of relationships which have characteristics transcending any single group's field of integration; e.g., the ethnosystem's political, educational, or economic subsystems (Solomon, 1976, p. 46).

Mental health educators and professionals could use the concept of ethnosystem in creating culturally sensitive Hispanic curriculum content and for providing services to Hispanics. Ethnosystems are the natural networks, the primary patterns of interaction, survival, and adjustment indigenous to societies. As used here, the concept of "natural networks" has its origins in several disciplines: social work, sociology, social psychology and anthropology, as well as in the mental health "community support–significant others" literature. Mental health curriculum developers need to familiarize themselves with the growing body of literature which provides information about natural networks and primary patterns of interactions among the Hispanics and their viability for providing knowledge of as well as access to members from different Hispanic groups.[5] Curriculum developers need to be aware, also, that these natural networks and primary systems exist apart from the usual modes of secondary interactions that Hispanics have developed for survival within Anglo-urbanized systems, including the mental health establishment. Obviously, there is a basic similarity between the ethnosystem with secondary interaction for coping with the Anglo society and the concept of two environments, the immediate or nuturing environment and the wider environment. When, as Norton notes, the larger societal system rejects the minority group's immediate environment or ethnosystem,[6] there is incongruence between the two, and power blocks are directed toward the minority individuals, groups and communities (Norton, 1978).

There are similar parallels between Norton's concept of "reversible thought," borrowed from Piaget (the ability and conscious motivation to think about the situation being observed and to look for points of conflict, difference and congruence with the larger society) and Solomon's idea of the nonracist practitioner as one who should "possess the ability to perceive in any behavior—other's or one's own—alternative ways to explain that behavior, particularly those which the self might most strongly reject as false" (Solomon, 1976, p. 313).

Likewise, these same themes are evident in the works of Valle (1979), who discusses the development of culturally plural curriculum content. Valle, as in Solomon's description of the nonracist practitioner, points out that "one must learn to look behind apparent actions in order to come to an appreciative understanding of a belief system's impact on pluralism and intergroup homogeneity." Thorough explorations of values and beliefs can show that similar actions may be based on quite different normative understandings. This explanation is an important point for mental health educators and practitioners if we are to break Anglo-bound interpretations in treating Hispanic clients. As Herskovitz says in delineating cultural relevance, "The very definition of what is normal or abnormal is relative to the cultural frame of reference" (Herskovitz and Herskovitz, 1972, p. 66). He warns mental health practitioners to proceed with caution in using the terminology of mental health, including such terms as *normal* and *abnormal*, because of their connotations of psychic instability, emotional imbalance and departure from normality. Herskovitz suggests using other words that do not invite such distortion of cultural reality. To avoid falling into the distorted-perception traps set by mental health terminology, a culturally relevant designation of "normal" would be useful.

One such designation, the concept of "empowerment" in Solomon's ethnosystem framework, holds interest for developing a paradigm for use in treating Hispanic and minority clients. Empowerment is the gaining of an ability "to manage emotions, knowledge, skills, or material resources in a way that makes possible effective performance of valued social roles so as to receive personal gratification" (Solomon 1976, p. 28). If these gains are made within the context of the ethnosystem of the specific Hispanic or minority culture, the individual patient and/or the groups of that culture may be seen in a positive light from the mental health practitioner's point of view. The natural network of ethnosystems and their empowerment of the individuals and groups within them should be utilized in treatment of Hispanic and minority clients. Social scientists with diverse perspectives—Edmonson, Suttles, and Kent, as well as Roth and Novak—all point to the extensive and well-organized indigenous or naturalistic coping systems utilized by Anglo- and Northern-European-style human service delivery systems as current examples of mutualistic institutions relying upon the combination of formal and informal resources in assisting clients (Valle 1979).

Just as important as understanding the impact of the ethnosystem on normative values and group homogeneity is the understanding of intergroup heterogeneity if we are to remove the stereotypes surrounding the various Hispanic cultures. Although Hispanic clients may appear to be homogeneous because of the commonalities in their background—the Spanish Catholic tradition, the colonial experience, the importance of family, the common language—they constitute a culturally heterogeneous population. Once we have penetrated below the surface of secondary values and norms, intergroup heterogeneity is very evident within even just one ethnic minority population. Individuals of each Hispanic population (e.g., Mexican or Cuban) vary in identity based on national origin and in sociocultural and demographic characteristics. The psychic structure must be understood in this context of diverse roots and different vernaculars. Recognition of this cultural heterogeneity is especially important when considering the provisions of mental health services and the development of a Hispanic cross-cultural paradigm (Bacarisse 1979).

Furthermore, intergenerational differences are important to keep in mind as well. As Romano (1969) has indicated, Mexican-Americans (Chicanos) can be said to live three histories at once. In this same context, for example, Issei and Nisei, first- and second-generation Japanese, are quite different groups within the same ethnic designation, namely, Japanese Americans. Each has had different mixes of psychohistorical experiences (Valle 1979). Spanish-speaking populations with different points of national origin are also quite different cultural subgroups. Cubans and Puerto Ricans have different national roots. Native Americans first and foremost stress tribal identities. Blacks are not at all culturally monolithic, but rather demonstrate considerable sociocultural diversity. Black ethnics of Caribbean origin cannot be automatically lumped with other Blacks, whose roots are primarily in highly industralized North American environments. One has only to explore the distinctly verifiable phenomena of Black and regional English to capture differentials in the normative outlooks of this ethnic minority cohort.

This last observation about dialect and language differences within the same, albeit heterogeneous, culture is a relatively unexplored theme that Valle advances as a ready access point for the development of culturally specific course content. Language holds considerable promise for the construction of culturally sensitive curriculum paradigms. For example, the cultural heroes and the folk art of specific ethnosystems and identity groups gives an appreciative understanding of the groups' uniqueness. Linguists, such as Sapir (1970) and Whorf (1971), have been keenly aware of the function of language and symbols in shaping perception (Valle 1979). Many groups in the United States, such as Latinos, still retain their language of origin with English as a second language. Within these ethnic languages, many clues to mutual relationships and group values can also be readily detected. For example, Spanish contains a variety of forms of address which can tell the culturally syntonic observer such things as the status differences between individuals, as well as relational closeness and social distance.

Language also yields significant understanding about ways of coping and helping by the tense, style and syntax of speech. In Spanish, one does not announce to others that one is there to help, rather one asks "permission" to be of help. "Let me be of help" does not translate culturally to *dejenos ayudarlos* but to *permítanos ayudarle*, with the accent on "permit us" to be of assistance. Subtle as they may appear, these nuances often provide the key to the professional's success in making contact with Hispanic clients and the client's willingness to utilize services. Such understanding is critical to the formation of culturally specific curricula.

Developing the Hispanic mental health curriculum means removing the Anglo assumptions and stereotypes embedded in our mental health models that do not apply to Hispanic populations. Constructing the curriculum requires that curriculum developers reestablish the foundations of mental health with paradigms particular to the Hispanic cultures they are intended to serve. Unbinding our thinking from Anglo components and using Hispanic norms calls for flexibility in our thinking and alternative ways of looking at behavior which utilizes cultural cues such as language. Curriculum developers should utilize the suggested frameworks presented by Solomon to build an awareness of not only the influence of ethnosystems upon each Hispanic culture, but also differences within each culture. Imparting Hispanic content within these frameworks would combine formal mental health training based on culturally relevant paradigms with training in the indigenous coping systems proven successful in the delivery of services for ethnic populations. Studying Hispanic content in a culturally specific framework will give students of social work the background and practice they need to assist the Hispanic populations that increasingly use their services.

Theory Development

Erecting the framework for Hispanic content obviously depends upon developing culturally relevant theories to contain that content within the boundaries of each specific ethnic group and to avoid irrelevant theories or insupportable generalizations about all Hispanics. Thus, our main need in terms of theory development is to clarify culture and remove long-standing confusion of culture with conditions visited upon and observed in, but not indigenous to, Hispanic ethnic cultures. The confusion of culture with the conditions of, for instance, poverty and race, has led to mistaken identities of ethnics by social scientists and consequent erroneous views of mental health among ethnic groups. Culture, as used in mental health circles, assumes a very restricted definition tied to the simplistic enumeration of stray ethnic minority-group behaviors. Ethnic minority curriculum paradigms cannot be appropriately developed if the distinctions are not made between cultural characteristics specific to the ethnic group and the distinctly different subsets within the group, such as social class or race. To clear up this confusion, we will, first, define culture as "that binding energy generated among individuals and groups on the basis of shared appreciative elements." Kluckhohn (1949) has succinctly described the thrust of this definition to include implicit as well as explicit patterns of behavior expressed in symbols, artifacts and the values attached to historically desired ideas. Second, we will draw the distinction between subsets within cultures and actual cultural characteristics. Third, we will isolate the cultural information, as stated in the definition, needed to build theory in a Hispanic mental health curriculum.

Poverty and Culture

Cassavantes, speaking specifically about Mexican-Americans, indicated that cultural variables need to be distinguished from socioeconomic indicators (Valle, 1979). Poverty and culture are not synonymous. Yet since the reification of the "culture of poverty" by social scientist Oscar Lewis, a multiplicity of conceptual problems have plagued strategies for change related to ethnic populations.

Reading Stephen Rose's *Betrayal of the Poor* makes one aware that reliance on the "culture of poverty" concept reversed the spirit of the Office of Economic Opportunity (OEO) social change experiment (Rose, 1972). Although development of cultural pluralism in a curriculum was not Rose's principal theme, it is clear to those directly familiar with the OEO experiment that the strategies used did not reflect an understanding of the different cultures of the ethnic populations involved. Poor Chinese, Blacks, Asians and Native Americans are not culturally identical. Each of these groups has what Alvarez terms separate psychohistorical experiences which are clearly not coequal just because the groups are poor (Valle 1979).

Social Class and Culture

Just as poverty is not synonymous with culture, neither is the concept of social class. Acquiring middle-class status is not the equivalent of losing one's ethnic heritage. It is, therefore, incorrect to cast upward mobility and cultural assimilation as synonymous. Nor is it supportable to state categorically that middle-class ethnics are ready to view social institutions that adhere to ethnic-majority formats as desirable or as necessarily sympathetic to their needs and value perspectives.

The concept of race also needs to be differentiated from culture. Conceptual distinction becomes immediately evident when a black-skinned, Spanish-speaking person from Latin America identifies as "Latino" rather than as "Black." The same applies when one encounters a very light-skinned Latino who will identify culturally as a Third World person and not as white. This is not to imply that races lack cultural heritage, but rather that specific cultures may well encompass many races.

Race and Culture

Now that we have defined what culture is and is not, we need to know what cultural information should be used in constructing theory for Hispanic content. Solomon's definition of the ethnosystem, quoted previously and described as the primary interaction pattern of the ethnic group, plus what Spicer (1971) terms as "persistent identity systems" may be useful in building theory. The Solomon ethnosystem pointed to the ethnic groups' variance in modes of communication, in their contact over material resources, and in the structure of the groups' internal relationships within a school organization as the building blocks of integrative curricula (Solomon, 1976). Spicer gives three criteria for discerning such ethnosystems or identity systems: (1) the language and symbols in use within particular groups; (2) the social relations and indigenous organizational structures, as well as the primary interactional processes of such groups; and (3) the shared values and belief systems of the particular groups.

Social Work Curriculum: Cross-Cultural Building Blocks

To paraphrase both authors, theory development requires learning the characteristics of the language, the meaning of symbols and the artifacts of the culture. More specifically, we will need to know how different Hispanic groups manage material goods, how each group is set up, how members identify themselves by culture and how status is differentiated among members of the culture. And we will need to know what beliefs and values members of different Hispanic groups have in common and their impact on the ethnosystem. In short, we distinguish one ethnic group from another by the cultural character-istics that meet Solomon's and Spicer's criteria. Acquiring the infor-mation on cultural charactertistics posed by these criteria will provide the material for developing theory within the ethnosystem framework for Hispanic content. It will also preserve intact the various distinctions between Hispanic groups. Developing theories along the lines of these cultural criteria will enable us to restructure the mental health curriculum paradigms using cultural information syntonic with each ethnic experience.

Similarly, accepting an Hispanic paradigm means that information brought to light by research is interpreted within the Hispanic cultural context and that this context is explained to and can be understood by non-Hispanics. The careful delineation among Hispanic cultures by Hispanic faculty will inculcate consciousness of ethnic distinctiveness among Anglo colleagues whose efforts to achieve cultural pluralism have been limited by Anglo-monocultural biases and by their lack of understanding of culture-specific differences.

Research

Research on the different Hispanic populations is needed in various areas. A subtask panel on Hispanic mental health found that, although the amount of research in the field has increased, much of it has been unsound (Special Populations Sub-Task Panel on Mental Health of Hispanic Americans, 1978). Padilla, Ruiz and Alvarez (1973) cite the weak methodological data, faulty analytic techniques, stereotypic interpretations, lack of replicability of findings and the absence of programmatic research. Quality has not kept pace with quantity, and even the increasing volume has left important areas untouched by research. Research is needed in the unstudied areas of health, sexuality, divorce and child abuse. The weaknesses and the enormous gaps in the available research show that Hispanic mental health knowledge has yet to become an integrated body of scientific knowledge.

For the mental health curriculum to be based accurately upon the Hispanic experience, research must avoid the pitfalls caused by the lack of knowledge and of understanding of the Hispanic culture and by the monocultural models of the Anglo's mental health system. Quality research will require development of knowledge based on reliable and valid information that is culturally sensitive and specific to Hispanics; and recognition of the diversity that exists among various populations with divergent sociocultural and demographic characteristics (Bacarisse 1979).

Subgroups of the Hispanic population—the undocumented aliens, the elderly, youth, and ex-offenders—require research to deliver a sound and complete picture of the diversity among Hispanic populations. Furthermore, investigation should include collection of information on the incidence and prevalence of Hispanic mental health disorders and should address complex problems of diagnosis and treatment approaches. As Arce (1979) stresses:

The question of relevance of services is nowhere more critical than in multicultural Hispanic content because diagnostic assessment tools and specific treatment interventions must account for the significant cultural differences if they are to be accessible and effective (p. 33).

It is incumbent upon our mental health curriculum developers to provide these necessary diagnostic assessment tools and treatment interventions. Creating the curriculum that will enable students of social work to provide the assessments and treatments needed by Hispanic clientele requires that we remove irrelevant Anglo-cultural components. We must realign the factual and value components of our judgments about mental health to fit a cross-cultural Hispanic paradigm that emerges from the shared intuitions and examples about the ethnic minority situation; draws from commonly understood and shared beliefs; utilizes similar symbolic generalizations; and is accorded an honorable place within the mental health disciplinary matrices.

In removing inappropriate Anglo-cultural components, curriculum developers need to be aware of the ways such components are contrary to the requirements of the Hispanic paradigm just described so as to avoid error. To begin with, the Anglo model of mental health presumes that mental health content is value-free information and is applicable across cultures. This idea follows Weber's (1949) methodology, which argues that we can keep our distance from the data and let the facts speak for themselves. It also holds that social inquiry proceeds best through the positing of ideal types and hypotheses, primarily using the deductive approach. Such ideas simply do not apply to a Hispanic paradigm. Even worse, they stand in the way of gaining any new understanding of the Hispanic populations (Valle 1979). The value-free pose is at odds with the outlook of the Hispanic professional who begins with the assumption that there is no escape from the biases he encounters everyday. The Hispanic professional sees prejudice on any number of levels and knows that "objective" or "value-free" information simply ignores reality. The Hispanic professional's own cultural background and outlook affect daily information-gathering, interpreting and reporting activities. Personal and enculturated values are inextricably tied to our assessments of mental health facts. In shaping the curriculum on the Hispanic paradigm, we are aware of the biases we bring to information and statistics.

Indeed, bias is everywhere evident to the Hispanic professional in the mental health profession because he is aware of his cultural duality by force of his own difference from the majority culture. Although it is easy to see the ethnic diversity, that diversity has not been behaviorally accepted or accurately reported. And while the profession has affirmed the value of cultural plurality, it remains more a goal than an accomplishment. The Hispanic professional has not seen acceptance of cultural plurality in terms of equal access to and impact upon mental health's knowledge, goals and resources, even though the wish is expressed by Anglo colleagues. Pantoja and Blourock (1975) have succinctly pointed out that, at the power level, well-meaning individuals have ignored the actual social reality of ethnic minority persons while pursuing the ideal of "cultural pluralism" (Valle 1979). Similarly, many scholars in social work have identified race as an important factor in the client-worker relationship, yet no studies or articles are devoted to describing the specific principles that would provide an understanding of racial issues. Nor has there been any research which systematically studies the characteristics of social workers who are preferred by Hispanic clients or the effects of ethnicity of the practitioner on the preferences and attitudes of Hispanic clients toward social workers (Salcido 1979a).

The phenomenon within the mental health profession of glossing over differences, or well-wishing, while actually ignoring the existence of cultural pluralism is cogently revealed in exchanges between majority-culture and Hispanic colleagues. When Hispanic colleagues attempt to impart to Anglo colleagues the meanings of primary-level relationships and belief systems unique to a Hispanic culture, Hispanics often find that ethnic distinctive aspects of behavior are downplayed. While Anglo as well as Hispanic colleagues may be aware of scholarship that supports the contention that ethnics of color do not "melt" into American culture, Hispanic colleagues are often frustrated by Anglos who, in the interest of "equity," deny the duality with which their Hispanic colleagues live. Yet an evaluation of the impact of culturally plural knowledge on the mental health establishment in social work and other fields shows that the attainment of equity and cultural pluralism is nowhere near the goal that is given so much lip-service.

In conclusion, to develop an integrated body of scientific knowledge upon which an Hispanic-culture paradigm can be based, we need to conduct systemic Hispanic mental health curriculum research. The research to come should avoid the pitfalls that characterized research of the past: fragmented knowledge base, lack of program, weak methodology and analysis that did not permit replication of findings but encouraged stereotypic interpretations. We recommend that research cover a full range of topics, not only in mental health but also in other health areas. Topics such as sexuality, familial patterns—including divorce and child abuse—the family as a support system, and use of medical services are examples of possible areas of research. Research should also cover all the significant subgroups among Hispanic populations. These include undocumented and documented aliens, youth, the elderly and ex-offenders. The information gained about these topics and their impact on the subgroups among the Hispanic populations will add substance to the true heterogeneity the mental health professionals encounter in clinics, with their increasing number of Hispanic clients.

Specific to the mental health profession itself, research should report the incidence and extent of mental health disorders among the various Hispanic populations. It will be particularly important to measure the effect of race upon the client–practitioner relationship, cited so often as a factor by social work scholars (Salcido, 1979a). Research should likewise assess the attitudes of clients toward mental health practitioners of the same and of different ethnic backgrounds. This may inform us about what characteristics clients prefer in their choice of mental health services. That same information should be incorporated in our mental health curricula to produce graduates able to relate to Hispanic clients of various origins. Research should be directed to the complex problems of diagnosis and treatment approaches among populations that require analyses based on the cultural context of the clients (Bacarisse 1979).

When adequate resources are allocated for research with and by Hispanics, and when the impacts of culture are studied as a regular part of the curriculum, we will believe that Hispanic cultural diversity is accepted as a part of the curriculum. A truly Hispanic curriculum will examine research in light of the cultural differences among Hispanic nations and clearly maintain the distinctions among them. Drawing these distinctions will equip social work students in the mental health curriculum with appropriate interpretations vested in the value and belief systems of different Hispanic nations.

As Hispanic cultural paradigms take the place of Anglo cultural ones, students will recognize the distinctions in the demographic and socio-cultural characteristics of each nationality. Using a Hispanic mental health paradigm requires that we adjust our thinking to make factual and not value judgments about mental health. A Hispanic cross-cultural mental health paradigm will start with "appreciative" assumptions that amount to an awareness of the cultural components shared by Hispanic cultures. Building the paradigm requires taking steps Schon advocates in basing the paradigm structure on information derived from linguistic and symbolic systems, their primary interactional behaviors, and their value and belief systems indigenous to the ethnic minority populations studied (Schon, 1963). The appreciative understandings of the paradigm acknowledge the assumptions inherent in the culture. Solomon's ethnosystem and Spicer's identity system essentially agree with the steps Schon advocates to integrate the curriculum. Curriculum developers have the responsibility of exposing the assumptions and values of language in marking the status of speakers and the use of symbols. It is also the job of curriculum developers to trace ethnosystems in main interactional patterns of Hispanic cultures. The development of these theories and research should take its rightful place within mental health disciplinary matrices.

Principles of Hispanic Integration

From the material presented previously, it is apparent that we must adhere to certain guidelines if we are to achieve a fully integrated Hispanic mental health curriculum. Listed below are four guidelines:

1. The full integration of the curriculum requires larger enrollment of Hispanic students, as well as more Hispanic faculty members, who should share in the responsibility for the development of curriculum. Significant numbers of students and faculty members are necessary to maintain the commitment to full integration of Hispanic content.

2. To be effective, Hispanic content must be based on cross-cultural Hispanic ethnic paradigms. The paradigms are syntonic with ethnic experience and establish appropriate standards of mental health for Hispanics.

3. Important distinctions among Hispanic cultures must be appreciated, including ethnosystems and values, belief systems of groups and language differences.

4. Research and faculty development are essential to the deepening of our knowledge of Hispanic cultural patterns.

Strategies for Institutional Change and Policy Recommendations

Education

Integration of Hispanic content into the mental health curriculum will require several strategies directed at education, training, delivery systems and funding. Social work educators in baccalaureate, master's, and doctoral programs located in areas where large concentrations of Hispanics form an integral part of the community should ensure that the programs include as one of their overall objectives the preparation of students for practice with Hispanics. The educational preparation of students in these programs should include content that enables them to demonstrate knowledge about the relevant minority population in the university service area. The social work curriculum offered by Arizona State University since 1978 is an example of an educational program that has included culturally relevant ethnic content (Salcido, 1979a). The commitment to this objective has been evident in the recruitment of ethnic minority faculty and students, with emphasis upon Indian, Chicano and Black populations, the inclusion of ethnic minority content in most classes and the provision of faculty development programs on ethnic minority content. We propose a similar program that includes recruitment drives to enroll more Hispanic students of all origins within the appropriate region and the awarding of teaching contracts to Hispanic faculty members. The Hispanic faculty members should take an active role not only in the development and implementation of a Hispanic curriculum offered in core course offerings but also in ensuring that appropriate Hispanic content is integrated into the curriculum. Minority content monitoring committees should be composed of the chairs of decision- and policy-making bodies and executives of agencies providing social services to Hispanic and other minority clients. It would be the responsibility of a monitoring committee to oversee the development of the minority curriculum; to provide guidance in research; to obtain feedback about the mental health curriculum from faculty, students and agencies serving Hispanic clients; and to evaluate the program. A "do-pass" would be necessary from the monitoring committee before approval of proposed courses in the mental health curriculum concerning Hispanics and other minorities.

In many instances policies need to be developed to implement these strategies and existing mechanisms need to be strengthened to ensure compliance. Council on Social Work Education (CSWE) standards for accreditation of B.S.W. and M.S.W. degree programs already exist, but compliance is spotty and enforcement by the CSWE is rare. Accreditation teams visiting program sites located in areas with large concentrations of Hispanics should always include a Hispanic. The council should also seek to broaden the representation of Hispanics on the board of directors, the Commission of Accreditation, various committees and in staff positions.[7]

Training

The second strategy requires the training of mental health practitioners, professionals and paraprofessionals, who are currently working with minorities, in particular with Hispanics, but who lack formal education and training to do so. Because a low level of cultural sensitivity exists among the majority of mental health service providers, training programs should be developed and made available on a regional, if not a national, basis. The training should include programs designed upon the Hispanic paradigm and developed from the Hispanic mental health curriculum. All assumptions made about these programs should be based upon requisite knowledge and skills essential to the provision of culturally relevant and appropriate mental health services for Hispanic populations.

Bilingual and Bicultural Model

The third strategy would restructure delivery systems on a bilingual and bicultural model. The restructuring would require organizing agency structures to ensure Hispanic representation on policy-planning and decision-making bodies. This might ease the organizational rigidity of mental health institutions which often hampers the development of appropriate services to Hispanic populations, discriminates against Hispanics seeking mental health services, and fosters the excessive use of treatment modalities that rarely take into consideration the realities of culture, language, mores, familial relationships, supports and so forth. The restructuring of delivery systems should combine a comprehensive range of services and geographic accessibility with equitable employment and development practices, service accessibility and acceptance by the Hispanic community, and immediate response to problems brought by community members. Service-delivery agency personnel should be fully integrated into the Hispanic communities they serve. Full integration means that members of the community may be utilized and that service-delivery personnel should be bilingual, with a working knowledge of the ethnosystems of cultures whose members are seen in the agencies. Such a model is currently used by El Centro Community Mental Health Center in East Los Angeles and the Miami Mental Health Clinic in Little Havana.

Funding

Of course, all of the previously described strategies will require that social work education programs be funded for developing the Hispanic mental health curriculum. Funds are also needed for research on theory and practice development, as well as on content development. Funding agencies need not only to provide incentives within selected grant programs to encourage these activities but also to develop mechanisms to ensure that funded programs are held accountable and to stop funding if programs are not meeting stated objectives.

Conclusion

Fully integrating Hispanic content through the mental health curricula in social work educational programs will require making changes on several levels. First, as educators we must realize that the Hispanic population increases substantially each year and will probably constitute the largest ethnic minority in the United States in the twenty-first century. The increasing number of Hispanics alone warrants that we as social work educators ensure that we are providing students with the necessary knowledge and tools to deliver culturally relevant and appropriate services to Hispanic populations. The majority of Hispanics work in high-risk occupations, are below the recognized poverty level, are poorly schooled, live in inadequate housing and in densely populated neighborhoods. These conditions threaten their sense of stability and mental health. Many Hispanics are turning to mental health clinics, but many more are inhibited from using mental health services that fail to address cultural factors and that lack mental health practitioners who are bilingual or trained to work primarily with Hispanics. One way to increase the potential for improved mental health service delivery and utilization by Hispanics is to train more culturally sensitive, bilingual and bicultural mental health workers.

Another is to recruit more students of Hispanic origin and to maintain a commitment to creating a fully integrated mental health curriculum in social work educational programs.

A large part of the responsibility for research will rest with Hispanic faculty members and students. Much empirical research is needed on demographic data, socioeconomic and cultural factors and other customary subjects of our profession. While our descriptive literature includes much of value in terms of racism and cultural differences, there are still large gaps that can be filled by research done by Hispanic students and faculty. With the increase in Hispanic students and faculty, research on Hispanic mental health will attain that presently far-off status of an integrated body of scientific knowledge on which we can draw to flesh out theories of behavior and practice.

Appendix 1
Articles with Chicano and Puerto Rican Content

Date	Author and Title	Publication Data
	CHICANO ARTICLES	
1971	Aguirre, L. R., The meaning of the Chicano movement	*Social Casework, 52* (5), 259-322
	Atencio, T. C., The survival of La Raza despite social services	
	Florez, J., Chicanos and coalitions as a force for social change	
	Garcia, A., The Chicano and social work	
	Knoll, F. R., Casework services for Mexican-Americans	
	Morales, A., The collective preconscious and racism	
	Ortega, P. D., The cultural renaissance	
	Solis, F., Socioeconomic and cultural conditions of migrant workers	
	Sotomayor, M., Mexican-American interaction with social systems	
1972	Aguilar, I., Initial contacts with Mexican-American families	*Social Work, 17* (5), 66–70
1973	Montiel, M., The Chicano family: A review of research	*Social Work, 18* (2), 11–23
1974	Maduro, R. J., & Martinez, C. F., Latino dream analysis: Opportunity for confrontation	*Social Casework, 55* (8), 461–69
	Souflee, F., & Schmitt, G., Education for practice in the Chicano community	*Journal of Education in Social Work, 10* (3), 75–84
1975	Santa Cruz, L. A., & Hepworth, D. H., News and views: Effects of cultural orientation on casework	*Social Casework, 56* (1), 52–57
	Boulette, T. R., Group therapy with low-income Mexican-Americans	*Social Work, 20* (5), 403–5
	Maldonado, D., The Chicano aged	*Social Work, 20* (3), 213–16
1976	Aguilar, I., & Wood, V. N., Therapy through a death ritual	*Social Work, 21* (1), 49–54
	Medina, C., & Reyes, M. R., Dilemmas of Chicano counselors	*Social Work, 21* (6), 515–17
1978	Morales, A., Institutional racism in mental health and criminal justice	*Social Casework, 59,* (7)
1979	Ebihara, H., A training program for bilingual paraprofessionals	*Social Casework, 60* (5), 274–81
1979	Salcido, R. M., Undocumented aliens: A study of Mexican families	*Social Work, 24* (4), 306–11
	PUERTO RICAN ARTICLES	
1972	Mizio, E., Puerto Rican social workers and racism	*Social Casework, 53* (5), 267–72
1973	De Rodriguez, L. V., Social work practice in Puerto Rico	*Social Work, 18* (2), 32–40
1974	Borrero, M., Cuadrado, L., & Rodriguez, E. R., The Puerto Rican role in interest-group politics	*Social Casework, 55* (2), 67–116
	Campos, A. P., Proposed strategy for the 1970s	

Date	Author and Title	Publication Data
	PUERTO RICAN ARTICLES (Cont.)	
	Delgado, M., Social work and the Puerto Rican community	
	Gonzalez, H., The struggle to develop self-help institutions	
	Longres, J. F., Jr., Racism and its effects on the Puerto Rican continentals	
	Mizio, E., Impact of external systems on the Puerto Rican family	
	Montalvo, B., Home-school conflict and the Puerto Rican child	
	Rivera, J. J., Growth of the Puerto Rican awareness	
1977	Delgado, M., Puerto Rican spiritualism and the social work profession	*Social Casework, 58* (8), 451–58
	Ghalig, J. B., Cultural sensitivity and the Puerto Rican	*Social Casework, 58* (8), 459–68

Notes

1. Our concern is with the integration of Hispanic content in social work education. Although all educational programs in social work should include substantial content on identifiable minorities, our recommendations are designed especially for areas in which students will have opportunities for field experience and subsequent employment with Hispanic populations. Obviously, a university in an area with a large concentration of a particular minority will be strongly influenced by its setting.

2. The articles are Knoll, F. R., Casework services for Mexican-Americans, in *Social Casework*, 1971, *52*(5), 259–322; Aguilar, I., Initial contacts with Mexican-American families, in *Social Work*, 1972, *17*(5), 66–70; Aguilar, I., & Wood, V. N., Therapy through a death ritual, in *Social Work*, 1976, *21*(1), 49–54.

3. The article is Souflee, F., & Schmitt, G., Education for practice in the Chicano community. In *Journal of Education for Social Work*, 1974, *10*(3), 75–84.

4. The article is Santa Cruz, L. A., & Hepworth, D. H., News and views: Effects of cultural orientation on casework. In *Social Casework*, 1975, *56*(1), 52–57.

5. This will be mentioned again in our discussion of the normative values and language limitations practitioners need to be aware of in treating the various Hispanic populations.

6. Solomon refers to this as negative valuation of a stigmatized collective.

7. The reporting procedure of the Council on Social Work Education needs to be improved. The council continues to recognize only two Hispanic groups, Puerto Rican and Chicano, making it impossible to report statistics on other Hispanic students or faculty members or to recognize the cultural plurality and identification with natural origin that may exist. The council should use the Equal Employment Opportunity Commission definition of *Hispanic*, which is used by the Census Bureau, the School Reporting Committee of the Office of Civil Rights, the National Center for Educational Statistics and others. Under that definition Hispanics are "persons of Mexican, Puerto Rican, Cuban, Central or South American, or other Spanish culture or origin—regardless of race." The present council practice of identifying only Puerto Ricans and Chicanos is resulting in a serious underreporting of Hispanic students and faculty members and the disenfranchisement of other Hispanic students and faculty members in constituent groups recognized by the council.

References

Arce, A. Mental health policy and the hispanic community. In J. Szapocznik (Ed.), *Mental health drug and alcohol abuse: An Hispanic assessment of present and future challenges.* Washington, D.C.: National Coalition of Hispanic Mental Health and Human Service Organizations, 1979.

Bacarisse, L. Y. Cultural diversity among Hispanics: Implications for social work education. Unpublished manuscript presented at the Mental Health Curriculum Development Conference held by Howard University School of Social Work, Chicago, Illinois, November, 1979.

Herskovitz, M., & Herskovitz, F. *Cultural relationism: Perspectives in cultural pluralism.* New York: Vintage Books, 1972.

Kluckhohn, C. *Mirror for man: The relation of anthropology to modern life.* New York: McGraw-Hill, 1949.

Norton, D. G. *The dual perspective: Inclusion of ethnic minority content in the social work curriculum.* New York: Council on Social Work Education, 1978.

Padilla, A. M., Ruiz, R. A., & Alvarez, R. Community mental health services for the Spanish-speaking/surnamed population, *American Psychologist,* 1973, *30,* 892–905.

Pantoja, A., & Blourock, B. Cultural pluralism redefined. In A. Pantoja, B. Blourock, & J. Bowman (Eds.), *Badges and indicia of slavery: Cultural pluralism redefined.* Lincoln, NB.: University of Nebraska, 1975.

Romano, O. The historical and intellectual presence of Mexican Americans. *El Grito,* 1969, *2* (2), 13–26.

Rose, S. M. *The betrayal of the poor: The transformation of community action.* Cambridge, MA.: Schenkman, 1972.

Salcido, R. M. Chicano content in social work: The state of the art. Unpublished manuscript presented at the Mental Health Curriculum Development Conference held by Howard University School of Social Work in Chicago, Illinois, 1979 (a)

Salcido, R. M. Undocumented aliens: A Study of Mexican families. *Social Work,* 1979, *24,* 306–11. (b)

Sapir, E., & Handlebaum, D. (Eds.). *Culture, language, and personality.* Berkeley, CA.: University of California Press, 1970.

Schon, D. *Displacement of concepts.* London: Tavis-stock Publications, 1963.

Solomon, B. *Black empowerment: Social work in oppressed communities.* New York: Columbia University Press, 1976.

Special Populations Sub-Task Panel on Mental Health of Hispanic-Americans. *Report to the President's Commission on Mental Health.* Los Angeles: Spanish-Speaking Mental Health Research Center, University of California at Los Angeles, 1978.

Spicer, E. H. Persistent cultural systems: A comparative study of identity systems that can adapt to contrasting environments. *Science,* 1971, *174* (4011), 795–800.

U.S. Bureau of the Census. Persons of Spanish origin in the United States: 1980. *Current population reports,* Series P-20, No. 328. Washington, D.C.: U.S. Government Printing Office, 1980.

Valle, R. Ethnic minority curriculum in mental health: Latino/Hispano perspectives. Unpublished manuscript presented at the Mental Health Curriculum Development Conference held by Howard University School of Social Work in Chicago, Illinois, 1979.

Weber, M. *The methodology of the social sciences.* Glencoe, IL.: The Free Press, 1949.

Whorf, B. T., & Carroll, J. B. (Ed.). *Language, thought, and reality.* Cambridge, MA.: M.I.T. Press, 1971.

Bibliography

Abrahams, R., & Troike, D. (Eds.). *Language and cultural diversity in American society.* Englewood Cliffs, N.J.: Prentice-Hall, 1972.

Alfero, L. Conscientizacion. In *New themes in social work education.* New York: International Association of Schools of Social Work, 1972.

Alvarez, S. Mexican American community organization. *El Grito* 1971, *4* (7), 68–77.

Alvarez, R. The unique psycho-historical experience of the Mexican American people. *Social Science Quarterly,* 1972, *52,* 15–29.

Cassavantes, E. *A new look at the attitudes of the Mexican American.* Albuquerque, N.M.: Southwest Cooperative Education Laboratory, 1969.

Centro del Barrio Bilingual-Bicultural Teaching-Learning Center. *Chicano culture and mental health.* San Antonio: Worden School of Social Service, Our Lady of the Lake University, 1978.

Clark, M., & Kierfer, C. W. Social change and intergenerational relations in Japanese and Mexican Americans. Unpublished paper, Langly Porter Neuropsychiatric Institute, San Francisco, 1973.

Colley, C. Primary groups. In P. H. Hare, E. Borgatta, & R. Bales (Eds.), *Small groups: Studies in social interactions.* New York: Alfred A. Knopf, 1955.

Dohrenwend, B. P., & Dohrenwend, Barbara S. *Social status and psychological disorders.* New York: John Wiley & Sons, 1969.

Edmonson, M. S. Los Manitos: A study of institutional values. In M. Edmonson, C. Madsen, & J. Collier (Eds.), *Contemporary American culture.* New Orleans: Middle American Research Institute, 1968.

Freire, P. *Education for a critical consciousness.* New York: Seabury Press, 1973.

Glaser, B., & Strauss, A. S. *The discovery of grounded theory.* Chicago: Aldine Publishing Company, 1967.

Hamilton, C. Black social scientists: Contributions and problems. In J. Ladner (Ed.), *The death of white sociology.* New York: Vintage Books, 1973.

Hamovitch, M. B. One school's attack on institutional racism. *Social Work Papers,* 1974, *12,* 1–8.

Harm, M. G. (Ed.). *A report of the Community Mental Health Practice-Education Project.* New York: Council on Social Work Education, 1978.

Herskovitz, M. *Man and his works: The science of cultural anthropology.* New York: Knopf, 1947.

Houston, S. H. Black English. *Psychology Today,* 1973, 6 (10) 45–48.

Ishizuka, K. The elder Japanese. Monograph, *Cross Cultural Minority Aged Series.* San Diego, California: Campanile Press, San Diego State University, 1977.

Kardiner, A. *The psychological frontiers of society.* New York: Columbia University Press, 1970.

Katz, A. J. (Ed.). *Community mental health.* New York: Council on Social Work Education, 1979.

Kent, J. A descriptive approach to a community. Videotape lecture at Boulder, Colorado, Western Interstate Commission on Higher Education, 1971.

Kuhn, T. *The structure of scientific revolutions.* Chicago: University of Chicago Press, 1970.

Kurtz, D. The rotating credit association: An adaptation to poverty. *Human Organization,* 1973, *32* (1), 49–58.

Latino Task Force on Community Mental Health Training. *Latino community mental health.* Monograph No. 1, Spanish-Speaking Mental Health Center, University of California at Los Angeles, 1974.

Leighton, A. *Studying personality cross culturally.* New York: Harper and Row, 1961.

Leighton, A. Cross cultural psychiatry. In J. Murphy, & H. Leighton (Eds.), *Approaches to cross cultural psychiatry.* Ithaca, NY.: Cornell University Press, 1965.

Lewis, O. The culture of poverty. *Scientific American,* 1966, *215* (4), 19–25.

Lurie, A., & Rosenberg, G. *Social work in mental health.* New York: Long Island Jewish-Hillside Medical Center, 1976.

Novak, M. *The rise of the unmeltable ethnics.* New York: McMillan Company, 1972.

Penalosa, F., & McDonaugh, E. C. Social mobility in a Mexican-American community. *Social Forces,* 1966, *44* (4), 498–505.

Press, I. The incidence of Compadrazgo among Puerto Ricans in Chicago. *Social and Economic Studies,* 1963, *12* (4), 475–81.

Rothman, J. *Planning and organization for social change.* New York: Columbia University Press, 1974.

Rubin, A. *Community mental health in the social work curriculum.* New York: Council on Social Work Education, 1979.

Salcido, R. M. Need: Hypertension research for Mexican-Americans. *Public Health Reports,* 1979, *94* (10), 372–75.

Salcido, R. M. Problems of the Mexican-American elderly in an urban setting. *Social Casework,* 1979, *60,* 609–15.

Seward, J. M., & Marmor, J. *Psychotherapy and culture conflict.* New York: Ronald Press, 1956.

Solomon, B., & Stanford, P (Eds.). *Growing old in the ethno-systems.* San Diego, CA.: San Diego State University, Campanile Press, 1974.

Suttles, G. *The social order of the slum: Ethnicity and territory in the inner city.* Chicago: University of Chicago Press, 1968.

Valle, R. Amistad-Compadrazgo as an indigenous webwork compared with the urban mental health network. Unpublished dissertation, Los Angeles, University of Southern California, 1974.

Valle, R. *The elder Latino.* San Diego, CA.: San Diego State University, Caminile Press,1978.

Vickers, G. *The art of judgement.* New York: Basic Books, 1965.

von Bertalanffy, L. System symbol and image of man: Man's immediate socio-ecological world. In I. Gladston (Ed.), *The interface between psychiatry and anthropology.* New York: Bruner/Mazel, 1971.

PART THREE

Psychiatry

CARL C. BELL   IRMA J. BLAND
EARLINE HOUSTON   BILLY E. JONES

CHAPTER 9

Enhancement of Knowledge and Skills for the Psychiatric Treatment of Black Populations

Curriculum Development and Implementation

Psychiatry, by definition, is the medical study, diagnosis, treatment and prevention of mental illness. A major development within psychiatry occurred at the close of the nineteenth century when Sigmund Freud conceptualized a relationship between mental illness and the unconscious, as well as stages of personality development. Freud's theories, which have become the cornerstone of modern psychodynamic and developmental theory, were based on clinical observation and treatment of patients from middle-class white European, Jewish backgrounds and stressed certain psychological requisites for the development of a healthy personality. The assumption that these theories and psychological requisites are applicable to all groups of people, regardless of ethnic or cultural differences, has not been adequately evaluated or assessed. When the treatments evolving from these theories do not help the patient, the conclusion generally reached is that the patient lacks those qualities necessary for successful therapy. Other conclusions, however, may be drawn: the theory may not be applicable across different cultural or ethnic groups; the psychiatrist applying the treatment may not know how to modify the theories for treatment of different cultural or ethnic groups; or the psychiatrist may have biases or prejudices that make it difficult for him to provide successful treatment.

The question of cross-cultural appropriateness of theories has particular implications for the treatment of Black psychiatric patients. The psychiatric profession must grow aware of the historic economic, social, political and cultural factors inherent in institutional racism and strive to neutralize the negative myths, stereotypes, and concepts concerning the mental health, personality development, and overall functioning of Blacks. For years, the Black psychiatric patient has been considered the antitheses of the ideal patient for psychotherapy, being viewed as nonverbal, hostile, unmotivated and impulse-ridden. In addition, there exist myths concerning the pathology of the Black family, the absence of Black cultural heritage, the rarity of depression or suicide within the Black community, and the lack of strength or ability to cope within the Black personality (Sabshin, Diesenhaus and Wilkerson, 1970; Bradshaw, 1978).

Psychiatry is being called upon to treat a greater number of Black people than ever before, but there is a lack of critical knowledge about Black people, their growth and development. The personality development, socioeconomic situations and idiosyncracies of individuals belonging to ethnic groups different from that of the traditional patient must be addressed by the profession, and behavior once defined as criminal or pathological must be recognized as being more suitably explained by social and economic conditions. Racism has been recognized by psychiatrists of color as the number one mental health problem in this country. The dynamics and treatment of racism and its effect in both the Black and white communities should be examined.

In developing Black curriculum content in psychiatry, the primary aim is to increase the quantity and improve the quality of instruction the resident receives about Blacks. Valid and reliable scientific knowledge about Black people should be provided, and residents should improve their ability to comprehend and evaluate experiences of Black patients, by working, for example, in community mental health settings that provide services to Blacks on a consulting-rotation basis (Bradshaw, 1978).

The experiences of Black psychiatric residents in predominantly white training institutions have demonstrated the need for faculty that is sensitive to minority issues (Jones, Lightfoot, Palmer, Wilkerson and Williams, 1970). In teaching residents, faculty must be able to show how to link psychotherapeutic issues of diagnosis and treatment with the socioeconomic and cultural conditions of the Black patient's experiences. Faculty must also be able to evaluate cultural adaptation and identification and distinguish it from pathology. Sensitivity to the problems of special countertransferences with Blacks is also required. This chapter, therefore, presents a framework for psychiatric residency programs, emphasizing the treatment of Blacks.

State of the Art

For many years manpower had been considered the answer to the critical issue of providing psychiatric services to the Black population. That approach, while limited, had its achievements, namely a relative increase in the numbers of Black psychiatrists; a somewhat increased awareness and sensitivity to needs of Black trainees by educational institutions; and the emergence of multiple social- and community-care delivery systems. The most serious limitation, however, has been the clear lack of responsibility of educators and institutions to provide trainees with the necessary minority content to deliver service to Black patients. The content for providing psychiatric services to Blacks has been primarily initiated outside of the educational institutions. Black Psychiatrists of America and the American Psychiatric Association Symposia and Seminars, for example, have been particularly active in the area of minority content. The hope that these efforts would stimulate training institutions to rectify their omission of minority content in their programs and in their thinking has not been fulfilled. In fact, there oftentimes has been overt resistance.

The setting, nature and orientation of psychiatric residency training programs vary. Core curricula generally include the following subjects: individual psychotherapy; group, family and child therapies; behavior modification; crisis intervention; consultation-liaison; community psychiatry; sexual dysfunction treatment; and pharmacological therapy. To a greater or lesser degree traditional psychotherapy retains its analytic core of thinking, its one-to-one supervision and its psychodynamically oriented case conferences. Many programs have added community psychiatry training and various subcultural orientations with varying degrees of success. In some instances such programs have merely reinforced disinclination of residents (Morrison, Share and Grabman, 1973) while in others they have resulted in positive changes in both attitude and practices (Yamamoto, Dixon and Bloombaum, 1972).

Significant progress will occur only when the core curriculum content of psychiatric education in our training institutions changes. We must make a start in effecting such changes and affecting the attitudes and pedagogical practices of future educators. Otherwise, untested assumptions determining attitudes and practices will continue from generation to generation of psychiatrists.

Problems are inevitable when new treatments of socioeconomically and culturally different populations are thrust upon trainees without internalization by the educators and institution and without adequate integration into the theoretical content of the core curriculum. Ambivalences in attitudes of the educators arouse anxiety and racial hypervigilance in the trainees. Differences in values and experiences become magnified beyond empathic understanding, and the distance between the psychiatric resident and the educators is accentuated. Inevitable transference and countertransference racial issues cannot be comfortably addressed and worked through in supervision.

To cope with this stressful dissonance as well as to modulate the "identity crisis" inherent in becoming a psychiatrist, the resident is

Psychiatric Education: An Analysis of Training Deficits

pushed into adopting a homogeneous focus, restricting himself to familiar, bourgeois ideology and experience. As Fromm (1970, p. 119) demonstrates, theory becomes absolute. There is little concern with the variety of life experiences, with socioeconomic or ethnologic realities. Attempts are made to transpose a theory that does not seem to fit, and ultimately the results are an analogy rather than an analysis. Analogy leads to gross misapplications of both theory and technique, erroneous assumptions and the continuous manufacture of myths and stereotypes. The burden of this dissonance inevitably falls on the patient (Yamamoto and Goin, 1965).

Indications are overwhelming that psychiatric practices are biased in favor of the white, upper classes of our society who share the values and traits often evidenced by the professional (Cole, Branch and Allison, 1962; Hollingshead and Redlich, 1958; Jones, 1974; Brill and Storrow, 1960). This is in large part due to educators who, because they lack knowledge about the treatment of Black people, are ill-prepared to change basic attitudes and pedagogical practices that influence residents in training and affect their understanding. This deficiency of information further distances the trainee from any impact efforts to enlighten the trainee may potentially have.

The exceptional resident is one who early in training recognizes, through his or her innate capacity for empathy, that he or she must not loose sight of the patient. Through his own efforts as an integrator and synthesizer, he focuses on the patient and moves toward an integration of theory and technique. He explores the inner-psyche to elucidate conflicts and pathological defenses. He further proceeds to incorporate an understanding of interacting psychic drives with the sociocultural realities of the patient. With an "accurate" sense of empathy as his primary, pivotal tool, he accepts the challenge to use his knowledge, expertise and self as a therapeutic instrument. Rather than attempting to make the patient fit a rigid framework, he has learned to deploy his skills creatively in accordance with the diagnostic situation and with the realities of the individual patient.

The traditional role of the psychiatrist, isolated within his office from the real world beyond, has in many ways protected him from exposure as a real person (Daniels, Abraham, Garcia, and Wilkinson 1977). Each psychiatrist must choose his own domain of professional involvement, considering himself and the professional mission he has undertaken. Psychiatric education, however, must integrate its endeavors with and be accountable to the real world and the people who wait to be served. By producing psychiatrists with expanded horizons and genuine interests in human-service delivery, psychiatry will be better able to use creatively theoretical knowledge and therapeutic skills to meet its professional task. A quality psychiatric training program is one that, despite a central theoretical orientation, encourages diversity. As Daniels (1973) so poignantly states:

The most important issue in residency training is bringing together the trainee, the patient and the teacher within an effective delivery system for the care of mental illness. . . . Although the ideal may not be attainable, it is short-sighted to ignore deficiencies in our current system and to foster training in which the trainee never confronts some of the real problems of mental illness service delivery.

Black Curriculum Content in Psychiatric Training

Blacks have long recognized the need to obtain better psychiatric treatment for their people. In an effort to bring attention to this need, many books, articles and research projects have been developed. Psychiatric treatment of Blacks is related to how residents are trained. Yet, it is clear that residents are not being prepared properly to treat Black populations. In 1972 the American Psychiatric Association (APA) Trustees recognized the need for minority curriculum content in residency training.

L. H. Rudy, M.D., executive director of the American Board of Psychiatry and Neurology, had the state of Illinois laws amended so that a Black resident could spend time in a Black treatment context with a Black supervisor as "the experience which was obtained was not available as part of the intramural curriculum" (Rudy and Rhead, 1973). He stated, "It was essential to continue to train individuals in the specialized problems of minority groups if the training program were to be considered truly relevant." It has further been recognized that residents in training go through a process of professional socialization during which residents assimilate values, attitudes and normative behavior of their professional group.

Thus it is felt that "those responsible for training programs should strive to design socialization routes which recognize the racial diversity of the body of trainees and to promote learning of behaviors and values which all affirm and reflect equally a reverence for black and white cultures" (Griffith and Delgado, 1979). The report of the APA's Task Force on the Delivery of Psychiatric Services to Poverty Areas recognized the need for training psychiatrists to better deal with minorities. The report states, "Racial and cultural struggles have inhibited effective planning, development, and delivery of psychiatric services in poverty areas" (Rae-Grant, Lightfoot, Becker, Bell, Jenkins, Harris and Foster, 1973). Further, they report, "Psychiatrists and other mental health disciplines were quite unprepared to recognize or deal with these issues and the situation remains relatively unchanged to date. Yet the success or failure of programs in poverty areas demands special attention to the influence of race and culture on the planning, appropriate modification on service delivery patterns, questions of fiscal and administrative control, and service priorities" (Rae-Grant et al., 1973).

While there is a recognition of the need for minority content in residency training programs, the Black Psychiatrists of America (BPA) found that little or no action was being taken to fill that need. The BPA was able to impress the need for minority attention upon the APA, which in response created the position of deputy medical director of minority affairs in the early 1970s. The director, in addition to having developed a bibliography of minority mental health issues, provides consultation to groups and individuals concerning minority affairs, raises minority issues at APA meetings, and forms liaisons with other groups. It was through this facility that the APA–NIMH Minority Fellowship Program was established in 1974 with the Center for Minority Group Mental Health Programs of the National Institute of Mental Health (NIMH). The center also initiated the Minority Biomedical Programs in 1974. Earlier, in 1971, the center had sponsored the first National Black Mental Health Conference. Through the center, funding has been made available for, among other subjects, the study of institutional racism; positive minority value systems; effects of social policy on minorities; and mental health service needs of minorities. A bibliography on racism was published in 1972.

The BPA also established the Solomon Carter Fuller Institute which, along with the Committee of Black Psychiatrists of the APA, brings a noted lecturer to the APA annual meetings for a special lecture on minority-related issues. The institute produces research relevant to the Black experience as it relates to psychiatry and has begun to compile a bibliography and information on the history of Black psychiatry. It recently sponsored a roundtable on the subject of foreign medical graduates and their need for training in issues related to the care of Black patients.

The BPA also began the Academy on Issues in Psychiatry for Black Populations in an attempt to correct the deficiencies in training regarding the treatment of Black populations. The academy produced an excellent paper, "Training Psychiatrists for Working with Blacks in Basic Residency Programs" (Bradshaw, 1978), which contains specific recommendations on integrating minority content into already-existing traditional residency programs. The intent of the academy is to identify unique curriculum needs of psychiatric residency programs regarding Black populations and to develop a model training program suitable for all residents but with emphasis on foreign medical graduates, as they tend to serve the majority of Blacks in state hospitals.

Another nationally based program addressing minority content in psychiatry is the National Medical Association's Section on Psychiatry and Neurology. It provides scientific reports at the association's annual national meeting. The papers of this section seek to deal with the dissemination of knowledge essential to the treatment of Blacks.

In spite of these nationwide efforts to fill the void in training geared toward the care of Blacks, the primary responsibility for obtaining that training remains with the resident. When institutions implement such content, it is often done on an individual basis and is geared only toward the Black resident in order that he may better treat the Black patient. Yet non-Black residents will also be treating significant numbers of Black patients and therefore need this "other than traditional" training. Because of the lack of a mandate from the national regulatory bodies demanding that programs have minority content, little has been done to ensure that residents receive training that will allow them to treat properly Black populations.

Theoretical and Content Needs

Premises of the "Dominant" Culture

In Freud's classical descriptions of his work with neurotic patients, the family and social setting of the patient were delineated but only as scenery on a stage on which the principle drama was the clash of intrapsychic forces (Arthur, 1975). Individual differences were viewed in terms of fortuitous traumas of individual men. Differences in external frames of reference essentially went unrecognized because of a narrow, homogeneous focus and a seemingly uncritical acceptance of the premises of a "dominant" culture.

With the devastating effects of World War I and the later experiences of World War II, psychoanalytic reductionism was forced to loosen its reigns. The recognition of social setting and phenomena in the origin, manifestation, course and treatment of emotional and mental illness led to significant influences and an in-rush of social psychiatric thinking. With the advent of chemotherapy in the 1950s, further exploration and therapeutic application of social thinking was facilitated. It led to the classical works of Maxwell Jones (1953) on the concept of therapeutic communities; Stanton and Schwartz (1954), who provided a conceptualization of the mental hospital as an integrated social system; and Hollingshead and Redlich (1958), who demonstrated the differential distribution of psychiatric disorders and availability of treatment services as associated with social class. Epidemiological studies, concerns about social class and attempts to harness social factors for therapeutic use resulted in both new ideas and legislative action that began to distance psychiatry from the premises of the "dominant" culture.

Currently in psychiatric education there is a focus on understanding both intrapsychic conflict as well as social phenomena. A change of emphasis, more or less, to an eclectic approach in both theory and practice has brought with it increasing complexity. One conceptualization of the nature of this growing complexity is that it represents the ambivalence and associated anxiety inherent in moving away from familiar, homogeneous suppositions based on the premises of a "dominant" culture. The lack of integration that has resulted from attempts to modify traditional theoretical models restricts psychiatry's ability to deal effectively with clinical issues, especially those arising out of heterogeneous, sociocultural and economic realities.

The hope for the future is to move forward with sincere efforts in research, theory and practice to a more adequate integration of biological, psychological and sociological data. Perhaps then psychiatry will be both theoretically and technically equipped to understand the true interplay of psychic drives for each individual patient. The challenge to psychiatric education is to adequately integrate the concept of heterogeneity into its theoretical framework and pedagogical practices so as to increase efficacy in the treatment and delivery of services to all segments of the heterogeneous population. Certainly the community mental health movement has made significant strides in this direction. Initiated at first by concern for the plight of the institutionalized, chronic patient, this movement has opened up a vast arena to social psychiatry. Community mental health addresses issues of social stratification and cultural and economic heterogeneity, and, in doing so, has uncovered the lack of integration of social issues in psychiatric education. As Shervington (1976) suggests, the crises surrounding the community mental health movement and its denigration in some departments of psychiatry are rooted in resistance due to racism, professionalism and elitism.

Because of the lack of integration of the realities of heterogeneity in psychiatric education, patients differing from the suppositions of homogeneity of a "dominant" culture may suffer from misdiagnosis, misapplication of theory and ultimately faulty treatment. Homogeneity disregards the heterogeneity of American culture. When confronted by social conditions different from the middle-class norm, disregard of those differences frequently causes failure to grasp medical issues.

The following section serves to demonstrate how built-in biases have laid the foundation for erroneous inferences and highlights some of the theoretical and content needs that a standard psychiatric residency fails to provide regarding the assessment and diagnosis of Black people. It is hoped that this information will facilitate the psychogenetic and dynamic aspects of behavior that dictate the directions of treatment of Blacks.

History of Racism and Psychiatry

Myths and Stereotypes of the Past. Historically, myths and stereotypes concerning the Black person in America have had both religious and scientific rationales as their foundation. Beginning in the seventeenth and eighteenth centuries, the concepts that Black men were born inferior to white men and had limited mental capacities took root. Psychiatry, along with other professional disciplines, consistently perpetrated myths and stereotypes that were necessary to justify slavery. Medicine and social sciences attempted to demonstrate that Blacks had smaller craniums and that Blacks who were not slaves had higher incidences of insanity. Statements such that the Black man belonged to a "lower race" that had not completely evolved and was childlike or juvenile in behavior, as cited in historical writings, (Stamps, 1956; Stanton, 1960) were typical. This primitive race of people (Blacks) could be content only when cared for. Evarts (1914) felt that Blacks could experience only dementia praecox, as depression was too advanced a mental illness for such an inferior people.

Particularly after Emancipation, census figures, later proven fabricated and questionable, were used to statistically confirm the increase in illness among Blacks not enslaved (Morais, 1967; Deutch, 1944). Eminent men, such as Carl Jung, were vocal in elaborating theories that demonstrated the need for segregation and control of Blacks (Jung, 1960).

During the nineteenth and early twentieth century physical inheritance and biological origins were thought to account for the presumed racial inferiority of the Black man. Behavioral characteristics were considered to be hereditary, and the Black race was believed to have many undesirable behaviors which needed to be repressed and channeled by the superior white race. Blacks were too emotional, they were sexually promiscuous, lazy, in need of authority, criminally inclined and unintelligent (Bevis, 1921). During the 1800s, with the establishment of mental hospitals in the United States, separate accommodations were provided for Blacks in the North by those few facilities that did accept Blacks. Otherwise, they were placed in jails or almshouses. There were no provisions for mentally ill slaves (Prudhomme and Musto, 1973). When it was noted that Blacks had a lower incidence of mental illness than did whites, this was attributed to the "simplicity of an uncivilized race" (Ray, 1856).

Contemporary Myths and Stereotypes. Racism in contemporary psychiatry involves certain eleborations of historical myths concerning mental illness among Blacks. Thomas and Sillen (1972) outlined the most current "themes or ideas" in psychiatry and psychology concerning the mental status of Blacks in our society: the genetic fallacy, the mark of oppression, the illusion of color blindness, the deficit model, the family problem and the sexual mystique.

The genetic fallacy holds that races differ in inherited mental qualities, with Blacks being inferior to whites in intellectual potential and achievement. This train of thought has been traditional in American scientific thought and has supported beliefs of Blacks' inferiority. The question of heredity versus environment in intellectual and psychological growth and development has become much more a question of how the two factors interact rather than a question of the degree of influence of one over the other. There are psychologists such as Anastasi (1976) who recognize the problems of intelligence testing and the environmental and cultural factors contributing to behavior. Then again, there is Jensen (1969), who has tried to find evidence for the unscientific genetic argument that intellectual differences between the races is predominantly due to heredity.

Blacks, because they have been oppressed, are believed by some to bear the mark of oppression: irreversible psychological damage that has left them humble, dejected, and crushed with low self-esteem and unbounded self-hatred. This belief does not acknowledge the strengths and positive responses Blacks have shown to the stresses of oppression. An opposite tendency within the behavioral sciences has been to deny (through the illusion of color blindness) the deleterious or crippling effects of racism. This view tends to ignore the social context of behavior, and proponents label as deviant responses behaviors that are in reality adaptive to a hostile environment.

The phrase "culturally deprived" has become synonymous with Black people. According to the deficit model, poverty is viewed as a result of psychological traits rather than as a result of environmental or sociological conditions. This emphasis shifts the concern from the conditions of poverty, such as poor housing, inadequate nutrition, insufficient medical care and so forth and allows the adherent to, in effect, blame the victim. Such a rationale also frees the believer from any guilt he may feel in not trying to eliminate the conditions of poverty.

Another theme in contemporary racism is the so-called pathology of the Black family. Some sociological and psychological analyses of the Black family have led to the erroneous premise of a Black matriarchy within the Black community. Black women are viewed as unfeminine, castrating to their men, promiscuous and, typically, on welfare. Black men are viewed as inadequate father figures, as emasculated men who are unwilling to provide for their families.

The sexual mystique would have it that a Black man is a sexual stud whose primary desire is to make love to a white woman. Both the Black male and Black female have been of considerable interest to whites from a sexual point of view, as evidenced by the miscegenation issue and the sexual stereotypes, which are rooted in racism.

Institutional Racism. Historically, psychiatry as a speciality has been least available to Blacks. Often the Black church has provided needed services to the Black psychiatric patient. Certain neglected areas of psychiatry are of particular concern to the Black community, for example, alcohol and drug addiction, mental health of children, mental health delivery systems, and the medical-legal aspect of psychiatry (Sabshin, Diesenhaus and Wilkerson, 1970). Those neglected problem areas are part of the institutional racism within the field of psychiatry. In addition, the limited types and numbers of mental health facilities available to Blacks and the limited number of Blacks entering psychiatry are further reflections of institutional racism (Williams, Ralph and Denham, 1978).

Epidemiological studies have proven questionable in their reliability and validity (Fischer, 1969). Erroneous conclusions are drawn concerning rates of admission and types of illnesses among Blacks (Crawford, 1969; Kramer, Rosen and Willis, 1973). The ethnocentrism of Western culture has caused the psychiatric profession to have great difficulty in coping with the heterogeneity of American culture (Bland, 1979).

Assessment and Diagnosis of Black Patients. In recent years, a growing bulk of literature has pointed to the lack of an accurate assessment of the psychiatric disorders of Black patients. As the problem continues, however, it seems evident that steps must be taken to educate psychiatrists as to the pitfalls in diagnosing Black people. Investigators have made sweeping generalizations about epidemiology of Black psychiatric disorders based on skimpy evidence, and all too often these speculations were used to reinforce racist concepts (Thomas and Sillen, 1972; Pasamanick, 1963, 1964). For example, Wilson and Lantz (1957) reported that a higher incidence of mental illness in Blacks at that time was attributable to a greater degree of freedom accorded Blacks then. One of the reasons Blacks outnumber whites in correctional institutions by nine to one is that racism has influenced the assessment of Blacks (Cannon and Locke, 1976; Lowe and Hodges, 1972; Comer, 1977).

In looking at the difference in diagnostic patterns between white and nonwhite patients at outpatient clinics, Cannon and Locke (1976) found that in both 1961 and 1969 nonwhites were assigned more serious diagnoses than whites. The leading diagnosis for white males being admitted to state and county hospitals was alcohol disorders (79.5 per 100,000) as compared with the leading diagnosis for Blacks males, which was schizophrenia (197.1 per 100,000). The second leading diagnosis in white males was schizophrenia (56.3 per 100,000), while in Black males it was alcohol disorders (122.0 per 100,000). The leading diagnosis among both Black and white females was schizophrenia. The rate per 100,000 white females was 42.8, however, compared with 118.2 in Black females. For discharge from general hospital inpatient services, the leading diagnosis in both white males and females was depressive disorders (65.3 and 131.3 per 100,000 per population respectively) as compared with schizophrenia in both Black males and females (119.3 and 117.8 per 100,000 per population respectively).

It has been repeatedly reported that Blacks have lower rates of affective illness when compared with whites. Earlier reports attributed this finding to Blacks' state of primitive mentality. In later reports, the etiology of the differences was explained using psychodynamic theory (Thomas and Sillen, 1972). There have been several studies that demonstrate the supposed lower prevalence of affective illness in

Blacks as compared with Whites (Malzberg, 1963; Prange and Vitols, 1962; Jaco, 1960; Johnson, Gershon and Hekimian, 1968).

In diagnosing schizophrenia there again appear to be racial differences, with Blacks exhibiting a higher rate (Malzberg, 1963; Faris and Dunham, 1939; Frumkin, 1954; Taube, 1971). While there have been several attempts to demonstrate that these diagnostic differences tend to reflect a subtle form of institutional racism, the lack of recognition that Blacks seem to have as high a rate of affective illness as do whites continues (Simon and Fleiss, 1973; Helzer, 1975; Bell and Mehta, 1979). Another study found that the differences in the incidence of psychosis between Blacks and whites was negligible (McLean, 1949).

With regard to the nonpsychotic disorders among Black patients, it has been shown repeatedly that as a rule they are related to supportive treatment and custodial care (Bell, 1979; Fiman, 1975; Jones et al., 1970; Spurlock, 1975; Sue, David, McKinney and Hall, 1974; Thomas and Sillen, 1972; Wilder and Coleman, 1963; Yamamoto and Goin, 1966; Gross, 1969). Regarding the assessment of the Black family, there has been much written that castigates the Black family as a "tangle of pathology" (Thomas and Sillen, 1972), primarily because of the effects of slavery and of economics (Davis, 1968). Thus, "the onus is placed on the Black family as a self-perpetuating source of pathology, rather than on the racist society which condemns most Blacks to poverty, slum housing, and inferior schools" (Thomas and Sillen, 1972). This view, however, has been seriously questioned (Spurlock, 1975; Billingsley, 1968; Hill, 1971; Staples, 1970; Herzog and Lewis, 1970; Ladner, 1971; and Gutman, 1976).

The assessment of children and adolescents is no different. Earlier, Bender made special note of the two features that were "characteristic" of the Black race, specifically the capacity for laziness and the special ability to dance (Spurlock, 1975). Black children have developed various survival techniques to minimize the consequences of discrimination, and these behavioral patterns have sometimes been viewed as maladaptive and pathologic by the majority of white culture. These children may exhibit problems such as mental retardation, learning disabilities or hyperactivity; they need special attention rather than relegation to custodial care (Bell, 1970; Bell, 1971; Crump, Horton and Ryan, 1957). Also, psychiatrists are likely to recognize and treat serious psychopathology in aggressive, antisocial white adolescents but tend to dismiss similar signs and symptoms in Black adolescents as culturally appropriate or evidence of character pathology and thus candidates for institutionalization (Lewis, Balla and Shanok, 1979). Certainly the statistics on the different rates at which white and Black juvenile delinquents are institutionalized bear this out.

From the evidence presented it is clear that the assessment and the diagnosis of Black patients are hampered by widespread racism and ignorance. This can be corrected only by minority curriculum content in the training of psychiatrists.

Dispelling Racial Stereotypes and Myths. The racial myths concerning the Black psychiatric patient are rooted in the pseudoscientific studies conducted on Blacks by behavioral and social scientists as well as in the limited clinical experiences of white psychiatrists with Black psychiatric patients. Among the most current stereotypes are those that describe the Black patient as nonverbal, unintelligent, concrete, nonintrospective and impulse-ridden. The Black patient is viewed as having character disorders that are ill-suited for therapy (Anderson, Lightfoot, Spiro and Tardy, 1976; Jones and Seagull, 1977).

Blacks and Dynamic Psychotherapy

The cultural-deprivation theories portray Blacks as low in self-esteem, hostile and defective. Among the other misconceptions that ensue from these theories are the following: there is little or no hope for Blacks because they are so downtrodden that their situation is self-perpetuating; the family life and child-rearing practices of Blacks are chaotic and because of the lack of good role models the children are damaged intrapsychically at an early age; within the family the Black female is a castrating, aggressive, domineering individual, while the male is an immoral, irresponsible, supersexual, but emasculated individual; and the children are raised in a violent, traumatic and cognitively unstimulating environment (Mental Health Committee Against Racism, 1974).

Blacks have as wide a range of behavior as any other racial or ethnic group. The question that needs to be addressed concerning behavior manifested by any oppressed group is whether the behavior is in response to conditions of the oppression experienced by members of the group. In certain instances behaviors previously designated "pathological" and unsuitable have been demonstrated to be appropriate and healthy responses to conditions of slavery and/or racism.

A Black psychiatric patient and a white psychiatrist come from two different cultures, and therefore two different realities, and this certainly has an influence on the therapeutic process. Schacter and Butts (1968) state that, although racial differences may in some instances catalyze analysis, obscuring or overestimating racial stereotypes may hamper analysis. Racial stereotypes may be ignored, and there may be overreaction to subculturally acceptable behaviors that have been viewed as pathological by the dominant culture. In order to be effective with Black clients white psychiatrists must uncover and recognize, examine and resolve their own conscious and unconscious biases and prejudices toward Blacks.

Confronting Denial of Black Identity. In dynamic psychotherapy with a Black patient the issue of race must always be addressed. To deny the significance of the race of a Black person as an immeasurable part of identity is to deny an important and overriding aspect of his or her being. The therapist must be comfortable in dealing with racial material and feelings; knowledgeable about and sensitive to the patient's customs and culture; and skillful in helping the patient to uncover and work through this material for the therapy to be successful.

In treatment, denial of Black identity may be exhibited by the patient or by the therapist. When the patient is unable to see himself and situations affecting him in the context of the identity, role and circumstances of Blacks in this society, he is denying his Black identity. This unconscious rejection is aimed at protecting the patient from the pain and hurt, rage and anger, impotency and frustration that comes with being a member of an oppressed, victimized people. Attempting to identify with the dominant (aggressor-oppressor) group is not only an attempt to ward off harmful forces and protect the self but also an attempt to prop up low self-esteem and image. The denial requires a rejection of a significant part of self, and hence is an unhealthy attempt at adjustment.

In treatment, the therapist aids the patient in recognizing the denial of his identity by helping him question and confront his perceptions and his use of denial. The therapist must assist the patient in uncovering, tolerating, and examining the fears, rage and frustrations underlying this defense. This is done by interpretations, guidance and use of transference in a supportive therapeutic relationship. As the reality is seen, the patient works through and resolves the conflicts and issues involved, and more appropriate mechanisms for coping are developed. With this comes the incorporation of a healthy Black identity.

When the therapist denies the significance of the identity of his Black patient, the therapist has unresolved conflicts regarding race. If the therapist is Black, it is most likely that the matter of being Black may not have been resolved by the Black therapist himself. The importance of the Black therapist working through and resolving any of his own conflicts over Black identity cannot be overstated. If the therapist has resolved his own feelings, he is then able to carry out his role in the therapeutic relationship.

When a white therapist denies the significance of the patient's Black identity, he has not resolved his own racism. This is usually apparent when the therapist sees the patient as "not as a Black, but just like everyone else." This phenomenon of "hallucinatory whitening" is a denial of the individual's Black identity (Jones et al., 1970). In such cases, for the white therapist to see and relate to the Black patient as a Black threatens the therapist's unresolved repressed racial conflicts. The belief in the stereotypes, the feelings of superiority, the acceptance of the sexual myths and the role played by members of the dominant (aggressor-oppressor) group can all be part of the repressed, uresolved racial material.

Meeting the Patients' Needs. The psychiatrist treating Black clients must develop a sensitivity to this client's needs and an appreciation and knowledge of his client's reality. He must be able to empathize but not overidentify with the Black struggle. Often Black clients may have immediate pressing problems that must be dealt with before intrapsychic exploration can occur. The psychiatrist must be able to ascertain emergency crisis situations such as a housing or child-care problem and be able to refer the client to an appropriate agency so that the problem can be resolved.

The white psychiatrist desiring to be effective with Black clients must anticipate some degree of distrust, given the racial situation. He must comprehend the sometimes subtle, sometimes overt differences in linguistic style. The patient should never have his beliefs or behavior ridiculed or debated because it is unorthodox or threatening to the psychiatrist's own belief system. Black clients have backgrounds as diverse as other clients, and the psychiatrist must be flexible enough in his treatment approaches to determine which method is best for which patient. For instance, a nondirective therapeutic approach may be unsuitable for a low-income person if he is accustomed to being directed by authority (Comer, 1977). White psychiatrists must understand the dynamics involved when traumatic racial experiences become intertwined with neurotic difficulties.

Black Patients' Expectations. A Black patient's expectations of the therapeutic process and of the white psychiatrist's role may often conflict with the psychiatrist's perceptions of the same. The Black patient may desire comfort and guidance and may expect the therapist to be assertive. He may need immediate relief from pressing problems of daily living and only after that will he be interested in the psychodynamics of his inner self. The patient may expect help in the form of medication and treatment in the office (Rosen and Frank, 1962). A suggestion of hospitalization can be interpreted as an act of prejudice. Black patients may be defensive, hostile and nonverbal. This is an adaptive style of defense to powerlessness (Jones and Seagull, 1977). There is fear, suspicion and distrust of the white therapist. If the Black patient believes the goal of therapy is to maintain the status quo, he will be suspicious of Black as well as of white psychiatrists.

Blacks never know how they will be received by whites, and so there is a resentful anxiety. The distrust results in an unwillingness to reveal weaknesses. The Black patient may appear sullen and reserved and exhibit self-hatred and exaggerated indifference (Rosen and Frank, 1962; Comer, 1977). Few Blacks have dealt with the issue of race in such a manner that they always are able to separate internal conflict from the external pressures of racism. This is difficult because the defensive and adaptive mechanisms involve the sociocultural milieu. Some Blacks may enter the therapeutic process with total abdication of responsibility for decisions and self-assertiveness (Pinderhughes,

1973). Other Black patients may have so suppressed the anger and rage that they are unable to manage acceptable self-assertive means of behavior (Carter, 1979).

It is imperative that the psychiatrist explain to the patient their respective roles in the therapeutic process. He should establish what the psychiatric treatment will entail for the patient and relate the importance of their relationship to the treatment. This must be done in language and terms familiar to and comfortable for the patient.

Successful Treatment Outcome. The successful outcome of treatment for a Black patient in dynamic psychotherapy consists of the resolution of underlying, problematic unconscious conflicts and the development and use of more appropriate and mature coping mechanisms. While these two elements are the product of good dynamic psychotherapy, a Black patient has unique conflict areas that should also be resolved.

Acceptance of and pride in one's Black identity should be a part of the posttreatment. The anger and rage that one feels as a member of an oppressed group must also have been uncovered and examined. Although the anger does not totally resolve, since it is related to reality and recurring situations, it is better understood and more appropriately directed and expressed. Blind rage and nondirected hostility are not part of the successfully treated Black; expressed anger and focused, directed hostility can be. The heightened sensitivity that is part of the protective warning system of Blacks, defined as cultural paranoia by Grier and Cobb (1968), remains and becomes better honed as a result of therapy. The need for a member of a nondominant (oppressed-victimized) group to constantly be on guard to ward off assault is a real protective need and function. With successful psychotherapy the Black patient should be a better integrated, productive, functional human being who enjoys his identity, expresses his heritage and copes with reality.

The Need for Research

Given the problems facing Black psychiatric patients as outlined in the previous sections, it is important to look at research areas that will enlarge the data base from which to treat Black populations and thus allow a more substantial education about Blacks.

Influence of Increased Mortality and Morbidity

Black people face twice the mortality and morbidity rates as whites with regard to neonatal death, cancer, maternal mortality and morbidity, prematurity, and many other variables that affect the quality and quantity of life (Barber, 1979). It has been posed that herein lies the cause of increased prevalence of Black-on-Black homicide, of young adult suicide, of drug abuse and of other forms of Black self-destructiveness. Every Black has experienced the fact that racism can kill dreams, and this experience has different effects on different persons. Blacks have sustained tremendous trauma to their ethnic heritage, family systems and psychological and physical well-being at the hands of the racist factions of this country. The capacity demonstrated by Blacks to adjust to the stressful circumstances placed on them surpasses survival. Black people have maintained their spirit, creativity, humor, intuition and ability to improve their condition both as individuals and as a group. Research on the capacity of Blacks for coping with oppressive forces will enable psychiatry to better strengthen these coping skills in Blacks as well as in others.

A humanistic attitude, that is, the warmth and conscience that many Blacks exhibit toward others (Staples, 1976), may have developed in reaction against the white stance of superiority (Grier and Cobb, 1968; Bell, 1978). Perhaps a good deal of the American Blacks' ability to maintain themselves in a racist society has to do with their African roots. African culture was handed down by word of mouth and emphasized the interconnectedness of life (Staples, 1976). Oral transmission of culture involved a village elder and as such was an interpersonal process that tended to support the concept of the extended family found in the Black family structure. In addition, a good deal of African wisdom is contained in the stories, which convey morals through metaphors. These stories are still poorly understood because we lack understanding of the inner meaning of their symbols. Also, possibly because of both the "spiritual" nature of the African heritage and American Blacks' cultural vestiges of that heritage, the Black church in this country plays a strong role in the lives of Black people. The African heritage and its reflection in Black peoples' lives in America must be researched as they relate to Black cognitive and coping styles, which are positive aspects of Black life and need to be defined and refined.

Child-Rearing Practices, Social Forces and Personality Development

Child-rearing practices of Blacks have been linked to certain degrees of instrinsic pathology within the Black family system and to deficits in the child's potential capacities (Kardiner and Ovesey, 1951; Seward, 1956; Ausubel and Ausubel, 1958). Yet comparative studies of Blacks and whites with equivalent socioeconomic status show fewer differences (Radin and Kamil, 1965; Schuster, 1968; Uzell, 1961; Davis and Havighurst, 1968). The extent to which child-rearing practices and the Black child's potential are affected by societal forces needs further elucidation. Among the questions to be addressed by further research are the following:

  • What are the differential influences of socioeconomic class versus ethnic and cultural membership as they impinge upon childrearing practices?

• Are societal forces that impinge upon masses of Black people with the effects of poverty, discrimination and the exclusion of opportunity the major culprits?

• Do these forces abort all efforts and good intentions of Black parents to provide a stable, secure and nurturant milieu for their children?

• How can Black families better insulate themselves from and counteract the negative forces of society that impinge upon their relationships with their children?

• What factors allow parents to foster positive self-esteem in their children despite the social realities?

• What accounts for the unique coping skills in some Black children that allow survival, adaptation and superior achievement in a hostile world that continuously denies them equal access to opportunity and rewards for their efforts?

To answer these questions, we must generate a more accurate theoretical framework from which to dictate therapeutic interventions and to formulate preventive strategies. This will require tremendous research efforts.

Epidemiology

Defining Mental Health and Diagnosing Mental Illness. In the field of psychiatric epidemiology, the study of mental illness among Blacks encounters a number of problems and issues. Psychiatric epidemiology has always grappled with the problem of defining mental illness and identifying mental disorders (Thomas and Sillen, 1972). Though most psychiatrists accept the classification of the *Diagnostic and Statistical Manual of the APA,* there is still disagreement on psychiatric diagnosis. Kramer, Rosen and Willis (1973) write, "Types of behavior that are considered to be psychiatrically abnormal by one racial or ethnic group are not always so considered by members of another group. Criteria which make it possible to determine when such behavior should be included as a mental disorder (e.g., personaltiy disorders) and when not must be developed."

Gary and Jones (1978) reviewed several definitions of mental health and mental illness. The most common theme deemed necessary for mental health is the ability to cope and adjust to the sociocultural, political, economic, and other forces of the total society, as well as to those of one's own subgroup within the total society. It has been established that similar symptoms may be diagnosed differently, depending on the race of the patient (Gross, Herbert and Knatterud, 1969). According to Kramer, Rosen and Willis (1973), there is, in addition to "reliable differential diagnostic technique," the need for standardized case-finding techniques "and methods for determining the onset and termination of illness."

Incidence and Prevalence Rates. The incidence of mental disorder in a given population is dependent upon the balance between the resistance of the population and the forces of stresses—biological, cultural, psychological, social, economic, and political—that produce mental disorder (Kramer, Rosen and Willis, 1973). The prevalence rate is a function of the incidence rate and the duration of the illness. In any discussion of incidence and prevalence of mental illness rates among Blacks, it is necessary to recognize that racism influences those factors that contribute to mental disorder as well as those that affect the duration and severity of an illness.

Absence of Reliable Research on Sociocultural Factors Affecting Mental Illness in Blacks. Although a major focus of epidemiological studies in psychiatry has been the difference in rates of mental illness between Blacks and whites, the findings of the studies have been ambiguous and contradictory. Dohrenwend and Dohrenwend (1969) reviewed eight field-survey studies designed to compare the prevalence of mental illness between Blacks and whites; half the studies found higher rates for Blacks and the other half higher rates for whites.

One weakness of such studies is the fact that the investigations are often conducted at the state or local level and use treated rates. There are variations in the number and types of psychiatric services available, the probability of a case being admitted and the time lag between onset of a disorder and contact at a psychiatric facility.

Thomas and Sillen (1972) observe that the Biometrics Branch of the National Institute of Mental Health questions the validity of data comparing Black and white incidence rates from different areas of the country. Among the factors influencing admissions rates are age distribution and hospital policy. The laws and practices in a particular locale and the extent of racial prejudices are also variables to be considered (Kramer, Rosen and Willis, 1973).

One of the variables that has been included in more recent studies of incidence rates of mental illness has been that of socioeconomic status (Hollingshead and Redlich, 1958). Warheit, Holzer and Arey (1975) found that the differences in mental health scores between Blacks and whites were largely insignificant when controlled for sociodemographic variables such as age and socioeconomic status. Psychiatric epidemiological studies conducted on Black mental health rates are contradictory, and no precise statement can be made until more rigorous investigations encompassing all the variables involved are performed.

Psychiatric training is designed to transmit the two components of psychiatry to the resident: the theory and the experience. Theoretical | **The Training Process** knowledge in itself does not make a balanced psychiatrist nor does experience without conceptualization enable one to practice the art of psychiatry. When a psychiatrist, trained in a standard psychiatric residency (i.e., one without minority curriculum content), treats a minority patient whose subculture is unfamiliar, he finds that his training did not prepare him properly. For training to be adequate, it must focus on two elements: the amount of minority content and the method by which that content was transmitted to the students. How the technical knowledge and skills are taught to psychiatrists in order for them to better treat Black populations is extremely important and entails such issues as the attitudes and values of the teacher, the type of professional socialization, the types of role models available and the context in which the learning experience occurs.

The training of psychiatrists to deliver psychiatric services to Black patients should be carried out in an area which has a high number of Black patients as its treatment population. Given the socioeconomic factors that impinge upon the mental health of Black patients, it is crucial for a psychiatrist to deal with limited resources as a part of his training in order to align his experience in coping with scarcity with the Black patient's real-life situation. Within this context (rare hospital beds; unavailability of places in half-way houses; difficulty in obtaining lithium levels; the absence of openings for insight-oriented, long-term cases; virtually nonexistent services for children and adolescents; and so forth), a different attitude is fostered in the physician. Such a context has a serious influence on the practitioner's level of comfort in certain surroundings.

As a result of the predominately white context of training in most residency programs, some Black psychiatrists lose the ability to communicate with Blacks. Many psychiatrists feel uncomfortable in the ghetto because the patients they encounter are different from the occasional Black patient who has been accepted by a training institute because he is an "interesting case." The patient population in the ghetto will more than likely reflect the pattern of mental illness that is prevalent in the area, and one will likely find a number of chronic debilitating disorders that make up the bulk of the treatment population at large. On one hand, it may be worthwhile to get experience in treating many different types of psychopathology. On the other hand, it can be argued that one needs to become an expert in the most prevalent psychiatric disorder, as that disorder demands the greatest attention from the therapeutic community.

Psychiatric trainees learn much more than theoretical and content areas from their teachers. They learn more subtle lessons regarding values, attitudes, professional mores and the like. They are exposed to what is considered to be the best bedside manner for a psychiatrist to have, the best way to dress, the best way to speak—all of which can be grouped under the category of best role model. Whether they embrace particular values depends on how they are thought of by their colleagues and by themselves.

Thus, the socialization process is extremely important in determining the outcome of psychiatric training. The least helpful of socialization processes is the disjunctive type, in which only one resident goes through training. The best process is the serial type, in which several residents train together and learn from each other's mistakes. Unfortunately, the socialization process experienced by most Black residents is usually the singular type in which the resident is the only one to have passed through in several years. This same liability of the disjunctive socialization process also holds true for the only white trainee who happens to get some training relevant to minorities from a community psychiatry tract as found in some residency programs. Clearly, the training of psychiatrists to deal with Black patients needs to be done in a serial fashion so that the experience will not be an alienating one (Griffith and Delgado, 1979).

The training should be conducted by people who are cognizant of the Black experience with both its positive and negative aspects. This will provide an attitudinal milieu quite different from the standard training of white residency programs in which the difference between the Black experience and the white experience is minimized by "hallucinatory whitening" (Jones et al., 1970). The training should also be conducted by persons who work in the Black community and who treat Black patients. It is more likely they will not harbor as many of the institutional racist values and attitudes that are implicitly transmitted to persons in training. The difference in language, the capacity to establish rapport with Black patients, the capacity to deal with Black patients' hostility toward the system—all of these need to be dealt with under supervision by an experienced therapist who is familiar with dynamics in the Black patient and how best to deal with them.

Training Strategies

At least two strategies are indicated to enhance knowledge and skills for the treatment of Black populations. First, the issues discussed in this chapter should be included in the training of residents. Such training is a suggested but often absent part of the residency curriculum. Second, an academy is needed to teach the teacher. The recently established Academy on Issues in Psychiatry for Black Population provides us with training models.

Residency Curriculum

Ideally, training focusing on treatment of Blacks should be an integral part of every psychiatric residency program located in an area with a significant Black population. To treat Blacks outside such an area subjects the resident and the patient to an unnecessarily frustrating experience, which can leave the patient confirmed in the view that another white institution has failed him. Also, the resident can become part of another generation of psychiatrists confirmed in the view that "those people" are untreatable. Those few residency training programs blessed with sufficient interest and expertise in the treatment of Black populations should be awarded grants to operate as pilot programs. Such pilot programs could demonstrate the utilization of more effective teaching and treatment. Over the course of four years, these programs could utilize experiential group training, didactic courses, field and clinical experiences, grand rounds and journal clubs.

Experiential Group Training. Both the Tavistock model—which focuses on group processes as influenced by the racial composition of the group members—and racial sensitivity groups could be used as weekly training experiences perhaps for periods of six months or so.

Didactic Courses. Didactic courses could include general works relating culture to psychology and specific information discussed under "Theoretical Content Needs" earlier in this chapter.

Field Experiences. Experiences in the field could include visits to families, to neighborhood churches and to other meeting places. The residents could be introduced to local ministers and lay persons who play a supportive role in the community.

Clinical Experiences. Clinical experiences should include treatment of Black patients of various ages and social classes. There is a need for training in therapies utilizing a systemic approach to treatment, where the emphasis is on rapid change in symptomatic behavior accomplished through alteration of the social context as agreed upon by the therapist and the family. Such an approach is in congruence with the holistic tradition of African folk healers and is more effective in crisis intervention than a lengthy investigation of causes of behavior. The urban poor majority of Blacks typically have little reason to trust or cooperate with a therapist who is primarily investigative in nature. This approach often reminds the Black patient too vividly of the repetitive "studies" of the various deficiencies of Black populations, without providing effective service.

Systemically based interventions for groups and families focus on the interactional processes of the group or family as the force that maintains symptomatic behavior. These interventions are similar to some practices of African medicine men. They address the symptomatic *behavior* more directly and rapidly than therapies which investigate the *cause* of the symptom through use of insight. The more immediate approach, designed for quick relief of symptoms with less emphasis on investigation of their cause, is less likely to be abandoned by the untrusting patient. Later, if there is still need, the initial success with symptom removal will make for a more effective therapeutic alliance in further treatment.

Live supervision and the use of videotape should be incorporated in the training procedure. There are at least two reasons for the use of live supervision and videotape in the teaching of the systemic approaches to treatment for Black populations. First, teaching is hardly possible without such supervision. The many interactions of a verbal and nonverbal nature are also impossible to describe adequately in the process notes typical of the individual interview. Much of the session will go unreported and, therefore, unsupervised. During live supervision the supervisor can make a number of interventions which will radically influence the success of the session, an impossibility for the trainee within the few sessions many families allow before dropping out.

Second, the live supervision allows the correction of various otherwise unreported behaviors on the part of the therapist having to do with stereotyping the Black individual or family, ignorance of Blacks in context different from that of service-receivers and anxiety about dealing with persons from a group different from that of the therapist. Anxiety alone often results in the inability of the therapist to do as well with Black patients as would be possible with patients from his own group.

Such anxiety is the great enemy of empathy. The patients, experiencing their own difficulties, are in no position to reassure the therapist. In fact, the therapist's anxiety is frequently misperceived by them as contempt. Surely, the paralysis of the therapist's capacity for empathy leaves him without a way to join the patient on an effective level, which leads to failure in treatment. This anxiety is often bound by the mechanism of projection: "It is they who are unsuitable for treatment, not I who am anxious and incompetent." This particular projection frequently operates at the institutional level and allows entire departments to turn their backs on the treatment needs of Black populations, relegating them to therapies requiring as little intense interpersonal contact as possible.

To this day, institutions or parts of institutions that do treat large numbers of Black patients frequently fall in status in the eyes of others because "everyone knows it is impossible." Further, the institution must struggle with inadequate third-party payment for the least restrictive treatment given and with many other manifestations of the indifference and hostility of society at large. In effect, the institution is "tarred with the same brush."

Grand Rounds. The use of grand rounds would give the resident a chance to observe the expertise of nationally prominent visiting professors for the benefit of his patient. More than that, however, is the chance to increase the prestige of therapeutic effort with Black patients in the eyes of teachers and residents inside and outside the psychiatry department.

Journal Clubs. Journal clubs can be used not only to explore the psychiatric literature relevant to Black patients but also to study literature about the Black experience. The works of Fanon, Baldwin and Ellison for example, would be included.

Workshop Curriculum

Unfortunately, the number of psychiatrists who are experts in treatment of Black patients is small. Thus a second training strategy teaching the teacher, becomes necessary. This strategy requires the training of residency training directors, their professors and their residents in a series of workshops designed to provide didactic material about Black individuals and families, experiential training in group process as it is influenced by racial composition and pre- and post-testing.

Didactic Material. The Academy on Issues in Psychiatry for Black Populations is already in operation. The first session of the academy will offer such courses as: Epidemiology of Mental Illness Among Blacks; Social Variables and Black Mental Health; Psychological Development of Black Children and Adolescents; The Black Family—Strengths, Weaknesses, Myths and Types; Treatment with Black Families; and Diagnosis and Individual Therapy of Black Adults. In addition there will be subject tracts on administration, mental health center operations, chronic patient care, academic psychiatry and problems of adolescence. The faculty will consist of many prominent Black and white psychiatrists who have skills in treating Black populations. In addition, the course will supply physicians with twenty-eight Category I, AMA continuing medical education credit hours. Repeated sessions will allow for a serial socialization process for those attending, as well as a growing forum for issues in Black psychiatry.

Experiential Training in Interracial Group Processes. As there are far too few psychiatrists available to treat Black populations, the burden of treatment must necessarily fall on those of other disciplines as well. One of the most effective ways of providing such treatment involves the use of a multidisciplinary team that includes psychologists, psychiatric nurses, social workers and paraprofessionals. Members of the mental health professions have received training relevant to, although different from, that of psychiatrists and which is enriching to the therapeutic effort. Similarly valuable in bridging the gap between the community and the professional is the paraprofessional mental health worker.

In addition to the usual training in diagnosis and the various therapeutic modalities offered by most programs, the study of the effect of covert group processes on individuals will serve the psychiatrist well. We refer here specifically to the type of training available in the "Tavistock" model for group relations conferences, where the objectives are to learn about covert group processes that cannot be explained simply as an aggregate of individual personality characteristics. Groups operating according to the dependent, pairing or fight-flight assumptions abandon their task in favor of pursuit of unconscious gratification of these urges. Further, groups can induce uncharacteristic behavior in individuals that may be inimical to the accomplishment of the group task through "group psychological role suction" described by Redl and Waltenberg in 1951. Through this projective mechanism, unwanted feelings and attributes are ascribed to the target individual who "carries" them for the group, as though none of the other group members possessed them.

Because of their visibility and the charged position they occupy in society, minority group members are more likely to be at the focus of irrational, unconscious group processes. These can be particularly strong when focused on a Black psychiatrist in the leadership position. Black women in the leadership position, for instance, may be the objects of frustrations and longings of a group operating on a basic assumption dependency mode. Indeed, they may be induced to behave as though they really were capable of gratifying such needs, to a degree inconsistent with reality. The inevitable exhaustion of the woman, the infantilization of the group and the abandonment of its task are all undesirable consequences of such unchecked processes. There is some indication that white women and Black men in the leadership position may be at the focus of dependency longings, the white woman because of what she represents as a mothering figure and the Black man because of his historical status of fellow traveller with those not in leadership. This is only one scenario, of course. Further study is needed regarding the projections customarily elicited by Black males and females versus white males in multidisciplinary teams.

Patients' positions in their work group will have a serious influence on the treatment. Experiential and cognitive learning about such group processes can be begun with a series of self-analytic group sessions in the course of the workshop.

Pre- and Post-testing. Pre- and post-testing, both for retention and comprehension of the didactic material and for change in racial attitudes, particularly as these influence perceptions of interpersonal distance, is indicated. The workshop should be both an educational and a research instrument; data from past workshops can be used to improve subsequent ones and to predict those aspects of training that would be most successful in other training settings.

Strategies for Implementing Minority Curriculum Content

Mandate from Accreditation Bodies

In order to be eligible to take the American Board of Psychiatry and Neurology, a psychiatrist must have spent three years in an accredited residency training program. Residency training programs, to be accredited, are reviewed by the Residency Review Committee of the American Medical Association (AMA). On this committee are representatives from the American Board of Psychiatry and Neurology and from the AMA Council of Medical Education. If the program meets the minimum requirements of the Residency Review Committee, the committee then makes a recommendation to the Liaison Committee on Graduate Medical Education of the AMA regarding accreditation of the residency training program. If the liaison committee approves the review committee's recommendation, the training program is accredited and anyone attending this residency program for three years can become eligible to take the American Board of Psychiatry and Neurology.

An inspection of this process shows that to have minority curriculum content in residency training programs, it will be necessary to have the Residency Review Committee of the AMA mandate minority curriculum content in its minimum requirements for a recommendation of accreditation. It also is essential to have a similar requirement from the Liaison Committee on Graduate Medical Education since it has the final authority to accredit a residency program.

Finally, as the Residency Review Committee of the AMA is composed of members from the AMA's Council of Medical Education, it would seem important to have the Residency Review Committee deliver a mandate to the national group of psychiatric residency training programs stating the need for minority curriculum content and implementation in their programs. The American Board of Psychiatry and Neurology as well as the AMA Council of Medical Education would have to recognize the importance of such a mandate and be willing to put it into effect. The need for minority curriculum content in psychiatric residency programs has long been recognized by the American Psychiatric Association and the American Board of Psychiatry and Neurology. Unfortunately, little has been done to put any "teeth" into the recommendations that would fill that need.

Only through a mandate from the bodies that accredit residency training programs in psychiatry will a minority curriculum tract be implemented and made available to residents who train to be psychiatrists. This is not to say that every residency training program would have to have a means of transmitting a minority curriculum tract to the residents, but it would mean that the various programs would be obligated to see that such a tract was made available to their residents. Either the resident could be sent to a program elsewhere or the tract could be sent to the resident's program from a nationally recognized teaching facility specializing in the teaching of issues relevant to the psychiatric care of Black patients.

Over the years, the spiraling cost of medical education has become a major public concern. The cost of training a resident in a quality program, whether in psychiatry or in any other specialty, is indeed expensive and includes not only the stipend or salary paid to the trainee but also the salary of teachers and supervisors. The hidden cost of support staff, facilities, equipment and operations must also be added. When all is calculated, the sum is staggering. The current mechanism available to fund residency training includes—

A Criterion for Funding Residency Training Programs

- the use of funds collected by the medical center for services rendered and interest and dividends from investments, property and so forth;
- the use of private donations, endowments and contributions;
- the use of grants and stipends from foundations and other nongovernmental institutions;
- the use of grants and stipends from governmental agencies (city, state and federal).

Governmental funds dispersed as grants, stipends and medicaid and medicare reimbursements should have certain attached requirements. As federal contracts and grants have an affirmative action, equal employment opportunity requirement as a criterion for eligibility, a similar requirement should exist for public funds used in residency training programs. Requiring minority curriculum content and its implementation as criteria for eligibility for public funds used in residency training would provide much needed support in getting this vital curriculum into the mainstream of psychiatric training. Such a requirement would provide the strategy and "teeth" needed to persuade the training programs to include minority curriculum content.

Most research in mental health in this country is funded by grants and by contracts from the federal government. Through the funding mechanism, the federal government, along with the mental health research community, sets priorities and to a large extent determines what gets researched. The fact that there is money available to study a particular subject that the government is concerned about is a legitimate means of stimulating and advancing knowledge in a particular field. It is an important role for government to play in funding research that will yield answers, solutions and a better life for its citizens.

A Criterion for Funding Research at Training Institutions

We are proposing a strategy in keeping with the role and responsibility of the federal government. We recommend that the government require, as criteria for eligibility for training centers applying for research funds, the development and use of a minority curriculum content in their training program. To qualify for research funds, a training center would have to have in place an acceptable minority curriculum.

These strategies of persuasion, if practiced by the federal government and the medical establishment as described in these pages, will clearly demonstrate the significance our society places on mental health and minority curriculum. This clear statement of importance will provide the strength needed to make minority content an integral part of the mental health curriculum.

References

Anastasi, A. *Psychological testing* (4th ed.). New York: McMillan, 1976.

Anderson, J. M., Lightfoot, O. B., Spiro, H. R., & Tardy, W. J. *The inner city Black.* Philadelphia: Smith Kline & French Laboratories, 1976.

Arthur, J. Social psychiatry. *Career Directions,* 1975, *4,* 28–38.

Ausubel, D. P. & Ausubel, P. Ego development among segregated Negro children. *Mental Hygiene,* 1958, *42,* 362–69.

Barber, J. President's inaugural address: Health status of the Black community. *Journal of the National Medical Association,* 1979, *71,* 87–90.

Bell, C. The effect of group size on bargaining outcome and interaction in a mixed motive game. *Dissertation Abstracts International,* 1970, Vol. 31 (5-B).

Bell, C. A social and nutritional survey of the population of the Children and Youth Center of Meharry Medical College of North Nashville, Tennessee. *Journal of the National Medical Association,* 1971, *63* (5), 397–98.

Bell, C. Narcissism, racism, and integrity. *Journal of the National Medical Association,* 1978, *70,* 89–92.

Bell, C. The need for psychoanalysis is alive and well in community psychiatry. *Journal of the National Medical Association,* 1979, *71,* 361–68.

Bell, C. Preventive psychiatry in the board of education. *Journal of the National Medical Association,* 1979, *72* (9), 881–86.

Bell, C., & Mehta, H. The misdiagnosis of Black patients with manic depressive illness. *Journal of the National Medical Association,* 1979, *72* (2), 141–45.

Bevis, W. M. Psychological traits of the southern Negro with observations as to some of his psychoses. *American Journal of Psychiatry,* 1921, *1,* 69–78.

Billingsley, A. *Black families in white America.* Englewood Cliffs, N.J.: Prentice-Hall, Inc., 1968, 39, 40.

Bland, I. J. The reality of heterogeneity: Consequence of its lack of integration in psychiatric education. Paper read at National Institute of Mental Health Conference on Development of Minority Curriculum Content, November 1979.

Bradshaw, W. H., Jr. Training psychiatrists for working with Blacks in basic residency training. *American Journal of Psychiatry,* 1978, *135,* 1520–29.

Brill, N. O., & Storrow, H. A. Social class and psychiatric treatment. *Archives of General Psychiatry,* 1960, *3,* 340–44.

Cannon, M., & Locke, B. Being Black is detrimental to one's mental health: Myth or reality? Presented at W.E.B. DuBois Conference on Health of Black Populations, Atlanta University, December 14, 1976.

Carter, J. H. Frequent mistakes made with Black patients in psychotherapy. *Journal of the National Medical Association,* 1979, *71,* 1007–9.

Cole, N. J., Branch, C. H., & Allison, R. B. Some relationships between social class and the practice of dynamic psychiatry. *American Journal of Psychiatry,* 1962, *118,* 1004–12.

Comer, J. What happened to minorities and the poor? *Psychiatric Annals,* 1977, *7* (10), 79–96.

Crawford, F. R. Variations between Negroes and whites in concepts of mental illness, its treatment and prevalence. In S. S. Plog, & R. B. Edgerton (Eds.), *Changing perspectives in mental illness.* New York: Holt, Rinehart & Winston, 1969.

Crump, E. P., Horton, C. P., & Ryan, D. K. Growth and development: Relation of birth weight in Negro infants to sex, maternal age, parity, prenatal care and socioeconomic status. *Journal of Pediatrics,* 1957, *51,* 678–97.

Daniels, R. S. Changing human service delivery systems: Their influence on psychiatry training. *American Journal of Psychiatry*, 1973, *130*, 1232–35.

Daniels, R. S., Abraham, A. S., Garcia, R., & Wilkinson, C. Characteristics of psychiatric residency programs and quality of education. *American Journal of Psychiatry*, March 1977 Supplement, *134*, 7–10.

Davis, A., & Havighurst, R. J. Social class and color difference in child rearing. In C. Kluckhohn & H. A. Murrar (Eds.), *Personality in nature, society and culture.* New York: Knopf, 1968.

Davis, E. The American Negro: From family membership to personal and social identity. *Journal of the National Medical Association*, 1968, *60*, 92–99.

Deutch, A. The first U.S. census of the insane (1840) and its use as pro-slavery propaganda. *Bulletin of the History Medicine*, 1944, *15*, 469–82.

Dohrenwend, B. P., & Dohrenwend, B. S. *Social status and psychological disorder.* New York: John Wiley and Sons, 1969.

Evarts, A. B. Dementia Praecox in the colored race. *The Psychoanalytic Review*, 1914, *1*, 388–403.

Faris, R., & Durham, W. *Mental disorders in urban areas.* Chicago: University of Chicago Press, 1939.

Fiman, B. Special report on inequities in mental health service delivery. Human services research prepared for National Institute of Mental Health, Center for Minority Group Mental Health Programs, March 28, 1975.

Fischer, J. Negroes and whites and rates of mental illness: Reconsideration of a myth. *Psychiatry*, 1969, *32*, 428–46.

Fromm, E. *The crisis of psychoanalysis.* New York: Holt, Rinehart & Winston, 1970.

Frumkin, R. M. Race and major mental disorders. *Journal of Negro Education*, 1954, *23*, 97–98.

Gary, L. E., & Jones, O. J. Mental health: A conceptual overview. In L. E. Gary (Ed.), *Mental health, a challenge to the Black community.* Philadelphia: Dorrance and Company, 1978.

Grier, W. H., & Cobb, P. M. *Black rage.* New York: Basic Books, 1968.

Griffith, E., & Delgado, A. On the professional socialization of Black psychiatric residency in psychiatry. *Journal of Medical Education*, 1979, *54*, 471–76.

Gross, H., Herbert, M. R., & Knatterud, G. L. The effects of race and sex on the variation of diagnosis and disposition in a psychiatric emergency room. *Journal of Nervous and Mental Diseases*, 1969, *148*, 638–42.

Gutman, H. G. *The Black family in slavery and freedom, 1750–1925.* New York: Pantheon Books, 1976.

Helzer, J. Bipolar affective disorder in Black and white men. *Archives of General Psychiatry*, 1975, *32*, 1140–43.

Herzog, E., & Lewis, H. Children in poor families: Myths and realities. *American Journal of Orthopsychiatry*, 1970, *40*, 375–87.

Hill, R. *The strengths of Black families.* Washington, D.C.: National Urban League, 1971.

Hollingshead, A. B., & Redlich, F. C. *Social class and mental illness.* New York: John Wiley and Sons, 1958.

Hsu, F. (Ed.). *Psychological anthropology.* Cambridge, MA.: Schenkman, 1972.

Jaco, G. *Social epidemiology of mental disorders.* New York: Russell Sage Foundation, 1960.

Jensen, A. R. How much can we boost IQ and scholastic achievement? *Harvard Educational Review*, 1969, *39*, 1–123.

Johnson, G., Gershon, S., & Hekimian, L. Controlled evaluation of lithium and chlorpromazine in the treatment of manic states: An interim report. *Comprehensive Psychiatry*, 1968, *9*, 563–673.

Jones, A., & Seagull, A. Dimensions of the relationship between the Black client and the white therapist. *American Psychologist*, 1977, *32*, 850–55.

Jones, B., Lightfoot, O., Palmer, D., Wilkerson, R. G., & Williams, D. H. Problems of Black psychiatric residents in white training institutions. *American Journal of Psychiatry*, 1970, *127*, 798–803.

Jones, E. Social class and psychotherapy: A critical review of research. *Psychiatry*, 1974, *37*, 307–20.

Jones, M. *The therapeutic community*. New York: Basic Books, 1953.

Jung, C. G. *Psychology and alchemy*. Princeton, N.J.: Princeton University Press, 1960.

Kardiner, A., & Ovesey, L. *The mark of oppression*. New York: W. W. Norton, 1951.

Kramer, M., Rosen, B., & Willis E. M. Definitions and distributions of mental disorders in a racist society. In C. V. Willie, B. S. Brown, & B. M. Kramer (Eds.), *Racism and mental health*, Pittsburgh: University of Pittsburgh Press, 1973, 353–462.

Ladner, J. A. *Tomorrows tomorrow*. Garden City, N.Y.: Doubleday and Company, Inc., 1971.

Lewis, D. O., Balla, D. A., & Shanok, S. S. Some evidence of race bias in the diagnosis and treatment of the juvenile offender. *American Journal of Orthopsychiatry*, 1979, *49*, 53–61.

Lowe, G., & Hodges, E. Race and the treatment of alcoholism in a southern state. *Social Problems*, 1972, *20* (2), 240–52.

Malzberg, B. Mental disorders in the U.S. In A. Deutsch & H. Fishman, (Eds.), *Encyclopedia of mental health* (Vol. 3). New York: Franklin Watts, Inc., 1963, p. 1051–66.

Mental Health Committee Against Racism. *The Culture of poverty revisited*. New York: Author, 1974.

McLean, H. V. The emotional health of Negros. *Journal of Negro Education*, 1949, *18*, 283–90.

Morais, H. M. *The history of the Negro in medicine*. New York: Publishers Co., 1967.

Morrison, A., Share, M. F., & Grabman, J. On the stresses of community psychiatry and helping residents to survive them. *American Journal of Psychiatry*, 1973, *130*, 1237–41.

Pasamanick, B. Some misconceptions concerning differences in the racial prevalance of mental disease. *American Journal of Orthopsychiatry*, 1963, *33*, 72–86.

Pasamanick, B. Myths regarding prevalance of mental disease in the American Negro. *Journal of the National Medical Association*, 1964, *56*, 6–17.

Pinderhughes, C. A. Racism and psychotherapy. In C. V. Willie, B. M. Kramer, & B. S. Brown (Eds.), *Racism and mental health*. Pittsburgh: University of Pittsburg Press, 1973.

Prange, A., & Vitols, M. Cultural aspects of the relatively low incidence of depression in southern Negroes. *International Journal of Social Psychiatry*, 1962, *8*, 104–12.

Prudhomme, C., & Musto, D. F. Historical perspective on mental health and racism in the United States. In C. V. Willie, B. M. Kramer, & B. S. Brown (Eds.), *Racism and mental health*. Pittsburgh: University of Pittsburgh Press, 1973.

Radin, N., & Kamil, C. The child rearing attitudes of disadvantaged Negro mothers and some educational implications. *Journal of Negro Education*, 1965, *34* (2), 138–46.

Rae-Grant, Q., Lightfoot, O., Becker, A., Bell, C., Jenkins, R., Harris, L., & Foster, D. Report from the Task Force on Delivery of Psychiatric Services to Poverty Areas.

Unpublished report, American Psychiatric Association, Washington, D.C., 1973. (Available on request)

Ray, I. Review of Jarvis, insanity and idiocy. *North American Review*, 1856, *82*, 78–100.

Redl, F., & Waltenberg, W. W. Mental hygiene in teaching. New York: Harcourt, Brace, 1951.

Rosen, N., & Frank, J. D. Negroes in psychotherapy. *American Journal of Psychiatry*, 1962, *119*, 456–60.

Rudy, L., & Rhead, C. Personal communication, November 13, 1973. (Available on request)

Sabshin, M., Diesenhaus, H., & Wilkerson, R. Dimensions of institutional racism in psychiatry. *American Journal of Psychiatry*, 1970, *127*, 787–93.

Schacter, J. S., & Butts, H. F., Transference and counter-transference in interracial analyses. *Journal of the American Psychoanalysis Association*, 1968, *16*, 792–808.

Schuster, J. W. The values of Negro and Caucasian children, do they differ? *Journal of Negro Education*, 1968, 37 (1), 90–93.

Seward, G. *Psychotherapy and culture conflict.* New York: Ronald Press, 1956.

Shervington, W. W. Racism, professionalism and elitism: Their effects on the mental health delivery system. *Journal of the National Medical Association*, 1976, *68*, 91–96.

Simon, R., & Fleiss, J. Depression and schizophrenia in hospitalized patients. *Archives of General Psychiatry*, 1973, *28*, 509–12.

Spurlock, J. Psychiatric states. In R. A. Williams (Ed). *Textbook of Black-related diseases.* New York: McGraw Hill, 1975.

Stamps, R. M. *The peculiar institution: Slavery in the ante-bellum South.* New York: Knopf, 1956.

Stanton, A. H., & Schwartz, M. D. *The mental hospital.* New York: Basic Books, 1954.

Stanton, W. *The leopard's spots: Scientific attitudes toward race in America, 1815–1859.* Chicago: University of Chicago Press, 1960.

Staples, R. E. Educating the Black male at various class levels for marital roles. *Family Coordinator*, 1970, 19(2) 164–67.

Staples, R. *Introduction to Black sociology.* New York: McGraw Hill, Inc., 1976.

Sue, S., & David, A., McKinney, H., & Hall, J. *Delivery of community mental health services to Black and white clients.* Seattle, WA.: University of Washington, 1974.

Taube, C. Admission rates to state and county mental hospitals by age, sex and color, United States, 1969. Department of Health, Education and Welfare, National Institute of Mental Health, Biometry Branch, 1971, Statistical Note 41, 1–7.

Thomas, A., & Sillen, S. *Racism and psychiatry.* New York: Brunner/Mazel, 1972.

U. S. Department of Health, Education and Welfare. *Bibliography of Racism.* DHEW Publication 73–9012. Washington, D.C.: Government Printing Office, 1972.

Uzell, O. Occupational aspirations of Negro male high school students. *Sociology and Social Research*, 1961, *45* (2), 202–4.

Warheit, G. J., Holzer, C. E., & Arey, S. A. Race and mental illness: An epidemiologic update. *Journal of Health and Social Behavior*, 1975, *16*, 243–56.

Wilder, J., & Coleman, M. The "walk-in" psychiatric clinic: Some observations and follow-up. *International Journal of Social Psychiatry*, 1963, *9*, 192–99.

Williams, W. S., Ralph, J. R., & Denham, W. Black mental health workforce. In L. E. Gary (Ed)., *Mental health: A challenge to the Black community.* Philadelphia: Dorrance & Company, 1978.

Wilson, D, & Lantz, E. The effect of cultural change on the Negro race in Virginia as indicated by a study on state hospital admissions. *American Journal of Psychiatry*, 1957, *114*, 25–32.

Yamamoto, J., Dixon, F., & Bloombaum, M. White therapists and Negro patients. *Journal of the National Medical Association*, 1972, *64*, 312–16.

Yamamoto, J., & Goin, M. K. On the treatment of the poor. *American Journal of Psychiatry*, 1965, *122*, 267–71.

Yamamoto, J., & Goin, M. K. Social class factors relevant for psychiatric treatment. *Journal of Nervous and Mental Diseases*, 1966, *142*, 332–39.

Bibliography

Beigel, A., Sarfstein, S., & Wolfe, J. Toward increased psychiatric presence in community mental health centers. *Hospital and Community Psychiatry*, 1979, *30* (11), 763–67.

Brown, B. S. The life of psychiatry. *American Journal of Psychiatry*, 1975, *133*, 489–95.

Greden, J. F., & Cassariego, J. I. Controversies in psychiatric education: A survey of residents attitudes. *American Journal of Psychiatry*, 1975, *132*, 270–73.

Gurel, L. Some characteristics of psychiatric residency training programs. *American Journal of Psychiatry*, 1975, *132*, 363–72.

Hsu, F. (*Ed.*). *Psychological anthropology*. Cambridge, MA.: Schenkman, 1972.

Official Position Statements of the American Psychiatric Association in Precis Form, 1948–1972. Washington, D.C.: American Psychiatric Association, 1972, 19.

NORMUND WONG   FRANCIS G. LU
STEVEN P. SHON   ALBERT C. GAW

CHAPTER **10**

Asian and Pacific American Patient Issues in Psychiatric Residency Training Programs

It was conservatively estimated that by 1980, the Asian and Pacific American (AAPA) population of the United States will exceed 3 million people (Owan, 1975). This is especially impressive when one considers that this population was reported to be only 1.5 million in 1970. This rapid increase has been particularly marked since 1965 because of changes in laws that shifted immigration away from Western Europe and predominantly toward Asia, the Pacific Islands and Latin America. During the first one hundred years, Asian and Pacific American immigrants to the United States were primarily Chinese, Japanese and Philipino. Over the past ten years there has been a dramatic increase in other Asian and Pacific American groups such as the Koreans, Samoans, Guamanians, East Indians and Indo-Chinese (Owan, 1975).

Earlier studies reporting on past immigrants may not apply to more recent immigrant groups. The Asian and Pacific American population is becoming more heterogeneous with the constant influx of recent immigrants. The continuing waves of immigrants have created conflicts and differences between the old and new Asian and Pacific Americans. There are varying degrees of acculturation. International relations have undergone vast changes, creating spin-offs in Asian and Pacific American communities and, in addition, immigrants from different sections of the same nation are arriving who are unable to communicate with their countrymen because of speech differences (President's Commission on Mental Health, 1978b). Although there may be some shared philosophical, religious, and other cultural commonalities, the differences among Asian and Pacific Americans may be as striking as the similarities. Deliverers of mental health services to Asian and Pacific Americans must be cognizant of the dissimilarities as well as the similarities, for what may be appropriate for one group may be inappropriate for another.

Rationale for
Including Asian
and Pacific
American Issues
in Psychiatric
Training
Programs

Convinced that this country lacked sufficiently trained mental health manpower, the federal government invested heavily in professional training programs, resulting in a marked increase in psychiatrists and other mental health personnel in both the public and private sectors. In the last twenty years, the supply of psychiatrists, psychologists, psychiatric social workers and psychiatric nurses has more than doubled. Financial support for mental health services increased from $1.7 billion annually in the late 1950s to approximately $17 billion by 1976. Nevertheless, many people in this country still receive inadequate care. Persons with chronic mental illness, children, adolescents, older Americans, the urban poor, migrant and seasonal farmworkers, rural inhabitants and racial and ethnic minorities are unserved or underserved (President's Commission on Mental Health, 1979).

The number of psychiatrists has increased from three or four thousand in the mid 1940s to approximately thirty thousand in 1980. In many large metropolitan cities, psychiatrists cannot maintain a full practice, and yet many patients are underserved in the same area. There is a vast maldistribution of psychiatrists as well as a large number of undertrained psychiatrists who are ill-equipped to treat the underserved populations. Most psychiatric residency programs have not provided the training or leadership to enable their graduates to work with these underserved groups.

The necessity of developing meaningful and effective mental health care programs for Asian and Pacific Americans and other minority populations has been recognized by the National Institute of Mental Health (NIMH). Since 1974, it has made stipends available through the American Psychiatric Association to increase the number of minorities in the mental health professions. In further recognition of this problem, the President's Commission on Mental Health (1978) designated a subpanel to study the mental health of Asian and Pacific American people. A number of investigators feel that psychopathology among this population has been vastly underestimated and that available resources for handling their mental health problems are inadequate (Berk and Hirata, 1973; Brown, Stein and Huang, 1973; Jacobs, Landau and Pell, 1971; Kitano, 1973; Sue and Frank, 1973; Sue and Sue, 1971; and San Francisco Chronicle, 1972).

Despite the fact that the Asian and Pacific American population is a heterogeneous and complex group of people with diverse religions, cultures, languages and histories, certain racial myths exist. Asian and Pacific Americans have been stereotyped as model citizens who are quiet, self-sufficient, industrious and well-adjusted to the American society (Abbot and Abbot, 1968; Kitano, 1962, 1967; Sue and Kitano, 1973; Sue and McKinney, 1975; U.S. News and World Report, 1966).

However, this image is being disspelled by epidemiologic studies. There is an increasing incidence of suicide, alcoholism, juvenile delinquency and drug addiction. Even taking into account the true incidence of mental illness and disorder among Asian and Pacific American people, it has been shown that they underutilize conventional mental health facilities in comparison with white patients (Sue and McKinney, 1975). When seen at traditional mental health centers, Asian and Pacific American patients appear to have a higher proportion of psychoses, are older and less educated, and have been more seriously disturbed for a longer period of time than non-Asian patients.

In the past, the majority of professional caregivers assumed that the underutilization of mental health services by the Asian and Pacific American population was due to a lack of need for mental health services. It is becoming increasingly evident that the Asian and Pacific American patients who use mental health services, even when attracted by bilingual and bicultural staffs, tend to be more chronically ill and more severely disorganized than the majority of white patients. The typical Asian and Pacific American patient will not seek mental health services unless there is an acute and direct need, which usually manifests itself as a social need. The patient may be creating a disturbance in the community, acting aggressively toward family members or causing property damage.

Different paradigms must be employed in the treatment of Asian and Pacific American patients because cultural factors may render the traditional mental health service approaches ineffective. The predominant psychiatric medical model draws heavily on a Western European philosophical base. It is a product of the scientific method whose developmental roots began in the age of rationalism in the sixteenth century. Scientific rationalism, and with it the scientific method, is reductionistic, i.e., in order to understand something, one attempts to break it down into its component parts. Orderly, natural laws are used to explain the actions and events of our environment.

The scientific approach has had a great impact on Western civilization and has contributed to our age of modern technology. It heavily influences the way we look at the world. In contrast, people from Asian and Pacific cultures come from traditions that trace back thousands of years as opposed to several hundred in the Western world. Their patterns of belief, value systems and perspective of the environment may and often do vary extensively from the way Westerners interpret the world. Unless cultural factors are taken into account, the judgments and interpretations that the majority of mental health professionals make about the Asian and Pacific American patients may be erroneous and inappropriate to the cultural context of the patients.

There are two significant areas where cultural bias frequently interfers with the delivery of psychiatric care to Asian and Pacific

American patients. The first area is in the lack of appreciation for the role of the family. In most Asian and Pacific American cultures, the family plays a far more important role than it does in contemporary American society where family bonds are looser and the nuclear family consists of the parents and children. Western society stresses ideals of individuality, and children are expected to leave the family to strike out on their own. Westerners see life as the individual life cycle, which begins with birth and ends with death. The emphasis is on the "here and now."

In contrast to Western society, most Asian and Pacific American cultures place far greater emphasis on the family and less importance on the individual. The family unit serves as the link between the past and future. It is the family name and not the achievements of the individual that has existed throughout history and will carry into the future. However, the individual's actions during his lifetime reflect on his ancestors and on all future generations. Thus, mental illness has a stigmatizing effect on the whole family line and, unless properly managed, Asian and Pacific American patients will not avail themselves of psychiatric care.

Furthermore, each family member has a specific role and function which is based on Confucian concepts dating back several thousand years. Members are interdependent upon each other. They are tied together throughout their lives, and different generations commonly live together in the same home. Majority mental health professionals seeing Asian and Pacific American families may label them as pathological, based on what they consider appropriate for mainstream, middle-class, white Americans. Asian and Pacific American children are frequently labeled as "dependent," family members as "overprotective" and relationships between family members as "symbiotic."

The second source for major potential misunderstanding is the mode of communication used by Asian and Pacific American people. American society values directness, openness and honesty in communication while in most Asian and Pacific American cultures, communication tends to be indirect and is governed by many complex variables. Among these are age, status, role, the sense of familiarity, the concepts of obligation, shame and "loss of face." Thus these patients are often mislabeled "quiet," "passive," "nonexpressive" and are termed "resistant" to psychotherapy. When observed with their children, Asian and Pacific American parents have been described as "uncaring" and "unloving" because they do not express feelings verbally or through physical contact in front of observers.

Support as well as pressure for the inclusion of minority content in all psychiatric training programs has come from federal and some state funding sources as well as from national bodies that accredit training. Although there is heated dispute over the number of psychiatrists actually needed in this country, there is no doubt that psychiatrists are maldistributed and many minority populations and areas are unserved and underserved. The report to the President's Commission on Mental Health (1978a) points out that racial minorities are greatly underrepresented in the field of psychiatry. Among its many recommendations, it urges that support be given for the training of minority personnel. It also recommends that NIMH fund the development of culturally relevant training materials and models via continuing education programs for mental health professionals.

The President's Commission on Mental Health (1979) acknowledged the differences between cultural groups and the way they define, tolerate and deal with deviant behavior, including mental illness. It called for the expansion of the Minority Fellowship Program funded by the American Psychiatric Association and NIMH. It called for the continuation of NIMH-funded special projects to enhance the capability of mental health personnel and community support systems to work more closely together. Also, it pointed out the need for developing relevant curricula and training materials in these priority areas.

The rationale for the inclusion of minority issues in the standard psychiatric training curriculum draws further support from the Interim Report of the Graduate Medical Education National Advisory Committee to the Secretary of HEW (1979). The report pointed out the relatively large role that foreign-trained physicians have played in nonmedical school affiliated hospitals that render services to minority groups. Foreign medical graduates have accounted for 39 percent of the total trainees in psychiatric residency programs and over 50 percent of the staff in many state mental hospitals. With the decrease in their numbers since the passage of the Health Professions Medical Assistance Act P.L. 94-484 restricting immigration of foreign medical graduates, underserved populations will receive even less psychiatric service. Therefore, it has been recommended that minority patient issues be included as part of all standard psychiatric curricula to enable American medical graduates to provide care for these groups.

The AMA Essentials of Accredited Residencies (1978) requires that "clinical and didactic teaching must be of sufficient breadth to ensure that all residents become thoroughly acquainted with the major methods of diagnosis and treatment of mental illness which are recognized as significant both in this country and abroad" and that "the curriculum must include adequate and systematic instruction . . . to help the resident understand the importance of economic, ethnic, social and cultural factors in mental health and mental illness." Furthermore, it mandates that residents in training must have "experience in the care of patients of both sexes . . . and patients from a wide variety of ethnic, social, and economic backgrounds." It also states the need for residency programs to "provide residents with instruction about American culture and subcultures" and mentions that "the curriculum should contain instruction about these issues adequate to enable the resident to render competent care to those patients from various cultural backgrounds for whom he has clinical responsibility in the course of his residency."

As of October 1979, the National Institute of Mental Health Division of Manpower and Training Programs Guidelines required that new priorities would have to be satisfied in order for psychiatric training programs to receive grant support. Among these requirements were the education and training of personnel to provide mental health services to unserved or underserved minority populations through the development of effective and efficient systems for mental health manpower development. Linkages between institutions that educate or train mental health personnel and agencies which utilize those personnel for the delivery of mental health services received more emphasis. Priority was also given to programs that would increase the supply of minority manpower for various roles in mental health service delivery systems.

Didactic teaching alone on specialized subjects has little or no impact on the practice of the trainees unless a sincere effort is made to integrate the teaching with actual clinical work. A logistical problem exists in that most Asian and Pacific American populations are clustered on the West or East coast, with the result that in many psychiatric training programs located elsewhere in the country, trainees have little contact with Asian and Pacific American patients. We take this factor into account and in this chapter suggest the inclusion of Asian and Pacific American curriculum materials that would be pertinent for all residency training programs. We recommend more detailed curriculum for a training program situated in a region with a large number of Asian and Pacific Americans.

Furthermore, while it may be possible within the standard residency period to train a resident to function adequately as a psychiatrist in an Asian and Pacific American community, it will probably require additional time and training to develop expertise in this specialized field. This is a situation similar to the training of residents who wish to practice child psychiatry. A specialized training program could be independent, but in all likelihood it would probably function best as a track system within a general residency program. A specialized residency training program for Asian and Pacific Americans should be significantly involved in rendering psychiatric services and be readily accessible to a large Asian and Pacific American population.

The desire to provide better patient care is a reason for inclusion of minority curriculum. A governmental mandate to render care to unserved or underserved minority populations is another. Intellectual curiosity, funding stipulations, a wish to develop a cross-cultural program, personal interests of residents or faculty, and the political advantages accrued to community and training centers are some more common reasons to justify the inclusion of minority patient issues including those of Asian and Pacific Americans in the formal curriculum. However, some guiding principles should be observed to make the teaching effective.

There should be a significant correlation between clinical practice and the didactic curriculum. To provide a meaningful learning experience for residents, a balance of clinical practice and didactic teaching is necessary. Competent individual, family or group supervision must be available for these patients. Residents should have the opportunity to work with Asian and Pacific American patients whenever possible. Training directors must be aware of the need of residents and faculty to see immediate gains in order to justify the use of curriculum time for the teaching of Asian and Pacific American issues over other subjects taught.

Both staff and residents need to be made aware that when they attempt to treat an Asian patient and his family, cross-cultural and cross-ethnic issues must be taken into consideration. It is important for psychiatrists to learn how to be comfortable and proficient with patients from different racial and ethnic backgrounds. Residents and faculty should appreciate the impact of racism and cultural and ethnic influences on the personality development and manifestations of psychopathology in Asian and Pacific American patients.

Because trainees learn best from models, we urge that there be suitable Asian and Pacific American professional faculty who are integrally involved in the teaching of minority curriculum and who can provide a unique understanding of their own ethnic or cultural groups. In addition, these teachers can render an important service in creating Asian and Pacific American teaching materials, which are still in the early stages of development. Non-Asian psychiatrists with expertise in Asian and Pacific American matters should also teach minority curriculum issues in order to avoid fragmentation of the faculty. Besides their involvement in didactic teaching, Asian and Pacific American faculty should be available for clinical supervision. They may provide the cultural expertise in psychodynamic, psychopharmacologic and psychosocial approaches as each appropriately relates to patient care.

It is imperative that the cross-cultural courses not be perceived as inferior to, or of lesser importance than, other subjects in the core

Guiding Principles for Developing and Integrating Asian and Pacific American Curriculum Content in Psychiatric Training Programs

curriculum. Teaching in this area should require the same standards of quality expected for all other courses. Course attendance should be mandatory and should include all trainees in the teaching program.

In order to address unconscious biases and prejudices and to develop greater sensitivity, faculty and trainees should engage in a group experience. The group sensitivity experience should be included as part of the core curriculum. Participants should consist of trainees, psychiatric faculty and members of all mental health disciplines with whom Asian and Pacific American patients have contact.

Visits to homes of Asian and Pacific American patients are an essential part of the educational process in that residents learn about the vastly different family orientations and traditions. The way Asian and Pacific American families cope with the stress of a mentally ill member, deal with issues of trust and "outsiders," struggle with the stigma of mental illness, attempt to maintain their cultural value systems, language and food concepts and yet retain their unique family dynamics are best seen and understood in the home setting. Residents will quickly come to appreciate the vital role the family occupies in the genesis as well as management of mental illness in a family member.

If trainees have frequent contact with a large number of Asian and Pacific American patients, they should be provided the opportunity to acquire conversational skills. Some familiarity with the spoken language, such as the conveyance of greetings and basic conversation in the patient's native tongue, goes far in establishing initial rapport and trust and conveys the immediate impression that the clinician is indeed interested in the patient.

Core Curriculum Content for All Psychiatric Residency Programs

This section specifically focuses on mental health issues of Asian and Pacific Americans in the context of a more encompassing cross-cultural curriculum that addresses the mental health care of all minority and subcultural groups for whom the resident may have clinical responsibility in the course of his training. The following curriculum takes into consideration the keen competition for teaching time, which many residency programs face. The content material is modified to reflect this reality.

Postgraduate Year One (PGY I)

Courses. There should be an introductory cross-cultural seminar on all the minorities in the United States. Asian and Pacific American cultural issues and how they affect mental health care should be included as part of this course. Asian and Pacific American mental health resources in the community should be identified and demonstration interviews of one or several patients from this group can be done.

Terminal Objectives. Trainees should acquire some historic knowledge of the Asian and Pacific American cultural groups, and they should be familiar with health and mental health resources in the community for this population. The trainees should possess a preliminary fund of knowledge about the influence of Asian cultures in the presentation of medical and psychiatric illness and gain an awareness of the coping mechanisms used by Asian and Pacific American families.

Attitudinal Learning. Residents should acquire sensitivity to existing cultural, ethnic and racial stereotypes and learn to counteract them in their contacts with patients. They should develop some sensitivity to the role occupied by the Asian and Pacific American family in coping with illness in its members.

Skills to be Acquired. The trainees should be able to elicit pertinent medical, personal, ethnic and cultural data when seeing Asian and Pacific American patients; deal with cultural, sexual, ethnic and racial biases which interfere with the patient–doctor relationship; and possess some skill in relating effectively to Asian and Pacific American families.

Courses. The cross-cultural seminar should be continued and should address issues in more depth. Specific Asian and Pacific American ethnic groups such as the Chinese, Japanese, Pilipinos, Koreans, Vietnamese or Pacific Islanders can be studied in greater detail. A sensitivity group should be started with focuses on racial, ethnic and sexual issues. Faculty members may also be encouraged to participate. The standard interviewing seminar course should include some Asian and Pacific American patients, and interpreters should be made available for non-English-speaking patients.

Postgraduate Year Two (PGY II)

If possible, residents should complete at least two psychiatric histories on Asian and Pacific American patients that incorporate culturally relevant factors, such as the patient's concept of illness, the significance of diet, mode of symptom presentation, family constellation and value systems. Home visits to Asian and Pacific American families are recommended.

Terminal Objectives. By the end of PGY II, the trainees should possess some knowledge about the following: cultural variations of psychopathology; culture-bound syndromes; the significance of foods and dietary habits; Asian and Pacific American concepts of mental illness; a preliminary knowledge of various Asian and Pacific American traditional, lay and contemporary healing systems; an awareness of the immigration experience of Asian and Pacific American groups to the United States; and the epidemiology of mental illness among Asian and Pacific American populations as compared with other cultures in this country and in the world.

Attitudinal Learning. The trainees should be aware of their own attitudes toward Asian and Pacific American patients. Hopefully, the resolution of racial prejudices will result in better and more effective ways of relating to these patients and their families.

Skills to be Acquired. Residents should be able to elicit meaningful psychiatric data from Asian and Pacific American patients and to better appreciate the role of cultural and ethnic factors in the production of the patient's mental illness. They should learn how to use an interpreter during interviews, when necessary. In their formulations of the patient's illness they should demonstrate an ability to incorporate significant sociocultural issues as they relate to the psychodynamics of Asian and Pacific American patients. Trainees are to demonstrate beginning skills in working with Asian and Pacific American families and be able to relate meaningfully to these patients and their families in the context of the various traditional and Western treatment methods.

Postgraduate Year Three (PGY III)

Courses. Seminars on normal and abnormal personality development, family and group therapy, child psychiatry and community consultation should include the impact of racial prejudice and discrimination on the subsequent development of the individual and family. The different patterns of child rearing and the manifestations of psychiatric illness among Asian and Pacific American populations should be taught. The influence of Asian and Pacific American culture upon group formation and the variations in family and group therapy of these patients must be emphasized. Elective seminars can be offered that deal with Asian and Pacific American literature, arts and medical literature. Elective language courses should be made available if trainees are in frequent contact with Asian and Pacific American patients. There should be periodic departmental conferences that deal with the influence of subcultures on the doctor–patient relationship, manifestations of psychiatric illness and the process of therapy. A weekend field experience of living with an Asian and Pacific American family can rapidly acquaint trainees with significant cultural and treatment issues. During PGY III a consultation experience in community agencies providing psychiatric, medical and adjunctive health care to Asian and Pacific American patients can be introduced.

Terminal Objectives. There should be an expansion and furthering of the objectives from the previous year. Trainees should be knowledgeable about the impact and influence of prejudice and racial discrimination on the development of the individual and community institutions and their subsequent effect on mental health and treatment. Residents should appreciate the complex interplay of culture on the psychological development and growth of Asian and Pacific American children. The trainees should be aware of some cross-cultural issues and how they affect psychiatric diagnosis and treatment.

Attitudinal Learning. There should be an increased sensitivity to the effects of cultural, racial, ethnic, sexual and class attitudes upon the doctor–patient relationship and the treatment process. Trainees should demonstrate greater comfort in relating to Asian and Pacific American patients, families and community agencies.

Skills to be Acquired. The skills acquired in PGY II should be further refined and expanded. Trainees should be able to provide appropriate consultation to social agencies and to their mental health colleagues in managing Asian and Pacific American patients, and should show greater proficiency in the diagnosis and treatment of Asian and Pacific American patients than in PGY II.

Postgraduate Year Four (PGY IV)

Courses. During the last year of residency training, the cross-cultural seminar should cover the traditional and modern concepts of health and disease. The seminar would also include a study of traditional, lay and Western mental health care systems and review the literature and research on traditional and modern methods of healing. The problems of the elderly Asian and Pacific American population, such as their adaptive patterns and styles, family breakdown, stresses created by an alienated society and ways of dealing with retirement, should be examined. There should be a study of mental health legislative and forensic issues to see how they affect Asian and Pacific American populations. The adjustment problems of recently arrived Asian and Pacific American immigrants and refugees are to be covered. Also included in this area are the adjustment and acculturation problems confronting the different generations.

Terminal Objectives. Knowledge should be acquired regarding historical, legal and political issues that have affected the immigration, adjustment patterns and coping styles of Asian and Pacific Americans and their communities. Trainees should be aware of the traditional and contemporary healing systems that are used by these patients. Trainees should be attuned to problems of the Asian and Pacific American elderly and the adjustment and acculturation problems of newly arrived immigrants and Asian and Pacific American youth, and their impact upon established Asian and Pacific American communities.

Attitudinal Learning. Residents should be knowledgeable in their role as consultants to Asian and Pacific American and non-Asian and Pacific American health agencies and their medical colleagues. They should be familiar with the non-Western healing practices used by Asian and Pacific American patients and be comfortable in functioning as therapists for these patients. They should be able to recognize and successfully manage transference and countertransference issues when doing psychotherapy with Asian and Pacific American patients.

Skills to be Acquired. The trainees should be able to provide effective program consultation on mental health issues confronting Asian and Pacific American patients to include the elderly immigrants and youth. They should be able to inform colleagues about the special aspects in the delivery of mental health services to these patients. Trainees should be able to formulate research designs that deal with mental health issues concerning Asian and Pacific American patients and should also have the capacity to pursue independent projects on mental health issues regarding Asian and Pacific American patients, families and communities.

Specialized Training in Regional Asian and Pacific American Mental Health Multidisciplinary Training Centers

Although we believe that Asian and Pacific American patient care issues should be included in the core curriculum of all psychiatric residencies, we also advocate the establishment of specialized electives for psychiatrists in regional Asian and Pacific American mental health multidisciplinary training centers. It is well known that psychiatric training programs retain individual strengths and features which distinguish them from other programs, in addition to meeting the required essentials of accredited residencies. No two psychiatric residency programs are alike. These differences are determined by the make-up of the faculty and staff, priorities of the department or the larger institution, funding sources and the patient population served.

The incorporation of minority patient care issues in all training programs would make residents better providers of care for these patients. However, it is unlikely that a psychiatrist graduating from the average residency program could render highly effective service to, or advance the current state of knowledge about, Asian and Pacific American patients unless he had sought additional and specialized training. For these reasons we urge support for the establishment of a selected number of regional Asian and Pacific American mental health multidisciplinary training centers that would be affiliated with a psychiatric residency and would be well-staffed by Asian and Pacific American professionals who are heavily invested in providing mental health services to these populations.

The need for such regional training centers that focus on training and service to Asian and Pacific American populations rests on three arguments. The pertinent mental health literature on the training of Asian and Pacific American social workers, psychologists and psychiatrists (Kushida 1976; Sue and Chin, 1976; Wong, 1978) and the Report of the Special Populations Subpanel on Mental Health of Asian/Pacific-Americans (President's Commission on Mental Health, 1978c) reported the following. First, there is a lack of clinicians, teachers, researchers and administrators in the three mental health disciplines who can render bicultural and bilingual services to Asian and Pacific American patients. There is clearly a need to increase the number of trainees and faculty to satisfy this demand. Second, there is an underutilization of mental health services by Asian and Pacific American patients despite the need because of barriers in the service delivery systems. These obstacles have been identified as cultural and linguistic constraints; lack of bilingual and bicultural staff; tokenism in the employment of bilingual and bicultural personnel; maldistribution of service providers; credentialing obstacles encountered by Asian and Pacific immigrant mental health care providers; rigid catchment area boundaries; and insufficient services due to inadequate funding by local, state and federal agencies. Third, there is a poor knowledge base about Asian and Pacific American patients.

Sue and Chin (1976) state that we must develop a body of didactic knowledge suitable for teaching trainees. Dissatisfaction exists with the traditional measures of personality and with culturally biased theories of behavior, and "we need to train astute observers, sophisticated and novel research strategists, and persons who understand their group." Because of a dearth of clinical research activity, the current didactic curricular content remains somewhat distant from clinical realities.

These problems and objectives could best be dealt with in a unified way as suggested in the Asian and Pacific American subpanel report to the President's Commission on Mental Health (1978b) through the creation of training centers with the following characteristics. There should be larger, regional centers, as opposed to smaller catchment area centers, in order to pool financial and personnel resources as well as the Asian and Pacific American patient population. In this manner the number of staff, faculty, patients and training opportunities would be increased, resulting in better mental health care. Such centers should be community-based service organizations, multidisciplinary in approach and affiliated with a major teaching institution such as a university or medical school. These centers should be open to visiting faculty and trainees who would take their acquired skills back to their own communities.

Guiding
Principles in
Developing
Asian and
Pacific
American
Curriculum
in Regional
Training
Centers

A regional Asian and Pacific American mental health multidisciplinary training center must adhere to certain principles in order to achieve its objectives. First, psychiatric training should be conducted in an interdisciplinary context. Both the social work and psychology disciplines have begun to develop training programs and curriculum for Asian and Pacific Americans. Because of the multifaceted problems confronting Asian and Pacific Americans which necessitate involvement with all the mental health disciplines, psychiatric trainees would best be taught in a multidisciplinary setting (see Figure 1).

Each discipline would maintain its own identity while benefiting from the sharing of an interdisciplinary focus on Asian and Pacific

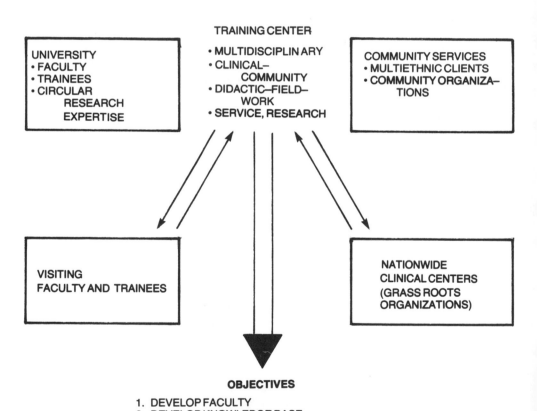

FIGURE 1

Proposed Asian and Pacific American Training Center

American issues. Supervision would be provided by members of the same discipline to afford trainees a role model, while didactic seminars on Asian and Pacific American issues could be taught in an interdisciplinary fashion. The interfacing of trainees from all the mental health disciplines in the clinical setting and seminars would lead to the optimal sharing of common experiences and problems encountered in working with Asian and Pacific American patients. Such an atmosphere would foster interdisciplinary collaboration in dealing with service needs and generating research.

Second, active and meaningful affiliation between organizations and major training centers should occur in teaching and research. In the past, there have been marked discrepancies between the didactic curriculum and clinical practice in training programs. The regional training center would be able to coordinate and integrate the didactic teaching and clinical experience. The faculty and staff of both institutions would maintain their clinical skills with Asian and Pacific American patients by providing direct and indirect services at the community service agency. They would also engage in clinical research which, in turn, would influence the formal curriculum. The teaching and research resources available from an academic teaching institution would promote clinical research and the development of curriculum appropriate to the Asian and Pacific American population.

Third, trainees working with Asian and Pacific American populations must develop not only culturally appropriate clinical skills but also must acquire consultation and teaching expertise in dealing with community institutions, agencies and lay groups in order to provide effective primary, secondary and tertiary care. Asian and Pacific American groups must be made aware of the mental health services available to them, and collaborative efforts are also necessary to create innovative, effective mental health approaches.

Fourth, service, training and research efforts must proceed simultaneously. The regional training center should deliver bicultural and bilingual services in an innovative fashion, develop new curriculum and training models and acquire new information. The interconnections between service, teaching and research must be readily apparent and viewed positively by the staff and faculty, trainees and the Asian and Pacific American community.

Last, but not least, in order to afford maximum cooperation between the academic center and regional training center, funds for training should also be granted directly to the training center.

Core Curriculum Content for Psychiatrists in Asian and Pacific American Training Centers

The specialized training program would probably function best as a track system within a general residency program, with clinical placements in community service agencies in Asian and Pacific American neighborhoods. The resident in such a training program should be regarded in the same light as the resident in child, forensic, community or research psychiatry. All are expected to possess a sound grounding in basic psychiatry on which is superimposed additional, specialized interests (Wong, 1978).

In the general residency program, the formal curriculum must provide courses in comparative psychopathology (focused on cultural and ethnic variations), cultural norms and anthropology, social psychology, religions and social issues of the ethnic group. In addition, seminars should deal with social problems and mental health issues of other minority groups. Research and teaching skills are to be encouraged. These courses should be taught throughout the four or more years of training rather than being relegated to any one time.

Any program specifically designed to train psychiatrists to work with Asian and Pacific American populations must meet the general requirements established for psychiatric graduate medical education. However, care must be taken to avoid overlapping of courses and clinical experiences in order not to impose hardships on the resident. While it may be possible within the standard residency period to train the resident to function as a competent psychiatrist in an Asian and Pacific American community, it may require additional time and training to attain the stated goals. Similarly, the trainee in child psychiatry may require extended training.

One or more ethnic training tracks may be situated in a training institution located, for example, in the San Francisco Bay area, where there are many Chinese, Japanese and Koreans. The requirements for each ethnic training program should be maintained whenever possible, for despite many similarities there are significant differences and needs among the groups. In addition, the ethnic training programs should be multidisciplinary to include training for Asian psychologists, psychiatric nurses and social workers within the same institution.

The core curriculum for psychiatric residents in regional training centers will differ from the cross-cultural curriculum mostly in the third and fourth postgraduate years of training. A fifth postgraduate year of training may be offered to produce a psychiatrist who is expert in working with Asian and Pacific American people and who will be capable of doing clinical practice, teaching and research. Psychiatric residents who elect training in Asian and Pacific American regional multidisciplinary training areas will be drawn from three groups. First, there will be residents who enter a psychiatric training program in a geographic area where there is a large Asian and Pacific American population and the trainees plan to specialize in working with this group. Second, during PGY IV, residents may elect six-month clinical rotations in Asian and Pacific American regional multidisciplinary training centers and, third, graduates may elect to do an additional year of postgraduate training (PGY V). There may also be residents who choose to come to a regional center from other residency training programs because they are interested in working with Asian and Pacific American populations. They fit into the second or third category of trainees.

It is assumed that residents in the first group will have had courses on minority issues in the general residency training program but, in addition, will have had actual patient experience with Asian and Pacific American populations. Residents in PGY IV may elect a clinical rotation such as the outpatient department, inpatient service, child and adolescent clinic and so forth where they will see primarily Asian and Pacific American patients and receive supervision by Asian and Pacific American faculty. During their clinical work they will continue to be in formal courses and clinical conferences where a greater emphasis will be placed on Asian and Pacific American cultural and treatment issues. They will have intimate contact with the following: current legislative issues; group, family and individual treatment issues as they apply to Asian and Pacific American patients; the application of relevant theory to the practice of child psychiatry; teaching in consultation to Asian and Pacific American health agencies; instruction in Asian and Pacific American languages; and experience in managing the acculturation problems faced by the different generations of Asian and Pacific American groups.

The PGY V fellowship would allow trainees greater freedom to concentrate in areas of selected clinical research, community organizational work, or curriculum development projects as well as a chance to further their clinical skills. Fellows could work with staff and faculty on ongoing projects and initiate their own research. Didactic teaching would consist of clinical conferences, tutorial and supervisory sessions and appropriate seminars that would further the trainee's skills as a clinical researcher, community organizer or teacher.

Trainee and Faculty Development

Training programs designated to educate Asian and Pacific American psychiatrists within a general residency should have at any one time a minimum of two Asian trainees. Peers learn from each other, apart from the formal instruction they receive, and they need a psychological and culturally similar base of support in a new environment. The presence of two or more culturally related Asian trainees, for example, two Japanese Americans or a Chinese American and a Japanese American, would help reinforce their ethnic identification and special training objectives. Ideally, for ease of training, the trainees should be members of that ethnic minority population served by the training institution or be culturally related to it. If an Asian applicant does not wish to enter this specialized track, he or she should not be counted as one of the two trainees deemed necessary to maintain such a program but should be considered instead as a regular resident (Wong, 1978).

Affirmative action recruitment of multidisciplinary Asian and Pacific American trainees and other trainees interested in working with Asian and Pacific American groups is essential. Such trainees should meet the other qualifications for the university residency program, have a personal commitment toward working with Asian and Pacific American populations and, preferably, have a bicultural and bilingual personal background. Financial stipend support from the federal government and state would greatly enhance trainee participation. Qualified trainees should be encouraged to assume teaching responsibilities and actively recruited to join the staff and faculty upon graduation.

While the Asian trainee must be exposed to the clinical experiences required of non-Asian trainees, he should participate especially in outreach and after-care programs. Above all, the trainee's patient load should not be restricted to Asian and Pacific American patients; he needs to be exposed to a wide variety of individuals with different clinical syndromes and requiring various treatment approaches. The trainee should be encouraged to try innovative therapies for Asian and Pacific American patients not fitting into clearly defined Western treatment categories.

Affirmative action recruitment of multidisciplinary Asian and Pacific American minority faculty is essential. To have maximum impact, the faculty should be full-time and on a regular tenure-promotion track. Community service staff, community leaders and visiting Asian and Pacific American consultants must be seen as vital elements of the training staff. Because of the recognized shortage of Asian and Pacific American academicians in the United States, existing and potential faculty in various training programs should be identified and a forum of support should be provided.

A national roster of names should be established. These academicians can serve as resources for teaching and provide consultation for the development of faculty, both Asian and non-Asian, and Asian curriculum content in local programs. Asian and Pacific and American psychiatrists should be encouraged to pursue research on minority mental health issues. They should participate in national organizations such as the Asian Caucus of the American Psychiatric Association, where Asians and non-Asians meet and provide intellectual stimulation and mutual support.

A number of national, federal and nonfederal psychiatric, medical and educational organizations have shown some receptivity for the inclusion of Asian and Pacific American psychiatrists in their ranks and have supported affirmative action in placing Asian and Pacific American psychiatrists in leadership roles. Political involvement in these groups is important both for the academic careers of psychiatrists and for the impact upon the home institutions. Prominent organizations include the American Association of Directors of Psychiatric Residency Training, National Institute of Mental Health, American Association of Chairmen of Departments of Psychiatry, American Association of Psychiatric Services to Children, Association of Directors of Medical Student Education in Psychiatry, American Academy of Child Psychiatry, American Medical Association and the American Board of Psychiatry and Neurology.

Institutional racism and the tendency to lump Asian and Pacific American psychiatrists together with the much maligned foreign medical graduates have raised barriers to the academic progression of many Asian faculty and discouraged potential faculty members. On the other hand, international politics and more effective lobbying by Asian and Pacific American groups have created the most favorable climate for Asian and Pacific American faculty and staff ever observed in institutions. Asian and Pacific American psychiatrists who previously denied their ethnic and racial heritage are more willing to be involved in Asian and Pacific American issues and should be encouraged to actively teach culturally relevant courses in psychiatric training programs. However, they must continue to be viewed as competent psychiatrists in their own right who are Asian and Pacific Americans by virtue of ethnic and racial origins and who may possess psychiatric expertise in cross-cultural issues. The stigma of being an Asian psychiatrist, a relative rarity, is disappearing.

During the past decade in particular, the number of nationally recognized Asian and Pacific American psychiatrists has increased, although they are comparatively few in actual numbers. The visibility of positive role models may encourage current trainees to seek an academic career, thus expanding the current supply of Asian and Pacific American faculty. However, the nation is experiencing a crisis in psychiatric recruitment—only 3 to 4 percent of all medical school graduates are entering psychiatry. Any significant increase in the number of Asian and Pacific American academicians will be long in coming. Along with their non-Asian and Pacific American colleagues, Asian and Pacific American psychiatrists will have to work on attracting high school and college students to the field of psychiatry.

Research

Basic and clinical research on Asian and Pacific American populations is crucial in the development of the curriculum and teaching materials. The body of Asian and Pacific American psychiatric literature is quite small. Because there is very little research that directly addresses treatment issues, the highest priority should be given to clinical studies that are relevant to the delivery of services. Such research should evaluate the effectiveness and theoretical validity of the current treatment approaches and help develop conceptual models for clinical practice based on sound knowledge. Asian and Pacific American research, academic curriculum and service delivery can be viewed as a tripartite model in which all three elements are intimately connected (see Figure 2). Ideally, in this model service delivery should rest upon the academic curriculum and research. At present, service needs greatly influence research and the academic curriculum content, in contrast to the usual psychiatric training programs where the delivery of service is subordinate to education and research. In practice there is an active exchange between the three components although in the regional center, at this time, we place the highest priority on the delivery of services.

It seems logical that research aimed at developing successful clinical interventions for Asian and Pacific American patients should take place within the service delivery agencies that have been most successful in meeting mental health needs of these patients. Over the past several years a number of Asian and Pacific American mental health agencies have been developed throughout the United States. They have generally been created because the mainstream mental health system has not been successful in treating Asian and Pacific American patients. These programs are usually community-based and staffed with service providers who themselves are Asian and Pacific Americans. Examples of such programs are the South Cove Community Mental Health Services in Boston, the Richmond Maxi-Center in San Francisco, the Northeast Chinatown Mental Health Services in Oakland, Asian Counselling and Referral Services in Seattle, and several others. Research on delivery of services by these programs and on the types of clinical interventions they have found successful would provide valuable knowledge for teaching.

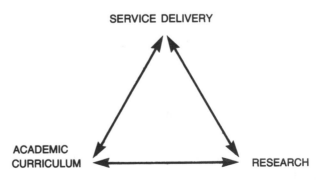

FIGURE 2

A Tripartite Model for Practice with Asian and Pacific Americans

The following fourteen research areas have been identified as high priorities in developing a body of theoretical knowledge regarding Asian and Pacific American patients.

1. The development of a clinically useful definition of culture would enable service providers to take into account the societal variations that influence psychodynamic formulations, diagnoses and treatment.

2. Basic epidemiological data regarding the various Asian and Pacific American cultures would include—

- patterns of utilization of mental health services;
- types of psychopathology identified with service providers;
- types of treatment given to Asian and Pacific American service seekers;
- outcome of treatment;
- differences in the above when service providers are Asians or Pacific-Americans themselves as compared with when they are not;
- differences in the above according to each of the identified Asian and Pacific American ethnic groups and different generations in each group.

3. The manifestations and conceptualization of mental illness, psychopathology and family and individual response to illness and treatment in Asian and Pacific American cultures should be studied.

4. Asian and Pacific American communication patterns, and especially nonverbal communication, should be considered. Most Western psychotherapies rely on verbal communication to express ideas and feelings. However, Asian and Pacific American cultures frequently utilize nonverbal communication to convey important messages in lieu of direct verbal expressions. These may be misunderstood or not noticed by Western therapists.

5. The applicability of psychoanalytic theory to Asian and Pacific American cultures is relevant. Research must address the modifications and necessary theoretical refinements if psychoanalytic approaches are to be effectively applied to people whose philosophical framework, sociocultural values and developmental patterns are quite different.

6. Genetic differences of Asian and Pacific American populations may account for different responses to alcohol, lithium and other psychotropic drugs. Empirically, it has been noted that Asian manic-depressive patients respond to a lower serum lithium level, require lower doses of phenothiazines, and may react adversely to alcohol. These are issues worthy of research.

7. Asian and Pacific Americans born in the United States may experience conflicts of growing up with dual and often contradictory value systems, resulting in generational and identity conflicts. The

problem of not feeling whole and well-integrated and the adaptive responses employed deserve more attention. In addition, Asian and Pacific American communities constantly struggle with the acculturation problems of first, second and third generation individuals, which are vastly different.

8. Specific Asian and Pacific American patterns of symptom formation and symptom constellations should be looked at. It has been noted that Asian and Pacific American patients have a high incidence of psychosomatic symptoms. Specific symptom patterns must be further elucidated and their symbolic and social meaning better understood.

9. Culture-bound syndromes should be clarified. Descriptions of specific culture-bound syndromes and their relation to recognized Western pathological syndromes should be explored.

10. The role of the family is much more significant in the Asian and Pacific American groups than in the majority American culture. A better understanding of the different Asian and Pacific American family constellations and their role in treatment is essential in the delivery of effective mental health services.

11. The role of indigeneous healing practices in treatment is important. Historically, the Asian and Pacific American cultures have employed acupuncture, herbs, massage, medication and so forth to treat mental health problems. A better understanding of these forms of treatment would be helpful along with the possibility of integrating them into Western mental health treatment.

12. Psychological assessment instruments should be analyzed for their cultural relevance and appropriateness. Our current psychological tests are culture-bound. The modification of existing assessment devices and the development of culturally relevant and appropriate instruments for Asian and Pacific American populations is necessary.

13. Approaches are needed for dealing with the culture shock and adjustment problems of newly arrived Asian immigrants. The United States has received large numbers of Asian immigrants within the past five years, and these people are undergoing considerable stress adapting to a vastly different way of life. Immediate strategies must be developed to help these immigrants cope and to prevent mental health problems from arising.

14. The following service delivery issues affecting Asians and Pacific Americans deserve attention from researchers:

> • the development of culturally congruent approaches to patient care;
> • effective methods of overcoming the stigma of mental health service utilization;
> • effective means of surmounting language barriers that may hinder effective mental health care and access to medical and psychiatric treatment.

In order to successfully implement the inclusion of Asian and Pacific American issues in psychiatric training programs, Asian and Pacific American psychiatrists must strive to assume meaningful academic, administrative, clinical and research roles in training programs. Although they may possess knowledge about cross-cultural psychiatry, they must first be recognized as competent psychiatrists to gain the respect of trainees and faculty and lend credence to the subjects they teach. There must be an adequate number of Asian faculty in such a training program. It is suggested that there be a minimum of three, key Asian faculty—a social scientist and two psychiatrists. One psychiatrist should be a significant figure in the didactic teaching program and the other a clinical supervisor. Part-time Asian faculty and consultants should be involved to further strengthen the didactic and clinical teaching.

Being an Asian should not be sufficient in itself to qualify the individual as a key faculty member for the special program. The person must know the cultural, social and philosophical aspects of his or her ethnic heritage; be able to communicate in the language; and have worked with Asian and Pacific American patients and community groups. Outside Asian and Pacific American faculty should be invited to teach in this specialized program. Because it may be difficult to find within a single institution sufficient, qualified faculty from these groups, it is essential to engage visiting consultants from other geographic locations in order to provide the program with breadth and depth (Wong, 1978).

Faculty members interested in introducing Asian and Pacific American content materials in residency programs should work within the existing institutional structure to formulate teaching materials and to negotiate for teaching time. The faculty initiator should present both the teaching material and an evaluation method to test the effectiveness of the teaching program. Consideration should be given to applying for funding from governmental agencies such as NIMH or from private foundations to help support the teaching of minority issues.

The teaching of Asian and Pacific American patient issues in most residency programs is best presented within the context of a cross-cultural seminar that addresses cultural issues in the delivery of mental health care to all minority groups. The inclusion of all ethnic patients in any training program's immediate service area gives added relevance to the systematic examination of cultural issues in mental health care. Staff and trainees can see the benefits of teaching that addresses patient issues they encounter daily. Some cross-cultural principles learned in the general seminar can be applied to all ethnic groups.

Several teaching institutions interested in cross-cultural psychiatric teaching programs can form a consortium to pool their resources. In this manner, they can secure a sufficient number of faculty, develop common teaching materials and work more effectively to secure funding from other sources. Above all, Asian and Pacific American

Implementation Strategies at the Institutional Level

psychiatrists should work closely with the other Asian mental health professionals so that cross-fertilization of ideas and dissemination of research findings and teaching materials can take place. An effort should be made to evaluate the quality and relevance of existing teaching materials with the aim of cataloging them for use in various training programs. There is still a paucity of published clinical and research papers that relate to mental health issues of Asian and Pacific American patients. More published data are needed if these issues are to successfully compete for teaching time in a residency program.

We recommend strong support for the concept of Asian and Pacific American multidisciplinary mental health training centers as they appear to be the model facility for developing the faculty, knowledge base, service delivery system and curriculum materials that will be useful for all psychiatric residency programs. To facilitate communication and dialogue between the training centers and other institutions and to demonstrate their educational commitment, we recommend the following:

- that these centers engage in the production of periodic newsletters, manuals of curricular development, clinical research findings and videotapes;
- that they make presentations regularly at scientific meetings and encourage visiting faculty and residents to participate in the programs;
- that they have continual liaison with other grass-roots service delivery systems to share their experiences and to provide additional fieldwork placements;
- that they establish additional training centers in other geographic regions.

Major Public Policy Recommendations

The report to the President's Commission on Mental Health has recommended many significant changes in the field of education and the delivery of mental health services. We urge that continuing support be given to these recommendations and that the National Institute of Mental Health continue to place high priority on training, delivery of services and research for each of the four identified ethnic minority groups. Similarly, the American Medical Association Essentials of Accredited Residencies has clearly elucidated the need for clinical and didactic teaching that takes into account the economic, ethnic, social and cultural factors in mental health and mental illness. It stresses the need for residents to be familiar with the various cultural backgrounds of patients for whom they have clinical responsibility in the course of residency training. It is urged that implementation of these recommendations be reviewed periodically by groups who have Asian and Pacific American representatives.

The NIMH Division of Manpower and Training Program Guidelines has placed into effect the new priorities that must be satisfied in order for psychiatric training programs to receive federal grant support. These follow closely the recommendations in the report to the President's Commission on Mental Health. Again, it is recommended that Asian and Pacific American psychiatric educators and clinicians serve on key review committees and site visiting teams to ensure that the NIMH program guidelines are followed when psychiatric training programs receive federal aid. Qualified Asian and Pacific American personnel should be considered for appointments to peer review groups operated by the National Institute on Drug Abuse.

The development and refinement of a model Asian and Pacific American core curriculum suitable for all psychiatric training programs should continue to have high priority. This is best done in the context of a cross-cultural seminar, which should be considered an essential part of all residency training programs. This item should be brought to the attention of the American Association for Directors of Psychiatric Residency Training, which should support its implementation.

In keeping with the concept of specialized research and training centers, the federal government should support the development of the regional multidisciplinary Asian and Pacific American mental health centers devoted to training, research and excellence in service. Such funding should be matched by state and local support. These centers would bring together experts on Asian and Pacific American educational, research and patient care issues and serve as a "think tank" for the development of faculty. Psychiatric graduates or trainees rotating through these centers could apply their expertise in their local areas.

We support the concept of a national registry or identified group of experts on Asian and Pacific American affairs, which would be available on a consultant basis to aid psychiatric training programs and community service agencies in improving services, research and training to Asian and Pacific American populations. Toward this end we recommend that training funds be granted directly to community-based training programs to help integrate didactic teaching and the delivery of services to minority populations. Last, we support the concept of funding special projects in training, research and service delivery to minority groups in the hope that their efforts can be disseminated to all psychiatric training programs in the United States.

References

Abbott, K., & Abbott, E. Juvenile delinquency in San Francisco's Chinese-American community. *Journal of Sociology*, 1968, *4*, 45–56.

American Medical Association's Essentials of Accredited Residencies. *1978–79 Directory of residency training programs*, Chicago, IL.: Author, 1978.

Berk, B. B., & Hirata, L. C. Mental illness among the Chinese: Myth or reality? *Journal of Social Issues*, 1973, *29*, (2), 149–66.

Brown, T., Stein K. M., & Huang, K. Mental illness and the role of mental health facilities in Chinatown. In S. S. Wagner (Ed.), *Asian-Americans: Psychological perspectives*. Palo Alto, CA.: Science and Behavior Books, 1973.

Center for Mental Health Services. Manpower research and demonstration guidelines. Department of Health Education and Welfare, July, 1979.

San Francisco Chronicle. Chinatown gangs. July 5, 1972, p. 3.

Graduate Medical Education National Advisory Committee to the Secretary, HEW. Interim Report. Department of Health Education and Welfare. Publication No (HRA) 79–633. Washington, D.C.: U.S. Government Printing Office, 1979.

Jacobs, P., Landau, S., & Pell, E. *To serve the devil: Vol. 2, Colonials and sojourners.* New York: Vintage Books, 1971.

Kitano, H. H. Changing achievement patterns of the Japanese in the United States. *Journal of Social Psychology*, 1962, *58*, 257–64.

Kitano, H. H. Japanese American crime and delinquency. *Journal of Psychology*, 1967, *66*, 253–63.

Kitano, H. H. Japanese American mental illness. In S. Sue & N. Wagner (Eds), *Asian-Americans: Psychological perspectives*. Palo Alto, CA.: Science and Behavior Books, 1973.

Kushida, A. H. A training program for Asian and Pacific Islander Americans. *Social Casework*, 1976, *57* (3), 185–94.

Owan, T. Asian Americans: A case of benighted neglect. Paper presented at the National Conference on Social Welfare, San Francisco, California, May 1975.

President's Commission on Mental Health. *Task Panel Reports*, Vol. 1. Washington, D.C.: U.S. Government Printing Office, 1978.(a)

President's Commission on Mental Health. *Task Panel Reports*, Vol. 3. Washington, D.C.: U.S. Government Printing Office, 1978.(b)

President's Commission on Mental Health. Report of the Special Populations Subpanel on Mental Health of Asian/Pacific Americans. In *Task Panel Reports*, Vol. 3. Washington, D.C.: U.S. Government Printing Office, 1978.(b)

President's Commission on Mental Health. *HEW Task Force Report*. Washington, D.C.: Department of Health Education and Welfare, Publication No. (ADM) 79–848, 1979.

Sue, D., & Frank, A. A typological approach to the psychological study of Chinese and Japanese American males. *Journal of Social Issues*, 1973, *29*, 129–48.

Sue, S., & Chin, R. Report on the National Asian American Psychology Training Conference, Long Beach, California, July 29–August 1, 1976.

Sue, S., & Kitano, H. Stereotypes as a measure of success. *Journal of Social Issues*, 1973, *29*, 83–98.

Sue, S., & McKinney, H. Asian-Americans in the community mental health care system. *American Journal of Orthopsychiatry*, 1975, *45*, 111–18.

Sue, S., & Sue, D. W. Chinese-American personality and mental health. *Amerasia Journal*, 1971, *1*, 36–49.

U.S. News and World Report. Success story of one minority group in the U.S. December 26, 1966, pp. 73–76.

Wong, N. Psychiatric education and training of Asian and Asian-American psychiatrists. *American Journal of Psychiatry*, 1978, *135*, 1525–29.

Bibliography

Abbott, K, & Abbott E. Juvenile delinquency in San Francisco's Chinese-American community: 1961–66. In S. Sue, & N. Wagner (Eds.), *Asian American psychological perspectives.* Palo Alto: Science and Behavior Books, 1973.

Abel, T., & Metrauz, R. *Culture and psychiatry.* New Haven: College and University Press, 1974.

Antunes, G. Ethnicity, socioeconomic status, and the etiology of psychological distress. *Sociology and Social Research,* 1974, *58,* 36–368.

Barth, F. *Ethnic groups and boundaries.* Boston: Little Brown, 1969.

Benedict, R. *The chrysanthemum and the sword.* Cambridge, MA.: The Riverside Press, 1946.

Berkeley, R. The new gangs of Chinatown. *Psychology Today,* May 1977, pp. 60–69.

Bott, E. *Family and social network.* New York: Free Press, 1972.

Bourne, P. Suicide among Chinese in San Francisco. *American Journal of Public Health,* 1973, *63* (8), 744–50.

Breslow, L., & Klein B. Health and race in California. *American Journal of Public Health,* 1971, *61*:763–75.

Carpenter, W., & Strauss, J. Cross-cultural evaluation of Schneider's first-rank symptoms of schizophrenia: A report from the international pilot study of schizophrenia. *American Journal of Psychiatry,* 1974, *131* (6), 682–87.

Carr, J. E., & Tan, E. K. In search of the true Amok: Amok as viewed within the Malay culture. *American Journal of Psychiatry,* 1976, *133* (11), 1295–99.

Caudill, W., & Weinstein H. Maternal care and infant behavior in Japan and America. *Psychiatry,* 1969, *32,* 12–43.

Chafetz, M. E. Consumption of alcohol in the Far and Middle East. *New England Journal of Medicine,* 1964, *271,* 291–301.

Chang, M. *Tides from the West.* New Haven: Yale University Press, 1947.

Chen, P. Samoans in California. *Social Work,* 1973, *18* (2), 41–48.

Chung, S. H., & Rieckelman, A. The Koreans of Hawaii. In W. S. Tseng, J. F. McDermott, & T. W. Maretzki (Eds.), *People and culture in Hawaii.* Honolulu: University of Hawaii Press, 1974.

Daniels, R. *The politics of prejudice.* Berkeley CA.: University of California Press, 1962.

Divine, R. A. *American immigration policy, 1924–1952.* New Haven: Yale University Press, 1957.

Dow, T. S., & Silver, D. A drug induced Koro syndrome. *Journal of the Florida Medical Association,* 1973, *60* (4), 32–33.

Edwards, J. G. The Koro pattern of depersonalization in an American schizophrenic patient. *American Journal of Psychiatry,* 1970, *126* (8), 1171–73.

Fujii, S. Elderly Asian-Americans and use of public services. *Social Casework,* 1976, *57* (3) 203–7.

Gaw, A. An integrated approach in the delivery of health care to a Chinese community in America: The Boston experience. In A. Kleinman (Ed.), *Medicine in Chinese cultures.* Department of Health Education and Welfare Pub. No. (NIH) 75–633. Washington, D.C.: Government Printing Office, 1975.

Gaw, A. (Ed.). *Cross-cultural psychiatry.* Littletown, MA.: Wright-PSG Publishing, 1982.

Gordon, M. *Assimilation in American life.* New York: Oxford University Press, 1964.

Ho, M., & Norling J. The helper principle and the creation of therapeutic milieu. *Child Care Quarterly,* 1974, (2), 109–18.

Hsu, F. L. *Americans and Chinese: Two ways of life*. New York: Schumann, 1953.

Ichihashi, Y. *Japanese in the United States*. Stanford, CA.: Stanford University Press, 1932.

Jew, C. C., & Brody, S. A. Mental illness among the Chinese, 1: Hospitalization notes over the past century. *Comprehensive Psychiatry*, 1967, 8, 129–32.

Kane, J., & di Scipio, W. J. Acupuncture treatment of schizophrenia: Report on three cases. *American Journal of Psychiatry*, 1977, 136, 297–302.

Kikumura, A., & Kitano, H. H. Interracial marriage: A picture of the Japanese Americans. *Journal of Social Issues*, 1973, 29, 67–81.

Kim, B. An appraisal of Korean immigrant service needs. *Social Casework*, 1976, 57 (3), 139–48.

Kinzie, J. D. A summary of literature on epidemiology of mental illness in Hawaii. In S. W. Tseng, J. F. McDermott, & T. Maretzki (Eds.), *People and cultures of Hawaii*. Honolulu: University of Hawaii Press, 1974.

Kitano, H. H. *Japanese Americans: The evolution of a subculture*. Englewood Cliffs, N.J.: Prentice Hall, 1969.

Kitano, H. H. Japanese-American mental illness. In S. Plog, & R. Edgerton (Eds.), *Changing perspectives on mental illness*. New York: Holt, Rinehart and Winston, 1969, 257–84.

Kitano, H. H., & Sue, S. Model minorities. *Journal of Social Issues*, 1973, 29 (2).

Kitano, H. H. *The Japanese American*. New York: Prentice-Hall, 1967.

Kora, P. Morita therapy. *International Journal of Psychotherapy*, 1964, (4), 611–40.

Kung, S. W. *The Chinese in American life*. Seattle: University of Washington Press, 1962.

Lebra, T. S. *Japanese patterns of behavior*. Honolulu: University of Hawaii Press, 1976.

Li, F., Schlief, Y., Chang, C. J., & Gaw, A. Health care for the Chinese community in Boston. *American Journal of Public Health*, 1972, 536–39.

Lim, K. B. Asian-Americans: No model minority. *Social Work*, 1973, 43–53.

Lin, T. A study of the incidence of mental disorder in Chinese and other cultures. *Psychiatry*, 1953, 16, 313–36.

Lin, T., & Lin, M. Service delivery issues in Asian-North American Communities. *American Journal of Psychiatry*, 1978, 135 (4), 454–56.

Liu, W., & Yamada, M. The Asian-American mental health research center. *Social Casework*, 1976, 56 (3), 139–48.

Lo, W. H., & Lo, T. A ten-year follow-up study of Chinese schizophrenics in Hong Kong. *British Journal of Psychiatry*, 1977, 131, 63–66.

Lott, J. Migration of a mentality: The Pilipino community. *Social Casework*, 1976, 57 (3), 165–72.

Lyman, S. Red Guard on Grant Avenue: The rise of youthful rebellion in Chinatown. In B. Lamond (Ed.), *Asian-American psychological perspectives*. Palo Alto, CA.: Science and Behavior Books, 1973.

Maretzki, T. W. What difference does anthropological knowledge make to mental health? *Australia and New Zealand Journal of Psychiatry*, 1976, 10, 83–88.

Marsella, A. J., Kinzie, D., & Gordon, P. Ethnic variations in the expression of depression. *Journal of Cross-Cultural Psychology*, 1973, 4 (4), 435–59.

McWilliams, C. *Factories in the field: The story of migratory farm labor in California*. Boston: Little Brown and Co., 1936.

Morales, R. F. *Makibaba: The Pilipino American struggle*. Los Angeles: Mountainview Publishers, 1974.

Reed, T. E., Kalant, H., Gibbins, R. J., Kapur, B. M., & Ranking, J. G. Alcohol and acetaldehyde metabolism in Caucasians, Chinese and Americans. *Canadian Medical Association Journal*, 1976, *115*, 851–55.

Reynolds, D. K. *Morita psychotherapy.* Berkeley, CA.: University of California Press, 1976.

Reynolds, D. K., & Yamamoto, J. East meets West: Moritist and Freudian psychotherapies, research and relevance. In J. Masserman (Ed.), *Science and psychoanalysis*, Vol. 21. New York: Grune and Stratton, 1972.

Sata, L. S., Wong, N., Nguyen, T. D., Okura, K. P., Kim, L. I. C., & Morales, R. F. The Asian-Pacific American. In *Cultural Issues in Contemporary Psychiatry*, Vol. 2. Continuing Education Service of Smith Kline Corporation, 1978. (Audiovisual material)

Schooler, C. Serfdom's legacy: An ethnic continuum. *American Journal of Sociology*, 1976, *81*, 1265–86.

Sue, D. W., & Kirk, B. A. Asian-Americans: Use of counseling and psychiatric services on a college campus. *Journal of Counseling Psychology*, 1975, *22*, 84–86.

Sue, S., & Sue, D. W. MMPI comparisons between Asian-American and non-Asian students utilizing a student health psychiatric clinic. *Journal of Counseling Psychology*, 1974, *21* (5), 434–37.

Sue, S., & Wagner, N. (Eds.). *Asian-Americans: Psychological perspectives.* Palo Alto, CA.: Science and Behavior Books, 1973.

Sung, B. L. *Mountain of gold: The story of the Chinese in America.* New York: MacMillan, 1967.

Sung, B. L. *Chinese American manpower and employment.* Report to Manpower Administration, U.S. Department of Labor, 1975.

Tseng, W. The development of psychiatric concepts in traditional Chinese medicine. *Archives of General Psychiatry*, 1973, *29*, 569–75.

Yap, P. M. Hypereridism and attempted suicide in Chinese. *Journal of Nervous Mental Disorders*, 1958, *127*, 34–41.

Yap, P. M. Koro—A culture-bound depersonalization syndrome. *British Journal of Psychiatry*, 1964, *111*, 43–50.

Yap, P.M. The culture-bound reactive syndrome. In W. Caudill, & T. Lin (Eds.), *Mental health research in Asia and the Pacific.* Honolulu: East-West Center Press, 1969.

JAMES W. THOMPSON   HENRIETTA B. BLUEYE
CARL R. SMITH   R. DALE WALKER

CHAPTER **11**

Cross-Cultural Curriculum Content in Psychiatric Residency Training

An American Indian and Alaska Native Perspective

The training of psychiatric residents is complicated and everchanging. A few short years ago it seemed enough to take young physicians interested in psychiatry and provide them with intensive didactic and clinical training in psychoanalytic theory and technique. This is not the case today, however. Biological psychiatry, emergency psychiatry, family therapy, group therapy, behavior modification, child psychiatry, and other areas have forcefully argued the necessity of their inclusion in residency training. To a great extent they have been successful. Conversely, the same has not been true of cross-cultural psychiatry and other minority-related content, even though the justification for including such content has certainly been present.

Incorporating minority-related (or cultural or cross-cultural) content in psychiatry residency training curricula is indicated by the Liaison Committee on Graduate Medical Education (LCGME). *The Essentials of Accredited Residencies of the LCGME* (1979) states:

> Residents must have experience in the care of . . . patients from a wide variety of ethnic, social and economic backgrounds . . . . The residency program should provide its residents with instruction about American culture and subcultures. (pp. 52, 53)

This is not, however, a strong statement, especially in the light of the use of the word *should*, rather than the obligatory *must*. Nevertheless, a mandate does exist for the inclusion of minority-related content in the training of psychiatrists. Another source of support for including such content is *A Resident's Guide to Psychiatric Education* (Thompson, 1979). A handbook meant "to offer the psychiatric resident some guidelines in the broad field of psychiatry," it states in the section on cultural anthropology the following objectives:

Changes in Psychiatry and Residency Training

269

To attain an understanding of some of the various concepts of
culture and of the idea that cultures have arrived at a variety of
greatly diverse solutions to the problems of survival and the
achievement of satisfaction.
   To learn the range and diversity of marital and family patterns
across cultures and the ecological forces that may determine them.
   To have an awareness of some of the research concepts related to
the mental health aspects of cultural change and migration. (pp. 30,
32)

Despite the LCGME mandate and the *Resident's Guide* objectives,
minimal attention is paid, in practice, to cultural content in psychiatic
residency training, even in locations where minority groups are very
much in evidence. For example, at a medical school located in a
southwestern state in which 100,000 Indians live, there is one lecture
to psychiatry residents on Indian medical concepts and human behavior
and four, 1½-hour colloquia related to Indians. At a medical school in
a western state in which 31,000 Indians live, residents participate in
three hours of colloquia related to Indians and can elect cross-cultural
seminars with lectures relating to American Indian mental health.

Federal legislation and special interest groups representing patients
have forced the health care system to be responsible for a great number
of patients with mental and "social" illnesses not previously seen as
appropriate for or amenable to psychiatric intervention. This was
accomplished through many avenues, including community mental
health legislation and deinstitutionalization. This new focus, combined
with advances in psychopharmacology and the growth of therapies
concentrating on the social milieu, brought several jarring revelations
to light, namely that—

- there are large underserved and unserved populations of
psychiatrically ill patients;
- our diagnostic system appears woefully inadequate;
- mental health, mental illness and psychiatric treatment
which may fit the majority culture do not necessarily fit other
cultures and subcultures;
- when patients fall into recognized diagnostic categories, the
"incurable" illnesses may not be so incurable after all.

Many of the patients suddenly "found" as a result of these new forces
in psychiatry were members of minority groups that had long been
"forgotten" until the social, legal and health care systems were
reexamined. Until recently, minority groups were usually thought of
as having the lowest status and as contributing the most problems
within these systems.

The changes in the mental health care delivery system have been
nothing short of revolutionary. But psychiatric residents (and the
patients treated) still find that they lack understanding of cultural

psychiatry. The culturally sensitive resident must "make do" with empathy and innate understandings, as illustrated in the following example. It is related by one of the authors:

> While on night call as a resident I was asked by an emergency room physician to see what he described as a "crazy Indian." As I recall it was very cold that night, and I was frightened as I walked across the street because I had never psychiatrically interviewed an Indian who was psychotic and was unsure what to expect and how I might react. I was aware of the phenomenon of countertransference, and also aware that I was about to experience this first hand. When I was ushered into the little interview room, a young male who appeared anxious and agitated was lying on a bed. The nurse had warned me that he was impulsive and potentially violent. He was strapped to the bed after being brought in by the police. Being unsure of myself and not knowing what else to say, I immediately told the man that I also was an Indian. He smiled, appeared to relax a bit and asked me to help him with his situation. I agreed to listen. He began to explain that his four-year-old son had been taken from him by white people; a judge had decided that the boy should be placed in a foster home with a white family. They did this, the patient said, because he had been found with the son one morning curled up against a building where they had spent the night after drinking a bottle of wine. It was a number of miles from home, and he and the boy were sleepy. They were accustomed to sleeping outside, so they "camped" for the night. They were "attacked" by the police, he was arrested for public drunkeness, and the boy was placed in a foster home. The patient had been unable to find his son. He stated that he was so outraged with the situation that he had threatened the judge who did this to him. He assured me that without his son he was ready to die and would be willing to "suffer the consequences" if only he could teach the judge the price of separating a man from his son.
>
> The patient went on to say that he had no job in the city and no place to live, but he had a few friends downtown who could temporarily give him a place to stay. He had no legal assistance, and being new to the city he did not know how to seek help. He was receiving no financial assistance and had never used welfare.
>
> In making my psychiatric assessment of this man's situation it was clear that I was not being asked to deal with "pure" psychopathology. This patient's treatment required the engaging of an array of public and social services, all directed at the most essential and basic needs. In addition, these services had to be made sensitive to the patient's specific needs. I knew that if this man had been seen by a doctor with no training in cultural psychiatry he might well have been diagnosed as psychotic and/or alcoholic, deemed dangerous to himself and others, and committed to a psychiatric ward. My task was to make his treatment and rehabilitation (if necessary at all) easier by inclusion of the appropriate services. As I contemplated this, I thought, "How can we expect a patient from another culture to understand all of these systems and make them work for him?"
>
> Seeing the inadequacies of our own hospital health care model, I knew that the patient could receive help only if he were referred to the local Indian health board or if I were to take the patient on

myself in individual crisis intervention. I was hopeful that he would agree to work with me, for I knew that I had much to gain in helping him. Not only could I learn more about the total treatment of such an "illness," but I also could begin to understand much more of my own countertransference.

The residents who are concerned with the issues illustrated in this example are forced to read on their own (if indeed they can find anything to read on the subject) and to "supervise" themselves. In addition, in many programs they are best advised not to discuss these issues too much with peers and professors, lest they be thought of as ignoring more important areas. Without information to the contrary the resident will be drawn into using understandings and procedures which militate against the best care of minority patients. For instance, many psychological testing instruments have not been validated as useful in the assessment of minority mental illness. Even the traditional mental status examination is of questionable usefulness to a nonculturally sensitive interviewer.

It is increasingly appreciated that the training of a modern psychiatric specialist must encompass a multitude of conceptual models, diseases, treatments and patient types. Greater diversity is finding its way into training programs. In the area of cultural content, however, curriculum content has lagged behind this trend. Why there is such minimal treatment of cultural issues in residency training, and what can be done to improve the situation are the subjects of this chapter.

The Lag in Content

There are several reasons for the lag in cultural curriculum content. One reason is the resistance to change that would follow such curriculum proposals for psychiatric training. The idea that there are patients for whom entirely new conceptualizations in diagnosis, treatment, and modes of practice must be developed is threatening for some. The tendency is to act as though these patients did not exist or to continue to try to fit them into old models. The "crazy Indian" discussed previously would still have to search long and hard to find a physician willing to deal with him as other than a psychotic, an alcoholic, a child abuser or a potential suicide victim or murderer. The minority person is stereotyped as being a "poor therapy candidate," "incurable," or "just bad."

Another reason for the lag in developing cultural curriculum content is the poor availability of information and teaching techniques. Even training programs that have an interest in providing such education may have difficulty finding materials, qualified teachers or appropriate teaching models. Even if there is a "local expert," presentations frequently are narrow, anecdotal and without unifying principles. The message to the trainee boils down to, "People in other cultures are somewhat different from one another (and from you), just in case you should happen to run into any."

The large number of minority cultures and subcultures in the U.S. and in the world is yet a third reason for the lag. There exists a bewildering array of minority subcultures in the United States alone. For example, there are at least 200 American Indian tribes in this country, all with different histories and cultures. In fact, two given Indian persons may have more varied backgrounds between them than do two given European persons (Levine and Lurie, 1970). Most tribes have developed some commonalities (the pan-Indian concept), but all are profoundly culturally different from the majority culture in the United States. This is not a problem related only to Indians; to some extent cultural diversity is found among Hispanics, Blacks, Asian Americans and other groups. Given this diversity, it is quite natural that a residency training director might opt to include no minority cultural content at all (or only token content) to avoid trying to decide which minority groups to include and exclude.

Addressing the Lag in Content

Dealing with resistance to changes in curriculum and psychiatric practice is a task of "consciousness raising" aimed at changing attitudes. This work must be done on multiple levels, involving, for example, the American Psychiatric Association and the American Association of Directors of Psychiatric Residency Training, licensing bodies such as the American Board of Psychiatry and Neurology, accrediting bodies (such as the LCGME), and local medical schools and training programs. The agents of such "consciousness raising" must be professionals who are themselves members of minority cultures or who are aware of and trained in cultural issues. These professionals can speak from positions within such organizations to bring cultural issues to the fore; propose and support position and policy statements; foster changes in standards and board questions; and provide information on the need for cultural curriculum content and the ways to provide it.

In addition, a challenge is posed by the lack of materials and the abundance of cultural diversity. A major task in cross-cultural psychiatric training is to introduce sufficient material into a training program to be meaningful, but not overwhelming, to the residents or the training program itself. In this chapter, we will attempt to speak to five key issues that must be addressed in teaching minority cultural content. These issues include (1) general vs. specific material; (2) factual vs. ideological content; (3) who the teachers of such curriculum content should be; (4) putting learning into practice; and (5) potential research areas.

General versus
Specific Content

General content here refers to content that speaks of no culture or minority in particular except as examples, focusing rather on normal variations in people and on distinguishing illness from cultural dissimilarity. *Specific content* refers to material related to a specific group. An example of specific content would be "the diagnosis and treatment of alcoholism in the Arapaho Tribe."

If one chooses a specific orientation in developing seminars on Indians, Blacks, Hispanics, Asian Americans, and so forth, there are definite advantages. More facts, figures and specific case examples can be provided, which allows psychiatrists to directly apply their learning to a person of a particular group. Groups can be considered on the basis of availability of relevant literature, and specific illnesses affecting specific groups can be studied. Finally, residents will feel that they have mastered a concrete body of knowledge.

A specific approach has some disadvantages. Residents may be trained to deal with groups that they will never see. This is true even if the groups chosen are those in the area where the residency program is located, for residents may choose to practice elsewhere. Second, some important groups are bound to be left out. And finally, even within a given group, subgroup variation within the group may render specific subject matter meaningless.

Use of the general approach also has some advantages. These include preparing the resident to deal with any person culturally different from himself or herself because the training is aimed at overall precepts rather than narrow specifics; encouraging educators to develop more adequate materials and techniques for teaching because they will not be relying only on multiple case examples without unifying principles; and training the resident to deal with the patient in a creative and individualized way with culture being only one portion of the diagnostic and therapeutic approach.

Disadvantages of the general orientation include the following. First, residents may be provided with so few specifics that the generalities are meaningless. Second, residents may get the idea that they know "all there is to know of importance" about other cultures and subcultures. And, third, there is the possibility of angering members of specific cultural minorities who wish also to be represented in curriculum content.

In this chapter we would argue for a general orientation to the teaching of the cultural aspects of mental health and illness. However, training that relies on multiple case examples with no conceptual framework would not only create a very chaotic training program but also leave the practitioner with, at best, spotty knowledge and skills for dealing with cultural matters. The modern psychiatrist deals with a wide range of patients and disorders. The psychiatrist of the future will be required to deal with ideas, illnesses, and treatments that are not even conceived of today. In addition, one can never hope to include in training programs material on all cultures. Instead of providing residents with a few blueprints, we need to teach them how to draw and use a blueprint. How such a blueprint or framework might be developed is shown through the examples to be presented. Although these examples are extensive, they are not intended to be a comprehensive treatment of cross-cultural psychiatry. Nor are the individual examples intended as finished products. They are included to illustrate how a general approach might be developed.

The examples used are of American Indian patients and are from the authors' combined experience. We would expect that all examples in a complete curriculum would *not* be of Indian patients, though we would hope that many would be. The cultural groups represented will vary with the program, its location and its patient population, as well as its professors and residents. But two things should in our opinion remain constant:

> • a focus on the precepts of dealing with patients culturally different from the resident, as opposed to a focus on the examples per se;
> • the inclusion of examples from a broad range of cultures, as opposed to the use of only one or two cultures for this purpose.

We believe that a case example–discussion format is most useful in presenting cross-cultural material. The topic does not easily lend itself to lectures, for the "body of knowledge" to be learned is simply not as structured as psychopharmacology. In this sense, teaching cross-cultural psychiatry is similar to teaching psychotherapy. Much of the educational process in this area is attitudinal in nature, calling for a forum in which attitude change can occur.

Steps in the Educational Process

We also believe that classroom work must be accompanied by clinical experience and supervision, a topic that will be addressed later in this chapter.

The steps in a case example–discussion format should include:

I. Areas of concern when dealing with a person culturally different from oneself
II. A clinical example illustrating these areas of concern
III. Discussion of the materials
IV. Key points, both didactic and attitudinal (Although attitudinal points may or may not be formally stated in the teaching session, it is assumed that they are present and very important.)
V. References for further reading

How these steps might be applied in the development of a blueprint or framework is illustrated in the following three examples.

Example 1

I. Areas of Concern
   1. How does religion interact with mental health?
   2. How does removal of a person from his home environment affect him psychologically?
   3. How can the psychiatrist effectively use native healers and the precepts of native healing?

II. Clinical Case
   In Alaska, a Native American medical student relates:

   A Native American boy, 12 years old, was brought to the hospital because he was not speaking. His parents had died when he was very young, and a Native American couple had "adopted" him. In his home village, 200 miles from Fairbanks, he had been doing well in school and leading the life that most adolescent boys lead—hunting and fishing. On the assumption that if he were moved to Anchorage he would be more successful, he was removed from his unofficial adoptive family and put into a Caucasian home in Anchorage. In school he did not do well academically, was the only Native American there and was taunted for being different. He was very much alone. He began to lock himself in his room and was violent toward his stepsiblings. Finally, when he got hold of a gun and threatened suicide, he was brought to the mental institution. This was three months prior to my arrival on the psychiatric unit. During that time the boy seemed out of touch and had not spoken a single word. During my month with him, he did not speak. He did begin to seem more in contact, though, and I distinctly began to feel that he looked forward to our meetings.
   My first thought was to see if a native healer could come to see him. That wasn't possible. My next thought was to send him home to his village and let him live the life that adolescent boys there lead. That wasn't possible either. After my month's rotation, I left him with a great feeling of sadness.

III. Discussion Questions
   1. As this student's resident, how would you have helped her deal with this problem?
   2. How might a native healer have been useful here?
   3. What was this patient's illness?
   4. Would sending the boy back to his village have helped? Made things worse?
   5. Were the student's suggested solutions indeed "impossible"?
   6. Did a move to a city per se contribute to the clinical picture?
   7. What within the Caucasian family may have contributed?

IV. Key Points (available to the discussion leader only)
   (Didactic)

1. In many cultures (including some Indian cultures) a native healer will not treat a patient in another culture's treatment setting.
2. To be "adopted" once, and then to be moved to Anchorage, may have meant many things to such a youth. He may have felt that this would be a continuing pattern; or he may have felt that his Native American family did not really want him and that he would never see them again.
3. He may have felt "contaminated" by white culture, and so unworthy to live. He may have believed that to live outside his culture was tantamount to death.

(Attitudinal—these may or may not be directly stated)
1. The youth had a strong cultural heritage which was not inferior to white urban culture (i.e., fishing and hunting are as "good" as school in the city.)
2. Native healers are not "quacks."
3. Speaking may not be the best form of communication in treating a patient.

V. References for further reading (see bibliography to this chapter)

Example 2

I. Areas of Concern
   1. What does "a visit to the hospital" mean to members of another culture?
   2. What is "child abuse and neglect" from a cross-cultural perspective?
   3. How might parenting be different in different cultures?

II. Clinical Case
   A female Yakima Indian infant was referred to Children's Orthopedic Hospital because of multiple birth defects involving the extremities. She was brought to the hospital by her unmarried mother and father, respectively sixteen and eighteen years old. After the child was admitted, the parents returned to their home on the Yakima Reservation, many miles away. A prolonged period of evaluation and therapy of the infant followed.

   Because the parents did not come to visit the child during this time, the pediatric residents and the social worker became convinced of familial neglect. Since the baby had failed to thrive, the staff concluded that the parents were probably too young, inexperienced and irresponsible to take the infant home and properly care for her. The staff began planning to place the infant in a foster home and to have her declared a ward of the state.

   A psychiatry resident trained in cross-cultural psychiatry was assigned to the ward about this time. She realized that a trip from the Yakima reservation was a long trip. She also knew that if she could bring the parents to the hospital, there might be changes made in the care of the infant. After calling the Indian Health Service physician who had sent the baby to Seattle, arrangements were made for the parents to come to the hospital. Upon the parents' arrival the baby brightened and began feeding better from her mother. The mother surprised the nurses by asking for a different and more effective nipple for the baby's bottle. The baby returned home with her parents and the Indian Health Service physician followed the baby's growth and her multiple birth defects.

III. Discussion Questions
1. What in the family and social history would have been helpful in this case, had one been taken?
2. If you had been the Indian Health Service physician, what would you have told the parents to encourage them to go to the hospital to see the child?
3. How might the parents have understood the etiology and nature of the baby's defects?
4. Assume the state had in fact taken custody of the child. How would you have dealt with the parents when they arrived if you had been the psychiatric consultant? If you had been the pediatric resident?

IV. Key Points (available to the discussion leader only)
(Didactic)
1. Marriage and parenting may be looked at very differently in different cultures. (For example, this mother was from a family of thirteen children and had cared for infants since age ten.)
2. For a poor, rural person of another culture to go to a city hospital, where people have different language and customs, may be a cultural shock which is profoundly disturbing.
3. A child with deformities may be seen very differently by parents of varying cultures. They may see the child as a curse or a blessing; they may understand the problem in mystical or biological terms.

(Attitudinal—these may or may not be directly stated)
1. Unmarried, young parents are not "bad" parents per se.
2. Not having the money to come visit a relative in the hospital, or being frightened of such a trip, is not evidence of being uncaring or uninterested.
3. Neglectful or abusive parenting is very different from parenting which does not agree with the mores of the majority culture. These must be clearly separated.

V. References for further reading (see bibliography to this chapter)

Example 3

I. Areas of Concern
   1. How does the picture of alcoholism differ in various cultures?
   2. What does drinking behavior mean in various cultures?
   3. Do the sexes within a culture differ with regard to drinking behavior?
   4. Are there different patterns of drinking behavior even within a culture?
   5. What concomitants to drinking behavior may be found in a given culture?

II. Clinical Case
   A 46-year-old Arapaho man is brought in by his family to the outpatient psychiatry clinic of the University Hospital. He is very drunk and has been drunk for several days. As the history unfolds, it becomes apparent that the patient's alcohol use is sporadic (with binges of 1 to 2 weeks, 8 or 9 times per year), but by no means is it a new phenomenon. What has led the family to bring the man for treatment are two new behaviors: (1) daily crying spells in a usually stoic individual and (2) abusive comments made to strangers (men and women), often of a sexual nature.

   The patient is a farmer, with a small acreage, on the same land his father farmed. He has always been a hard worker and has provided for his family. He is married and has three children—a son, age 26, and two daughters, age 23 and 13. The son has an alcohol problem and has been in minor trouble with the law but holds a steady job. The older daughter is married and works as a laboratory technician at the Indian Hospital. The patient is brought in by the younger daughter and the wife.

III. Discussion Questions
   1. Is this patient an alcoholic? Why?
   2. What might the family constellation have to do with the presentation and dynamics of the case?
   3. Why the change in the patient's behavior?
   4. What sociocultural history would you like to have concerning this case? What data about the man's cultural environment?
   5. How would you approach this case?

IV. Key Points (available to the discussion leader only)
   (Didactic)
   1. Alcoholism differs greatly from culture to culture, even among tribal groups. Alcoholism in an Arapaho looks very different from alcoholism in a Seminole.
   2. "Severity" of alcoholism in a given culture is in part based on an internal comparison within that culture (e.g., in Arapaho culture this patient may be regarded as having a mild problem with alcohol.)
   3. A heavy drinking pattern in Indians may be associated with the following:
      • a dependency conflict

- anxiety
- feelings of powerlessness
- a change from an economy based on hunting and gathering
- a low degree of social complexity

4. Another view of Indian alcoholism is that it is the result of the position of Indians in America. Being in a disadvantaged position leads to alienation and a feeling of being deprived and frustrated in attempts to reach their goals.
5. There may be a genetic predisposition to alcoholism in some cultural groups that is greater than in some other groups.
6. Cultures in a state of transition between a traditional culture and a new, predominant culture may be at higher risk for problems like alcoholism.

(Attitudinal—these may or may not be directly stated)
1. All alcoholics are not alike (even within a culture).
2. "Chronic" alcoholism should not blind the clinician to other aspects of a case (e.g., recent changes, family dynamics, and so forth).
3. Drinking behavior is not a moral weakness.

V. References for further reading (see bibliography to this chapter)

The third example differs from the first and second in that it relates to a problem which to some extent is unique to American Indians. Alcoholism in Indians is *very* different from that in other cultures, in genetics, presentation, etiology, severity and prognosis. Because the example does deal so specifically with one group, it represents an exception to our theme. It is included to illustrate that there are problems that may be so specific to a culture and so great a concern to the clinical psychiatrist that individual curriculum content is necessary. Even so, the basic stance of general cultural content should be intertwined in the specific case example. For instance several of the key points in example three could easily be applied to any culture, and should be so applied within the discussion. The basic message should be that there are ways of understanding and dealing with alcoholism taking cultural differences into account, and, in addition, there exist particular cultures that need to be specifically understood in relation to alcoholism.

Much work is needed to develop this five-step educational format. Areas of concern must be identified which speak to a wide range of cultures; examples and discussion questions must be developed that effectively bring out important issues; key points must be written that capture the essence of what is to be learned; and references for future reading must be researched to allow the resident to easily pursue a given topic. These references should be carefully chosen to accurately portray cultural diversity.

A major conflict arises between those who would present curriculum content with regard to epidemiology, diagnosis, treatment and research (the "academic" group) and those who would use curriculum time to espouse a particular ideology with regard to minorities or a particular minority (the "ideologic" group). The academic group might present data as to incidence and prevalence of illness *A* and its symptoms, treatment and prognosis in various minority groups, stressing how cultural, sociological, economic and political factors influence each of these. The ideologic group might discount all these data in favor of a position that the patient is simply a victim of racism and that appropriate treatment is the fighting of that racism. This can be a very heated issue for teachers and curriculum planners, as the academic group may feel that the other is trying to suppress data and facts that do not fit into their ideological framework, and the ideologic group may feel that the former is co-opted and racist because they ignore the social ills that are expressed in the patient's difficulties. Resolution of this issue must precede any substantive efforts in curriculum development (Saur, 1979).

We agree that racism exists, and that it plays a large part in some patients' difficulites. Psychiatrists must understand the difference between individual psychopathology and reactions having a base in racism. But psychiatrists do not need to be sent to deal with this area with zealousness but no facts. This in the long run can be another form of racism wherein the patient is made to suffer for the sake of an ideology espoused by the physician.

Factual versus Ideological Content

The Teachers

Who should teach minority and cultural material? Some would say that a minority person should be the teacher, while others insist that this is not necessary. The argument of the former group reduces to: "The only one who can understand Indians and teach about them is another Indian." This position has several pitfalls. The greatest is that taken to extreme, it becomes ridiculous. The reductio ad absurdum would be: "The only one who can understand me is me because no one else is me, and therefore only I can teach me about how to deal with me." Another pitfall is that there are simply not enough minority teachers to do the job and probably never will be. Even if there were enough, it would be hoped that they would not be relegated to only the area of cross-cultural psychiatry, each becoming a mere "token Indian" on the faculty. This is a possible outcome if all such teaching were to be done by them. Finally, to be a minority person does not guarantee the appropriate training or attitude necessary for the job.

We contend that it is better to have no formal minority curriculum at all than to have a curriculum tainted with ignorance or racism.

Fortunately, the choice of teacher becomes much less important when a general content model such as the one described is used. The basic precepts taught are the same, regardless of who teaches them. Minority professors will undoubtedly teach all or part of the cross-cultural curriculum in some locations. But our model more easily allows them to resist having total responsibility for this area, which in turn allows them to develop professionally in other areas. Professors from the majority culture may also participate in the training process, further broadening the number of informed, aware and sensitive teachers.

Putting Learning into Practice

No area of psychiatric education is totally didactic. Psychotherapy is not learned apart from relating to patients in an appropriate setting. Biological psychiatry is not learned without the administration of psychopharmacologic agents to patients. The same is true with regard to the inclusion of cultural content in the curriculum. Clinical work is imperative to translate the general precepts learned in the classroom into interaction with real people. It is not adequate for clinical experiences to be presented within the confines of Anglo medical settings. While it is true that people carry their cultural background with them, even into "alien" circumstances such as an emergency room or university outpatient clinic, much cultural background may be suppressed when the patient comes face to face with a white psychiatry ward in a white hospital with white doctors.

Because the patient does not readily present a specific culture, the psychiatric resident may come to feel that it is not important or that it does not even exist outside the classroom. Cultural material important to diagnosis and treatment will be given most freely in settings concordant with that culture. The resident will more fully experience the plight of patients from another culture when they are seen in the settings of the minority culture and can then be more empathetic toward these patients when they are seen in the medical settings of the majority culture. Finally, field training is necessary for the proper presentation of cultural material because much of this material must be gleaned from participant observation. The knowledge will not be shared directly or verbally.

A caution we would give with regard to field work is to emphasize that learning should take place on two levels: (1) education as to the generalities of working with those of other cultures, which is the most important task; and (2) education as to the specifics of the culture where the field placement occurs. If this distinction is not made, the residents may feel that they have seen all there is to see and have learned all there is to learn. In addition, residents may try to apply specific learnings from one culture to another culture, and not understand why it "doesn't work" in the second culture, unless both levels of learning are approached in supervision.

Another caution is to follow the precepts of good community consultation-liaison programing and practice when setting up such field placements. These include relationship building at all levels, as discussed by Hollister and Miller (1977); organizational agreements and understandings at all levels; mechanisms for the resolution of problems which may arise; a continuous and regular relationship with the field site; and regular onsite and "back home" supervision for the trainee (Hollister, 1977). These are important in any setting, but especially important when dealing with a group which finds the majority culture and its representatives "alien."

Potential Research Areas

Clearly, these issues point to areas of needed research. A wide variety of cultures and minorities needs to be studied to understand commonalities that could be included in a general approach to curriculum content. Differences should also be identified so as to provide examples of exceptions to general principles.

An overriding research question would be to discover what content, if any, leads to better treatment for a minority patient. A related question is whether this is different, and in what ways, from content that leads to better treatment for patients in general. Another area of research would be to discover whether teaching by a minority person does make a difference in understanding of the material by residents and the likelihood that they will later use the material effectively.

Finally, does a general or a specific approach, as previously defined, lead to better understanding of the material by residents, better usage of the material and improved patient care?

Institutional Change and Faculty Development

While planning a curriculum for minority content in residency training, we must not forget that the institutions with which we are dealing are themselves cultures with their own beliefs, rituals, language, customs and pathologies. Any strategy to change these institutional cultures and their people (e.g., faculty, residents, students) must take cultural matters into account, just as these matters would be taken into account in changing an individual. A few suggestions on how to deal with teaching institutions include the following:

• Make all efforts scholarly activities, at least in part. It is very difficult for those in an academic culture to reject genuine efforts toward scientific inquiry and scholarship.

• Involve the leaders of the institutional culture.

• Identify those from various cultural and ethnic backgrounds, even though they may not be members of a recognized minority. Use their understandings in the formulation of such curricula.

• Stress through research and example that improved training and patient care will result.

• Tie inclusion of cultural content to monetary or other rewards.

These suggestions are consistent with organizational development of any kind. Major planning time spent early in the process to develop such strategies with full participation of those familiar with organizational development is the key to the success of effective minority curriculum development.

Cross-Cultural Curriculum Development as a Public Policy Issue

At first reading, the content of this chapter may not seem to relate to public policy. Rather, core curriculum content for psychiatric residency training may seem to be very nonpublic. This is not the case, however. Whether one takes a broad view of "public," or a narrow one, the topic at hand is in fact very much related to policy formulation.

Earlier we alluded to policy formulation in organizations which could well be considered public in a broad sense. These were professional organizations, licensing bodies, accrediting bodies, and local medical schools and training programs. Certainly these bodies are a part of and relate to the public as a whole, as well as the portion of the body politic which is made up of minority cultures and subcultures. Also, influencing these groups to include certain curriculum material in turn influences the practice of psychiatry (both within the training institutions and among their graduates), and leads to more complete and sensitive patient care. (We would hold that this is true of care for *all* patients, not just those who are members of recognized minority cultures.)

Such curriculum change is also a public policy issue in the more narrow sense of policy made by governments. We need to look no further than the Bureau of Indian Affairs and the Indian Boarding Schools to see how a public policy ("acculturation") has led to deculturation, displacement and misery for the "beneficiaries" of this policy (Hammerschlag, Alderfer, and Berg, 1973). The examples are numerous, and any minority culture can cite many. What is important in the present context is to be sure that public policy formulations in the area of curriculum development are such that minority content is supported and mandated. The direct benefit of such formulations is the actual inclusion of such content. The indirect benefits are no less profound. Such benefits include:

- "consciousness raising" within the governmental structures themselves;
- a "spillover" effect, wherein policy in one area may affect policy formulation in other areas;
- the creation over time of a body of "enlightened" professionals, who will exert no small effect on future policy formulation.

Activity in this area is not only desirable, but absolutely necessary if the curriculum changes proposed in this chapter are to come to fruition, or have more than limited success.

We have identified further work which needs to be done to develop minority or cultural curriculum content in psychiatric residency training programs. The guiding principles which we have identified are:

- General schemata for training should be developed that speak to understanding and dealing with people of different cultural backgrounds.
- Specifics of a particular culture should be used as examples, not as the core content.
- While ensuring that social ills, including racism, are dealt with, material should be scholarly rather than ideological.
- Teachers should be chosen on the basis of their knowledge and attitudes with regard to cultural issues, rather than because of minority cultural identification per se.
- Didactic learning must be put into practice both in medical settings of the majority culture and in settings culturally different from that of the resident.
- Field placements should be developed using the principles of effecitive community consultation-liaison programing and practice.
- Institutional change strategies must take place at multiple levels and take the institutional culture into account.
- Attempts to affect public policy, both in a broad and in a narrow sense, are absolutely necessary for curriculum change strategies to have the greatest chances for success.

References

Hammerschlag, C. A., Alderfer, C. P., & Berg, D. Indian education: A human systems analysis. *American Journal of Psychiatry*, 1973, *1311* (10), 1098–1102.

Hollister, W. G. University of North Carolina School of Medicine, Division of Community of Psychiatry, Chapel Hill, N.C., Personal communication, 1976.

Hollister, W. G., & Miller, F. T. Problem-solving strategies in consultation. *American Journal of Orthopsychiatry*, 1977, 47 (3), 444–50.

Levine, S., & Lurie, N. O. (Eds.). *The American Indian today.* Baltimore: Penguin, 1970.

Liaison Committee on Graduate Medical Education. *Essentials of accredited residencies, revised to March 30, 1979.* Chicago: American Medical Association, 1979.

Saur, W. University of North Carolina School of Social Work, Chapel Hill, N.C., Personal communication, 1979.

Thompson, M. G. G. *A resident's guide to psychiatric education.* New York: Plenum, 1979.

Bibliography

American Psychiatric Association. *Psychiatric education: Prologue to the 1980's.* Washington, D.C.: Author, 1975.

American Psychiatric Association. *The working papers of the 1975 Conference on Education of Psychiatrists.* Washington, D.C.: Author, 1975.

Attneave, C. L., & Kelso, D. R. (Eds.). *American Indian annotated bibliography of mental health: Volume 1.* Seattle: University of Washington Press, 1977.

Bacon, M. K. The dependency conflict hypothesis and the frequency of drunkenness: Further evidence from a cross-cultural study. *Quarterly Journal of Studies on Alcohol,* 1974, *35,* 863–76.

Bergman, R. L. A school for medicine men. *American Journal of Psychiatry,* 1973, *130,* 663–66.

Brode, P. M. Alcoholism as a mental health problem of Native Americans. *Archives of General Psychiatry,* 1975, *32,* 1385–91.

Cahn, E. S., & Hearne, D. W. (Eds.). *Our brother's keeper: The Indian in white America.* New York: New American Library, 1969.

Caplan, G. *Principles of preventive psychiatry.* New York: Basic Books, 1964.

Carlson, E. J. Counseling in a Native context. *Canada's Mental Health,* 1975, *23,* 7–9.

Citizens Commission on Graduate Medical Education. *The graduate education of physicians.* Chicago: American Medical Association, 1966.

Coles, R. *Eskimos, Chicanos, Indians: Volume IV of children of crisis.* Boston: Little, Brown, 1977.

Dohrenwend, B. P. Socio-cultural and social-psychological factors in the genesis of mental disorders. *Journal of Health and Human Behavior,* 1975, *16,* 365–92.

Feldman, S. D., & Thielbar, G. W. (Eds.). *Life styles: Diversity in American society.* Boston: Little, Brown, 1972.

Ferguson, F. N. Navajo drinking: Substantive hypotheses. *Human Organization,* 1968, *27,* 159–67.

Frank, J. D. *Persuasion and healing.* New York: Schocken, 1963.

Goodtracks, J. G. Native American non-interference. *Social Work,* 1973, *18,* 30–34.

Halleck, S. *The politics of therapy.* New York: Science House, 1971.

Hallowell, A. I. Psychic stresses and culture patterns. *American Journal of Psychiatry,* 1936, *92,* 1291–1310.

Hollingshead, A. B., & Redlich, F. C. *Social class and mental illness: A community study.* New York: John Wiley and Sons, 1958.

Jewell, D. P. A case of a "psychotic" Navaho Indian male. *Human Organization,* 1952, *11,* 32–36.

Kiev, A. *Transcultural psychiatry.* New York: The Free Press, 1972.

Kleinman, A., Eisenberg, L., & Good, B. Culture, illness, and care: Clinical lessons from anthopologic and cross-cultural research. *Annals of Internal Medicine,* 1978, *88(2),* 252–58.

Levy, J. E., & Kunitz, S. J. *Indian drinking: Navajo practices and Anglo-American theories.* New York City: Wiley-Intersciences Publishers, 1974.

Peretti, P. O. Enforced acculturation and Indian-white relations. *Indian Historian,* 1973, *6,* 38–52.

President's Commission on Mental Health. *Task panel report: Special populations.* Washington, D.C.: U.S. Government Printing Office, 1978.

Schwab, J. J., & Schwab, M. E. *Socio-cultural roots of mental illness: An epidemiologic survey.* New York: Plenum, 1978.

Shore, J. H. Psychiatric epidemiology among American Indians. *Psychiatric Annals,* 1974, *4,* 56–66.

Spiegel, J., & Papajohn, J. (Eds.). *Transactions: The interplay between individual, family, and society.* New York: Science House, 1971.

Thomas, A., & Sillen, S. *Racism and psychiatry.* New York: Brunner/ Mazel, 1972.

Torrey, E. F. *The mind game.* New York: Bantam, 1972.

Townsley, H. C., & Goldstein, G. S. One view of the etiology of depression in the American Indian. *Public Health Report,* 1977, *92* (5), 458–61.

Usdin, G. (Ed.). *Psychiatry: Education and image.* New York: Brunner/Mazel, 1973.

U.S. Department of Health, Education, and Welfare. *Suicide, homicide, and alcoholism among American Indians: Guidelines for help.* Washington, D.C.: U.S. Government Printing Office, 1973.

Walker, R. D. Alcoholism: Treatment program considerations for the American Indian. National DWI Conference, Falls Chruch, Virginia, December 1979.

Walker, R. D. Treatment strategies in an urban Indian alcoholism program. *Journal of Studies on Alcohol,* Suppl. No. 9, 1981.

Walz, G. R., & Benjamin, L. *Transcultural counseling: Needs, programs, and techniques.* New York: Human Sciences Press, 1978.

Wangler, D. G. Science, magic, and culture. *American Indian Culture and Research Journal,* 1974, *1,* 14–16.

Weslager, C. A. *Magic medicines of the Indian.* New York: Signet, 1973.

ANTONIO ARCE   MANUEL DIAZ
RICARDO GALBIS   RODOLFO GARCIA

CHAPTER **12**

Development of Hispanic Curricula in Psychiatric Residency Programs

Regardless of the predominant theoretical orientations of their curricula, psychiatric residency programs do not alone determine the quality of mental health services in their settings. The curriculum and the services components, which are both elements of a community's mental health service delivery system, are part of a large social organization that may act to facilitate or to deter improvements in training or service delivery. Other elements in the system include the psychiatric resident, the residency program, the medical school department of psychiatry, the environmental and sociopolitical context of the community and the local mental health authorities and organizations of community residents. These elements also determine the receptiveness to change in training and program development within a residency program.

The relationship, therefore, between the content of a psychiatric residency training curriculum and the quality of the services ultimately provided is exceedingly complex. Unfortunately, few residency programs have any focused minority content at all, and fewer still emphasize the Hispanic content (Gurel, 1975). In addition, some programs are resistant to any change in their curricula that is perceived as originating outside their own institution.

For many residents, psychiatric residency training is an intense, often very stressful, experience. Residents in psychiatry face amibiguity more often than residents in other areas of medicine that deal with well-described disease entities. Because psychiatry is concerned with behavior, psychiatrists encounter less clearly defined syndromes where the diagnosis does not automatically lead to a treatment plan as specific as in internal medicine. While there is little debate in medicine about the validity of major disease processes, psychiatry is in the midst of an identity crisis; advocates of one side say that mental illness is not a disease, and others equally rigidly proclaim that psychopharmacology is the primary basis of the psychiatrist's knowledge. Additionally, sensitivity groups and personal psychotherapy or psychoanalysis emphasize the personal growth and self-understanding of residents in training.

Many resident applicants to psychiatry training programs come into psychiatry with the idea of wanting to work with patients within a personal relationship. Many have a liberal, socially conscious, political orientation. Hispanic medical school graduates with this orientation tend to go into family practice because they want to work in the community treating people with whom they identify. They may see general practice as more directly fulfilling this goal than a career in mental health.

Hispanics are grossly underrepresented in medical school. The low number of Hispanic residents in training programs is one of the most important variables affecting services to Hispanic patients. Hispanics in the United States are largely urban dwellers of lower socioeconomic status who, as a group, defy categorization because of heterogeneity not only in national origin, customs and level of acculturation but also in kinds of mental health problems they present (Karno and Edgarton, 1969). All too common characteristics of many Hispanics are poverty and underemployment, which force heavy reliance on public mental health clinics (Rosenthal and Frank, 1958). In many cases these are clinical facilities of a university hospital medical center (Karno, 1966), where residents have a major role in service delivery. The stress of heavy service demands and the lack of other bilingual treatment staff and supervisors can make the resident's job more difficult. The resident's frustrations can sometimes take the form of cursory histories and overreliance on medication for Hispanic patients.

One way to increase the number of Hispanics in residency programs is to make quality services for Hispanics a high priority. Affirmative action efforts can attract Hispanic medical school graduates and recruit Hispanic psychiatrists to their attending staff. Across the entire range of the allied behavorial science professions, and in mental health in particular, the degree of representation of Hispanics is extremely important in the provision of services. In addition to conveying the message that discrimination is not practiced in institutional hiring, the accessibility of services for the monolingual patient becomes directly proportional to the number of Spanish-speaking staff.

With regard to curriculum, the extent to which the residency program director follows a traditional approach becomes important in the development of curriculum content relevant to Hispanics. By traditional approach, we mean the idea that curriculum development begins with the question, "What should be taught?" rather than with, "What should the observable competencies be by the end of the training experience?" The former approach leads to the development of *teaching* objectives, while the latter leads to the development of *learning* objectives that are measurable and observable. The emphasis of a program bears on services for Hispanics, particularly in the area of clinical diagnosis. Data from multiple settings and from various other minority groups have shown that minorities tend to receive less precise and more pathological initial diagnoses and fewer referrals to outpatient psychotherapy clinics (Morales, 1971; Rosenthal and Frank, 1958; Brill, 1960; Yamamoto, Bloombaum and Hattem, 1967).

The extent to which residency programs are oriented toward curriculum based on learning objectives will influence their participation in the development of quality-assurance mechanisms. So far, the impetus for the development of quality-assurance mechanisms has sprung from local and state mental health authorities that fund or otherwise regulate public mental health clinics and hospitals. Increasingly, residency programs that operate mental health clinics feel themselves being pressured because of periodic reviews by these mental health authorities. The residency program oriented toward measurable quality standards would be far more likely to adopt a leadership position and further develop and implement quality control mechanisms for clinical services rather than a program based on teaching objectives that would see monitoring as a necessary evil that had to be lived with. If a quality-assurance mechanism is realistic and fully implemented with the support of the residency director and the department chairperson, it should be capable of identifying gaps and deficiencies in clinical services for Hispanics, thereby helping to prevent and correct dual standards of quality. The data obtained from identifying services deficiencies can then be used to further refine and modify the training curriculum and to allow evaluation of its effectiveness in improving services. This chapter will focus, therefore, on issues relevant to Hispanic curriculum development and integration.

The first section in this chapter begins with an overview of recent developments in minority content development in psychiatric training. "Hispanic Content in Curriculum Development" examines different approaches to minority content development and discusses innovative programs and training groups. This section leads to a conceptualization of a framework for minority content development that is then elaborated upon in the subsequent sections.

The second section, "Clinical Services for Hispanics," starts with a brief overview of the current state of mental health services that are available to Hispanics. The major thrust of this section is to outline theoretical issues that have direct practical implications for the delivery of clinical services. An example of this is in the very concept of "minority." The authors demonstrate that when this concept is understood in a purely descriptive fashion, the implication is that each "minority" group requires vast ethnographic studies in order for psychiatrists to know how to make services more relevant to members of a "minority." On the other hand, if the problems that Hispanics face in receiving services from mental health providers are understood as resulting primarily from interpersonal interactions with treatment staff, then delivery can be formulated in terms of the dynamics of the psychotherapeutic relationship. Much has been learned in psychiatry about the essential characteristics of successful doctor–patient relationships. The implications for training are significant. Residency directors would then stress fundamentals of clinical interviewing with special attention given to how transference and countertransference can be affected if the patient is Hispanic, rather than stressing anthropological-ethnographic information or hypotheses about personality factors that are supposedly common to all Hispanics.

Later in this section, a clinical interaction model of the initial interview is presented. This is used to illustrate the dynamics of interaction and to outline those interactions that are most likely to contribute to the success of the interview with Hispanic and other minority patients. A useful framework has been described recently by Engel (1980) in his article on the clinical application of the biopsychosocial model, which he describes and contrasts with the biomedical model. He maintains that the theoretical flaw in the biomedical model is the reductionism whereby personal and social data from the patient must first be reduced to a system level of biochemical–physical characteristics before it can have clinical meaning. Conversely, the clinical application of the biopsychosocial model illustrates how other elements in the treatment course of the individual patient are clinically significant because they affect the person's total response to the health care system.

A general systems framework, such as the biopsychosocial model, provides a useful way of conceptualizing the relationship among the curriculum, the treatment setting and the characteristics of the therapist and patient. When the role of the curriculum within a service program is seen from this perspective, it becomes clear that the characteristics of the patient most important to the clinical outcome are the person's personal past experiences and that these data are obtained through the two-party system that includes the doctor and the patient. Furthermore, clinical stereotypes derived from literature on what Hispanics are like as a group may not be relevant to any one particular patient. In fact, stereotypes of this kind might act to selectively screen out information regarding the patient that does not fit the stereotype in the resident's mind.

The third section, "Training Curriculum Model," includes a sample training seminar syllabus. The purpose is to illustrate one approach in developing a training seminar that begins with a clear statement of aims and contains specific learning objectives. Furthermore each of the five seminar sessions has specific learning objectives that enable the instructor to measure desired competencies under stated conditions. In addition, videotapes of clinical interviews would permit measurement of the resident's clinical behavior. The content of the seminar is focused on the interactional process between the clinician and the patient and the possible distortions produced by transference and countertransference issues brought into play by stereotypical perceptions between them.

Although the focus is on process, specific attention is given to understanding the unique experiences that Hispanics and other groups have endured in this country at various times in history. Another thrust of the seminar is to enhance the residents' awareness of ideologies. Ideological trends, as Schwebel (1975) has shown, inevitably are represented in the professional literature wearing the mantle of objective scientific truth. Thomas and Sillen (1972) have developed this point thoroughly in their book *Racism and Psychiatry*. Research regarding Hispanics is particularly prone to this kind of veiled racism because of the heavy reliance on earlier anthropological studies that employed methodologies not applicable to complex urban milieus and which assumed a group homogeneity in Hispanics simply not borne out in reality (Vaca, 1970).

The fourth section, "Quality Assurance," illustrates a sample quality-assurance program that was designed for use in a community mental health center outpatient service. It includes a rationale, a procedure and a checklist for use by a multidisciplinary committee to assess quality of services based on clinical documentation in the chart. Additional features that are described are training aids such as guideline questions and a sample clinical history complete with an appropriate treatment plan using a problem-oriented approach.

The last section, "A Perspective for the Development of Minority Content in Psychiatry," is relevant for Hispanic clinical services. A series of concluding statements follow regarding broader issues of theory development, research needs and strategies for change and policy implementation.

Hispanic Content in Curriculum Development: Problems and Issues

Overview

An approved training program in psychiatry must provide residents with—

- a well-balanced presentation of all generally accepted theories, schools of thought and diagnostic and therapeutic procedures;
- adequate and systematic instruction in the basic sciences and the social and behavioral sciences to help the resident understand the importance of economic, ethnic, social and cultural factors in mental health and mental illness;
- experience in the care of patients of both sexes, of various

age groups and of a wide range of ethnic, social and economic backgrounds;

• continuous review and assessment of their language and other communication skills;

• instruction about American cultures and subcultures, their attitudes, values and social norms;

• oversight by a faculty that includes representatives of major mental health disciplines.

The actual operational practice of these principles to minority curriculum content leaves much to be desired. Despite a rapidly growing body of literature on the cultural aspects of psychiatry, the integration of sociocultural dimensions into psychiatric training curricula has yet to be accomplished. There is virtually no consensus among psychiatric educators about what material should be presented and in what kinds of courses.

In 1975, Gurel published an analysis of characteristics of psychiatric residency training programs. Curriculum content was one of those characteristics examined. Of the 288 accredited programs, only 105 (36 percent) addressed the issue of specific training efforts in furthering understanding of minority groups of foreign cultures. But among those 105 respondents, 46 relied on experiences derived from exposure to minority group members in the course of everyday contacts with patients and staff, and 59 indicated explicit efforts through didactic instruction alone or didactic instruction coupled with exposure to patients in community settings. In other words, only one out of every five residency training programs in the United States appears to be addressing the issue of cultural aspects of psychiatry with any degree of academic responsibility. Unfortunately, Gurel's report does not describe the extent or intensity of such training.

Trends in Curriculum Development

Efforts to develop a framework for minority content in psychiatric training curricula are beginning to come to the fore. The American Psychiatric Association has recently established a Task Force on Cultural and Ethnic Factors in Psychiatry. Among its goals are the inventorying of the curricula of residency training programs to ascertain if cultural and ethnic subject matter is included; the development of model courses and bibliographies for use in training programs; the dissemination of information on the specifics of culturally differentiated diagnostic and treatment techniques for various ethnic groups; and the correlation of a multiethnic and culturally appropriate mental health approach with other medical specialities.

Another effort in this direction was a series of workshops sponsored by the Boston University School of Medicine and the Veterans Administration Hospital at Bedford, Massachusetts, in April 1979. The aims here were the development of a model curriculum; the field testing of the curriculum; and the development of evaluative instruments to assess the impact of the introduction of such a model curriculum into existing programs. The workshop focused on cultural conceptions of mental health and mental illness; cultural aspects of psychopathology; cultural patterns in the family response to mental illness; and cultural aspects of treatment approaches (including psychotherapy). The latter included not only the modification of treatment techniques but also the character of culturally sanctioned treatment seeking behaviors, especially the folk-belief system and the utilization of folk-healers.

Bernal y del Rio and Associates at the Puerto Rico Institute of Psychiatry have been active in this regard (American Medical Association, 1978). They have designed two model programs: a Laboratory of Socio-cultural Detoxification (LSD) and a Selective Recruitment Program. The objective of the LSD program is to stimulate change within organizational structures that comprise the mental health delivery system by influencing policy makers. The Selective Recruitment Program is based on the resident-exchange concept in which mainland institutions and the Puerto Rico Institute exchange residents for one year. This gives the non-Hispanic psychiatrist direct exposure to "bicultural psychiatry."

Rationale for Minority Content

The goals for undertaking any type of training are the acquistion of knowledge and the acquisition of skills. Training methodologies utilize didactic and experiential approaches to impart knowledge and skills. The two approaches complement each other. A considerable amount of collateral knowledge can be acquired in the process of practice, and, theoretically at least, the greater the amount of knowledge acquired the more skillful the practitioner.

From the standpoint of psychiatry as a medical speciality, exposure to social, cultural and ethnic factors in health and disease should begin in undergraduate medical school training. Most medical schools rely heavily on minority populations to provide the clinical material for practical experience in the management of patients. Indoctrination of medical students in the value systems, family structure, cultural patterns, child-rearing practices, nutritional factors and so forth of the minorities will set the foundations for future practice.

The basic knowledge thus acquired will be of even more relevance to those physicians who ultimately become psychiatrists. According to the American Medical Association (1978), a comprehensive four-year curriculum in any accredited psychiatric residency training program should include at appropriate times during the training period the following:

• required readings in the scientific literature on relevant aspects of anthropology, sociology, psychiatric epidemiology, racism and so forth;

• supplementary lecture series by representatives of various cultural groups;

• seminars on aspects of interracial, interethnic and intercultural processes;

• a group experience aimed at inducing insight, correcting stereotypic and prejudicial misconceptions and modifying behaviors;

• instruction and supervision in the management of patients from other cultural backgrounds, by members of the faculty who belong to the respective ethnic or racial group;

• instruction in communication theory with opportunities for acquiring the necessary language skills or, at least, knowledge about the language of the minorities represented in the geographic area of the training facility.

In developing training curricula with special reference to Hispanics, a crucial issue is their cultural heterogeneity. While all Hispanics share a common language and Spanish heritage, each subgroup has incorporated them within its own developing culture in degrees which are qualitatively and quantitatively different. As a result, each group (Mexican, Puerto Rican, Cuban and so forth) has maintained its cultural identify and is clearly distinguishable from the others. Each has its own lifestyle; its own social context; its idiosyncratic patterns of thinking, feeling and behaving; and its own linguistic forms. Each group's motivations in migrating to the United States are also clearly different. The upper-class Cubans coming to the United States in the 1960s faced a different set of adjustment problems than lower-class rural Mexicans walking across the border during the "bracero" or "green card" years.

Similarly, the past experiences of Hispanics of Mexican descent during the riots or the mass deportations of the 1940s are different from the institutionalized racism in parts of southern Texas in the late 1960s (Morales, 1972). These historical circumstances have required different adaptive responses and subsequently different attitudes toward societal institutions and feelings of integration within society among Hispanics. While all groups face basically similar problems in American society and have limited alternatives, each arrives at different solutions. This monolingual, multiculturalism distinguishes the Hispanic group from American Indians, Asian Americans and Blacks.

Evaluating the quality and effectiveness of care is a complex task. The evaluation of mental health care in general is beset with numerous pitfalls given the state of our knowledge, the incredible intricacy of the problem, the difficulties in defining "success" in therapy and the need to control numerous variables. For the Hispanic population, these problems are compounded by the lack of basic knowledge on Hispanics and the cultural heterogeneity of their population.

The initial interview in which a patient comes in contact with a psychiatrist in a clinic marks the formal beginning of the doctor–patient relationship and influences subsequent impressions of the patient toward the treatment facility. The complex interaction between doctor and patient determines subsequent treatment planning by the doctor and treatment compliance by the patient. Similarily, clinical contact with other mental health professionals will act to reinforce or negate attitudes developed in the patient's relationship with the treating physician or the identified primary therapist. The initial interview, when understood as a two-party interactional system, can serve as a model to conceptualize intervening determinants in clinical services for Hispanic and other minority patients. Frank (1967) describes how various determinants of both individual and sociocultural natures influence the psychotherapeutic relationship between patient and doctor. When the patient is of Hispanic and of other minority status, additional determinants from various sources can selectively influence the dynamics of the psychotherapeutic relationship. We will explore such influences that include environmental, social and ideological stereotypes and then describe a clinical interview model.

Environmental and Social Determinants. Current mental health services for Hispanics are, in summary, restricted to the public sector primarily, largely inaccessible and piecemeal rather than comprehensive. Numerous authors (e.g. Thomas and Sillen, 1972) have documented the lack of quality services that often means that Hispanic and other minority-status patients are less carefully assessed and more often hospitalized than they are referred for outpatient services. Furthermore, when referred they are more often assigned to less experienced therapists, are seen less frequently and are more often medicated and generally offered treatment modalities that involve less of a personal relationship with the therapist. Moreover, these deficiencies reflect the broad inequities that lower class people of minority status perennially endure in society. The issue of mental health services and minority status is only part of a larger set of conditions that includes inequalities in general health care delivery, justice, employment and political representation (Morales, 1972).

Ideological Determinants. Ideology is inevitable in psychological theory because it influences the basic assumptions upon which theories

Clinical Services for Hispanics: Determinants and a Clinical Model

The Initial Interview

rest and from which testable research hypotheses are derived. Schwebel (1975) has shown that historically, theory development in psychology and education has been imbued with the same prejudices and stereotypes prevalent in society at the time. Thomas and Sillen (1972) in *Racism and Psychiatry* illustrated how racist ideas have often been given scientific legitimacy through their expression in scientific articles and prestigious professional journals in psychiatry and psychology. Kuhn (1962) has conceived the questioning and testing of a priori basic assumptions as an essential element in scientific revolution because of the potential effect on how future data and experience are organized.

Perhaps because of their long historical presence in this country and the fact that vast numbers of them are of low socioeconomic status, Hispanics have been the objects of numerous stereotypes. Clinicians often subscribe the same stereotypic views of lower class Hispanics to the general population as Lopez (1977) has shown.

The ideological orientation we propose is *structural environmental determinism*, as described by Levi-Strauss (1963). This position assumes that the most important factors influencing a given interpersonal phenomenon are the circumstances and interplay of the elements of the actual interaction. This contrasts sharply with *cultural determinism* (Kardiner and Ovesey, 1962) which stresses a person's cultural background as a more significant determinant in a given interpersonal interaction than the particular circumstances or context of the situation. *Biological determinism* (Newby, 1965) differs from this in that the key variables would be posited in the patient's genes instead of his "cultural heritage." The orientation one assumes will certainly influence the formulation of theoretical problems in clinical services and the kind of changes needed to bring about positive change.

Implications of "Minority" as an Inherent Quality. Whether the concept of "minority" is understood as an inherent quality—that is, that there is such a thing as group psychology or group character—or as more clearly an ascribed status will influence the development of training and service goals.

The first position implies that racial or ethnic groups differ significantly from each other in that their members have certain more or less uniformly distributed psychological traits that occur in a group independently of current circumstances. These recurring traits are sufficiently characteristic of each group as to distinguish each group from the other irrespective of similarities or differences in shared environmental conditions. Environmental conditions would include such things as crowded housing, underemployment, rural–urban migration, low education, and other stresses of life.

When groups of people are found having many of these demographic characteristics, who in addition share a racial or ethnic similarity, their behavior tends to be understood as not being responsive or interactive with these environmental conditions. Viewing "minority" as an inherent quality tells us nothing of how life's stresses affect human behavior, growth and family functioning. Rather conclusions are drawn about supposed "normative behaviors" and "group traits" for this particular minority group. The assumption is made that such similarities in behavior are more expressions of a group's "traditional culture and values" and are predictable behaviors that might be demonstrated by any group having similar socioeconomic character-istics and similar historical circumstances. For example, often in research studies the control groups differ not only ethnically but also socioeconomically. Yet differences in the results tend to be overtly attributed to membership in the racial or ethnic group.

This position leads to further attempts to develop behavioral ty-pologies or clinical stereotypic notions of what the Hispanic personality or the Hispanic family is like, while ignoring the individual variance among so large a group of people. To the extent that Hispanics are seen as possessing some basic personality type or group character, the focus will be on understanding more about their culture and normative behaviors and seeing problems in clinical services as primarily cases of cultural conflict, differing value orientations and expressions of maladaptive, culturally derived personality traits.

A greater conceptual problem is that culture cannot be discussed independently from socioeconomic class without running the risk of attributing factors that are more properly determined by socioeconomic status rather than by supposed "cultural traits." A further problem with this point of view is that it makes an assumption of group homogeneity that does not stand up to the clinical experience of a number of Spanish-speaking clinicians, including the authors, who have simply not found the typical Mexican or Puerto Rican or Cuban. In working with individuals, the psychiatrist finds the person's personal history yields far more useful clinical information than an attempt to fit an individual into a priori notions of Hispanic culture.

Implications of "Minority" as an Ascribed Position. Understanding and formulating clinical service problems from this perspective places greater emphasis on understanding interaction between the minority patient and the clinician. Factors that may influence this complex interpersonal relationship are sought from data on the interactive process rather than from supposed characteristics or traits about the minority status of the individual. In other words, an ascribed status implies an ascriber, a two-party system. An individual's status cannot be understood without understanding the context in which that person behaves toward others and in which others behave toward him or her.

The most important implication of this point of view is that there need be no assumptions made about any group psychology that connotes an identifiable personality type for members of the group by virtue of their sharing any racial or ethnic characteristic. Rather, the relationship between any individual patient's personality structure is assumed to be much more influenced or determined by the specific life experiences and developmental variables in that person's history and much less influenced by mere membership in the racial or ethnic group. From this it would follow that the more identifiable, segregated and subjected to scorn a group is in society, the more that group's basic needs will be frustrated. The result of this frustration, however, is more accurately understood as derived from their status than from any intrinsic group traits other than their ability to be easily identified by physical or linguistic characteristics.

The assumption is made that there are fundamental human needs present in all of us and that the search to gratify these needs is influenced, shaded, colored and given expression differently by different minority groups (Sullivan, 1954). Furthermore, this assumption maintains that despite the differences that exist between groups in terms of preferences for food, customs and recreational activities, when ill or in a state of upset, members of different groups will more closely resemble each other than members of their own groups who are not in turmoil.

Cultural Stereotypes as Determinants. An example of the importance of the perspective of the observer is found in an article on ethnicity as a factor in mental health services delivery (Karno, 1966). The observation was made of a Hispanic man with a confused, lost expression on his face wandering the maze of hallways in a large psychiatric institute. One could interpret this observation in two ways. On one hand, the man's confusion could be explained in terms of his "traditional Mexican cultural values" that places more importance on "personalismo" and personalized one-to-one systems of health care rather than on large impersonal health institutions; one would say that this was a case of "culture shock." Conversely, one could say that this anecdote illustrates that people from rural backgrounds who are used to a smaller scale are more likely to experience stress in large institutions. Following this reasoning, an Appalachian Anglo in similar circumstances would be expected to react similarly and little would be attributed to any notion of what "traditional Anglo culture" is like.

A more dramatic example of the significance of basic assumptions about whether people of minority status are understood as people of a certain *kind* or people in a certain *status* is the following case of Mrs. Hernandez. Mrs. Hernandez was a patient hospitalized at a large university teaching hospital in Los Angeles a few years ago. Mrs. Hernandez was then a 34-year-old housewife, mother of two small children, who was an undocumented person and who was hospitalized for psychotic symptoms of a schizophrenic nature of two months duration. She was acutely delusional and paranoid on admission according to the admission note.

After a two-week trial of major antipsychotic agents she remained frightened and psychotic with no significant improvement. The psychiatry resident, somewhat frustrated by her lack of progress, heard that a *curandero* (healer) was available to visit patients. He arranged through a well-meaning nurse's aid at the general hospital for a particular *curandero* to visit Mrs. Hernandez.

It would perhaps have been different if after interviewing her and her family he had learned that she believed in and had used *curanderos* in the past. Even if that had been the case, however, the use of *curanderos* with psychotic patients is highly questionable. What actually happened, however, was that the patient had not even been consulted about the visit because of the stereotype prevalent on the ward at that time that "most Mexicans believe in *curanderos* whether they admit it or not." In any case, the patient was brought into a room where after a few minutes the *curandero* performed a ritual *limpia* or "spiritual cleansing." Several nurses, medical students and other residents gathered to watch the ceremony.

The following day one of the authors interviewed the patient for the first time in Spanish and found her to be quite delusional and paranoid. She made specific comments about "evil spirits" and "the devil." Her chart did not mention specific references to the devil in her delusional thinking previously. After three weeks more of continued medication she cleared sufficiently to give more history. She stated that she had been preoccupied with the feeling that people around her might try to harm her and that "when that man talked to me of chasing away the devil I really got scared and felt that he could control my thoughts." It would certainly appear that if her physician's knowledge of her as an individual and of schizophrenia as a clinical syndrome had been greater he would not have been swayed by the promise of a quick resolution through the simplistic approach of having a *curandero* "cleanse" her.

It is clear that the approach that was followed derived from a stereotypic notion of what "these kind of people are like," which can lead to indifference in understanding an individual's specific circumstances. This does not imply that knowledge of *curanderos*, faith healers and other significant cultural experiences of particular groups is irrelevant for the clinician. This knowledge might be particularly useful in understanding the circumstances of early family life and the development of the individual. The interjection of a *santero* (middle priest of the Yoruba religion), *curandero*, or other nonmedical, non-Western therapist into the treatment plan has to be carefully thought out and understood in the context of the individual patient's clinical situation. Except in hospitals where they are indigenous and form a part of a treatment team (such as the Aro Hospital in Nigeria, where Professor Lambo has conducted a series of experiments in different modalities of treatment delivery systems), the introduction of a misunderstood and sometimes suspected *curandero* may be a great mistake.

The young resident in training does not have to become a *santero* anymore than he has to become Jewish or Catholic to treat patients of those religions; but he should know that these beliefs exist, and there should be a supervisor who does know the traditional beliefs in depth to explain his doubts if needed. The psychiatrist taking a postgraduate fellowship in transcultural psychiatry should have a course in comparative religions of his area of interest. You cannot assess a transcultural situation without full knowledge of all the variables.

Many psychiatrists have the notion that anthropology deals mainly in the study of quaint or primitive tribes in faraway places. While this is partly true, an increasing number of young anthropologists are forming part of inner-city or rural health treatment teams. Their work is important and psychiatrists should be aware of the Society of Medical Anthropology and its journal and the contributions of such leading persons as Geza Roheim, Claude Levi-Strauss, Roger Bastide and Lydia Cabrera.

A provocative thought was raised by Fuller Torrey (1973) when he spoke of *curanderos.* He questions who is going to license, regulate and identify valid practitioners. Who are charlatans and rip-offs? We believe that healers must have a solid reputation in the community where they work and open lines of communication to the psychiatry "establishment." Those that charge exorbitant fees, do not refer patients they cannot handle to the medical treatment facility and offer a mixture of "cures" of their own creation are apt to be charlatans. The traditional Latin *yerberos* or herb doctors should not be confused with the other variety of more or less effective folk healers. The *yerberos* throughout Mexico, the Caribbean and South America possess a vast amount of popular botanical lore and should be further studied.

More important, awareness of significant historical circumstances of various groups is often helpful because it gives the clinician a common base for accurate empathy. Many white clinicians have forefathers who faced similar circumstances fifty or seventy-five years ago during the great European migrations. The point is, however, that attributes of the particular patient must be given primary importance over characteristics that may or may not be present but that are based on presumed knowledge of the patient's racial or ethnic group.

The Initial Interview as a Clinical Model

The interview is a two-person system model of people interacting with each other. It has as its central figures the clinician, acting in the role of therapist, and the person, in the role of patient. They can be said to be in dynamic interaction because the therapist does not merely elicit "data" from the patient with cool scientific objectivity, but rather the observations of the therapist are influenced by his or her own behavior in eliciting the behavioral data. This was described by Sullivan (1954) as "participant-observation." Engel (1980) has elaborated this idea further, stating that the data of a personal nature is obtained from the patient through a two-party system—the doctor–patient relationship—and is therefore influenced by the characteristics of that system. Similarly, the patient is forming his or her own impression of the personality characteristics of the therapist while participating in these observations through his or her behavior. Frank (1967) has discussed similar ideas as part of his studies on features common to all psychotherapeutic relationships.

Certain general forces will be operating even before the patient and therapist meet:

- The patient must partially believe that he has come to the right place for relief of emotional distress, that the place is culturally sanctioned.
- The physical and interpersonal setting in the office or emergency room will have an effect; the setting may be inviting, neutral, stressful or chaotic.
- The outside environment will confer some degree of status to each member according to how mental illness and the profession of psychiatry are currently perceived as well as the current status of any minority group that the clinician or client may belong to. An example of this would be the middle-aged, white-haired psychiatrist of northern European background or the patient who is brought in by the police in handcuffs. Either one of these situations might be expected to elicit stereotyped responses in the other person.

The *content* of the verbal exchange between the two participants could be understood by reading a transcript of the discussion. It would contain specific references to either one or the other participant and historical data regarding the patient. The *process*, however, would not be limited to the verbal exchange but would also include the nonverbal exchange as well as the subtle inflections in the tone and other voice characteristics of both. The *process* refers to not only what is said but how it is said and otherwise communicated, the meaning of which reveals the participant's underlying attitudes about each other.

In an optimal situation such as when the therapist is well trained, skilled, empathetic and the environmental forces are minimally interfering, the following might be expected to occur:

The Therapist. The therapist sees the patient as "worthy" and there is a minimum of social distance. This was defined operationally in Yamamoto's studies (1967, 1978) of psychiatric residents' patient-treatment behavior using the Bogadrus scale. The greater the social distance between therapist and patient, the less likely the resident was to recommend a treatment modality that involved personal engagement or intensive psychotherapy. Freud alluded to the same kind of thing when he wrote, "This procedure . . . presupposes in the physician a personal concern for the patients. . . . I cannot imagine myself to delve into the psychical mechanisms of a hysteria in anyone who struck me as low minded and repellent and who on closer acquaintance, would not be capable of arousing human sympathy" (Frank, 1967).

The therapist feels that he has a theory capable of explaining the patient's behavior. The therapist feels able to relate the patient's patterns of behavior to some kind of theoretical framework that allows him to explain it and make it meaningful. By being able to understand the situation of the patient in terms of a body of theoretical knowledge that has been previously learned, the therapist's own anxiety in the face of human suffering is lessened. This process of conceptualizing the patient's problem in terms of a previously mastered theoretical framework is also important when the patient does not improve. As one therapist remarked, "One still has the feeling that one is doing the right thing even if the patient is not getting better." Obviously this could be misused as a rationalization, but the idea is that if the therapist is able to conceptualize the patient's behavior and relate it to a knowledge base, he is in a better position to convey his understanding to the patient.

The therapist is then in a position to convey to the patient an alternative explanation for what has happened to him. The word *alternative* is used because often the patient already has explained the situation to himself in terms of a fundamental unworthiness of being loved or a moral "badness." Often some variety of projection on the circumstances is used: "If only such and such were different I would not be in this situation." This explanation is also important because it can represent the therapist's "badge of competence," that he knows what he is doing and that the client indeed has come to the right place. But perhaps the most important result of this process is that the client then can begin to feel that the therapist has an understanding of his situation and therefore merits faith in the expectation of emotional relief.

The therapist is then able to outline a treatment approach for the patient. This will include something of the tasks necessary to bring about improvement in the situation. The course will be influenced by the particular school of thought and orientation of the therapist. Interestingly, this step is shared by therapists the world over, including shamans in remote tribes and far-off island "witch doctors." Even contemporary therapists have analogues in seemingly very primitive situations. So while a behaviorist may do a behavioral analysis, a Rogerian reflect back feeling, and a psychodynamically oriented therapist identify conflict and analyze resistance, the underlying process offers the patient a path to improvement and engages him at some personal level to assist in its accomplishment. The stereotype of the nonemotional analyst is illusory if one considers that for several hours each week the analyst and the patient lock themselves up in a quiet room and the analyst devotes his attention to trying to make sense out of the patient's associations. This can be a very intimate process of human engagement.

In summary, then, from the therapist's perspective, the therapist engages the patient and feels comfortable in understanding the patient with the theoretical tools at his disposal. By communicating his understanding of the meaningfulness of the patient's behavior a positive expectation of emotional relief can be aroused in the patient. This has sometimes been referred to as faith (Frank, 1967).

The Patient. On the patient's side of the diagram we can see an analogous series of psychological processes and behaviors that may occur under optimal circumstances. The patient feels that he is accepted by this higher-status expert, the therapist, and that this acceptance is nonjudgmental and nonmoralistic despite the therapist hearing the negative side of patient's past behavior. The patient may begin to see that the therapist not only doesn't judge the patient as morally bad but instead sees him as a person in a struggle with certain conflicts, feelings or impulses that have so far been counterproductive to the problem's resolution. The patient begins to feel that he has not only come to the right place but that in the act of coming to meet with this stranger he has already taken the first step in mastering some of the problems that beset him. The patient may feel the therapist can offer an explanation of questions such as, "Why do I do what I do?", "How did I get in this present situation?", and "What must I do to get out from under?". The patient will think about some of the things the therapist has said. The patient may not be persuaded that the therapist's plan or approach may lead to improvement, but he is influenced by the sincerity, calmness and empathy evidenced in the therapist.

In summary, under optimal circumstances the patient begins to feel that he can place his emotional reliance on the therapist for some expectation of relief.

The foregoing was a brief schema of a complex human interaction—the encounter between patient and therapist for an initial interview. It may be sufficient to illustrate some points that may be selectively inferred if there is a social or ethnic difference between the therapist and patient, e.g., when the patient is a lower income Hispanic.

The therapist might actually believe that somehow Hispanics do not really have the same psychological structures, feelings and aspirations as others. He may believe that they are different human beings by virtue of having a different set of "values" and deep-rooted "cultural traditions" and that in some way they should be shown respect by "preserving" them from change. Once seen as fundamentally different, the therapist's own attitudes toward this different group becomes more operational and can range from "I must save these unfortunates" to "It's really their own fault entirely" to, finally, "But they are happy that way, that's all they know and it's their lot" (Butts and Schrachter, 1968). The major problem then becomes the therapist's perception of the individual patient's personal characteristics, which are obscured by stereotype.

Equally important is that once a therapist sees a group as fundamentally different psychologically, he is less likely to see a group member as understandable within a known theoretical framework. The result is a certain anxiety in the therapist, as if he were faced with a problem for which his theoretical tools were not relevant. The belief in the inappropriateness of the therapist's theoretical framework is further fostered by psychiatric literature that borrows heavily from anthropological research of many years ago that studied relatively isolated tribes in far-off places. Kardiner and Ovesey (1962) and others have contributed to development of stereotypes that have been inappropriately applied to clinical practice. The result can be that the therapist says to himself, "I'm not an anthropologist anyway, and my theoretical school is based on middle-class values. I am irrelevant to these people for any kind of relationship-oriented psychotherapy."

The therapist may then communicate a certain helplessness, anxiety and hopelessness to the patient, which he may try to mask by a patronizing attitude, by overreliance on medication and by choosing treatment modalities based on a less-than-comprehensive assessment of the patient. Often this results in prescriptions for treatment that have in common a lack of personal engagement between the patient and therapist. This is not to say that treatment recommendations other than intensive one-to-one psychotherapy are second-class, only that patients seeking and capable of responding to such treatment are too often referred to long-term patient groups or brief medications clinics.

The preceding illustration of the initial interview can be understood as a complex two-party system with forces in dynamic interaction that include not only the larger societal factors but also elements such as the psychiatric literature available to residents and the role of prejudicial attitudes.

We believe that the focus for psychiatric training and quality control should be on the interaction between therapist and patient because of the importance of the initial interview in determining the accuracy of the diagnosis and the kind and quality of care the patient will receive. This shift from the characteristics of the patient to the characteristics of the interaction is analogous to what has occurred in research in school behavior. For many years the lowered performance of the children of minority status was explained by looking at the children and their parents' values, IQ's and cultural background, and not too amazingly many theories and explanations were based on the data thus derived. Under the U.S. Civil Rights Commission (1971) a massive study, based on Flander's (1970) report, took place in 493 classrooms throughout the Southwest. The subject of the study was not solely the children but rather the interactional process between them and the teachers and the classroom itself. Through a complex methodology designed to examine the actual interaction the study found that Mexican-American children received significantly more "reminders of the teacher authority," while Anglo children received, usually from Anglo teachers, more statements rated as "supportive." This study found a different set of intervening variables that were measurable and clearly influential in affecting the attitude and performance of students. As long as only the children's supposed cultural characteristics were studied, the implications for change were projected into some future time when parental values might change, and thereby change the children's cultural background. Because of the widened focus of study, recommendations for change were reformulated in terms of substantive issues such as greater numbers of bilingual teachers and the identification of teachers with frankly racist attitudes and behavior.

Somewhat in a similar fashion psychiatric education ought to focus more on observable and measurable behaviors where they matter most. There is great need to explore quality assurance mechanisms that can be implemented in clinics and hospitals. This is needed to monitor quality in clinical services so that it can be related to the terminal learning behavioral objectives in the training curriculum of the residency program.

Training Curriculum Model

The training curriculum described here is designed for first-year psychiatry residents as a part of a three- to four-year program. It includes supervised clinical experiences with Hispanic individuals, families and groups as well as a more structured seminar oriented on experiences of the type described in this chapter. The curriculum should be a part of basic residency experience. Residents interested in more comprehensive or specialized transcultural learning could be offered electives aimed at developing a solid research orientation. The present curriculum, however, illustrates several key ideas summarized in the following way.

The Aim Is Clearly Stated and Clinically Oriented. The stated aim of the seminar is "to enhance the residents' ability to maximally utilize their basic clinical skills for psychiatric patients regardless of racial, economic or ethnic difference."

This statement reinforces the philosophy that problems in quality services for Hispanics and other minority-status patients can be best understood as clinical skill problems (when language is not an obstacle) in the clinician's interaction with the patients. Furthermore, this is a responsibility of the supervising clinicians. This is not to say that knowledge from other fields such as anthropology and sociology is irrelevant, only that the clinical application of this knowledge falls mainly in the mental health clinical arena and should not be delegated to nonclinicians in other behavioral science fields.

The Curriculum Has Terminal Learning Objectives that are Behaviorally Stated, Measurable and Observable. The first terminal objective is that the resident will list significant elements of the basic assumptions, experimental design and hypotheses with 75 percent agreement with a prepared list when presented with three studies regarding mental health issues and minority patients. This terminal learning objective is cognitive since it requires the resident to demonstrate particular knowledge when presented with specific materials. Also, it fulfills the goal of having stated objectives in that the resident must meet a predetermined percentage of acceptable responses. To achieve success the resident must have a critical regard for the psychiatric literature involving minority issues and patient care.

The second terminal learning objective is that the resident, when presented with a videotape interview of a therapist with a minority-status patient, will be able to identify stereotypic responses or behaviors of the patient and of the therapist with 75 percent agreement with the prepared list. The achievement of this objective would mean that the resident has sufficient clinical skills to be aware of transference and countertransference manifestations of stereotypic thinking and behavior that would be detrimental to the development of a positive doctor–patient relationship. This objective is also attitudinal in that the resident's responses and sensitivity to positive and negative attitudes expressed in the clinical interview would permit inferences regarding his own attitudes toward patients of minority status. An alternative approach to measuring the achievement of this objective is a direct supervision of the resident carrying out a clinical evaluation with a minority patient. This approach, however, presents a difficulty in drawing comparisons, since each interview would be different depending on the patient and on the particular resident.

The Training Curriculum Is Programmatically Related to Quality-Assurance Mechanisms. The basis for integrating the training curriculum into a quality-assurance program is to incorporate the use of clearly stated, expected behavior outcomes. Therefore the terminal learning objectives previously stated, to the extent that they are achieved, will be reflected in the clinical record and will serve as minimal accepted standards of quality clinical services.

The Process of the Interview as Manifested by the Interaction Between Doctor and Patient is Emphasized. The first two sessions cover the basics of the interpersonal dynamics between doctor and patient with specific emphasis on those interactions most likely to be negatively affected when there is a social class or ethnic difference between doctor and patient. Basic concepts of interpersonal psychiatry as well as anthropology and sociology are covered with special attention given to the discussion of the clinical application of these terms within the framework of a two-party system composed of minority-status patients and the physician. General systems theory and the biophysic social model framework (Engel, 1980) are used to conceptualize both the relative importance, of dealing with any one individual minority patient, and the individual's past personal experiences as determinants in his clinical situation, instead of stereotypic notions based on supposed personality traits in the patient's reference group. Emphasizing the clinical process between doctor and patient increases sensitivity to the patient's status, and the new information and skills acquired enhance the doctor's effectiveness with patients of different minority groups.

The Specific Content Regarding Hispanics and Hispanic Subgroups Is Included Together with Information Regarding Other Groups. Specific information regarding the cultures of the Hispanic population, both as part of their historical experiences in this country as well as the customs of their country of origin, are regarded as essential. We feel, however, that because of the heterogeneity of Hispanics, it is less useful for the resident to obtain this information as part of the clinical history on each Hispanic patient. Also, the acquisition of knowledge of the histories of minorities is clearly within the scope of psychiatric residency education. Specific information is provided regarding the historical experiences of Hispanics as well as Blacks, Chinese, Japanese, Jews and others. An article is included on Appalachian Anglos, for instance, to illustrate that lower class Anglos living in rural poverty experience similar adjustment problems when they migrate to the large urban centers.

The aim of the course would be to enhance the resident's ability to utilize to the maximum extent basic clinical skills with psychiatric patients regardless of racial, economic or ethnic differences. The goals would enable the resident to—

General Orientation and Overview of Course

• acquire critical regard for the psychiatric literature in the area of mental health issues regarding minorities and understand the underlying theoretical bases and assumptions implicit in the literature;

• acquire an understanding of the relative importance of racial or cultural characteristics of the patient vs. the clinical skills of the therapist;

• acquire a greater understanding of the differences and similarities in the experiences of minorities in this country.

The overall course objectives would consist of the following:

• When presented with three studies regarding mental health issues of minorities, the resident will be able to list significant elements of the basic assumptions, experimental design and hypotheses with 75 percent agreement with a prepared list.

• When presented with a videotaped interview of a therapist with a minority patient, the resident will be able to identify stereotypical responses or behavior of the patient and therapist with a 75 percent agreement with a prepared list.

• When presented with a written clinical summary of a patient, the resident will be able to identify areas of the content that are particularly helpful or unhelpful in the assessment and treatment of minority patients with a 75 percent congruence with a prepared sample.

Sample of Course Outline for First-Year Psychiatric Residents

The curriculum would include five sessions, delineated as follows:

• Session 1: brief review of general principles of the psychiatric interview;

• Session 2: definition of basic concepts and terms useful in clinical practice;

• Session 3: discussion of common underlying ideologies as trends in the scientific literature and review of representative sample articles;

• Session 4: review of classic epidemiological studies and relationship of ethnicity and socioeconomic status variables;

• Session 5: review and discussion of data on historical experience of various minority groups in this location.

Session 1

1. *Brief Review of General Principles of the Psychiatric Interview*

• Clarification of situation—formal inception
• Reconnaissance
• Detailed inquiry
• Termination

2. *Learning Objectives of this Session*

After this session, the resident should be able to (1) discuss several social and scientific developments that influenced the changing role of the psychiatrist regarding minorities; and (2) describe how a racial or cultural difference between therapist and patient may selectively affect different parts of the diagnostic psychiatric interview.

3. *Recommended Reading*

Franklin, J. D. Dynamics of the psychotherapeutic relationship. In T. J. Scheff (Ed.), *Mental illness and social process*. New York: Harper & Row, 1967.

Psychiatric anthropology, transcultural psychiatry: The past. In G. Dubreuil, & E. D. Wittkower (Eds.), *Transcultural psychiatric research*, Vol. 2, April, 1974, pp. 7–10.

Sullivan, H. S. *The psychiatric interview.* New York: W. W. Norton Co., 1954.

Tiger L., & Fox, R. Good Grooming. In *The imperial animal.* New York: Holt, Rinehart, Winston, 1971.

Ziferstein I. The role of the psychotherapist in a changing society. *Psychotherapy & Psychosomatics*, 1975, *25*, 283–86.

1. *Examples of Basic Definitions and Variations in Meanings*   *Session 2*

- Group personality characteristics and traits
- Normality
- Deviancy
- Human behavior
- Culture
- Cultural values
- Social class
- Subculture
- Prejudice
- Stereotype
- Motivation
- Adaptation
- Anthropoernic vs. anthropophagic values
- Ethnocentrism, nationalism, racism

2. *Relevance of These Concepts for the Psychiatric Assessment of Particular Patients*

- Dynamic

- Statistical
- Behavioristic points of view
- Prognostic
- "Treatability"

3. *Learning Objectives of this Session*

After this session, the resident should be able to define and explain key terms relevant both to the social sciences and psychiatry.

4. *Required Reading*

Roheim, G. Modern nations. In *Psychoanalysis and anthropology.* New York: International Universities Press, 1968, pp. 361–69.

Thomas, A. & Sillen S. Myths from the past. In *Racism and psychiatry.* New York: Brunner/Mazel, 1972, pp. 1–22.

5. *Recommended Reading*

Devos, G. A. Minority group identity. In J. C. Finney (Ed.), *Culture change, mental health, and poverty.* New York: Simon and Schuster, 1970, pp. 81–96.

Goetzi, G. Mental illness and cultural beliefs in a southern Italian immigrant family: A case report. *Canadian Association Journal,* 1970, *18,* 219–29; Abstract in *Transcultural Psychiatric Research Review,* 1974, *10,* 88–89.

Kelleher, M. J. Gross national (Anglo-Irish) differences in obsessional symptoms and traits of personality. *Psychological Medicine,* 1972, *2,* 33, 41.

Session 3

1. *Overview of Theoretical Trends in the Social Science Literature Regarding Minorities*

- Biological determinism
- Structural-environmental determinism
- Cultural determinism

2. *Review of Research Representative of Different Trends in Theory and Discussion*

3. *Learning Objectives of this Session*

After this session the resident should be able to describe significant basic theoretical assumptions, values and methodologies in representative samples of psychiatric research regarding minorities.

4. *Required Reading*

Prince, R. Psychotherapy and the chronically poor. In J. E. Finney (Ed.),
    Culture change, mental health, and poverty. New York: Simon and
    Schuster, 1970, pp. 20–41.

5. *Recommended Reading*

Kuhn, T. S. *The structure of scientific revolutions.* Chicago: University
    of Chicago Press, 1962, pp. 91–109.

Lewis, O. A Puerto Rican boy. In J. C. Finney (Ed.), *Culture change,
    mental health and poverty.* New York: Simon & Schuster, 1970,
    pp. 149–72.

Ryan, W. Learning to be poor: The culture of poverty cheesecake. In
    Blaming the victim. New York: Vintage Books, 1971, pp. 117–141.

Schnabel, M. The inevitability of ideology. In *Psychological theory.
    International Journal of Mental Health,* 1975, *3* (4), 4–25.

Vaca, N. C. The Mexican American in the social sciences. *El Grito,*
    1970, *3* (3), 3–24.

U.S. Civil Rights Commission. *Teachers and students: Differences in
    teacher interaction with Mexican-American and Anglo students.*
    Report 5, Mexican-American Education Study. Washington, D.C.:
    Author, 1970.

1. *Classic Epidemiological Studies Regarding Minorities and Mental   Session 4
   Health*
   - Mid-Town Manhattan study
   - Hollingshead and Redlich study of psychopathology in New
     Haven
   - Other more specialized studies

2. *Concept of Psychopathology and Its Various Ways of Being Deter-
   mined*
   - Race and psychopathology
   - Sex and psychopathology
   - Socioeconomic status and psychopathology

3. *Learning Objectives of this Session*

After this session, the resident should be able to discuss significant
aspects of the assumptions and methodology in several large scale
epidemiological studies of mental illness.

4. *Required Reading*

Nathan, P. E., & Harris, S. E. (Eds.). *Psychopathology in society.* New
    York: McGraw-Hill, 1975, pp. 27–53.

5. *Recommended Reading*

Cohen, J. Social work and the culture of poverty. In F. Reissman, J. Cohen, & A. Pearl (Eds.), *Mental health and the poor.* London: The Free Press of Glancoe, Macmillan Co., 1964.

Hollingshead, A. R., & Redlich, F. C. *Social class and mental illness.* New York: John Wiley and Sons, 1958.

Langner, T., & Michaels, S. *Life stress and mental health: The Midtown Manhattan study.* New York: The Free Press, 1963.

Ryan, W. *Blaming the victim.* New York: Vintage Books, 1971, pp. 136–63.

Session 5

1. *Historical Data on the Experience of Different Minority Groups in this Country*

Subjective and Objective Accounts

- Blacks
- Chinese
- Japanese
- Jews
- Mexican-Americans
- Other, including white Anglo-Saxon Protestants

2. *Discussion and Comparison with Minorities That Are No Longer Regarded As Such*

- Irish-Americans
- Other immigrant groups

3. *Learning Objectives of this Session*

After this session the resident should be able to discuss the historical experiences of various minority groups in this country and particularly contemporary social interaction with the majority.

4. *Required Reading* (any of the following)

Anderson, C. H. *White protestant Americans: From national origins to religious group.* Englewood Cliffs, N.J.: Prentice-Hall, 1970, p. 13.

Campbell, A. The nature of white attitudes. In *White attitudes toward Black people.* Ann Arbor: University of Michigan Press, 1971, pp. 1–20.

Fitzpatrick, J. P. The problem of color. In *Puerto Rican Americans.* Englewood Cliffs, N.J., Prentice-Hall, 1971, pp. 101–14.

Giffin, R. Newcomers from the southern mountains. In A. M. Rose &
    C. B. Rose (Eds.), *Minority problems.* New York: Harper & Row,
    1965, pp. 55–61.

Handlin, O., & Handlin, M. F. Origins of anti-semitism in the United
    States. In A. M. Rose & C. B. Rose (Eds.), *Minority problems.* New
    York: Harper & Row, 1965 pp. 17–25.

Kitagawa, D. The American Indian. In A. M. Rose & C. B. Rose (Eds.),
    Minority problems, New York: Harper & Row, 1965, pp. 26–34.

Morales, A. *Ando sangrando (I am bleeding): A study of Mexican
    American-police conflict.* La Puerte, CA.: Perspective Publications,
    1972, pp. 33–46.

Statement of the Japanese American Citizens League for the Jonas
    Subcommittee on Claims. The evacuation of the Japanese-Ameri-
    cans and its aftermath. In A. M. Rose & C. B. Rose (Eds.), *Minority
    problems.* New York: Harper & Row, 1965, pp. 186–194.

Quality Assurance

Quality assurance consists of a mechanism to measure the extent to which clinical services reflect the level of quality described as optimal by a clinic or hospital. This most often includes the random selection of clinical records that are reviewed in accordance with a prepared list of items and evaluated as to whether quality care is reflected in the clinical record. Quality assurance is significantly different from program evaluation in that quality assurance involves ongoing observations of clinical records through various treatment components of the clinic rather than measuring the overall impact of the program over a given period of time. Another important distinction is that quality assurance provides ongoing data that can be used by program directors to modify program policy and training activities in order to address the clinical service deficiencies identified.

The sample quality-assurance mechanisms that are included in Appendices 1 through 4 consist of the following components, briefly described.

> • An overview of rationale and procedure: This explains to the clinic staff the purpose and rationale for quality assurance. The composition and functions of the quality-assurance review committee are discussed. Special attention is given to prescribing the organizational role of the quality-assurance committee to ensure that the data obtained from the review of treatment charts is coordinated by the clinical director and fedback to appropriate agency administrative bodies. In this way quality assurance serves as a needs-assessment instrument for determining training and program policy and procedure modifications.

• Guideline questions for taking and recording clinical history: This form is an example of a problem-oriented approach for record keeping that may be useful as a quality assurance mechanism. The guideline questions include some important areas in the clinical history that are specifically relevant for Hispanic patients. The clinical history form illustrates how the information can be organized into "the treatment plan" section of the clinical history form that is used to synthesize the clinical assessment of the patient into specific and behaviorally stated problems and treatment goals.

• Clinical history and treatment plan of a hypothetical patient: A hypothetical patient's clinical history is filled out on the form to illustrate the development of a treatment plan that is problem-oriented and behaviorally stated. There is a place for the patient to sign, if appropriate, and will help develop a better therapeutic alliance. During training of staff, these forms are used in workshops where the clinician fills out a written clinical history from a videotape clinical interview simulation of this particular hypothetical patient. Other staff can be shown the videotape and, in addition, be given the written clinical history and asked to write out a treatment plan. Afterward, the completed treatment plan can be distributed and small group discussion used to enhance skills in writing behaviorally oriented treatment plans.

• Sample of review items in the quality review form: This is a sample checklist of items that can be used to review outpatient clinical records. Each item is relevant to different sections of the clinical record. Space is provided to indicate if the information is available and to comment on the quality of the clinical notation. Each clinician whose records are reviewed receives a copy of the form that has been filled out, along with the pertinent comments. The clinician's supervisor is asked to review this with the clinician or psychiatric resident and then return the form along with additional comments to the chairperson of the quality assurance committee.

The principal supervisor of the clinician whose chart has been reviewed receives the reviewed checklist form. He is expected to discuss the findings with the clinician during their usual supervisory sessions.

By instituting an ongoing, agencywide mechanism to examine random samples of clinical charts, data are obtained that can then be analyzed to see if there is a relationship between the ethnicity of the patient and specific patterns of deficiencies in the various sections of the clinical history treatment plans and clinical outcomes as recorded in the chart.

There are three main factors to keep in perspective when developing minority content for residency curricula as expressed in this chapter. First, the training curriculum of residency programs is best understood as an element in a system composed of characteristics of the institution and of the community. The clinical service component of the program and the changes proposed in the curriculum should take into account these variables in the training system.

Second, Hispanic content in training curricula is best developed through the interpersonal nature of clinical service provision, typified in the one-to-one initial clinical interview. It is vital to realize that processes of the interview may be complicated by differences in the socioeconomic, ethnic and cultural backgrounds of the doctor and patient. By conceptualizing the interview in terms of specific dynamics that are selectively affected by the impact of these variables and by recognizing transference and countertransference issues in the interactive process, psychiatrists can develop curricula with specific behavioral outcomes in mind.

Third, minority curriculum development is most effective when it is based on stated performance outcomes articulated with an ongoing quality-assurance mechanism that is sufficiently sensitive to identify deficiencies in clinical services provided to Hispanics and other patients of minority groups.

A Perspective for the Development of Minority Content in Psychiatry

Further development of minority content, given the concepts outlined in the chapter, requires, one, that a theoretical framework be developed that leads to measurement of the achievement of terminal learning objectives regarding clinical interventions with Hispanics and other minority status patients. The technical difficulty in designing sophisticated clinical simulations that illustrate common clinical pitfalls are considerable. Two, there is ample evidence that clinicians maintain a priori notions about Hispanics and other minority patients which are similar to prevailing prejudices in society and which operate as clinical stereotypes to negatively affect the quality of services provided.

Theoretical Needs to Further Minority Content Development

An assumption made in this chapter is that Hispanic individuals are as different from each other as are members of any other group and that stereotypic thinking is detrimental to conceptualizing, developing and providing mental health services to this group. A derivative of this assumption is the idea that there exists no "traditional Hispanic culture" that is independent from the adaptational process of this group to varied historical circumstances. Research is needed to test these assumptions and to develop the methodology necessary to

Research Required to Accomplish Theory Development

examine cultural group membership separately from socioeconomic factors.

Research, both basic and applied, of the Hispanic community is virtually unexplored territory. A vast need exists for intensive and extensive research into the Hispanic experience and its application to the delivery of mental health services. A cataloging could include literally every phase of mental health: normative behaviors; coping styles; ecological and epidemiological studies; improved research methodologies; development of appropriate screening and testing instruments; differential patterns of service utilization; the impact of acculturation on presenting problems and engagement in various treatment modalities; the effect of therapist ethnicity on responses to treatment; and so on. The implications of this very basic kind of knowledge for the correct assessment of behavior patterns and dynamics and the development of appropriate interventive techniques are obvious. Further research on the interpersonal manifestations of such stereotypes needs to be conducted under experimental conditions relevant to particular clinical situations and settings.

The development of instruments useful in measuring and identifying different types of interactions between doctor and patient during the interview are badly needed; up to now, only simple checklists have been used. In the 1970 Civil Rights Commission study of the interaction between Hispanic children and Anglo teachers in the classroom, the Flanders Interaction Scale was used. Development of similar kinds of instruments would be useful in making structured observations regarding the interaction between the doctor and the Hispanic patient. Such instruments would enable training directors to develop baseline data on interactive clinical behavior necessary in formulating terminal learning objectives for the training curriculum. These data would also provide a way of testing hypotheses regarding the relationship between demographic characteristics of patient and therapist and the outcomes of clinical interviews.

Strategies for Institutional Change and Faculty Development

The training mission of the residency program should be integrated into the overall service role of the program. In this way the terminal learning objectives of the residency program can incorporate expected competencies in the clinical interaction with Hispanics. The stated standards of clinical training can then be integrated into the clinic's quality assurance program. This goal can be achieved only if the various accrediting bodies, the leadership of the institution, and the training directors agree on a common statement of purpose. Such a statement of purpose would include the idea that quality of services and training includes a single standard for all patients including those of diverse cultural, racial and ethnic groups, especially in areas where there are substantial numbers of Hispanics. The ethnicity of administrative and service program personnel should reflect the population being served. Programmatic linkages and joint training and service ventures between residency programs and community-based agencies are fostered by creative funding arrangements that promote interdependence rather than competition for scarce funds.

Major Public Policy Recommendations at the Federal and State Levels

There are currently a host of advisory bodies to the National Institute of Mental Health at the national and regional levels as well as to state and county governments. These advisory groups often have to learn much about the public service agencies in order to provide coherent and realistic advice. Efforts should be directed to synthesizing the resulting advisory input in order to identify common themes and issues. This will provide a broader understanding of these problems and focus attention in order to monitor change.

Appendix 1
Quality Assurance Review Process
Adult Psychiatric Clinic

Purpose

The quality review process has as its primary goal to monitor the treatment services provided to patients of the adult psychiatric clinic by way of self-evaluation, in order to maintain a high quality of professional services. This process has the mechanism to monitor the propriety, effectiveness, and quality of patient care services. It will improve clinical skills, determine in-service needs and will offer an input for the designing of a workable, accessible and effective treatment system.

Meetings

The quality assurance teams will meet weekly and will serve as quality assurance subcommittees as well as utilization review committees.

Team Members

The teams will consist of interdisciplinary staff including a psychiatrist, psychologist and psychiatric social worker. Each team will have a team leader who will have coordinating and tracking responsibilities. The team leaders will be responsible to the chairperson of the quality assurance system. The chairperson will have access to all information reported by the teams. It will be the responsibility of the chairperson to identify themes and issues that indicate a need for in-service or the need to initiate modifications in the delivery system. The chairperson will be responsible to the clinic director.

The Review Process

1. The primary source of information to be utilized in the review process will be the individual clinical record.

2. Open and closed charts will be selected by patient file number by a random system devised by the clinic administrator (about 32 charts a month, 90 percent open, 10 percent closed).

3. The clinic administrator (or designee) will assign charts to teams according to the existing mechanism to avoid charts being assigned to the same team responsible for treating the patient.

4. Each team leader will receive the list of charts to be reviewed by the team members each week. The team leader will assign the charts to be reviewed. Full time staff will review two charts, part time staff will review one chart each week.

5. The team leader will keep a log of the charts to be reviewed.

6. The team members will review the charts and will prepare the quality assurance check lists prior to the next meeting.

7. The team members will discuss their check lists and impressions during the quality assurance team meeting. Among the issues to be considered will be: Was the admission appropriate? Was adequate information gathered prior to the formulation of the treatment plan? Was the treatment plan logical and feasible? Was the treatment plan acceptable in terms of clinical and ethical issues? Does the patient's improvement, from a clinical judgment sense, appear to be related to the treatment services provided? Does the termination appear

to be logical and timely? Were adequate and feasible aftercare plans formulated and implemented?

8. The team leader will record committee comments on the quality assurance report form during the meeting and will attach this report to the review check list.

9. The team leader will place the check list in the box of the administrative supervisor.

10. The administrative supervisor will utilize the information from the quality assurance report and check list to take remedial action or to provide appropriate reinforcement. The administrative supervisor will document action taken on the quality assurance report.

11. The administrative supervisor will return the report and the review check list to the team leader.

12. The team leader will date the return of the forms on the log sheet.

13. The chart review check list and the quality assurance team report will be clipped together and filed under the therapist's name. The information will be confidential and will be accessible only to administrative and supervisory staff.

14. The chairperson will periodically review and analyze the quality assurance reports and comments on themes and trends and will share a summary of the issues and trends with the clinic director during the administrative meeting.

15. The summary will be discussed in the administrative meeting for the purpose of identifying and implementing needed modifications in the delivery system and for the purpose of identifying staff training needs.

Appendix 2
Sample Patient Clinical History Form and Guideline Questions

I. Identifying Data

Name: _____

Sex: _____ Age: _____

Living Situation: _____

_____

Marital Status: _____

Occupation: _____

Means of Support: _____

_____

Date: _____

Date of Evaluation: _____

Person(s) Interviewed: _____

_____

Referral Source: _____

Phone: _____

II. Presenting Problem
   • Why did client come?
   • Why did client come now?
   • Client's own statement of the problem (quote).

III. History of the Present Problem
   • Date of onset. How is problem manifested? Are there or have there been any variations? What impact has there been on the client's social functioning? What interventions have been attempted, by whom, and what have been the results of these interventions? What does the client/family expect of the clinic? What does the client/family think would be a satisfactory resolution? What does the client/family see as the cause of the problem? What does the client/family think contributes to the problem? How does the client/family understand the problem?

IV. Biomedical & Psychiatric History
   • Are there any significant medical problems or disabilities (e.g. history of heart disease, tuberculosis, diabetes, respiratory problems, cancer, epilepsy, development disabilities, neurological problems)?
   • Any operations, injuries, or hospitalizations? Are there any allergies to medication, allergies which affect functioning? Has there been any contact with mental health services (e.g. psychiatric medications, rehabilitation services, therapy, hospitalizations, special treatments such as ECT)? Regarding psychiatric hospitalizations: dates, duration, reasons, age, number of times, names of facilities.
   • Any life threatening behavior, history of violence, suicide attempts?
   • Client's assessment of own health, any ongoing medical treatments. Date of/need for physical exam and/or psychological testing.

V. Medications (Past & Present)
   • List all medications, dosage, and purpose.
   • Identify reactions to psychotropic medications and side effects. Client's assessment of medications' effectiveness, how they work and lethality.
   • Other drug use history—illicit street drugs, amount, type, frequency, length of use, when begun, when stopped.

VI. Family History
  • Birth place—family origin, rural or urban background; family structure, composition, intactness; significant moves or changes. What were significant family members like? How were decisions made? Occupational history and lifestyle of parents.
  • Extended family—What was it like growing up in the family? Relationship with others in the family. Ethnic/National/Religious characteristics. Assimilation/Acculturation status.
  • History of mental health problems (including drugs and alcoholism) in the family.
  • Major diseases in family.
  • Personality problems in family.
  • Attitude toward children and self as parent.
  • Living situation—decision making patterns, educational status, child–bearing/childrearing status.
  • History of significant psychiatric, medical, marital, sexual-physical abuse, neglect, and occupation problems in family.

VII. Social History
  Achievement of Significant Development Milestones (Erickson Attachment).
  • Formal and informal affiliations (school, work, leisure time activities).
  • Level of social functioning.
  • Level of assimilation/acculturation.
  • Sexual history.
  • Educational/occupational/work history.
  • Marital history—number, type, age, problems, strengths, attitudes.
  • Where does person live and what are his/her supports—resources?

VIII. Mental Status
  • Appearance.
  • Behavior (See attachments for MS Behavioral descriptions).
  • Feeling.
  • Perception.
  • Thinking.
  • Suicidal-Homicidal ideation.

IX. Diagnostic Impression (DSM III) Manifested by: G.A.S.

X. Dynamic Formulation
  The formulation should be a brief narrative that expresses a working hypothesis of the nature of the person experiencing the stated problem. It should address—
  • the background and development of the person;
  • the strength that the person has brought to his or her life situation;
  • the stresses, both from within (conflict) and external family, social cultural factors that have shaped the current problem situation.

XI. Special Diagnostic Studies Needed or Performed
  • Psychological—purpose needed or performed.
  • Physical Exam.
  • Neurological.
  • Education.

Signatures: _____   Title: _____

_____   Date: _____

G.A.S. Score: _____

Appendix 3

Clinical History and Treatment Plan of a Hypothetical Patient

I. Sex: Female   Age: 20 years
   Marital Status: Means of Support:
   Living Situation: 20 year old single, unemployed female, living at home
                      with her mother and father
   Occupation: Secretary   Phone: Home: _____
                                              Work: _____
                                       Person(s) Interviewed: Client

II. Presenting Problem
    Complains "I'm depressed and nervous, I feel like crying all the time."
    Used to like being with people but now prefers staying at home. Fearful
    of crowds. No longer drives her car—too frightened. Lacks self-confidence.

III. History of Present Problem
     Client expresses embarrassment at having to seek help for her emotional
     problems, but her condition has become increasingly worse and her
     medical doctor finally recommended that she come to the clinic. Client
     alleges that up to about 18 months ago she was cheerful, out-going and
     self-confident. She has no idea what caused the drastic change. She
     denies prior emotional or physical problems. She was hospitalized about
     18 months ago for a "flu" condition, developed pneumonia, became very
     ill and remained in the hospital for 15 days. She recuperated slowly.
     Although medically recovered, she remained fearful that she might again
     become sick and have to go to the hospital. Client describes onset of
     depressive feelings approximately 17 months ago. She noticed that she
     began to wake up at dawn and also began to lose her appetite. She has
     not worked since being hospitalized, and has remained at home with
     both parents and a younger brother.

IV. Biomedical & Psychiatric History
    Patient denies any serious illness other than the above. Client has had
    an 18 lb. weight loss over the last 6 months. Client's only hospitalization
    was at _____ hospital 18 months ago. Client denies history of
    significant allergies or hypertension, tuberculosis, high blood pressure,
    heart disease, or alcoholism.

V. Medications (past & present)
   Has been taking valium 5 mg., 5 times daily prescribed by the family
   physician for about 8 months. For some time she has taken up to 5 per
   day.

VI. Family History
    Client is next to the youngest of 5 siblings, 2 girls (18, 22) and 2 boys
    (24, 26) and is living at home with both parents and the youngest brother.
    The older siblings are married and have left home. One of the sisters
    has been hospitalized for a mental condition and is having problems
    with her marriage. With this exception, family psychiatric history is
    denied. Both parents were born in Mexico and came to the United States
    at an early age. There are few relatives who live in the area. The client

and siblings were born here. While the parents are bilingual, the primary language spoken at home is English. The father works in a blue collar job. He is currently unemployed. One sibling has completed high school. According to the client, her mother is against the recommendation because the client "is not crazy" and does not need this kind of help. The father, on the other hand, she feels, is very supportive and encourages her to get help. Client feels that her mother is objecting because she also is ashamed. She feels much closer to her father whom she describes as quiet, gentle, and supportive, and someone "I can talk to without getting into an argument." Her description of her relationship with her mother is just the opposite. "I can't talk to her. We get into an argument and then I start screaming at her." She describes her relationship with her siblings as good with the exception of the sister with the psychiatric history. The relation with her is primarily one of avoidance.

VII. Social History (including cultural factors)
Client reports a normal childhood and denies any serious problems. She states that she has always been heavy but it has not been a serious concern for her, although she has dated infrequently. She was an average student and graduated from high school 3 years ago. Shortly thereafter, she got a job as an office clerk for a large insurance company. She got along well with her co-workers and enjoyed her job until she became sick and was hospitalized. Until this illness she spent much time with girl friends going to movies. Client has never visited Mexico, nor had contact with relatives in Mexico. She has had no intimate relationships.

VIII. Mental Status
She is moderately obese and is the only one in the family who is overweight. Patient is casually but neatly dressed in skirt and blouse. Her behavior is subdued. She sits quietly with occasional movement of her hands to express a point but generally lacks animation. Her voice is low and soft with little variation in tonal quality. She looks sad and periodically becomes tearful.

Patient is oriented in all spheres and denies delusions and hallucinations. However, she gets nervous in crowds and then has the feeling that people are watching her. Her intelligence is average.

There is no evidence of impairment in her thinking. Attention and memory are intact. No disturbances in associations noted. Has had occasional suicidal thoughts but has not progressed to the point of developing a plan to carry out the thoughts. Patient is not considered suicidal at this time.

IX. Diagnostic Impression (DSMIII)
Major affective disorder (296.2). Manifested by dyphoric mood, with frequent tearful episodes. Poor eating and sleeping patterns and phobias (fear of crowds and driving her car).

X. Dynamic Formulation
The client is a young woman who was born into a family situation where father and mother were both uneducated immigrants. Mother is more traditionally oriented than father who may be seen by client as warm but ineffectual. Further stresses were large numbers of siblings, poverty and mental illness in one sibling. The client grew up with a self-image of herself as a person "who can make it" and able to make decisions for herself despite their being contrary to her mother's values.

When she became ill with pneumonia (perhaps aggravated by the experience of being helpless in hospital) she may have sustained a threat to her developing identity with a subsequent period of crisis and one month later developed illness with psychomotor retardation and vegetative signs.

XI. Special Diagnostic Studies
Not available.

Signatures: _____   Title: _____

_____   Date: _____

G.A.S. Score: _____

APPENDIX 3 (cont.)
Treatment Plan

Client Name _____ Number _____ Therapist _____

Problem	Approach	Goals	P—Partially U—Unattained D—Deferred Outcoming Data
Problem no. 1 Date of Entry: 12-11-79 Date of Onset:	Suicidal Ideation with crying spells 8 Individual treatment sessions	30 consecutive days with no reported suicidal ideation or crying spell Enhance client understanding of previous illness and mastery of issue	Attained—A 2-8-80
Problem no. 2 Date of Entry: 12-11-79 Date of Onset: 18 mos. ago (6-78)	Vegetative Signs of Depression Medication evaluation by psychiatrist Contact family physician for medical records and history	30 consecutive days of normal sleep pattern 10 pound weight gain over 30 days	Attained—A 2-8-80
Problem no. 3 Date of Entry: 12-11-79 Date of Onset: 18 mos. ago (6-78)	Fearfulness Individual treatment session for 8 sessions which support and encourage positive moves along hierarchy of social behaviors Attend evaluation session with Vocational Rehab.— T. L'Esperance	Begin driving car 2 times a week to clinic Contact two friends a week and have one social outing within 30 days Gainful employment within 60 days	Partially Attained— 2-8-80 Attained—A 3-2-80
Problem no. 4 Date of Entry: Date of Onset:	Frequent hostile outbursts toward mother 4 family treatment sessions with father, mother and siblings as appropriate, focusing on communication skills and behavioral contracting	To report three incidents of appropriate assertive behavior within 30 days 30 consecutive days of no inappropriate hostile outbursts with mother Reports of harmonious relationship with mother	Unattained—U 2-8-80 Deferred—D 3-2-80

Client's
Signature: _____

Date: _____

Therapist's
Signature: _____

Medical Doctor's
Signature: _____

Appendix 4
Quality Assurance Review Log Sheet

Team Leader _____

Therapist	Administrative Supervisor	Chart Name	Patient File No.	Date Discussed	Date Returned

Appendix 4 (cont.)
Quality Assurance Committee Report

Therapist's
Name _____

Patient's
Chart Name _____

Date _____

Members
Present _____

_____

_____

_____

_____

Committee Comments

Signature _____
                    Chairperson

Supervisor's Intervention

Date _____   Signature _____
                                        Supervisor

References

American Medical Association. *Directory of residency training programs*. Chicago: Author, 1978.

Brill, N. Q., & Stornow, H. A. Social class and psychiatric treatment. *Archives of General Psychiatry*, 1960, 340–44.

Butts, H. F., & Schrachter, J. S. Transference and countertransference in interracial analysis. *Journal of the American Psychoanalytical Association*, 1968, 792–808.

Engel, G. L Clinical application of the biopsychosocial model. *American Journal of Psychiatry*, 1980, *137* (5), 535–44.

Flanders, N. A. *Analyzing teaching behavior*. Menlo Park, CA. Addison-Wesley, 1970.

Frank, J. D. The dynamics of the psychotherapeutic relationship. In T. J. Scheff (Ed.), *Mental illness and social processes*. New York: Harper and Row, 1967.

Gurel, L. Some characteristics of psychiatric training programs. *American Journal of Psychiatry*, 1975, *132*, 363–72.

Kardiner A., & Oversey, L. *The mark of oppression*. New York: World Publishing Co., 1962.

Karno, M. The enigma of ethnicity in a psychiatric clinic. *Archives of General Psychiatry*, 1966, *14*, 516–20.

Karno, M., & Edgarton, R. B. Perception of mental illness in a Mexican American community. *Archives of General Psychiatry*, 1969, *20*, 233–38.

Levi-Strauss, C. *Structural anthropology*. New York: Basic Books, 1963.

Lopez, S. Clinical stereotypes of the Mexican American. In L. L. Martines (Ed.), *Chicano psychology*. New York: Academic Press, 1977.

Morales, A. The impact of class discrimination and white racism on the mental health of Mexican Americans. In N. N. Wagner, & M. J. Haus (Eds.), *Chicanos, social and psychological perspectives*. St. Louis: C. V. Mosby, 1971.

Morales, A. *Ando sangrando (I am bleeding): A study of Mexican American-police conflict*. La Puerte, CA.: Perspective Publications, 1972.

Newby, I. A. *Jim Crow's defense*. Baton Rouge: Louisiana State University Press, 1965.

Rosenthal, D., & Frank, J. D. The fate of psychiatric clinic outpatients assigned to psychotherapy. *Journal of Nervous and Mental Disease*, 1958, *127*, 330–43.

Schwebel, M. The inevitability of ideology in psychological theory. *International Journal of Mental Health*, 1975, *3* (4), 4–26.

Sullivan, H. S. *The psychiatric interview*. New York: W. W. Norton Co., 1954.

Thomas, A., & Sillen, S. (Eds.). *Racism and psychiatry*. New York: Brunner/Mazel, 1972.

Torrey, E. F. *The mind game: Witch doctors and psychiatrists*. New York: Aronson, 1973.

U. S. Civil Rights Commission. *Teachers and students: Differences in teacher interaction with Mexican American and Anglo students*. Report Number 5. Washington, D.C.: Author, 1971.

Vaca, N. A. The Mexican American in the social science, Part 2. *El Grito*, 1970, *4*, 17–25.

Yamamoto, J. Research priorities in Asian American mental health delivery. *American Journal of Psychiatry*, 1978, *135* (4), 457–58.

Yamamoto, J., James, Q. C., Bloombaum, M., & Hattem, J. Racial factors in patient selection. *American Journal of Psychiatry*, 1967, *124*, 630–36.

Bibliography

Arce, A. A. Ethnicity, Hispanic communities and issues in mental health. *Proceedings of the Puerto Rican Conference on Human Services.* Washington, D.C.: COSSMHO, 1975.

Arce, A. A.: Psychiatric training issues: The Puerto Rican perspective. *American Journal of Psychiatry.* (forthcoming)

Bloombaum, M., Yamamoto, J., & James, Q. Cultural stereotyping among psychotherapists. *Journal of Consulting Psychology,* 1968, 32–99.

Bradshaw, W. H. Training psychiatrists for working with Blacks in basic residency programs. *American Journal Psychiatry,* 1978, *135,* 1520–24.

Grinker, R. R. The future educational needs of psychiatrists. *American Journal of Psychiatry,* 1975, *132,* pp 259–62.

Kaplan, A. The conduct of inquiry. In *Methodology for behavioral science.* Scranton, PA.: Chandler Publishing Co., 1964.

Kuhn, S. The structure of scientific revolutions. In O. Neurath (Ed.), *Encyclopedia of Unified Science,* Vol. 2. Chicago: University of Chicago Press, 1962.

Madsen, W. Value conflicts and folk psychiatry in south Texas. In A. Kiev (Ed.), *Magic, faith and healing.* New York: The Free Press, 1964.

Miranda, M. R. *Psychotherapy with the Spanish speaking: Issues in research and service delivery.* Monograph No. 3, Spanish Speaking Research Center, University of California at Los Angeles, 1976.

Padilla, A. M. Psychological research and the Mexican American. In M. J. Haus, & N. N. Wagner (Eds.). *Chicanos social and psychological perspectives* (2nd ed.). St. Louis: C. V. Mosby, 1976.

Padilla, A. M., & Aranda, P. *Latino mental health: Bibliography and abstracts.* Department of Health, Education and Welfare Publication No. (ADM) 76–317, Superintendent of Documents, Washington, D.C., 1976.

Padilla, A. M., Olmedo, E. L., Lopez, S., & Perez, R. *Hispanic mental health bibliography II.* Monograph No. 6, Spanish Speaking Mental Health Research Center, University of California at Los Angeles, 1978.

Padilla, E. R., & Padilla, A. M. (Eds.). *Transcultural psychiatry: An Hispanic perspective.* Monograph No. 4, Spanish Speaking Mental Health Research Center, University of California at Los Angeles, 1977.

Padilla, A. M. & Ruiz, R. A. *Latino mental health: A review of the literature.* Department of Health, Education and Welfare Publication No. (ADM) 76–113, Superintendent of Documents, Washington, D.C., 1976.

Roheim, G. *Modernations.* In G. Roheim (Ed.), *Psychoanalysis and anthropology.* New York: International Universities Press, 1968, pp. 361–69.

Simmons, O. G. The mutual images and expectations of Anglo Americans and Mexican-Americans. In N. N. Wagner, & M. J. Haus (Eds.), *Chicanos: Social and psychological perspectives.* St. Louis: C. V. Mosby, 1971.

Terestman, N., Miller, J. D., & Weber, J. J. Blue collar patients at a psychoanalytic clinic. *American Journal of Psychiatry,* 1974, *131,* 3.

PART FOUR

Psychiatric Nursing

OLIVER OSBORNE   CAROLYN CARTER
NORMA PINKLETON   HILDA RICHARDS

CHAPTER 13

Development of African American Curriculum Content in Psychiatric and Mental Health Nursing

Psychiatric and mental health nurses are the largest group of psychiatric and mental health workers. They provide services in a wide variety of mental health settings, including state mental hospitals, community mental health centers, inpatient psychiatric units in general hospitals, mental retardation centers and in private practice. They also provide services in health care settings not specifically dedicated to the care of the mentally ill. They serve as mental health consultants in acute, intermediate and long-term facilities as well as in public health agencies and schools. They also provide consultation and support to private physicians. Despite their ubiquitous service, most psychiatric and mental health nurses have not been adequately prepared to deliver quality psychiatric and mental health services to African Americans. One vital reason for this incapacity has been a conspicuous absence of African American content in the literature and curricula of psychiatric and mental health nursing. Because social and cultural factors are involved in the genesis of mental illness, professionals who treat African Americans must understand the values, beliefs and norms that may affect the sickness and the well-being of African Americans. This means that nurse educators must develop culturally relevant educational programs.

The primary objective of the nursing curriculum is to prepare competent professional practitioners. Competency includes the ability to identify and use a variety of strategies to reach a given goal; the ability to use the resources of a variety of social systems, which include ethnic and racial subsystems within the society; the ability to engage in effective reality testing, which includes a sophisticated understanding of the world; and the ability to learn from and respond to changing situations.

The roles of the nurse include teaching, learning, advocating and facilitating individual and social change. To perform these roles, nurses

335

must know themselves, their feelings, attitudes, biases, prejudices, responses and reactions.

Definition of Terms

Throughout this chapter, where possible, the term *African American* rather than *Black* has been used. The authors contend that for the future, the term *Black* is inadequate to theory and curriculum building by mental health and other professionals who wish to enhance the life circumstances of African Americans. The term itself is merely an anglicized version of the Latin word *niger*. Its variances include the familiar *nigger, nigra, negre* and *Negro*. To consider *Black* a significant advance over *Negro* is to be deluded. The term *Black* did have some utility during the 1960s and 1970s through its association with the concept of "Black power." This phrase captured the imagination of Americans when, in 1966, in support of James Meredith's Freedom Walk, Stokely Carmichael urged:

> The only way we gonna stop them white men from whuppin us is to take over. We have been saying freedom for six years and we ain't got nothin'. What we gonna start sayin now is Black Power."
> (Chambers, 1968, p. 216)

The call for Black power recognized that a dominant American political and economic reality is ethnicity. It was in the recognition of this tradition that African Americans were called upon to come together as a political force to achieve their legitimate ends. The media as well as white supremacists interpreted the call for Black power as Black racism.

Although the term was useful as a rallying cry for the revolutions of the 1960s and the early 1970s, its limitations must now be confronted. It is not only a variation of the term *Negro*, but more important, it has limitations in the area of psychology and, more specifically, psycholinguistics. In the historical and social context of America's imagery, binary opposition means conflict. In Western culture the color black has been associated with darkness, ignorance and evil, while the color white has been associated with brightness, cleanliness and good. The developing fields of social linguistics, psycholinguistics, linguistic anthropology and cognitive anthropology suggest that words in themselves are not as important as the underlying concepts or conceptual themes that these words represent. In speaking of ignored, but consequential, issues in speech, Bernstein (1961) stated, "The error . . . seems largely due to the superficial focus upon the spoken details of the true codes rather than the broader conception of the codes as referring to the transmission of the basic or deep meaning structures of a culture or subculture."

The term *African American* provides opportunities for mental health and other professionals to develop in the minds of African Americans, no matter what their contemporary condition, a sense of their cultural heritage and values in a society which has traditionally devalued them. The term *African American* as a conceptual and psychotherapeutic strategy can be rooted in the rich cultural heritage of the African American, which by definition goes beyond the mundane, too often punitive, urban and rural American experience to include the perspective of African Americans as participants in a vital African reality as it exists, not only in Africa but also in the Caribbean, South America, African enclaves of Europe and even Melanesia and Polynesia. The accomplishments of this strategy facilitate the African American's awareness of his or her personal condition as a legitimate representation of the plight of all oppressed people and not of his or her own personal failure. It facilitates the development of the conceptual tools proposed by Roger Clark Wilcox (1971). Although the authors recommend an African American conceptual strategy to psychiatric mental health professionals, they recognize and accept that because of its verbal simplicity and historical and political relevance, the term *Black* will have continuing popularity.

Cultural Pluralism and Curriculum Development

An examination of the concept of cultural pluralism is important to the development and integration of African American content into nursing curricula. First, it must be noted that African Americans were the only group of Americans brought forcibly to America. For them the melting-pot theory of assimilation never pertained. Second, African Americans used the social rebellions of the 1960s to demand social and economic equality, and other minorities followed their lead. Third, although these surfacing subcultures indicated that the United States was a multicultural rather than a melting-pot society, no clearly accepted state of cultural pluralism has been achieved.

Cass (1969) observed the failure to achieve an integrated pluralistic society in his analysis of issues that motivated Black student unrest on college campuses during the 1960s. There was the naive belief that with increased minority enrollment "close acquaintance with white students and extended exposure to white culture would lead automatically to assimilation. The melting pot would function, in the new context, as it had in the folklore of the past. The realities proved more complex. . . . Proximity accentuates differences as often as it fosters assimilation."

The burden of assimilation, Cass remarked, was on the group to be assimilated.

> It is the black who is expected to do most of the accommodating. After all, it is he, the minority, who is being invited to enjoy the

benefits of membership in the established society of the majority. The black student's options were limited. He could deny his blackness and become as white in thought and action as his talent allowed; or he could follow the more difficult course of accepting the white man's offer of skills and knowledge, while fighting to retain his own sense of black identity.

By the mid-1960s, disenchantment with the potential benefits of integration had set in, and Black solidarity became apparent on white campuses. "The heart of the message from black campus leaders," stated Cass, "was that blacks have a valid culture of their own, separate from and, in some respects, superior to white culture; that to achieve their fullest human development blacks must become proud of their blackness . . . and stop trying to become white men with black skins."

This need for personal and social validity sometimes led to the demand for separateness of such things as study programs and living facilities. What they really wanted, according to Cass, "was to emerge from their collegiate years not only with the intellectual skills required for success in the white world, but also with deeper knowledge of their own people and a continuing commitment to the black community."

Moorman (1969) pointed out that "unrest among blacks on campuses . . . should be viewed as the legitimate and logical product of the functioning of the American higher educational system in its truest and most honored of tradition. . . . If a higher education does nothing else, if it fails in all other respects, it should awaken the educated person to the realities of his environment." Moorman continued that "education should guide the student in the acquisition of the necessary cognitive and evaluative tools to make a clear determination about the world in which he lives and to develop a system of values for coping with that world." Moorman felt that the education of Black Americans had a dimension beyond that of the average American student, "that of providing for heritage identification and enculturation," the dual imperatives involved in the education of Black Americans. This "duality of response" discussed by Cass and Moorman in the context of higher education is central to understanding the psychological dynamics of the African American and is discussed in some detail later in this chapter.

Trends in Professional Organizations and the Literature

Traditionally nurses have comprised, and still do, the largest single professional group of health care practitioners. Yet recent studies show a decline in the number of African American registered nurses (L. Robinson, 1972; Burgess, 1978). The Black movement of the 1960s did not help increase the number of African Americans in nursing. Burgess cited evidence that African American nurses have increased only 1.2 percent in ten years. In nursing education diploma programs had the smallest Black enrollment, associate degree programs the largest, while baccalaureate degree programs maintained a constant Black enrollment.

Most concerned nurses recognize the appropriateness of the resolution passed by the 1972 American Nurses Association (ANA) House of Delegates to create and implement programs designed to bring more African Americans into the profession. Today, its Human Rights Commission's affirmative action program has an impact on all structural units of the association. The commission consistently prods these units to include ethnic nurses of color as program participants and fosters culturally diverse curriculum content in schools of nursing and continuing nursing education programs. A unit assessment form developed by the commission allows it to monitor the ANA's commitment to cultural pluralism in the nursing care delivery system. A number of other regional and local nursing organizations also have participated aggressively in the development of affirmative action programs and pluralistic curriculum content. Foremost among these has been the Western Interstate Commission on Higher Education in Nursing (WICHEN) project.

In general, despite these efforts, safe nursing care for ethnic people of color continues to be an unmet need.

> African Americans and other ethnic people of color (Hispanics, American Indians, Asian Americans) represent only 6.2% of the 1,401,633 actively licensed Registered Nurses in this country (ANA Statistics Report, 1979).

The dearth of African American nurses and other nurses of color in the United States suggests the need to have all nurses learn how to provide quality nursing care, including psychiatric nursing care, to ethnic people of color.

Nurses of color who were members of the National Association of Colored Graduate Nurses before its 1951 merger with the ANA were concerned about the care of their brothers and sisters. This group believed that the merger would enable African American nurse members to participate in the total ANA program and would ensure that the programs sponsored by ANA would contribute to the welfare of all African American nurses. This commitment by the ANA was not met, and a number of local and national Black nursing associations continued to exist, committed to achieving objectives that were not being met by other nursing organizations. Twenty years after the 1951 merger, the National Black Nurses Association (NBNA) was formed to focus more attention upon the professional development of African American nurses and on the health requirements of African American people. These goals were articulated in the objectives of the NBNA:

- Define and determine nursing care for Black consumers for optimum quality of care by acting as their advocates.
- Act as change agents in restructuring existing institutions and/or helping to establish institutions to suit their needs.
- Serve as the national nursing body to influence legislation and policies that affect Black people, and work cooperatively and collaboratively with other health workers to this end.
- Conduct, analyze, and publish research to increase the body of knowledge about health care and health needs of Blacks.
- Compile and maintain a National Directory of Black Nurses to assist with the dissemination of information regarding Black nurses on national and local levels by the use of all media.
- Set standards and guidelines for quality education of Black nurses on all levels by providing consultation to nursing faculties, and by monitoring for proper utilization and placement of Black nurses.
- Recruit, counsel and assist Black persons interested in nursing to insure a constant progression of Blacks into the field.
- Act as the vehicle for unification of Black nurses of varied age groups, educational levels, and geographic locations to insure continuity and flow of our common heritage.
- Collaborate with other Black groups to compile archives relevant to the historic, current, and future activities of Black nurses.
- Provide the impetus and means for Black nurses to write and publish on an individual or collaborative basis.

Communication is the tool used by all helping professions. Hildegard Peplau, some thirty years ago, recognized communication as central to the process of nursing in her statement that "the nursing process is educative and therapeutic when nurse and patient *can come to know and to respect each other, as persons who are alike* (Peplau, 1952).

The effort to respect persons who are both alike and different is the challenge that nursing is still struggling to meet. There is a slow but constant push in nursing education to incorporate curriculum content on ethnicity, which is often relegated to one or two class sessions usually entitled "Caring for Patients with Culturally Different Backgrounds." Although few nursing curricula have an entire course devoted to minority health care issues, such a course has been a regular part of the undergraduate curriculum at the College of Nursing, University of Cincinnati. Even rarer is the curriculum that integrates relevant content on ethnicity throughout the entire program. One such program is the associate and baccalaureate ladder program at Medgar Evers College, City University of New York, in Brooklyn.

The nursing literature reveals that African American nurses, as well as other ethnic nurses of color, have historically noted deficits in the nursing profession's capability to respond to the health requirements of nonwhite populations. Traditionally, nursing has treated health matters as if racial, ethnic and socioeconomic differences either did not exist or had no impact upon health care practices. Consequently, nursing education has been singularly devoid of information about the nursing needs of people of color, and nursing texts have also ignored such issues. Only recently have these issues begun to appear in the nursing literature.

The psychiatric nursing literature, which began to develop in the late 1920s, provides a particularly revealing example of this myopia. The early psychiatric nursing textbooks reflected the knowledge and traditions of hospital psychiatry (Bailey, 1939; Carmichael and Chapman, 1936; Karnosh, Gage, and Mereness, 1944; Noyes and Haydon, 1940; Sands, 1941). They contained some information about personality development but mainly discussed the organic and traumatic psychoses. The conception of nursing care was the maintenance of the patient's safety and physical well-being.

In the 1950s, following the leadership of Peplau (1952), emphasis on interpersonal relationships, personality development and principles of psychiatric nursing increased (Brown and Fowler, 1971; Matheney and Topalis, 1970; L. Robinson, 1972). The explication of organic psychiatry, psychiatric nursing as hospital nursing and concerns with diagnoses became of lesser concern than the developing emphasis on growth and development, interpersonal relationships, communication, interviewing, the therapeutic nurse–patient relationship and the view of patient problems as in process rather than as static, diagnosed categories of behavior. By the 1970s some psychiatric nursing texts had begun to incorporate considerations of the community, including psychiatric care programs in the community; the community mental health movement; community problems of children, youth and adults; family disorganization; mental retardation; crisis intervention; and the social aspects of mental health.

It is important to note that since the 1920s, when the first psychiatric nursing texts appeared, very little has been mentioned about the psychiatric nursing needs of racial and ethnic minorities. There has been no evidence of a concern with social organization, culture or high-risk populations. Psychiatric nursing has not benefited from the increasing number of psychiatric nurses who have taken advanced degrees in sociology and anthropology nor from the sociopolitical upheaval of the 1960s and 1970s. An exception to this dismal record is the work of Davis (1974), which discussed at length the needs of African Americans and other ethnic racial groups as well as the issues of ethics and social structure as they relate to mental health nursing. Although Leininger's *Contemporary Issues in Mental Health Nursing*

(1973) included discussion of anthropological and sociological issues in mental health nursing, the contributing authors focused upon the general issues of these disciplines as they relate to nursing rather than on pragmatic issues of the mental health needs of traditionally disadvantaged populations.

The award-winning Wilson and Kneisl text (1979) does devote a few pages to the mental health needs of racial and ethnic minorities, but these considerations are almost lost among the many topics contained in this 855-page text. Their comments are suggestive but by no means comprehensive.

Little more than two decades have elapsed since the first serious attempts to develop mental health nursing theories. Currently there are several theoretical approaches to organizing thinking about the profession.

Since Peplau's (1952) landmark book explicating the importance of interpersonal relations in nursing, psychiatric nurses have been concerned with investigating the great variety of conceptual and practice possibilities within and related to this framework. As an approach, interpersonal relations focuses more on the nurse–patient relationship than on the totality of human functioning and factors which affect such functioning. Therefore, several theoretical frameworks have been utilized for broadening the base of understanding in psychiatric nursing. Throughout the literature there is a fundamental dedication to a holistic perspective to nursing (Levine, 1971). Examples are Roger's (1970) unitary human conceptualization, Orem's (1971) self-care conceptualization adaptation theory as set forth by Roy (1976), and the increasingly popular systems approach.

Each approach attempts to capture the whole of the human experience. Roger (1970) sees nursing as concerned with unitary humans as they interact with their environments. The importance of culture is deemphasized in this approach. Similarly, Orem's (1971) emphasis on self-care primarily relates to enhancement of individual psychological and physiological states. The self-care orientation may facilitate understanding of individual psychology and physiology but not of the impact of society and culture on the individual. The adaptation approach incorporates culture and society as important variables in understanding human functioning; however, it implies an underlying conservative character to human interaction with the environment. It does not easily accommodate innovation and command of social, cultural and environmental circumstances.

At this time, given the dearth of nursing knowledge about the care of African Americans, it appears that the systems approach may be most useful for the study of issues related to the development of mental health curricula sensitive to the needs of African Americans. This approach has as its basic premise change in the individual, family or social group due to the impact of society as well as culture. The systems approach has implications for a wide range of academic, clinical and administrative services of concern to nurses and is most useful when combined with the holistic orientation of nursing. Indeed, in the nursing literature it is very difficult to distinguish the holistic from the systems orientation.

The humanistic approach may be as important as the systems and holistic orientations, particularly for conceptualizations of nursing for African Americans. Humanism allows the introduction of history, ethics and metaphysics into psychiatric and mental health nursing. Within this complex of the holistic perspective, systems orientation and humanism, the philosophy and clinical applications of an African American psychiatric and mental health nursing curriculum may be developed.

The transcultural nursing movement, a consequence of the increasing number of nurses who have taken doctoral degrees in anthropology, may have instructive value for us as we attempt to develop content for curricula sensitive to the needs of minorities. Although transcultural nursing literature is a general health literature, review of this material suggests the potential for increasing nursing knowledge about the mental health needs of African Americans. As are other areas of the developing nursing science, however, the field is in its formative stage.

Since the mid-1970s, monographs and reports on minority issues in nursing have appeared. Foremost among these are *Providing Safe Nursing Care For Ethnic People of Color* (Branch and Paxton, 1976); *Models for Cultural Diversity in Nursing: A Process for Change* (Branch, 1978); and *Models for Cultural Diversity in Nursing Curriculum* (Branch, 1978). Thirty-nine schools participated in this latter study. The following major topics were recommended for inclusion in multicultural nursing curricula:

- historical perspectives and origins
- language and communication style
- nutritional preferences and taboos
- religious styles and rituals
- family dynamics and values
- health and illness belief systems and cultural medicine
- disease predisposition and resistance related to ethnic groups
- physical assessment (including color and development differentials) and mental health assessment (including environmental factors, patterns of behavior and beliefs)
- community structures and dynamics (rules, habits, morals, customs, ways of living, art, music and philosophy of life)
- factors affecting health in ethnic communities
- attitudes, self-awareness and philosophy

(See Appendix 1 for a list of cultural content areas for a multicultural curriculum.)

The Special Projects Section of the Division of Nursing of the National Institutes of Health and the Nurse Education Branch of the National Institute of Mental Health have funded projects for the recruitment and retention of minority nurses. These projects usually involve integrating cultural components into the curriculum. For example, under the Carter administration funds were allocated for two projects—the Minority Nurse Recruitment, Training and Manpower Project at the College of Nursing, University of Cincinnati, and the Disadvantaged Nurse Recruitment, Training, and Manpower Project at the University of Pittsburgh School of Nursing. Both projects featured recruitment and retention components, curriculum mechanisms for integrating ethnic content into the curriculum and faculty and staff minority awareness workshops.

Theoretical Needs

Because nursing theory is fledgling, theoretical issues of psychiatric and mental health nursing care for African Americans and general nursing theory will develop concurrently. As they develop, each stream of theory will inform the other.

In particular, there will be a need to enrich the literature with theoretical materials that speak to the mental health of African Americans. Roger Clark Wilcox (1971) provided ten indicators of African American mental health, summarized here, that can be used as therapeutic tools to foster a conscious awareness in African American patients of—

1. the hostility toward their existence in this society;
2. their ability to function under constant states of dynamic tension;
3. their ability to exercise power from a presumed powerless state;
4. their lack of desire to oppress, be oppressed, abuse or be abused;
5. their need to shape and control their own destiny;
6. their steady involvement in self-confrontation before societal confrontation;
7. their deep, heart-felt knowledge of and identification with their own culture, history and values;
8. their knowledge of society's destructive forces (i.e., racism, classism, sexism);
9. their ability to perceive the humanity of oppressed people as well as the relationship between exploiters and the exploited; and
10. their desire to think, feel and act in fluid motion, rather than fragment themselves emotionally.

These indicators can instruct all therapists engaged in treating African Americans. They have a special relevance, however, for African American therapists who treat African Americans, for they require these therapists to examine their roles as community leaders and their psychological identity with and accountability to the African American community. These indicators allow therapists and their clients to strive collaboratively to change the invidious political, economic, social and cultural conditions that interfere with the emotional well-being of African Americans.

There is an extensive literature that implicates a relationship between race, poverty and poor health (Bullough and Bullough, 1972; Norman, 1969; Allen, 1970; Kosa and Zola, 1969). Among the most pointed concerns of this literature are the difference in quality of medical care for whites and for African Americans; the organizational structures of the health care delivery systems that are disadvantageous to African Americans; the poverty which is related to powerlessness; the ability to control events within the health care delivery system; and the relationship between poverty and illness, particularly as it affects children.

To be of use to nursing, statements about mental health care of African Americans must be subject to examination from the holistic, systems and humanistic perspectives that are central to nursing orientations toward health and sickness. Because nursing is a fledgling discipline, it has the opportunity to go beyond established thinking about the delivery of psychiatric and mental health care to African Americans. The authors posit that there is an urgent need for nursing to develop theoretical and curriculum approaches to psychotherapy for African Americans and, at the same time, recognize that psycho-therapy is, by definition, remedial. The primary emphasis must be upon prevention, that is, on mental health. For African Americans this means understanding that the major and refractory cause of psychological and physiological disease among African Americans is institutional racism.

Parameters of Research

To a large extent, African American nursing research will always be economically and conceptually linked with all nursing research. There-fore, African American nurse researchers, together with all nurse researchers, must define and expand the parameters of nursing research. Yet, African American nurse researchers understand that, because institutional racism remains a dominant American social fact, research into racism and its mental health costs will often be considered suspect and, thereby, depreciated.

For example, the American Nurses Association maintains a racial-ethnic research fellowship program. Advisory committee members for this program regularly make site visits to universities at which research fellows are studying. They expect that these students will research problems of racial-ethnic minorities. On one visit, a student was found to be engaged in a study which did not involve racial-ethnic minorities. When the site visitor raised the question the dissertation advisor sharply criticized that such program criteria would confine research fellows to an academic ghetto. In effect, he was saying that dedication to the study of the health care needs of minorities is a narrow, unproductive and dishonorable enterprise which may well hinder the fellows' careers.

Review of the literature suggests that professional concerns with psychological and interpersonal relationship incompetencies, although important, are not the core psychiatric and mental health issues for African Americans. The literature defines the core issues as racism and its concomitants: poverty, poor education and racial restrictions upon full participation in the opportunity structure of American society. In addition, Bush, Ullom and Osborne (1975) found that African American definitions of mental health differ from those of mental health specialists. The definitions of mental health professionals were rooted in traditional concerns with psychology and interpersonal relationships. Those of the African Americans included issues of survival, food, clothes, shelter, education, support from loved ones and religion. Thomas and Sillen (1972) placed psychiatric problems among African Americans in the context of racism, examining traditional myths of racial inferiority. Wilcox (1971) presented a collection of research done by African American psychologists entitled *Psychological Consequences of Being a Black American*. The essays focused upon issues of cultural and racial disadvantage, problems of racial integration, racist impacts upon academic and social situations, biases of intelligence tests against nonwhites and matriculation in higher education.

Issues in Need of Research

Of the many research issues of consequence to African American nurse researchers, three reflect the authors' concern with identifying research strategies that are congruent with the conceptual themes of this chapter.

First, those researchers who believe that the fundamental factor hindering the psychological, social and cultural development of African Americans is institutional racism must be prepared to study this problem. Although all nurse researchers are encouraged to study issues of institutional racism, for African American researchers their work in this nontraditional direction reflects the reality that their very presence in nursing is long overdue.

Collegial, resource, environmental and political circumstances may militate against direct research on institutional racism, but the subject can be studied as parallel or ancillary to other problems. Epidemiological and ethnographic studies using independent variables—such as the interactions of African Americans with major institutions of our society; employment, job advancement and salary; migration; the criminal justice system; school dropouts, and so forth—might examine such dependent variables as life stress, adaptation, coping, mental illness, high blood pressure, and child-rearing practices.

Second, there is a need for beginning study of those African Americans who have progressed and even thrived in a hostile society. Such studies will provide mental health professionals with alternative and positive theories of the African American. It would be instructive to determine what regularities in thinking about and negotiating with racist institutions characterize the "successful" African American. Are the same skills useful across institutions or are they institution-specific?

Third, recognition that there are always large numbers of African Americans emotionally damaged by their interactions with institutional racism and other invidious environmental factors requires research to define modal psychopathological responses of African Americans (Osborne, 1979), to identify effective therapeutic interventions and to determine the impact of mental illness upon the family and primary groups.

Specific Curriculum Aims

In fostering the development and integration of African American curriculum content into the nursing curriculum, the composition of the faculty must be taken into account. A fundamental aim is to increase the number of African American nursing faculty. A second aim is to encourage these faculty to use their knowledge and perspectives to further enrich the ethnic and intellectual diversity of the faculty, student and curriculum. A third aim is to provide explicit information about America as a multicultural society and about the relationship between social and cultural facts and health states. In this effort, health education guides, resource materials and cultural orientation seminars are useful, as are audiovisual materials such as audio-cassettes, films, filmstrips and videotapes. African American psychiatric nurses could be shown caring for a variety of ethnic and racial patients in traditional and nontraditional settings. This would advance content development and allow its integration. A fourth aim is to provide information about the effect of racism on the delivery of health services to African Americans. A fifth is to develop successful African American student recruitment and retention mechanisms, including the provision of adequate tuition and monthly stipends for undergraduate and graduate studies. A sixth aim is to require evaluation of the progress of African Americans from admission through graduation in educational programs. The results of such evaluation can be used to improve the capacity of nurse education programs, increase the number of African American nurses, retain these nurses in their programs, enrich the cultural content of their curricula and, thereby, improve the quality of nursing services delivered in this multicultural society.

Principles Inherent in Minority Curriculum Content

A number of principles are particularly germane to curricula designed to improve mental health services to African Americans. They include the following.

Self-Concept. In using patients' strengths to enhance their self-concepts, psychiatric nurses seek to be sensitive to the feelings, experiences and aspirations of African American patients. The development of such sensitivity requires the systematic and objective assessment of the level of acceptance clients have for themselves. In this regard Cross's (1972) Negro to Black Conversion Scale is of interest. The scale provides both a means of assessing an African American's level of self-acceptance and a therapeutic tool to assist patients to gain self-acceptance. This scale and its underlying conceptualization has a potential—similar to the developmental schemes of Maslow and Erikson—for the analysis and treatment of developmental deficits in African Americans. Banks and Grambs (1972) have contributed an important volume to the sparse literature on Black self-concept.

As a contribution to the general literature on cultural patterning of human deprecation, Goffman (1963) describes how stigmatized individuals learn how to cope and how to help others who are stigmatized to cope. The means for transcending the stigmatized state is neither smooth nor clear. However, it is the psychiatric nurse's responsibility to gain an understanding of this state in the African American patient. The psychiatric nurse can assist the patient in developing coping strategies.

The Dilemma of Duality. Essien-Udoms (1962) concept of the dilemma of duality is a particularly important contribution to the psychiatric literature on African Americans. This concept suggests that African Americans must choose to act in one of two ways: "the Black way," which reflects their socialization in the Black community; or the "non-Black way," which reflects expectations of the non-Black community. According to this concept, high-level anxiety, maladjustments, neuroticism and rejection by others all reduce African Americans' sense of control over their environment. The dilemma is resolved by distinguishing between one's self and one's role. Essentially, African Americans can only have a healthy self-concept if they accept the dilemma of duality.

Institutional and Personal Racism. Institutional racism is the systematic subjugation, oppression, and forced dependence of a people that is developed and reinforced by institutional operating policies, priorities, values and normative patterns. Personal racism refers to behavior by individuals or groups that is rooted in beliefs of racial superiority. Personal acts of racism can thrive only if there is sanction or legitimation of such behavior by institutional racism.

Ethnicity. This concept refers to the study of ethnic people of color. Psychological adjustment, conditions of acculturation, patterns of ethnic behavior, identity, lifestyles, value systems, traditions, rules, family life and communication structures are some of the issues studied. The mental health problems associated with these lifestyles and with relationships between people of color and people of noncolor in the community are of particular relevance.

Aggressions. There is the adage, "Sticks and stones may break my bones but names will never harm me." This adage is reflected in Pierce's (1969) distinction between microaggressions and macroaggressions. Microaggressions, such as name calling, snubs, and stereotypic phrases, do hurt people's self-esteem and capacity to achieve. Macroaggressions are direct actions that constitute impediments to adaption and mobility or a direct threat to the survival of the indiviudal.

Dilution-Denial-Projection Syndrome. These concepts have been used by Pierce (1969) to describe how credit or value is systematically removed from contributions, statements and the like made by Blacks. Together, the microaggressions, macroaggressions and the dilution-denial-projection syndrome offer a system by which to record and study various methods used to place Blacks in subordinate positions. Psychiatric nurses must obtain knowledge and skills to assist Blacks in overcoming attempts to make them subordinate.

Socialization Theory. The unique experiences of African Americans suggest the need for more research on the socialization of African Americans' identity. Poussaint and Atkinson (1972) described three needs that motivate behavior and generate emotions in the socialization process: achievement, self-assertion and approval. Psychiatric mental health nurses, in their concern for the enhancement of the socialization and educational programs of schools that serve African American communities, might consider the following questions:

- Are students punished for assertive, as distinguished from aggressive, behavior that is culturally appropriate?
- Are African American students shifted into the demanding curricula?
- Are African American students allowed to graduate without proper reading, writing and mathematical skills?

Status. Ascribed status is an important content concern. The Sizemore scale (1972) describes the ascribed value given to individuals based on the variables of race, sex, money and education. This scale reveals that African American females are consistently at the bottom, while white males are at the top. The inclusion of research data of this nature in psychiatric nursing curricula will make clear the realities of institutionalized racism and help nurses become more sensitive and understanding of the relationship between racism and mental health.

Family Themes. There is a social science literature that describes the African American family as disorganized and neglects the strengths of African American families (Staples, 1971; Hill, 1972). It ignores the unique adaptive characteristics of single-parent, nuclear and extended families, of the role of godparents and other adopted relatives, of the importance of fathers and the influence of mothers, of the interchange-ability of parental roles, and of the dedication of unmarried parents. Billingsley (1968), Hill (1972) and Gutman (1976) have written extensively about the strengths of the Black family. Psychiatric and mental health nurses who understand the multifaceted characteristics of the African American extended family will contribute more to African American mental health than those who view the African American family as disorganized.

Assessment. An assessment of African American adaptations and psychopathology will include consideration of sociology as well as psychology. For example, paranoia can be seen as both a survival mechanism and a symptom of illness. Assessments of African Americans can also be enriched by study of the institutions that comprise the African American community. Also, the Black church remains a significant influence and an important assessment consideration in the treatment of the African American individuals, families and groups. It has been more than a religious institution; for people whose individual resources have always been limited, it has been the community and economic center. It has taught positive African American concepts, has influenced and provided community leadership, and has been a showcase for individual talent and a resource for people in need. The Black church is a cultural, political, economic and psychological resource for the African American community.

Primary Prevention. The idea of primary prevention provides a conceptual basis for aiding African Americans to overcome life's stresses and make satisfying adaptations. Adequate housing, meaningful employment, safe health care, quality education, sound nutrition and the opportunity for individual achievement remain unmet goals for most African Americans. Access to community media and ownership of community businesses also play a role in prevention. Support of community leaders and participation in local and political institutions contribute to positive mental health.

Secondary and Tertiary Prevention. Programs of secondary prevention are characterized by early diagnosis and treatment; tertiary prevention is characterized by the early return of patients to the community. These prevention strategies require special sociological and cultural considerations for African Americans. Appropriate treatment will always include awareness of the many ways racism intrudes upon treatment and prevention programs.

Corrections System. A particularly vital concern is the large number of African Americans in prisons. Mentally ill prisoners often remain untreated or mistreated. All prisoners should have opportunities to develop positive self-concepts, socially acceptable and responsible behaviors and improved economic and political skills.

Ethnonursing. Ethnonursing includes individualized care by a nurse who uses knowledge of and sensitivity to the ethnicity of clients and patients so that they may maintain their ethnic identity and cultural and historical values and commitments.

A Framework for African American Content

In psychiatry, empathy is considered the essential ingredient in a therapeutic relationship. Empathy is defined as the intellectual identification with or vicarious experiencing of the feelings, thoughts or attitudes of another and involves an appreciation of the way people communicate.

Language, according to Lewis (1939), is a "type of social action which was developed by man in his relations with other men." The function of the verbal expression is the transmission of some thought or feeling pertinent to the moment. Utterance and situation are bound up intimately with each other. The problem is how to help people understand, to empathize with one another; how to create empathetic psychiatric nursing clinicians.

Chestang (1972) presents a conceptual model for African American development in a hostile environment that is useful for structuring African American content in the psychiatric and mental health curriculum. Chestang believes that to try to understand the African American condition outside of the social context will be to ignore "the peculiar nature of the black experience and its impact on character development and transracial interaction." He differentiates between "the *black experience*, which is as unique and as varying as black people, and the *black condition*, which is similar to all." He states that there are only two relevant scientific paradigms operating in the social system:

- the individual deficiency model, which holds that problems are caused by deficiencies in the individual;
- the dysfunctional social systems model, which holds that problems are caused by deficits in the social system.

The former fits the Western puritanical viewpoint, as well as the underpinnings of Freudian psychoanalysis. It supports the view that there is a universal personality and that "pathology" consists of the deviations from that norm. The individual deficit model is the institutionalized school of thought supported nationally under the guise of "democratic pluralism."

The latter model falls in the province of sociology, and for decades sociologists argued that the African American social structure was dysfunctional. Ladner (1973) pointed out, however, that "traditional sociological analyses have failed to explore the unique experiences and culture of Blacks when they were the subject of investigation, and have excluded Blacks from the general framework of American sociology. The refusal to address Black culture and experience has caused the distortion that we see today in sociological literature."

In his review of the two models, Chestang concluded that the dysfunctional social systems model allowed for an appropriate understanding of the Black condition, characterized by the following:

- social injustice—the unfairness, inequality and denial of legal rights, which tends to be impersonal and diffuse;
- societal inconsistency—use of double standards for Blacks and whites;
- personal impotence—the externally imposed inability of Blacks to remove either of the above conditions.

The concept is diagramed in Figure 1.

Chestang found that "the experience and condition of being black in American society has resulted in the development of two parallel and opposing thought structures—each based on values, norms and

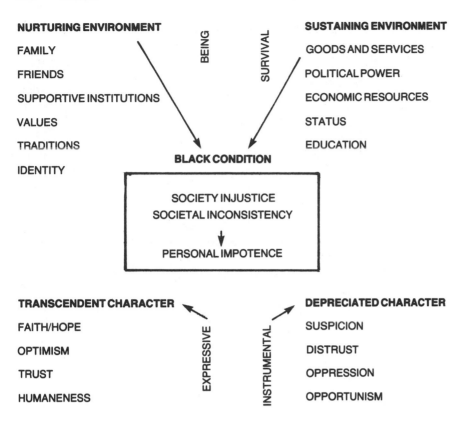

FIGURE 1

Interactional Model (Chestang, 1975)

beliefs and supported by attitudes, feelings, and behaviors—that imply feelings of depreciation, on the one hand, and a push for transcendence on the other." The depreciated character is one who "stoops to conquer," using masking to survive. Although this has negative connotations, persons of this type are forced to develop instrumental relationships to survive. The transcendent character attempts to participate in a society that doesn't want him. The feelings engendered are similar to loving but not being loved in return.

In order to integrate both the dominant and minority cultures in his character, the African American must maintain his contacts with his roots while using coping strategies learned in a hostile environment. Although Moynihan (1965) assumed that enslavement and poverty had to shatter Black family ties, Gutman (1976) found that most slaves maintained powerful familial and kin associations and that these associations sustained the developing African American culture. Rethinking the untruths that have been systematically taught will illuminate the appropriateness of two different sets of responses to what seems like the same circumstances. For example, Richards (1976) found that there were different variables predicting success among white and Black nursing students.

Ascribed Values

In the American culture, variables such as sex, money and education are closely related to ethnicity. Carter (1966) has modified Sizemore's (1972) chart of ascribed positions to include education, demonstrating the distinct oppressions of African Americans and the ascription of the lowest position to African American women. These realities surface in the dynamics surrounding the treatment of African Americans (see Table 1).

Chestang's model can be used as the basis for organizing a culturally sensitive curriculum for its content relates to many different ethnic and racial groups. Chestang states, "The concepts may be applicable to other groups that must negotiate a hostile environment. . . . The commonality of human experience precludes an interpretation pertaining exclusively to blacks." The interweaving of Chestang's theory with clinical experiences would help produce professionals who understand the duality of experience of the African American.

TABLE 1

Ascribed Value of Humans

	Race (White Superiority)	Sex (Male Superiority)	Money	Education	Total Points
White male	x	x	x	x	4
	x	x	x	—	3
	x	x	—	x	3
	x	x	—	—	2
Black male	—	x	x	x	3
	—	x	x	—	2
	—	x	—	x	2
	—	x	—	—	1
White female	x	—	x	x	3
	x	—	—	x	2
	x	—	x	—	2
	x	—	—	—	1
Black female	—	—	x	x	2
	—	—	x	—	1
	—	—	—	x	1
	—	—	—	—	0

Source: Carter, C. M. Social science and education for a Black identity. In J. Banks and J. Grambs (Eds.), *Black self concept.* New York: McGraw-Hill, 1972, page 148.

Psychiatric and mental health nurses must be skilled listeners to pick up problems of identity, dignity and self-esteem; of misdirected aggression and violence; of impulse control; and of disordered behavior. Nurses must recognize the relationships between social and cultural events and know that these are common problems which any client brings to the worker. Chestang hypothesizes that the African American client will bring more of them and that they will be of a different nature.

The components of African American cultures affect the therapeutic relationship. These components include philosophy of life, music, patterns of behavior, religion, morals, habits, rules, knowledge, art, language, beliefs, customs and ways of living. To assess and intervene in the treatment of African Americans, psychiatric nurses must understand the principles previously described. For example, if the therapist fails to understand the role of the Black church for the client seeking treatment, the total treatment program could fail because of lack of sensitivity and understanding regarding collaborative networks and support systems.

Psychiatric Nursing Curricula as Related to the Therapeutic Process

An understanding of the African American community contributes to the level of crisis intervention treatment that the psychiatric nurse can offer. Since crisis care is a form of brief treatment, knowledge of personal groups, family and community supports broadens possible nursing intervention options. Here, sensitivity, awareness and understanding of African Americans continues to be the vital ingredient for quality psychiatric nursing care to African American patients.

The advent of the community mental health movement, which was legislated in 1963, offered an opportunity for African American citizens and mental health professionals to combine forces for positive mental health. Primary prevention programs continue to be necessary for African Americans to overcome life's stresses and to make satisfactory adaptions. The psychiatric nurse should act as a community advocate in these areas.

Finally, psychiatric nurses must be sensitive, aware caregivers whose special knowledge and skills are appreciated in health care agencies. Because most of these clinics and agencies offer a myriad of services, psychiatric nurses can contribute formal and informal information and utilize unique and varied skills and knowledge to facilitate treatment and rehabilitation.

Psychiatric and mental health nurses should also begin to offer explicit information on Anglo-Saxon culture and then to expand the cultural context by giving culture-specific information regarding ethnic groups of color. Theoretical frameworks for studying cultural diversity and cultural pluralism should be presented.

Institutional Change and Faculty Development

A number of strategies for changes in institutions and faculty can be developed to facilitate the integration of African American content in the psychiatric and mental health curriculum. Administrative strategies would include assessment of the school's commitment to incorporate cultural diversity in its faculty, student and curriculum structures. Other specific administrative issues are the following: the school's philosophy and goals; dean's self-concept and relationship to the faculty and university president; degree of support from the university and the community; degree of autonomy; the flexibility of the budget; and previous successes with innovative programs. Deans who are committed to cultural diversity and who have been successful in these areas are more likely to participate in programs of institutional change and development of cultural diversity in curriculum content than deans who are not commited or who have had more troublesome administrative careers. Of course, the dean's leadership in the recruitment of an ethnic and racially diverse faculty is essential.

The engagement of faculty in programs to increase the school's cultural diversity begins with the identification of representatives from these groups who are committed to these changes. Provision of opportunities for faculty to meet regularly to develop appropriate, culturally diverse content and support to integrate such content into the curriculum are essential administrative strategies. Additional strategies for institutional change and faculty development include faculty activities designed to (1) increase the awareness and appreciation for ethnic people of color; (2) facilitate the recruitment, admission or employment and retention of ethnic and racially diverse student, faculty and staff populations; (3) develop and implement academic and clinical experiences that allow necessary learning experiences in providing quality nursing care to ethnic people of color; (4) support nursing research into issues of cultural diversity which impart health; (5) develop forums and seminars for presentation of research and theory on cultural diversity in health care; and (6) model humanistic attitudes toward all people. Enlightened faculty groups fully supported by academic administrators represent the greatest potential for identification, development and implementation of strategies for institutional and faculty change and for the attainment of a culturally diverse curriculum.

If today the concept of the "universal personality" is an invalid one, then the use of universal admission "standards" is also invalid. The literature states that predictors for student success relate to the father's income and father's education. Richards (1976) found that while these factors may be related to success of white students, a different clustering of factors must be understood for Black students. She found that—

- social class was not a relevant predictor;
- age, work experience and value placed on education were relevant factors in success;
- past experience seems related to present perceptions of the college experience (i.e., number of positive experiences in college, view of appropriateness of education demands);
- the "streaming" (grouping) systems and/or friendship systems experienced in elementary and high school are related to success in college;
- educational preparedness for college and post-high school training (particularly, practical nurse education) is related to success;
- achievement-orientation of family is related to present student success;
- place of attendance of elementary and/or high school is related to success (students who attended school outside the New York area had a better chance of being selected);
- religious orientation of family of origin is related to present religiosity and to student success for West Indian students but not for American-born students;
- positive self-concept is related to student success;
- cohesion of community in which reared is related to later student success;
- the presence of supportive persons in the community is related to success; and
- factors identified as family strengths are related to success.

These findings may need to be refined for use in the traditional admission–selection process of students. Yet the simple act of giving faculty more information about what is possible can allow for their change of behavior. Indeed, interwoven into any faculty development work must be mechanisms aimed at the reduction of hopelessness and low self-concept on the part of the faculty.

Although academic institutions exist to provide students with educational services, too often students stand at the lower end of the hierarchy. Undergraduate and graduate student committees can be effective advocates for institutional change and for the development of a culturally diverse curriculum. Student groups may function as a part of the official graduate and undergraduate student nursing organizations or as distinct groups organized for such advocacy. In most progressive nursing schools, students sit on development committees for curriculum, faculty and staff. The student advocate agenda in each committee would request implementation of cultural diversity in curriculum content and faculty-staff structures. Students must have administrative and faculty support and guidance to achieve their goals and avoid retaliation by threatened faculty and staff.

The community can also participate in programs of institutional and faculty change designed to include cultural diversity in the curriculum. Their interests lie in the creation of a health care delivery system that reflects and respects the multicultural characteristics of America. Social activists working with university administrators and faculty are not to be ignored. The political and business communities can also be enlisted to support institutional change and curriculum revision. African American churchs and other African American community organizations are vitally interested in the health care delivered to the African American community. They can participate as advocates and workers for change. Community involvement in these issues will galvanize the faculty's attention and ensure discussion of the curriculum defects.

Policy Recommendations to the National Institute of Mental Health

Historically, the National Institute of Mental Health has underwritten part or all of the cost of psychiatric nursing programs. Therefore, the authors believe that NIMH is in the position to exercise considerable influence on program implementation and student selection. In that light, we make the following recommendations:

- NIMH should review and change the term *minority*, wherever it occurs, to a more edifying and therapeutically useful term.
- All research and training grant applications should contain affirmative action plans. These plans should be sensitive to the objectives of the grant, and those grants that are funded should be audited for compliance with such plans.
- NIMH should continue and increase funding for traineeships for ethnic and racial students.
- NIMH should increase funding for (1) ethnographic and epidemiological research around ethnic and racial mental health issues; (2) research to identify therapeutic modalities appropriate to ethnic and racial people; and (3) research designed to identify, describe, classify and explain the functioning of folk healers, traditional healers, *curanderos* and so forth.
- NIMH should require that ethnic and racial content be included in the nursing curricula and that such content reflect the following principles: (1) that cultural content can be meaningful only when there are credit hours attached and requirements made for graduation and (2) that cultural content can be valid only when content and process are in terms defined by the community.

Appendix 1

List of Cultural Content Areas for a Multicultural Curriculum

I. Historical Perspectives
   A. Origins
      1. Anthropological Myth
      2. Creation Myth
   B. Presentation
      1. Migration (past)
         a. Generation (when)
         b. Geographical (where)
      2. Migration (present)

II. Language and Communication
   A. Historical Influence
   B. Verbal Communication
      1. Dialects (Ebonics, etc.)
      2. Effects of Acculturation and Assimilation on Communication
      3. Expression of Emotions
      4. Humor
   C. Nonverbal Communication
      1. Body Language (posture, grimaces, gestures, behavior, expression of emotion)
      2. Touch
      3. Eye Contact
      4. Space and Territoriality (proximity to others)
      5. Humor
   D. Sexual Connotation
   E. Therapeutic Communication (interviewing techniques)
   F. Interpersonal Dynamics

III. Nutritional Preferences
   A. Ethnic Preference
      1. Regular (adult and child)
      2. Therapeutic
         a. Medical (exchange groups)
         b. Ethnic
   B. Customs (special occasions, festivals)
   C. Taboos (food)
   D. Rituals
   E. Psychosocial Importance of Food
   F. Preparation of Food

IV. Religious Styles
   A. Rituals
   B. Codification (written or unwritten)
   C. Significant Other
   D. Religious Expressions, Practices, Rituals, Ceremonies, or Symbols in Relation to:
      1. Birth/Fertility Symbols
      2. Puberty
      3. Death
         a. Rituals

        b. Taboos
        c. Symbols
    E. Importance of Special Occasions
        1. Weddings
        2. Deaths
        3. Births
        4. Baths
    F. Rites of Passage (puberty)
    G. Coping Mechanisms (use of religion)

V. Family Dynamics
    A. Interaction of Family and Society
        1. Institutional Relationships and Ramifications
            a. Social
            b. Political
            c. Educational
            d. Religious
            e. Economic
        2. Influences of Sociocultural Trends
            a. Historical
                (1) Place of Origin
                (2) Immigration
                (3) Acculturation
                (4) Analysis of Important Trends
            b. Present
                (1) Society at large
                (2) Immediate Cultural Group
    B. Roles and Functions
        1. Sexual Role Expectations
        2. Lines of Authority
        3. Socialization
            a. Values
            b. Attitudes
        4. Roles
    C. Family Organization
        1. Size
        2. Lines of Descent
            a. Matrilineal
            b. Patrilineal
        3. Kinship Patterns
        4. Type
            a. Extended
            b. Nuclear
            c. Other
        5. Alternative Types
        6. Setting
            a. Urban
            b. Rural
    D. Interaction Patterns
        1. Communication
            a. Types
            b. Family Patterns
        2. Decision Making
        3. Problem Solving
        4. Lines of Authority

    5. Psychodynamics
        a. Strengths
        b. Weaknesses
        c. Deficits
        d. Power Structure
E. Socialization
F. Developmental States of Families
    1. Beginning
    2. Expectant
    3. Childbearing
    4. Childrearing
    5. Launching
    6. Middle Age
    7. Aging
G. Crises
    1. Type
        a. Developmental
        b. Situational
    2. Coping Mechanisms
        a. Strengths
        b. Weaknesses
        c. Deficits
H. Traditions and Customs

VI. Health/Illness Belief System, Folklore and Folk Medicine
A. Folk Medicine Practices
    1. Definition
    2. Overview (historical and legal aspects)
    3. Therapeutic
        a. Valuable
            (1) Black
            (2) Asian
            (3) Native American
            (4) Chicano (Mexican American)
        b. Harmful (nursing therapeutics)
            (1) Black
            (2) Asian
            (3) Native American
            (4) Chicano (Mexican American)
        c. Detrimental (life threatening)
            (1) Black
            (2) Asian
            (3) Native American
            (4) Chicano (Mexican American)
B. Scientific Rationale for Folk Medicine Practice
    1. Resources for Validation
        a. Practitioner
        b. Indigenous Population
        c. Clinical Data (case histories)
    2. Scientific Principles
    3. Psychosocial Aspects
C. Nursing Intervention
    1. Assessment
    2. Plan
    3. Action (referral)
    4. Evaluation

VII. Specific Diseases Related to Ethnic Group
  A. Respiratory
  B.. Cardiovascular
  C. Gastrointestinal
  D. Muscle/Skeletal
  E. Neurological
  F. Endocrinological
  G. Genitourinary
  H. Sensory

VIII. Assessment
  A. Physical Health (subjective and objective)
    1. Color (cyanosis, jaundice)
    2. Dermatological
    3. Growth and Development ("norms")—diagnostic and clinical lab values, what is normal, what is abnormal
  B. Mental Health
    1. Definition of Mental Health Vs. Mental Illness
    2. Emotional Growth and Development
    3. Adequacy and Relevance of Evaluation Tests
      a. Stanford-Binet
      b. Weschler, Vineland
      c. Roch Test

IX. Community Dynamics
  A. Community Structure
    1. Formal
      a. Urban
      b. Rural
    2. Informal
      a. Urban
      b. Rural
  B. Leadership Styles of Ethnic Groups
    1. Styles of Leadership
      a. Democratic
      b. Laissez-faire
      c. Authoritarian
    2. Function of Leadership
      a. Integrative
      b. Instrumental
    3. Advantages and Disadvantages of Leadership Styles
    4. Ethnic Group Preferences
      a. Decision-making Process
      b. Lines of Communication
      c. Power Structure
    5. Process of Developing Leadership Qualities (traditional and acquired)
    6. Factors Involved in the Identification of a Leader

X. Factors Affecting Health in Ethnic Communities

XI. Attitudes, Self-awareness, and Philosophy
  A. Historical Implications and Current Health Care Practices
    1. Development of Attitudes
      a. Disruption of Roots
      b. Societal Alienation
      c. Family Influence

    2. Societal Trends
      a. Recognition of Uniqueness of Health Care Needs of Ethnic Groups of Color
        (1) Consumer Awareness
        (2) Implementation of Cultural Content
      b. Implementation of Prejudice
B. Dynamics of Prejudice
    1. Image of Self
      a. Feeling of Worth
      b. Feeling of Rejection
      c. Feeling of Self-esteem
      d. Feeling of Powerlessness/Alienation
      e. Ego Strength
      f. Recognition of Self-limitations
    2. Perception of Others
      a. Types and Effects of Stereotyping
        (1) Black
        (2) Asian
        (3) Native American
        (4) Chicano (Mexican American)
C. Philosophy Consistent with Safe and Equitable Care
    1. Maintenance of Professional Deportment
      a. Consistent Peformance
      b. Competence
    2. Respect of Patient's Bill of Rights
      a. Observance
      b. Integration into Delivery of Health Care
    3. Evaluation of Self and Peers
      a. Ongoing
      b. Critical
      c. Holistic Approach
    4. Personal Growth
      a. Attendance at Workshops
      b. Self-evaluation
      c. A Plan for Staff Development

References

Allen, V. *Psychological factors in poverty.* New York: Academic Press, 1970.

American Nurses Association. Commission on Human Rights Unity Assessment Conference, Albuquerque, New Mexico, June 1979.

Bailey, H. *Nursing mental diseases* (4th Ed.). New York: Macmillan, 1939.

Banks, J., & Grambs, J. *Black self concept.* New York: McGraw-Hill, 1972.

Billingsley, A. *Black family in white America.* Englewood Cliffs, N.J.: Prentice Hall, 1968.

Bernstein, B. Social structure, language, and learning. *Educational Research,* 1961, *3,* (3) 163–76.

Branch, M. *Models for cultural diversity in nursing: A process for change.* Boulder, CO.: Western Interstate Commission on Higher Education in Nursing, 1978.

Branch, M., & Paxton, P. *Providing safe nursing care for ethnic people of color.* New York: Appleton-Century-Crofts, 1976.

Brown, P., & Fowler, G. *Psycho-dynamic nursing: A biosocial orientation.* Philadelphia, PA.: W. B. Saunders Company, 1971.

Bullough, B., & Bullough, V. *Poverty, ethnic identity and health care.* New York: Appleton-Century-Crofts, 1972.

Burgess, A. Baccalaureate nursing education and minority nurses. *Urban Health,* July–August 1978, 35–44.

Bush, M., Ullon, J., & Osborne, O. H. The meaning of mental health: A report of two ethnoscientific studies. *Nursing Research,* 1975, Vol. *24* (2), 130–38.

Cass, J. Can the university survive the Black challenge. *Saturday Review,* June 24, 1969, 68.

Carmichael, F., & Chapman, J. *A guide to psychiatric nursing.* Philadelphia, PA.: Lea and Fabiger, 1936.

Carter, C. *Negro uninvolvement in psychiatric after care.* Unpublished master's thesis, University of Pittsburgh, School of Nursing, 1966.

Chambers, B. *Chronicles of Black protest.* New York: Mentor Books, 1968.

Chestang, L. Character development in a hostile environment. Monograph 3. *University of Chicago, School of Social Service Administration (Occasional Paper),* 1972.

Cross, W. *Stages in the development of Black awareness: An exploratory investigation in Black psychology.* New York: Harper and Row, 1972.

Davis, A. Environmental influences on mental health and mental illness. In M. Falkman, & A. Davis (Eds.), *New dimensions in mental health-psychiatric nursing.* New York: McGraw-Hill, 1974.

Essien-Udom, E. *Black nationalism.* New York: Dell, 1962.

Goffman, E. *Stigma.* Englewood Cliffs, N.J.: Prentice-Hall, 1963.

Gutman, H. *The Black family in slavery and freedom—1750–1925.* New York: Pantheon Books, 1976.

Hill, R. *The strengths of Black families.* New York: Emerson Hall, 1972.

Karnosh, L., Gage, E., & Mereness, D. *Psychiatry for nurses.* St. Louis, MO.: C. V. Mosby, 1944.

Kosa, J., & Zola, I. *Poverty and health: A sociological analysis.* Cambridge, MA.: Harvard University Press, 1969.

Ladner, J. *The death of white sociology.* New York: Vintage Books, 1973.

Leininger, M. *Contemporary issues in mental health nursing.* Boston: Little, Brown and Company, 1973.

Levine, M. Holistic nursing. *Nursing Clinics of North America*, 1971, 6 (2), 253–63.

Lewis, N. Preface. In J. Kasanin (Ed.), *Language and thought in schizophrenia*. New York: W. W. Norton, 1939.

Matheney, R., & Topalis, M. *Psychiatric nursing*. St. Louis.: C. V. Mosby, 1970.

Moorman, E. The benefit of anger. *Saturday Review*, June 21, 1969, pp. 72–73, 84, 85.

Moynihan, D. *The Negro family: The case for national action*. Washington, D.C.: U.S. Government Printing Office, 1965.

Norman, J. *Medicine in the ghetto*. New York: Meredity Corporation-Appleton-Century-Crofts, 1969.

Noyes, A., & Haydon, E. *A textbook of psychiatry*. New York: MacMillan, 1940.

Orem, D. *Nursing: Concepts of practice*. New York: McGraw-Hill, 1971.

Osborne, O. H. Conceptualizing ethnic research for quality in nursing care. Paper presented at the Conference of Ethnic Nurses for the Advancement of Health Care, Los Angeles, California, April 1979.

Peplau, H. *Interpersonal relations in nursing: A conceptual frame of reference for psychodynamic nursing*. New York: G. P. Putnam's Sons, 1952.

Pierce, C. Violence and counter violence: The need for a children's domestic exchange. *American Journal of Orthopsychiatry*, 1969, *39* (4), pp. 553–68.

Poussaint, A., & Atkinson, C. Black youth and motivation. In J. Banks, & J. Grambs (Eds.), *Black self concept*. New York: McGraw-Hill, 1972.

Richards, H. *An assessment of factors related to success in inner-city nursing programs*. Unpublished dissertation, Columbia University, New York City, 1976.

Robinson, L. *Psychiatric nursing as a human experience*. Philadelphia, PA.: W. B. Saunders, 1972.

Roger, M. *An introduction to the theoretical basis of nursing*. Philadelphia, PA.: F. A. Davis, 1970.

Roy, C., Sr. *Introduction to nursing: An adaptation model*. Englewood Cliffs, N.J.: Prentice-Hall, 1976.

Sands, I. *Nervous and mental diseases for nurses*. Philadelphia, PA.: W. B. Saunders, 1941.

Sizemore, B. Social science and education for a Black identity. In J. Banks, & J. Grambs (Eds.), *Black self concept*. New York: McGraw-Hill, 1972.

Staples, R. (Ed.). *The Black family: Essays and studies*. Belmont: Wadsworth, 1971.

Thomas, A., & Sillen, S. *Racism and psychiatry*. New York: Brunner/Mazel Publishers, 1972.

Wilcox, R. C. *The psychological consequences of being a black American: A source book of research by Black psychologists*. New York: John Wiley and Sons, 1971.

Wilson, H., & Kneisl, C. *Psychiatric nursing*. Menlo Park, CA.: Addison-Wesley Publishing, 1979.

Bibliography

Adams, D., Bella, T., Chow, E., & Martinez, L. Objectives and radical diversity model. In M. Branch, & P. Paxton, (Eds.), *Providing safe nursing care for ethnic people of color*. New York: Appleton-Century-Crofts, 1976, 204–59.

Allport, G. *Personality: A psychological interpretation*. New York: Holt, Rinehart and Winston, 1937.

Allport, G. *Becoming*. New Haven, CT.: Yale University Press, 1955.

Allport, G. *Pattern and growth in personality*. New York: Holt, Rinehart and Winston, 1966.

Argyle, F. *The self-concept of Negro and white school beginners*. Paper presented at the annual meeting of the American Educational Research Association, Chicago, Illinois 1968.

Arnez, N. Enhancing the Black self concept through literature. In J. Banks & J. Grambs (Eds.), *Black self concept*. New York: McGraw-Hill, 1972, pp. 93–116.

Ausubel, D. *Ego development and the personality disorders*. New York: Greene and Stratton, 1952.

Babcock, R. S. Commentary: Who should attend college? In P. R. Rever (Ed.), *Open admission and equal access*. Iowa City, IA.: The American College Testing Program, 1971.

Ballard, B. *The education of Black folk*. New York: Harper and Row, 1973.

Bane, M., & Jencks, C. The school and equal opportunity. *Saturday Review*, October, 1972, 37–42.

Banks, J. *Teaching the Black experience*. Belmont, CA.: Fearon Publishers, 1970.

Banks, J. Race prejudice and the Black self concept. In J. Banks & J. Grambs (Eds.), *The Black self concept*. New York: McGraw-Hill, 1972, pp. 5–36.

Banks, J. *Teaching strategies for ethnic studies*. Boston: Allyn and Bacon, 1975.

Banks, W. The Black client and the helping professionals. In R. Jones (Ed.), *Black psychology*. New York: Harper and Row, 1972, pp. 205–11.

Bass, E. J. An investigation of changes in selected ninth grade students' concept of self and of others after interaction with selected materials taught in intergrated and segregated groups. *Dissertation Abstracts International*, 1969, 29, 2992-A.

Bayer, A. E., & Boruch R. F. Black and white freshmen entering four-year colleges. *Educational Record*. Washington, D.C.: American Council on Education, Fall, 1969, pp. 371–86.

Bayley, D., & Mendelsohn, H. *Minorities and the police: Confrontation in America*. New York: The Free Press, 1968.

Bayton, J. A., & Lewis, H. O. Reflections and suggestions for further study concerning higher education of Negroes. In R. C. Wilcox (Ed.), *The psychological consequences of being a Black American*. New York: John Wiley and Sons, 1971, pp. 186–197.

Bayton, J., & Muldrow, T. Interaction variables in the perception of racial personality traits. *Journal of Experimental Research in Personality*, 1968, 3, 38–44.

Bernard, J. *Marriage and family among Negroes*. Englewood Cliffs, N.J.: Prentice-Hall, 1966.

Bernstein, B. Language and social class. *British Journal of Sociology*, 1960, 11, 271–76.

Bernstein, B. A sociolinguistic approach to socialization: With some reference to educability. In F. Williams (Ed.), *Language and poverty: Perspectives on a theme*. Chicago: Markham Publishing Company, 1970.

Bessent, H. *A Curriculum design for disadvantaged students in a baccalaureate nursing program*. Unpublished doctoral dissertation, University Microfilm, Ann Arbor, Michigan, 1970.

Black admissions aides advise on competition for Ivy League. *New York Times*, Sunday, May 18, 1975, p. 2.

Burgess, A. *Racially differentiated student withdrawal from the baccalaureate nursing majors as related to faculty and empathy, 1971-1972*. Doctor of Education Project Report. Teachers College, Columbia University, New York, 1974, pp. 8–14.

Burgess, M., Duffey, M., & Temple, F. G. Two studies of prediction of success in collegiate programs of nursing. *Nursing Research*, 1972, *21* (4), 365–66.

Caplin, M. D. The relationship between self-concept and academic achievement and between level of aspiration and academic achievement. *Dissertation Abstracts International*, 1966, *27*, 979–80.

Caplin, M. D. The relationship between self-concept and academic achievement. *The Journal of Experimental Education*, 1969, *37*, 13–16.

Carnegie Commission on Higher Education. *A chance to learn: An action agenda for equal opportunity in higher education*. New York: McGraw-Hill, 1970.

Carnegie, M. E. *A comparative study of two groups of socioeconomically disadvantaged students in programs leading to registered nurse licensure*. Doctoral dissertation. Graduate School of Public Administration, New York University, 1972.

Carnegie, M. E. Editorial: ANA directory identifying minority nurses with doctorates, *Nursing Research*, 1973, *23*, 483.

Carnegie, M. E. Disadvantaged students in R.N. programs. *League Exchange*, 1974, *100*, 1–118.

Carter, C. M. Community mental health and the elderly. In *Nursing Clinics of North America*. Philadelphia, PA.: Saunders Co., 1976, pp. 125–34.

Chestang, L. W. The black experience: Character development in a hostile environment. Paper presented at the Center for Continuing Education, University of Chicago, 1975.

Cicourel, A., & Kitsure, J. The school as a mechanism of social differentiation. In S. Sieber & D. E. Wilder (Eds.), *The school in society*. New York: The Free Press, 1973.

Clark, K. American education today. In M. Weinberg (Ed.), *Integrated Education*. Beverly Hills, CA.: The Glencor Press, 1968, pp. 2–15.

Clark, L., & Clark, M. The development of consciousness of self and emergence of racial identification in Negro preschool children. *Journal of Social Psychology*, 1939, *10*, 591–99.

Cleary, T. A. Test bias: Prediction of grades of Negro and white students in integrated colleges. *Journal of Education Measurements*, 1968, *5* (2), 115–24.

Coleman, J. C. Implications of the findings on alienation. *American Journal of Sociology*, 1964, *70*, 76–78.

Coleman, J. S. The adolescent subculture and academic achievement. *The American Journal of Sociology*, 1960, *65*, 337–47.

Coleman, J. S. The concept of equality of educational opportunity. *Harvard Educational Review*, 1968, *68*, 7–22.

Coles, R. It's the same but its different. In T. Parsons & K. Clark (Eds.), *The Negro American*. Boston: Houghton-Mifflin, 1966.

Combs, N. *The Black experience in America*. New York: Hippocrene Books, 1972.

Comer, J. "White Racism: Its root, form, and function. In R. Jones (Ed.), *Black psychology*. New York: Harper and Row, 1972, p. 316.

Comer, J., & Cauderwell, T. Racism and health services. In C. Willie, B. Kramer, & B. Brown (Eds.), *Racism and mental health.* Pittsburgh: University of Pittsburgh Press, 1973, pp. 165–81.

Comitas, L., & Lowenthan, D. *Slaves, free men, citizens: West Indian perspectives.* New York: Doubleday, 1973.

Crawford, C. *Health and the family: A medical-sociological analysis.* New York: MacMillian, 1971.

Cross, K. *Beyond the open door.* San Francisco: Jossey-Bass, Inc., 1972.

Cross, K. P. *The junior college student: A research description.* Princeton, N.J.: Educational Testing Service, 1968.

Current Population Reports. *The social and economic status of the Black population in the United States, 1972.* U.S. Department of Commerce, Social and Economic Statistics Administration, Bureau of the Census, 1973. Series P 23, No. 46.

Curtis, L. Digest of research studies on self-concept. *Graduate Research in Education and Related Disciplines,* 1963–1967, 3, 82–88.

Doyle, B. *The etiquette of race relations in the south: A study in social control.* New York: Schocken Books, 1971.

Drake, S., & Cayton, H. *Black metropolis: A study of Negro life in a northern city* (Rev. Ed.), 2 vols. New York: Harper and Row, 1962.

Duncan, O. D. Social stratification and mobility: Problems in the measurement of trend. In E. B. Sheldon & W. E. Moore (Eds.), *Indicators of Social Change.* New York: Russell Sage Foundation, 1968.

Elkins, S. *Slavery: A problem in American institutional and intellectual life.* Chicago: University of Chicago Press, 1968.

Epps, E. G. Education for Black Americans: Outlook for the future. *School Review,* 1973, 81 (3), 315–27.

Fanon, F. *Black skins, white masks.* New York: Grove Press, 1967.

Fensham, P. J. (Ed.). *Rights on inequality in Australian education.* Melbourne: Cheshire Ltd., 1970.

Ferguson, C. The new world of nursing. *The Black Collegian,* 1979, 10 (1), 112–17.

Flaugher, R. *Testing practices, minority groups, and higher education: A review and discussion of research.* Research Bulletin No. 70-41, Princeton: Educational Testing Service, 1970.

Foner, N. *Status and power in rural Jamaica.* New York: Teachers College Press, 1973.

Foward, J., & Williams, J. Internal-external control and Black militancy. *Journal of Social Issues,* 1970, 26, 75–92.

Frazier, E. F. *The Negro family in the United States.* Chicago: University of Chicago Press, 1939.

Frazier, E. F. *Negro youth at the crossroads.* Washington, D.C.: American Council on Education, 1940.

Frazier, E. F. *Black bourgeoisie.* New York: Collier, 1962.

Frazier, E. F. *The Negro church in America.* New York: Schocken Books, 1974.

Freeman, H. F., Armor, D., Ross, M. J., & Pettigrew, T. F. Color graduation and attitudes among middle-income Negroes. *American Sociological Review,* 1966, 31, 365–74.

Fried, Marc. Social differences in mental health. In J. Kosa & I. Zola (Eds.), *Poverty and health: A sociological analysis.* Cambridge, MA.: Harvard University Press, 1969, pp. 113–67.

Froe, O. D. A comparative study of a population of "disadvantaged" college freshmen. *Journal of Negro Education,* 1968, 37 (4), 370–82.

Ginzberg, E., Vincent, B., Hamilton, G. T., Herma, J. L., & Yohalem, A. M. *The middle-class Negro in the white man's world.* New York: Columbia University Press, 1967.

Gittel, M., Berube, M., Gottfried, F., Guttentag, M., & Spier, A. *Local control in education—three demonstration school districts in New York City.* New York: Praeger Publishers, 1972.

Goode, W., & Hatt, P. K. *Methods in social research.* New York: McGraw-Hill, 1952.

Goodman, J. Institutional racism: The crucible of Black identity. In J. Banks & J. Grambs, *Black self concept.* New York: McGraw Hill, 1972, pp. 117–40.

Gordon, E. W. Some theoretical and practical problems in compensatory education as an antidote to poverty. In V. L. Allen (Ed.), *Psychological factors in poverty.* Chicago: Markham Publishing Company, 1970.

Gordon, E. W. Commentary: Inertia and higher education. In P. R. Rever (Ed.), *Open admissions and equal access.* Iowa City, IA.: The American College Testing Program, 1971.

Gordon, M. *Assimilation in American life.* New York: Oxford University Press, 1964.

Goveia, E. V. *Slave society in the British leeward island at the end of the eighteenth century.* New Haven: Yale University Press, 1965.

Grambs, J. The self-concept: Basis for reeducation of Negro youth. In W. Kvaraceus, J. S. Gibson, F. Patterson, B. Seasholes, & J. Grambs (Eds.), *Negro self-concept: Implications for school and citizenship.* New York: McGraw-Hill, 1965.

Green, R. L. The Black quest for higher education: On admissions dilemmas. *Personnel and Guidance Journal,* 1969, *47* (9), 17.

Green, R. L., & Farquhas, W. W. Negro academic motivation and scholastic achievement. *Journal of Educational Psychology,* 1965, *41,* 241–43.

Greenwald H. J., & Opppenheim, D. B. Reported magnitude of self-miseducation among Negro children: Artifact? *Journal of Personality and Social Psychology,* 1968, *8,* 49–52.

Greer, C. *The great school legend: A revisionist interpretation of American education.* New York: Basic Books, 1972.

Guggenheim, F. Self-esteem and achievement for whites and Negro children. *Journal of Projective Techniques and Personality Assessment,* 1969, *33,* 63–71.

Gurin, P., Gurin, G., Lav, R., & Beattie, M. Internal-external control in the motivational dynamics of Negro youth. *Journal of Social Issues,* 1969, *25,* 29–53.

Hadley, C. V. D. Personality patterns, social class, and aggression in the West Indies. *Human Relations,* 1949, *2* (4), 349–62.

Hamilton, C. V. *Black power: The politics of liberation in America.* New York: Vintage Books, 1967, pp. 46–47.

Hargreaves, D. *Social relations in a secondary school.* London: Rutledge and Kegan Paul, 1967.

Harris, J., & McCullough, W. D. Quantative methods and Black community studies. In J. A. Ladner (Ed.), *The death of white sociology.* New York: Vintage Books, 1973.

Hazzard, M. (Ed.). Symposium on a systems approach to nursing. *The nursing clinics of North America,* 1971, *6* (3), 385–93.

Healy, T. S. Commentary: Who should attend college? In P. R. Rever (Ed.), *Open admission and equal access.* Iowa City, IA.: The American College Testing Program, 1971.

Henry, J. *On education.* New York: Vintage Books, 1972.

Herleston, B. W. Higher education for the Negro. In R. C. Wilcox (Ed.), *The psychological consequences of being a Black American.* New York: John Wiley and Sons, 1971.

Hess, R., & Shipman, V. Early blocks to children's learning. *Children*, 1965, *12*, 189–94.

Hraba, J., & Grant, G. Black is beautiful: Pre-examination of racial preference and identification. *Journal of Personality and Social Psychology*, 1970, *16*, 398–402.

Hyman, H. H., & Reed, J. S. "Black matriarchy" reconsidered: Evidence from secondary analysis of sample surveys. *Public Opinion Quarterly*, 1969, *33*, 346–54.

Illich, I. Schooling: The ritual of progress. *New York Review of Books*, December 3, 1970.

Jackson, J. J. Black women in a racist society. In C. Willie, B. Kramer, & B. Brown (Eds.), *Racism and mental health*. Pittsburgh: University of Pittsburgh Press, 1973, pp. 185–268.

James, C. L. R. *Party politics in the West Indies*. Tabago, West Indies: Vedic Enterprises, 1962.

Jencks, C. Social stratification and higher education. *Harvard Educational Review*, 1968, *38*, 277–316.

Jencks, C., Smith, M., Acland, H., Bane, M., Cohen, D., Ginitis, H., Heyns, B., & Michelson, S. *Inequality: A reassessment of the effect of family and schooling in America*. New York: Basic Books, 1972.

Jenkins, M. D., & Randall, C. M. Differential characteristics of superior and unselected Negro college students. In R. C. Wilcox (Ed.), *The psychological consequences of being a Black American*. New York: John Wiley and Sons, 1971, pp. 198–215.

Jersild, A. *Child psychology*. Englewood Cliffs, N. J.: Prentice-Hall, 1960.

Kasanin, J. S. (Ed.). *Language and thought in schizophrenia*. New York: W. W. Norton, 1964.

Katz, M. C. *Bureaucracy and schools: The illusion of educational change in America*. New York: Praeger Publishers, 1971.

Keddie, N. Classroom knowledge. In M. F. D. Young (Ed.), *Knowledge and control*. London: Collier and McMillan Publishers, 1971, pp. 133–60.

Kendrick, S. A. The coming segregation of our selective colleges. *College Board Review*, 1967–68, *66*, 6–12.

Kendrick, S. A., & Thomas, C. L. Transition from school to college. *Review of Educational Research*, 1970, *40* (1), 151–79.

Kerlinger, F. N. *Foundations of behavioral research*. New York: Holt, Rinehart, and Winston, 1973.

King, I. *Toward a theory of nursing*. New York: John Wiley and Sons, 1971.

Klass, M. *East Indians in Trinidad: A study of cultural persistence*. New York: Columbia University Press, 1961.

Kleinfeld, J. The relative importance of teachers and parents in the formation of Negro and white students' academic self-concept. *Journal of Educational Research*, 1972, *65* (5), 211–12.

Knopf, L. *From student to RN: A report of the nurse career-pattern study*. Division of Research, United States Department of Health, Education and Welfare, Division of Nursing, National Institute of Health, DHEW Publication No. (NIH) 72–130, 1972.

Kramer, B. Historical Perspectives on mental health and racism. In C. Willie, B. Kramer, & B. Brown (Eds.) *Racism and mental health*. Pittsburgh: University of Pittsburgh Press, 1973, pp. 3–57.

Kramer, M., Rosan, B., & Willis, E. Definitions and distributions of mental disorders in a racist society. In C. Willie, B. Kramer, & B. Brown (Eds.), *Racism and mental health*. Pittsburgh: University of Pittsburgh Press, 1973, pp. 353–459.

Kvaraceus, W., Gibson, J., Patterson, F., Seasholes, B., & Grambs, J. *Negro self-concept: Implications for school and citizenship*. New York: McGraw-Hill, 1965.

Lacey, D. *The white use of Blacks in America.* New York: McGraw-Hill, 1972.

Lacy, L. A. *The rise of the proper Negro.* New York: MacMillan Co., 1971.

Ladner, J. A. *Tomorrow's tomorrow: The Black woman.* Garden City, N.Y.: Anchor Books, Doubleday, 1971.

Lansman, M. The relation of self-image to Negro achievement and attendance in a racially integrated elementary school. *Dissertation Abstracts International,* 1968, *29,* 442–43.

Lar, R. Internal-external control and competitive and innotive behaviors among Negro college students. *Journal of Personality and Social Psychology,* 1970, *14,* 263–70.

Lavin, D. E. *The prediction of academic performance.* New York: Russell Sage Foundation, 1965.

Lavin D. E., & Jacobson, B. *Open admission at the City University of New York: A description of academic outcomes after three semesters.* Office of Program and Policy Research, City University of New York, April 1973.

Lavin, D. E. *Open admissions at the City University of New York: A description of academic outcomes after four semesters.* Office and Program and Policy Research, City University of New York, 1974.

Lavin, D. E., & Silberstein, R. *Student retention under open admissions at the City University of New York: September 1970 enrollees followed through four semesters.* Office of Program and Policy Research, City University of New York, February, 1974.

Leininger, M. *Nursing and anthropology: Two worlds to blend.* New York: John Wiley and Son, 1970.

Leininger, M. *Transcultural nursing: Concepts, theories, and practices.* John Wiley and Sons, 1978.

Lessing, E. Racial differences in indices of ego functioning related to academic achievement. *Journal of Genetic Psychology,* 1969, *115,* 153–57.

Levy, G. E. *Ghetto school.* New York. Pegasus Press, 1970.

Lewis, H. *Black ways of Kent.* Chapel Hill, N.C.: University of North Carolina Press, 1955.

Lewis, H. E. A descriptive study of self-concept and general creativity of southern and northern undergraduate students. *Dissertation Abstracts International,* 1967, *27,* 3625–3626.

Lewis, O. The culture of poverty. In J. P. Spradely & D. W. McCurdy (Eds.), *Conformity and conflict.* Boston: Little, Brown and Company, 1974, pp. 303–13.

Liebow, E. *Talley's corner.* Boston: Little, Brown and Company, 1967.

Lincoln, C. E. *The Black church since Frazier.* New York: Schocken Books, 1974.

Lipscomb, L *Racial identity of nursing school children.* Paper presented at the annual meeting of the American Sociological Association, New Orleans, Louisiana, August 1972.

Long, G. H., & Henderson, E. H. Self-social concepts of disadvantaged school beginners. *Journal of Genetic Psychology,* 1968, *113,* 41–51.

Long, G. H., & Henderson, E. H. Social schemata of school beginners: Some demographic correlates. *Merrill-Palmer Quarterly of Behavior and Development,* 1970, *16,* 305–24.

Longstreet, W. *Aspects of ethnicity.* New York: Teachers College Press. 1968.

Lowenthal, D. *West Indian societies.* New York: Oxford University Press, 1972.

Lowenthal, D., & Comitas, L. *Consequences of class and color: West Indian perspectives.* New York: Doubleday, 1973.

Lowenthal, D., & Comitas, L. *The aftermath of sovereignty: West Indian perspectives.* New York: Doubleday, 1973.

Maslow, A. *Motivation and personality.* New York: Harper and Row, 1954.

Maslow, A. Personality problems and personality growth. In C. Moustakas (Ed.), *Exploration in personal growth.* New York: Harper and Row, 1956.

McCandles, B. *Children: Behavior and development.* New York: Holt, Rinehart and Winston, 1967.

McCord, W., Howard, J. Frieberg, B., & Harwood, E. *Life styles in the Black ghetto.* New York: W. W. Norton and Co., 1969.

McDill, E., Rigsby, L. C., & Meyers, Jr., E. D. Educational climates of high school: Their effects and sources. *American Journal of Sociology,* 1969, *74,* 567–68.

McDonald, R. L., & Bynther, M. D. Relationship of self and ideal-self descriptions with sex, race, and class in southern adolescents. *Journal of Personality and Social Psychology,* 1965, *1,* 85–88.

McDonald, R. L. Effects of sex, race and class on self, ideal-self and parental ratings in southern adolescents. *Perceptual and Motor Skills,* 1968, *27,* 15–25.

McGhee, P., & V. C. Crandall. Beliefs in internal-external control reinforcements and academic performance. *Child Development,* 1968, *39,* 91–102.

McKelpin, J. P. Some implications of the intellectual characteristics of freshmen entering a liberal arts college. *Journal of Educational Measurement,* 1965, *2,* 161–66.

Merton, R. K. *Social theory and social structure.* New York: The Free Press, 1957.

Miller, M. On Blacks entering nursing. *Nursing Forum,* 1972, *11* (3) 248–63.

Miller, S. M. The American lower class: A typological approach. In A. B. Shostak & W. Gomber (Eds.), *Blue-collar world.* Englewood Cliffs, N.J.: Prentice-Hall, 1964, pp. 9–23.

Moore, W. *Against the odds.* San Francisco: Jossey-Bass, Inc., 1970.

Mosteller, F., & Moynihan, D. (Eds.). *On equality of educational opportunity.* New York: Random House, 1962.

Munday, L. Predicting grades in predominately Negro colleges. *Journal of Educational Measurement,* 1965, *2,* 157–60.

Murdoch, K. A., & Kluckorn, C. (Eds.). *Culture: A critical review of concepts and definitions.* New York: Random House, 1963.

Murillo-Rohde, I. Family life among mainland Puerto Ricans in New York city slums. *Perspectives on Psychiatric Care,* 1976, *14* (4), 174–9.

Murillo-Rohde, I. Unique needs of ethnic minority clients in a multiracial society: A socio-cultural perspective. *ANA Publication* (M-24), 19–25, 1976.

Office of the Chancellor, City University of New York. *Nursing programs of the City University of New York.* Unpublished Manuscript, 1974.

Ogletree, E. Skin color preference of the Negro child. *Journal of Social Psychology,* 1969, *79,* 143–44.

Ordway, John. Some emotional consequences of racism for whites. In C. Willie, B. Kramer, & B. Brown (Eds.), *Racism and mental health.* Pittsburgh: University of Pittsburgh Press, 1973, pp. 123–45.

Osborne, O. Aging and the Black diaspora: The African, Caribbean, and African-American experience. In M. Leininger (Ed.), *Transcultural nursing.* New York: John Wiley and Sons, 1978, pp. 317–33.

Owen, S. V., & Feldhusen, J. F. Effectiveness of three models of multivariate predictions of academic success in nursing. *Nursing Research,* 1970, *19* (6), 517–25.

Palmer, R., & Masling, R. Vocabulary for skin color in Negro and white children. *Developmental Psychology,* 1969, *1,* 396–401.

Parker, S., & Kleiner, R. J. *Mental illness in the urban Negro community.* New York: The Free Press, 1966.

Perlmann, J. *Open admissions at City College: A report after two years.* Office of Open Admissions Coordinator, City College of New York, August 1972.

Pettigrew, T. Racism and the mental health of white American: A social psychological view. In C. Willie, B. Kramer, & B. Brown (Eds.), *Racism and mental health.* Pittsburgh: University of Pittsburgh Press, 1973, pp. 269–98.

Pinderhughes, C. Racism and psychotherapy. In C. Willie, B. Kramer, & B. Brown (Eds.), *Racism and mental health.* Pittsburgh: University of Pittsburgh Press, 1973, pp. 61–121.

Plog, S., & Edgerton, R. (Eds.). *Changing perspectives in mental illness.* New York: Holt, Rinehart and Winston, 1969, pp. 242–56.

Powell, G. Self concept in white and Black children. In C. Willie, B. Kramer, & B. Brown (Eds.), *Racism and mental health.* Pittsburgh: University of Pittsburgh Press, 1973, pp. 299–319.

Powell, G. J., & Fuller, M. The variables for positive self-concept among southern Black adolescents. *Journal of the National Medical Association,* 1972, *64* (6), 522–26.

Purkey, W. *Self-concept and school achievement.* Englewood Cliffs, N.J.: Prentice-Hall, 1970.

Rainwater, L. Crucible of identity: The Negro lower class family. *Daedalus,* 1966, *95,* 172–216.

Rever, R. (Ed.). *Open admissions and equal access.* Iowa City, IA. The American College Testing Program, 1971.

Robinson, A. Black nurses tell why so few are in nursing. *RN Magazine,* July 1972, pp. 35–41, 70–73.

Rogers, C. *Client-centered therapy.* Boston: Houghton-Mifflin, 1951.

Rogers, M. *An introduction to the theoretical basis of nursing.* Philadelphia, PA.: F. A. Davis. 1970.

Rosenberg, N. *Society and the adolescent self image.* Princeton: Princeton University Press. 1965.

Rosenberg, B., & Simmons, R. *Black and white self-esteem: The urban school child.* Washington, D.C.: American Sociological Association, 1971.

Rosenfeld, G., *Shut those thick lips!* New York: Holt, Rinehart and Winston, 1971.

Rubin, V., & Zavalloni, M. *We wish to be looked upon.* New York: Teachers College Press, 1969.

Ryan, W. *Blaming the victim.* New York: Vintage Books, 1971.

Safa, H. The matrifocal family in the Black ghetto: Sign of pathology or pattern of survival? In C. O. Crawford (Ed.), *Health and the family.* New York: MacMillan, 1971.

Soares, A. T., & Soares, L. M. *A comparative study of the self-images of disadvantaged children.* Paper presented at American Educational Research Association, Los Angeles, California, February, 1969.

Soares, A. T., & Soares, L. M. A comparative study of the self-perceptions of disadvantaged children in elementary and secondary schools. *Proceedings of American Psychological Association,* 77th, 1969, *4,* 659–60.

Soares, A. T., & Soares, L. M. *Differences in self-perceptions of disadvantaged students.* Paper presented at American Educational Research Association, Minneapolis, Minnesota, March, 1970.

Soares, A. T., & Soares, L. M. Critique of Soares and Soares Self-perceptions of culturally disadvantaged children—A reply. *American Educational Research Journal,* 1970, *7,* 631–35.

Soares, A. T., & Soares, L. M. Interpersonal and self-perceptions of disadvantaged and advantaged high school students. *Proceedings of American Psychological Association*, 78th, *170* (5), 457–58.

Soares, A. T., & Soares, L. M. Self-concepts of disadvantaged and advantaged students. *Child Study Journal*, 1970, *2*, 69–73.

Sowell, T. *Black Education—Myths and tragedies*. New York: David McKay Company, 1972.

Spurlock, J. Some consequences of racism for children. In C. Willie, B. Kramer, & B. Brown (Eds.). *Racism and mental health*. Pittsburgh: University of Pittsburgh Press, 1973, pp. 147–163.

Stafford, W. W., & Ladner, J. Comprehensive planning and racism. *Journal of American Institute Planners*, 1969, *35*, 68–74.

Staples, R. The myth of the Black matriarchy. In R. Staples (Ed.), *The Black family: Essays and studies*. Belmont, CA.: Wadsworth Publishing Company, 1971, pp. 149–59.

Strauss, S. The effect of school integration on the self-concept of Negro and Puerto Rican children. *Graduate Research in Education and Related Disciplines*, 1967, *3*, 63–76.

Stroud, F., & Bellow, T. Community nursing in racially oppressed communities. In S. Archer & R. Fleshman (Eds.), *Community health nursing*. North Satuate, MA.: Duxbury, 1975.

Taylor, C. P. Some changes in self-concept in the first year of desegregated schooling: The outward walls and the inward scars. *Dissertation Abstracts International*, 1968, *29*, 821–22.

Thomas, C. L., & Stanley, J. C. Effectiveness of high school grades for predicting college grades of Black students: A review and discussion. *Journal of Educational Measurement*, 1969, *6* (4), 203–15.

Thompson, W. *Correlates of the self concept*. Nashville: Counselor Recordings and Tests, Dede Wallace Center, June 1972.

Trowbridge, N. Self concept and socio-economic status in elementary school children. *American Educational Research Journal*, 1972, *9* (4), 525–37.

Wendland, M. M. Self-concept in southern Negro and white adolescents as related to rural-urban residence. *Dissertation Abstracts International*, 1969, *29*, 2642-B.

Wilcox, P. Positive mental health in the Black community. In C. Willie, B. Kramer, & B. Brown (Eds.), *Racism and mental health*. Pittsburgh: University of Pittsburgh Press, 1973.

Williams, E. *History of people of Trinidad and Tobago*. London: Deutsch, 1964.

Williams, R. L., & Byars, H. Negro self-esteem in a transitional society. *Personnel and Guidance Journal*, 1969, *47*, 120–25.

Williams, R. L, & Byars, H. The effect of academic integration on the self-esteem of southern Negro students. *Journal of Social Psychology*, 1970, *80*, 183–88.

Williams, R. L. & Cole, S. Scholastic attitudes of southern Negro students. *The Journal of Negro Education*, 1969, *38* (1), 74–77.

Winch, R. F. *Identifications and its familial determinants*. Indianapolis: Bobbs-Merrill, 1962.

Wittmeyer, A. L., Camiscioni, J. S., & Purdy, A. A longitudinal study of attrition and academic performance in a collegiate nursing program. *Nursing Research*, 1971, *20* (4), 339–47.

Woodson, C. *Miseducation of the Negro*. Washington, D.C.: The Associated Publishers, Inc., 1933.

Wright, R. *The ethics of living jim crow*. New York: Harper and Row, 1937.

Wylie, R. C. *The self-concept.* Lincoln, NB.: University of Nebraska Press, 1961.

Wylie, R. C., & Hutchins, B. Schoolwork ability estimates and aspirations as a function of socio-economic level, race and sex. *Psychological Reports,* 1967, *21,* 781–808.

Wyne, M., White, P., & Coop, R. *The Black self.* Englewood Cliffs, N.J.: Prentice-Hall, 1974.

Zirkel, P. A., & Moses, E. G. Self-concept and ethnic group membership among public school students. *American Educational Research Journal,* 1971, *8* (2), 253–65.

SUMIKO FUJIKI   JENNIE CHIN HANSEN
ANNA CHENG   YA-MEI LEE

CHAPTER **14**

Psychiatric-Mental Health Nursing of Asian and Pacific Americans

The objective of this chapter is to delineate the issues and factors that demonstrate the need for psychiatric-mental health nursing curricula culturally sensitive to Asian and Pacific Americans (AAPA). In addition, we aim to examine the training and manpower needs of psychiatric-mental health nurses caring for these populations. We believe these needs are salient because we are humanists, have respect for individuals of our own ethnic backgrounds and believe that it is the right of any individual to have sensitive and appropriate health and mental health care.

There are approximately three million Asian and Pacific Americans in the United States (Owan, 1975). This figure is impressive in that the 1970 census estimated a population of one and one-half million. The doubling of this figure has been greatly influenced by the relaxation of immigration laws which in 1965 went from the bias of higher European quotas to a more open immigration system. In addition, since 1975 there has been and continues to be, a steady influx of Indochinese refugees. These demographic changes in the Asian and Pacific American population present the challenge for the discipline of nursing to ensure that its practitioners are prepared and the tenets of its practice are broad enough to effectively meet the needs of Asian and Pacific Americans.

Psychiatric-mental health nursing as an area of practice within nursing is based upon providing a three-level prevention system of mental health care to the general population: primary, secondary and tertiary prevention. In primary prevention, the discipline concerns itself with promoting mental health behavior toward high-level functioning. In secondary prevention, concern is directed toward early case-finding and treatment systems to prevent the mental health problem from further deteriorating. In tertiary prevention, focus shifts to a rehabilitative situation that will bring the treatment population to its

Statement of
the Problem

377

most effective level of functioning and further maintain that degree of efficacy (Caplan, 1961). It follows that since the primary treatment population has been the dominant society, the approaches to the levels of treatment have been geared toward the amalgamated "American" or the Western culture mode.

This normative approach has its origins in the period of the melting-pot ideology. As the numbers of various ethnic peoples of color have increased, however, the concept of cultural plurality has been acknowledged to a greater extent. Unfortunately, the head-nodding acknowledgement of this concept has not always been translated into operational recognition of the differing needs of the various populations.

The fact that ethnic minorities have tended not to exert any major degree of sociopolitical force upon American society further underscores their limited influence in having their general needs recognized, to say nothing of their mental health needs. The Asian and Pacific American populations, having been greatly affected by various historically documented institutional racist practices in America, have become perhaps that much more of a "silent" minority. So often in the past, the lack of assertive verbalization by this group has stereotypically been attributed to strictly intrinsic cultural traits. This type of labeling easily leads to the condoned oversight of what actually constitutes culture as contrasted with a phenomenon of cultivated survival strategies.

It is also imperative to examine the heterogeneity of Asian and Pacific Americans. Often the term *Asian and Pacific American* conjures up images of a classic typology of a group or an individual. Although there are some broad similarities, there are significant intergroup variances that need to be understood. For example, the group comprises Chinese, Japanese, Filipinos, Koreans, Vietnamese, Cambodians, Laotians, Samoans, Guanamians, Thais, Burmese, Hawaiians or any other people who live in the geographic areas near the Pacific Basin. Each group has a distinctive culture and a unique history with regard to their immigration to the United States. Some groups have memories of discriminatory laws that excluded recognition of their rights for a defined period of time. In addition, the family histories of some of the groups, especially the Chinese and Japanese, may extend back as many as five generations in America. Others have immigrated more recently, especially the Indochinese, who have left their homelands because of political persecution. Ironically, in America some subgroups are seen as one, merged group, whereas in their homelands, these same subgroups would have been inveterate enemies. Suffice it to say that the unique patterns of immigration and the experiences of acculturation in America create different mental health issues for different groups of Asian and Pacific Americans.

The interface between psychiatric nursing and the fulfillment of the Asian and Pacific American mental health needs emanates indirectly from the basic tenets of service delivery in the nursing profession. The organization that sets guidelines for psychiatric-mental health nursing practice is the Division on Psychiatric and Mental Health Nursing of the American Nurses Association. This organization developed a *Statement on Psychiatric Nursing Practice* (American Nurses Association, 1976). Containing the philosophical assumptions for this area of nursing practice, this statement commits the discipline to holistic and humane care at all levels of prevention and, furthermore, advocates attention to environmental considerations and continuity of care that would maintain the dignity of the consumers' health care. Within this statement much is also written of the profession's concern for quality of service as well as concern for collaboration and coordination with other disciplines for the delivery of mental health care services. These philosophical assumptions do not delineate specific concern for ethnic people of color, but they are written broadly enough to allow such interpretation if one wishes.

The implicit assumptions of nursing practice provide the basis for sensitive care. However, these assumptions tend only to acknowledge the need for cultural diversity and, in general, are not operationalized in curricula. The information presented under the rubric of "culture" frequently lends itself to furthering stereotypes rather than truly fostering cultural sensitivity. In recognition of this failing Branch (1978), in a project of the Western Interstate Council on Higher Education in Nursing (WICHEN), developed models for the systematic incorporation in curricula of concepts and content that reflect cultural diversity. The amassed products of these efforts have been available, but there is a lag in the use of such materials.

It appears that part of the reason for the difficulty in incorporating culturally relevant materials rests with underlying differences in perception of the world. The Western approach uses a strict rational methodology to explain phenomena; the Eastern perception explains phenomena by systems not considered "scientific" by Western standards (Tashima, 1976). These perceptual differences have implications for nurses, many of whom define illness and wellness in middle-class as well as in Western terms. The Asian and Pacific American client, on the other hand, who often is more ethnocentric and of a different class, perceives these psychiatric concepts and treatment approaches from a different perspective.

This disparity has obvious implications for the utilization of available services by the ethnic minorities and for the delivery of services by the health care providers. When Asian and Pacific American clients have appeared for services, frequently they have already reached a point of severe crisis. Service providers, who as a group value early case finding and treatment, find themselves frustrated by the extreme degree of illness at which a client comes to the attention of the mental health system. Sue's (1977) study of Seattle mental health facilities demonstrated that Asian and Pacific Americans were diagnosed as "psychotic" in a proportion greater than any other group. This diagnosis was found in 22.4 percent of Asian and Pacific Americans, as compared with 13.8 percent of Blacks, 14.5 percent of Hispanics, 17.6 percent of American Indians and Alaska Natives and 12.7 percent of the Caucasian patients. Whether this finding reflects a use of other support systems before entry into the mainstream mental health system, a high level of pathology or a potential for misdiagnosis is subject to question.

The general impression that Asian and Pacific Americans do not utilize mental health care services is borne out in various studies (Miranda and Kitano, 1976). Sue's examination of seventeen community mental health centers during a three-year period, for example, reflected only a 0.7 percent usage of service by Asian and Pacific Americans relative to 2.4 percent Asian and Pacific American population. This finding has been replicated in the Los Angeles area where there was a 4 percent Asian and Pacific American population and only a 0.9 percent utilization of patient services (Hatanaka, Watanabe, and Ono, 1975). Again, there are different ways to interpret such findings. Whether the clients tended to use more informal networks rather than mainstream services or whether there were barriers to service delivery are reasonable questions. An interesting exception to studies reporting low utilization is the study by Berk and Hirata (1973), which found that during the 1855–1955 period there was a higher rate of admission of Chinese to state mental hospitals in California than would be indicated by their numbers in the general population. One potential conclusion to draw from this information is that many of these admissions (who were single men) resulted from the lack of informal supportive networks during that period in history.

Cultural influence is an important variable when looking at utilization patterns. Asian and Pacific Americans have frequently been found to use self-care or alternative or nontraditional modes of treatment before seeking a physician's care for symptom relief (Haung and Grachow, 1974). The use of traditional mental health "talk" therapies may not have great relevance for most Asian and Pacific American persons, as suggested by Okano (1976), who found that 235 Japanese Americans negated the relevance of mental health concepts and further interpreted mental disorder in terms of extreme deviance.

Another concept that must be placed in perspective is that of "face" in Asian and Pacific American groups. This concept emphasizes the control of expression and feeling. Such control, then, becomes a reflection of the person's maturity and is further related to the proscriptive concepts of shame and pride (Ho, 1976). These proscriptions for behavior are still viable and prevalent. They should not be used in and of themselves, however, to explain the lack of effort made by Asian and Pacific Americans to avail themselves of mental health services. Stress and mental illness prevail regardless of cultural variables. The point is that efforts to ensure the availability of services are needed, but from a perspective that is culturally consistent with the group served.

Allusions have been made to the barriers to service for Asian and Pacific American groups in connection with nonutilization of services. The *Report of the Special Populations Subpanel on the Mental Health of Asian/Pacific Americans* (1978) specifically outlines several barriers:

> (1) cultural linguistic constraints, (2) lack of bilingual/bicultural personnel, (3) tokenism in employment of bilingual/bicultural personnel, (4) obstacles to credentialing/licensing of personnel among Asian and Pacific immigrants, (5) catchment area confinement, and (6) insufficiency of services due to inadequate funding by local, state, and federal agencies (p. 791).

Cultural and Linguistic Constraints. The previous discussion of Western and Eastern cultural differences posited that people's differing perceptions of the world affect their basic approach to mental health and illness. Service providers who are not familiar with their target population's belief and thinking systems will often have difficulty perceiving the problem. Linguistic differences may further compound the cultural differences. For example, Gaw (1981), in his work as a bilingual-bicultural psychiatrist, was referred to a monolingual Asian patient who was exhibiting seemingly bizarre behavior. Upon questioning, he recognized that her stress-reducing behavior had been culturally based and was not totally inappropriate, as had been originally perceived.

Unless the therapist understands the patient's thoughts and feelings, pathology or beginning mental health problems can go unrecognized. Without linguistic consistency between the therapist and client very little mental health assessment can occur. There may well be true pathology in the individual which cannot be recognized for what it is unless the illness is seen in the context of the person's culture, which means that the therapist must have access to the information that makes communication linguistically possible.

The effect of cultural differences upon mental health service delivery and client acceptance was also reflected in Sue and McKinney's (1975) study on Asian and Pacific American utilization of Seattle community mental health services. They found that in traditional agencies the initial dropout rate was extremely high (52 percent) and that therapy sessions were being provided when treatment was pursued. There certainly exists the tendency to view the patient who terminates therapy as noncompliant instead of viewing the treatment model as irrelevant to certain populations. Furthermore, the literature has pointed to the fact that Asian and Pacific Americans and other minority group clients received less "preferred" forms of mental health treatment

than did their Anglo counterparts (Yamamoto, James and Pallcy, 1968).
All of the foregoing examples infer how the cultural variable affects
standard therapy and may not benefit many Asian and Pacific American
populations. The Yamamoto, James and Palley (1968) findings also
point to potential issues of discrimination and institutional racism,
which are so deep-seated as to be beyond the realm of influence that
the inclusion of minority curriculum content can provide.

Bilingual-Bicultural Personnel. With the passage of PL 94-63, there
was hope that opportunities for Asian and Pacific Americans to receive
bilingual-bicultural personnel when seeking mental health services in
community mental health centers would increase. This law mandated
that community mental health centers serving communities with a
"substantial portion of individuals with limited English speaking
ability" have a culturally responsive method to provide care as well
as an identified bilingual staff member (*Report of the Special Populations Subpanel*, 1978). Since compliance is not always monitored,
infractions occur, and thus a barrier to access to services still prevails.
This lack of legal compliance also, in effect, denies opportunities for
employment to Asian and Pacific Amerian bilingual-bicultural personnel (Nguyen, 1977).

Token Bilingual-Bicultural Personnel. Token employment of Asian
and Pacific Americans can be examined from two perspectives. First,
when employment does occur, bilingual-bicultural personnel are frequently hired as supportive rather than as therapeutic staff. Many an
anecdote has been told of the housekeeping or clerical staff person
who is used to interpret. Not only are such persons often professionally
equipped for such roles, but they are also used in capacities beyond
those they are expected or paid to fill. Second, when appropriate
personnel are employed, they are often so widely dispersed in the
structure that their net effect is minimal.

A contrasting effective approach was demonstrated by Sue and
McKinney (1975), who showed the increase in mental health service
usage by Asian and Pacific Americans when an Asian American
counseling and referral service was made available in Seattle. They
specifically found, that in a one-year period, the numbers of Asian and
Pacific Americans using this one service approximated the number of
Asian and Pacific Americans using services in eighteen community
mental health centers over a three-year period. Similar patterns in
ethnic-specific program availability and consequent usage by Asian
and Pacific Americans were found in Oakland (True, 1975) and San
Francisco (Wong, 1977). In summary, models that effectively circum-
vent traditional barriers to service are available.

Credentialed and Licensed Personnel. In nursing, there is an apparent
shortage of Asian and Pacific American psychiatric and mental health

nurses. This lack can be examined from different perspectives. Asian and Pacific Americans who have entered the profession of nursing tend not to enter the psychiatric and mental health areas of practice. The reasons for this have not been formally examined. One of the authors of this chapter, however, has consistently heard from her dominant-culture faculty colleagues that foreign-born Asian and Pacific American students "always have a difficult time with psychiatric nursing."

Also, when looking at Asian and Pacific American communities, it is readily apparent that some groups are more recent arrivals than others. The Indochinese, Samoans and Guanamians, for example, have a much more recent immigration history than many other Asian and Pacific American groups. As a result, fewer individuals from these groups have had the opportunity for education and training in the mental health field (Nguyen, 1977). There are individuals who have come from their native country with previous nursing background and education, but many are unable to qualify for licenses in the United States until future coursework is completed. The entire issue of foreign nurse graduates continues to be thought provoking and controversial (Wong, 1977). Of course, professional standards of care must be maintained for all concerned, but methods to facilitate entry into practice must also be addressed. Since it is these individuals who are most likely to sensitively serve their own populations, both the profession and the identified population would benefit if these nurses had access to the profession.

Catchment Area Confinement. The original concept of "catchment area" was to provide individual, geographic accessibility to mental health services. Theoretically, this concept is viable, but when there are minimal numbers of an ethnic-specific population, the catchment concept, in effect, becomes a barrier to service. To overcome this barrier, recommendations have been made that would enable individuals to cross catchment boundaries to receive more ethnic-specific mental health services. Inherent in this recommendation is a remodeling of current administrative program and fiscal arrangements to make such access feasible (*Report of the Special Populations Subpanel,* 1978, p. 795).

Local, State and Federal Funding Agencies. Admittedly, there has been an increase during recent years in the numbers and types of agencies that focus on Asian and Pacific American health and mental health concerns. However, services consistently appear to operate on minimal funding periods and budgets, fear of termination and an overall lack of true commitment by the funding sources (Wang, 1977). In this era of budgetary cutbacks at all levels, there is the added concern that these types of services will be severely, if not totally, cut back. In general, when fiscal cutbacks are ordered, the first services to feel the bite are supportive services, and mental health and health care become primary target areas for trimming. Taking this scenario one step further, mental health and health care programs that might service more special populations, for example, programs that are ethnic-specific, become more likely targets because these groups, as mentioned earlier, tend to have less political impact on the funding sources. Given these programmatic barriers to service, it becomes obvious that more reliable methods of ensuring ethnic-specific commitment are needed. One method of achieving this goal is the enactment of legislation that addresses issues of minority mental health.

It has become quite evident that there is a need for curricula that are sensitive, accurate and related not only to Asian and Pacific American populations but to other minority groups as well. The issues explored thus far—the tenet of the division of nursing most likely to provide service related to mental health needs and the range of issues influencing utilization of mental health and illness services—bears out this conclusion. Furthermore, the barriers to service cited earlier point not only to the additional need for knowledgeable and sensitive service providers but, perhaps more cogently, to the urgent need for more Asian and Pacific American psychiatric-mental health nurses. The subsequent discussion will outline the authors' recommendations for conceptual development and ways to influence systems that have a bearing on curricula issues and manpower development related to Asian and Pacific Americans.

Framework for Curriculum Content in Psychiatric-Mental Health Nursing

The psychiatric-mental health nursing perspective we will set forth was developed from our collective knowledge and from our experiences in working with the Asian and Pacific American population. Basic for anyone working with Asian and Pacific Americans would be a sensitive humanistic approach, which requires knowledge about the people served as well as knowledge about psychiatric-mental health nursing practice. It has been our experience that Asian and Pacific American clients have certain expectations of the professionals and of the services they offer. They anticipate respect for themselves as human beings and expect staff to be well-informed, capable professionals who are able to prescribe directions as to what they, the clients, should do. They tend to drop out of treatment programs if such services are not forthcoming. This attitude, coupled with some basic, culturally influenced fears of mental illness among many Asian and Pacific Americans, indicates an urgent need for psychiatric-mental health nurses to begin developing client-centered nursing practices based upon sound theoretical premises; understanding of Asian and Pacific American clients and their close interpersonal contacts with families and other significant groups; and understanding of the intricacies of Asian and Pacific American communities.

Since humans are born into specific communities and cultures, it becomes important that the impact of cultural, historical, political and socioeconomic influences be considered when identifying factors that shape Asian and Pacific Americans as they live and develop throughout their lives. In arriving at a framework for viewing Asian and Pacific American clients, we adopted a basic format. The individual, family and community were selected as major, independent variables that influence and are influenced by each other. Other variables such as cultural, socioeconomic and political forces and historical events are critical shaping and influencing forces. These major forces are dynamic and continually affect the individual, family and the community throughout the lifecycles of Asian and Pacific Americans. The family and other significant persons refers to the individual's role status at a particular time or at the time he or she is being assessed or studied. The variable of community relates to the geographical location (region) as well as to the composition of the people who live in the community (ethnicity). Furthermore, the framework specifies the kind of community, whether rural, urban or suburban. Figure 1 provides a view of the cultural, socioeconomic, political and historical variables that influence the developing individual, family or community. This framework serves to delineate the parameters that must be considered in clinical practice, curriculum content development and research. The arrows on the top of the figure show the dynamic nature of the variables' influences on each other.

Cultural Influences

Specific cultural practices, beliefs, customs, values, religions and folk practices of the respective Asian and Pacific American groups must be identified, particularly because they comprise the characteristics of the people and influence the mental status of group members. Some culturally proscribed attitudes may be in conflict with mental health treatment goals as prescribed by Western therapists (Kitano, 1970). Some attitudes and behaviors that may be diagnosed as pathological or deviant may be accepted and even sanctioned in some cultures. For some, the demands of two cultures become insurmountable obstacles.

The cultural influences that affect how one copes with life's stresses also affect how one responds to crises. For many Asian and Pacific Americans, this becomes complicated by the value of family and the need to save the family's reputation. The strong influence of Asian and Pacific American nuclear and extended families cannot be over-emphasized. Family pride, self-pride and shame are powerful forces in the individual's life. Thus, in times of trouble, it becomes important not to bring shame to the family or to cause it to lose face. In order to save face, families may hide their ill members who continue to

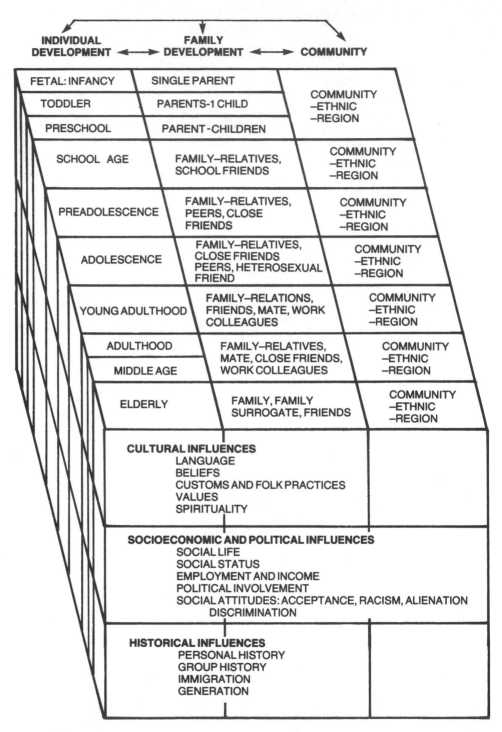

FIGURE 1

Framework for Content Basic to Psychiatric-Mental Health Nursing of Asian and Pacific Americans

deteriorate. At the point at which mental health services are obtained, the client has undergone tremendous suffering and has become pathological. An understanding of this strong cultural expectation in Asian and Pacific American societies might aid the nurse in practicing preventive psychiatric nursing. Indications of mental and emotional difficulties might be identified early, particularly the Asian and Pacific American clients' tendency to withdraw and to attempt to solve problems alone.

Asian and Pacific American citizens live within the boundaries of two major cultures which oftentimes are very diverse, and the conflicts created by such existences sometimes become insurmountable problems. For instance, current social issues such as the women's movement and the move to ratify the Equal Rights Amendment encroach upon sensitive, culturally sanctioned practices. Traditionally, and to this day, in many Asian and Pacific American cultures, women assume subservient, submissive roles to men (Welty, 1976). Certain human actions carry heavy penalties for those whose behavior is counterculture. In the Peoples Republic of China, divorce by women is not an approved practice. Women who leave their husbands become ostracized and are seen as outcasts (Welty, 1976). Those Chinese American women who divorce often experience the same ostracization as practiced in China.

Even though the Asian and Pacific American population is small in numbers and comprises less than 5 percent of the American population, the diversity among the groups is great (Kim, 1979). Cultural diversity is seen among people from the same ethnic group. These people may have different dialects, everyday practices and separate lifestyles even though they are from the same country. The geographical origins of the immigrants provide clues as to the variances in cultural, social and economic characteristics. There are noticeable regional within-group differences in language and culture among people of Chinese, Japanese, Korean and Filipino ancestry, among others. The diversity in ideologies within groups can be extreme. Chinese from the mainland of China differ from those whose homeland is Taiwan, Hong Kong or Singapore. Among the early Japanese immigrants, the provincial area of Japan they came from provided the basis for some social gatherings. Closeness and a sense of "family" became established for these people through their common origin. Thus, Japanese from Hiroshima would participate in the "Hiroshima Ken-Kai."

Historical Influences

Asian and Pacific American citizens have other differences that mental health professionals must recognize. One critical area is whether a person is American-born or an immigrant. If a client is an immigrant, it becomes important to know the reasons for immigration, when it took place, what the entry was like and with whom the person immigrated. The experiences of the recent Indochinese and Vietnamese immigrants would be different from those of someone who entered this country through the immigration quota system. The experiences of immigrants who arrived prior to the 1924 Exclusion Act are far different from the experiences of immigrants who arrived after World War II (Hundley, 1976). Significant numbers of the newly arrived immigrants come for reasons other than finding new homes and lives. There are those who come for educational purposes or who are sent by companies such as Toyota or Sanyo (Kim, 1979). These newly arrived people come from countries whose social and political mores are far different from those memories of the earlier immigrants from those countries, especially China, Japan, Korea and the Phillipines. These earlier immigrants are now elderly and bear scars of alienation, discrimination and racism.

The earliest Asian and Pacific American immigrants were Chinese, who first arrived around 1840. They were followed by groups of their countrymen who came to work as laborers for the Union Pacific Railroad and helped to develop the early West. Many of the early twentieth-century arrivals who came prior to the 1924 Exclusion Act are still alive. Many of them are bachelors who were denied the privileges of marrying and having families. These prohibitions were accomplished through U.S. legislative acts which prevented intermarriages and prohibited bringing brides into America. Today, many of these elderly Chinese men live in the ghettos of the West Coast and have become bitter, disillusioned and paranoid elderly people (Lyman, 1970).

The experiences of the early Japanese immigrants were similar except that they arrived with brides and families. Many of these immigrants came from rural agricultural and fishing villages; therefore, they moved into similar areas in this country. Strong political and social resistance to their presence created hardships, discriminatory legislation and confrontations for the Japanese immigrants. Agriculture and labor as well as fishing restrictions created much difficulty and anguish (Kitano, 1979).

The early Filipino immigrants arrived in the 1920s. Their American experiences were similar to those of the early Chinese immigrants in that Filipino women were not allowed citizenship privileges. In 1925 legislaton was enacted which stipulated that Filipinos had to serve in the U.S. Navy three years before they could become citizens (Rabaya, 1971). A majority of these people became farm laborers and their history is etched in unfair labor practices and bloodshed. Today, many of these Filipino bachelor immigrants who worked as farm laborers in their youth survive much as their Chinese counterparts: as bitter, paranoid, disillusioned elderly men in ghettos of large urban areas (Melendy, 1976).

Korean immigration occurred between 1903 and 1924. Most of the immigrants were of the Christian faith and were students and farm laborers. They, too, arrived with families and wives, preserving the family unit. The Korean immigrants were unique in that shortly after their arrival to the United States in the early nineteenth century, they became isolated from their homeland when Korea was annexed by Japan. As a result of their plight, the Koreans in America became determined to maintain their culture in their new land. This was an extremely difficult undertaking in the face of mounting discriminatory practices and laws (Houchins and Houchins, 1976).

Among more recent immigrants, the Pacific Islanders, such as the Samoans, immigrated westward lured by the Western cultures that infiltrated their countries. Religious converts comprise many of their numbers. Some have come to the United States in quest of a better life, much like the immigrants who have come before them. Many have become disillusioned as they have found themselves poorly equipped to compete in this highly technical, organized society. Oftentimes they lack work and language skills, are unemployed, live in poverty and experience cultural conflicts (Chen, 1973). The recent immigration of Vietnamese and Indochinese has brought another issue of importance to the attention of mental health professionals. As we know, these recent immigrants left their homelands to avoid political persecution. They have arrived in this country, however, at a time of rampant inflation and financial and unemployment crises, which tend to fan the flames of prejudice, discrimination and rioting in those who are without.

The srong roots of the elderly immigrants shaped their attitudes and, in turn, colored the attitudes of their offsprings. Challenges for psychiatric-mental health nursing lie in developing nursing strategies that help these individuals overcome the pains created by past experiences. Not only must the strategies address these past experiences but they must also consider the basic needs and longings of the early immigrants, who have been away for many years from their homelands and the families they left behind. Many of these elder Asian and Pacific American citizens were disillusioned upon visiting their homelands for the first time after years of absence; the past simply did not exist as they remembered it. One of the concerns of mental health professionals must be to help these people to adjust to the reality of the present and to give up dreams of bygone days.

The unique patterns of immigration and experiences of acculturation to the United States create different mental health issues. Often, mental health professionals are remiss in assessing this aspect of the psychosocial and historical background of the Asian and Pacific American clients and, inadvertently, provide less than sensitive mental health services.

Socioeconomic and Political Influences

The events and social climate of a given period play an important part in shaping Asian and Pacific Americans. For all groups, difficulties arose when each group became large in numbers and threatened other Americans in the job market. These events often led to legislative actions that had an impact upon the various groups as a whole. The Japanese American's experience of World War II was such an occurrence. The American-born Japanese, Nisei (second generation) and Sansei (third generation) were interned in concentration camps with their noncitizen parents, the Issei (first generation). These people were noncitizens not by choice, but because legislation denied them citizenship (Daniels, 1976). The disruption of family life and the enforcement of involuntary communal living or living outside of camps under curfew could not but result in serious mental health problems. The impact of such experiences requires serious consideration when developing nursing curriculum content.

DeVos (1973) found that third-generation Japanese Americans were more like their American peers than like their age mates in Japan. Chang (1979) found that the adolescents in Chinatown, San Francisco, had attitudes toward the elderly which were counterculture to the traditional piety and respect toward the elderly. In addition, generational conflicts emerge when the offsprings use English as a major language, fail to learn the parent's tongue and attempt to be like their counterparts in the greater society.

Guiding Concepts for Content Development

The actions of nurses should be based upon some identifiable theoretical and conceptual framework. Interpersonal theory is a strong component of this framework, and the nurse's ability to engage in therapeutic interpersonal processes is basic (Sullivan, 1953; Fromm-Reichmann, 1950). It provides a way of understanding human beings as they develop their aspirations, motives and needs. The basic concepts of interpersonal theory would provide roots for consideration of cultural diversity. The following selected concepts that form the basis of psychiatric-mental health nursing will be discussed with reference to the cultural impact whenever possible.

Nurse–Patient Relationships

Much has been written about nurse–patient relationships over the past three decades (Brown and Fowler, 1971; Kalkman and Davis, 1974; Peplau, 1952). The nursing of Asian and Pacific American peoples should be based upon respect for the clients and their individual and collective lifestyles. To accomplish this, it is essential that nurses know about folk practices, belief systems and taboos, particularly in the mental health area. The meanings and practices of life events such as pregnancies and births, rites of passage and psychosocial and biological development, identified in Figure 1, are important considerations. Perspectives on mental health and illness as well as special dietary and folk healing practices require consideration.

Differences in the perception of mental health and illness have to be understood clearly by both the nurse and the client. Oftentimes, Western ideas of mental health and mental illness are not consistent with those of the client's culture. For example, to be assertive toward one's parents would be incompatible with the values held by many Asian and Pacific American immigrants. The nurse's skill lies in knowing how to help reticent Asian and Pacific Americans become assertive so as to participate more fully and successfully in the greater society and to be able to make adaptations which compensate for weaknesses. Learning to be assertive in situations outside the familial context may make adaptation to the wider society more congruent with the expectations of society while lessening feelings of conflict over appropriate assertive behaviors.

Empathy as a Basic Therapeutic Tool

When Asian and Pacific American clients have language and conceptualizing difficulties nurse–patient interactions may become problematic. A concentrated effort must be made if nurse and client are to arrive at similar meanings of spoken words. Without such an effort, it is impossible for English-speaking nurses to provide psychotherapeutic treatment to clients who do not understand the English language.

In the face of language and cultural barriers, nurses must show empathy for their client. When languages and customs remain unintelligible, nurses must continuously rely on their sensitivity to the client's present state and recognize what feelings are being expressed (Zderad and Patterson, 1978).

Self-Concept and Self-Awareness

One of the major goals of Asian and Pacific American psychiatric-mental health nursing is to help clients strengthen and maintain their concept of self. This becomes a challenge when the client comes from a culture where individual needs are submerged because of family and group expectations (Kitano, 1979). The nurse is also challenged by clients whose self-concepts have been affected by life-long experiences of discrimination and alienation. Self-awareness is equally important for nurses who work with the Asian and Pacific American client. Nurses need to be aware of their own biases and prejudices if such exist. Especially needed is the separation of one's own feelings from those of the Asian and Pacific American clients, who may have contrasting fears, aspirations and beliefs (Fromm-Reichman, 1951). For the Asian and Pacific American these contrasts would include developing a sense of belonging to two cultures, accepting both statuses and finding peace and contentment as such a person. To deny one's origin and ethnicity would engender conflict about one's self and identity (Reik, 1949). For some Asian and Pacific American clients, programs that encourage acceptance of one's unique values and traditions and that help the young, especially, to identify and absorb with pride a sense of greater self-worth are essential.

In addition to a clear sense of self-worth, nurses must have considerable knowledge of theories about individuals, groups of people, families and communities. Also essential is knowledge about various therapies and treatment goals. Nurses working with Asian and Pacific American clients should be adept at using basic psychiatric-mental health nursing skills, which include communication, assessment, interview, interpersonal relationships and participation in individual, group and family therapies. Utilizing one's knowledge of the Asian and Pacific American client's culture is basic to program or treatment plans. For the traditional Asian and Pacific American clients, Western psychotherapy may not be effective if their cultural demands are not considered.

Assessments

Some means of assessing the degree of impact a client's culture has upon him or her should be employed. Sue and Sue (1971) identified three typological characters of Chinese American personalities: the traditionalist, nonassimilator; the marginal man, who favors dominant-society norms but has not attained total assimilation; and the American Asian, who maintains an intermediate course. Chang (1980) has conceptualized four major typological characters who adapt certain values and reject others and, as a result, become Asian traditionalists and adopt Asian values and behaviors, as seen in first generation immigrants; Americanized Asians who adopt dominant Western values and behavior usually associated with white, middle-class America; Asian Americans who have integrated values and behaviors from both cultures; and alienated Asians who reject both traditional Asian and dominant Western values (see Figure 2).

The mental health problems of any of these "types" of Asian and Pacific American citizens would reflect their particular development. Knowledge of theories of personality development and of group and community processes would be basic to understanding the impact of cultures on the Asian and Pacific American.

Intervention and Treatment Processes

Mental health services for Asian and Pacific Americans should be made available in culturally sensitive ways. In our experiences, many of the new immigrants respond to community-based programs and outreach endeavors. For example, at the Richmond Maxi Clinic in San Francisco, group therapy that used nonthreatening familiar topics was

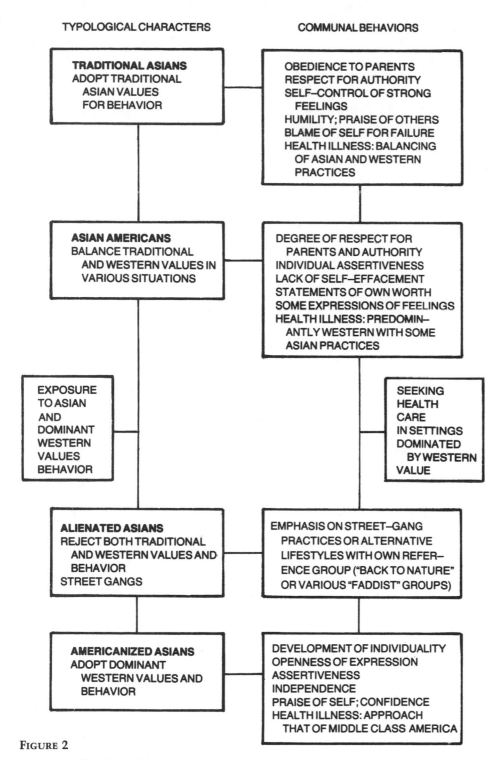

TYPOLOGICAL CHARACTERS   COMMUNAL BEHAVIORS

TRADITIONAL ASIANS
ADOPT TRADITIONAL
ASIAN VALUES
FOR BEHAVIOR

OBEDIENCE TO PARENTS
RESPECT FOR AUTHORITY
SELF–CONTROL OF STRONG
    FEELINGS
HUMILITY; PRAISE OF OTHERS
BLAME OF SELF FOR FAILURE
HEALTH ILLNESS: BALANCING
    OF ASIAN AND WESTERN
    PRACTICES

ASIAN AMERICANS
BALANCE TRADITIONAL
    AND WESTERN VALUES IN
    VARIOUS SITUATIONS

DEGREE OF RESPECT FOR
    PARENTS AND AUTHORITY
INDIVIDUAL ASSERTIVENESS
LACK OF SELF–EFFACEMENT
STATEMENTS OF OWN WORTH
SOME EXPRESSIONS OF FEELINGS
HEALTH ILLNESS: PREDOMIN–
    ANTLY WESTERN WITH SOME
    ASIAN PRACTICES

EXPOSURE
TO ASIAN
AND
DOMINANT
WESTERN
VALUES
BEHAVIOR

SEEKING
HEALTH
CARE
IN SETTINGS
DOMINATED
  BY WESTERN
VALUE

ALIENATED ASIANS
REJECT BOTH TRADITIONAL
    AND WESTERN VALUES AND
    BEHAVIOR
STREET GANGS

EMPHASIS ON STREET–GANG
    PRACTICES OR ALTERNATIVE
    LIFESTYLES WITH OWN REFER–
    ENCE GROUP ("BACK TO NATURE"
    OR VARIOUS "FADDIST" GROUPS)

AMERICANIZED ASIANS
ADOPT DOMINANT
    WESTERN VALUES AND
    BEHAVIOR

DEVELOPMENT OF INDIVIDUALITY
OPENNESS OF EXPRESSION
ASSERTIVENESS
INDEPENDENCE
PRAISE OF SELF; CONFIDENCE
HEALTH ILLNESS: APPROACH
    THAT OF MIDDLE CLASS AMERICA

FIGURE 2

Conceptualization of Four Typological Characters of Asians in the United States (Conceptualized by Dr. Betty T. Chang, R.N., D.N.S.)

successful. Some Asian and Pacific American clients may be more responsive to problem-oriented therapies than to client-centered therapy. This would be true especially when there is a strong cultural force to avoid centering upon one's own self or to avoid discussing one's own problems outside the family.

Asian and Pacific Americans may respond most postively to therapeutic processes that include the following considerations:

- Clarification of role expectations, both in therapy and in the clients' personal lives;
- Avoidance of situations where parents act out their personal problems before their children—separate talks for such problems might work better. For some, intense feeling such as anger would be counterculture;
- Assistance to families to structure more successful approaches to problem solving;
- Assistance to children to develop culturally in the two cultures with the least amount of conflict;
- Assistance to families to learn how to establish equilibrium as they live in two cultures;
- Provision of programs that become community-supported endeavors, making it much easier for clients to participate in mental health programs;
- Recognition of and provision of help for clients with psychopathologies regardless of the severity of symptoms;
- Utilization of ethnic and cultural communities, experts and programs to assist Asian and Pacific American clients.

Skills in both group and individual therapy would be helpful whether the nurse uses group treatment to move clients into individual therapy or moves clients from individual therapy to group treatment. As mentioned before, many Asian and Pacific American clients become very ill before seeking mental health assistance and often are no longer able to function adequately by themselves, in their families or community or in groups. Bringing strangers together to discuss nonthreatening topics has created an atmosphere whereby these lonely, suffering clients have become able to discuss and work out mental health problems with others. Respect for the clients' strong cultural need to "save face" is central to treatment programs.

Research

There are many critical areas of psychiatric-mental health nursing that require research. There remains a dearth of information about mental health problems related to psychiatric mental health nursing.

There is an urgent need for descriptive studies, as well as for the development of tools that measure or determine culturally relevant facts. From such studies and tools, theories can evolve and be tested. We have identified the following research needs:

- development of mental status assessment tools appropriate for Asian and Pacific American individuals;
- development of family assessment tools appropriate for measuring conflicts, mental illness and mental health of Asian and Pacific American individuals;
- development of specific interventions for specific mental health problems experienced by Asian and Pacific American individuals, such as alienation and discrimination;
- development of research that identifies the impact diverse cultures have on the Asian and Pacific American individual, with consideration of the developmental stages of life;
- identification of the effects of diverse culture on families and their development;
- identification of the extent of historical experience upon individual lives and on Asian and Pacific American groups;
- identificaton of the early signs of stress and of problems of maladaptation peculiar to Asian and Pacific American individuals;
- identification of the early signs of familial stress and problems of maladaptations;
- identification of the early signs of community stress and problems of maladaptation;
- identification of behavioral characteristics reflective of Asian and Pacific American peoples;
- identification of behavioral characteristics that are not consistent with accepted norms for Asian and Pacific American peoples;
- identification of culturally sanctioned behaviors that create mental health problems for Asian and Pacific Americans as they live in the United States.

Asian and Pacific American literature reveals individual and, to some extent, group American experiences (DeVos, 1973; Kim, 1979; Kitano, 1980; Sue and Sue, 1971). Research to identify pertinent variables that reflect the Asian and Pacific American peoples and their American experiences seems essential. Understanding their world views, hopes and aspirations would be tremendously helpful. Descriptive and experimental studies are needed for nurses to develop measures that test nursing approaches. Oftentimes, inappropriate tools are used in cultural studies. They are ineffective when Asian and Pacific

American cultural variables play an important part. Thus, we see a great need for the development of appropriate mental health measures for Asian and Pacific Americans.

Levels of Policy Influence

What is meant by policy influence? It is increasingly recognized that the person who provides services operates under not only an organization but also under professional standards of practice. For consistency in practice, standards must be prescribed from a source of control higher than the individual practitioner (e.g., the professional organization or the agency). Thus, to truly affect the type of mental health care a client receives, it is necessary to influence various levels of policy determination that oversee the mental health arena.

We will look at the national, state and local levels of policy making that would have impact on the nursing practitioner from a multifaceted standpoint, since there are many variables affecting policy making. We have one policy suggestion, however, that crosses all levels of policy influence.

It would be impossible to have Asian and Pacific American culturally based learning experiences of a consistent caliber at every geographical setting. For those ethnocentric communities with distinctive cultures or languages, however, there should be a system whereby professional expertise and supervision is available in close by, multidisciplinary training centers. Not only would broad federal funding be needed for such a program but also state recognition by the regulatory bodies of the validity of such training and education. This would then allow individual schools to contract for such learning experiences for students especially interested in bicultural-bilingual mental health care delivery. The strategy behind a multidisciplinary approach accomplishes several objectives. First, the geographic location would be in an area that had access to the ethnocentric population under study. Second, there would be available professional staff with past and current expertise in working with ethnocentric clients to assist in the supervision of students. There also would be an interdisciplinary focus to the operation of such a center, which would provide much more realistic and effective case management of individuals in psychosocial need. In short, when speaking of working sensitively with Asian and Pacific American clients in need of bilingual-bicultural mental health care, it is reasonable to acknowledge not only the shortage of persons who are bilingual and bicultural but also to acknowledge methods that would provide the most effective training modality.

Nursing at the National Level

At the national level are the two major nursing organizations: the National League of Nurses (NLN) and the American Nurses Association (ANA). The NLN, comprising both nurses and consumers of care, ensures that certain curricular standards of nursing education and practicing standards of health care agencies are maintained before providing its valued accreditation approval. Its range of influence extends from agencies that provide home health care to professional nursing education programs offering graduate degrees. Since the NLN's accreditation is highly regarded, potential members are interested in meeting the organization's expectations. This national organization offers standardized tests by which the individual school of nursing can determine where it stands in relationship to other schools of nursing. It is obvious that the NLN has direct influence on individual practitioners and therefore on client care, which makes the organization an important policy structure. If the organization recognizes that cultural diversity is a major factor of the health care system, each of its three components—educational standards, testing and accreditation—should then reflect that belief. The NLN should be asked to solicit input from the major minority nursing organizations regarding curriculum, service and testing issues as they pertain to ethnic people of color. If the NLN incorporates such input, then faculty and staff development relative to cultural content and issues should be required.

The other major national organization of nurses, the ANA, is considered the primary professional organization for discipline and concerns itself with planning, establishing and maintaining standards of practice within the profession of nursing. In the past, the organization has provided support for the recruitment of minority individuals into the profession at the undergraduate and graduate levels. In particular, the minority doctoral fellowships have provided direct financial support for a certain number of students. Another project, "Breakthrough," intended to facilitate recruitment of minority individuals into the profession was funded for a period of time and was coordinated with the nursing student preprofessional organizations. However, the funding for this project has since been terminated. The Commission on Nursing Education (1980) put forth a resolution at the 1980 ANA national meeting entitled, "Minority Representation in Nursing Education," reflecting concern at the limited numbers of minority individuals in nursing programs. The resolution is supportive but needs more specificity as well as financial backing in order to effect a tangible rather than a philosophical change.

Besides greater recruitment of individuals into the profession, there are two other policy issues to be addressed at this national level of influence. One of the issues concerns mobility within the profession. Frequently, ethnic persons of color are counseled into the nursing arena via levels lower than the baccalaureate entry (e.g., two-year programs). It is well known that the majority of ethnic nurses of color tend to predominate the licensed vocational levels or registered nurse levels—without baccalaureate or further degrees. The profession continues to wrestle with the issues of career mobility balanced with standards of practice, also evidenced by some of the 1980 resolutions

(Commission on Nursing Education, 1980, p. 15). The fact remains that there are few Asian and Pacific American nurses at the baccalaureate and higher levels of nursing.

The other policy issue, also related to career mobility, concerns the testing and licensing of foreign nurses. The issue of foreign nurses is an ongoing one, but it is a major concern for Asian and Pacific American populations, especially the Filipino and Korean nurses who have been educated abroad. Ironically, these nurses, because of their bicultural and bilingual abilities, would most likely be more effective practitioners with their respective populations. There continues to be a shortage of licensed psychiatric-mental health nurses to work with Asian and Pacific American populations; yet there is a multitude of foreign-educated nurses who cannot practice because of institutional barriers. The authors do not advocate a totally different standard of nursing practice measurement for foreign nurses, but we do support the effective and efficient evaluation and implementation of these nurses and their abilities. There is such a great need for bilingual and bicultural Asian and Pacific American nurses. A major policy recommendation is that the major nursing organizations work not only with the national testing system, but also with the major minority nursing organizations who are concerned with such issues as well as the state licensing boards, which ultimately make the decisions to accept practitioners.

Nursing at the State Level

At the state level, the formal licensing agency would be the nursing state board which prescribes the role and functions of the registered nurse. Relatedly, the regulatory board decides upon and administers the minimal acceptable practice and educational levels of the registered nurse (and oftentimes the licensed vocational and practical nurse). The board is most evident in the administration of tests and consequent bestowal of the license to practice in the discipline of nursing. Nurses who already have licenses from other states or countries would come under this agency's purview. Those nurses from Asian and Pacific Asian countries who desire to practice in a particular state would have to take supplementary courses and pass an English-equivalency exam and the basic nursing board exam. It is interesting to note that the required psychiatric nursing courses are those that are consistently found to be deficient in the foreign nurses' backgrounds.

The state board of nursing also accredits all its schools of nursing. To receive such accreditation, there are particular expectations to be met by each school that demonstrate compliance with the statutory regulations. This function of the state board is very important from the standpoint of ensuring content in ethnic sensitivity. Unfortunately, sensitivity is often so broadly written that accountability to such a statement could easily be met at minimal and inconsistent levels, which is what frequently occurs. A policy recommendation here is that state boards of nursing seriously evaluate their intent to provide culturally sensitive care to their populace and that they follow up on those organizations that have developed the means to systematically incorporate cultural content into nursing curricula (Branch, 1978).

While the previous discussion addressed the statutory regulatory bodies, it is still important to promote culturally relevant mental health care through policy development at state-level voluntary nursing organizations, for example, the state-level organization of the ANA or NLN. Often there is a great deal of communication between the voluntary and official systems regarding standards of practice. Therefore, a concerted effort by the culturally sensitive state voluntary agencies would affect not only its constituent members but also the more official agencies.

Schools and Universities. It is imperative that the philosophies of schools of nursing posit their commitments to culturally relevant care in a measurable manner. Because of the hierarchy that exists at universities, it is furthermore necessary that the universities themselves, as well as the particular colleges, have philosophies that allow for curricula that address both the overall professional skills and the focus on individualized care that characterize the discipline.

Nursing at the Local Level

The faculty are critical to determining whether a program supports ethnically sensitive care, particularly in mental health. Because of the present small number of graduate psychiatric-mental health nurses of Asian and Pacific American background in teaching positions, recruitment of these nurses will continue to be necessary. In the past, concepts of Western psychiatric treatment were foreign to Asian and Pacific American nurses, and, hence, this field was not as attractive as others. Until the number of Asian and Pacific American psychiatric nurses increases, faculty from other groups will be placed in the position of teaching about cultures other than their own. Those who espouse the desire to help their students provide sensitive care should be encouraged. We need faculty who are perceptive and open to different modes of addressing mental health care. They should be supported by the director or dean of the program.

It is of strategic importance to attain a position on the decision-making body that develops the program or school's curriculum. From such a position, one can influence the focus of the program and determine the best criteria for evaluating the curriculum in terms of its accountability to program objectives. Assuming there is a commitment to provide a culturally sensitive nursing program, part of this curriculum body's function should be to monitor this commitment.

At the school level, there has only been an allusion to the fact that there are changes that need to be effected at all levels of nursing education. In particular, affirmative action in the recruitment of students and faculty who are Asian and Pacific American and who are bilingual and bicultural has been lacking. It is incumbent upon nursing professionals who are already practicing to recognize the unique contribution Asian and Pacific American students and personnel can provide and to support such diverse thinking and practice in order to meet the needs of the clients we purport to serve.

Other Areas of Influence

The last areas for potential policy changes involve two separate but influential professional segments of society that indirectly but most assuredly shape policy. First are the publishers which, by virtue of what they accept for publication, determine what information is disseminated to large populations. Second are the funding agencies which, by virtue of what they decide to fund, determine what research is performed.

Publishers. A strategy to influence publishers involves the requesting of more articles related to ethnic-sensitive care. What are needed are articles by individuals with the true credentials to write authoritatively on such areas; stereotyping, which has occurred so often in the past, is to be avoided. The major national nursing organizations could purposely stay in close contact with the editors of psychiatric-mental health journals.

Funding agencies. In the arena of national-level grants, the authors recommend that not only should ethnic-sensitive individuals participate on grant review panels but that grant proposals be evaluated on their own merit for ethnic sensitivity. Considered in this measure would be the track record of the submitter in demonstrating cultural relevance and sensitivity to mental health in the past. So often it is the political process that influences the grant awards rather than the merit of the grant proposal itself, especially when the applicant is a "lesser" known school or organization.

In summary, policy at all levels must be changed in order to effect a true improvement in the nature and type of mental health care available to Asian and Pacific American populations. Policy on an international level must also be considered, given the pool of skilled individuals who would very likely be culturally sensitive practitioners. The question becomes one of how to most efficiently and effectively incorporate these persons while maintaining professional standards. The question of sensitive person power is pervasive. Not only do we need more Asian and Pacific American nurses, but given the lack of such professionals at this point, we also need to effect changes in the educational and delivery systems that shape the type of care all clients receive.

References

American Nurses Association. *Statement on Psychiatric Nursing Practice.* Kansas City, MO.: Author, 1976.

Berk, B., & Hirata, L. C. Mental illness among the Chinese: Myth or reality. *Journal of Social Issues,* 1973, *3* (2), 149–66.

Branch, M. *Models for cultural diversity in nursing: A process for change.* Boulder, CO.: Western Interstate Commission on Higher Education in Nursing, 1978.

Brown, M. M., & Fowler, G. R. *Psychodynamic nursing: A biosocial orientation.* Philadelphia: W. B. Saunders Co., 1971.

Caplan, G. *An approach to community mental health.* New York: Grune and Stratton, 1961.

Chang, B. L. *A study of attitudes towards the elderly.* Unpublished paper supported by the Institute of American Cultures through the Asian American Studies Center, University of California at Los Angeles, 1980.

Chen, R. N. Samoans in California. *Social Work,* 1973, *18,* 41–48.

Chuman, F. F. *The bamboo people: The law and Japanese-Americans.* Del Mar, CA.: Publisher's Inc., 1976, p. 54.

Commission on Nursing Education. Resolution put forth at the 1980 American Nurses Association national meeting. *American Nurse,* 1980, *12* (4), p. 14.

Daniels, R. American historians and East Asian immigrants. In N. Hundrey (Ed.), *The Asian American: The historical experience.* Santa Barbara: Clio Press, 1976.

DeVos, G. *Socialization for achievement: Essays on the cultural psychology of the Japanese.* Berkeley: University of California Press, 1973.

Fromm-Reichmann, F. *Principles of intensive psychotherapy.* Chicago: University of Chicago Press, 1951.

Gaw, A. Considering cultural diversity: A key to astute psychiatry. In the *Roche Report: Frontiers of Psychiatry,* March 1, 1981, 12–13.

Hatanaka, H. K., Watanabe, B. Y., & Ono, S. The utilization of mental health services in the Los Angeles area. In W. H. Ishikawa & N. H. Archer (Eds.), *Service delivery in Pan Asian communities.* San Diego: Pacific Asian Coalition, 1975.

Haung, C., & Grachow, F. The dilemma of health services in Chinatown, New York City. Paper presented at the annual conference of the American Public Health Association, New Orleans, Louisiana, October, 1974.

Ho, M. K. Social work with Asian Americans. *Social Casework,* 1976, *57* (3), 195–201.

Houchins, L., & Houchins, C. The Korean experience in America, 1903–1924. In N. Hundrey (Ed.), *The Asian American: The historical experience.* Santa Barbara: Clio Book Press, 1976.

Hundley, N. (Ed.). *The Asian American: The historical experience.* Santa Barbara: Clio Book Press, 1976.

Kalkman, M. E., & Davis. A. J. *New dimensions in mental health-psychiatric nursing* (4th ed.). New York: McGraw-Hill, 1974.

Kim, B. C. *Asian Americans: Changing pattern, changing needs.* Chicago: Association of Korean Christian Scholars, 1979.

Kitano, H. *Japanese-Americans: The evolution of a subculture.* Englewood Cliffs, N.J.: Prentice Hall, 1979.

Kitano, H. *Race relations.* (2nd ed.) Englewood, N.J.: Prentice-Hall, 1980.

Lyman, S. M. Redguard on Grant Avenue: The rise of youthful rebellion. In *The Asian in the West.* Reno: Western Studies Center, University of Nevada, 1970, pp. 99–118.

Melendy, H. B. Filipinos in the United States. In N. Hundley (Ed.), *The Asian American: The historical experience.* Santa Barbara: Clio Book Press, 1976.

Miranda, M. W., & Kitano, H. Mental health services in Third World communities. *International Journal of Mental Health,* 1976, *5* (2), 39–49.

Nguyen, T. D. Mental problems and service needs of Indo-Chinese refugees. Paper prepared for the President's Commission on Mental Health, Sub-Panel on Mental Health of Asian/Pacific Americans, 1977.

Okano, Y. *Japanese-Americans and mental health: An exploratory study of attitudes.* Unpublished doctoral dissertation, California School of Professional Psychology, Los Angeles, 1976.

Owan, Tom. *Asian-Americans: A case of benighted neglect.* Paper presented at the National Conference of Social Welfare, San Francisco, May 13, 1975.

Peplau, H. E. *Interpersonal relations in nursing.* New York: G. P. Putnum's Sons, 1952.

Rabaya, V. Filipino immigration: The creation of a new social problem. In A. Tachiki, E. Wong, F. Odo, & B. Wong (Eds.), *Roots: An Asian American reader.* Los Angeles: University of California at Los Angeles, 1971.

Reik, T. *Listening with the third ear.* New York: Farrar, Strauss, 1949.

Rogers, Carl. *Client-centered therapy.* Boston: Houghton-Mifflin Company, 1951.

Report of the Special Populations Subpanel on the Mental Health of Asian/Pacific Americans, President's Commission on Mental Health. Washington, D.C.: U.S. Government Printing Office, 1978.

Sue, S. Psychological theory and implications for Asian-Americans. *Personnel and Guidance Journal,* 1977, *55,* 381–89.

Sue, S., & McKinney, H. Asian Americans in the community health care system. *American Journal of Orthopsychiatry,* 1975, *45*(1), 111–18.

Sue S., & Sue, D. W. Chinese-American personality and mental health. *Amerasia Journal,* 1971, *1* (2), 36–39.

Sullivan, H. S. *The interpersonal theory of psychiatry.* New York: W. W. Norton, 1953.

Tashima, N. *Asian American mental health: A cultural perspective.* Unpublished master's thesis, San Diego State University, 1976.

True, R. H. Mental health services in a Chinese American community. In H. Ishikawa and N. Hayashi (Eds.), *Service delivery in pan Asian communities.* San Diego, California, Pacific Asian Coalition, 1975.

Wang, L. Chinatown, San Francisco: A few mental health issues. Written testimony presented on behalf of the Northeast Mental Health Center, San Francisco, to the President's Commission on Mental Health, San Francisco, California, June 21, 1977.

Welty, P. T. *The Asians.* New York: J. B. Lippincott, 1976.

Wong, H. L. Community mental health services and manpower and training concerns of Asian Americans. Paper presented on behalf of the Richmond Maxi-Center, San Francisco, California, to the President's Commission on Mental Health, June 2, 1977.

Yamamoto, J., James, Q. C., & Palley, N. Cultural problems in psychiatric therapy. *General Archives of Psychiatry,* 1968, *19,* 45–49.

Zderad, L., & Patterson, J. *Humanistic nursing.* New York: John Wiley and Sons, 1976.

Bibliography

Brown, W. Japanese management: The cultural background. *Monumenta Nipponica*, 1966, *21*, 47–60.

Caplan, G. *Principles of preventive psychiatry.* New York: Basic Books, 1964.

Daniels, R. *The politics of prejudice.* New York: Atheneum, 1970.

Kitano, H. Mental illness in four cultures. *Journal of Social Psychology*, 1970, *80* (2), 121–34.

Sue, S., & Wagner, N. (Eds.). *Asian Americans: Psychological perspectives.* Palo Alto: Science and Behavior Books, 1973.

Sue, S., & Sue, D. W. Comparison between Asian-American and non-Asian students utilizing a student health psychotric clinic. *Journal of Counseling Psychology*, 1974, *21* (5), 423–27.

/

JANICE KEKAHBAH   PATRICIA SILK WALKER
AUDRA PAMBURN   ROSEMARY WOOD

CHAPTER 15

Development of American Indian and Alaska Native Curricula Content in Psychosocial Nursing

An analysis of the psychosocial needs of American Indians and Alaska Natives, minority content in professional nursing curricula, and theories of human development reflects three problems:

1. The mental health needs of American Indians and Alaska Natives are as great, if not greater than, those of other cultures (President's Commission on Mental Health, 1978).

2. Colleges of nursing are not educating members of American Indian and Alaska Native communities who might meet the needs (American Indian/Alaska Native Nurses Association [AIANNA], 1978).

3. Other mental health professionals are not prepared to provide services to American Indians and Alaska Natives because they hold values that are mismatched with the values of these groups and do not recognize the role those values play in the success or failure of treatment (Benedict, 1934; Kekahbah and Wood, 1971; Kluckhohn, 1974; Levine, 1971).

The following terms are used throughout this chapter:

American Indian and Alaska Native—"An individual who is of American Indian or Alaska Native descent, who is recognized by the United States government and/or the Indian/Native community as being Indian or Alaska Native, and who identifies him/herself as an Indian/Alaska Native" (Kekahbah and Wood, 1971).

Indian Community—"A group of individuals who share bonds of kinship, value sets, social structure and may or may not share a common territorial area. Indian people living within an urban area may constitute an Indian community though they may not live in the same neighborhood or may not have the same tribal affiliation" (Kekahbah and Wood, 1971).

Professional Nurse—An individual who has completed a prescribed course of study in baccalaureate nursing, has taken and passed the state board examination for registered nurses and has graduate level preparation in the area of psychosocial nursing.

Health—"A state of complete physical, mental and social wellbeing, and not merely the absence of disease or infirmity" (World Health Organization, 1956).

White—"An abstraction—a composite of social, political, and economic attitudes by certain people, whose skin is usually whiter than most of the world's population and who behaved in a certain way toward primitive peoples wherever they were encountered around the globe. The White is a colonizer who early developed an advanced technology; he is an exploiter of human and natural resources; he has destroyed, often intentionally, almost every alien culture he has come in contact with; and he has imposed an iron rule on the remnant peoples of these cultures" (Farb, 1969, p. 24).

Reality Shock—A startling discovery and reaction to the discovery that school-bred values are in conflict with work-world values (Kramer, 1970).

Cultural Shock—A state of anxiety precipitated by the loss of familiar signs and symbols of social intercourse when one is suddenly placed in a cultural system markedly different from familiar surroundings (Kramer, 1970).

Career Mobility—"A general category that designates movement from any one level to another level in an occupational field" (Lenburg, 1975, p. 26).

Open Learning—"Educational approaches designated to permit . . . flexibility and individualization of learning and to emphasize the role of the learner in the educational process" (Lenburg, 1975, p. 26).

Rationale for Indian Content

Rationale for Mental Health Needs

If one of the goals of nursing education is to prepare psychiatric nurses to meet the needs of society, it is necessary for curriculum content to reflect those needs. The inclusion in curricula of content relevant to American Indians and Alaska Natives is clearly warranted. According to certain contemporary social indicators, the incidence of mental-health-related problems among American Indians and Alaska Natives is unusually high when compared with majority group norms (Cahn, 1969). During the past twenty years, self-participated deaths for American Indians and Alaska Natives accounted for a disproportionate number of deaths relative to those reported for the general population, as shown in Table 1. Self-participated deaths include deaths due to

TABLE 1

Selected Causes of Death Among Indians and Alaska Natives in Reservation States, 1955 and 1975 (per 100,000 population)

	Crude Death Rates		Percentage Change
	1955	1975	
All causes	972.2	691.8	−25
Accidents	155.6	150.5	−3
Diseases of heart	133.8	115.6	−13
Malignant neoplasms	59.1	60.9	+3
Cirrhosis of liver	14.2	42.5	+199
Cerebrovascular diseases	46.4	34.9	−25
Influenza and pneumonia	89.8	33.7	−62
Certain causes of mortality in early infancy	67.6	20.4	−70
Diabetes mellitus	13.9	17.4	+25
Homicide	15.9	22.2	+40
Suicide	8.7	21.6	+148
Congenital anomalies	19.0	9.1	−52
Tuberculosis	55.1	7.7	−86
Arteriosclerosis	NA	8.4	
Nephritis and nephrosis	NA	4.2	

Note: NA indicates not available.

Source: IHS Nursing Newsletter, vol. I, 1977, Vital Events Branch, OPS/DRC/IHS, 11-15-76.

suicide, homicide, accidents, uncontrolled diabetes, hypertension and cirrhosis of the liver.

Table 1 compares fourteen leading causes of death in 1955 and in 1975, with a total crude death rate for 1977 of 691.8. According to the table, of the fourteen listed causes of death, four—self-participated death categories—account for 237 deaths per 100,000 population or 34 percent of the crude death rate for all causes. The breakdown is as follows: accidents, 105.5; cirrhosis of the liver, 42.5; homicide, 22.2; and suicide, 21.6, for a total of 236.8. Accidents continue as the leading cause of death in the American Indian and Alaska Native population. Some 22 percent of all deaths in this population result from an accident. Diseases of the heart and malignant neoplasm are the second and third causes of death among this population. These two classifications are ranked first and second in the total U.S. population. Cirrhosis of the liver, fourth leading cause of death in the American Indian and Alaska Native population, is the seventh leading cause of death in the United States. The crude death rate for cirrhosis of the liver has increased 200 percent since 1955. Suicide and homicide have also increased considerably in their crude death rates during this period. Diabetes mellitus and malignant neoplasms are the other disease categories with higher rates in 1975 than in 1955. Major

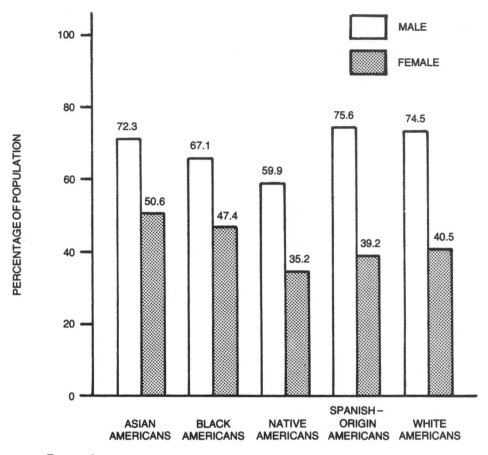

FIGURE 1

Percentage of Population by Sex, Age 10 and Over in Civilian Labor Force, U.S. 1970 (American Public Health Association, Minority Health Chart Book, 1974)

reductions have been noted for tuberculosis, influenza and pneumonia, certain causes of mortality in early infancy, and congenital anomalies. In the twenty-year period 1955–1975 there has been a 25 percent reduction in the crude death rate among American Indian and Alaska Native people.

Deaths that have some degree of human participation are also, to some degree, related to alcoholism. Alcoholism and/or self-destruction (conscious or unconscious) is related to poverty, unemployment and feelings of frustration, anger and despair.

Furthermore, failure to thrive economically and educationally is disproportionately high for the American Indian and Alaska Native population when compared with other segments of the population, as is documented in Figure 1 and Figure 2. Figure 1 clearly shows that a

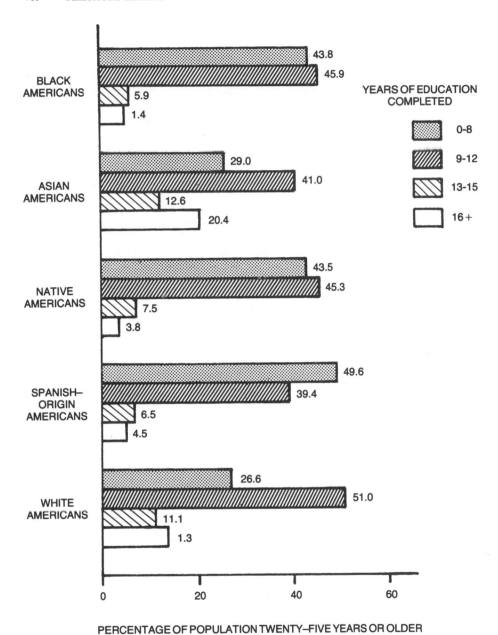

FIGURE 2

Years of School Completed for Individuals 25 Years of Age and Older (American Public Health Association, Minority Health Chart Book, 1974)

smaller percentage of the American Indian and Alaska Native population was employed in 1970 than any other ethnic and racial group, with 59.9 percent of males and 35.2 percent of females in the civilian labor force. The two groups with the next lowest percentage of population employed were Black males at 67.1 percent, followed by Spanish-speaking females at 39.2 percent.

According to Figure 2, a smaller percentage of the American Indian and Alaska Native population (3.8 percent) twenty-five years and older had completed sixteen years of education than any other ethnic and racial group of comparable age. The next highest percentage reported was for Black Americans at 4.4 percent. Asian and Pacific Americans comprised the highest percentage of the population twenty-five years and older reported to have completed sixteen years of education: 20.4 percent.

The data shown in Figure 1 and Figure 2 reveal that the psychosocial needs of American Indians and Alaska Natives are as great as if not greater than any other group in society. If schools of nursing are to prepare practitioners to address the needs of the total society, the greatest needs within that society, those of American Indians and Alaska Natives, must be addressed in nursing curricula.

College-Level Preparation

Although the psychosocial needs of the American Indian and Alaska Native population are greater than in any other group, the numbers of American Indians and Alaska Natives prepared to meet these needs are fewer than in any other group. The American Nurses Association (ANA) has set the basic level of psychiatric nursing practice at the master's degree level. However, according to the American Indian Nurses Association, there are only six American Indian nurses with master's degrees in psychiatric or mental health nursing. The immediate future holds little hope for a reversal of this shortage.

The AIANNA is currently conducting a survey of all graduate schools of psychiatric and mental health nursing which are either funded or not funded by the National Institute of Mental Health (NIMH) but which are in either case accredited by the National League for Nursing (NLN). The results of this survey will provide additional data on the state of the art in the training of American Indian and Alaska Native psychiatric and mental health nurses. Partial data results indicate the almost total absence of American Indians and Alaska Natives in graduate nursing education.

The long-range picture for a lessening of the shortage of American Indian and Alaska Native psychiatric nurses is as bleak as at present. In order to enter graduate studies, the nurse first must obtain a bachelor's degree. Table 2 shows data on American Indians in basic nursing education programs from a 1975 survey of all NLN accredited nursing programs.

TABLE 2

American Indians in Basic Nursing Education, 1975

Number of Indian Students	Number of Schools of Nursing
1	37
2	25
3	11
4–6	11
7–14	8
15–24	7

Source: American Indian and Alaska Native Nurses Association School of Nursing Survey, 1975.

According to Table 2, there could have been no more than 466 and no fewer than 325 American Indian and Alaska Natives enrolled in basic nursing education programs, that is, diploma, associate degree, and bachelor's degree programs. Of these, only 66 were enrolled in baccalaureate programs. In 1978 AIANNA repeated the school of nursing survey. As of 1978, there were only 96 American Indian and Alaska Native Nurses with bachelor's degrees. There were only 92 American Indian and Alaska Native students reported enrolled in all schools of nursing. These data document the dramatic present and future shortage of American Indian and Alaska Native psychiatric nurses and graphically demonstrate the failure of nursing education to prepare nurses from these groups to meet the great need in this society.

Mental Health Professionals and Service Delivery

Early investigations of culture were conducted by social anthropologists. Margaret Mead was one of the first to document through field work the culturally relative nature of value sets, mores and folkways. By the mid-1930s, social scientists from various disciplines were working together and borrowing intradisciplinary concepts, particularly anthropological and psychoanalytic theories, in an attempt to better understand the human condition. Benedict (1934), in her well-known *Patterns of Culture*, compared the universal and cultural definitions of normal and abnormal. Erik Erikson (1963) observed and analyzed differences in personality development and identity among Sioux Indians. Similarly, Devereaux (1951) defined cross-cultural psychotherapy as a situation "in which the therapist's knowledge of his . . . patients' culture . . . was exploited for therapeutic ends." According to Devereaux, in order to conduct psychotherapy, the therapist must have knowledge of both psychiatric theory and of the particular culture of the patient.

In addition to psychotherapy, there are other interventions available to the psychiatric-mental health nurse for which a knowledge of culture is equally as important. Moreover, the practice of psychiatric-mental health nursing is an intrapersonal process that involves the nurse, as a person, as well as the client.

Every human being is a product of some culture which dictates how that individual perceives and interprets the world around him (Benedict, 1934). That health care deliverers and social scientists are not immune to defining the world in terms of their own culture has been documented. Torrey (1970), Menninger (1971), and Bergman (1971) have discussed erroneous labeling by white scientists regarding the use of *peyote.* Torrey, in comparing the actual effectiveness of Indian medicine men and women and the white psychiatrist, claims that perceived effectiveness has been more in terms of the observer's culture than in terms of actual effectiveness. Medicine men and women have the same rate of success as do white psychiatrists when each works within their respective cultures. In a content analysis of Bureau of Indian Affairs literature and literature by Indian authors, Levine (1971) demonstrates a wide divergence between the two in terms of describing American Indians. Kekahbah and Wood (1971) demonstrated via in-depth interviews a mismatch between non-Indian deliverers and Indian consumers of health in attitudes toward cultural values. Levine (1971) discussed the fact that most therapists are products of the white culture and that the professional's culture affects his or her ability to function in a different culture.

> The majority of psychotherapists are persons who have been social-ized in the Protestant ethic of middle to upper socio-economic status. This culture, having its own value systems, biases, and life styles, requires the therapist to find ways to transcend and over-come his experiences and thereby relate to a different culture and values. If the therapist does not make a meaningful attempt to do this, he is limited in his ability to understand another way of life (p. 10).

Levine cites studies that indicate that value congruence determines, at least in part, treatment of choice, judgment of progress and whether the patient is "popular" with the therapist (1971, p. 11). Also cited are studies that indicate that therapists' attitudes and emotions are related to, among other factors, race and social class and that "what is called 'transference problems' may really be the therapist's attitude and behavior toward the patient." Levine (1971) also cites Block's statement that before therapists judge the behavior of clients as being inappro-priate, they should be sure that patients are not realistically responding to some deprecatory attitude on the part of the therapists. Health professionals must be aware of the role their own culturalization has played in forming their attitudes and patterns of relating (Kekahbah and Wood, 1971). The problem arises when therapists attempt to work within a culture different from their own and fail to deal with the cultural differences. Failure to account for cultural variables leads to misunderstanding and misinterpretations of the client's thoughts, feeling and behavior due to different value sets, lifestyles and biases.

It seems obvious from the preceding discussion that in order to practice psychiatric nursing among American Indians and Alaska Natives, it is necessary for nurses to understand the part played by both their own culture and that of the clients in the nurse–client relationship. However, surveys of both graduate and undergraduate nursing education reveal a lack of cultural content, as illustrated in Table 3.

Table 3 was taken from the AIANNA 1975 School of Nursing Survey which included all NLN accredited schools of basic nursing education.

Of the 235 responding schools, 137 (58 percent) included nothing specific to the health care of American Indians; 71 schools (30 percent) included 1 to 2 hours; 12 schools (5 percent) included 3 to 4 hours and 15 schools (6 percent) included 5 to 6 hours in their respective curricula to connect specifically with the health care of Indian people.

The AIANNA survey of graduate programs asked for the number of credit hours devoted to each ethnic and racial group. Of the 42 questionnaires returned, 8 were not applicable, 5 responded to a postcard stating they had not received the questionnaire and 29 were tabulated. Of the 29 school responses tabulated, 6 reported having no hours of ethnic and racial health courses; 9 reported courses of a general nature but none that were ethnic- and racial-specific; and 14 reported curriculum content that was specific to the various ethnic

TABLE 3

Hours of Curricula Content Devoted to Health Care of American Indians

Number of Hours	Number of Schools
0	137
1–2	71
3–4	12
5–6	15
Total	235

Source: American Indian/Alaska Native Nurses Association School of Nursing Survey, 1975.

TABLE 4

Hours Devoted to Ethnic and Racial Health in Graduate Schools of Psychiatric Mental Health Nursing

School	American Indian	Asian American	Black American	Spanish-Speaking	Other
1	2	2	2	10	0
2	0	0	4	3	4
3	0	0	10	0	0
4	0	0	10	30	0
5	0	2	4	2	0
6	1	0	15	1	0
7	0	9	9	9	0
8	10	10	10	5	0
9	5	4	4	4	4
10	1	1	1	1	0
11	0	0	2	2	0
12	1	1	3	3	0
13	0	0	6	6	0
14	4	2	8	2	2
Total	24	31	88	78	10

and racial groups. Table 4 shows the number of hours reported by 14 graduate schools as being devoted to ethnic and racial health care.

According to Table 4, of the 14 graduate schools including ethnic and racial content in the curriculum, fewer hours are devoted specifically to the health of American Indians (24 hours) than to any other group.

Trends in Developing American Indian Content

The data presented thus far reveal that the presence of American Indian and Alaska Native content in nursing curricula is far from adequate. However, the presence of some content in the majority of graduate programs, as indicated by AIANNA surveys, can be interpreted as an extremely positive trend.

Papers written by American Indian and Alaska Native nurses in the early 1970s focused primarily on replacing the melting pot theory with that of cultural pluralism as a theoretical reference within nursing and nursing education (Kekahbah, 1975; Primeaux, 1975; Wood, 1974, 1975(a), 1975(b)). Less than ten years ago, based on the melting pot theory, the health care of the white population was considered "the norm" with members of the other ethnic and racial groups being viewed as individual deviants. That American Indian and Alaska Native content is included at all indicates a recognition by nursing education that norms are set by each ethnic and racial group and that individuals are measured against the normative values specific to each group.

According to discussions with nurse educators, there does seem to be a trend toward including anthropology as a prerequisite in prenursing at the undergraduate level. This trend indicates that nursing educators are beginning to understand that cultural concepts are as important to understanding the human condition as are concepts of physiology, anatomy, sociology and psychology. Nurses are now being prepared to do research and theory development—which are crucial to understanding minority content issues in nursing curriculum.

Today university programs include research as a requirement for the B.S.N. degree. This trend, together with an increase in the numbers of schools that require cross-cultural courses, is considered quite positive.

Another positive trend is a majority movement toward the acceptance and practice of holistic principles of health promotion. It is congruent with traditional American Indian and Alaska Native values and should be capitalized upon to decrease the mismatch between non-Indian provider and Indian recipient of health care. Also, within the majority culture, a greater number of single mothers are keeping their children—long a practice within American Indian and Alaska Native communities—rather than giving them up for adoption. Although it has yet to be reflected in nursing curricula, social scientists are beginning to recognize "single-parenting" as an alternate lifestyle and to develop social institutions to provide support systems to families with such lifestyles. Another phenomenon that is occurring within the majority culture is the involvement of the father in child care and concerns the option for fathers to assume legal custody in divorce actions.

Like the trend toward holistic health care, these two trends (single mothers keeping their children and single fathers assuming custody of their children) are congruent with traditional Indian values. As stated previously, white mental health professionals have an established pattern of ignoring the influence of culture on their behavior as well as on the behavior of their clients. Mental health professionals tend to automatically interpret the behavior of their clients based on their own culture and not the client's culture. Where the culture of the client does not match the culture of the therapist the probability is great that the therapist will misunderstand and misinterpret the behavior of the client. Although trends discussed previously do not directly influence the established pattern of ignoring cultural differences, they do indicate a lessening of the cultural differences themselves (at least in three areas).

The National Institute of Mental Health (NIMH) and other government agencies have stimulated program development relative to diverse culture. Further, the NIMH Minority Center has established doctoral fellowships for ethnic people of color. In addition to the immediate benefits brought about by these programs, NIMH has emphasized the importance of all cultures in society. The institute has been responsive to the needs of society and supportive of those institutions whose goals are to address those needs. The center's efforts have produced a greater number of American Indian and Alaska Native mental health professionals; decreased the probability of misunderstanding and misinterpretation between the therapist and the client; and stimulated efforts—vis-à-vis research, conferences and curricula development—to change the pattern of mental health professionals ignoring the influence of culture on the therapist–client relationship.

Framework for Developing American Indian Content

The field of nursing and the orientation of the American Indian and Alaska Native both involve an active process of recognizing and dealing with the many systems that combine to make up the human life experience. Concepts inherent in both orientations go well beyond the physical and affective, to the environmental domains, and reflect values that are now popularly referred to as "holistic." Another concept inherent in both nursing and American Indian and Alaska Native orientations is that of the life-span process, which is at all times flexible and responsive to the environmental system. In short, both groups have, as overriding themes, interest in and concern for the richness of humankind's experience in the environment.

In graduate psychosocial nursing curriculum, one sees these orientations reflected in the study of systems theory, as students elaborate upon undergraduate content in the areas of human development (intrapersonal, interpersonal, psychosocial, cognitive and physiological) and intervention levels (primary, secondary and tertiary). The focus moves beyond the individual to the couple, the family system, social system (group) and the community system (culture). Further, the educational arenas expand to include research juxtaposed with theory and practice, as students attempt to develop higher levels of clinical and academic competence.

Today nursing is an applied profession in the process of theory building, and the work of mental health professionals in other disciplines provides a theoretical framework for incorporating curriculum content in nursing on American Indians and Alaska Natives. Given the overall orientations of nursing and of American Indians and Alaska Natives, it seems appropriate to utilize the ecosystem framework as a basis for the curriculum task, as an ecosystem matrix is based upon systems research.

Trimble and Medicine (1976) have carefully reviewed the theory and process associated with their suggestion of the ecosystem matrix as an alternative model for the theoretical considerations in the mental health of Indians. They also point out that "the needs of the theorist may determine which levels are employed [on the matrix]" (p. 183). Similarly, the needs of the profession might also alter the matrix. As psychosocial nursing is an applied profession that uses many sciences, it seems feasible to develop two independent and interrelated ecosystems from which nurses extrapolate a cell or cells to meet their needs in understanding and providing quality care.

Psychosocial nursing deals with the social and psychological issues that clients and treatment environments present. Psychosocial nurses working with American Indians and Alaska Natives must address two other issues if they are to provide quality care: cultural concerns and tribal group—the latter being one of much potential confusion for novices, who have little knowledge of the many different tribes (and therefore cultures) which they erroneously combine to be "the American Indian culture."

The authors contend that the first ecosystem matrix for psychosocial nursing would have the following three dimensions: (1) the "linguistic family" level, which provides a manageable arena within which to process various tribes; (2) "cultural components"; and (3) "social status." The three dimensions of the matrix together with their subcomponents are presented in Table 5.

The first two levels are well reviewed in their respective bodies of literature (Gibson, 1980; Josephy, 1968; Swanton, 1946). Graduate student nurses will probably have had course work directed at level two in their undergraduate programs—either as an elective or as a requirement for the nursing degree. The University of Washington, for example, has an undergraduate course that addresses global cultural issues as they relate to health seeking and health care delivery behaviors. The components of the second level would not be new concepts to the graduate of that basic program. However, the first and third levels of analysis present components that represent alien terri-

TABLE 5

Dimensions of the Matrix

Levels of Analysis	Components
Linguistic family (Gibson, 1980)	Algonkian, Iroquoian, Siouian, Caddoan, Uto-Aztecan, Athapascan, Muskhogean, Tonoam, Salish, Shahaptian-Nez Perces.
Cultural variables	Values, Taboos, Customs, Sentiments
Social statuses (Parsons, 1953)	
Qualities	Intelligence and birthright
Performance	Roles in community and achievement
Possessions	Talents and skills and property

tory to the graduate. For example, the linguistic families level (first) represents an area of study that is not reflected in nursing curriculum—at any level. An occasional student might be enterprising enough to explore electives in the field of linguistics or in American Indian studies. By far, however, the majority will be unaware of this possibility for grouping the large number of American Indian and Alaska Native tribes. There are those who would advocate a "cultural areas" point of reference for this issue of grasping tribal groups. Wissler (1966) has been the primary advocate for this approach with Spencer and Jennings (1965) supporting the concept. Others (Josephy, 1968; Medicine, 1972) have criticized the latter approach as an artificial approach with negative consequences for the image of the Indian.

The third level—social statuses—is different from the Hollingshead (1959) socioeconomic scales well known to social science professionals. Hollingshead's groupings, however, are not adequate in understanding and working with American Indians and Alaska Natives. Within the Indian communities, social status is based not upon economics but upon local prestige. A review of the sociological literature reveals that Parsons (1953) presented a functional approach to stratification and that Davis and Moore (1949) had earlier discussed the functional importance of different positions (Reissman, 1959). Parsons's (1953) division of statuses into three categories seems to have promise for nurses who are attempting to understand and work with American Indians and Alaska Natives. Parsons's work outlines and defines the major categories as qualities, performances and possessions. He goes on to define qualities as "those properties of a unit which can be evaluated independently of any change in its relations to objects in its situation, but may be ascribed to the unit as a whole" (p. 94).

Reissman (1959) defines qualities as those "characteristics that are ascribed . . . such as intelligence or birthright" (p. 72). Performances are judgments of one's activity as compared with others—or one's achievements. Finally, possessions include objects that are owned or controlled (possessions and skills are included here by Reissman). Elaboration upon these three categories relative to American Indian and Alaska Native communities could logically include six variables useful in judging and ranking status. Those six variables are (1) intelligence; (2) birthright (qualities); (3) roles in the community; (4) achievements (performances); (5) talents and skills; and (6) property (possessions). From this three dimensional matrix, with its variables, one develops a $10 \times 4 \times 6$ cube of 240 cells from which to develop components of nursing curriculum. Figure 3 demonstrates the matrix graphically.

Figure 4—The Nursing Education Matrix—embodies the elements of professional nursing and is likewise three dimensional. The result is a $5 \times 3 \times 3$ cube of 45 cells from which the nurse can extrapolate

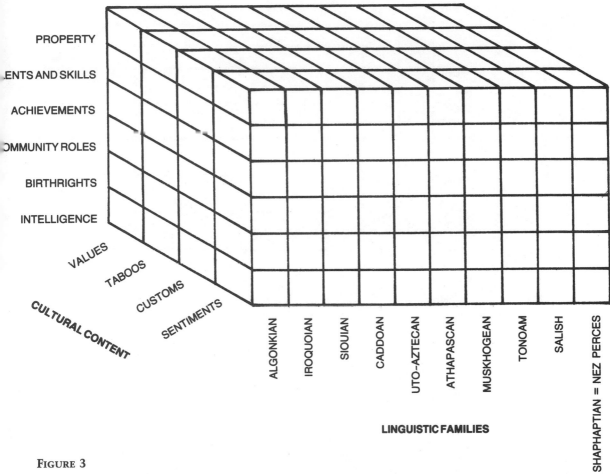

FIGURE 3

American Indian Matrix

cells to meet her academic and practice needs. Figure 4 reflects the matrix with its variables along each axis. The treatment focus variable reflects those natural groupings of persons with whom the psychosocial nurse interacts. These elements are also the predominant areas explored within graduate nursing curriculum. The intervention levels axis is reflective of Caplan's (1961) notions—concepts which are well integrated into practice at both the undergraduate and graduate levels of *all* nursing practice. Finally, the value of the education component variable cannot be stressed enough as critical to practice and theory building. It is from this axis that nursing will increase its movement into the arena of an independent science and become a model for other professions.

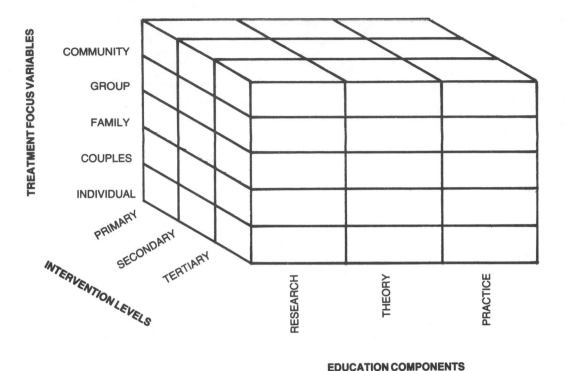

FIGURE 4

Nursing Education Matrix

Guiding Principles

The surrounding community of a college of nursing provides the population from which the students are drawn and to which graduates of nursing programs must respond when practicing nursing care. Because individuals behave in the phenomological set of their specific culture—a factor which has a profound influence upon one's response to health and illness—curricula must be responsive to the differing needs of different communities. Communities are formed for the purpose of providing people with a way to meet their common needs for shelter, health, protection, education and general welfare. A college of nursing is a community agency organized as a means for meeting specific needs of that community. In order to respond to those community needs adequately, the school of nursing must assess the specific health needs of the particular community in which it is located. Therefore, the curriculum is designed to provide nurse practitioners who can meet these needs.

For those communities of which American Indians and Alaska Natives are a part, schools of nursing must assess the specific health needs and design curricula to train nurse practitioners who can meet these needs. American Indian and Alaska Native cultural content can be said to be present in curriculum only when it can be identified, named, described and measured. Such cultural content can be said to be a meaningful, integral or important part of curriculum only when there are credit hours attached or a requirement is made for graduation and is valid only when content and process are in terms defined by the American Indian and Alaska Native communities in addition to those defined by the nursing community.

The following are factors that may serve to further American Indian and Alaska Native content development and integration and are presented in outline form.

Strategies for Institutional Change and Faculty Development

Social Factors

- revitalization of individual ethnic identity while continuing the process of cultural integration or developing a common world culture
- revolution in values
  - —emphasis on health and health care as an inalienable human right
  - —equal and comprehensive care and treatment for all people
  - —greater tolerance for individual differences
  - —changing standards of communication
  - —changing views of morality
- change in family structure
  - —family unit changes
  - —family member role changes
  - —meaning of marriage changing
- education level
  - —increase in education level of the population
  - —decrease in social and educational deprivation
  - —increase in equal opportunity for all people
  - —more efficient uses of human resources

Political Factors

- redistribution of governmental controls and resources in order to bring about equitable sharing of power among all people in society
  - —reduction of industry and business influence and controls over resources
  - —increase in support of health and health agencies, e.g.,

prepaid insurance coverage, control over standards of health care, education and training of health workers, larger, more efficient health care systems with more flexible and mobile subsystems

• increase in organized citizens' groups, e.g., Indian Coalition of Tribes; exertion of pressure by power groups to effect change; increased involvement of public in social, health, and political issues; organization of women into a powerful force

Environmental Factors

• population shifts to new urban centers

• crowding—causing increases in psychiatric problems, thought and behavior disorders, suicide, drug abuse, alcoholism, battered children

• encroachment on Indian lands

• exploitation of mineral, water and land resources by industrialists

Technological Factors

• more sophisticated use of computers and information banks

• more sophisticated technology for diagnosis and treatment of health problems

These factors occur in the course of the life span of a student in nursing and have definite implications for minority curriculum content. For each factor isolated, the curriculum builder needs to answer questions such as the following:

• What are the nursing curriculum commitment implications of this factor?

• What are the nursing behaviors that will be necessary for the nurse to function within the ramifications of this factor?

• What content will enable the nurse to develop the desired behaviors?

The answers to these questions should provide the college of nursing with a set of theoretical curriculum framework implications; terminal behaviors; and essential content that will be a source of reference for structuring courses.

Strategies to initiate curriculum change and faculty development can be approached by having a task force of American Indian and Alaska Native professional nurses advise the institutions of higher learning on specifics pertaining to the culture of American Indians and Alaska Natives. The approach would not be as difficult as many educators and curriculum developers may think. The courses that are required to obtain a degree in psychiatric nursing could be modified to include cultural specifics on American Indian and Alaska Natives.

There isn't any possible way to include all the traditions and value systems of the many different tribal and native groups, but many common traditions prevail which could be incorporated into the curriculum that would provide the student with knowledge of the American Indian and Alaska Native culture. Specific skills could be learned that could be applied by the students in working with this particular population.

Faculty having difficulty locating resource material for content development are encouraged to utilize the National Center for American Indian and Alaska Native Mental Health Research and Development in Portland, Oregon. They have an extensive annotated bibliography which nursing faculty can use. Another strategy is the inclusion of American Indian and Alaska Native nurses on the faculty. The difficulty of utilizing this strategy is recognized in view of the extreme shortage of American Indian and Alaska Native nurses. In the absence of available American Indian and Alaska Native nurses for full-time faculty appointments, it is possible to utilize them for consultation in curriculum development. Resource people can be located through the Registry of the American Indian and Alaska Native Nurses Association.

Faculty can be developed through organized "in-service" programs wherein American Indian and Alaska Native nurses work with faculty both individually and in groups. The goals of these work sessions should be the following:

- to increase knowledge of the role of culture and the human condition;
- to increase sensitivity of faculty for cultures other than their own;
- to assist with problem solving relative to a specific and immediate problem such as
    —a "problem" faculty member(s) who seems insensitive
    —a student who is in danger of failing
    —intrafaculty cross-cultural conflict.

The knowledge base of the faculty can be increased through attendance at conferences such as those sponsored by the American Indian and Alaska Native Nurses Association. Formal papers are presented during these annual conferences by American Indian and Alaska Native health professionals and other health professionals experienced in working with Indian people.* Presentations are made by highly re-

* Continuing education units are usually awarded by the state nurses association where the conferences are held.

spected members of the American Indian and Alaska Native community such as tribal chairmen, medicine men and women and community health representatives. Members from the general community who have knowledge of and influence over government and social factors affecting economic, health and educational conditions of American Indians are present and active. Attendance at one of these conferences would most likely provide the only opportunity for most non-Indian faculty members to meet American Indians and Alaska Natives in a sociocultural environment more Indian than white.

Theoretical Needs

There is a need to develop theory for American Indians in the following areas:

- growth and development, development and use of defense mechanisms, family dynamics, group dynamics;
- cross-cultural interpersonal relationships and application of the various treatment modalities;
- child-care patterns and cultural values; and
- relationship between cultural identity and mental illness.

Research Needs

The following areas of research are needed for theory development:

- the extent to which various modalities of psychotherapy are applicable to American Indians and Alaska Natives;
- relative success rate of psychotherapists who are of the same culture as the patient and of those who are not;
- the effect of cultural values of the therapist on her or his ability as a therapist;
- effectiveness of different treatment modalities by tribe;
- epidemiological variables by tribe; and
- definition of mental health by tribe.

Recommendations

We recommend that: American Indian and Alaska Native Nurses be members on the National League of Nursing and state board examination committees; cross-cultural material become part of the graduate nursing program curriculum content; standards of nursing practice include cross-cultural values; psychiatric nursing students be placed with American Indian and Alaska Native programs for their practicum; a task force be formed of American Indian and Alaska Native people to develop specific cultural content for curriculum developers to integrate into the nursing courses; and a model curriculum be developed and piloted by American Indian and Alaska Native nurses and made available to schools of nursing for implementation and utilization nationally.

Federal and private monies need to be utilized in those colleges, universities and organizations that have "track records" of producing American Indian and Alaska Native nurses and nurses capable of working in the Indian community. These monies should not be misused by bribing various colleges and universities to give "lip service" of interest only as long as the monies are there.

References

American Indian/Alaska Native Nurses Association. Survey of schools of professional nursing, 1974–75 (repeated 1978). Unpublished manuscript, American Indian/Alaska Native Nurses Association, Norman, Oklahoma.

Benedict, R. *Patterns of culture.* Boston: Houghton-Mifflin, 1934.

Bergman, R. L. Boarding schools and the psychological problems of Indian children. Unpublished manuscript, University of New Mexico, 1971.

Cahn, E. S. *Our brother's keeper.* New York: World Publishing, 1969.

Caplan, G. *An approach to community mental health.* New York: Grune and Stratton, 1961.

Davis, K., & Moore, W. E. Some principles of stratification. In L. Wilson & W. L. Kolb (Eds.), *Sociological analysis.* New York: Harcourt, Brace, 1949.

Devereaux, G. *Reality and dream: The psychotherapy of a Plains Indian.* New York: International University Press, 1951.

Erikson, E. *Childhood and society.* New York: W. W. Norton, 1963.

Farb, P. *Man's rise to civilization.* New York: Avon Books, 1969.

Gibson, A. M. *The American Indian: Prehistory to the present.* Lexington, MA.: D. C. Health, 1980.

Hollingshead, A. Three-factor index of social position. Unpublished manuscript, Yale University, New Haven, Connecticut, 1959.

Josephy, A. M., Jr. *The Indian heritage of America.* New York: Bantam Books, 1968.

Kekahbah, J. Nursing research in the Indian community. Paper presented at the meeting of the American Indian/Alaska Native Nurses Association, Lawrence, Kansas, 1975.

Kekahbah, J., & Wood, R. A study of the patterns of relating between the deliverers of health care services and the consumers of health care services within the Indian community. Unpublished manuscript, American Indian/Alaska Native Nurses Association, Norman, Oklahoma, 1971.

Kluckhohn, C. *Mirror for man: Survey of human behavior and social attitudes.* New York: Whittlesey House, 1949.

Kramer, J. R. *The American minority community.* New York: Thomas Y. Crowell, 1970.

Lenburg, C. B. *Open learning and career mobility in nursing.* New York: C. V. Mosby, 1975.

Levine, F. An exploratory study of the accuracy of the Bureau of Indian Affairs: A representative of the American Indian. Unpublished manuscript, Rutgers University, New Brunswick, New Jersey, 1971.

Medicine, B. The anthropologist as the Indian's image maker. In J. Henry (Ed.), *The American Indian reader.* San Francisco: Indian Historian Press, 1972.

Menninger, K. Discussion. *American Journal of Psychiatry,* 1971, *128* (3), 699.

Parsons, T. A revised analytical approach to the theory of social stratification. In. R. Bendix & S. M. Lipset (Eds.), *Class, status, and power.* Glencoe, IL.: Free Press, 1953.

President's Commission on Mental Health. *Task Panel Reports,* Appendix 3. Washington, D.C.: U.S. Government Printing Office, 1978.

Primeaux, M. Indians in nursing education. Paper presented at the meeting of the American Indian/Alaska Native Nurses Association, Lawrence, Kansas, 1975.

Reissman, L. *Class in American society.* Glencoe, IL.: Free Press, 1959.

Swanton, J. R. *The Indians of the Southeastern United States.* Washington, D.C.: U.S. Government Printing Office, 1946.

Torrey, E. F. Mental Health services for American Indians and Eskimoes. *Community Mental Health*, 1970, 6 (6), 455–63.

Trimble, J. E., & Medicine, B. Development of theoretical models and levels of interpretation in mental health. In S. Tax (Ed.), *World anthropology*. The Hague: Mouton Publishers, 1976.

Wissler, C. *Indians of the United States.* New York: Doubleday, 1966.

Wood, R. Change through affirmative action within a health care delivery system. Paper presented at the meeting of the American Indian/Alaska Native Nurses Association, San Francisco, California, 1974.

Wood, R. A cross-cultural approach to health care. Paper presented at the meeting of the Oklahoma American Public Health Association, Tulsa, Oklahoma, 1975. (a)

Wood, R. Ethnicity and health care: The American Indian and health. Paper presented at the meeting of the National League for Nurses, New Orleans, Louisiana, 1975. (b)

World Health Organization. Report of the World Health Organization, United States Committee on World Health Organizations, New York, 1956.

Bibliography

Allport, G. *Becoming.* New Haven: Yale University Press, 1955.

Allport, G. *The nature of prejudice.* Boston: Beacon Press, 1954.

American Indian/Alaska Native Nurses Association. *Health careers.* Department of Health, Education and Welfare, Indian Health Service (contract no. 246-75-C-2302), Norman, Oklahoma, 1976.

Attneave, C. *Mental health of American Indians: Problems, prospects, and challenges for the decade ahead.* Paper presented at the meeting of the American Psychological Association, Honolulu, Hawaii, September, 1972.

Auchlmayr, R. Cultural understanding: A key to acceptance. *Nursing Outlook,* 1969, *17,* 20–23.

Bain, H. W., & Goldthorpe, G. Sioux lookout project—A model of health care delivery. *Canadian Medical Association,* 1972, *107,* 523.

Bettleheim, B. & Janowitz, M. *Dynamics of prejudice.* New York: Harper, 1950.

Bettleheim, B. *The children of the dream.* London: The Macmillan Company, Collier-Macmillan Ltd., 1969.

Branch, M., & Paxton, O. *Providing safe nursing care for ethnic people of color.* New York: Appleton-Century-Crofts, 1976.

Brink, P. (Ed.). *Transcultural nursing, a book of readings.* Englewood Cliffs, N.J.: Prentice Hall, 1976.

Buckley, W. *Modern systems research for the behavioral scientist: A sourcebook.* Chicago: Aldine, 1968.

Campbell, T., & Chang, B. Health care of the Chinese in America. In B. Spradley (Ed.), *Contemporary community nursing.* Boston: Little, Brown & Co., 1975.

Ciba Foundation Symposium. *Transcultural psychiatry.* Boston: Little, Brown & Co., 1965.

Cohen, Y. *Man in adaptation: The cultural present.* Chicago: Aldine, 1968.

Cooper, J. B., & Singer, D. N. The role of emotion in prejudice. *Journal of Social Psychology,* 1956, *44,* 241–47.

Cox, O. *Caste, class, and race.* New York: Doubleday, 1948.

Damon, A. Race, ethnic group, and disease. *Journal of Social Biology,* 1969, *16* (2), 69–71, 73–75, 77.

Eiduson, B. T. The commune-reared child. In J. D. Noshpitz (Ed.), *Basic handbook of child psychiatry, I.* New York: Basic Books, 1979.

Fellow, D. *Mosaic of America's ethnic minorities.* New York: John Wiley & Sons, 1972.

Franklin, J. H. *From slavery to freedom.* New York: Knopf, 1967.

Fuchs, E., & Havighurst, R. J. *To live on their earth.* Garden City, N.J.: Anchor Press/Doubleday, 1973.

Hall, E. T. *Beyond culture.* New York: Anchor Press/Doubleday, 1976.

Henle, M., & Hubbell, M. B. Egocentricity in adult conversation. *Journal of Social Psychology,* 1938, *9,* 227–34.

Hilgard, J. R., Newman, M. F., & Fisk, F. Strengths of adult ego following childhood bereavement. *American Journal of Orthopsychiatry,* 1960, *30,* 788–98.

Hoebel, E. A. *Anthropology: The study of man.* New York: McGraw-Hill, 1966.

Honigmann, J. *Culture and personality.* New York: Harper and Brothers, 1954.

Hsu, F. *Aspects of culture and personality.* New York: Abelard-Schuman, 1954.

Humphrey, P. Learning about poverty and health. *Nursing Outlook,* 1974, *22,* 7.

Hunt, R. *Personality and culture.* New York: The Natural Museum Press, 1967.

Jilek, W. G. Indian healing power: Indigenous therapeutic practices in the Pacific Northwest. *Psychiatric Annals*, 1974, *4*, 13–21.

Jiron, P. Diabetes and the American Indian. Lawrence, KS.: American Indian Nurses Association, 1975.

Johnson, C. Nursing and Mexican-American folk medicine. *Nursing Forum*, 1964, *3*, *104–113*.

Kiev, A. *Magic, faith, & healing: Studies in primitive psychiatry today*. New York: The Free Press, 1964.

Kiev, A. *Transcultural psychiatry*. New York: The Free Press, 1972.

Kluckhohn, C., & Murray, H. (Eds.) *Personality in nature, society, and culture*. New York: Knopf, 1967.

Kniep-Hardy, M., & Burkhardt, M. A. Nursing the Navajo. *American Journal of Nursing*, 1977, *77*, 95–96.

Kosa, J., & Zola, I. K. *Poverty and health: A sociological analysis* (Rev. Ed.). Cambridge, MA.: Harvard University Press, 1975.

Leninger, M. *Towards conceptualization of transcultural health care systems: Concepts and a model*. Philadelphia, PA.: F. A. Davis, 1976.

Leninger, M. *Nursing and anthropology*. New York: John Wiley & Sons, 1970.

Leninger, M. The cultural context of behavior: Spanish-speaking Americans and nursing care. In B. Spradley (Ed.), *Contemporary community nursing*. Boston: Little, Brown & Co., 1975.

McCauley, M. A. Indian nurse considers cultural traits. *American Nurse*, 1975, 7 (5), 5, 15.

Mead, M. Review of contributions to anthropology/psychoanalytic psychotherapy: Major contributions from 1936 to 1966. In G. Devereaux (Ed.), *Reality and dream: The Psychotherapy of a Plains Indian*. New York: International University Press, 1951.

Mead, M. *New lives for old*. New York: Dell Publishing Co., 1956.

Murray, R., & Zenther, J. *Nursing concepts for health promotion*. Englewood Cliffs, N.J.: Prentice-Hall, 1975.

Opler, M. K. *Culture, psychiatry, and human values*. Springfield, IL.: Charles C. Thomas, 1956.

Opler, M. K. (Ed.). *Culture and mental health*. New York: Macmillan, 1959.

Powdermaker, H. *Probing our prejudice*. New York: Harper & Row, 1941.

Primeaux, M. Caring for the American Indian patient. *American Journal of Nursing*, 1977, *77*, 91–94.

Rakin, A. I. *Growing up in the Kibbutz*. New York: Springer, 1965.

Robertson, H. R. Removing barriers to health care. *Nursing Outlook*, 1969, *17* (9), 43–46.

Rubel, A. J. Concepts of disease in Mexican-American culture. *American Anthropology*, 1960, *62*, 795–814.

Saunders, L. *Cultural differences and medical care*. New York: Russell Sage Foundation, 1954.

Shore, J. H., & Von Fumetti, B. Three alcohol programs for American Indians—642 cases. *American Journal of Psychiatry*, 1972, *128*, 1450–54.

Sohier, R. Gaining awareness of cultural differences: A case example. In M. Leninger (Ed.), *Transcultural health care issues and conditions*. Philadelphia, PA.: F. A. Davis, 1976.

Spector, R. E. *Cultural diversity in health and illness*. New York: Appleton-Century-Crofts, 1979.

Spiro, M. *Children of the Kibbutz*. Cambridge, MA.: Harvard University Press, 1958.

Spradley, B. W. (Ed.). *Contemporary community nursing.* Boston: Little, Brown & Co., 1975.

Starlie, F. *Nursing and the social conscience.* New York: Appleton-Century-Crofts, 1970.

Suchman, E. A. Sociomedical variations among ethnic groups. *American Journal of Sociology,* 1964, *70,* 319–331.

Suchman, E. A. Social patterns of illness and medical care. *Journal of Health and Human Behavior,* 1965, *6,* 2–16.

Symposium on Cultural and Biological Diversity in Health Care. *Nursing Clinics of North America,* 1977, *12,* 1.

Trimble, J. E. Value differences of the American Indian: Concerns for the concerned counselor. In P. Pedersen, W. Lonner, & J. Drapuns (Eds.), *Issues in cross-cultural counseling.* Honolulu: University Press of Hawaii, 1975.

von Bertalanffy, L. *General system theory.* New York: George Braziller, 1968.

Welch, S., Comer, J., & Steinman, M. Some social and attitudinal correlates of health care among Mexican-Americans. *Journal of Health and Social Behavior,* 1973, *14,* 205–13.

Werner, E. E. *Cross-cultural child development: A view from the planet earth.* Monterey, CA.: Brooks/Cole, 1969.

HECTOR GONZALES   JANIE WILSON
ELSIE GILDE-RUBIO   BERTA A. MEJIA

CHAPTER **16**

Hispanic Psychiatric-Mental Health Nursing

It is projected that by 1980 Hispanics will constitute the largest ethnic group in the United States. Compared with the general population, less than 50 percent of Hispanics utilize existing mental health services. The major factors responsible for underutilization of services are inaccessibility, unavailability, unacceptability and sociocultural inconsistency of delivery. Whenever Hispanics do receive them, mental health services are often of inferior quality. Frequently treatment is given exclusively by paraprofessionals in understaffed clinics (Casas and Keefe, 1978). There is a serious shortage of mental health professionals adequately prepared to provide culturally consistent services. If such services are to be rendered, professionals must develop a knowledge base that includes a thorough understanding of and sensitivity to the linguistic and sociocultural characteristics of their clients.

A growing body of literature addresses ethnic issues pertaining to nursing in general, at times including concepts relevant to psychiatric-mental health nursing (e.g. Branch, 1976; Brink, 1976; and Brownlee, 1978). However, a comprehensive text that addresses systematic psychiatric-mental health nursing assessment, treatment and evaluation models for any ethnic group and Hispanics in particular has yet to be written.

Culturally consistent information about Hispanics at all levels of education of psychiatric-mental health nurses is urgently needed. If there is to be change in direct and preventive services to Hispanics, particular attention needs to be given to graduate programs. Graduates from these programs, in addition to being prepared to deliver direct care, are also potential faculty members as well as candidates for positions in administration, policy making and management. These professionals would increase the potential for providing culturally consistent psychiatric-mental health nursing care to Hispanics. The need for doctorally prepared nurses to research the interaction of

431

cultural variables with mental health and psychopathology is also of vital importance.

Because of the national trend toward integrating psychiatric-mental health nursing content in undergraduate curricula, young graduates tend not to view psychiatric-mental health nursing as a specialty. Such an outlook has resulted in declining enrollments in graduate psychiatric-mental health nursing programs. This decline further diminishes the number of prospective Hispanic students and, consequently, the availability pool of Hispanic psychiatric nurses.

In designing psychiatric-mental health nursing curriculum content relevant to Hispanics, we will consider nursing-related, nursing-process, and nursing-occupation content (Gonzalez, 1966). Nursing-related content incorporating anthropology, sociology, psychology, ethnomedicine and other disciplines and their contributions to the study of Hispanics should be examined so as to further determine what additional content should be included in nursing courses. The content should bear particular relation to nursing practice, ethics, legal aspects and setting. Nursing-process content includes concepts which will meet the specific needs of Hispanics. Concepts that may be specific, but not limited, to psychiatric-mental health nursing may include Hispanic family values and structures, cultural beliefs, ethnopsychiatric practices and folk health beliefs, child-rearing practices and values, language and communication patterns and psychodynamics of the acculturation process. Nursing-occupation content includes concepts in nursing courses which explain the ethics, legal aspects, history and self-development necessary for an effective nurse. Included is the so-called bedside manner inherent to all nursing practice, but which is of greater importance in psychiatric nursing. This bedside manner should be consistent and reflect knowledge of Hispanic cultures.

Content that addresses attitudes, prejudice, bias, racism, cultural differences and the various cultures, including one's own, should be incorporated into nursing curricula. Students should be taught to meet the psychiatric-mental health needs of Hispanic clients and should be evaluated in both theoretical and clinical terms. Psychiatric-mental health nursing content dealing with the needs of Hispanics should be institutionalized as an integral component of the curriculum in a nursing school.

This chapter is concerned with the development of Hispanic psychiatric-mental health nursing content for inclusion in nursing curricula and focuses on (1) trends and deficits in the state of the art of Hispanic content integration into psychiatric-mental health education in nursing; (2) a framework of theoretical content needs in Hispanic curriculum development; (3) research needs; (4) guiding principles for Hispanic content development and integration into nursing curricula; (5) strategies for better integration of Hispanic content in psychiatric-mental health curriculum development; and (6) policy recommendations at federal, state and institutional levels.

Culturally consistent psychiatric nursing care to Hispanics refers to nursing care that incorporates and is in consonance with the psychological and sociological referents of the Hispanic client. In a sense, this type of care is descriptive rather than prescriptive.

Hispanic subgroup refers to those persons whose ethnic heritage can be traced to Mexico, the Dominican Republic, Puerto Rico, Cuba, Central America, South America or Spain and who are now residing in the United States. The term may also embrace those persons who represent an amalgam of these origins and, in some instances, whose heritage overlaps with American Indian culture. The latter would most likely include those persons of Mexican origin residing in the southwestern region of the United States.

Concepts and Terms

To meet the psychiatric-mental health needs of Hispanics, culturally consistent assessment, evaluation and treatment skills, as well as theoretical content must be included in nursing curricula. The Western Interstate Commission for Higher Education in Nursing (WICHEN) developed a project called "Models for Introducing Cultural Diversity in Nursing Curricula." Forty schools of nursing and eight health service agencies in the western part of the United States participated. The activities of these schools and agencies were shared through workshops offered at seven sites across the United States. The workshops were concerned with changing, updating or revising significant parts of the overall curriculum through instruction and experiences that prepared students to provide nursing intervention to persons from specific ethnic groups (WICHEN, 1977).

Another effort toward the inclusion of minority content in nursing is the book, *Providing Safe Nursing Care for Ethnic People of Color* (Branch, 1976). The book, a collective effort, was planned and developed by a group of ethnic nurses of color. The authors argue that the deficit-deficient concept as related to people of color has resulted in the denial of the positive aspects of cultural health traditions and systems. The authors describe a set of new approaches to nursing care the outcomes of which are redirected toward enhancing a state of wellness for people of color. Additionally, the authors present models designed to supplement existing curricula. Although the WICHEN project and Branch addressed the need for minority content, neither of the two projects relates specifically to the Hispanic client.

Trends and Deficits in the State of the Art

Trends

Deficits

An extensive review of the literature did not reveal any studies directly related to the identification of the psychiatric-mental health perceptions or needs of Hispanics, nor to the provision of psychiatric-mental health nursing care to Hispanic clients. In one investigation, Wilson (1978) studied the perception, causation, and resolution of illness in a group of Mexican Americans and, from the data obtained, hypothesized that mental illness is perceived as *mal puesto* (a folk term for illness) by that group. There is no evidence in the literature that the hypothesis has been tested.

A review of the literature also failed to provide information about the number of psychiatric nurses who would qualify as providers of socioculturally consistent psychiatric-mental health nursing care to Hispanic clients. One might surmise that nurses of Hispanic heritage might have a bicultural-bilingual orientation that may make them culturally sensitive to their Hispanic clients' needs. There are no data, however, to indicate that their education or life experiences have adequately prepared them to understand how Hispanic culture interacts with intrapsychic, interpersonal and psychosocial variables to produce mental health or psychopathology. This is not to deny that a Hispanic bilingual-bicultural nurse would not have a better understanding of the cultural referents. But no data were identified to support the notion that Hispanic nurses provide better psychiatric-mental health nursing care to Hispanic clients than do non-Hispanic nurses. Investigations need to be conducted with both groups of nurses.

Framework for Curriculum Development

The importance of including culturally specific content about Hispanics in nursing curricula has been previously addressed. A structural framework that could be utilized by schools of nursing to incorporate curriculum content dealing with the psychiatric-mental health nursing care needed by Hispanics is presented in Figure 1. Following Figure 1 is a taxonomical elaboration and description of the content identified in the model. This taxonomical elaboration is not intended to be limiting or exhaustive in its analysis. Schools of nursing are encouraged to conduct further interpolation or extrapolation. Whether some factors in Figure 1, which is a guide, are applicable depends on the Hispanic subgroup under consideration and its degree of acculturation.

A Taxonomical Elaboration of Figure 1

Our framework addresses a totality of life experiences necessary to a thorough understanding of issues of Hispanic mental health. It provides concepts relevant to psychiatric-mental health nursing practices with Hispanic clients and allows for formulating culturally sensitive tools for use with these clients. In outline form, it forms a base from which to integrate curriculum materials on Hispanics. The material may be

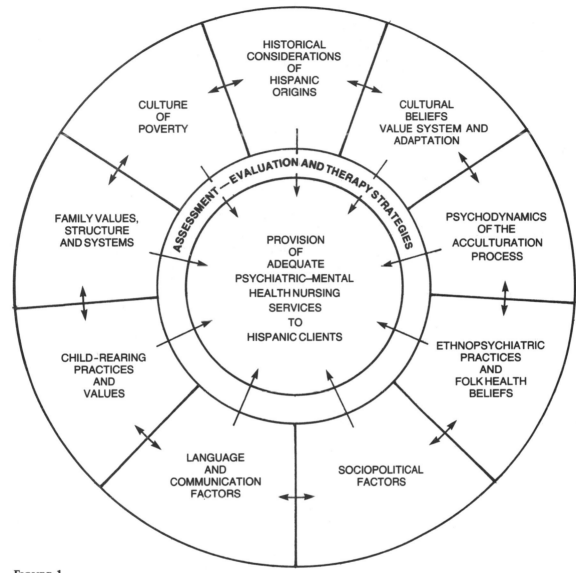

Model Depicting Culturally Consistent Curriculum Content in Psychiatric-Mental Health Nursing for Hispanics

modified or updated as more information is made available on Hispanic subcultures.

Historical Considerations of Hispanic Origins

- Hybrid ethnic origins
- Racial compositions
- Previous religious orientation

- Previous value systems
- Previous world view perspective
- Previous health beliefs

Culture of Poverty

- Substandard housing
- Underemployment
- Unemployment
- Prejudice
- Racism

Cultural Beliefs, Value System and Adaptation

- Sociological dynamics of acculturation and assimilation
- Value orientation variants as determined by urban or rural environment orientation and/or social class membership
- Process of acculturation and its contribution toward family unity or disruption
- Social pressures within the Hispanic culture that encourage nonacculturation
- Social pressures outside the Hispanic culture that discourage acculturation
- Determinants of positive cultural adaptation in the face of negative social forces, i.e., discrimination or rejection
- Evaluation of bicultural-bilingual adaptation and its contribution to positive self-image

Psychodynamics of the Acculturation Process

- Theoretical understanding of the process of psychological ego identity and its relationship to development of cultural identity
- Theoretical psychodynamics of the failure to establish cultural identity and the possible adoption of a "screen identity"
- Psychodynamic treatment approach to cultural identity disorders

Language and Communication Factors

- Conceptual and semantic differences between Spanish and English
- Failure to adopt English as a second language and its correlation with adherence to psychopathologic symptomatology

Family Values, Structure and Systems

- Hispanic authoritarian family pattern and its similarity to the lower-class white American authoritarian family pattern

    —Role assignments

    —Value system

- Psychodynamics of the roles "machismo" and "marianismo" and the maintenance of these roles
- Values of family cohesiveness and interdependency vs. the American cherished values of individual autonomy, independence and emphasis on achievement

Ethnopsychiatric Practices and Folk Health Beliefs

- Hispanic folk medicine and herbs
- *Curanderismo* (healer that uses herbs)
- *Espiritismo* (spiritual healer)
- *Santeria* (healer)
- *Dichos/Consejos* (advisor who speaks the language)

Childrearing Practices and Values

- Cultural value placed on obedience, politeness and respect toward adults vs. the devaluation of equalitarianism: contribution toward the development of learned compliance vs. assertiveness and passive aggression vs. competitiveness
- Value placed on family honor and responsibility and its contribution toward developing values that are group-oriented, and group controlled vs. individual satisfaction and achievement
- Understanding conflicting values
  - —Expectation that children will adhere to a strict disciplinary code while expecting the development of autonomous behavior
  - —Expectation that a child will learn to take responsibility through independent exploration while offering minimal adult control and support
- The Psychodynamics of the Sex Role Socialization Process
  - —Mother's role in inducting her son into the "macho" role and her daughter into the acceptance of the role of abnegating female
  - —Father's role in maintaining the system
- Accelerated acculturation rate of children as compared with their parents and the subsequent conflicts that arise as a result of these acculturation gaps
  - —Parental reaction to perceived loss of control, i.e., stronger adherence to cherished cultural values
  - —Rejection of cultural values by the child
- Determination of who actually sets disciplinary standards in the case of an extended family living arrangement

Sociopolitical Factors

- Bilingual education
  —Research
  —Legislation
- Development of culturally sensitive assessment tools for reliability and validity
  —IQ tests
  —Developmental assessment tools
- Utilization of mental health facilities by Hispanics
- Education of culturally sensitive mental health clinicians

Research Needs in Hispanic Curriculum Development

Considering the dearth of research related to psychiatric-mental health nursing and Hispanic clients in both nursing education and practice, research is needed in all areas. In particular, investigations need to be directed toward clients, faculty, student educational outcomes, practice outcomes and attitudes of health providers toward Hispanics.

Clients

Research with clients should be directed toward ethnopsychiatric practices and folk health beliefs; language and communication factors, cultural beliefs, family values and structures; child-rearing practices and values; sociopolitical factors; and the psychodynamics of the acculturation process. The approach to be taken for research of this nature has been described by Frake (1968). The ethnoscientific research approach allows clients to relate their experiences from their own points of view and is therefore recommended for obtaining data when appropriate. This research approach was used by Bush, Ullom and Osborne (1975) to explore the definition of *mental health* as conceptualized by central city residents and psychiatric-mental health professionals. An example of a Black female who resided in a central city area was selected for presentation in this chapter.

The question was asked, "What does the term *mental health* bring to mind?" (p. 132). The informant concluded that, in her terminology, the equivalent of *mental health* was *feeling good*. She proceeded to provide other terms or labels as appropriate to include groups of experiences or ideas related to *feeling good*. Examples were praying, having kids and having friends. The authors concluded that both psychiatrists and community mental health professionals used an "abstract, specialized, and 'intellectual' terminology which often resulted in vagueness and ambiguity" (p. 136). Psychiatrists also almost exclusively employed terminology that reflected an illness orientation. However, both female and male residents of a central city area used "concrete, down-to-earth terms" in defining mental health and were able to distinguish mental health with terms that reflected an absence of illness orientation. The authors asserted that "data from these studies point out incongruences in cognitive sets of professionals and recipients of mental health care" (p. 138). Although the sample size was very limited and the findings cannot be generalized, the study is significant because the authors reported perceptions of mental illness from the clients' point of view. Perhaps studies of this type would yield useful data related to the Hispanic client.

Faculty

The degree of sensitivity among faculty in schools of nursing to the need for teaching culturally consistent content related to psychiatric-mental health nursing of Hispanic clients needs to be investigated. Several pertinent questions need to be addressed. The first among them is, "Are faculty exposed to continuing education experiences that broaden their knowledge of the needs of Hispanic clients"? These data could be obtained by simply counting and reporting the number and kinds of experiences. A second question is, "How are these experiences being taught to students"? This evidence could be sought through content analysis of course outlines, texts and syllabi, which form the basis for communicating curriculum content to students. Such action-oriented research may enhance faculty awareness about the extent of Hispanic psychiatric-mental health nursing content in a curriculum. A third question is, "What are the attitudes of faculty toward including psychiatric-mental health content about Hispanics"? Attitudinal statements could be developed and pilot-tested and a Likert-type scale utilized to obtain the data. Differences in attitudes between Hispanic and non-Hispanic faculty members could be analyzed.

Student Educational Outcomes

Student educational outcomes could be investigated using several methods. A content analysis of unit and comprehensive examinations for culturally consistent items related to psychiatric-mental health nursing of Hispanics could be conducted. Once the items are identified, an item analysis could be done to determine the number of correct and incorrect responses. Attitudinal questions similar to those used to obtain data about faculty could be used to determine student attitudes about Hispanic psychiatric-mental health content. Again, differences between Hispanic and non-Hispanic students could be analyzed.

Practice Outcomes

Practice outcomes need to demonstrate concrete evidence that the psychiatric-mental health nursing needs of Hispanic clients are being met. Activities that can be readily observed and achieved by the client or the family could be evaluated. Questionnaires could be developed to determine whether the care being given was perceived by clients as being culturally consistent and whether it was meeting their needs.

Attitudes of Health Providers

Attitudes of health providers caring for clients with psychiatric-mental health needs are important attributes that need to be measured. Attitude scales about providing culturally consistent, psychiatric-mental health nursing care to Hispanic clients could be developed and used to gather data about providers. Differences between Hispanic and non-Hispanic providers would be useful information.

Once data in these five areas of research are collected and analyzed, conclusions should be synthesized. A framework that conceptualizes psychiatric-mental health perceptions and needs of Hispanic clients should be developed and integrated into the nursing curricula. Ultimately, these concepts should be integrated into the practice of nursing with the psychiatric-mental health Hispanic client.

Guiding Principles for Hispanic Curriculum Development

Guidelines or principles that should form the basis for action are developed around two points that are intimately related in schools of nursing: faculty concerns and dynamics and curriculum concerns. While the general principles for curriculum development are, in effect, nonspecific to the subject matter under examination, there are some specific principles that nursing faculty need to consider. A basic principle is that faculty must have an internalized commitment to include culturally consistent psychiatric-mental health nursing care in its curriculum. Subsequent to this basic curricular premise are the following:

- Faculty must identify validated knowledge and content about Hispanics and their psychiatric-mental health needs that are related to the nursing process and the nursing occupation.
- Faculty must decide what of this identified content is teachable.
- Faculty should become sensitive to presenting culturally consistent psychiatric-mental health content in such a way that it will provide a positive student experience and result in a graduate who can provide culturally therapeutic services to Hispanics.
- Course content should include objectives in the cognitive, affective and psychomotor domains and include real clinical experiences with Hispanic clients if possible, as well as video-taped recordings and films.

• Content should be specific to the predominant Hispanic subgroup in the school of nursing's region. Figure 1 is recommended for developing subgroup-specific Hispanic content.

The integration of Hispanic psychiatric-mental health nursing content must occur at the nurse-training level and also at the level of continuing education for current nurses. At the training level, the integration of Hispanic psychiatric-mental health nursing is influenced by both external and internal factors.

Among the external forces having an impact on schools of nursing are agencies that regulate nursing schools; voluntary nursing associations; employers of graduates; and registered nurses or individuals in the community. They have a great impact on changing the internal activities of schools of nursing by the nature of their recommendations, requests, suggestions and desires.

Regulatory Agencies. The most notable agencies that regulate schools of nursing and their activities are state boards of nursing. State boards of nursing can be encouraged by interested citizens to begin looking at the degree to which concerns of Hispanics are reflected in the curriculum and among the faculties and students in schools of nursing. Since state boards of nursing are an arm of the state legislature and hence responsive to the needs of their constituents, questions may be raised by individuals (both nurses and nonnurses) about the extent and the degree to which either state boards of nursing or the schools they regulate address Hispanic concerns appropriate to that state. For example, in California, Texas, Florida and New York, where there is a significant number of Hispanics, residents can ask, "What efforts can be documented by either schools of nursing or their approving state boards of nursing to show direct benefit to the Hispanic population of the state?" The legislature, its state board of nursing or its schools of nursing can be influenced so that they offer a curriculum that is relevant to the Hispanic community, attracts Hispanic students and numbers Hispanic nurses on the faculty.

Federal agencies also play a role in the effort to improve nursing services to Hispanics, for example, through the enforcement of current civil rights laws or through requirements for funding. If a school of nursing chooses to be unresponsive to the Hispanic community in which it is situated, then the federal government should not be an accomplice—through funding—of such unresponsiveness. With respect to the delivery of psychiatric-mental health nursing care to Hispanics, the Psychiatric Nursing Education Branch of the National Institute

Strategies for Faculty and Institutional Change

External Factors

of Mental Health should be continually on the alert to avoid this type of accusation. Progress reports indicating the extent to which schools of nursing are initiating or increasing their activities are one way to demonstrate evidence of responsiveness to the Hispanic community.

Voluntary Nursing Associations. Although there are over sixty national nursing associations in the United States, the National League for Nursing (NLN) is recognized by the Council on Postsecondary Accreditation as the national accrediting agency for nursing education, and the American Nurses Association (ANA) is recognized as the agency representing registered nurses. Both of these associations have great influence on what schools of nursing and registered nurses think and do. The NLN, through its accrediting processes, can effect changes that will be beneficial to Hispanic communities in which schools of nursing are located. One criterion accepted as part of the accreditation criteria by the Council of Associate Degree Programs of the NLN states:

> The program of learning provides learning experiences which develop specific knowledges, concepts, understanding, skills, and facts pertaining to cultural diversity (National League for Nursing, 1977.)

The key factor in this criterion is that those schools offering the associate degree in nursing and seeking accreditation must provide evidence about the way in which they meet this criterion. Phrased differently, cultural diversity in general and the concerns of Hispanics in particular have become institutionalized in the accrediting process of a component council of the NLN. In addition, the NLN has offered programs dealing with Hispanics as part of its convention activities at each national convention since 1973. One of the contributors to this chapter is currently on the board of directors of the NLN.

The ANA has also attempted to address the concerns of minorities in general. Among a group of papers on cultural differences in nursing presented at the 1972 convention was one citing Hispanic attributes. At that same convention, Hispanic nurses began to express the need for forming a caucus. This caucus was formed at the 1974 convention and has since formed its own organization, the National Association of Hispanic Nurses. The ANA, again at the 1972 convention, created the Affirmative Action Task Force, which was changed in 1976 to the Commission of Human Rights. The change in name has been interpreted as a change in focus by some minority nurses. The ANA, with the aid of the federal government, has developed a fellowship program designed to increase the number of doctorally prepared minority nurses in the United States. One of the authors of this chapter has since earned the doctorate under this program. Unlike the NLN, there are no Hispanic nurses on ANA's board of directors.

Both ANA and NLN have taken some positive actions and positions toward increasing the number of minority nurses and have moved toward teaching and practicing more culturally consistent nursing care. However, a cursory review of the literature of both organizations failed to provide specific insights into the provision of culturally consistent psychiatric-mental health nursing care for Hispanics. Both these and other nursing organizations could assume more imposing postures in this area.

Employers of Graduates. Employing agencies could express their concerns to those schools of nursing that are their main source of registered nurses. Solicited and unsolicited statements that express whether graduates are being prepared to provide culturally consistent psychiatric-mental health nursing care to Hispanics could be forwarded to schools of nursing. Since many schools of nursing do follow-up studies of their graduates, this process also facilitates direct input into schools of nursing from employing agencies. If a school is not preparing nurses who exhibit beginning competency in providing culturally consistent psychiatric-mental health nursing care to Hispanics, perhaps then the school could be encouraged to make attempts to recruit Hispanics into their program.

Registered Nurses and Individuals in the Community. Registered nurses can affect a school of nursing's continuing education offerings. The majority of the continuing nursing education programs offered by schools of nursing are based on the philosophical assumption that they will meet perceived needs of registered nurses who are enrolled. Consequently, registered nurses—singly, in groups or through their local nursing associations—need to express their desire for courses aimed at developing their expertise in providing Hispanic psychiatric-mental health nursing care.

Also, individuals in the community in which a school of nursing is situated can request that the school begin or continue to address the needs of the community through such offerings for its nurses or through courses dealing with consumer health education. Courses on consumer health education need a great deal of further study and development by schools of nursing. Consumer health education courses in Hispanic psychiatric-mental health should be developed on such topics as: value of *curanderos, santeras* and *espirituistas;* health beliefs of Hispanics; how to deal with bicultural pressures; the phenomena of bilingualism; illness beliefs; and so on. Interested Hispanics and Hispanic political action groups in the community can approach schools of nursing in their area for the purpose of obtaining information about the school's efforts, identifying the school's interest in meeting psychiatric-mental health needs of Hispanics, making the school aware of its need to provide a positive response to the Hispanic needs in the community and establishing communications between the Hispanic community and the school.

Internal Factors   Internal factors affecting the integration of psychiatric-mental health for Hispanics into the curricula of schools of nursing include (1) the parent institution; (2) the chief executive officer of the school of nursing; and (3) the faculty in the school of nursing.

Parent Institution. The parent institution or the college or university with which the school of nursing is affiliated should take the initiative to actively and positively encourage its various educational components to include Hispanic concerns in their educational programs. Universities and colleges can encourage their school of nursing to address Hispanic curricular concerns through their educational philosophy as published in their college bulletins; their continuing education programs about Hispanics; and their periodic reports about the progress made toward an institution-wide affirmative action plan or toward a similar school-wide plan. A university or college commitment of this nature may provide the consciousness raising needed by its educational components. Such a commitment may also provide evidence that the university is responsible to social concerns. This evidence may be used by these educational institutions to ensure compliance with various regulatory agencies, but more important, it will establish that the educational institution is seeking means by which to achieve social relevancy.

Chief Executive Officer of the School. The chief executive officer of the school of nursing bears the ultimate responsibility for the conduct of overall activities and offerings in a given school. Consequently, the chief executive officer can affect the extent to which a school considers Hispanic content a vital part of its operations. In those communities in which there is a significant proportion of Hispanics, the chief executive officer should assume the leadership in incorporating appropriate activities associated with Hispanic concerns into the day-to-day operations and activities of the school of nursing.

Faculty in the School of Nursing. By far, the most influential group that can advance the concerns of Hispanics in a school of nursing is the faculty. Including Hispanic curriculum content, sensitizing students to Hispanic concerns and fostering a positive climate for Hispanic faculty and Hispanic issues are among the factors that a responsive nursing school faculty can address in their endeavor to align themselves with Hispanic concerns in their community. In addition, the faculty could assign students to Hispanic clients, encourage research about Hispanic psychiatric clients and design learning experiences that deal with Hispanics.

The use of an Hispanic advisory group to determine current community needs and to obtain feedback about the school's efforts is another possible means by which faculty could address concerns of

Hispanic psychiatric-mental health needs. The use of consultants is another means by which this effort could be approached.

The general aim of continuing nursing education is to further refine and increase the skills, knowledge and attitudes acquired at the preservice level and at the occupational level. Thus, one of the purposes of continuing nursing education, relative to psychiatric-mental health nursing may be considered to be the promotion of the skills, knowledge and attitudes the registered nurse displays to the Hispanic client receiving psychiatric-mental health nursing care.

Continuing Education for Nurses

Promoting these attributes about Hispanic clients is easier said than done, easier to idealize than operationalize. Nevertheless, it is a process that must be weighed carefully and deliberately with the expressed intention of improving the quantity and quality of the psychiatric-mental health nursing care received by the Hispanic client. If this expressed intent becomes the outcome measure by which continuing nursing education efforts are evaluated, a major step toward ensuring the implementation of culturally consistent psychiatric-mental health nursing care for Hispanics will have been achieved.

How can this expressed intent—the improvement of the quality and quantity of psychiatric-mental health nursing care for the Hispanic client—be implemented and better integrated in the current system of nursing practice? Implementation could occur through three distinct but philosophically related areas in three different settings. These three are (1) staff development in health service agencies; (2) continuing education offerings by schools of nursing; and (3) educational programs by nursing associations.

Staff Development in Health Service Agencies. The staff development officer can develop a program that would assist the nursing staff to increase its ability to provide culturally consistent psychiatric-mental health nursing care to their Hispanic clients. A program of this nature should not be a one-time effort but should be a sustained, continuing program with specific objectives to be accomplished over time. This program can deal with the knowledge, skills and attitudes that registered nurses should have so that their psychiatric-mental health nursing care would be relevant, valid and culturally consistent to their Hispanic clientele. But a critical question for any staff development officer in a health service agency is: How does one go about designing, implementing and evaluating such a program?

First, an accurate analysis of the racial and ethnic compositions of the health service agency's clientele and its employees should be conducted. An author-modified instrument entitled "Data Sheet for Health Service Agencies to Determine their Hispanic Clientele/Employees," which can be self-administered, was based on one originally developed by WICHEN during its project, "Models for Cultural Diversity in Nursing" (see Appendix 1). Data culled by this instrument can be used by a staff development officer to determine the health service agency's status quo. In a sense, to get "a lay of the land" becomes vital to making decisions about the approach needed in developing a staff program for any particular health service agency. The instrument will also assist in identifying the agency's ethnic resources with respect to its employees so that these resources may be used as appropriate in designing the staff development programs.

The "Agency Questionnaire," also originally developed by WICHEN and modified by these authors to make it Hispanic-specific, could be used by the staff development officer to rate the health service agency's philosophy, hiring policies, staff development programs and various other factors (see Appendix 2). The purpose of this instrument would be to permit an interested health service agency to self-evaluate various aspects of its activities with respect to meeting the needs of its Hispanic clientele. A rating scale that could be used by a health service agency for self-assessment is presented in Table 1.

Both instruments can be used on a periodic basis to provide evidence of a health service agency's progress or its changing patterns. Since the purpose of these two instruments is to design staff development programs that are relevant and up-to-date, it behooves the staff development officer to periodically update the information by use of the instruments. The data derived from these instruments would provide guidelines for identifying specific content for staff development programs.

A workbook developed by WICHEN (1977) is designed to assist

TABLE 1

Interpretation of a Health Service Agency's Responsiveness to its Hispanic Clientele

Health Service Agency's Score	Interpretation
35–41	Represents a health service agency that has made a highly positive and comprehensive response to its Hispanic clientele
28–34	Represents a health service agency that is making strides toward providing a positive response to its Hispanic clientele
21–27	Represents a health service agency that needs to improve its response to its Hispanic clientele
14–20	Represents a health service agency that responds erratically to its Hispanic clientele
13 or less	Represents a service agency that is unresponsive to its Hispanic clientele

persons responsible for staff development and is useful for identifying content to be included in a staff development program based on need as determined by the two previously discussed instruments. It becomes useful if the findings of the two instruments are used as the basis for making decisions about selecting content from the workbook or other sources.

Health services agencies can also collaborate with local schools of nursing with the aim of offering joint programs or requesting them to offer courses dealing with psychiatric-mental health nursing care of Hispanics. Requesting assistance from local schools of nursing may be of great aid to those health services agencies whose size is such that they do not employ a staff development officer. Contacting the local schools of nursing located in community colleges may be more economical, because the continuing education offerings of these schools generate their own contact hour reimbursement, enabling them to charge lower fees.

Continuing Education by Schools of Nursing. If a local school of nursing views itself and its continuing education offerings as vehicles for effecting subtle, but positive, change in the day-to-day clinical practice of nurses in their community, then the school may initiate continuing education courses reflective of the Hispanic needs in the surrounding community or region.

Continuing nursing education courses designed to develop or enhance the local nurse's ability to provide culturally consistent psychiatric-mental health nursing care to Hispanics should be an integral part of a school of nursing situated in a city or region where Hispanics are a significant part of the population. Curriculum content for these courses includes topics in the areas of racism, discrimination, the various origins of and the differences among Hispanics, thinking-communication patterns of Hispanics, health beliefs of Hispanics, the function of folk healers in the Hispanic community and the views of Hispanics about mental illness and of the mentally ill. In addition to curriculum content about the Hispanic client, courses should be offered encompassing topics dealing with, among others, the nurse's own perceptions, overt and covert discriminatory practices at both the individual and institutional level and the more recent phenomenon of *victimology*, a term signifying the belief that the victim is to be blamed for his or her condition or life situation. For example, the unemployed, if they really wanted, could find a job; rape victims must have done something to "incite" the attack on them; and if Hispanics really needed health care, they would seek it.

Programs by Nursing Associations. Some nursing associations—of which there are over sixty in the United States—have, from time to time, offered as part of their convention activities, programs dealing with Hispanics. Also, some of these organizations have offered regional programs focusing on Hispanic concerns. The need to institutionalize Hispanic concerns as integral educational activities of these organizations needs to be further developed. The programs about Hispanics offered by these nursing associations have tended to be general and comprehensive in scope rather than to deal with the specific psychiatric-mental health needs of Hispanics.

The programs offered by these associations need to be structured so as to offer techniques useful to nurses interested in implementing culturally consistent psychiatric-mental health nursing care to Hispanics. Care needs to be exercised so that these programs avoid the pitfalls of Hispanic stereotyping and of attracting those nurses whose interest in Hispanics is one of morbid curiosity because Hispanics are "different."

Recommendations

Using the premises of this chapter as probable cause, the following policy recommendations are made:

- That the federal government incorporate into its initiative the expansion of psychiatric-mental health services to Hispanics.
- That the federal government incorporate into its initiatives the expansion of psychiatric-mental health education about Hispanics.
- That the federal government require its grantees to demonstrate evidence about the extent to which an approved affirmative action plan with respect to Hispanics has been implemented, especially with those grantees located in cities with significant Hispanic populations.
- That the National Institutes of Health encourage research about the psychiatric-mental health of Hispanics.
- That research be encouraged to identify, describe and evaluate ethnic therapeutic modalities used by Hispanics.
- That federally sponsored special projects that foster the exploration of techniques by which nursing students could become culturally sensitive to the needs of Hispanics be encouraged.
- That *curanderismo, santerismo* and *espiritismo* be researched with the aim of identifying, describing, classifying and explaining their function in the mental health of Hispanics.
- That accrediting agencies in nursing be encouraged to seek advice of Hispanics relative to appropriate concerns, especially

in those states in which there is a significant Hispanic population.

• That schools of nursing establish methods by which their faculty could initiate, maintain, expand and evaluate in their curricula the psychiatric-mental health issues of Hispanics.

• That the federal government and state boards of nursing examine and explore facilitative means by which nurses from Hispanic countries immigrating to the United States could be assisted to become licensed.

• That accrediting agencies for health services incorporate in their accrediting criteria statements relative to the provision of culturally consistent nursing services.

• That boards of nursing include in their criteria for approval of schools of nursing statements concerned (1) with developing culturally consistent curriculums and (2) with recruiting Hispanic students.

• That serious consideration be given to further subdividing the Hispanic cell to incorporate the specific Hispanic subgroups under study, i.e., Mexican Americans, Cubans, Puerto Ricans and South Americans.

• That regional education boards, such as the Western Interstate Commission for Higher Education in Nursing, the Southern Regional Education Board and the New England Board of Higher Education be funded to provide programs dealing with content about Hispanics.

Appendix 1

Data Sheet for Health Service Agencies to Determine Their Hispanic Clientele/Employees

For Year 19____

Directions: Please write in the information as accurately as possible.

Date Completed: _____ Completed by: _____

	Total	Hispanics
I. Information about clientele		
A. Population in catchment area served	_____	_____
B. Number of clientele seen annually by agency	_____	_____
II. Information about employees		
A. Number of agency employees	_____	_____
B. Number of nursing staff (includes RN, LPN/LVN, Nursing Attendants)	_____	_____
Number of Registered Nurses	_____	_____
Number of LPN/LVN	_____	_____
Number of Nursing Attendants	_____	_____
C. Number of nursing staff leaving agency for whatever reason	_____	_____
Number of Registered Nurses	_____	_____
Number of LPN/LVN	_____	_____
Number of Nursing Attendants	_____	_____
D. Number of new nursing staff hired by agency	_____	_____
Number of Registered Nurses	_____	_____
Number of LPN/LVN	_____	_____
Number of Nursing Attendants	_____	_____

Appendix 2
Agency Questionnaire

Agency: _____ Date Completed: _____ Assessment by: _____

Directions: Please write in the information for your agency. For the following
questions, if your answer is no, place an 0 in the box at the right.
If your answer is yes, place a 1 in the box at the right.

I. The following questions deal with your agency's philosophy:

A. Is there a specific statement in your philosophy of
providing care to Hispanics? ☐

B. Is there an affirmative action plan for hiring Hispanics? ☐

C. Has the affirmative action plan been implemented? ☐

Total the above section ☐

II. The following questions deal with your agency's hiring
policies:

A. Are there Hispanics on selection committees or who are
involved in the hiring process of new employees? ☐

B. Is evidence of staff sensitivity to the needs of Hispanics a
criterion for hiring? ☐

C. Is performance in Hispanic studies courses used as a
criterion for hiring? ☐

D. Is bilingualism a criterion for hiring? ☐

Total the above section ☐

III. The following questions deal with your agency's commitment
to retaining Hispanic staff:

A. Upon hiring, is the new employee oriented to the program,
etc.? ☐

B. Are there inservice education sessions which emphasize
cultural components? ☐

C. Is inservice education mandatory for retention or
promotion? ☐

D. Are courses or learning experiences about Hispanics
encouraged as part of the inservice education program? ☐

E. Is learning a second language considered part of the
inservice education program? ☐

F. Is bilingualism used as a criterion for promotions? ☐

G. Is performance in Hispanic studies courses or in relevant
learning experiences with Hispanics used as criteria for
promotions? ☐

H. Is the ability to relate to Hispanics clients used as a criterion for evaluation and promotions?

Total the above section

IV. The following questions deal with your agency's dismissal or firing policies:

A. Are employees allowed to file a grievance procedure with the executive director of the board of directors?

B. Are there Hispanics on grievance committees?

C. Is written warning given prior to dismissal?

D. Are employees given warning or terminated for persisting in giving culturally inconsistent care?

Total the above section

V. The following questions deal with your agency's commitment to quality of care standards:

A. If your clientele is Hispanic, are there signs, permission forms and teaching materials in Spanish?

B. Are there specialized services for Hispanics with unique needs?

C. Do you have an aggressive referral system with other community agencies and organizations?

D. Does your public relations program exhibit sensitivity to the unique needs of Hispanics?

E. Is there a patient advocate or ombudsperson in your agency?

F. Are there inservice sessions where Hispanic clients act as teachers?

Total the above section

VI. The following questions deal with bilingual services:

A. Are bilingual services available for Hispanics?

1) Signs translated?

2) Permission forms translated?

3) Menus translated?

B. Are professional translators/intepreters available for Hispanic clients?

C. Are translators/interpreters compensated?

1) Salary differential?

2) Time compensation?

Total the above section

VII. The following questions deal with community relations:

   A. Is a community relations office available for patients who have questions and/or complaints about services in your health service agency?   ☐

   B. Is there an outreach section of your services?   ☐

   Total the above section   ☐

VIII. The following questions deal with inservice needs:

   A. Do you teach your personnel the significance of proper skin assessment for Hispanics?   ☐

   B. Are you teaching your staff that specific disease processes are more prevalent in Hispanics?   ☐

   C. Do you know the consequences that can result if you are unaware of the Hispanics' beliefs about causes of disease?   ☐

   D. Are you teaching your staff about different folk practices that affect the Hispanics' acceptance or denial of the sick role?   ☐

   E. Do you teach your staff the variations in communication concepts that exemplify the verbal, nonverbal, and other preferences for modes of communication preferred by Hispanics?   ☐

   Total the above section   ☐

	Maximum Score	*Your Agency Score*
Total I	3	☐
Total II	4	☐
Total III	8	☐
Total IV	4	☐
Total V	6	☐
Total VI	8	☐
Total VII	2	☐
Total VIII	6	☐
Grand Total	41	☐

References

Branch, M. F., & Paxton, P. P. *Providing safe nursing care for ethnic people of color.* New York: Appleton-Century-Crofts, 1976.

Brink, P. J. *Transcultural nursing.* Englewood Cliffs, N.J.: Prentice-Hall, 1976.

Brownlee, A. *Community culture and care.* St. Louis, MO.: C. V. Mosby, 1978.

Bush, M. T., Ullom, J. A., & Osborne, O. H. The meaning of mental health: A report of two ethnoscientific studies. *Nursing Research,* 1975, *24,* 130–38.

Casas, J., & Keefe, S. E. *Family and mental health in the American community.* Monograph No. 7, Spanish Speaking Mental Health Research Center, Los Angeles, California, 1978.

Frake, C. O. The ethnographic study of cognitive systems. In M. H. Fried (Ed.), *Readings in anthropology* (Vol. 2). New York: Thomas Y. Crowell, 1968.

Gonzalez, H. H. *An identification and description of curriculum content in twenty-eight randomly selected pre-service nursing programs leading to the associate degree.* Unpublished masters dissertation, Catholic University of America, Washington, D.C., 1966.

National League for Nursing. *Criteria for the evaluation of educational programs in nursing leading to an associate degree.* New York: Author, 1977.

National League for Nursing. *Position on nursing's responsibility to minorities and disadvantaged groups.* New York: Author, 1979.

Western Interstate Commission for Higher Education in Nursing. *Workbook: An instructional program for health service agencies.* Boulder, CO.: Author, 1977.

Wilson, J. An ethnoscientific study to determine the perception, description, causation, resolution, and categorization of the illness domain for Mexican Americans. Unpublished doctoral dissertation, University of Texas, Austin, Texas, 1978.

Bibliography

Abad, V., Ramos, J., & Boyce, K. Clinical issues in the psychiatric treatment of Puerto Ricans. In E. R. Padilla, & A. M. Padilla (Eds.), *Transcultural psychiatry, an Hispanic perspective.* Monograph 4, Los Angeles: University of California Spanish Speaking Mental Health Research Center, 1977.

Abril, I. Mexican-American folk beliefs that affect health care. *Arizona Nurse*, May–June, 1975, pp. 14–20.

Aguilar, I., & Wood, V. Therapy through death ritual. *Social Work*, 1976, (1), 49–54.

Alers, J. O. *Puerto Ricans and health.* Hispanic Research Center, Fordham University, New York, 1978.

American Nurses Association. *Affirmative action: Toward quality nursing care for a multiracial society.* Kansas City, MO.: Author, 1976.

Baca, J. E. Some health beliefs of the Spanish-Speaking. *American Journal of Nursing*, 1969, *69* (10), 2172–76.

Bello, T. The third dimension: cultural sensitivity in nursing practice. *Imprint*, 1976, *23*, 36–38.

Casavantes, E. Pride and prejudice: A Mexican-American dilemma. *Civil Rights Digest*, 1970, *3* (1), 22–27.

Clark, M. *Health in the Mexican-American culture* (2nd ed.). Berkeley: University of California Press, 1970.

Concha, P., Garcia, U., & Perez, A. Cooperation vs. competition: A comparison of Anglo-American and Cuban American youngsters in Miami. *Journal of Social Psychology*, 1975, *95*, 273–74.

Davis, A., & Havighurst, R. J. Social class and color differences in child rearing. In C. Kluckhorn, H. Murray (Eds.), *Personality in nature society and culture.* New York: Knopf, 1948, 308–20.

DeTornyay, R. Cultural diversity and nursing curricula. *Journal of Nursing Education.* 1976, *15* (2), 3–4.

Diaz-Guerrero, R. Socio-cultural premises, attitudes and cross-cultural research. *International Journal of Psychiatry*, 1967, *2* (2), 79–87.

Edgerton, R. B., & Karno, M. Mexican-American bilingualism and the perception of mental illness. *Archives of General Psychiatry*, 1971, *24* (3), 286–90.

Edgerton, R., Karno, M., & Hernandez, B. Curanderismo in the metropolis. *American Journal of Psychotherapy*, 1970, *24* (11), 124–34.

Fitzpatrick, J. P. The adjustment of Puerto Ricans to New York City. In M. Arnold & C. B. Rose, (Eds.), *Minority problems: A textbook of readings in intergroup relations.* New York: Harper and Row, 1965, pp. 42–43.

Foster, G. M. Relationships between Spanish and Spanish-American folk medicine. *Journal of American Folklore*, 1953, *66*, 201–17.

Gaitz, M., & Scott, J. Mental health of Mexican Americans: Do ethnic factors make a difference? *Geriatrics*, 1974, *29* (2), 103–10.

Garner, V., & Merrill, E. A model for development and implementation of cultural content in the nursing curriculum. *Journal of Nursing Education*, 1976, *15* (2), 30–34.

Gibson, G. An approach to identification and prevention of developmental difficulties among Mexican-American children. *American Journal of Orthopsychiatry*, 1978, *48* (1), 96–112.

Gillin, J. Magical fright. *Psychiatry*, 1948, *11*, 387–400.

Gomez, E., & Cook, K. *Chicano culture and mental health: Trees in search of a forest.* San Antonio: Worden School of Social Service, 1978.

Gomez, R. *The changing Mexican American.* Boulder, CO.: Pruett, 1972.

Gonzalez, H. H. Health beliefs of some Mexican-Americans. In *Becoming aware of cultural differences in nursing.* Kansas City, MO.: American Nurses Association, 1973, pp. 1–2.

Gonzalez, H. H. Health care needs of the Mexican-American. In *Ethnicity and health care.* New York: National League for Nursing, 1976, pp. 21–28.

Graves, T. Psychological acculturation in a tri-ethnic community. *Southwestern Journal of Anthropology*, 1967, *23*, 337–49.

Grebler, L., Moore, J., & Grezman, R. *The Mexican-American people; The nation's second-largest minority.* New York: The Free Press, 1970.

Harwood, A. The hot-cold theory of disease. *Journal of the American Medical Association*, 1971, *216*, 1153–58.

Hernandez, C., Haug, M., & Wagner, N. *Chicanos: Social and psychological perspective.* St. Louis, MO.: C. V. Mosby, 1976.

Hollingshead, A. B., & Redlich, F. C. Social stratification and psychiatric disorder. In N. J. Smalser (Ed.), *Personality and social systems.* Wiley: New York, 1970.

Johnson, L. *East Harlem community health study.* New York: Mt. Sinai School of Nursing, 1972.

Kiev, A. *Curanderismo—Mexican American folk psychiatry.* New York: The Free Press, 1968.

Kluckhohn, F. R. Dominant and variant value orientation. In C. Kluckholn & H. Murray (Eds.), *Personality in nature, society and culture.* New York: Knopf, 1967.

Kreisman, J. The curandero's apprentice: A therapeutic integration of folk and medical healing. *The American Journal of Psychiatry*, 1975, *132* (1), 81–33.

Latino Task Force on Community Mental Health Training. *Latino community mental health.* Spanish Speaking Mental Health Research and Development Program, University of California at Los Angeles, 1974.

Leininger, M. Becoming aware of types of health practitioners and cultural imposition. In *Becoming aware of cultural differences in nursing.* Kansas City, MO.: American Nurses Association, 1972, pp. 9–15.

Leininger, M. The significance of cultural concepts in nursing. In *Transcultural nursing.* New York: Wiley, 1978.

LeVine, E. S., & Bartz, K. Comparative child-rearing attitudes among Chicano, Anglo and Black parents. *Hispanic Journal of Behavioral Sciences*, 1979, *2*, 165–78.

Lewis, O. Culture of poverty. *Scientific American*, 1966, *2* (15), 19–25.

Lewis, O. *LaVida: A Puerto Rican family in the culture of poverty.* New York: Random House, 1966.

Ludwig, E., & Santibanez, J. *The Chicanos: Mexican American voices.* Baltimore: Penguin Books, 1971.

Madsen, W. Value conflicts and folk psychotherapy in South Texas. In A. Kiev (Ed.), *Magic, faith, and healing,* New York: The Free Press, 1964, pp. 420–40.

Madsen, W. *Mexican-American of South Texas.* New York: Holt, Rinehart, and Winston, 1967.

Madsen, W. Society and health in the lower Rio Grande Valley. In J. H. Burma (Ed.), *Mexican-Americans in the Southwest.* Cambridge, MA.: Schenkman Publishing, 1970.

Maduro, R. J. Journey dreams in Latino group psychotherapy. *Psychotherapy: Theory, Research and Practice*, 1976, *13* (2), 148–55.

Maldonado, D. The Chicano aged. *Social Worker*, May, 1975, 213–16.

Martin, P. (Ed.). *La Frontera perspective: Providing mental health services to Mexican Americans.* Tuscon: La Frontera Center, 1979.

Martinez, A. *Rising voices.* New York: New American Library, 1974.

Martinez, C. Community mental health and the Chicano movement. *American Journal of Orthopsychiatry*, 1973, *43* (4), 595–601.

Martinez, C., & Martin, H. W. Folk disease among urban Mexican-Americans. *Journal of the American Medical Association*, 1966, *196* (2), 161–64.

Martinez, R. (Ed.). *Hispanic culture and health care: Fact, fiction, folklore.* St. Louis, MO.: C. V. Mosby, 1978.

McWilliams, C. *North from Mexico.* New York: Greenwood Press, 1968.

Mexican American Policy Research Project. *The health of Mexican Americans in South Texas.* Austin: The Lyndon B. Johnson School of Public Affairs, 1979.

Moquin, W. *A documentary history of the Mexican Americans.* New York: Praeger Publishers, 1972.

Montiel, M. Social science myth and the Mexican American family. *El Grito*, 1970, *4*, 56–63.

Murrillo, N. The Mexican American family. In *Chicanos social & psychological perspectives.* St. Louis, MO.: C. V. Mosby, 1971.

Murrillo-Rhode, I. Family life among Mainland Puerto Ricans in New York City slums. *Perspectives in Psychiatric Care*, 1976, *14* (4), 174–79.

National League for Nursing. *Cultural dimensions in the baccalaureate nursing curriculum.* New York: Author, 1977.

Olmedo, E., & Lopez, S. (Eds.). *Hispanic mental health professionals.* Monograph No. 5, Spanish speaking Mental Health Research Center, University of California at Los Angeles, 1977.

Padilla, A., Ruiz, R. A., & Alvarez, R. Community mental health services for the Spanish speaking/surnamed population. *American Psychologist*, 1975, *30*, 892–905.

Parres, R., & Santiago, R. Social tensions in relationships of Mexicans and North Americans. In J. Masserman (Ed.), *Science and psychoanalysis: Psychoanalysis and social process.* New York: Grune & Stratton, 1961.

Peck, H. B., Kaplan, S., & Roman, M. Prevention, treatment and social action: A strategy of intervention in a disadvantaged urban area. *American Journal of Orthopsychiatry*, 1966, *36*, 57–69.

Penalosa, F. Mexican family roles. *Journal of Marriage and the Family*, 1968, *11*, 680–88.

Phillipus, M. J. Successful and unsuccessful approaches to mental health services for an urban Hispano American population. *Journal of Public Health*, 1971, *61* (4), 820–31.

Pinderhughs, C. Ego development and cultural differences. *American Journal of Psychiatry*, 1974, *131* (3), 171–76.

Ramirez, M. Identification with Mexican family values and authoritarianism in Mexican Americans. *Journal of Social Psychology*, 1967, *73*, 3–11.

Ramos, R. A case in point: An ethnomethodological study of a poor Mexican-American family. *Social Science Quarterly*, 1973, *53* (4), 905–19.

Robinson, S., & Paxton, P. Continuing education needs of nurses serving minorities and the poor. *Journal of Continuing Education in Nursing*, 1974, *5* (2), 12–17.

Rogler, L., & Hollingshead, A. Puerto Rican spiritualist as a psychiatrist. *American Journal of Sociology*, 1961, *5* (6), 17–21.

Roman, M., & Kaplan, S. *The organization and delivery of mental health services in the ghetto.* New York: Praeger Press, 1973.

Romano, O. I. Charismatic medicine, folk healing and folk-sainthood. *Anthropology,* 1965, *67,* 11–52.

Rubel, A. J. Concepts of disease in the Mexican-American culture. *American Anthropologist,* 1960, *62,* 793–814.

Samora, J. *La Raza: Forgotten Americans.* London: Notre Dame Press, 1966.

Sanchez, A. J. The definers and the defined: A mental health issue. *El Grito,* 1971, *4* (4), 4–11.

Saunders, L. Healing ways in the Spanish Southwest. In E. G. Jaco (Ed.), *Patients, physicians, and illness.* New York: The Free Press, 1958. pp. 189–206.

Serrano, A. C., & Gibson, G. Mental health services to the Mexican American community in San Antonio, Texas. *Journal of Public Health,* 1973, *63* (2), 1055–57.

Seward, G. H. *Psychotherapy and culture conflict in community mental health* (2nd ed.). New York: The Ronald Press Company, 1972.

Simmons, O. G. The mutual images and expectations of Anglo-Americans and Mexican-Americans. *Daedalus,* 1962, *91,* 286–99.

Special Populations Sub-Task Panel on Mental Health of Hispanic Americans. *Report to the President's Commission on Mental Health.* Reprinted by the Spanish Speaking Mental Health Research Center, Los Angeles, California, 1978.

Spector, R. *Cultural diversity in health and illness.* New York: Appleton-Century-Crofts, 1979.

Spicer, E. H. (Ed.). *Ethnic medicine in the Southwest.* Tuscon, AZ.: The University of Arizona, 1977.

Steiner, S. *La Raza, the Mexican Americans.* New York: Harper and Row, 1968.

Stevens, E. Machismo and Marianismo. *Society,* 1975, *9,* 57–62.

Tamez, E. G. Curanderismo: Folk Mexican American health care system. *Journal of Psychiatric Nursing and Mental Health Services,* 1978, *16,* 34–39.

Torrey, E. F. The case for the indigenous therapist. *Archives of General Psychiatry,* 1970, *20* (3), 365–73.

Torrey, E. F. What western psychotherapists can learn from witchdoctors. *American Journal of Orthopsychiatry,* 1972, *42* (1), 69–76.

Valentine, C. *Culture and poverty.* Chicago: University of Chicago Press, 1968.

Western Interstate Commission for Higher Education in Nursing. *Models for cultural diversity in nursing: A process for change.* Boulder, CO.: Author, 1977.

Western Interstate Commission for Higher Education in Nursing. *Workbook for an instructional program for curriculum change.* Boulder, CO.: Author, 1977.

Western Interstate Commission for Higher Education in Nursing. *Workbook for a single course.* Boulder, CO.: Author, 1977.

White, E. Giving health care to minority patients. *Nursing Clinics of North America,* 1977, *12* (1), 27–40.

Yamamoto, J. Optimal treatment for patients of all races and social classes in a Los Angeles clinic. In *Psychiatric care of the underprivileged international psychiatric clinics* (Vol. 8). Boston: Little Brown, 1971, pp. 143–66.

Yamamoto, J., James, Q. C., & Palley, N. Cultural problems in psychiatric therapy. *Archives of General Psychiatry,* 1968, *19,* 45–49.

Contributors

Arce, Antonio, M.D.
Professor and Deputy Chairman
Department of Mental Health
Sciences
Hahneman Medical College
Director
Hahneman Community Mental
Health/Mental Retardation Center
Philadelphia, Pennsylvania

Bacarisse, L. Yvonne, M.S.W.
Associate Professor and
Chairperson
Department of Social Work
Florida International University
Miami, Florida

*Bell, Carl C., M.D.
Associate Director
Division of Behavioral and Psycho-
dynamic Medicine
Outpatient Behavioral Medicine
Jackson Park Hospital
Chicago, Illinois

Bennett, Maisha, Ph.D.
Director
Outpatient Behavioral Medicine
Jackson Park Hospital
Chicago, Illinois

Bernal, Guillermo, Ph.D.
Assistant Professor of Psychiatry
University of California
San Francisco, California

Bernal, Martha E., Ph.D.
Associate Professor
Department of Psychology
University of Denver
Denver, Colorado

Bland, Irma J., M.D.
Assistant Professor of Psychiatry
Northwestern University Medical
School
Chicago, Illinois

Blueye, Henrietta B., M.D.
Resident in Psychiatry
Cambridge Hospital
Seattle, Washington

*Brown, Eddie F., D.S.W.
Director
Office of Intergovernmental
Operations
Arizona Department of Economic
Security
Mesa, Arizona

*Bush, James A., D.S.W.
Assistant Professor
Social Work and Mental Health
Education Consultant
Charles R. Drew Medical School
Los Angeles, California

Carter, Carolyn, Ph.D.
Assistant Professor
Nursing Graduate Program of
Psychiatric Mental Health
Director, Minority Affairs
University of Pittsburgh
Pittsburgh, Pennsylvania

Cheng, Anna, M.S.
Nurse Practitioner
Peninsula Hospital
San Pedro, California

Chunn, Jay C., II., Ph.D.
Dean
School of Social Work
Project Director
Interdisciplinary Curriculum
Development
Howard University
Washington, D.C.

Compton, John (Ph.D. candidate)
Assistant Professor
School of Social Work
University of Denver
Denver, Colorado

Diaz, Guido, M.D.
Associate Professor
Department of Psychiatry
University of Miami School of
Medicine
Miami, Florida

Diaz, Manuel, M.S.W.
Associate Professor
Fordham University
New York, New York

459

Dunston, Patricia J., Ph.D.
　　Assistant Professor and Project
　　　Coordinator
　　Interdisciplinary Curriculum
　　　Development
　　Howard University
　　Washington, D.C.

France, Gary A., Ph.D.
　　Director
　　Edmond Guidance Center
　　Adjunct Professor of Clinical
　　　Psychology
　　Oklahoma State University
　　Edmond, Oklahoma

*Fujiki, Sumiko, Ph.D.
　　Associate Professor
　　Graduate Program in Psychiatric
　　　Mental Health Nursing
　　University of Colorado
　　Denver, Colorado

Galbis, Ricardo, M.D.
　　Executive Director
　　Andromeda Hispano Mental
　　　Health Center
　　Senior Attending Psychiatrist
　　Washington Hospital Center
　　Washington, D.C.

*Garcia, Rodolfo, M.D.
　　Private Practitioner
　　Los Angeles, California

*Gaw, Albert C., M.D.
　　Assistant Professor of Psychiatry
　　Boston University School
　　　of Medicine
　　Staff Psychiatrist
　　Bedford V.A. Hospital
　　Bedford, Massachusetts

Gilde-Rubio, Elsie, R.N.
　　Assistant Professor
　　New York Medical College
　　New York, New York

*Gonzales, Hector, Ph.D.
　　Professor and Chairperson
　　Department of Nursing Education
　　San Antonio College
　　San Antonio, Texas

Hansen, Jennie Chin, M.S.
　　Research Associate
　　Onlok Senior Health Services
　　Assistant Professor of Nursing
　　San Diego State University
　　San Francisco, California

Houston, Earline, M.D.
　　Clinical Director
　　North Unit
　　Philadelphia State Hospital
　　Philadelphia, Pennsylvania

Jones, Billy E., M.D.
　　Director
　　Lincoln Hospital Department
　　　of Psychiatry
　　Bronx, New York

Kekahbah, Janice, M.A.
　　Executive Director
　　AIANNA
　　Editor
　　American Indian/Alaska Native
　　　Nurses Publishing, Co.
　　Norman, Oklahoma

Kim, Luke I.C., Ph.D.
　　Chief of Professional Education
　　California Medical Facility
　　Vacaville, California

*King, Lewis M., Ph.D.
　　Director
　　Fanon Research and Development
　　　Center
　　Professor of Psychiatry
　　UCLA and Drew Medical School
　　Inglewood, California

Kuramoto, Ford H., D.S.W.
　　Director
　　Hollywood Mental Health Services
　　Los Angeles, California

LaFromboise, Teresa D., Ph.D.
　　Assistant Professor of Counseling
　　　Psychology
　　University of Nebraska
　　Lincoln, Nebraska

Lee, Ya-Mei, M.S.
　　Psychiatric Nurse Consultant
　　Richmond Maxi Center
　　San Francisco, California

Lewis, Ronald G., Ph.D.
　　Director
　　American Indian Training Program
　　University of Wisconsin—Mil-
　　　waukee
　　Milwaukee, Wisconsin

Lim, Donald T., Ph.D.
　　Director of Training in Psychology
　　Veterans Administration Medical
　　　Center
　　Palo Alto, California

Lu, Francis G., M.D.
  Assistant Professor in Residence
  Department of Psychiatry
  University of California
  San Francisco, California

Mackey, Duane H., Ed.D.
  Assistant Professor
  School of Education
  University of South Dakota
  Vermillion, South Dakota

Mackey, John E., M.S.W.
  Community Development
    Specialist
  Indian Public Health Service
  Portland, Oregon

Martinez, Angel C., Ph.D.
  Co-Director
  Services for the Hispanic
    Population
  William Alanson White Institute
  Adjunct Assistant Professor
    of Clinical Psychology
  New York University
  New York, New York

Mejia, Berta A., M.S., R.N.
  Assistant Professor and Coordinator
  Child Psychiatric Nursing Track
  Yale University
  New Haven, Connecticut

Moody, Sarah, Ph.D.
  Visiting Assistant Professor
  Department of Psychology
  University of New Orleans
  New Orleans, Louisianna

*Morales, Royal F., M.S.W.
  Director
  Asian American Community
    Mental Health Training Center
  Los Angeles, California

Morishima, James K., Ph.D.
  Associate Professor
  University of Washington
  Seattle, Washington

Munoz, Faye U., D.S.W.
  Project Director
  Minority Mental Health Training
  Boulder, Colorado

Murase, Kenji, D.S.W.
  Professor
  Department of Social Work
    Education

San Francisco State University
  Principal Investigator
  Pacific/Asian Mental Health
    Research Project
  San Francisco, California

Norton, Delores G., Ph.D.
  Associate Dean for Curriculum
  Associate Professor
  University of Chicago
  Chicago, Illinois

*Olmedo, Esteban L., Ph.D.
  Administrative Officer for Ethnic
    Minority Affairs
  American Psychological
    Association
  Washington, D.C.

*Osborne, Oliver, Ph.D.
  Professor and Chairman
  Department of Psycho-Social
    Nursing
  University of Washington
  Seattle, Washington

Pamburn, Audra
  Program Analyst
  White Cloud Center
  University of Oregon Health
    Sciences Center
  Portland, Oregon

Pinkleton, Norma, Ed.D.
  Assistant Health Commissioner
  Cincinnati Health Department
  Cincinnati, Ohio

Richards, Hilda, Ed.D.
  Dean
  College of Health and Human
    Services
  Ohio University
  Athens, Ohio

Ross-Sheriff, Fariyal, Ph.D.
  Associate Professor and Consultant
  Interdisciplinary Curriculum
    Development Project
  Howard University
  Washington, D.C.

*Salcido, Ramon M., D.S.W.
  Assistant Professor
  University of Southern California
  Los Angeles, California

Sanders, Charles L., D.P.A.
  Associate Professor and Acting
    Chairman of Macro Area

School of Social Work
Howard University
Washington, D.C.

Santisteban, David, Ph.D.
Associate Director
Spanish Family Guidance Center
Coral Gables, Florida

Shon, Steven P., M.D.
Psychiatrist
San Francisco, California

Silva, Juliette S., Ph.D.
Associate Professor
School of Social Work
University of Denver
Denver, Colorado

Smith, Carl R., M.D.
Psychiatrist
Midwest City, Oklahoma

Solomon, Barbara B., D.S.W.
Professor
University of Southern California
Los Angeles, California

*Thompson, James W., M.D., M.P.H.
Research Psychiatrist
Division of Biometry
and Epidemiology
National Institute of Mental Health
Rockville, Maryland

Thompson, Odessa, Ph.D.
Assistant Professor and Chairperson of Human Behavior Sequence
School of Social Work
Howard University
Washington, D.C.

**Trail, Ira, Ph.D.
Dean

School of Nursing
University of Oklahoma
Norman, Oklahoma

*Trimble, Joseph E., Ph.D.
Associate Professor of Psychology
Western Washington University
Bellingham, Washington

Walker, R. Dale, M.D.
Assistant Professor of Psychiatry
University of Washington
Seattle, Washington

Walker, Patricia Silk, M.S.
Instructor
Department of Psycho-Social
Nursing
Seattle, Washington

Wilson, Janie, Ph.D.
Assistant Professor
San Antonio College
San Antonio, Texas

Wong, Herbert Z., Ph.D.
Executive Director
Richmond Maxi Center
San Francisco, California

*Wong, Normund, M.D.
Director
Department of Education and the
Menninger School of Psychiatry
Clinical Professor of Psychiatry
University of Kansas Medical School
Topeka, Kansas

*Wood, Rosemary, M.S.
Clinical Program Consultant
Office of the Director of Indian
Health Service
Lawrence, Kansas

* These individuals took on the tremendous task of serving as leader for each of the groups.
** This individual served as a consultant to the American Indian and Alaska Native nursing cell.

Index

Abbott, 240
Abnormal (term), 183
Abraham, 208
Academy on Issues in Psychiatry for Black Populations, 210, 225, 228
Accidents, as a cause of death, 407
Accreditation process, 146–147, 149–150, 157, 158, 230–231, 284, 448, 449. *See also* Licensing bodies.
Accreditation Standard 1234A, 158
Acculturation, definition of, 78–80; and Asians, 129, 134, 135, 139, 143, 145–146, 239, 260; and Hispanics, 81, 436
Adolescents. *See* Youth.
Affective illness, 215–216
Affirmative action programs, and nursing, 339, 400; and social work, 110
Affirmative Action Task Force, 442
Africa, and America, 7
African (term), 6
African-American (term), 336–337
African culture, influence of, 221
Aggression, 349
Aging, 131, 242. *See also* Elderly.
"Ain't it awful," syndrome, 101
Alaskan natives, 158, 159. *See also* American Indians.
Alcohol, Drug Abuse, and Mental Health Administration (ADAMHA), 24, 61, 87, 88, 89–90
Alcoholism, and American Indians, 44, 60–61, 279–280, 408; and Asians, 35, 241; and Blacks, 214, 215
Alderfer, 284
Alexander, 99
Aliens, Hispanic, 188, 190. *See also* Immigrants.
Allen, 345
Allison, 208
Alpert, 72
Alvarez, 186, 188
American Academy of Child Psychiatry, 257
American Association of Chair-

men of Departments of Psychiatry, 257
American Association of Directors of Psychiatric Residency Training, 257, 273
American Association of Psychiatric Services to Children, 257
American Black Psychology Association, 7
American Board of Psychiatry and Neurology, 209, 230, 257, 273
American Indian and Alaska Native (term), 405
American Indian/ Alaska Native Nurses Association (AIANNA), 405, 413, 414
American Indian Nurses Association, 410, 411
American Indian studies programs, 44–45, 418. *See also* Culture.
American Indians, and psychiatric nursing, 405–427; and psychiatry, 269–288; and psychology, 43–63; and social work, 157–176
American Medical Association, 257, 295–296; Council of Medical Education, 230; Essentials of Accredited Residencies, 243, 262
American Nurses Association, 339; 410; Hispanics, 442; and nursing policy, 379, 396; and research, 346
American Nurses Association Statistics Report, 1979, 339
American Psychiatric Association, 210, 240, 243, 273, 294
American Psychiatric Association Symposia and Seminars, 207
American Psychiatric Association Trustees, 209
American Psychology Association, 23, 49–51, 66, 87, 89
Anastasi, 213–214
Anderson, 217
Anthropology, and mental health issues, 43–44, 45, 46, 296, 302, 308, 309, 415
Appalachian-Anglo, 309
Aranald, 71
Arce, 86, 188–189
Archives, Black nurses, 340

Arey, 223
Argentinians, 74
Arizona State University, 162, 192
Armas, 79
Arnalde, 83
Aro Hospital, 301
Arthur, 211
Asian-American (term), 24, 27
Asian American Community Mental Health Center (Los Angeles), 30, 130, 137, 138, 147
Asian-American movement, 127
Asian-American Psychological Association, 24
Asian American Social Workers Association, 128
Asian-American studies program, 127
Asian American Task Force in Social Work Education, 130, 131
Asian and Pacific American (term), 128, 130, 378
Asian and Pacific Americans, and psychiatric nursing, 377–401; and psychiatry, 239–268; and psychology, 23–41, and social work, 127–155
Asian Caucus of the American Psychiatric Association, 256
Asian Community Mental Health Services (Oakland), 34
Asian Counselling and Referral Services (Seattle), 258
Assessment, patient, 215–217, 260, 297, 311–312, 350–351, 392, 438
Association of Directors of Medical Student Education in Psychiatry, 257
Atkinson, 349
Atlanta University School of Social Work, 108, 109
Attneave, 46, 47, 52
Aylesworth, 26

Bacarisse, 184, 188, 191
Bailey, 341
Bakan, 85
Baldwin, 228
Balla, 216

463